Managing Organizations

A Systems Perspective

SECOND EDITION

Packianathan Chelladurai

Holcomb Hathaway, Publishers
Scottsdale, Arizona 85250

Library of Congress Cataloging-in-Publication Data

Chelladurai, P.
    Managing organizations for sport and physical activity : a systems perspective / Packianathan Chelladurai.— 2nd ed.
    p. cm.
Includes bibliographical references and index.
ISBN-13: 978-1-890871-62-8
    1. Sports administration. 2. Physical education and training—Administration. I. Title.
    GV713.C52 2005
    796'.06'9—dc22

                          2005006713

Copyright © 2005, 2001 by Packianathan Chelladurai

Holcomb Hathaway, Publishers, Inc.
6207 North Cattletrack Rd.
Scottsdale, Arizona 85250
480-991-7881
www.hh-pub.com

10 9 8 7 6 5 4 3

ISBN 978-1-890871-62-8

All rights reserved. No part of this publication may be reproduced, in any form or by any means, without permission in writing from the publisher.

Printed in the United States of America.

About the Author   xii
Preface   xiii

INTRODUCTION

Sport Management: Its Past, Present, and Future   1

Manage Your Learning ■ *Strategic Concepts*   2
MANAGEMENT THEN AND NOW   2
EMERGENCE OF SPORT MANAGEMENT   3
THE PAST   3
    Landmark Thrusts   4
THE PRESENT   4
    Professional Status of Sport Management   4
    Economic Significance of the Sport Industry   6
CAREER OPPORTUNITIES IN SPORT MANAGEMENT   13
    Organizational Contexts   13
    Activity/Job Types   13
THE FUTURE OF SPORT MANAGEMENT   14
Summary   17
Developing Your Perspectives   17
References   18

1   Defining the Field of Sport Management   19

Manage Your Learning ■ *Strategic Concepts*   20
THE FIELD DEFINED   20
SPORT INDUSTRY PRODUCTS   22
    Products as Goods and Services   23
    Services and Their Attributes   24
CONSUMER, PROFESSIONAL, AND HUMAN SERVICES   28
    Consumer Service   28

      Professional Service   29
      Human Service   29
CLIENT MOTIVES FOR PARTICIPATION   31
      Pursuit of Pleasure   32
      Pursuit of Skill   32
      Pursuit of Excellence   32
      Pursuit of Health/Fitness   33
CLASSIFYING SPORT SERVICES   33
      Participant Services   34
      Spectator Services   35
      Sponsorship Services   38
      Donor Services   40
      Service to Social Ideas   40
      Production and Marketing of Sport Services   41
RELATIONSHIPS AMONG SPORT PRODUCTS   41
PRIMARY AND ANCILLARY (SATELLITE) SPORT PRODUCTS   42
SPORT MANAGEMENT AS COORDINATION   44
      Human Resources   45
      Technologies   46
      Support Units   46
      Context   46
DEFINITION OF SPORT MANAGEMENT   48
Summary   *51*
Developing Your Perspectives   *52*
References   *52*

2 Classical View of Organizations   55

Manage Your Learning ■ *Strategic Concepts*   56
IMPORTANCE OF ORGANIZATIONS   56
DEFINING ORGANIZATIONS   57
ATTRIBUTES OF ORGANIZATIONS   57
      Identity   58
      Instrumentality   58
      A Program of Activity   58
      Membership   58
      Clear Boundaries   59
      Permanency   59
      Division of Labor   59
      Hierarchy of Authority   60
      Formal Rules and Procedures   60
ATHLETIC TEAMS AS ORGANIZATIONS   61
CLASSIFYING ORGANIZATIONS   63
      Profit Orientation   63
      Source of Funding   65
      Prime Beneficiary   66
      Employee–Customer Interface   67

    Volunteer Participation   68
Summary   68
Developing Your Perspectives   69
References   69

3 Systems View of Organizations   71

Manage Your Learning ■ Strategic Concepts   72

ORGANIZATIONS AS OPEN SYSTEMS   72
PROPERTIES OF ORGANIZATIONS AS OPEN SYSTEMS   74
    Subsystems and Boundaries   74
    External Environment   75
    Internal Environment   78
PROCESSES IN OPEN SYSTEMS   79
    Negative Entropy   79
    Equifinality and Multifinality   81
ORGANIZATIONS AS SYSTEMS OF INPUTS–THROUGHPUTS–OUTPUTS AND FEEDBACK   82
    Inputs   83
    Throughputs   83
    Outputs   83
    Feedback   84
THE SYSTEMS APPROACH IN OVERVIEW   85
ENVIRONMENTAL INFLUENCES ON ORGANIZATIONS   86
    Stakeholder Theory   86
    Institutional Theory   92
    Resource Dependence Theory   94
Summary   95
Developing Your Perspectives   95
References   96

4 Meaning of Management   99

Manage Your Learning ■ Strategic Concepts   100

MANAGEMENT DEFINED   100
THE FUNCTIONS OF MANAGEMENT   102
    Planning   102
    Organizing   103
    Leading   104
    Evaluating   105
THE SKILLS OF MANAGEMENT   106
    Technical Skills   106
    Human Skills   107
    Conceptual Skills   107
THE ROLES OF A MANAGER   108
    Interpersonal Roles   110
    Informational Roles   110

      Decisional Roles   110
      Managerial Roles and Managerial Levels   112
      Managerial Roles in Athletic Contexts   112
THE MANAGEMENT PROCESS IN OVERVIEW   113
THE UNIVERSAL NATURE OF THE MANAGEMENT PROCESS   114
Summary   117
Developing Your Perspectives   118
References   118

5 Planning   121

Manage Your Learning ■ Strategic Concepts   122
THE PLANNING FUNCTION   122
DEFINITION OF PLANNING   123
STEPS IN THE PLANNING PROCESS   124
      Specifying Goals   125
      Identifying Opportunities   126
      Identifying Constraints   127
      Generating Alternate Courses of Action   129
      Establishing Performance Criteria to Evaluate Alternatives   130
      Evaluating Alternatives   131
      Selecting an Alternative   132
      The Plan Document   132
STRATEGIC PLANNING   133
      Mission and Mission Statement   135
TACTICAL/OPERATIONAL PLANNING   137
PLANNING AND BUDGETING   138
RATIONAL PLANNING AND ORGANIZATIONAL GOALS   140
      Stated Goals   141
      Real Goals   142
      Goals and Constraints   149
      Rational Planning and Information Gathering   149
DIRECTIONAL PLANNING   154
      Directional Planning and Stated Goals   156
      Directional Planning and Information   156
Summary   157
Developing Your Perspectives   157
References   158

6 Managerial Decision Making   161

Manage Your Learning ■ Strategic Concepts   162
THE SIGNIFICANCE OF DECISION MAKING   162
OPPORTUNITIES AND PROBLEMS   164
STEPS IN DECISION MAKING   164
      Problem Statement/Framing the Problem   164

      Generating Alternatives   166
      Evaluating Alternatives   166
PROGRAMMABILITY AND SIGNIFICANCE OF DECISIONS   166
      Programmed and Nonprogrammed Decisions   167
      Significance of Decisions   167
RATIONALITY IN DECISION MAKING   169
      Economic Person Model   170
      Bounded Rationality   171
      Administrative Person Model   171
      Implicit Favorite Model   173
DECISION MAKING AS A SOCIAL PROCESS   176
      Advantages of Participative Decision Making   177
      Disadvantages of Participative Decision Making   178
      Decision Styles   178
Summary   184
Developing Your Perspectives   184
References   185

7 Principles of Organizing   187

Manage Your Learning ■ *Strategic Concepts*   188
ORGANIZING DEFINED   188
CLASSICAL PRINCIPLES   190
      Specialization   190
      Span of Control   190
      Departmentation   192
      Unity of Command   196
      Responsibility and Authority   196
BUREAUCRACY   197
      Tenets of a Bureaucracy   197
      Criticisms of Bureaucracy   199
      Bureaucracy in a Democracy   202
      Bureaucracy in Sport Organizations   204
Summary   205
Developing Your Perspectives   205
References   206

8 System-Based Organizing   207

Manage Your Learning ■ *Strategic Concepts*   208
ORGANIZING: OPEN SYSTEMS PERSPECTIVES   208
      The Lawrence and Lorsch Model   210
      The Thompson Model   215
      The Parsonian Model   218
      Comparison of the Thompson and Parsons Models   220
      Technical Core in Service Organizations   223
AUTHORITY STRUCTURE IN SERVICE ORGANIZATIONS   224

NETWORK ORGANIZATIONS   226
   Internal Networks   227
   External Networks   229
   Interorganizational Networks   231
Summary   *237*
Developing Your Perspectives   *237*
References   *237*

9 Motivational Basis of Leading   239

Manage Your Learning ■ *Strategic Concepts*   *240*
LEADING AND MOTIVATING   240
MOTIVATION DEFINED   241
NEED-BASED (OR CONTENT) THEORIES   242
   The Need Hierarchy Theory   243
   The Two-Factor Theory: Motivation–Hygiene Theory   247
   Implication of Need-Based Theories for Sport Managers   251
PROCESS THEORIES   252
   Vroom's Expectancy Theory   252
   Adams' Theory of Inequity   256
   Justice and Fairness Theories   259
AN INTEGRATIVE FRAMEWORK: THE PORTER AND LAWLER MODEL OF MOTIVATION   261
   Effort–Performance Relationship   261
   Performance–Reward Relationship   263
   Reward–Satisfaction Relationship   263
   Feedback Loops   264
MOTIVATION IN SPORT ORGANIZATIONS   264
   Professional Service versus Consumer Service Organizations   265
   Volunteer Organizations   266
Summary   *267*
Developing Your Perspectives   *268*
References   *269*

10 Behavioral Process of Leading   271

Manage Your Learning ■ *Strategic Concepts*   *272*
THE LEADING FUNCTION   272
LEADERSHIP DEFINED   273
THE TRAIT APPROACH   275
THE BEHAVIORAL APPROACH   275
   Ohio State Studies   275
   Michigan Studies   276
   Limitations of Ohio State and Michigan Studies   278
SITUATIONAL THEORIES OF LEADERSHIP   278
   The Contingency Model of Leadership Effectiveness   279
   McClelland's Model of Managerial Motivation   284
   Comparing Fiedler's and McClelland's Views   287

The Path–Goal Theory of Leader Effectiveness　288
The Adaptive-Reactive Theory　293
Summary　296
Developing Your Perspectives　297
References　297

11　Contemporary Approaches to Leadership　301

Manage Your Learning　■　Strategic Concepts　302
EVOLUTION OF CONTEMPORARY THEORIES OF LEADERSHIP　302
TRANSACTIONAL THEORY　303
　Leader–Member Exchange Theory　303
　Transactional versus Transformational Leadership　305
TRANSFORMATIONAL LEADERSHIP　305
CHARISMATIC LEADERSHIP　310
AN INTEGRATIVE FRAMEWORK: THE MULTIDIMENSIONAL MODEL OF LEADERSHIP　311
　Required Leader Behavior　311
　Preferred Leader Behavior　314
　Actual Leader Behavior　315
　Performance and Satisfaction　316
　Transformational Leadership Within the Multidimensional Model　317
Summary　318
Developing Your Perspectives　318
References　319

12　Program Evaluation　321

Manage Your Learning　■　Strategic Concepts　322
EVALUATION DEFINED　322
　Individual-, Unit-, and Organizational-Level Performances　323
　Organizational Units and Programs　324
PROGRAMS DEFINED　324
　Planning and Programming　325
　Programs versus Projects　326
　Public and Nonprofit Programs　326
　Programs in the Commercial/Profit Sector　328
　Programs in Small Organizations　328
PROGRAMS FROM A SYSTEMS PERSPECTIVE　329
　Outputs and Impacts　330
　Programs as Social Interventions　331
PROGRAM EVALUATION　331
　Purposes of Program Evaluation　333
　Program Profile　334
　Standards of Evaluation　334
Summary　340
Developing Your Perspectives　340
References　341

Organizational Effectiveness   343

Manage Your Learning ■ Strategic Concepts   344

EFFECTIVENESS AND EFFICIENCY   345
ORGANIZATIONAL EFFECTIVENESS: THE ULTIMATE CONCERN   346
GOALS MODEL   348
    Need for Clear Goals   349
    Need for Measurable Goals   350
    Substitution of Surrogate Measures   350
SYSTEM RESOURCE MODEL   351
    System Resource versus Goals Model   354
    Obtaining System Resources as an Operative Goal   354
    Applicability of System Resource Model   355
PROCESS MODEL   357
    Pros and Cons of the Process Model   358
MULTIDIMENSIONALITY OF ORGANIZATIONAL EFFECTIVENESS   359
THE MULTIPLE-CONSTITUENCY MODEL   362
MULTIDIMENSIONALITY PERSPECTIVE VERSUS MULTIPLE-CONSTITUENCY MODEL   367
COMPETING VALUES MODEL   368
    Internal versus External   368
    Flexibility versus Stability   369
    Means versus Ends   369
PARADOXICAL NATURE OF ORGANIZATIONAL EFFECTIVENESS   371
PRIMACY AMONG MULTIPLE PERSPECTIVES   372
    Relativistic Perspective   373
    Power Perspective   373
    Social Justice Perspective   374
    Evolutionary Perspective   374
PRIME BENEFICIARY APPROACH   374
AN OVERVIEW OF ORGANIZATIONAL EFFECTIVENESS   377
Summary   378
Developing Your Perspectives   379
References   379

Managing Diversity   383

Manage Your Learning ■ Strategic Concepts   384

ORGANIZATIONS AND DIVERSITY   384
DIVERSITY DEFINED   386
DIMENSIONS OF DIVERSITY   387
DIFFERENCES VERSUS DEFICITS   389
WHY THE CONCERN WITH DIVERSITY?   389
BENEFITS OF MANAGING DIVERSITY   391
COSTS OF MANAGING DIVERSITY   392
PERSPECTIVES ON MANAGING DIVERSITY   392

OPTIONS FOR HANDLING DIVERSITY   397
CONCEPTUAL FRAMEWORKS OF DIVERSITY IN SPORT   401
AN INTEGRATIVE FRAMEWORK   404
    Competence as the Cornerstone   404
    Forms of Diversity   404
    Diversity Management Strategies   406
    Task Factors   408
    Time Factor   410
A CONTINGENCY PERSPECTIVE   411
ACTUALIZATION   414
Summary   414
Developing Your Perspectives   415
References   415

AUTHOR INDEX   418

SUBJECT INDEX   421

Packianathan Chelladurai, or "Chella" as he is most widely and affectionately known, has clearly established himself as one of the preeminent scholars in sport management. Chella has left an indelible mark at two world-class universities, the University of Western Ontario, London, Canada, and the Ohio State University. Throughout his career, he has directly influenced aspiring scholars at both institutions and broadly influenced all of us within the field of sport management through his insightful writing, research, and counsel.

Chella's contributions have been recognized worldwide. Over the past three decades, Chella has become sport management's "international spokesperson." He has been invited to speak and consult on a worldwide basis, presenting at national and international conferences held in the Republic of South Africa, Korea, the Netherlands, Japan, Hungary, France, England, Spain, Taiwan, India, and Poland, among other countries. His influence has been felt in sport management associations in India, Japan, and Europe, in addition to his significant contributions in both Canada and the United States.

Chella has established a prolific publishing record over the past 30 years. His articles have appeared in issues of the *Journal of Sport Management, Journal of Sport and Exercise Psychology, Research Quarterly for Exercise and Sport,* and others. Chella's first textbook, *Sport Management: Macro Perspectives,* published in 1985, represented a clear departure from the norm of earlier texts in the field; it was marked, and uniquely so at the time, by an integration of management theory with clear, practical applications for the field of sport management. Chella is also the author of *Human Resource Management in Sport and Recreation* (Human Kinetics, 1999).

The marriage of sound theory and excellent practice in the field of sport management has long been talked about but rarely achieved. Chella has dedicated his professional career to this goal, and this most recent book, *Managing Organizations for Sport and Physical Activity: A Systems Perspective,* Second Edition, represents a giant step toward its achievement.

GARTH PATON
Kinesiology, University of New Brunswick, Canada
North American Society for Sport Management

This book is an effort to facilitate a full understanding of management by bringing relevant theories and concepts to bear upon the issues we face in managing organizations that deal with sport and physical activity. In essence, the book describes and discusses sport and physical activity organizations and their management from a systems perspective, as indicated in the title. Of course, most of the chapters in the book are devoted to management and its functions as outlined below.

I have attempted to incorporate the perspectives and models most relevant to managing sport and physical activity organizations. In the Introduction, I provide a brief historical view of the emergence of the field of sport management. In addition, I discuss the economic impact of the sport industry and its components. The immensity of the sport industry highlights the significance of managing the organizations that produce the sport product/services. I provide a comprehensive description of the field in Chapter 1 in terms of the services produced and marketed in the field. Chapter 2 is devoted to defining organizations and to a description of their attributes and forms. In Chapter 3 I discuss the concept of systems and systems thinking and present the perspective of organizations as open systems. In Chapter 4 I describe management in terms of its functions, skills necessary for effective management, and the roles of managers.

After describing the field of sport management, the concept of organizations, the systems perspective, and the process of management in the first four chapters, I move on to discuss the four major functions of management in Chapters 5–13. While outlining the process of planning in Chapter 5, I also discuss the issues associated with organizational goals, the generation of information needed for effective planning, and the relationship between planning and budgeting. As almost every aspect of management is concerned with making decisions, Chapter 6 is devoted to managerial decision making and various models of decision making. I also discuss the social processes of decision making and the appropriateness of varying degrees of member involvement in decision making under diverse conditions.

Chapters 7 and 8 deal with the function of organizing. In Chapter 7, I briefly describe the classical principles of organizing, then delve into Weber's bureaucracy as a popular form of organizing—both its strengths and weaknesses. I also highlight the significant and complementary place of bureaucracy in a democracy. Chapter 8 outlines the systems perspectives on organizing and the need for differentiation and integration within organiza-

New to This Edition

- Updating to include new research and developments in the industry.
- Updated discussion of organizational forms, with new information on contemporary organizations that includes internal, external, and interorganizational networks.
- New material on management competencies, biases in decision making, and the resource-based view of organizations.
- A new section on environmental influences on organizations, including expanded information on stakeholders and discussions of institutional and resource-dependent theories.
- New sidebars—on such topics as outsourcing coaching and stakeholder influence on college football—that further apply the book's concepts to the sport industry.
- New and updated case studies in the instructor's manual.

Instructor's Manual and PowerPoint presentation are available to adopters of this book.

tions. It also highlights the importance of boundary-spanning units of an organization in its interactions with its environment.

While the functions of planning and organizing are more conceptual or cerebral in nature, the function of leading is relatively more interpersonal. Because the leading function is oriented toward influencing and motivating members, it is essential that we gain insight into individual motivation. Thus, Chapter 9 addresses individual motivation. I describe the more significant and popular theories of motivation focused on the *content* as well as the *process* of motivation. I conclude the chapter with a description of an integrative theory of motivation. Chapter 10 discusses the critical interpersonal and behavioral process of leadership. I describe the classical theories of leadership that focus on the leader, the members, and the situational elements. In Chapter 11, I discuss the more contemporary approaches to leadership, including transformational and charismatic leadership and the leader–member-exchange theory (LMX). I conclude the chapter with a description of my own Multidimensional Model of Leadership as an integrative framework.

The next two chapters expand on the managerial function of evaluation: program evaluation and assessing organizational effectiveness respectively. The other significant aspect of performance appraisal, the evaluation of individual performance, is covered in my companion book, *Human Resource Management in Sport and Recreation* (Human Kinetics, 1999). Chapter 12, on program evaluation, deals with purposes and processes of evaluating various programs of a sport or physical activity organization. Chapter 13 emphasizes organizational effectiveness as the ultimate dependent variable of any organizational analysis or managerial action. I present the problems associated with defining and measuring the concept of organizational effectiveness as political and scientific issues. The political aspect of organizational effectiveness refers to the question of whose views should prevail in the effectiveness judgments. In addition to the various perspectives advanced in this debate, I describe the "prime beneficiary" approach to resolving the issue of whose views should hold in the assessment of organizational effectiveness.

In the final chapter, I discuss the emergent concerns with managing diversity. As the American population becomes more and more diverse, the clients/customers and employees of sport and physical activity organizations also become more diverse. Accordingly, I discuss the issues associated with diversity and the approaches to managing diversity. In the process, I highlight the notion that management is fundamentally concerned with coordinating the diverse elements in its domain (i.e., its human and material resources, the various organizational processes, the products, the stakeholders, and other environmental elements). Thus, the chapter serves to synthesize the essential thrusts of the previous chapters.

Each of the chapters contains learning objectives, key terms, illustrative diagrams, boxed summaries of key concepts titled "In Brief," and sidebars offering significant statements and excerpts from theorists or theories. At the end of each chapter I provide a comprehensive list of references and a list of issues and questions under the heading "Developing Your Perspectives." Readers and instructors should find these learning aids useful. Readers will recognize that this book does not provide details for "how to" carry out certain managerial activities. There are two reasons. First, as noted in Chapter 3 on the systems view of organizations, there is no "one best way" to carry out the managerial activities. Second, a prescription of one way of doing things might lead readers to form habits. This would be fine with simpler and noncritical tasks. But as Vroom (2003) pointed out, "habits typically reflect the learning environment at the time the habit was formed. As long as the environment is unchanging, this property is fine. But in a changing world, such as that which most managers currently experience, habits can be troublesome" (p. 977).

The most obvious audience for this book is among students in sport management, broadly defined to include physical education, high school and collegiate athletics, campus recreation, community recreation, club management, aquatics management, and such other fields concerned with sport and physical activity. Further, because athletic coaching is a form of management, teachers of coaching courses may also find most of the content of the book relevant to their courses. Readers will find the content of the book straightforward. Teachers will have the flexibility to choose or emphasize specific chapters and introduce their own material to supplement the text.

The theories and models I have included may reflect my preferences, and the interpretations of them may be a function of my biases. This sets the stage for instructors and readers to debate contentious issues and to generate alternate views and solutions.

While acknowledging my debt to my reviewers, colleagues, and co-investigators and to my students, who over the years have shaped my thoughts and perspective on sport management, I have one request for the readers of the book: When you find conceptual or technical flaws in the text, please let me know. If you are pleased with the book, please tell others.

Reference

Vroom, V. H. (2003). Educating managers for decision making and leadership. *Management Decision, 41* (10), 968–978.

ACKNOWLEDGMENTS

I would first like to express my gratitude to my mentors and benefactors, Dr. Earle Zeigler and Dr. Garth Paton, who lured me into sport management inspired me with their enthusiasm and love for the field, and groomed me to be a professional in the field. I thank my doctoral advisor Dr. Shoukry Saleh of the University of Waterloo for being a role model of patience, friendship, and scholarship. Terry Haggerty, who befriended me when I was a struggling student and helped me sustain the rigors of higher education in Canada at the University of Western Ontario, deserves a special thanks.

I am grateful to Dr. Dorothy Zakrajsek, who recruited me to the Ohio State University, and to Dr. Mary Daniels, who was the first teacher to prescribe my first book as the required text for her class.

I am also thankful to the host of my students who provided valuable comments and insightful questions. My special thanks go to Harold Riemer, Kyungro Chang, Hasan Birol Yalcin, Brian Turner, and Marlene Dixon, who read the entire manuscript or parts of it and provided valuable feedback. I owe my gratitude to my learned colleagues Shirley Cleave, George Cunningham, Karen Danylchuk, and Aubrey Kent for their valuable input into this work. I am also thankful to Jordon Hamson, Brian Turner, and Carla Costa, who reviewed the revised edition and provided valuable feedback. My thanks are due to my current students Gonzalo Bravo, May Kim, Dave Shonk, Doug Stevens, Doyeon Won, and Zhu Zhang for their input into this revised version.

I am indebted to Colette Kelly and Gay Pauley of Holcomb Hathaway for the contract to write the text. Their insight and expertise in publishing as well as management have been valuable in editing the manuscript. While they deserve the credit for shaping my manuscript into publishable text, I am responsible for any remaining conceptual lapses and technical errors in the text. I also wish to thank Harold Reimer and Aubrey Kent for their work in preparing the Instructor's Manual, and Dianna Gray for her contribution to the book's PowerPoint presentation.

Since I left India 32 years ago, my roots in my Indian past have been slowly withering away, and new roots in North America have taken over in the form of my association with the community of sport management scholars and students. Even more significantly, the emotional roots are represented by my grandchildren, Jason, Shane, Daniel, Andrew, and Michelle, and their parents, Ruban and Karen, and Chandran and Sally. These delightful families and the bunch of boisterous kids keep my wife and me very happy and busy. They make me want to do more to be worthy of their affection and respect.

Of course, no words can express the depth of my gratitude to my wife, Ponnu, who has over the years tolerated my foibles and helped me in all my efforts. Her love, patience, and support sustain me in all spheres of my life.

This book is dedicated to the women in my life:

Sornammal	*My mother*
Kanagammal	*My mother-in-law*
Ponnuthai	*My wife*

INTRODUCTION

Sport Management: Its Past, Present, and Future

MANAGE YOUR LEARNING

After completing this introduction you should be able to:

- Understand the historical roots of sport management.
- Describe the current status of sport management.
- Explain the economic significance of sport.
- Know the career opportunities in sport management.
- Understand the prospects for sport management.

STRATEGIC CONCEPTS

administration of physical education
career opportunities
gross domestic sports product
job types
organizational contexts
participant sport
professional association
segments of sport industry
size of sport industry
sport industry
sport tourism

MANAGEMENT THEN AND NOW

An indelible mark of civilization has been the pooling and management of human effort. Indeed, the progress of the human race has been based on various forms of management through which the efforts of people have been channeled in specific ways. Numerous examples can be drawn from early history to show the historical contributions of management. Black and Porter (2000) note that management was thought about and practiced even in the centuries before Christ by the Mayans, Greeks, and Romans. As early as 1000 B.C., Chinese officials were said to have written on how to manage and control human activity. Black and Porter suggest that many features of early Chinese management resemble the tenets of modern-day bureaucracy (to be discussed in Chapter 7): "It is clear that even four thousand years ago, [Chinese] rulers searched for efficient and effective ways to manage people. In some respects, they came up with answers that sound very familiar today" (p. 33).

Robbins (1976) cites an example from Exodus in the Bible. When Moses was overburdened with administrative and judicial duties, his father-in-law advised that Moses should appoint able men as "rulers of thousands, and rulers of hundreds, rulers of fifties, and rulers of tens . . . and it shall be, that every great matter they shall bring unto thee, but every small matter they shall judge: so shall it be easier for thyself, and they shall bear the burden with thee" (Exodus 18:

17–23). This is, in essence, the institution of a hierarchy and the delegation of authority—managerial processes that are much touted in modern literature.

Although the study and practice of management can be traced to earliest times, intense and thorough investigation, as well as propagation of the art and science of management, began in the early part of the 20th century. Today, almost every university in North America offers programs in Business Administration, Public Administration, Hospital Administration, and other such specializations.

EMERGENCE OF SPORT MANAGEMENT

Even more recent is the emergence of a specialized field of management called sport management. As sport and physical activity have become dominant features of North American society, and indeed around the world, the number and types of organizations whose major domain of operation is sport and physical activity have multiplied dramatically over the past 30 years. In addition to the traditional concerns associated with the manufacture and retailing of sporting goods, various other organizations deal with sport and physical activity. A sampling of these organizations would include those that:

- offer the use of their facilities and equipment for sport and physical activity, as in health clubs,
- schedule activities, as in youth sport leagues,
- offer instruction in specific activities, as in municipal recreation departments,
- organize competitions and promote excellence, as in university intercollegiate programs, and
- regulate the affairs of the sport or activity within the state, province, or nation, as in national Olympic associations.

These various kinds of organizations that deal with sport and physical activity need to be managed effectively, hence the importance and emergence of sport management.

THE PAST

The field of sport management as we know it today had its beginnings in the educational institutions. It was then called organization and **administration of physical education.** Zeigler (1951) notes that a course in organization and administration of physical education and athletics was offered even as early as 1890. The subject matter of early courses was mostly concerned with maintenance of sport facilities in educational institutions, purchase and care of equipment, and organizing and conducting sport events.

The major impetus for sport becoming a dominant feature of American society was high-school and collegiate sports. As we all know, no other country in the world places such emphasis on sports in educational institutions as the United States. The sport facilities in many high schools in America would be the envy of some of the larger universities around the world. As another example, the annual budget of the intercollegiate athletic departments in many major universities amounts to about 30 million dollars. That is more than what many governments around the world spend on all of their sport and physical education programs.

With the increasing popularity of educational sports, including intramural sports and the associated financial outlay, came the emphasis on management of that phenomenon. Several universities began offering programs on administration of high-school athletics and intercollegiate sports. We have such programs even today. These professional preparation programs have been primarily confined to preparation of administrators or managers of sport in the educational institutions.

Landmark Thrusts

About 40 years ago, two significant moves came about to foster the emergence of sport management as we know it today. First, Dr. James G. Mason at Ohio University began a program of training for managers of professional sports. Although the program started in 1966, the idea was said to have been originally proposed to Dr. Mason in 1957 by Walter O'Malley, president of the Brooklyn Dodgers, a professional sport franchise (Stier, 1999). Many of the alumni of the program are now employed in various professional sport franchises. With that broad and deep network, the program is still going strong.

The other significant thrust moved toward the academic study of sport management, spearheaded by Dr. Earle F. Zeigler in the 1960s (Paton, 1987). He and his students at the universities of Michigan, Illinois, and Western Ontario formed the vanguard of the academic study of sport management. They continue to be significant contributors to the field. In recognition of Dr. Zeigler's leadership and contribution, the North American Society for Sport Management (NASSM) has instituted an award in his name to be presented to outstanding individuals in the field.

In Brief

The field of sport management has grown from earlier fields of administration of physical education and athletics. Sport management is broader in scope, and it includes the earlier fields.

THE PRESENT

I describe the present status of sport management in two sections: the professional status of the occupation of sport management and the economic status of the sport industry. We need to consider both of these aspects because the occupation of sport management is concerned with managing the sport industry.

Professional Status of Sport Management

The professional status of any occupation is defined by several factors. The following section outlines three significant factors elevating the status of sport management: degree programs, professional associations, and scholarly journals.

Sport Management Degree Programs

At the moment, more than 200 universities in North America offer sport management degree programs at the bachelor's, master's, and doctorate levels. It is among the fastest growing areas of study in American universities. More and more students want to enroll in these programs, and universities, starving for students, are expanding their programs to accommodate this great demand. For instance, it was reported that 210 entry-level faculty positions were open during 1997–1999 (Mondello, Mahony, Hums, & Moorman, 2002). Many doctoral students are able to find a teaching job in a university before or immediately after graduating. As another example of the growth of sport management, many universities and governments in Europe and the European Union have endorsed a program for a European master's degree in sport management.

Professional Associations

The maturity of a profession is indicated by the existence of a **professional association** that brings together scholars and practitioners to exchange ideas and generate guidelines for self-regulation of the profession and its members. The NASSM (www.nassm.org) has been in existence since 1985. The joint task force set up by the National Association of Sport and Physical Education (NASPE, www.aahperd.org/naspe) and NASSM has developed a set of curricular guidelines for baccalaureate, master's, and doctoral degree programs in sport management. It has also put in place a process for approving new programs (NASPE/NASSM Joint Task Force, 1993). The Sport Marketing Association (SMA, www.sportmarketingassociation.com) was founded in 2002 and held its first annual meeting in November 2003.

Beyond North America are several other organizations. Japan can boast of two: the Japanese Society of Sport Management (JSSM) and the Japanese Society of Sport Industry (JSSI). These societies have annual conferences and their own publications. The European Association of Sport Management (EASM), formed in 1993, has grown to hold considerable influence in the field. Australia and New Zealand have joined hands to form the Sport Management Association of Australia and New Zealand (SMAANZ). The Asian Association for Sport Management was founded in 2003. Even more recently, the Sports Tourism International Council has been formed with its headquarters in Ottawa, Canada.

Journals in Sport Management

Another hallmark of a profession's growth is the publication of scholarly and trade journals. The journals dedicated to sport management in North America are the *Journal of Sport Management*, first published in January 1987, and the *Sport Marketing Quarterly*, first published in 1992. The *International Journal of Sport Management* was launched in 1999. Beyond North America, the *European Journal of Sport Management* (currently named *European Sport Management Quarterly*) began publication immediately after the EASM's inauguration in 1993. The *Journal of Sport Sponsorship* was introduced in the United Kingdom in 1999. As noted earlier, the Japanese associations have their own publications. The SMAANZ began publishing its own journal, *Sport Management Review*, in 1999. The *Journal of Sport Tourism* began publication in 2003. These publications will go a long way to sustain and advance the study and practice of sport management. They also indicate the growth of sport management as a profession.

In addition to these dedicated journals, several other journals and trade publications publish sport management–related articles. These include *Athletic Administration, Fitness Management, Interscholastic Athletic Administration, Journal of American Fitness Association, Journal of Leisure Research, Journal of the National Intramural Recreation Sports Association (NIRSA), Journal of Parks and Recreation Administration, Athletic Business, Athletic Management, Club Industry, Corporate Fitness and Recreation,* and *Fitness Management.* A more significant publication dedicated to the sport business is *Street & Smith's SportsBusiness Journal,* which began publication in 1998. It is an important source of current information on many matters related to sports as a business.

In Brief

The professional status of sport management as an occupation is indicated by the number and quality of degree programs offered by universities, the professional associations, and the number of journals published.

Economic Significance of the Sport Industry

The foregoing developments in terms of degree programs, professional associations, and journal publications are only a reflection of the economic significance of sport. There are several estimates on the **size of the sport industry**. They differ not only in the time frame for the estimate (e.g., year 1995 versus 1999), but also in what they include as part of the **sport industry**. Despite these differences, they all show that the sport industry is a vibrant and growing one, ranking among the top 10 industries in the United States. For illustrative purposes, I summarize two recent estimates in the following sections.

Size of the Sport Industry

There have been various estimates of the size of sport industry in the United States. Brown (2002) noted that among the various estimates of the size of the sport industry, Meek's (1997) was the most accurate as it encompassed all forms of sport participation, and as it followed the Federal guidelines on estimating an industry size. Meek (1997) reported that the size of the sport industry was $152 billion in 1995. He labeled this amount the **gross domestic sports product** (GDSP). Meek applied the same rules and methodology used by the U.S. Department of Commerce in calculating the gross domestic product (GDP). The breakdown of the $152 billion is shown in Exhibit 1.1.

The GDSP of $152 billion represents the final consumption of sport products and services. Any intermediary transactions between production and final consumption are not included in this figure (Meek, 1997). For example, the $80 price for a tennis racket includes the price the retailer paid for the racket and all the expenses incurred in transporting, storing, and displaying the racket. Meek cautioned that including those expenses would amount to "double" counting. However, he also notes that such transactions do constitute economic activity. His estimate of the additional economic activity supported by the sport industry was another $259 billion in 1995. Thus, the sport industry accounted for more than $400 billion of economic activity in the nation.

Exhibit 1.1 Meek's (1997) economic value of the sport industry in 1995 (in billions of dollars).

A. SPORTS CONSUMPTION

1. Entertainment and Recreation

Participation in leisure sports	32.000	
Admission to spectator sports	5.300	
Pari-mutuel net receipts	3.300	
Concessions, souvenirs, etc.	3.400	
Other	.173	
Total		44.173

2. Products and Services

Equipment, apparel, & footwear	71.000	
Sports medicine	18.500	
Trading cards, videos, books, etc.	3.500	
Other	.153	
Total		93.153

3. Nonsport-related Advertising   7.522

Total Sports Consumption   144.848

B. SPORTS INVESTMENTS

Infrastructure Investments   11.816

C. SPORTS NET EXPORTS

Imports	10.151
Exports	4.544
International Licensing	1.000
Net (Exports and Licensing minus Imports)	(4.700)

Total Gross Domestic Sports Product (GDSP)   151.964

From: Meek (1997).
Note: Totals subject to rounding errors.

What is even more impressive is that according to Meek (1997), the sport industry ranked 11 among the top 25 industries in the United States in 1995. It was ranked higher than, for example, chemicals and allied products ($141 billion), electronic and electrical equipment ($138.5 billion), and industrial machinery and equipment ($123.3 billion).

The latest estimate as of writing this chapter comes from *Street & Smith's SportsBusiness Journal* in its last issue for the year 1999 (December 20–26). Defining the sport industry as "money generated by organized sports" (Broughton, Lee, & Nethery, 1999, p. 23), it proclaimed that the sport industry was worth $213 billion. Exhibit 1.2 shows the breakdown of the **segments**

Exhibit I.2 *Street & Smith's SportsBusiness Journal* estimate of economic value of the sport industry in 1999 (in billions of dollars).

A. ADVERTISING
1. Network telecasts	5.66	
2. National cable	1.39	
3. Regional	.47	
4. Print	1.8	
5. Stadium/arena signs	16.68	
6. Radio	2.25	
TOTAL		28.25

B. ENDORSEMENTS
Top 80 athletes	0.486	
Projected total for all		.73

C. ACTIVE EQUIPMENT/APPAREL/FOOTWEAR
Used in Competition
1. Sportswear	8.73	
2. Footwear	6.93	
3. Equipment	9.28	
TOTAL		24.94

D. FACILITY CONSTRUCTION
1. Stadium/track	1.70	
2. Arena	0.79	
TOTAL		2.49

E. INTERNET
1. Advertising	0.295	
2. Access fees	0.005	
TOTAL		0.3

F. LICENSED GOODS
1. Apparel/footwear	8.8	
2. Home (housewares, furniture, etc.)	0.99	
3. Media (electronics, software, etc.)	3.63	
4. Miscellaneous	1.68	
TOTAL		15.1

G. MEDIA BROADCAST RIGHTS
1. Big four pro leagues	8.87	
2. Collegiate telecasts	0.987	
3. Other telecasts	0.270	
4. Radio	0.443	
TOTAL		10.57

H. PROFESSIONAL SERVICES
1. Agents	0.223	
2. Marketing agencies	2.37	
3. Facility management	5.74	
4. Financial, legal, insurance	5.70	
TOTAL		14.03

Continued.

Exhibit I.2

I. SPECTATOR SPORTS		
1. General admissions	10.47	
2. Premium seating	3.25	
3. Game day concessions, etc.	8.84	
TOTAL		22.56

J. SPONSORSHIPS		
Events/teams/leagues		5.09

K. MEDICAL TREATMENT		
1. Baseball	1.45	
2. Football	1.16	
3. Basketball	0.759	
4. Soccer	0.314	
5. Softball	0.150	
6. Other	0.267	
TOTAL		4.10

L. TRAVEL		
1. Spectators	40.82	
2. Colleges	1.09	
3. Big four pro leagues	0.295	
4. Other	2.26	
TOTAL		44.47

M. PUBLICATIONS/VIDEOS		
1. Magazine	0.922	
2. Videos/video games	0.752	
3. Books	0.450	
TOTAL		2.12

N. GAMBLING		
1. Legal sports wagers	2.30	
2. Horses/greyhounds, jai alai	15.33	
3. U.S. Internet	0.920	
TOTAL		18.55

O. TEAM OPERATING EXPENSES		
1. Big four pro league player salaries	5.24	
2. Big four pro league operating expenses	7.00	
3. Colleges	4.30	
4. Others	2.69	
TOTAL		19.23

Grand Total for the Sport Industry	213.00

From "The answer: $213 billion," by Broughton, Lee, & Nethery. *Street & Smith's SportsBusiness Journal, 2* (35), December 20–26, 1999. All rights reserved. Used with permission.

Note: Totals are rounded figures.

of the sport industry and their worth. *Street & Smith's SportsBusiness Journal* boasted that the sport industry was bigger than

communications ($212 billion)	mining ($121 billion)
public utilities ($210 billion)	motor vehicles and equipment ($85 billion)
agriculture ($132 billion)	motion pictures ($31 billion)

According to this estimate, the only industries that were bigger than the sports industry were

real estate ($935 billion)	banking ($266 billion)
retail trade ($713 billion)	transportation ($256 billion)
health care ($460 billion)	

The figures provided by Broughton, Lee, and Nethery (1999) are very impressive indeed, considering that they do not include some of the segments included in the Meek (1997) report. (See Sidebar 1.1 for some of the exclusions.) Students must take note of the fact that the travel expenses of spectators and teams amounted to $44.47 billion, which is 20 percent of the total for the sport industry. Thus, it is not surprising that a specialized field of study labeled **sport tourism** has emerged, bridging areas of sport management and tourism. Gibson (2003) refers to three types of tourism: "(a) active sport tourism where participants travel to take part in sport; (b) event sport tourism where participants travel to watch sport; and (c) nostalgia sport tourism where participants visit sports-related attractions such as halls of fame, famous stadia, or sports-themed cruises" (p. 207). Courses in sport tourism are being introduced in many degree programs. Many scholars are researching this topic, and some have written textbooks (e.g., Standeven & De Knop, 1999).

In Brief

The sport industry is larger than many established industries. The estimates of the economic worth of the industry vary from $150 to $213 billion.

Here are some more impressive figures. The CBS television network paid the NCAA over $500 million per year to televise the annual men's basketball tournament, and the ABC television network gave $100 million a year for the rights to telecast the four games of Football's Bowl Championship Series (*By the Numbers*, 2002). The 115 NCAA Division I-A athletic departments had combined annual expenditures of $2.3 billion (Fulks, 2002). Mahony and Howard (2001) report that $16 billion was spent on new arenas and stadiums during the 1990s and that, in 1998, 5,000 companies spent $5.1 billion on sponsoring sporting events and teams in the United States and Canada. The sale of sport-licensed products amounted to $11.45 billion in 2000. The International Health, Racquet & Sportsclub Association (IHRSA) reports that at the end of 2001, 33.8 million Americans were members of 18,203 clubs, which had a combined total revenue of $12.3 billion (IHRSA, 2004).

Participant or Recreational Sport

The foregoing impressive figures include elite sport offered by organizations such as the professional sport leagues and the NCAA Division I schools. But the expenses incurred for participation are even more impres-

Packing List

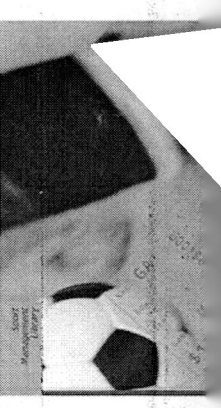

Order Date	2008-11-30 10:20:22
Amazon Order #	058-2557619-8314956
Go4Books Reference #	22203
SKU Locator #	9781885693389 howard
Requested Ship Method	standard
	Media Mail
Email	heather_cornett@mail.msj.edu

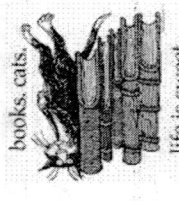

books. cats.
life is sweet.

Heather Cornett
2222 S GREENWOOD DR APT 13
Johnson City, TN 37604-7055

Quantity   *1*
Book Title   *Financing Sport, Second Edition (Sport Management Library) [Hardcover] by...*
Author   *Dennis R. Howard*

Thanks for your order!

We strive to provide the best possible customer service! If you were completely satisfied with this order please give us a 5 star review on Amazon. If you were not completely satisfied, please email us and tell us why at:

Financing Sport
2nd Edition
Dennis R. Howard
John L. Crompton

The contemporary sport manager must be an entrepreneur who uses marketing and financing skills to yield optimum social and economic benefits. Financing Sport Second Edition provides the most in-depth exploration of traditional and innovative revenue acquisition methods for sport organizations. The first edition of this groundbreaking text published in 1995 has been adopted in universities throughout the world and has been translated into Chinese and Japanese. Rather than simply updating sections of various chapters—common to most new editions—the authors approached each chapter as though writing the book for the first time. The business of sport is fast paced and ever changing. The content of the Second Edition captures the many new and creative ideas managers in sport organizations have implemented in response to their dynamic work environment. The second edition also

Don't be shy to include any suggestions as to how we may improve our customer service. We are here to serve you!

Returns Policy: "If your return is due to a mistake on our part we will refund you 100% of the total you paid. If you need to return the book for any other reason you may do so, but we charge a 40% restocking fee."

Returns Address:

213 Oak Street SE
Minneapolis, MN 55414

*** Be sure to include the order number shown below with any return so we'll know who to credit!

Order Number 058-2557619-8314956

Sidebar

As noted, the various estimates of the size of the sport industry differ in what they include (or do not include) as part of the sport industry. The following are some of the exclusions in the estimate provided by *Street & Smith's SportsBusiness Journal*.

> The most visible exclusion from our study was that of recreational pastimes. Fishing, hunting, camping, and personal fitness generate billions of dollars, but until corporate America starts sponsoring your personal weight regimen, or a major network pays for broadcast rights to your next hunting expedition, we'll stay focused on organized sports. We also sought to clarify past categories. In previous studies, spectator sports was a massive section because it included all money involved with being a viewer of sports, whether you were listening to a game while lounging in your hammock or were actually at the ball yard. It included ad revenue and broadcast fees. . . . At the risk of sounding like sports snobs, we say that if you haven't paid for a ticket—if there's no chance of you catching a foul ball or high-fiving a mascot—you're a viewer, not a spectator. Our spectator category covers game-day, on-site expenditures. This does not negate past studies; it simply breaks the category down a bit. (Broughton, Lee, & Nethery, 1999)

sive. The sum of $32 billion spent for participation and the $71 billion spent on equipment, apparel, and footwear (i.e., $103 billion) constitute more than 60 percent of the money Americans spent on participation in sport. That is, nearly two-thirds of the sport industry is represented by participant sport (Chelladurai, 1999). Viewed from another perspective, **participant sport** is the core of the sport industry, which spawns the spectator sport, which, in turn, supports (and is supported by) other related industries (see Exhibit 1.3).

As one example, consider that 40 million U. S. youth participate in various sports outside of the programs organized by educational institutions (National Council of Youth Sports-NCYS, 2001). Ferguson (1999) provided estimates for participation in various sports at the youth level, per youth per year, with some examples of those expenses shown in Exhibit 1.4. Note that hockey, the most expensive sport, is not included, although Ferguson refers to a family spending $4,500 for their son's participation in hockey. At any rate, the overall average expenditure for the selected sports varies from a minimum of $628 to $1889 per person. Taking into account the inflation since 1999, we can make a modest estimate of $1000 per participant. If we take this average and multiply it by the 40 million youth participating in sport, the value of the youth sport segment of the sport industry would be $40 billion. We should also consider student participation in athletics at the elementary, middle, and high school levels, and the vast number of athletes in non-revenue sports in collegiate athletics.

SPORT MANAGEMENT: ITS PAST, PRESENT, AND FUTURE 11

Exhibit I.3 Segmentation of sport industry.

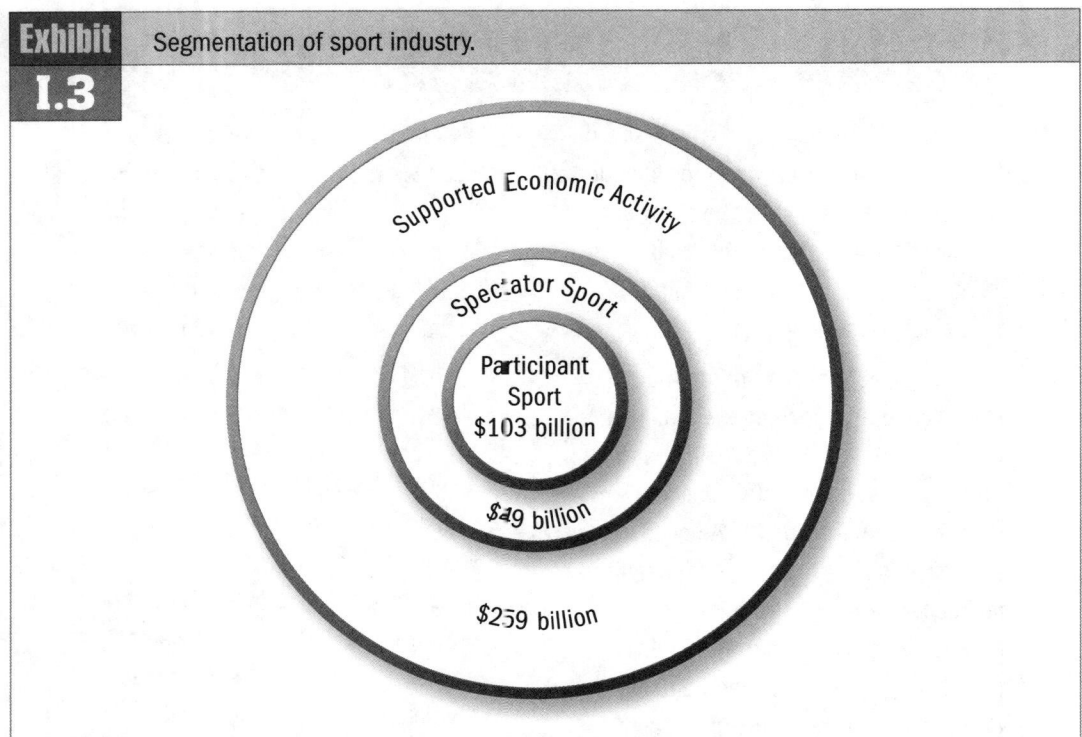

From: Chelladurai (1999). *Sport management: Quo vadis?* Keynote presentation at the 7th Congress of the European Association for Sport Management. Thessaloniki, Greece. September 16–19, 1999.

Exhibit I.4 Cost of participation in U. S. youth sports, per youth per year.

Sport	EQUIPMENT		CLUBS		TRAVEL		CLINICS		TOTAL	
	Min	Max	Min	Max	Min	Max	Min	Max	Min	Max
Track and Field	600	1,500	100	100	100	500	50	100	850	2,200
Soccer	85	265	30	400	50	250	400	600	565	1,515
Basketball	200	395	12	150	60	210	100	400	372	1,155
Baseball	150	450	25	150	10	100	200	600	385	1,300
Tennis	130	750	50	700	100	1,500	600	900	880	3,850
Swimming	45	100	25	450	40	150	600	600	710	1,300
Overall Total	1,210	3,460	242	1,950	360	2,710	1,950	3,200	3,762	11,320
Overall Average	201.66	576.66	40.33	325.00	60.00	451.66	325.00	533.33	627.00	1,886.66

*Cost per clinic single session; no information regarding number of clinics attended.

CAREER OPPORTUNITIES IN SPORT MANAGEMENT

The foregoing account of the economic significance of the sport industry also underscores the wide variety of **career opportunities** available in the sport industry. Meek (1997), who estimated the gross domestic sport product to be $152 billion in 1995, also estimated that the sport industry provided employment for nearly 2.32 million people in direct activity in generating the GDSP. This employment yielded a household income of $52 billion. In addition, another 2.33 million people were employed in the economic activities supported by the sport industry. This employment added $75 billion to household incomes. Overall, the sport industry facilitated the employment of 4.65 million people for a total household income of $127 billion.

Organizational Contexts

These employment opportunities are offered by different kinds of organizations pursuing different goals and employing different processes to achieve their goals within the sport domain. The following is a partial list of **organizational contexts** involved in sport:

- educational institutions, including elementary and high schools, colleges, and universities
- professional sport teams
- nonprofit organizations that offer sport, fitness, and wellness services, such as the YMCA and Boys and Girls Clubs
- profit-oriented firms dealing in sport, fitness, and wellness services
- corporate fitness and wellness units
- profit-oriented firms providing consulting, legal, agency, and marketing services
- government agencies such as city recreation departments and state parks and recreation departments
- the U.S. Armed Forces
- sport-governing bodies at the national and state levels (e.g., the United States Basketball Association, the United States Lawn Tennis Association, the Ohio State Volleyball Association)
- international sport-governing bodies such as the International Federation of Basketball Associations (FIBA) and International Federation of Football [Soccer] Associations (FIFA)
- umbrella sport organizations such as the National Collegiate Athletic Association and the U.S. Olympic Committee

Activity/Job Types

Careers in sport management can also be broadly classified on the basis of specific activities or **job types.** These activity/job areas include:

- event management
- facility management
- ticketing operations

- licensing operations
- concession operations
- legal issues
- scheduling of facility/equipment
- programming
- rental operations
- scheduling of games/activities
- tournament operations
- parking operations
- marketing operations
- public relations
- personnel management
- budgeting and accounting

Note that not all of the above classes of activities will be relevant to all organizations. For example, ticketing operations are meaningful only where sport is offered as entertainment for a fee. Also, within any type of activity area, there may be different levels of jobs arranged in a hierarchical order. For instance, in a large university athletic department, there may be a director of ticketing operations with one or more assistant directors who, in turn, may supervise several ticketing clerks. Similarly, the employees maintaining a city's ballparks usually are organized into two or more hierarchical levels. The aerobics instructors in a fitness club may be supervised by a higher-ranking person.

THE FUTURE OF SPORT MANAGEMENT

Pitts and Stotlar (1996) reported that the size of the sport industry was $47.3 billion in 1986, which jumped to $50.2 billion in 1987 and to $63.1 billion in 1988. They predicted that at an average growth rate of 6.8 percent, the industry would grow to be worth $139 billion. As noted, this figure was surpassed even in 1995 according to Meek (1997). The latest estimate by *Street & Smith's SportsBusiness Journal* (Broughton, Lee, & Nethery, 1999) shows the sport industry to be even larger at $213 billion in 1999. Despite the discrepancies in what is included in the sport industry and how they are estimated, these figures do indicate substantial growth. We could also expect that at some point the sport industry might hit a plateau. In fact, Mahony and Howard (2001) caution that such growth may not be experienced in future years. They noted that the boom of the 1990s may indeed place the industry in a precarious position. The issues they identify are:

- The continuing and growing disparity between large- (e.g., New York Yankees) and small-market (Pittsburgh Pirates) teams. Although small-market teams may be able to close the gap by building new stadiums, their glamour fades away in about three years. Thus, the small market teams still lag in their capacity to generate revenues. For instance, Mahony and Howard (2001) point out that when the Los Angeles Dodgers team could charge $375,000 a year for their luxury suites, the Pittsburgh Pirates could charge only $175,000 a year.

- Public support for teams to build new facilities waned toward the end of the 1990s. Thus, some teams have had to shell out enormous amounts of money themselves to build those facilities. This meant that the cost of servicing their debts proportionately increased. According to Mahony and Howard, this debt service could cost as much as $30 million for some teams.
- In an attempt to make up for the increasing costs, professional franchises have begun to increase ticket prices. As a consequence, attendance at games has begun to dwindle.
- Further, expecting corporations to continue to lease the luxury suites also poses problems. When the economy takes a downturn, corporations may shy away from these arrangements.

Mahony and Howard do have some suggestions for managers of professional sports on how to remain viable. The first suggestion is for professional sport franchises to exploit Web technology to market themselves, sell their tickets and licensed merchandise, and communicate with the public. Their second suggestion is that the managers should exploit big events (e.g., Super Bowl and World Cup), rivalries between teams (e.g., New York Yankees and Boston Red Sox), and stars (e.g., Lebron James). The NCAA effectively exploits its annual basketball tournament (the so-called March Madness). Mahony and Howard suggest that if the NCAA adopted a national play-off format for football (i.e., creating a new and more significant and prolonged event), it could generate even more publicity, prestige, and wealth. Other suggestions include tapping new markets (as in the NFL expanding into Europe) and reconnecting with traditional fans (as when universities cater to students), creative financing (as in selling shares or bonds), cutting budgets (i.e., reducing costs), and seeking synergy (i.e., merging with or acquiring other agencies). Although Mahony and Howard (2001) present a somewhat gloomy picture of the future of sport business, their description is confined to professional sport. As noted earlier, professional sport is only a small portion of the sport industry.

Now to a more optimistic forecast of the future of sport industry. In forecasting the patterns of economic growth in the next thousand years, Molitor (1996) proposed that economic growth will be powered by the "big five" engines: leisure time era, life sciences era, mega-materials era, new atomic age, and new space age. These eras are described in Exhibit 1.5. What is most relevant to us is that Molitor predicts that the engine behind the economic growth in the near future (i.e., by the year 2015) will be the leisure time era. In his view, this sector would account for 50 percent of the American GNP (gross national product). The sector would include, among several other activities, recreation, entertainment, gambling and wagering, travel, tourism, adventure-seeking, sports, exercising, and outdoor activities. These activities are similar to those included in the estimates of the size of the sport industry. Extrapolating from Molitor's perspective, we

> **In Brief**
>
> The future of sport management looks bright because the prospects for the sport industry itself are promising. Increasing leisure time, the popularity of women's sports, and globalization of sport are the bases for this optimism.

> **Exhibit I.5** Molitor's (1996) "big five" engines of economic growth in the next thousand years.
>
> 1. **LEISURE TIME ERA** (by 2015). Hospitality, recreation, and entertainment. Leisure time pursuits have been a part of human activity from the very outset. The change about to be fully felt occurs when "free time" dominates total individual lifetime activity.
>
> 2. **LIFE SCIENCES ERA** (2100). Bio-tech, genetics, cloning, genetic engineering, transgenics, and "pharming," among others. Theoretical underpinnings trace back more than a century. The pace began to accelerate with the human genome project, and it reached a dramatic turning point with the cloning of Dolly.
>
> 3. **MEGA-MATERIALS ERA** (2200–2300). Quantum mechanics, particle physics, nano-technologies, isotopes/allotropes/chirality, superconductors, and microscopic imaging systems constitute the major core technologies. This sector began to take off with the development of plastics, bulletproof Kevlar, ceramic engineering, high-strength alloys, composites, silicon, super-alloys, high-temperature superconductors, crystallography, cryogenics, semiconductors, time/temperature/pressure variable materials, designer materials.
>
> 4. **NEW ATOMIC AGE** (2100–2500). Thermonuclear fusion, hydrogen and helium isotopes, and lasers constitute the key technologies upon which almost every energy-dependent activity will depend. Paramountcy of these activities looms ever-closer as finite fossil fuels—first petroleum then natural gas, and finally coal—are depleted. This era reaches its apex a century or more into the future. Roots of coming change, however, trace far back in time. Commencing with theoretical foundations, this early phase came of age with "splitting the atom." Early experiments soon led to atomic fission, followed by development of thermonuclear explosives. Breakthroughs essential to harnessing fusion center on advances in magnetohydrodynamics, laser-induced implosion, and quantum physics.
>
> 5. **NEW SPACE AGE** (2500–3000). Astrophysics, cosmology, spacecraft development, exploration, travel, resource-gathering are pivotal activities propelling this stage of development. Beginnings for this sector trace back to gunpowder and rockets—developments over 2,000 years ago. World War II rockets and jet aircraft accelerated the pace. Sputnik, spy satellites, manned space missions, extra-planetary probes, and telescopic arrays that pierce the outermost limits of the universe are among the activities contributing to the conquest of space.

can say that the sport industry itself would be a driving force in the economic growth in the United States.

Molitor (1996) also notes that "leisure time, continuing to steadily increase, very soon will account for over 50 percent of lifetime activities in advanced-affluent nations" (p. 159). The increase in leisure time would be facilitated by shorter workdays and workweeks, increased number of holidays, longer vacations, increased leaves of absence, and early retirement. All of these scenarios augur well for the growth of the sport industry and sport management. We should also note two significant trends that affect sport management. The first significant emerging trend is the attraction of women's sports. Consider the Women's World Cup in soccer, held in the United States in 1999. If the unprecedented attendance rate and television audience are any indication, the boom in women's sports is going to be phenomenal. Concomitant with the increase in spectator appeal of women's sports, there will be an even greater demand for sport services that promote more—and more intensive—participation by women and girls. The second significant trend is the globalization of sport.

SUMMARY

The extent and significance of the sport industry are impressive. We must realize, however, that the sport industry did not just happen. Considerable entrepreneurial and managerial talents and efforts have fueled the phenomenal growth of the sport industry. Many organizations, both profit and nonprofit, have been and are responsible for the growth and sustenance of sport. These organizations produce and market sport-related products, and the extent of consumption of those products determines the size of the sport industry. The focus of this book will be on managing those organizations and coordinating the processes of producing and marketing sport products. Accordingly, the ensuing chapters will provide a more detailed description of several processes of managing those organizations.

DEVELOPING YOUR PERSPECTIVES

1. Consider Meek's (1997) estimate of the size of the sport industry in 1995 and Broughton, Lee, and Nethery's estimate in *Street & Smith's SportsBusiness Journal* for the year 1999 (see Exhibits I.1 and I.2). Compare and contrast the categories of industry segments employed in the two estimates. Identify the overlaps among them.

2. This Introduction presented a list of organizational types that offer job opportunities in sport as well as a list of job or activity types in sport management. Would you add anything to those two lists? What kind of job would you like, and in what type of organization? Explain.

References

Black, J. S., & Porter, L. W. (2000). *Management: Meeting new challenges.* Upper Saddle River, NJ: Prentice Hall.

Brown, M. (2002). The size of the sport industry in the United States: Understanding the methodologies. Paper presented at the 10th Congress of the European Association for Sport Management. Jyväskylä, Finland, Spetember 4–7.

Broughton, D., Lee, J., & Nethery, R. (1999, December 20–26). The answer: $213 billion. *Street & Smith's SportsBusiness Journal, 2,* 23–29.

By the Numbers. (2002). Charlotte, NC: Street & Smith.

Chelladurai, P. (1999). *Human resource management in sport and recreation.* Champaign, IL: Human Kinetics.

Ferguson, A. (1999). Inside the crazy culture of kids sports. *Time, 154* (2), 52–80. (July 12, 1999).

Fulks, D. L. (2002). *Revenues and expenses of Divisions I and II intercollegiate athletic programs: Financial trends and relationships—2001.* Indianapolis, IN: National Collegiate Athletic Association.

Gibson, H. J. (2003). Sport tourism: An introduction to the special issue. *Journal of Sport Management, 17,* 205–213.

IHRSA. (2004). Industry statistics. http://cms.ihrsa.org/IHRSA/viewPage.cfm?pageId=149. Retrieved on January 4, 2004.

Mahony, D. F., & Howard, D. R. (2001). Sport business in the next decade: A general overview of expected trends. *Journal of Sport Management, 15,* 275–296.

Meek, A. (1997). An estimate of the size and supported economic activity of the sport industry in the United States. *Sport Marketing Quarterly, 6* (4), 15–21.

Molitor, G. T. T. (1996). The next thousand years: The "big five" engines of economic growth. In G. T. Kurian & G. T. T. Molitor (Eds.), *The 21st century.* New York: Simon & Schuster Macmillan.

Mondello, M. J., Mahony, D., Hums, M., & Moorman, A. (2002). A survey of search committee chairpersons: Candidate qualifications preferred for entry-level tenure track sport management faculty positions. *International Review of Sport Management, 3,* 262–281.

NASPE/NASSM Joint Task Force on Sport Management Curriculum and Accreditation (1993). Standards for curriculum and voluntary accreditation of sport management education programs. *Journal of Sport Management, 7,* 159–170.

Paton, G. (1987). Sport management research: What progress has been made? *Journal of Sport Management, 1,* 25–31.

Pitts, B. G., & Stotlar, D. K. (1996). *Fundamentals of sport marketing.* Morgantown, WV: Fitness Information Technology.

Robbins, S. P. (1976). *The administrative process: Integrating theory and practice.* Englewood Cliffs, NJ: Prentice Hall.

Standeven, J., & De Knop, P. (1999). *Sport tourism.* Champaign, IL: Human Kinetics.

Stier, W. F. (1999). *Managing sport, fitness, and recreation programs: Concepts and practices.* Boston: Allyn and Bacon.

Zeigler, E. F. (1951). *A history of professional preparation for physical education in the United States, 1861–1948.* Unpublished doctoral dissertation. University of Oregon.

CHAPTER 1

Defining the Field of Sport Management*

*The contents of this chapter are largely drawn from Chelladurai (1992, 1994).

MANAGE YOUR LEARNING

After completing this chapter you should be able to:
- Describe the differences between goods and services.
- Distinguish among consumer, professional, and human services.
- Discuss the motives for participation in sport and physical activity.
- Analyze the distinctions among participant, spectator, sponsorship, and donor services.
- Describe the primary purpose of sport management.

STRATEGIC CONCEPTS

consumer services
coordination
human resources
human services
management
marketing
participant services

production
professional services
service attributes
spectator services
sponsorship services
support units
technology

THE FIELD DEFINED

The growth of sport management and its present scope were described in the Introduction. The figures provided to underscore the economic significance of the sport industry were all quite impressive. Despite the enormous progress described in the Introduction, there is no comprehensive and coherent description of our field. Some of the definitions that have been advanced show a divergent or fragmented view of sport management. For example, Chelladurai (1985) defines sport management as

> management of those organizations whose major domain of operation is sport and physical activity. (p. 4)

Similarly, Slack (1997) defines a sport organization as

> a social entity involved in the sport industry; it is goal directed with a consciously structured activity system and a relatively identifiable boundary. (p. 5)

Parks and Quarterman (2003) refer to DeSensi, Kelley, Blanton, and Beitel (1990) in defining sport management as an area that includes a wide variety of sport-related careers. (p. 8)

They also note that

sport management is also the name given to many university-level academic programs designed to prepare students to assume positions in the sport industry. (p. 8)

Their book includes contributions from other scholars who have focused on specific organizational contexts, such as intercollegiate athletics, or functional areas, such as sport marketing, where such career opportunities exist. Focusing on the academic units in colleges and universities, the NASPE/NASSM Joint Task Force on Sport Management Curriculum and Accreditation (1993) defines sport management as

the field of study offering the specialized training and education necessary for individuals seeking careers in any of the many segments of the industry. (p. 159)

Mullin (1980) defines a sport manager as

a person whose job entails planning, organizing, staffing, directing, and controlling to be performed within the context of an organization whose primary or predominant product or service is sport and sport-related. (p. 3)

In Brief

The various definitions of sport management differentially emphasize sport organizations, careers in sport management, and the sport industry. In all these cases, the focus ultimately turns to sport products.

Students must note the emphasis on sport or sport-related products. Yet another definition was offered by the founders of the North American Society for Sport Management (NASSM), including the venerable Dr. Earle F. Zeigler, considered by many as the father of sport management. The constitution of NASSM (n.d.) states that

The purpose of the Society shall be to promote, stimulate, and encourage study, research, scholarly writing, and professional development in the area of sport management (broadly interpreted).

It goes on to say that

the members of this Society are concerned about the *theoretical* and *applied* aspects of management theory and practice specifically related to sport, exercise, dance, and play as these enterprises are pursued by all sectors of the population.

The inclusion of "exercise, dance, and play" in the above definition is noteworthy. In a similar vein, Pitts and Stotlar (1996) define the sport industry as

the market in which the products offered to its buyers are sport, fitness, recreation, or leisure-related and may be activities, goods, services, people, places, or ideas. (p. 3)

Note the reference to the term *industry* in the definitions offered by Pitts and Stotlar (1996), Slack (1997), and NASPE/NASSM (1993). Many scholars and practitioners tend to use the term *industry* in its singular form. When we consider that an industry is a group of organizations that produce the same or similar products that are substitutable for each other (such as the paper

Sidebar

The definitions given in this chapter view sport management as a field concerned with several forms of participation in physical activity including recreational sport and fitness activities. The term *sport* in sport management is used in a generic sense to include all of these forms of participation. Unfortunately, a misconception exists that sport management in the United States is concerned only with elite sport such as intercollegiate athletics and the professional and semiprofessional sports. This is not the case. Most practitioners and scholars would subscribe to the inclusive nature of sport management, and this text is based on the broader view of sport management. Readers will encounter references to recreational agencies, fitness clubs, sport clubs, and other such agencies and programs. There are also specialized fields such as recreation administration and fitness management, and most of what is taught and practiced in those fields would parallel what is described in this text.

industry and automobile industry) the question arises whether we are indeed a single industry. Are the products of a university recreation department substitutable for the products of a professional sport franchise? From this perspective, Mullin (1980) noted that "we have a collection of sport management occupations. The sports industry is fragmented. It is in fact a number of sports industries" (p. 8). If sport management is concerned with different industries, then it is useful to describe the field in terms of the products those industries produce. The rest of the chapter is devoted to describing these products.

SPORT INDUSTRY PRODUCTS

Chelladurai (1993, 1994) defines the sport management field more comprehensively by cataloging and classifying its products, alluded to by various scholars (e.g., Mullin, 1980; Mullin, Hardy, & Sutton, 2000; Pitts & Stotlar, 1996). The logic behind his definition and description of the field is described below.

It has been argued that developing a classification of the observed phenomena is fundamental to any form of scientific inquiry. "To classify things is to bring parsimony and mental order to one's view of them" (Hambrick, 1984, p. 27). It is a fundamental characteristic of humans to gain a better understanding of the nature around them by classifying things.

The need to begin with the classification of the products of sport management rather than the organizations themselves comes from the growing interface between management and economics. The recent interest of management scholars in applying economic principles to the study of organizations, and of economists to look at their field from a managerial perspective, has resulted in a body of knowledge known as *organizational economics*. The major propositions of organizational economics are that (a) organizations are mechanisms that have evolved to facilitate the process of exchange of products, and (b) the organizational arrangements needed to support any particular exchange will depend on the inherent characteristics of the exchange (Hesterly, Liebeskind, & Zenger, 1990).

Consider the case of (a) a professional sport club, (b) a profit-oriented fitness club, and (c) a city recreation department. The professional sport club produces entertainment in the form of sport excellence and exchanges that product with the public for the price of admission to the game. The profit-oriented fitness club maintains the facility and equipment and rents them to its customers in exchange for a fee. It may also provide expert consultation, instruction, and leadership in fitness activities in exchange for a fee. The city recreation department maintains the playing fields and the arenas. What it offers is the use of those fields and arenas by the public at large. What the public offers in exchange is not so direct as in the previous two examples. Here, the exchange is in the form of taxes paid by members of the community, but the idea is the same—that is, somebody pays a price in exchange for the consumption of a sport product or service.

By the same token, these three organizations are structured and managed differently. For instance, the entertainment value of professional sport is a function of the competitiveness of the teams involved. To ensure competitiveness, professional leagues have rules for drafting and movement of players from team to team. The leagues also set salary caps for teams. League rules govern the individual clubs. The schedule of games is also largely left to the league. In contrast, a fitness club is autonomous from other fitness clubs. The owners can decide on the services to be offered and prices for those services based on market conditions. They can also set the schedule of activities. The city recreation department is a unit of the city government, which is controlled by elected representatives from various parts of the city. The department is normally structured to be responsive to the city council and its members. The variations in the structure and processes of these three different sport organizations reflect the products they exchange and the nature of that exchange.

From this perspective, the question of what is being exchanged becomes critical. What are the entities involved in the exchange that is being facilitated by sport organizations? If we can define, describe, and classify the products of exchange within the context of sport and recreation, then we should be able to capture the essential nature of the field and its boundaries.

Products as Goods and Services

The products of any organization may be goods or services or both. A good is a physical object that can be produced at one time and used later. In contrast, a service is an *intangible occurrence, process, or performance* that is produced and consumed simultaneously (Gronröös, 1990; Sasser, Olsen, & Wyckoff, 1978). In our context, the goods include all the equipment needed to engage in various kinds of sports and physical activity (e.g., golf clubs, tennis balls, soccer shoes, weight-training sets). In addition, promotional materials and merchandise (e.g., T-shirts, caps, banners) can also be included in the list of goods produced in the context of sport.

It should be pointed out that goods might be used in the production of services. For example, a fitness specialist may use highly sophisticated and expensive equipment to assess an individual's fitness status and then prescribe a suitable exercise program for that person. The equipment (i.e., goods) facilitates the service. In other words, the client has not bought the equipment, only the use of it by the specialist. A recreation department may use computers to assign participants randomly to various teams and draw up a schedule of competitions. The computer facilitates the service provided by the department. When a racquetball court is rented, the service involved is related to the renting of the court, an expensive good. A scoreboard (a piece of equipment) in an arena enhances the game experiences of the spectators (the service). These goods are properly called *facilitating goods and facilities* (Chelladurai, Scott, & Haywood-Farmer, 1987). Another example occurs when a baseball glove is purchased in a sport shop. The majority of the cost is for the glove (the good), but some of the cost is associated with the service rendered by the retailer, who purchased the good from the manufacturer and displayed it for the customer's convenience. The difference between the wholesale price and the retail price is the cost of the service to the customer.

> **In Brief**
>
> Every organization is a mechanism for exchange of one or more products with other elements in society. Thus, an understanding of the products of an organization is necessary to understand the organization itself.

According to the criterion of whether an organization is producing goods or services, almost all sports and recreation organizations can be classified as service organizations. Departments of sport management provide expert teaching in related subjects; athletic programs provide expert coaching for selected athletes; intramural programs provide opportunities for participation and competition among the general student population. Professional sport teams provide entertainment for the public. Government agencies, such as municipal recreation departments, may offer the use of facilities and opportunities to participate in organized competitions. Before we go on to describe and catalog the various services within sport and recreation, let us look in greater detail at the definition and description of services in general.

Services and Their Attributes

Earlier in the chapter, a service was defined as an *intangible occurrence, process, or performance* that is produced and consumed simultaneously. The nature of a service is better understood by highlighting its pertinent attributes (characteristics). The **service attributes** most frequently discussed are *intangibility, perishability, heterogeneity,* and *simultaneity* (Gronröös, 1990; Lovelock, 1991; Sasser et al., 1978; Schneider & Bowen, 1995).

A service is *intangible* in the sense that the client or customer cannot judge the quality of the product before actually obtaining it. The customer usually is guided by previous experience, the reputation of the organization, or the person(s) delivering the service. An athlete might base her choice of a university on the reputation of the coach or of the university itself or even on the recommendation of a friend. However, the athlete does not really know how good the service (i.e., the coaching and academic counseling) is until she experiences it. Similarly, clients have to experience the leadership of a fitness instructor or the lessons of a tennis pro before they can judge their quality. Intangibility stems from the sensual and psychological benefits that customers derive individually from a service. Feelings of comfort, status, and a sense of well-being are individualistic, so the services offered remain intangible.

Services are also *perishable*. It was noted earlier that a service could not be produced and stored for future use. If no customer reports to a fitness consultant during a two-hour period, whatever services the consultant could have provided during that period have been lost. Similarly, if a racquetball court is not rented, the service (i.e., the use of the court during that period) has vanished. In contrast, a manufacturer can continue to produce goods and inventory even though there are no sales at any given moment.

Heterogeneity refers to the fact that while goods, such as a particular brand of tennis rackets, are usually of uniform quality (whether good or bad), services are relatively more variable in quality. There are three reasons for this:

- First, individual differences among service providers in terms of personality, experience, and expertise result in different experiences for the clients. For instance, the leadership offered by different fitness leaders or the lessons of different tennis pros may vary.
- Second, the same employee may not provide the same level of service from one time to another. For example, a tennis instructor's lessons may vary in quality from day to day. This could be a function of the instructor's level of motivation and fatigue (teaching the eighth class of the day), stress (pressures affecting family life), and other such factors.
- Third, the quality of the experienced service can be affected by the consumer's psyche—a service may be judged good or bad depending upon the consumer's frame of mind. If motivation, fatigue, and stress can affect the service provider, the same factors could also affect the clients. For instance, a client of a fitness club who has just learned that his child is not progressing well in school may not be appreciative of the pleasant and warm greetings from the receptionist. On the other hand, heterogeneity may not be as pronounced in the case of the rental of a tennis court, where it will basically be the same day in and day out.

Simultaneity refers to the fact that a service has to be consumed as it is produced. When a coach is instructing, the athletes must be present. Because the production and consumption of a service are simultaneous, the interface between the employee (the producer of a service) and the client (the consumer of that service) becomes extremely important. In contrast, the production of tennis rackets happens at a place and time far removed from the customers. Thus, the interface between the producer and the consumer is much more important in the exchange of services than of goods. The term *inseparability* is also used to refer to this attribute, indicating that the production and consumption of a service cannot be separated.

Recently, Lovelock and Gummesson (2004) have argued that the attributes of intangibility, heterogeneity, simultaneity (inseparability of production and consumption), and perishability are not sufficient to distinguish a service from a good. In their view, the growth of telephone ordering and ecommerce means that the prepurchase judgments about a good (e.g., a trampoline for the playground) cannot be made because the customer cannot touch it, feel it, or test it before the purchase. That is, the concept of intangibility extends to goods also. More-

> **In Brief**
>
> A service is intangible because it cannot be scrutinized before purchase; it is perishable because it cannot be stored for future use; it is heterogeneous because it is variable from time to time; and its production and consumption occur simultaneously.

over, some services can be verified before actual purchase, making the attribute of intangibility invalid in relation to that service. Suppose you plan on joining a fitness club to work out on your own. You may go to one or more fitness clubs to check the quality and layout of the equipment, parking facilities, locker room facilities, and similar items of concern to you. Based on these evaluations, you may join a particular club. The club's service to you is in fact the rental of its facility and equipment. Intangibility does not apply because you can test the equipment.

The concept of heterogeneity or variability loses its relevance in services where the process of service delivery is highly routinized and mechanized. Consider the case of club orientation in the fitness club. If the orientation is presented by several different employees, their mannerisms, attitudes, and behaviors may vary, thus making their services variable. Suppose the fitness club decides to educate new members using a video showing the facilities and equipment demonstrations. In such a case, there is little variability in the orientation process. As for inseparability, Lovelock and Gummesson (2004) point out that there are several *separable* services such as dry cleaning your clothes and changing the oil in your car. In these cases, you do not get involved in the dry cleaning process or the oil change, which are the core of these services. Stringing a tennis racket and sharpening skates would be examples of separable services in our context. As for perishability, Lovelock and Gummesson note that the concept is multidimensional in that it may refer to the actual *product* or service being perishable (e.g., tomatoes going bad or a professor giving a lecture that ends once class ends), or the *productive capacity* being perishable, as when a factory is shut down due to a power failure and its capacity to produce at that time perishes. In both of these perspectives, the concept of perishability applies both to goods and services. Some information-based services may not be perishable after all because they can be recorded and replayed later. For instance, if you take a video camera to your class and record the lectures of your professor (with permission of the instructor), his or her service in delivering the lecture is no longer perishable. Therefore, even perishability is not a good criterion to be used in distinguishing a service from a good.

Given the inadequacy of the four attributes to clearly delineate the boundaries of goods and services, Lovelock and Gummesson propose an alternative criterion to distinguish a service from a good—the *transfer of ownership*. Their essential argument is that in a service operation, there is no transfer of ownership of the service per se. They note that "marketing transactions that do not involve a transfer of ownership are distinctively different from those that do" (p. 34). Further, they argue that "services involve a form of *rental* or *access* in which customers obtain benefits by gaining the right to use a physical object, to hire the labor and expertise of personnel, or to obtain access to facilities or networks" (p. 34). Within this nonownership framework they identify five broad categories of services.

1. *Rented goods services.* These services allow the customers the use of a physical good for a set time for a fee. For example, golf courses let the golfers rent the golf cart and bowling alleys rent shoes to their customers.

2. *Place and space rentals.* In this service, a customer gets to use a specified place or space for a fee. When I buy my season tickets for OSU Buckeye

football games, I am allowed to occupy a particular seat number in a particular row in a particular section for the duration of the game. From this perspective, I am renting the space defined by that seat. This is exactly what happens when you park a car in a commercial parking lot; you rent the space and pay a certain amount for the period of time you occupy that space.

3. *Labor and expertise rentals.* In this form of service, the client simply rents the labor or expertise of another person or firm to carry out certain activities. The simplest example is when you or I hire somebody to mow the lawn in our yard. When a city recreation department hires a local marketing firm to survey the citizens on their sport and physical activity preferences, the department is renting the expertise residing in the marketing firm. When someone pays for knee surgery, the payment includes the fee for the expertise of the surgeon and the surgical team.

4. *Physical facility access services.* When someone buys a ticket to the Hall of Fame in a given sport, the person receives access to the facility and the exhibits therein. Some famous sport *venues* sell tickets for access to their facilities; for example, Yankee Stadium does so. In contrast to buying a ticket for a game where a seat is guaranteed, the client purchases general access to the facility.

5. *Network access and usage.* In this form of service, a client rents the right to participate in a network such as "telecommunications, utilities, banking, insurance, or specialized information services." Some of the sports-related websites (e.g., NCAA, IEG) store enormous amounts of information and data. While the information on some of the websites is free to access (e.g., NCAA), other commercial websites (e.g., IEG) do charge a fee for access to their websites.

Lovelock and Gummesson's (2004) introduction of the new criterion of *transfer of ownership* (or absence of transfer of ownership to be more correct) as the defining characteristic of a service represents a basic shift in assumptions. The former assumption that the four attributes of intangibility, heterogeneity, inseparability, and perishability distinguish services from goods is replaced by the new assumption that what makes a service unique from a good is that there is no transfer of ownership in the case of a service but only the rental of or access to an object, labor and expertise, facility, or network.

While Lovelock and Gummesson (2004) have made a logical argument for a more definitive distinguishing attribute of a service, they have not suggested the abandonment of the other four attributes as guiding managerial thought and actions but argue that they are not sufficient to define a service. If we accept their basic argument for *transfer of ownership* as the dividing line between a good and a service, we can also recognize that most services do differ from most goods on the four attributes. That is, most services are characterized by intangibility, heterogeneity, inseparability, and perishability. By the same token, we must understand that various services may differ among themselves in the degree of relevance of each of the four attributes. It would be very useful for us to conceive of four continuums representing the four attributes as shown in Exhibit 1.1.

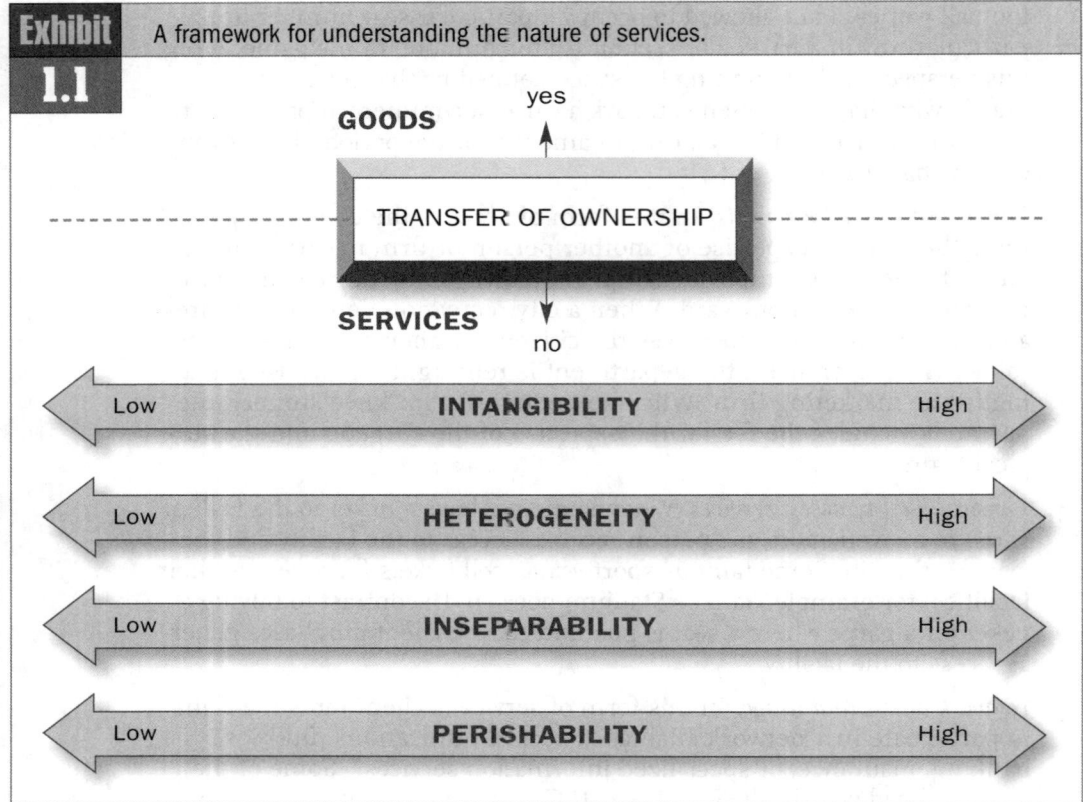

Exhibit 1.1 A framework for understanding the nature of services.

CONSUMER, PROFESSIONAL, AND HUMAN SERVICES

While the attributes given above are applicable to all services, we can also make distinctions among services based on their nature. The nature of the service provided is defined by what actually happens in the service provider–client interface. A significant aspect of the service provider–client interface is the amount and type of information exchanged between the client and provider in the production of the service (Gronröös, 1990; Mills & Margulies, 1980; Sasser et al., 1978; Schneider & Bowen, 1995). Sasser and colleagues (1978) used this construct to categorize services into consumer and professional services. In this section, both service categories will be discussed as well as human services, a subcategory of professional services.

Consumer Services

Consumer services are largely based on low-skilled and routine services including renting of facilities and retailing of goods. For example, when a university permits its students to use its gymnasium and playing fields on a drop-in basis, it is offering a consumer service. A racquetball club may restrict its operations to rental of its courts and sales of sporting goods in its pro shop. Such services require very little expertise on the part of the service providers who interact with the clients. A reception clerk need only know the appropriate reservation procedures for the facilities or equipment, and guidelines for their use. Similarly, a locker room attendant need only know who is eligible for what equipment, and the procedures to sign out the equipment.

Professional Services

Professional services are largely based on knowledge, expertise, and special competencies of the employee (the service provider). For example, an exercise physiologist's services and a tennis pro's instructions are based on their respective expertise and knowledge. Similarly, a university provides a professional service when it offers expert coaching in various sports to selected students. In our context, the critical difference between a consumer service and a professional service is the direct and active leadership provided by the service worker in the assessment of clients' needs, the specification of appropriate activities, and the guidance and coaching provided during participation.

> **Sidebar**
>
> Schneider and Bowen (1995) in contrasting a professional service with a fix-it service (i.e., to get a malfunctioning device working again) suggest that "a professional service is a highfalutin' synonym for a fix-it service provided by someone with a degree or license. Doctors, stockbrokers, architects, bankers, and professors deliver professional services. They also build things as well as fix things: stockbrokers build financial reserves, doctors build health, architects build buildings, and so forth" (p. 191).

It is very likely that an agency would offer both consumer and professional services to varying degrees, as in a university's intramural and intercollegiate athletic programs. A commercial fitness club may rent its facilities and equipment and, at the same time, offer professional services in the form of fitness testing, exercise prescription, and consultation.

Professional services themselves can be categorized into two major types: services involving something in which a client is interested and services involving the transformation of a client. For instance, lawyers, architects, accountants, and stockbrokers provide complex professional services to their clients/customers. By the same token, teachers, guidance counselors, and the clergy also provide professional services. But there is a distinction between these two types of services. The former type involves knowledge and guidelines regarding *something* in which the clients are interested (e.g., a legal issue, a building, or an investment). In contrast, the latter type is engaged in transforming in some way the *people* themselves (e.g., educating the child, guiding the students, and enhancing the spiritual life) (Hasenfeld, 1992; Hasenfeld & English, 1974). The latter services are human services.

Human Services

Human services "define or alter the person's behavior, attributes, and social status in order to maintain or enhance his well being." Also, the "input of raw material are human beings with specific attributes, and their production output are persons processed or changed in a predetermined manner" (Hasenfeld & English, 1974, p. 1).

Thus, human services compared to the other professional services are unique because:

- the input (that is, the raw materials) is humans.
- the input/raw material is variable in terms of age, gender, health, fitness level, and so on.
- the processes cannot be standardized because the input/raw material is variable.
- while client expectations are legitimate, only professional experts decide on the service to be provided (for instance, a coach decides on the strategies to be employed in a game; a fitness specialist decides on the exercise regimen).
- the clients who are the input get actively involved in the process of producing the relevant service. (Chelladurai, 1996; Williamson, 1991)

The last factor is problematic in two different ways. First, a client's active involvement may hinder the employee's activities and judgment. For example, a client in an aerobic class who grunts too loudly while performing the routine, or one who shows off too much during the routine, may disrupt the activities of the instructor. The other problem is that the clients may not be compliant to expert directions (Hasenfeld, 1983, 1992). These two issues are accentuated in the sport context because the production of some of our services requires our clients to engage in quite *agonistic* (that is, painful) and *prolonged* activities. The provision of fitness- and health-oriented services, for example, is dependent on the extent to which the clients will adhere to the service provider's guidance and participate in vigorous activities. Similarly, pursuit of excellence in a sport requires the client to undergo strenuous practice sessions while forgoing other more pleasurable activities. These unique characteristics of human services in sport and recreation highlight the significance of ensuring that our service providers are professionally competent and, at the same time, skilled in social interactions.

Hasenfeld's (1983) three-level classification of (a) *people-processing,* (b) *people-sustaining,* and (c) *people-changing* functions of human services helps us to elaborate further on the nature of human services in sport and recreation organizations.

- **People-processing.** This function refers to testing or screening people and placing them in a particular class based on some specified criterion. Fitness-testing laboratories perform this function when they rate their customers on a scale of relative fitness. Classifying promising athletes after extensive assessment of their psychomotor abilities would be a people-processing service. Similarly, testing athletes for drugs would also be designated as a people-processing service.
- **People-sustaining.** Another function of human service organizations may be to sustain people (that is, prevent or delay the decline in the welfare or status of the clients). This is the major function of welfare departments, nursing homes, and hospital chronic wards. In our context, cardiac rehabilitation programs and physical therapy and athletic injury clinics provide people-sustaining services.
- **People-changing.** People-changing services aim at some changes in the clients or customers in terms of one or more of the biophysical, psychological, or social attributes. For example, sport management degree programs change their clients into more knowledgeable persons in the field; fitness programs make people healthier; recreational programs make

their clients more relaxed and energized; and coaching programs and sports camps make the clients better performers.

Hasenfeld's three-level classification of human services can be easily mapped onto sport and physical activity services in general. However, because in sport and physical activity services our focus is on those services that involve the active participation of the clients, the people-processing services become less germane, and the people-sustaining and people-changing services more pertinent.

In Brief

Services can be broadly classified as consumer and professional services. Human services, a subcategory of professional services, may involve processing, sustaining, and/or changing people.

CLIENT MOTIVES FOR PARTICIPATION

While the description of the types of services is critical for developing managerial guidelines, it is equally important that we identify the motives of the clients who participate in our services. As noted before, participant services in sport require the active involvement of clients. Thus, the clients contribute as much as the service employees to the nature of the service.

While the notion of consumer involvement is generic to the production of many services, it is of greater importance in our context because the production of a sport or recreation service often depends upon active *physical exertion* on the part of the consumer. As mentioned earlier, the efforts of an exercise leader will result in a service only if the clients physically participate in the exercise regimen. Hasenfeld (1983), referring to human services in general, noted that "Patients may refuse to comply with a physician's orders; students may ignore their teachers; and clients may resist discussing their interpersonal problems. . . . Consequently, the control of the client and the need to elicit conformity are critical issues in human service organizations and consume much of the efforts of their practitioners" (pp. 122–123). Getting the clients to participate in the sport and physical activity programs becomes problematic for the service providers.

The relative ease or difficulty of securing client motivation in sport and physical activity services varies from one context to another. The psychological dynamics of client motivation are best understood if we consider clients' motives for participation in physical activities. Several schemes have been proposed to classify participant motives and attitudes in (a) youth sports (Gill, Gross, & Huddleston, 1983); (b) school physical education (Jewett, 1987); (c) college physical activity classes (Mathes & Battista, 1985); (d) older adults (Heitmann, 1986); and (e) various life stages (Vuolle, 1987).

Ellis (1988) proposes a continuum of goals for activity and leisure in the community ranging from health care through health enhancement to enjoyment. These are further broken down into cure, rehabilitation, wellness promotion, self-expenditure on work/service, and self-actualization. In more recent years, Pelletier, Fortier, Vallerand, Tuson, and Briere (1995) developed the Sport Motivation Scale (SMS) to measure three forms of intrinsic motivation, three forms of extrinsic motivation, and amotivation (i.e., being neither intrinsically nor extrinsically motivated to participate). Roberts (1993) and

Duda (1994, 1996) refer to two orthogonal goal orientations of participants in sport. *Task orientation* refers to success being judged on the basis of task mastery and personal improvement, and *ego orientation* refers to success being judged on the basis of one's performance relative to other performances.

For our purposes, we can group the motives, attitudes, and goals outlined by these scholars into (a) pursuit of pleasure, (b) pursuit of skill, (c) pursuit of excellence, or (d) pursuit of health/fitness.

Pursuit of Pleasure

People may participate in sport and physical activity because they enjoy the kinesthetic sensations or the competition provided by, say, a game of squash. The pleasures they seek can be enjoyed only during participation; that is, they are not seeking any other benefits outside of actual participation itself. It is easier to secure client motivation when such pleasure seeking is the basis for participation; that is, the clients are intrinsically motivated. Thus, the elementary school teacher is not much concerned about motivating the children during recess. Similarly, fitness club employees need not focus on motivating those who participate in squash or tennis for the pleasure of it.

> **Sidebar**
>
> Sasser et al. (1978) note with reference to professional services, "while employees may be replaceable, every replacement alters the nature of the organization . . . and the nature of the product" (p. 401). That is, the employees themselves define the organization, particularly a professional service organization. Thus, when a professor of sport management leaves a university, the course offerings in that field alter, the research thrust also changes, and, in sum, the service product in the area becomes different. This scenario is often repeated in the context of elite sport coaching. Every replacement of the head coach is followed by a different coaching philosophy and different strategies (that is, a different product).

Pursuit of Skill

The desire to acquire physical skills may compel people to participate in sport and physical activity. Individuals may focus on perfecting their skills through continued vigorous physical activity. Organized physical activity classes (such as wall climbing and judo, as well as sports camps and clinics) aim at imparting skills in various sports to members of the community. The popularity of such programs among people of all ages attests to the pervasiveness of the desire to learn skills.

Pursuit of Excellence

People may also participate in some form of sport or physical activity in pursuit of excellence in that activity. Pursuit of excellence is broadly defined as the effort to win in a contest against a standard. The standard may be your own previous performance, somebody else's performance, or simply winning against an opponent. Those who pursue excellence prepare for the contests and are willing to comply with the instructions of the coach or teacher. The scenario of athletes going through painful exercises chanting the motto "no pain, no gain" aptly illustrates the pursuit of excellence. Note that acquisition and mastery of skills are prerequisites for the pursuit of excellence.

Pursuit of Health/Fitness

Some others may participate in sport and physical activity mainly for those health-related benefits (such as fitness, stress reduction, longevity, etc.) that result from such participation. In other words, the benefits of participating are extrinsic to the activity itself. They reside outside the actual physical activity and are derived after prolonged physical activity.

In this regard, Hasenfeld's (1983) distinction between those functioning adequately and those functioning below an adequate level has relevance for us. That is, many individuals who are sufficiently fit and healthy would like to maintain that level of fitness and health; therefore, they continue to participate in sport and physical activity. Such motives may be labeled *sustenance* motives. On the other hand, some others may participate in physical activity to improve fitness and health that has been judged inadequate. These motives may be labeled *curative*.

Although these motives are distinct from each other, the activities that people select to satisfy any one of these motives may result in other outcomes as well. For example, those who play squash in pursuit of pleasure may also gain in fitness and may also enhance their performance capabilities. Similarly, those who run for the sake of fitness may learn to enjoy the kinesthetic sensations as well as the sense of achievement in running farther or at a faster pace. However, it is critical from a managerial perspective that the primary purpose for participation in a program of sport or physical activity be established so that its development and implementation will be smooth and coordinated. For instance, the need for motivating clients before and during participation would vary with the purposes of such participation. In pursuit of pleasure, the activity itself is the reward, and therefore it acts as the motivator for the participants. The service provider's role is then restricted to providing facilities and equipment, scheduling activities, and giving general supervision. On the other hand, in pursuit of excellence, skill, or fitness and health, the reward will not be immediate, and therefore the agency has a greater responsibility in motivating the participants.

> **In Brief**
>
> The reasons why people participate in sport and physical activity may be broadly classified as (a) pursuit of pleasure, (b) pursuit of skill, (c) pursuit of excellence, and (d) pursuit of health and fitness. Activities chosen to satisfy one motive may yield other outcomes as well.

CLASSIFYING SPORT SERVICES

Based on the distinctions among consumer, professional, and human services and on the motives of participants, the services (products) within the domain of sport management can be broadly classified into *participant services, spectator services, sponsorship services* (including licensing and merchandising), *donor services,* and *social ideas.* These are explained in the following sections. Some of these broad areas can be further broken down into specific services as shown in Exhibit 1.2. The manufacture and sale of sporting goods is a sport product that is relatively self-explanatory and will not be discussed here.

Exhibit 1.2 Classification of sport services.

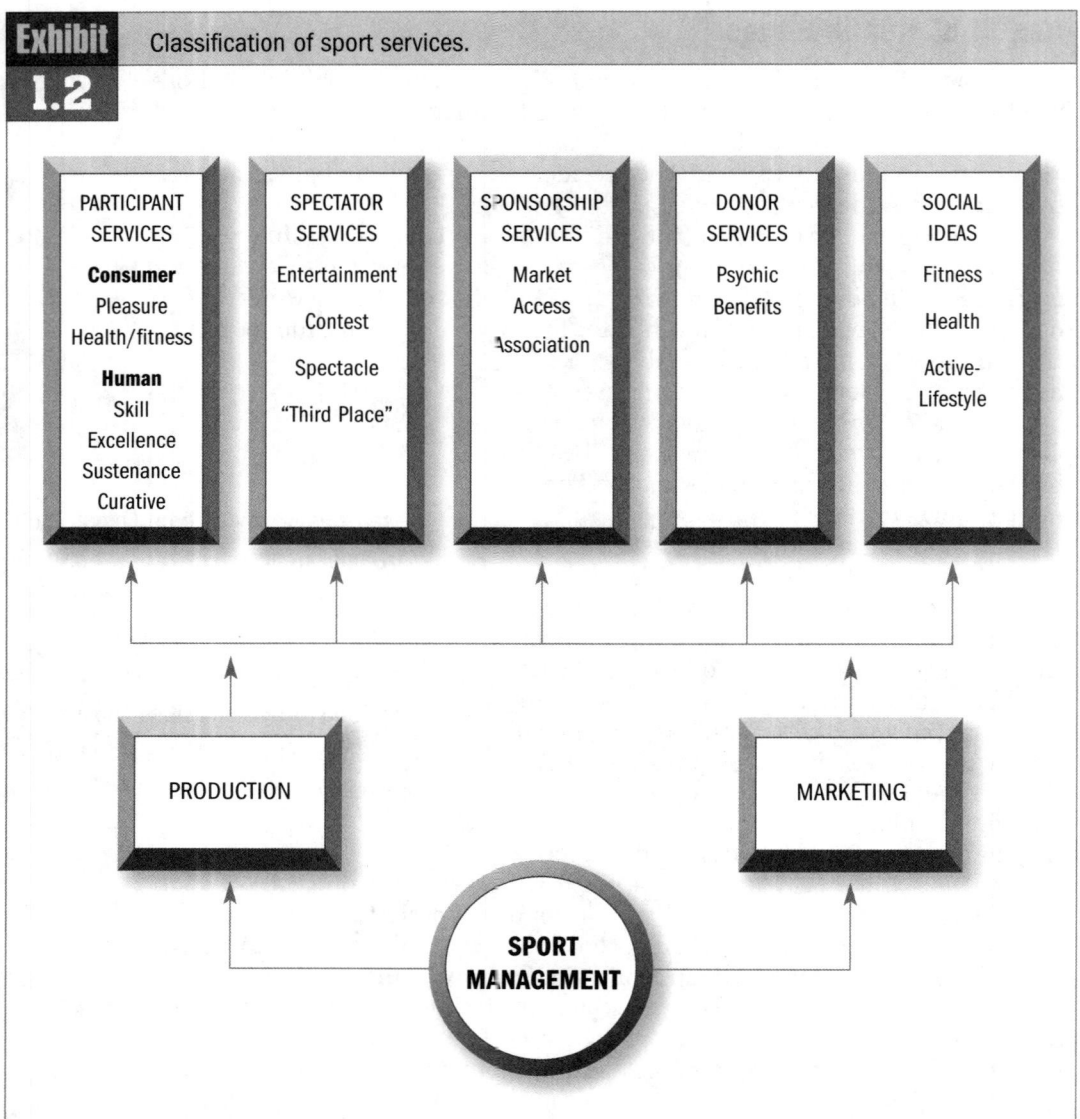

Participant Services

Participant services are those services that we offer in order for clients to engage physically in some form of sport or physical activity. A combination of the types of services (consumer and human) and client motives (pursuit of pleasure, health/fitness, skill, and excellence) yields six types of participant services: *consumer-pleasure, consumer-health/fitness, human-skill, human-excellence, human-sustenance,* and *human-curative* (Chelladurai, 1992). The descriptions of these participant services are as listed below:

- *Consumer-pleasure* services refer to the scheduling or reserving of facilities or equipment as requested by clients who seek pleasure in physical activity. This class of service includes organizing and conducting different kinds of competitions for clients.

- *Consumer-health/fitness* services involve scheduling or reserving facilities or equipment to satisfy clients' desire to maintain their fitness and health.

The next set of services includes human services that involve instruction, guidance, or coaching by experts.

- *Human-skill* services refer to the expert application of teaching technology and leadership in developing the skills (including techniques and strategies) of the clients in various forms of sport and physical activity.
- *Human-excellence* services provide expert guidance and coaching for clients in their pursuit of excellence in a chosen physical activity.
- *Human-sustenance* services are the organization and conduct of exercise and fitness programs on a regular basis under the guidance and supervision of an expert leader, as in the case of aerobic instructors leading a group of clients.
- *Human-curative* services involve designing and offering physical activity programs to rehabilitate those in need of improvement in fitness, health, or physical appearance in such areas as cardiac rehabilitation, relaxation and stress reduction, and weight loss.

> **Sidebar**
>
> Each sport, of course, has its own special features that make it especially attractive to certain consumers. For instance, basketball has speed, agility, physical contact, power, and grace. Stars like Michael Jordan and Shaquille O'Neal are recognized instantly by almost everyone. However, often the intricacies of a sport are either not well understood or not easily communicated to the public. Many Americans expect anyone kicking a ball to "boot" it like an NFL place-kicker or punter. Thus, U. S. audiences may not appreciate the graceful soccer pass that is cleverly "chipped" over and around defenders. Similarly, the crowd gives less approval to the most skillful ice hockey play than to a crude "check" into the boards. Anyone who disputes this claim can simply monitor crowd noises and excitement levels at a hockey game (Mullin et al., 1993, p. 139).

Spectator Services

Spectator services refer to the entertainment we provide to our clients. Not all sports have the same degree of entertainment value for all people. For instance, although soccer is the most popular sport in the world, it does not generate the same level of excitement in the United States. Similarly, cricket is quite popular in the British Commonwealth countries while remaining virtually unknown in the United States. These differences are a function of culture and tradition. Even within one country or cultural context, individuals may be attracted to specific features of a sport. While the rough-and-tumble of football may be attractive to some, the quiet and finesse of golf may appeal more to others. Our concern here is not with the entertainment value of a single sport but of sports in general.

The entertainment value of sport may be generated by two different ventures with different goals and processes. The primary purpose of professional sports is to make a profit through providing entertainment to the public. Therefore, pro leagues recruit excellence produced elsewhere and parade it before the paying public in the form of organized competitions.

> **Sidebar**
>
> In Broyles and Hay's (1979) view, "competitive athletic events are part of the entertainment business. Athletes are brought together to create a social event that is exciting and valuable to fans. These events are marketed to attract customers" (p. 3). And, "the primary objective of a successful business organization is to produce a quality product and/or service to satisfy the needs of the customers; similarly, the main goal of a successful athletic program is to produce a winning team to satisfy some of the entertainment needs of the fans. By winning more than half of its competitive events, an athletic program establishes itself as a winner. Winning is the name of the game for athletic administrators" (p. 27).

They ensure that the teams are of similar caliber so that the outcome of a competition is relatively unpredictable. In contrast, there are those organizations that pursue the goal of excellence—for example, the traditional role of intercollegiate athletics in the United States. These athletic programs also organize competitions, though mainly to promote and prove excellence. In the process, they may also produce entertainment value for their publics. Such entertainment may be viewed as a by-product of the pursuit of excellence. This is not to deny that the provision of entertainment and generation of revenue may indeed be the primary objectives for some universities. In fact, some authors maintain that intercollegiate athletics should be run as businesses that provide entertainment and generate revenue. For instance, Broyles and Hay (1979) explicitly state that the prime objective of intercollegiate athletic programs is to satisfy the entertainment needs of fans. Now many athletic departments openly proclaim and pursue the entertainment perspective.

The entertainment value of sport competitions stems largely from three different sources—*contest, spectacle,* and *third place experience.*

The Contest

The entertainment value of a sport contest lies in (a) the excellence exhibited by the participants, (b) the unpredictability of the outcomes of a contest, and (c) the loyalty and attachment of people to certain sports, teams, and athletes. Thus, the higher the level of excellence, the higher the entertainment value. Contests of the Olympics, World Cup, and professional sports are more attractive to watch than high-school contests. Next, the entertainment value of a contest increases if the outcome is not a foregone conclusion. Normally, the unpredictable nature of the contest stems from the equality of resources, such as skill, size, strength, and training, between the contestants, and from the element of luck (the bounce of the ball, or a referee's mistakes). Spectators are more interested in watching a game between two top-ranked teams than between a high-ranked team and a team in the cellar. The Dream Team (the U.S. team for the Barcelona Olympics in 1992) was loaded with so much talent that every contest turned out to be a "no contest." However, in this case, it was not the competitions per se that were attractive but the ensemble of the most excellent talent in the sport.

The third element of the contest as a source of entertainment is the loyalty or attachment of individuals (the fans) to a particular sport, team, or ath-

lete. There are those who like baseball and hate basketball; those who love the Blue Jays and think less of the New York Yankees; and those who admire Anastasia Myskina or Andy Roddick and those who adore Lindsay Davenport or Roger Federer. Thus, it is not surprising that considerable effort and money are spent in promoting (a) a sport (hence the National Basketball Association's commercial slogan, "I Love This Game"); (b) a team (the promotion of the Dallas Cowboys as America's team); and (c) an athlete (the efforts to name a successor to Michael Jordan).

> **In Brief**
>
> The elements that characterize spectator sports are (a) the contest itself, (b) the spectacle, and (c) the stadium/arena serving as a "third place."

The Spectacle

While the contest forms the core of the event, spectacle is also a part of these contests. The opening and closing ceremonies of the Olympics, and the parades and half-time shows of football games in America are added elements of the entertainment package (i.e., product extensions, in marketing terminology). The cheerleaders and the marching bands are also part of the spectacle. In fact, some of the more famous cheerleading squads (e.g., the Laker Girls of the Los Angeles Lakers basketball team) may be invited to perform during periods in a hockey game in a remote city. In 2004, the organizers of the Madrid Masters tennis tournament hired fashion models as ball girls for one televised match each day to add to the entertainment value (*Columbus Dispatch*, October 19, 2004). Being skeptical about fashion models in skimpy outfits on the sidelines of a tennis court, Andre Agassi, a contestant in the tournament, noted, "I think it's important for our sport to understand its product clearly. And I'm not quite convinced it's part of our product" (*Columbus Dispatch*, October 20, 2004; p. E2). However, for some of the paying public these elements are as important as the contest itself.

The "Third Place" Experience

An equally important aspect of sport as entertainment was highlighted by Melnick (1993), who argues that the forces of urbanization, individualism, interpersonal competition, technology, and geographical mobility have made the primary social ties with family and friends tenuous. Individuals in these contexts seek to satisfy their social needs in less personal ways. The venues where such associations can take place are called "third places" (as distinct from the home and workplace). Third places offer opportunities for "casual encounters with strangers of a quasi-primary kind" (p. 49). Thus, "sports spectating has emerged as a major urban structure where spectators come together not only to be entertained [by the contest] but to enrich their social psychological lives through the sociable, quasi-intimate relationships available" (p. 44). Melnick goes on to argue that sport managers may benefit by emphasizing this particular service—the availability of a third place. The notion of a third place may extend beyond the stadium and arena into bars, restaurants, and even shopping malls where a group of individuals can watch a game on television.

The third place experience as defined above also serves as a forum for BIRGing—Basking In Reflected Glory (Cialdini et al., 1976; Wann & Branscombe, 1990)—and CORFing—Cutting Off Reflected Failure (Snyder, Lassegard, & Ford, 1986; Wann & Branscombe, 1990). BIRGing refers to the tendency for people to publicize their connection with others who have been successful (Cialdini et al., 1976). These authors note that college students tend to wear school-identifying apparel after their college football teams' victories and use the pronoun "we" when the team was victorious, thus strengthening their connection with the winning team. CORFing is the distancing of oneself from the failure of others (Snyder et al., 1986). People tend to increase distance between themselves and others who have been unsuccessful. It is argued here that the presence of quasi-intimate relationships in a third place permits both unmitigated expression of reflected glory and distancing from reflected failure.

Sponsorship Services

Corporate sponsorship is one of the fastest growing and richest areas within sport management. Shank (2005), citing IEG Sponsorship Report (2004), reports that worldwide corporate sponsorship has been estimated to total $28 billion. This amount includes an estimated $10.25 billion in the United States alone, of which $7.25 billion was devoted to sponsoring events. Among the various sports worldwide, soccer accounted for the largest share at $1.9 billion, reflecting its popularity around the world.

Why would corporations spend so much money on sponsoring sporting events and teams? What do they gain in return? The definition of sponsorship offered by Mullin et al. (2000) provides the answer to this question. They define sponsorship as "the acquisition of rights to affiliate or directly associate with a product or event for the purpose of deriving benefits related to that affiliation or association. The sponsor then uses this relationship to achieve its promotional objectives or to facilitate and support its broader marketing objectives" (p. 254). In a similar vein, both Shilbury, Quick, and Westerbeek (1998) and Milne and McDonald (1999) view sponsorship as a business reciprocal relationship in which the sponsor provides funds for a sports event or organization in return for the rights of association, which can be used for commercial advantages. In Shank's (2005) view, sponsorship is "investing in a sports entity (athlete, league, team, or event) to support overall organizational objectives, marketing goals, and promotional strategies" (p. 330). Shank (2005) lists the following as the sponsorship objectives:

1. Creating awareness of the sponsor's products and services, and/or corporate name;
2. Competing with other companies;
3. Reaching new target markets composed of people of similar activities, interests, and opinions;
4. Establishing long-term relationships with clients;
5. Building up the image of the sponsor; and
6. Increasing sales.

Amis, Pant, and Slack (1997) list the following as additional objectives of sponsorship:

1. Linking with local businesses and political communities;
2. Entertaining corporate customers;
3. Improving employee relations; and
4. Testing of company products under "real-life" conditions.

The above definitions incorporate two significant elements: *market access* and *association*.*

Provide Market Access

The major service offered to the sponsors is the access to communication with a specific market (the direct and indirect consumers of a sport). With such access, sponsors are able to pursue their promotional and marketing objectives. When a footwear company offers millions of dollars to promote a tournament, it gains in exchange the access to millions of spectators and TV viewers who watch the game. The significance of this market access for the corporate sector is reflected in the millions if not billions of dollars spent on sponsorships in the United States, in Europe, and throughout the world.

> **Sidebar**
>
> According to Howard and Crompton (1995), "Voluntary exchange is the central concept underlying both sponsorship and donations. The concept requires something of value to be offered in exchange for something else of value. Before an investment or donation is made, the contributor is likely to ask two questions, 'What is in it for me?' and 'How much will it cost me?' The trade-off is weighted between what will be gained and what will have to be given up. Both sponsorship and philanthropy offer sources of funds, resources, and in-kind services to sport organizations, but they differ in the nature of what they expect in exchange" (p. 226).

Although corporations spend huge amounts on sponsorship of elite sports (professional sports, intercollegiate athletics, and Olympic events), the idea and practice of sponsorship is spreading to other sporting contexts as well. For example, the American Youth Soccer Organization was sponsored in 1998 by more than 15 corporations including Lever Brothers, Sunkist, and Quaker Oats (*Columbus Dispatch*, 1998). Little League, the American Youth Soccer Organization, and Pop Warner Football are said to have generated six-figure revenues each in 1998 through sponsorship (*Columbus Dispatch*, 1998). The basic reason why corporations are eager to sponsor these youth sports enterprises is the access they gain to a market of millions of children and their households. It should also be recognized that many organizations sponsor some of the not-so-popular sports because of their sense of social responsibility.

---

*Some authors have identified hospitality services as a component of sponsorship (e.g., Howard & Crompton, 1995). While it is true that corporations use those services to entertain their significant customers and employees, such services are usually generated by the sponsors themselves; that is, the sport organization itself is not providing those services. Therefore, hospitality services are not emphasized in this section.

Create Association

A related outcome of sponsorship is the *image building* or *image projection* by association for the sponsoring corporation. The image promoted may be related to the concept of social responsibility (as in corporations sponsoring specific teams for the Olympics) or to the idea of excellence (corporations identifying with winning teams or excellent athletes).

Donor Services

The products we propose to exchange when we seek a donation are merely the sources of *psychic benefits*. Such psychic benefits may be altruistic (the good feeling of having supported a worthy venture), or they may be egoistic (the personal gratification in seeing one's name on the list of donors). Two points are worth noting here. First, these psychic benefits are self-administered by the donors themselves. The sport organization simply provides a basis from which these benefits can be derived. Second, an act of donation may engender both altruistic and egoistic benefits simultaneously. Consider a donor giving millions of dollars for the construction of an arena to be named after her. The generous offer is born out of both real concern to fulfill the need of the community (altruistic benefit) and the desire to leave behind something bearing her name (egoistic benefit).

The foregoing is not to deny that some donors may have other ulterior motives in giving donations. For example, donors to political parties may do so with a view to gain access to decision-makers. In a similar manner, a donor may give a sizable donation to a sport-governing body in the hope that the decision-makers will be inclined to select the donor's son or daughter to the national team. As another example, a person may give a huge donation to the local YMCA's sports program with a view to influence the decision on a construction contract. You may also recall that the Salt Lake Olympic Committee members made donations to the projects of some of the members of the International Olympic Committee (IOC). While such donations did help those projects and their intended clients, they were still questionable because they were made with a view to influence the IOC members to vote in favor of awarding the Olympic event to Salt Lake City. Illegitimate and corrupt efforts of influence should not be considered donations in the true sense.

Service to Social Ideas

Some sport organizations are also engaged in promoting social objectives such as fitness and health through physical activity. The TRIM movement in Europe and PARTICIPACTION (a term coined to indicate participation and action) in Canada are good examples of such organizations. The National Association for Sport and Physical Education (NASPE) in the United States promotes the idea of "quality sport and physical education" in the form of posters, brochures, press releases, and meetings. While some may view this campaign as an effort to promote the profession itself, the underlying theme is participation in sport and physical activity. Similarly, Nike's advertising slogan "Just Do It" promoted the idea of participation in physical activity while at the same time promoting its own corporate image. All these efforts are aimed at exchanging with the public the social idea and practice of participation in physical activity, and the benefits of such participation.

Production and Marketing of Sport Services

An important element in Exhibit 1.2 is the emphasis on both the **production** and **marketing** of the various services. Consider, for example, some of the significant activities of a typical university athletic department. It is heavily engaged in recruiting high-quality coaches and athletes, facilitating their training by maintaining and scheduling facilities, allotting a budget to every team to cover its expenses, and organizing and conducting the contests. Through these processes the department produces excellence and entertainment. In addition, the department also engages in promotional and advertising campaigns to highlight its products—setting up an elaborate scheme to distribute the tickets for the contests, and engaging in public relations efforts to justify the department, its processes, and its products. These are the marketing efforts of the department. In a similar manner, a city recreation department prepares and maintains the playing facilities, organizes youth leagues, schedules the games, and recruits volunteers as coaches and referees. These are the factors that go into the production of that particular service. The department may also publicize the existence of its sport programs through the media, billboards, and mailings in order to attract more participation by community members. These efforts are marketing-oriented. Thus, sport management as a field is engaged in both the production and marketing of sport products.

In Brief

Sport management is concerned with both the production and marketing of various sport services.

RELATIONSHIPS AMONG SPORT PRODUCTS

Although the various sport products have been described separately, they are intricately related, as shown in Exhibit 1.3. For example, consider participant services. Those who engage in a sport for the pleasure of it (consumer-pleasure service) may become highly skilled in that sport, which is the goal of human-skill service. Those who are pursuing skills in a sport may also become excellent in that sport (the goal of human-excellence service). Similarly, those who engage in a sport in pursuit of pleasure, skill, or excellence may also enhance their fitness and health (the goal of consumer-health, human-sustenance, and human-curative services).

Next consider spectator services. The product that is being exchanged is entertainment, but entertainment is a function of contests among excellent teams or athletes. That is, the entertainment value of sport increases as excellence in the sport increases. Thus, spectator services are an offshoot of human-excellence services. Further, spectator services imply that there are a host of fans of a sport (basketball), a team in a sport (Philadelphia 76ers), or an athlete (LeBron James). These fans constitute a market—a market attractive to some corporations. These corporations, in turn, are willing to sponsor a competition, a team, or an athlete in return for access to the market. Thus, sponsorship services are born out of spectator services. Similarly, licensing services are also a function of spectator services. As noted earlier, sponsorship services are also applicable to participant services related to specific sports insofar as the partic-

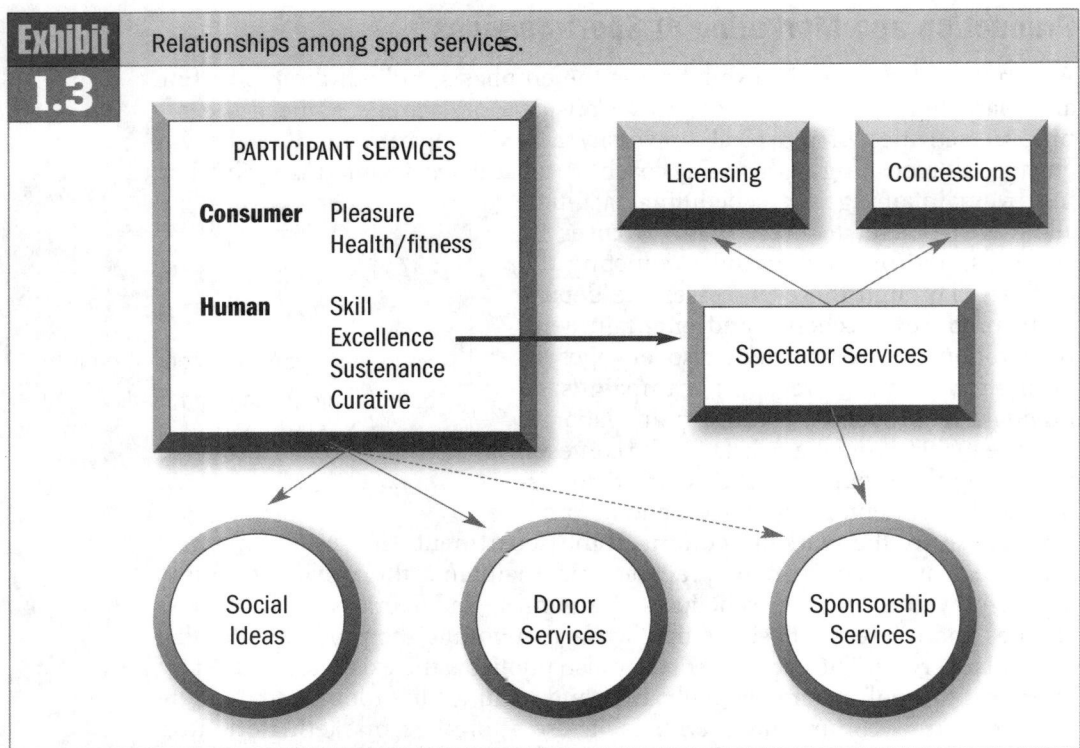

Exhibit 1.3 Relationships among sport services.

Modified from P. Chelladurai, "Sport management: Its scope and career opportunities." In *The management of sport: Its foundation and application*, B.L. Parkhouse (Ed.). Copyright © 1996, Mosby. Used with permission of the McGraw-Hill Companies.

ipants themselves constitute a sizable market, as with Little League, the American Youth Soccer Organization, and Pop Warner Football.

PRIMARY AND ANCILLARY (SATELLITE) SPORT PRODUCTS

The classification presented in this chapter (see Exhibits 1.2 and 1.3) lists the primary products of our field. There are, however, other significant products associated with sport. As noted in the Introduction, *Street & Smith's SportsBusiness Journal* includes the following as major segments of the sport industry: advertising, endorsements, equipment/apparel/shoes, facility construction, media broadcast rights, professional services, medical treatment, travel, publications/videos, and gambling (Broughton, Lee, & Nethery, 1999). The satellite operations associated with the primary products of participant and spectator sport are shown in Exhibit 1.4. These satellite services are noteworthy in that they are generated by the primary services while also facilitating the production and marketing of the primary services. Consider, for example, the player agency services. A player agent represents one or more athletes in bargaining with a professional team over the athlete's salary and contract. Player agents exist because professional teams produce spectator services and seek outstanding athletes. Player agents greatly facilitate the professional team's efforts to recruit and retain outstanding athletes. Similarly, several legal firms specializing in sport law provide very critical services to sport organizations in terms of risk manage-

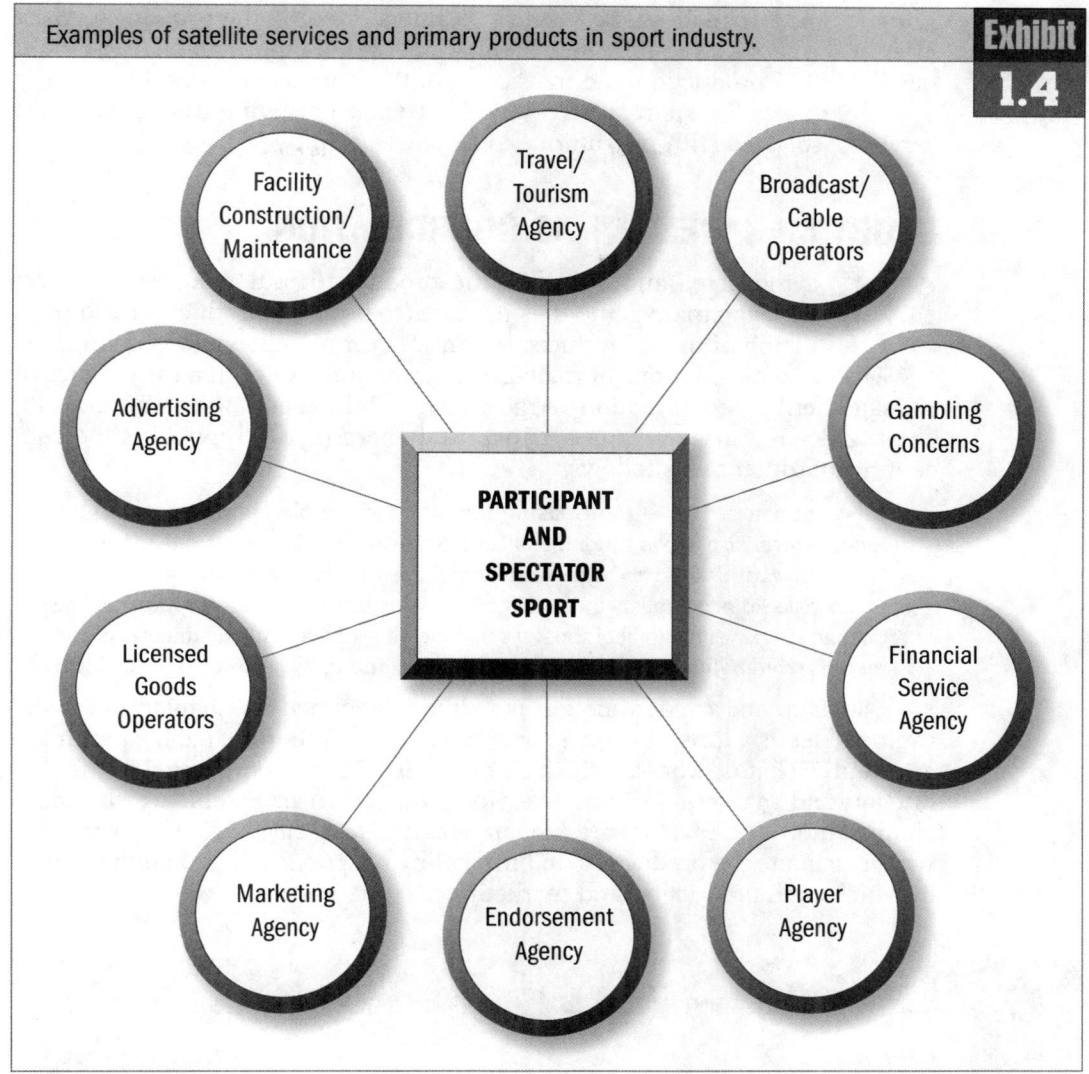

Exhibit 1.4 Examples of satellite services and primary products in sport industry.

ment and avoidance of legal liability. The broadcasting media exist as a segment of the industry only because there are organizations such as the professional sport leagues and intercollegiate athletic leagues, which produce the excellence and entertainment in sport. In turn, the entertainment value and the prestige of the leagues are enhanced by the broadcast services.

In another example, a local university may hire the services of consultants in event management to run a weeklong program of basketball clinics for the youth of the locality (a human-skill service). The consultants bring their expertise in staging the event. They recruit renowned basketball players and instructors to run the clinics and volunteers to assist in the clinics, and they recruit participants and assign them to various ability or age groups. The consultants also schedule the clinics and secure the use of facilities. In addition, they may also undertake to secure sponsorships to finance as well as publicize the clinics. These consultant services became necessary only because of the decision to provide the primary human service oriented toward skill development.

Thus, as sport managers, we need to be able to identify the primary services offered in the field of sport management, as well as those ancillary services needed in the production and marketing of the primary services. Most of the ancillary or satellite sport services may be seen as springing from participant service associated with pursuit of excellence.

SPORT MANAGEMENT AS COORDINATION

Having listed and classified the products in our field, we will next describe management as it relates to both the production and marketing of those products. When we examine the various definitions and descriptions of management, we quickly see that the essence of **management** is **coordination** (Argote, 1982; Mintzberg, 1989; Thompson, 1967; Zalesny, Salas, & Prince, 1995). Mintzberg (1989) highlights the concept of coordination as follows:

> Every human activity—from making of pottery to the placing of a man on the moon—gives rise to two fundamental and opposing requirements: the division of labor into various tasks to be performed and the *coordination* [emphasis added] of those tasks to accomplish the activity. The structure of an organization can be defined simply as the total of the ways in which it is divided into distinct tasks and then its *coordination* [emphasis added] achieved among those tasks. (pp. 100–101)

Management as coordination is further elaborated in Chapter 4. For the moment, let us address the question, "What is being coordinated in sport management?" That is, what are the factors that need to be coordinated in the production and marketing of sport services? As shown in Exhibit 1.5, the more significant of these factors are *human resources, technologies,* and *support units,* which facilitate the production and marketing of sport services, and the *context* in which such production and marketing take place.

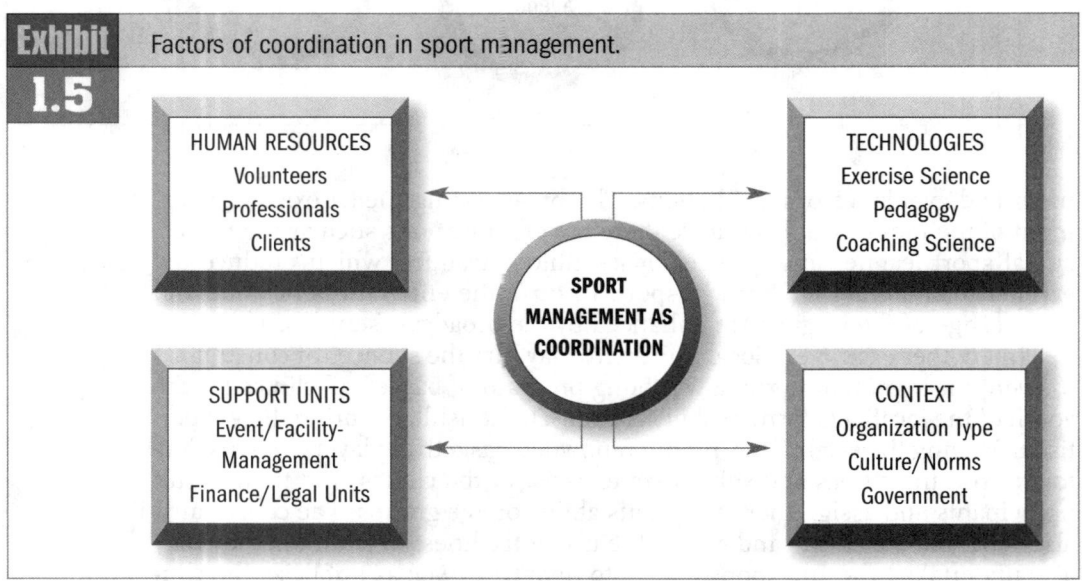

Exhibit 1.5 Factors of coordination in sport management.

Modified from P. Chelladurai, "Sport management: Its scope and career opportunities." In *The management of sport: Its foundation and application,* B.L. Parkhouse (Ed.). Copyright © 1996, Mosby. Used with permission of the McGraw-Hill Companies.

> **Sidebar**
>
> The categorization of human resources of a sport organization into clients, employees, and volunteers is meaningful in most cases, but the athletes in American intercollegiate athletics do not fit neatly into one of these categories. University athletes are first and foremost clients of the university athletic department. Further, their participation is voluntary. The scholarship assistance provided to athletes facilitates their academic pursuits and does not represent payment for athletic contributions. However, when thousands of spectators watch a game in which these athletes participate, they become service providers in creating the entertainment. From this perspective, the athletes become volunteer employees of the athletic department. The athletes in professional sport teams are, of course, professional employees of the franchise because they are paid for their contributions.

Human Resources

The most significant factor that needs to be coordinated is the **human resources**—that is, the people involved in the production of the sport services. The people are the clients, the paid employees, and the volunteer workers.

Clients. The human resource of any venture offering sport and physical activity service will necessarily involve the clients of that service, because the service cannot be produced without the active participation of those clients (Chelladurai, 1992, 1999). Clients may vary in their orientation toward sport and physical activity and in their degree of commitment to such programs. Motivating the clients and gaining their compliance is a challenge to the service providers.

Employees. The next kind of human resources is the service employees. As noted earlier, employees may further be classified into consumer service or professional service employees. Consumer service employees engage in simple, routine activities requiring little training, whereas professional service employees provide complex, knowledge-based, and individualized service to their clients.

Volunteers. Heavy involvement of volunteers is also characteristic of sport organizations. These volunteers are the mainstay of such projects as the Special Olympics and youth sport organized by recreation departments in many cities. The conventional approaches to managing paid workers must be considerably modified in the case of volunteers. The coordination of the contributions of volunteers with those of paid employees is a critical area of sport management. In sum, motivating these differing types of employees and coordinating their activities is a very significant component of sport management that offers both a challenge and an opportunity for sport managers.

> **In Brief**
>
> Sport management is concerned with coordinating the activities of three sets of human resources: clients, paid workers, and volunteer workers.

Technologies

"**Technology** is the systematic application of scientific or other organized knowledge to practical purposes and includes new ideas, inventions, techniques, and materials" (Byars, 1987, p. 28). The technologies associated with the production of our services are generated by disciplinary fields such as exercise physiology, sport medicine, sport psychology, sport pedagogy, coaching education, health science, sport nutrition, and so on. The success of our endeavor depends on the proper use of the knowledge generated in those subdisciplines. Consider, for example, the services offered by a fitness club. The knowledge generated by exercise physiologists will determine the appropriateness of a particular exercise regimen for a particular group of clients. Similarly, the information generated by sport/exercise psychologists on factors that contribute to adherence (or nonadherence) to exercise programs has implications for sport managers. When sport sociology determines which groups of people tend to participate in what kinds of activities, this knowledge should affect marketing strategies and practices. Sport philosophy may guide us in ethical and moral issues concerning the management and delivery of our services. In addition to the sport-based subdisciplines, sport management may also draw on the knowledge generated in such fields as management science and consumer psychology.

The relative significance of these technologies clearly varies from service to service and also varies with the quality levels expected of a service. For example, the importance of exercise physiology would be higher in human-curative services than in consumer-pleasure services. Following this argument, we can expect a high-school coach to be more highly trained than a volunteer youth coach. At high levels of performance, as in pursuit of excellence, we may even have specialists and experts such as a team doctor and team psychologist assisting the coach. Note that the concept of coordination of technologies implicitly refers to the coordination of the activities of those individuals or groups who actually use those technologies in producing the services. In other words, the sport manager does not have to be an expert in all the technologies associated with the production and marketing of the services offered by the organization. However, the manager must have a rudimentary knowledge of these technologies so that she can effectively coordinate the activities of the experts in their respective fields.

Support Units

Sport management is also concerned with the coordination of the **support units** that facilitate the production of a given service. These support units may deal with facility management, event management, personnel management, financial management, public relations, labor relations, sport law, and sport finance. The production and marketing of any product cannot be effectively achieved without the efficient and coordinated activities of the support units. The significance of these support units is reflected by the extent to which courses dealing with these support units are mandatory in almost all sport management degree programs. In fact, the NASPE/NASSM guidelines specify that a degree program will be certified only if it includes courses on these topics.

Context

An important aspect of sport management as coordination is the context in which production and marketing take place. In this phase, the sport manager is concerned with coordinating the production and marketing processes with the external forces represented by the interorganizational networks, market conditions, and government, culture, and community.

Interorganizational Networks

Interorganizational networks such as the National Collegiate Athletic Association (NCAA) in the United States and the Canadian Intercollegiate Athletic Union (CIAU) link those organizations that produce the same services with similar goals and operate in comparable organizational contexts. For example, all universities that offer athletic programs do so with education and pursuit of excellence as the major goals. The NCAA acts in support of this endeavor and provides the supervision and regulation necessary to ensure that the educational purposes are maintained by the entire membership. In a similar manner, the professional leagues such as the NFL, NBA, and NHL also ensure that their members adhere to commonly agreed rules and regulations to govern their respective organizations. You may be familiar with similar bodies that govern high-school sports at the state and national levels. One of the important responsibilities of the sport manager is to coordinate the activities of his own organization with the requirements of the appropriate interorganizational network.

Market Conditions

The context also includes market conditions such as changes in the demand for services and in the organizations competing for the same clients/customers and resources. Thus, a professional sport franchise has to coordinate its own activities, tactics, and strategies to counteract those of its competitors, such as another sport franchise (which provides the same or similar service) or a theater (which provides a substitute service).

Government, Community, and Culture

Our operations should be consistent with government regulations, cultural norms, and societal expectations. The well-publicized difficulties often encountered by industry and business in establishing a branch in another country point to the challenge of coordinating organizational activities with the requirements of the situation. Even within a national context, changes in societal expectations may occur frequently. The recent societal thrusts in favor of diversity and gender equity have affected the practice of management in general and sport management in particular. The growing sport management literature on considerations of gender equity is a case in point, emphasizing the need for sport managers to alter their employment practices. For example, it is unlawful and bad managerial practice to inquire about the gender of an applicant for a job when gender does not have a bearing on the job. Similarly, gone are the days when management paid higher salaries for male aerobic instructors than for female instructors.

The need to coordinate the operations of a sport organization with the local community's interests and desires is illustrated by the influence exerted by alumni associations in intercollegiate athletics. Similarly, professional sport franchises depend on local governments for building or renting stadiums and arenas. Even smaller sport organizations look to the local community for concessions and tax exemptions.

DEFINITION OF SPORT MANAGEMENT

From what has been outlined so far, sport management can be defined as "a field concerned with the coordination of limited human and material resources, relevant technologies, and situational contingencies for the efficient production and exchange of sport services" (Chelladurai, 1994, p. 15). The essential elements of this definition are illustrated in Exhibit 1.6.

According to this definition, management encompasses both the production and marketing (exchange) of sport services. Note also that the definition includes three distinct forms of endeavor: the *study,* the *teaching,* and the *practice* of sport management. Further, according to the definition, sport management is not restricted to any organizational context. That is, different types of organizations may be involved to varying degrees in the production and marketing of one or more sport services.

Finally, the definition emphasizes the notion of coordination as the primary purpose of management. The coordination of various elements within and outside organizations, as described above, points to the enormity and complexity of the managerial job. The complexity may indeed lead to paradoxical situations where the manager is forced to carry out contradictory activities to satisfy various constituencies of the organization that have conflicting needs or expec-

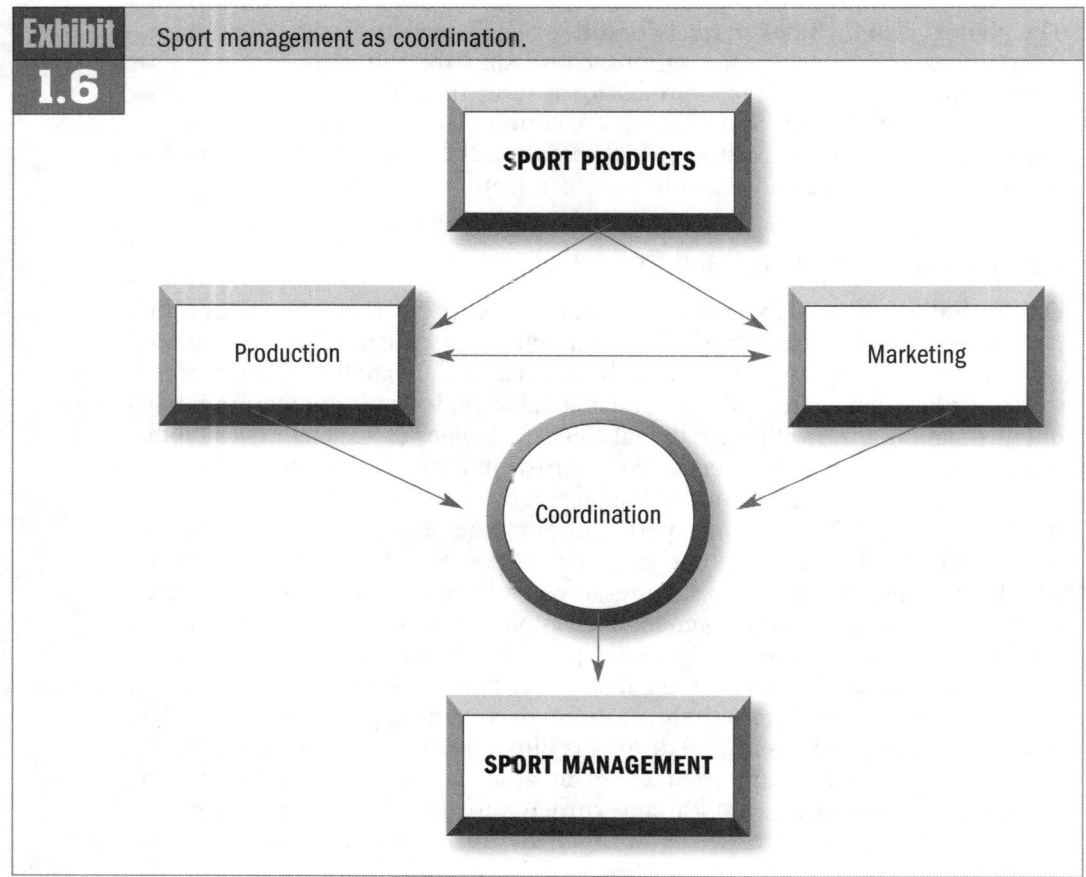

Exhibit 1.6 Sport management as coordination.

tations. Under these circumstances, the meaning of managing shifts from control and coordination to *coping*, where the manager attempts continually to overcome problems of contradictory demands and claims (Lewis, 2002).

The following chapters define and describe the managerial functions through which such coordination is achieved. The concept of organizations *per se* is explained in Chapters 2 and 3. An outline of the concept of management itself is provided in Chapter 4. Then follow descriptions of the functions of planning in Chapter 5, decision making in Chapter 6, organizing in Chapters 7 and 8, leading in Chapters 9, 10, and 11, program evaluation in Chapter 12, organizational effectiveness in Chapter 13, and diversity management in Chapter 14. These managerial functions are in essence aimed at coordinating the factors of production and marketing toward the achievement of organizational goals with limited resources.

Sidebar

Recall from the Introduction that Meek (1997) estimated the worth of satellite economic activities at about $260 billion. Our interest in these satellite activities is threefold. First, several aspects of these activities facilitate and promote our own services. When television networks broadcast certain sports programs, they do so to increase their share of television audience, and thus their profitability. In the process, they promote that particular sport event, the athletes involved, and the organizations that stage the event. Consider the enormous publicity boost that the Wimbledon and U.S. Open tennis tournaments receive during the telecasts of those tournaments. The footwear produced by Nike, Reebok, Adidas, and other firms facilitate our participant sport services. In a similar manner, travel agencies, player agencies, and advertising agencies contribute to our efforts, albeit indirectly.

Second, satellite activities constitute a reservoir of financial resources that we may tap into. For instance, corporations such as General Motors, Coca-Cola, and Visa spend millions of dollars advertising their products.

According to *Street & Smith's SportsBusiness Journal*, total advertising funds spent on sport in the year 1999 were $28.25 billion (Broughton, Lee, & Nethery, 1999). These organizations also like to promote themselves by associating with products and athletes. Hence, they have huge budgets for sponsorship of sport events, sport organizations, and athletes. *Street & Smith's SportsBusiness Journal* estimates sponsorship to be worth $2.4 billion (Broughton, Lee, & Nethery, 1999). Thus, it is not surprising that sport advertising and sport sponsorship are hot topics of discussion within sport management.

Third, satellite activities offer more than 2 million jobs that graduates from academic programs can potentially occupy (Meek, 1997). Some critical areas of concern for sport management degree programs are (a) finding internship and practicum opportunities for the students, and (b) placing graduates in meaningful employment. The satellite operations provide such opportunities.

The relationships among sport organizations, sport industry, and satellite organiza-

Sidebar

tions can also be illustrated through Knoke's (2001; p. 39) three-level scheme of organizations. The first level, the *organizational society,* consists of all organizations in a nation. All sport organizations, manufacturing organizations, business concerns, political organizations, charitable organizations, governments, military units, and the endless list of other organizations in a country constitute the organizational society. At the second level is the *organization population,* which is "a homogeneous set consisting of all organizations of a specific type or form, such as restaurants, newspapers, or hospitals" (p. 39). An organizational population is the same as an industry, where the organizations within an industry produce the same or similar products (e.g., professional sport leagues). The third level, the *organizational field,* is represented by different organizations from different industries that carry out different activities that are functionally interconnected. Knoke gives the example of all corporations, interest groups, and government agencies that are involved with national defense. In our context, intercollegiate athletic departments, the NCAA, the local and national media, local businesses including hotels and tourism businesses, relevant government agencies (e.g., police controlling traffic for an event), other sport organizations in the community, interest groups, faculty, students, alumni, and such other vested interests constitute an organizational field. Exhibit 1.7 illustrates the relationships among organizational populations and organizational fields. Sport managers need to be attuned to the factors within an industry that affect their organizations, as well as the factors from their organizational field that impinge on their organizations.

Given the significance of the satellite economic activities, the study and analysis of that domain are meaningful and necessary (Slack, 1997). In Chapter 3, we will discuss organizations as open systems. In that view, an organization is engulfed by its environment, consisting of other organizations that have an impact on the focal organization, including television networks, footwear manufacturers, travel and advertising agencies, and so on. From this perspective, it is imperative that we understand this part of our environment and cultivate our ability to communicate with it.

But at the same time, we should not let that interest determine how we define sport management. A case in point: The game of golf is not defined by the millions of dollars General Motors is willing to pay Tiger Woods to endorse the Buick line of cars. By the same token, General Motors and the automobile industry are not defined by the celebrities who endorse their products. Closer to home, Nike's or Reebok's sponsorship of our athletes, teams, or projects does not define our core products or our field. Thus, it is necessary to separate our field, defined by what we produce, from those enterprises that would buy and use our products or gain access to our markets for their own ends. While we need to understand how these elements in the environment influence our operations, and how our products influence them, we also need to understand that those elements do not define our field.

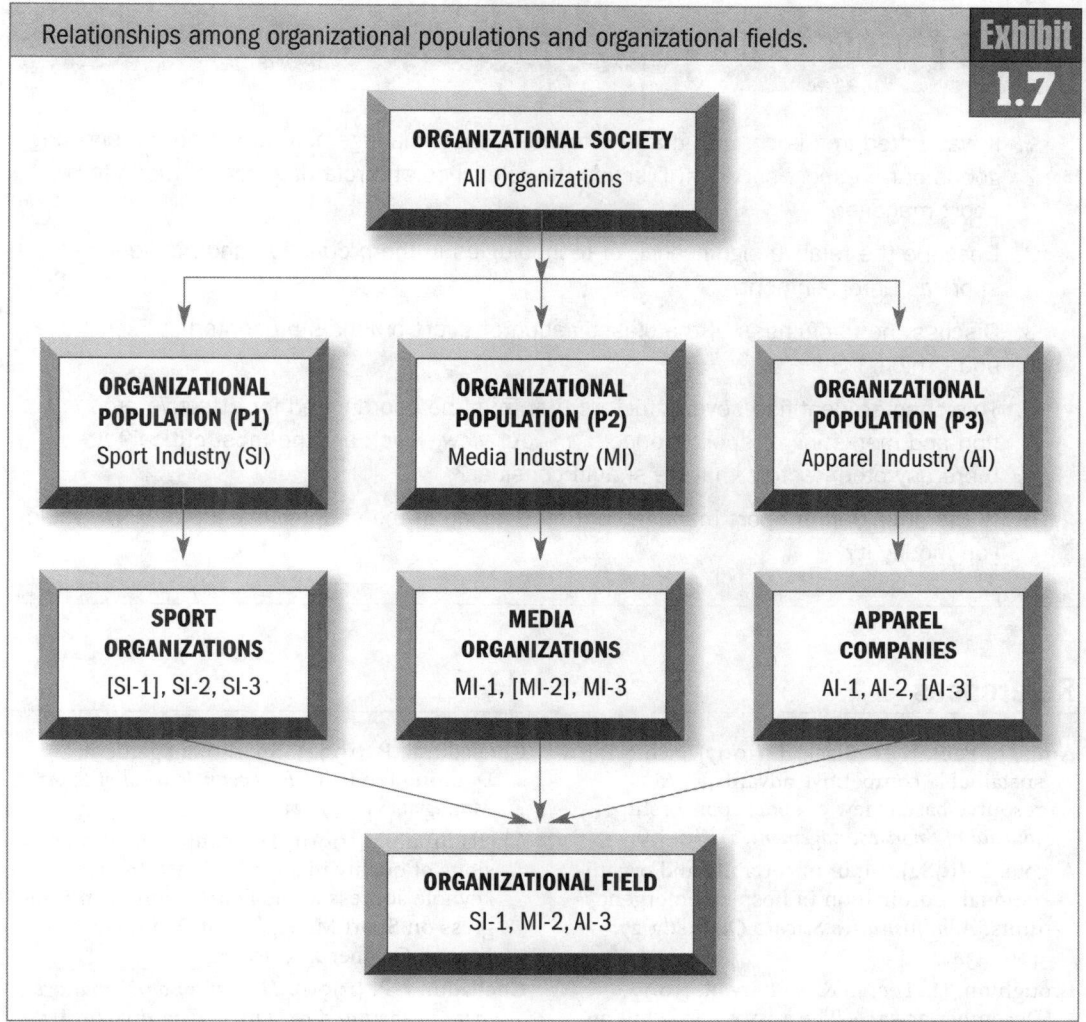

Relationships among organizational populations and organizational fields.

Exhibit 1.7

Source: Modified from Knoke (2001, p. 40, Figure 2.1).

SUMMARY

This chapter has outlined the significant sport products within the purview of sport management: participant services, spectator services, sponsorship services, donor services, and social ideas. Participant services were in turn classified into six classes based on the distinctions between consumer and human services and participant motives. We noted that other significant products such as sport tourism, advertising, and endorsement flow from these primary products. As noted in the Introduction, these satellite segments contribute much to the sport industry. The chapter also described the factors that must be coordinated in the production and marketing of sport products. These factors include human resources, technologies, support units, and contextual factors. Finally, a definition of sport management was offered, emphasizing both the production and marketing of sport products as well as the essential nature of management as coordination.

DEVELOPING YOUR PERSPECTIVES

1. It was noted in this chapter that the focus of sport management is not on the sporting goods but on sport services. Discuss the relevance and role of sporting goods to a sport manager.
2. Describe the relative significance of technologies in the production and marketing of sport as entertainment.
3. Discuss the usefulness of the classification of sport products presented in Exhibit 1.2 and Exhibit 1.3.
4. This chapter identified several factors that must be coordinated for effective production and marketing of sport products. In your view, which are the most critical? Are there any other factors that we should consider?
5. Is the definition of sport management as outlined in the chapter adequate? How would you modify it?

References

Amis, J., Pant, N., & Slack, T. (1997). Achieving a sustainable competitive advantage: A resource-based view of sport sponsorship. *Journal of Sport Management, 11,* 80–96.

Argote, L. (1982). Input uncertainty and organizational coordination in hospital emergency units. *Administrative Science Quarterly, 27,* 420–434.

Broughton, D., Lee, J., & Nethery, R. (1999, December 20–26). The answer: $213 billion Street & Smith's SportsBusiness Journal, 2, 23–29.

Broyles, J. F., & Hay, R. D. (1979). *Administration of athletic programs: A managerial approach.* Englewood Cliffs, NJ: Prentice Hall.

Byars, L. L. (1987). *Strategic management: Planning and implementation.* New York: Harper & Row.

Chelladurai, P. (1985). *Sport management: Macro perspectives.* London, Canada: Sports Dynamics.

Chelladurai, P. (1992). A classification of sport and physical activity services: Implications for sport management. *Journal of Sport Management, 6,* 38–51.

Chelladurai, P. (1993). Sport management: Defining the field. Invited inaugural address at the First European Congress on Sport Management of the European Association of Sport Management, University of Groningen, Netherlands. September 22–25, 1993.

Chelladurai, P. (1994). Sport management: Defining the field. *European Journal of Sport Management, 1,* 7–21.

Chelladurai, P. (1996). The nature and dimensions of quality in sport services. Invited keynote address at the Fourth European Congress on Sport Management. Montpelier, France. October 2–5, 1996.

Chelladurai, P. (1999). *Human resource management in sport and recreation.* Champaign, IL: Human Kinetics.

Chelladurai, P., Scott, F. L., & Haywood-Farmer, J. (1987). Dimensions of fitness services: Development of a model. *Journal of Sport Management, 1,* 159–172.

Cialdini, R. B., Borden, R. J., Thorne, R. J., Walker, M. R., Freeman, S., & Sloan, L. R. (1976). Basking in reflected glory: Three (football) field studies. *Journal of Personality and Social Psychology, 34,* 366–375.

Columbus Dispatch (May 2, 1998). Corporate sponsors' pitches hit home with youth sports leagues.

Columbus Dispatch October 19, 2004, E1.

DeSensi, J. T., Kelley, D. R., Blanton, M. D., & Beitel, P. A. (1990). Sport management curricular evaluation and needs assessment: A multifaceted approach. *Journal of Sport Management, 4,* 31–58.

Duda, J. L. (1994). A goal perspective theory of meaning and motivation in sports. In S. Serpa (Ed.), *International perspectives on sport and exercise psychology* (pp. 127–148). Indianapolis, IN: Benchmark Press.

Duda, J. L. (1996). Maximizing motivation in sport and physical education among children and adolescents: The case of greater task involvement. *Quest, 48,* 290–302.

Ellis, M. J. (1988). *The business of physical education.* Champaign, IL: Human Kinetics.

Etzioni, A. (1973). The third sector and domestic missions. *Public Administration Review,* July–August, 314–327.

Gill, D. L., Gross, J. B., & Huddleston, S. (1983). Participation motives in youth sports. *International Journal of Sport Psychology, 14,* 1–14.

Gronröös, C. (1990). *Service management and marketing: Managing the moment of truth in service competition.* Lexington, MA: Lexington Books.

Hambrick, D. C. (1984). Taxonomic approaches to studying strategy: Some conceptual and methodological issues. *Journal of Management, 10* (1), 27–41.

Hasenfeld, Y. (Ed.). (1992). *Human services as complex organizations.* Newbury Park, CA: Sage Publications.

Hasenfeld, Y. (1983). *Human service operations.* Englewood Cliffs, NJ: Prentice Hall.

Hasenfeld, Y., & English, R. A. (1974). Human service organizations: A conceptual overview. In Y. Hasenfeld & R. A. English (Eds.), *Human service organizations: A book of readings* (pp. 1–23). Ann Arbor, MI: The University of Michigan Press.

Heitmann, H. M. (1986). Motives of older adults for participating in physical activity programs. In B. D. McPherson (Ed.), *Sport and aging* (pp. 199–204). Champaign, IL: Human Kinetics.

Hesterly, W. S., Liebeskind, J., & Zenger, T. R. (1990). Organizational economics: An impending revolution in organization theory? *Academy of Management Review, 15* (3), 402–420.

Howard, D. R., & Crompton, J. L. (1995). *Financing sport.* Morgantown, WV: Fitness Information Technology.

IEG Forecast: Sponsorship spending growth will slow in 2001. (2000, December 18). *IEG Sponsorship Report, 19,* 1, 4–5.

IEG Sponsorship Report (2004). Bi-weekly report published by www.iegsr.com and http://www.sponsorship.com.

Jewett, A. E. (1987). Participant purposes for engaging in physical activity. In G. T. Barrette, R. S. Feingold, C. R. Rees, & M. Pieron (Eds.), *Myths, models, & methods in sport pedagogy* (pp. 87–100). Champaign, IL: Human Kinetics.

Khandwalla, P. N. (1977). *The design of organizations.* New York: Harcourt, Brace, Jovanovich.

Knoke, D. (2001). *Changing organizations: Business networks in the new political economy.* Boulder, CO: Westview Press.

Kuzma, J., & Shanklin, W. (1994). Corporate sponsorship: A framework for analysis. In P. J. Graham (Ed.), *Sport business: Operational and theoretical aspects* (pp. 82–87). Madison, WI: Brown & Benchmark.

Lewis, M. (2002). Exploring paradox: Toward a more comprehensive guide. *Academy of Management Review, 25,* 760–776.

Longhurst, K., & Spink, K. S. (1987). Participation motivation of Australian children involved in organized sport. *Canadian Journal of Sport Sciences, 12,* 24–30.

Lovelock, C. H. (1991). *Services marketing* (2nd ed.). Englewood Cliffs, NJ: Prentice Hall.

Lovelock, C., & Gummesson, E. (2004). Whither services marketing? In search of new paradigm and fresh perspectives. *Journal of Service Research, 7 (1),* 20–41.

Mathes, S. A., & Battista, R. (1985). College men's and women's motives for participation in physical activity. *Perceptual and Motor Skills, 61,* 719–726.

McGill, M. E., & Wooten, L. M. (1976). Management in the third sector. In J. L. Gibson, J. M. Ivancevich, & J. H. Donnelly (Eds.), *Behavior in organizations: Behavior, structure, processes.* Dallas, TX: Business Publications.

Meek, A. (1997). An estimate of the size and supported economic activity of the sport industry in the United States. *Sport Marketing Quarterly, 6* (4), 15–21.

Melnick, M. J. (1993). Searching for sociability in the stands: A theory of sport spectating. *Journal of Sport Management, 7* (1), 44–60.

Mills, P. K., & Margulies, N. (1980). Toward a core typology of service organizations. *Academy of Management Review, 5,* 255–265.

Milne, G. R., & McDonald, M. A. (1999). *Sport marketing: Managing the exchange process.* Sudbury, MA: Jones & Bartlett Publishers.

Mintzberg, H. (1989). *Mintzberg on management: Inside our strange world of organizations.* New York: The Free Press.

Mullin, B. J. (1980). Sport management: The nature and utility of the concept. *Arena Review, 4* (3), 1–11.

Mullin, B. J., Hardy, S., & Sutton, W. A. (2000). *Sport marketing* (2nd ed.). Champaign, IL: Human Kinetics.

NASPE/NASSM Joint Task Force on Sport Management Curriculum and Accreditation (1993). Standards for curriculum and voluntary accreditation of sport management education programs. *Journal of Sport Management, 7*, 159–170.

North American Society for Sport Management (n.d.). *Constitution.* Retrieved January 24, 2004 from www.nassm.com/constitution_a.htm.

Parks, J. B., & Quarterman, J. (2003). *Contemporary sport management* (2nd ed.). Champaign, IL: Human Kinetics.

Pelletier, L. G., Fortier, M. S., Vallerand, R. J., Tuson, K. M., & Briere, N. M. (1995). Toward a new measure of intrinsic motivation, extrinsic motivation, and amotivation in sports: The Sport Motivation Scale (SMS). *Journal of Sport and Exercise Psychology, 17*, 35–53.

Pitts, B. G., & Stotlar, D. K. (1996). *Fundamentals of sport marketing.* Morgantown, WV: Fitness Information Technology.

Robbins, S. P. (1976). *The administrative process: Integrating theory and practice.* Englewood Cliffs, NJ: Prentice Hall.

Roberts, G. (1993). Motivation in sport: Understanding and enhancing the motivation and achievement of children. In R.N. Singer, M. Murphey, & L. K. Tennant (Eds.), *Handbook of research on sport psychology* (pp. 405–420). New York: Macmillan.

Sasser, W. E., Olsen, R. P., & Wyckoff, D. (1978). *Management of service operations.* Rockleigh, NJ: Allyn and Bacon.

Schneider, B., & Bowen, D. E. (1995). *Winning the service game.* Boston: Harvard Business School Press.

Shank, M.D. (2005). *Sports marketing: A strategic perspective* (3rd ed.). Upper Saddle River, NJ: Prentice Hall.

Shilbury, D., Quick, S., & Westerbeek, H. (1998). *Strategic sport marketing.* St. Leonards, NSW: Allen & Unwin.

Slack, T. (1997). *Understanding of sport organizations: The application of organization theory.* Champaign, IL: Human Kinetics.

Snyder, C. R., Lassegard, M. A., & Ford, C. E. (1986). Distancing after group success and failure: Basking in reflected glory and cutting off reflected failure. *Journal of Personality and Social Psychology, 51*, 382–388.

Thompson, J. D. (1967). *Organizations in action.* New York: McGraw-Hill.

Vuolle, P. (1987). Social motives as determinants of physical recreation at various life stages. In G. T. Barrette, R. S. Feingold, C. R. Rees, & M. Pieron (Eds.), *Myths, models, & methods in sport pedagogy* (pp. 169–179). Champaign, IL: Human Kinetics.

Wann, D. L., & Branscombe, N. R. (1990). Die-hard and fair-weather fans: Effects of identification on BIRGing and CORFing tendencies. *Journal of Sport and Social Issues, 14* (2), 103–117.

Williamson, J. (1991). Providing quality care. *Human Services Management, 87* (1), 18–27.

Zalesny, M. D., Salas, E., & Prince, C. (1995). Conceptual and measurement issues in coordination: Implications for team behavior and performance. *Research in Personnel and Human Resources Management, 13*, 81–115.

Zeithaml, V. A., Parasuraman, A., & Berry, L. (1985). Problems and strategies in services marketing. *Journal of Marketing, 49*, 33–46.

CHAPTER 2

Classical View of Organizations

MANAGE YOUR LEARNING

After completing this chapter you should be able to:

- Define an organization.
- Identify and describe significant attributes of an organization.
- Describe the ways in which organizations can be classified and the significance of such classifications for management.

STRATEGIC CONCEPTS

attributes of an organization	identity
boundaries	instrumentality
business concern	mutual benefit association
commonweal organization	organization
cooperative unit	permanency
coordinated effort	prime beneficiary
division of labor	profit orientation
employee–customer interface	service organization
goal-realizing unit	source of funding
hierarchy of authority	voluntary associations

IMPORTANCE OF ORGANIZATIONS

In Chapter 1, we defined and described the field of sport management from the perspective of the products (services) produced and marketed in the field. That approach was based on the notion that **organizations,** including sport organizations, are simply mechanisms for the exchange of products. If organizations are responsible for the production and marketing of sport products, then it is useful to gain an understanding of organizations and their properties. This chapter focuses on defining and describing organizations in general and sport organizations in particular.

Management, defined and described in the next chapter, is relevant only in the context of organizations. Therefore, it is necessary to clarify the meaning of the term *organization,* its attributes, and its functions in the societal context. Moreover, since the methods and content of the four functions in the managerial process—that is, planning, organizing, leading, and evaluating—vary with differences between organizations, it is essential to analyze various organizations in terms of their similarities and dissimilarities. Then, these various organizations can be grouped according to some specific characteristics.

The chapter begins with a description of the critical elements included in various definitions of organizations. This is followed by an elaboration of the attributes that set an organization apart from other social entities.

DEFINING ORGANIZATIONS

The term *organization* has been defined by a number of authors. The following definitions are typical:

An organization is the rational coordination of the activities of a number of people for the achievement of some common explicit purpose or goal, through the division of labour and function, and through a hierarchy of authority and responsibility. (Bowman & Jarrett, 1996, p. 5)

An organization is a **cooperative goal-realizing unit** in which participants consciously enter into a mutual relationship and work together in order to attain common goals. (Keuning, 1998, p. 11)

An *organization* is a deliberate arrangement of people to accomplish some specific purpose. (Robbins, Coulter, & Stuart-Kotze, 2003, p. 13)

[An organization is a] social entity brought into existence and sustained in an ongoing way by humans to serve some purpose, from which it follows that human activities in that entity are normally structured and coordinated towards achieving some purpose. (Rollinson, 2002, p. 4)

An organization is a group of people working together in some type of concerted or **coordinated effort** to attain objectives. (Rue & Byars, 1992, p. 228)

In Simon's (1997) view:

The term organization refers to the pattern of communications and relations among a group of human beings, including the processes for making and implementing decisions. This pattern provides to organization members much of the information and many of the assumptions, goals, and attitudes that enter into their decisions, and provides also a set of stable and comprehensive expectations as to what the other members of the group are doing and how they will react to what one says and does. The sociologist calls this pattern a "role system"; we are concerned with [the] form of role system known as an "organization." (pp. 18–19)

All of the definitions for an organization essentially incorporate four elements:

1. More than one person is needed.
2. The members' contributions are specialized.
3. These specialized functions are coordinated.
4. A common end/goal is being sought.

ATTRIBUTES OF ORGANIZATIONS

The foregoing definitions imply several **attributes of an organization**. A clearer understanding of an organization can be gained by probing further into these attributes: identity, instrumentality, program of activity, membership, clear boundaries, permanency, division of labor, hierarchy of authority, and formal rules and procedures.

Identity

The **identity** of the organization is separate from the identities of the members who make up that organization. That is, an organization has its own identity without reference to who the members and/or office-bearers are. For instance, while the mayor and council members are in overall charge of the city recreation department, they may change after every election. Similarly, the directors and assistant directors of the department may also leave for one reason or another. However, the department remains and is known as the recreation department based on its activities rather than on which individuals are in charge or are carrying out the activities. Thus, the identity of a city recreation department is not bound by the identity of the participants, the employees, or the decision-makers. Similarly, a university athletic department has its own organizational identity independent of its directors, coaches, and athletes. In legal parlance, this concept of separate identity is referred to as the "corporate identity." According to Sofer (1977), the corporate identity "helps to separate the personal possessions and obligations of the main body of members from those they acquire in their collective capacity and *only* in that collective capacity" (p. 3). To gain such a legal status, however, an organization must be registered according to the laws of the land.

Instrumentality

An organization is **instrumental** in achieving goals that are beyond the capacity of the individual members. This is the fundamental basis for an organization. If organizations were not the means to some end, there would not be any need for individuals to join an organization. For example, an individual joins a local sports club because it is instrumental in securing the necessary facilities, in providing expert training and coaching, and in bringing together people of similar interests and skills.

A Program of Activity

The notion that an organization is instrumental in achieving certain specific goals implies that the organization is involved in specific activities. For example, a fitness and tennis club is recognizable by the fact that it provides facilities for physical activities including tennis, it schedules those activities and competitions, and it offers instructions in those activities. On the other hand, a firm retailing sporting goods is involved in the purchase, promotion, and sales of sporting goods. These programs of activities define, in part, the goals of the organization and the domain in which it operates.

Membership

Organizations tend to define who can have membership. They also establish procedures to replace members who leave for one reason or another. For example, to become a member of a university, one must either have a high academic degree (such as a Ph.D.) to be a faculty member, or have a high academic high-school record to be a student. In a similar manner, membership in a university athletic department either as an administrator, coach, or athlete is contingent upon the individual possessing the requisite qualifications. Employees of a firm specializing in sport law are expected to have some training and education in law, specifically pertaining to sport law. Fitness clubs hire as fitness specialists only those who have had training in exercise physiology. This attribute ensures that the organization's members have the skills and expertise to carry out at least some of the activities undertaken by the organization.

In some sport organizations, the notion of membership may be restrictive in the sense that only members with certain assigned attributes (usually demographic characteristics) would be accepted as participants. For instance, the participants in Little League have to be within a certain age range. Several sports leagues offer competitions for different groups based on age and/or gender classification. These restrictions are attempts to ensure equality in maturity and development of the participants, but they also define who can be members of what teams or leagues.

Clear Boundaries

An organization's **boundaries** are defined by the attributes described above. That is, an organization's goals, its program of activity, and its roster of members clarify its boundaries in terms of its area of operation, its personnel, and its customers or clients. For example, a university's boundaries are defined by the activities that are carried out (teaching, research, service), its members (teachers and support staff), and its clients (the students). The boundaries defining a university athletic department or a department of recreational sports are their respective activities, personnel, and client groups. Similarly, a commercial fitness club's boundaries are defined by its fitness programs, its staff, and its clients. The distinction between a public golf course and a private nonprofit golf course is based on who can use the facilities and who the managers are.

Permanency

Generally speaking, an organization is relatively more permanent than the members who compose it. The Roman Catholic Church, government bureaucracies, large industrial and business corporations, universities, and voluntary organizations like the sport governing bodies and Olympic associations are examples in which this attribute is clearly evident. The former president of the International Olympic Committee, His Excellency Samaranch, who made the IOC into a financial giant, has retired, as have several other members of the Committee. While officers come and go, the Committee itself survives and thrives. Similarly, a golf club is likely to continue to exist despite turnovers in personnel—managers, professionals, and groundskeepers. There is **permanency** to these organizations, which outlast the transfers, resignations, and deaths of individual members. It is conceivable, however, that smaller and not so well-established organizations could collapse with the departure of significant members.

Division of Labor

Division of labor and its consequence, specialization, makes the organization an efficient entity. As noted in the previous chapter, the managerial process of organizing should ensure that the division of labor is rational and consistent with the selected goals and programs of activities, which in turn should make for efficiency. In a department of sport management, for example, the division of labor among the faculty members will most likely fall along the lines of teaching in subject areas such as management, marketing, and finance, as well as the supervision of internships and research in specific areas. The existence of special units in an athletic department to manage facilities, events, ticketing, and marketing indicates the extent of division of labor in that department. A fitness club may divide its operations into specialized units for aerobics, weight training, swimming, tennis, and squash. A national sport-governing body may divide its total work into specific domains such as selection and training of national teams, training of coaches and officials, programs for mass participation, and marketing of its programs. Thus, every organization is characterized by division of labor.

Hierarchy of Authority

The coordination of individual members and their tasks requires a scheme in which one or more individuals specialize in coordinating the work of others. Moreover, persons in these positions of control and coordination must have the necessary authority. Thus, an organization is characterized by a **hierarchy of authority** and a table of organization that specifies who has authority over whom and for what purposes. This obviously results in unequal distribution of power, authority, influence, and status among organization members. In a department of sport management, the hierarchy of authority is represented by the positions of president and vice-presidents of the university, the dean and assistant deans of the college, and the chair of the department. We can identify the positions arranged in a hierarchical manner in any athletic department, professional sport franchise, city recreation department, private golf club, or similar sport organization. Because the hierarchy of authority is necessary for the control and coordination of the activities of the members, it also carries with it the power to schedule the activities, allocate funds to the various programs, and monitor activities in general.

In Brief

Organizations are characterized by nine attributes: a separate identity, instrumentality, a program of activities, a roster of members, clear boundaries, permanency, a division of labor, a hierarchy of authority, and formal rules and procedures.

Formal Rules and Procedures

A dominant attribute in any organization is the presence of explicit rules and procedures to direct and control the behavior of members (employees as well as customers). For instance, the constitution and bylaws of a sport-governing body stipulate who can be office-bearers, and how and by whom they are selected. These rules also articulate the specific responsibilities of each office-bearer. Members of a tennis club are given a set of rules to follow in reserving a court and using the facilities of the club. The NCAA is notorious for its voluminous set of rules relating to recruiting and eligibility. The purpose of rules is to ensure that the actions of individual members are consistent with the goals of the organization and coordinated toward the attainment of those goals. An equally important outcome of rules is that all clients of the organization are treated equally and fairly.

In summary, the above attributes are present to a greater or lesser extent in all organizations. While various organizations—businesses and industries, hospitals, the military, athletic departments, volunteer organizations like the Red Cross, and educational institutions—possess these attributes, some are quite distinct from others in many respects. For example, the Red Cross and the military are recognized as dissimilar entities because they pursue different goals, carry out different activities, and adopt different internal processes. On the other hand, organizations such as universities and high schools can be very similar to each other because their main purposes and activities (the educating of individuals) are comparable.

ATHLETIC TEAMS AS ORGANIZATIONS

The above description of organizations is broad enough to include athletic teams as well as universities and industrial corporations. Ball (1975) pointed out that while athletic teams possess all the attributes of an organization, they are also unique in terms of (a) the constant roster size of members across teams in the same sport, (b) the codification of the activities of the team in rule books, and (c) the public and precise record of performances of the team. These attributes facilitate organizational analyses of teams, particularly in comparative and cross-cultural contexts.

In fact, many research efforts relating to athletic teams are based on the notion that athletic teams are similar to conventional organizations in many respects. This basic premise has led several authors to employ theoretical models from industry and business in the study of athletic teams and their effectiveness. For instance, Chelladurai's (1978, 1993) multidimensional model of leadership was developed for applicability to athletic teams. This model, which will be discussed in detail in Chapter 11, was a synthesis and modification of leadership models in business and industry.

Riemer and Chelladurai (1998) developed a scale for measuring the satisfaction of athletes. This scale, known as the Athlete Satisfaction Questionnaire (ASQ), is based on the premise that athletic teams are organizations as already defined. The focus of the investigation was athletics in educational institutions. The ASQ relies on a conceptual framework derived from other satisfaction models in business and industry (Chelladurai & Riemer, 1997). According to the authors, there are two perspectives on athletes as members of the athletic team. In the first perspective, athletes are the clients or beneficiaries of the athletic team as the organization. Consistent with the recent emphasis in general management on client/customer satisfaction, measuring athlete satisfaction would be a measure of organizational effectiveness. The second perspective on the athletes stems from the notion that athletic teams are providers of entertainment to the public. In this scenario, the athletes produce the entertainment through their excellent performance. Therefore, the athletes resemble the employees in business and industrial organizations. Thus, measuring athletic satisfaction would be akin to measuring job satisfaction of regular employees. In either perspective, the athletic team is seen as an organization in itself.

Similarly, MacLean and Chelladurai (1995) and MacLean and Zakrajsek (1996) were concerned with evaluating the performance of coaches of athletic teams. Their analysis of coaching performance was based on models of evaluation from business and industry. Chelladurai and Ogasawara (2003) investigated the satisfaction of coaches in intercollegiate athletics. Similarly, Turner and Chelladurai (in press) explored the extent to which intercollegiate athletic coaches were committed to their occupation and to their organization. These works were based on models of job satisfaction found in industrial and organizational psychology literature. The basic assumption in these investigations is that the coach is the manager of the athletic team—an organization in its own right.

Not only sport scientists view athletic teams as conventional organizations. Organization theorists have also noted how the various sport teams such as baseball, football, and basketball teams constitute ideal prototypes of organizations. For instance, Drucker (1995) compares work teams in organizations to three different types of sport teams. He notes that:

> "Team-building" has become a buzzword in American business. The results are not overly impressive. . . . One reason—perhaps the major one—for these near failures is the all-but-universal belief among executives that there is just one kind of team. There actually are three—each different in structure, in the behavior it demands from its members, in its strengths, its vulnerabilities, its limitations, its requirements, but above all, in what it can do and should be used for. (pp. 97–98)

Drucker (1995) views an open-heart surgical team and an automobile assembly team as similar to baseball teams in that each member in these teams has a fixed position (e.g., second baseman and pitcher in baseball, and the anesthesiologist and the surgical nurse in the surgical team). Thus, "the players play on the team; they do not play as a team" (p. 98). Drucker compares the football team to the hospital unit that rallies around a patient who goes into shock, where the players play as a team despite their fixed positions. Finally, the tennis doubles team is compared to a musical band and to senior executives in a big company, where "players have a primary rather than a fixed position. They are supposed to 'cover' their teammates, adjusting to their teammates' strengths and weaknesses and to the changing demands of the 'game'" (p. 99). Drucker's essential point is that because the dynamics of each type of team are different, their success depends on how that type of team is composed and managed.

In Brief

Athletic teams are organizations in their own right, possessing the same attributes as conventional organizations. Their uniqueness lies in the limited and specified membership roster and activities, as well as the publicity of their performance.

In a similar vein, Keidel (1985) based a book of management on the archetypes of a baseball team, a football team, and a basketball team. He notes that the three teams differ in the performance required of each team member, the degree of interdependence among the members and their tasks, the type of coordination appropriate to each team, the characteristics of individual performers, and the rationale for recruiting and selecting members. Keidel's basic argument is that all organizations can be categorized into three types, each resembling one of the three types of sport teams. He goes on to suggest that some of the practices of high-performing sport teams can be implemented in conventional organizations.

CLASSIFYING ORGANIZATIONS

It has been argued that "classifying things is perhaps the most fundamental and characteristic activity of the human mind, and underlies all forms of science" (Crowson, 1970, p. 1). In emphasizing the need for the development of an organizational typology (that is, a classification), Mills and Margulies (1980) stated:

> Typologies play an important role in theory development because valid typologies provide a general set of principles for scientifically classifying things or events. What one attempts to do in such endeavors is to generate an analytical tool or instrument, not only as a way of reducing data, but more significantly to stimulate thinking. (p. 255)

The significance of a typology for practicing managers was further highlighted by McKelvy (1975) as follows:

> Organization science, and especially the application of its findings to the problem of organizations and managers, is not likely to emerge with viable laws and principles until substantial progress is made toward an acceptable taxonomy and classification of organizations. The basic inductive–deductive process of science does not work without the phenomena under investigation being divided into sufficiently homogeneous classes. Managers cannot use the fruits of science unless they first can discover which of all the scientific findings apply to their situation. (p. 523)

Some of the criteria for classifying organizations that are more germane to sport/physical activity organizations are summarized in Exhibit 2.1 and described below.

Profit Orientation

It is traditional to categorize organizations on the basis of whether their purpose is to make a profit. An individual business providing fitness services is an example of a profit organization (even if it does not actually make a profit), whereas a university intramural department offering the same services is an example of a nonprofit organization (even if its receipts exceed expenses). Similarly, a professional sports club is a profit-oriented organization, while a national sport organization is not. All government agencies are nonprofit organizations. There is a debate over the use of the terms *profit* and *nonprofit*.

Exhibit 2.1

Criteria for classifying an organization relevant to sport management.

1. **Profit orientation:** Is the organization's purpose to make a profit?
2. **Source of funding:** What is the source of its funding?
3. **Prime beneficiary:** Who benefits from the organization?
4. **Employee–customer interface:** What type of interaction occurs between the customer and the employee?
5. **Volunteer participation:** Is it a voluntary association?

Some feel that it is more appropriate to use the terms *for-profit* and *not-for-profit* to indicate the **profit orientation** of the organization. In this view, if any profit-oriented organization fails to make a profit, it would be labeled as nonprofit. However, the terminology of *profit* and *nonprofit* is most commonly used by scholars and practitioners.

A more serious issue than the labels attached to them is the similarity in structures and processes of the two types of organizations, profit and nonprofit. One complaint relating to NCAA Division I athletics is that several of the athletic departments run their programs in such a way as to maximize their revenues. While some of their methods may be unacceptable in a nonprofit and educational context, the idea of maximizing revenue should not be held against such institutions. A critical function of management is to ensure the survival of the organization. Such survival is based on securing resources not only for current operations but also for future operations. Thus, even managers of nonprofit sport organizations, including university athletic departments, are required to maximize their revenue to ensure the survival of their respective organizations and the continued provision of their respective services. If such maximization efforts result in an excess over expenses, such excess funds are rightly labeled *surplus* rather than *profit*. The surplus is, in fact, a reserve for a rainy day.

> **In Brief**
>
> Organizations can be classified as profit or nonprofit based on their orientation to make profit. The excess of income over expenditures incurred by a nonprofit organization is considered a surplus that can be used only to further its goals.

From a different perspective, many university athletic departments can generate revenue only on the strength of the popularity of certain sports, such as football and basketball. For instance, the football team of Ohio State University, where this author teaches, generates nearly $20 million per year—more than it costs to run the football program. The excess funds are used to support teams in more than 30 other sports for both men and women. If it were even remotely concerned with profit, the athletic department in the university would not support the other nonrevenue sports. This practice is consistent with Reynold's (2001) position that "The term *nonprofit organization* is used to refer to entities formed to provide social services rather than being formed to seek a profit. . . . The organizations do not have owners, and the ownership interest cannot be sold or traded. While the organization's revenues may exceed expenses, the excess must be used for the common good of society. It cannot directly benefit the members, and it cannot be referred to as profit" (pp. 432–433). Hopkins (2001) notes that from a legal perspective nonprofit organizations are distinguished from for-profit organizations by the doctrine of *private inurement*. The doctrine states that for a nonprofit to be tax exempt it "must be organized and operated so that no part of its net earnings inures to the benefit of any private shareholder or individual" (p. 900). Viewed from this perspective, it could be argued that revenue maximization is not only justified but also required.

Miller and Fielding (1995) provide another good example of a nonprofit organization engaging in revenue-generating activities. They document the history of the YMCA from its birth as a "noncommercial, protestant, religious organization endeavoring to spread the word of god through religious outreach, welfare, and relief-oriented activities" (p. 11). They describe the current status of many branches of the YMCA that offer similar or identical services to those of profit organizations. For example, many YMCAs offer fitness programs that do not differ much from those found at a privately owned profit-oriented fitness club. Referring to these YMCA branches as the "commercial YMCAs," Miller and Fielding (1995) point out that these YMCAs not only offer the same programs as the profit-oriented organizations, but they also offer them to the same market segment, comprised of those who can pay for these services. They also note that these YMCAs use the revenue generated by some of their activities to fund other nonrevenue-producing activities in the service of the community. From this perspective, the excess revenues are considered surplus rather than profit.

The growth in the number and size of nonprofit organizations has been considerable in the past few decades. It is estimated that their operating expenses make up 6 percent of the U.S. gross national product (Pappas, 1996). Given the immensity of these operations, it has become commonplace to speak of a *nonprofit sector* as contrasted with the *public* (or government) and *private* (restricted to profit-oriented businesses and industries) sectors (Pappas, 1996).

Source of Funding

The major **source of funding** has also been used to classify organizations broadly into private and public organizations. Those organizations that depend on private contributions or capital investments for their operation and survival are categorized as private organizations. Public organizations are those that are funded by tax monies at the national, state or provincial, or municipal level. Thus, all government agencies involved in the promotion of sport and physical activity are public sector organizations. All other sport organizations can be designated as private sector organizations.

A number of authors such as Etzioni (1973) and McGill and Wooten (1976) have noted the emergence of a new class of organizations, which they call third sector organizations. The essential feature of a third sector organization is the partnership or collaboration between traditional private and public sector organizations. This partnership usually takes the form of financial support from the public sector, with the private sector being charged with the management of the organization toward well-defined purposes.

There are two specific ways in which third sector sport organizations may come about. First, the government or its agencies may create a new organization in the third sector. In Canada, for example, the federal government launched Participaction Canada for the specific purpose of propagating fitness among the general public. The government provided a block grant of $500,000 and invited certain prominent members of the community, including business leaders, to carry out the functions outlined. Thereafter, the organization was left to its own devices to promote fitness. The government's contribution continued to be strictly monetary, but even that became negligible in comparison to the millions of dollars' worth of media advertisement generated by Participaction Canada. Amtrak in the United States is another example of a third sector organization. When the railway industry was

> **In Brief**
>
> Organizations can be classified as public (funded by government taxation), private (funded by private capital), and third sector (subsidized by government finances).

> **Sidebar**
>
> Fottler (1981) identified four types of organizations based on a combination of profit motive and source of funding. These four classes are (1) private for-profit organizations (which are the businesses and corporations whose capital is provided by investors); (2) private nonprofit organizations (which are supported by donations, endowments, and government grants); (3) private quasi-public organizations (which are created and partly funded by government and authorized to provide particular goods or services); and (4) public organizations (whose primary form of financing is taxation).

experiencing difficulties, the U.S. Government stepped in to create Amtrak and funded it initially to sustain the viability of the industry.

The second way for a third sector organization to emerge is when the government begins to provide funds to private sector organizations in support of specific functions. For example, Sport Canada will be spending $100 million Canadian in 2005 to support national sport organizations and their programs (Sport Canada, 2005), whereas the government's contribution was $20 million in 1983. As contributions from government increase, the sport-governing bodies become more and more third sector organizations.

Thus, the distinction among public, private, and third sector organizations can be narrowed down to the extent to which funding for these organizations is supplied through legislation of a senior-ranking organization. If this criterion is used, a university athletic department, which is financed by student fees on a schedule set and approved by the university senate, is similar to a third sector organization. On a higher level, the university itself is a third sector organization if it is heavily funded by the government—even though it retains autonomy in its management.

Prime Beneficiary

Blau and Scott (1960) referred to four types of organizations based on the criterion of **prime beneficiary** of the organization. In their view, while several groups may benefit through an organization, one of those groups can be identified as the primary group for whose benefit the organization exists. For example, while the faculty, staff, and students benefit from a university, it is the students who are the prime beneficiaries of the university because they are the reason the university exists in the first place. In fact, the benefits that accrue to the faculty and staff may be viewed as costs a university incurs in order to serve the students. Based on this notion of prime beneficiary, Blau and Scott (1960) classified organizations as follows:

1. **Mutual benefit associations,** in which the members or rank-and-file participants are the prime beneficiaries, as in player unions and private nonprofit golf or tennis clubs
2. **Business concerns,** in which the owners or managers of the organization are the prime beneficiaries, as in commercial fitness or golf clubs and professional sport franchises
3. **Service organizations,** in which the clients or the public-in-contact are the prime beneficiaries, as in athletic and recreational departments in educational institutions, city recreation departments, YMCA sports departments, and sport governing bodies

4. **Commonweal organizations**, in which the public-at-large is the prime beneficiary, as in prisons and police departments

Commonweal organizations are very few in society, and almost nonexistent in sport. Of course, some may see a summer sports camp as one way of "keeping the kids off the street" for the benefit of the other citizens. In this perspective, summer camps could be considered similar to commonweal organizations.

As we will discuss later in the book, the criterion of prime beneficiary is the best basis for many organizational decisions where several groups are likely to be affected.

> **In Brief**
>
> Organizations can be classified as mutual benefit associations existing for the primary benefit of members, business concerns for the benefit of owners, service organizations for the benefit of their clients, and commonweal organizations for the benefit of the public.

Employee–Customer Interface

In Chapter 1 we described several classes of sport services. One of the factors that differentiate among various forms of services is the type of interaction between the customer or client and the service employee. Based on what takes place in the **employee–customer interface** and the importance of the information component in that interface, Mills and Margulies (1980) classified service organizations as maintenance-interactive, task-interactive, and personal-interactive. In *maintenance-interactive* types of organizations, the information processed by the employee is rather limited, and the decisions he makes are simple. Consider, for example, the employee who handles the membership and reservations of a racquetball club. Each transaction with a customer involves little time, simple decisions, and minimal information processing. The services offered by this type of organization are usually consumer services as discussed in Chapter 1.

In *task-interactive* service organizations, there is more time involved, the decisions are more complex, and the employee has more information. As a consequence, the employee also has more power than the customer, who knows what she wants but not how to get it. For example, an entrepreneur, after deciding to build a new racquetball-fitness facility, must depend on an engineering and construction firm for a plan and the eventual construction of the facility. The entrepreneur—that is, the customer—depends on the construction firm employee's expertise and knowledge about the specific tasks to be completed. The services of this kind of organization are professional services as discussed in Chapter 1.

In *personal-interactive* service organizations, the clients or customers are "typically unaware or imprecise about *what* will best serve their interest and *how* to go about remedying a situation" (Mills & Margulies, 1980, p. 264). A fitness consulting firm or an athletic injuries clinic is an example from the field of sport/physical activity. Although the clients or customers may provide detailed information about their fitness level or the source and nature of their ailments, the employee processes this information and makes decisions. The customers may not be even aware if quality service is being provided. Note that the services of this type of organization are human services as described in Chapter 1.

Volunteer Participation

Most sport governing bodies and their local units are **voluntary associations**—organizations run by volunteers. Sills (1972) defined a voluntary association as:

> an organized group of persons (1) that is formed in order to further some common interest of its members; (2) in which membership is voluntary in the sense that it is neither mandatory nor acquired through birth; and (3) that exists independently of the state. (p. 363)

More recently, Knoke (1990) described volunteer associations as "collective action organizations [that] (1) seek nonmarket solutions to particular individual or group problems; (2) maintain formal criteria for membership on a voluntary basis; (3) may employ persons under the authority of organizational leaders; and (4) provide formally democratic procedures to involve members in policy decisions" (p. 7). These associations are differentiated from primary groups (such as social circles, friendship cliques, and families) because the latter groups do not have clearly stated purposes and specific criteria for membership. Volunteer associations also differ from regular work organizations such as governments and business organizations, which are characterized by rigid hierarchical authority systems and a contract between labor and the organization in the form of financial compensation for full-time work (Knoke, 1990).

These definitions are broad enough to include not only sport governing bodies and local sport clubs but also players' unions and referees' unions. However, the purpose of the unions is to protect the economic welfare of their members, whereas the former two—the truly voluntary associations—are not concerned with "making a living for the members" as Sills would put it. Further, for an association to be legitimately called voluntary, the volunteers (as opposed to paid staff) must constitute the majority of the participants. For example, the board of governors of a university or a hospital consists of volunteer members. However, the proportion of other paid participants, such as professors, doctors, or staff, is much larger; therefore, these types of institutions lose the true flavor of voluntary associations. In contrast, in sport governing bodies and their local units, almost all activities—top management as well as front-line activities—are run by volunteers. (A recent trend, however, has been to hire more and more paid staff to carry out the ever-increasing activities of sport organizations.) The presence of volunteers and their influence on organizational purposes and processes make the management of those organizations distinct from the management of other organizations. These differences in managerial processes are pointed out in subsequent chapters.

SUMMARY

In this chapter, we defined the organization as a social entity and described its characteristics. We discussed the significant attributes of an organization—identity, instrumentality, program of activity, membership, boundaries, permanency, division of labor, hierarchy of authority, and formal rules and procedures. We compared athletic teams to an organization as defined and described above. We noted that organizations can be classified on the basis of (a) profit orientation (profit and nonprofit organizations); (b) source of funding (public, private, and third sector organizations); (c) prime beneficiaries (mutual benefit, business, service, and commonweal organizations); (d) employee–customer interface (maintenance-interactive, task-interactive, and personal-interactive organizations); and (e) volunteer membership and governance (volunteer organizations). These classifications and the criteria on which they are based provide the sport manager with some insights regarding the context and people he is dealing with.

The various classifications of organizations are not mutually exclusive. The classification based on profit motive and that based on sources of funding are not independent of each other. For example, government (public) organizations are not profit-oriented. Similarly, most third sector organizations are nonprofit in nature. Organizations could be placed in different classes of organizations proposed by Blau and Scott (1960) and Mills and Margulies (1980). For example, a university, which is a nonprofit, third sector organization, is also a service organization (Blau & Scott) providing personal-interactive services (Mills & Margulies). On the other hand, a sports arena run by a city is a public, nonprofit, service organization providing a maintenance-interactive service.

The above classification systems provide some insight into the types of products produced by different classes of organizations, and the nature of the exchange of those products with their respective client groups. They also highlight the specific constraints and exigencies faced by different kinds of organizations. Thus, an understanding of these classifications can help sport managers adapt to the specific organizational contexts they manage.

DEVELOPING YOUR PERSPECTIVES

1. Consider the various definitions of an organization provided at the beginning of the chapter. Discuss the relative emphasis each one places on goals, people, specialization, and coordination.

2. This chapter describes several attributes of an organization. Select two sport organizations and describe them in terms of those attributes.

3. Considering the same two organizations, classify them according to the criteria provided in the chapter—profit orientation, sources of funding, prime beneficiary, and employee–customer interface.

References

Ball, D. W. (1975). A note on method in the sociological study of sport. In D. W. Ball & J. W. Loy (Eds.), *Sport and social order*. Reading, MA: Addison-Wesley.

Blau, P. M., & Scott, W. R. (1960). *Formal organizations: A comparative study*. San Francisco: Chandler.

Bowman, C., & Jarrett, M. G. (1996). *Management in practice: A framework for managing organizational change* (3rd ed.). Oxford, U.K.: Butterworth-Heinemann.

Chelladurai, P. (1978). *A contingency model of leadership in athletics*. Unpublished doctoral dissertation, University of Waterloo, Waterloo, ON, Canada.

Chelladurai, P. (1993). Leadership. In R. N. Singer, M. Murphy, & K. Tennant (Eds.), *The handbook on research in sport psychology* (pp. 647–671). New York: Macmillan.

Chelladurai, P. & Ogasawara, E. (2003). Satisfaction and commitment of American and Japanese collegiate coaches. *Journal of Sport Management, 17,* 62–73.

Chelladurai, P., & Riemer, H. (1997). A classification of facets of athlete satisfaction. *Journal of Sport Management, 11,* 133, 159.

Crowson, R. A. (1970). *Classification and biology* New York: Atherton Press.

Drucker, P. F. (1995). *Managing in a time of great change.* New York: Truman Talley Books/Dutton.

Etzioni, A. (1973). The third sector and domestic missions. *Public Administration Review,* July–August, 314–327.

Fottler, M. D. (1981). Is management really generic? *Academy of Management Review, 6,* 1–12.

Hopkins, B. R. (2001). Law and taxation. In T.D. Connors (Ed.), *The nonprofit handbook: Management* (3rd ed., pp. 893–921). New York: John Wiley & Sons.

Keidel, R. W. (1985). *Game plans: Sports strategies for business.* New York: Dutton.

Keuning, D. (1998). *Management: A contemporary approach.* London: Pitman.

Knoke, D. (1990). *Organizing for collective action: The political economies of associations.* New York: Aldine de Gruyter.

MacLean, J. C., & Chelladurai, P. (1995). Dimensions of coaching performance: Development of a scale. *Journal of Sport Management, 9,* 194–207.

MacLean, J. C., & Zakrajsek, D. (1996). Factors considered important for evaluating Canadian university athletic coaches. *Journal of Sport Management, 10,* 446–462.

McGill, M. E., & Wooten, L. M. (1976). Management in the third sector. In J. L. Gibson, J. M. Ivancevich, & J. H. Donnelly (Eds.), *Readings in organizations: Behavior, structure, processes.* Dallas: Business Publications.

McKelvy, B. (1975). Guidelines for the empirical classification of organizations. *Administrative Science Quarterly, 20,* 509–525.

Miller, L. K., & Fielding, L. W. (1995). The battle between the for-profit health club and the "commercial" YMCA. *Journal of Sport and Social Issues, 19* (1), 76–107.

Mills, P. K., & Margulies, N. (1980). Toward a core typology of service organizations. *Academy of Management Review, 5,* 255–265.

Pappas, A. T. (1996). *Reengineering your nonprofit organization: A guide to strategic transformation.* New York: John Wiley & Sons.

Reynolds, R. G. (2001). Nonprofit organizations as entrepreneurs. In T.D. Connors (Ed.), *The nonprofit handbook: Management* (3rd ed., pp. 432–442). New York: John Wiley & Sons.

Riemer, H. A., & Chelladurai, P. (1998). Development of the Athlete Satisfaction Questionnaire (ASQ). *Journal of Sport & Exercise Psychology, 20,* 127–156.

Robbins, S. P., Coulter, M., & Stuart-Kotze, R. (2003). *Management* (7th ed.). Toronto: Prentice Hall.

Rollinson, D. (2002). *Organisational behaviour and analysis: An integrated approach* (2nd ed.). Harlow: Financial Times Prentice Hall.

Rue, L. W., & Byars, L. L. (1992). *Management: Skills and application.* (6th ed.). Homewood, IL: Irwin.

Sills, D. L. (1972). Voluntary associations: Sociological aspects. In *International encyclopedia of the social sciences* (vol. 16). New York: Crowell, Collier, and Macmillan.

Simon, H. A. (1997). *Administrative behavior: A study of decision-making behaviors in administrative organizations* (4th ed.). New York: The Free Press.

Sofer, C. (1977). *Organizations in theory and practice.* New York: Basic Books.

Sport Canada (2005). Introduction. Retrieved January 19, 2005 from www.pch.gc.ca/progs/sc/pubs/tablesrondes-roundtables/synopsis/2_e.cfm.

Turner, B. A., & Chelladurai, P. (in press). Organizational and occupational commitment, intention to leave and perceived performance of intercollegiate coaches. *Journal of Sport Management.*

CHAPTER 3

Systems View of Organizations

ANAGE YOUR LEARNING

After completing this chapter you should be able to:

- Explain the processes associated with an open system, and compare an organization to an open system.
- Describe the inputs, throughputs, and outputs of an organization from a systems perspective.
- Understand the significance of the environment for organizational survival and growth.
- Explain three theories of the environmental influences on organizations.

STRATEGIC CONCEPTS

coercive isomorphism
demand-side stakeholder
environment
equifinality
inputs–throughputs–outputs
institutional isomorphism
involuntary stakeholder
mimetic isomorphism
multifinality
negative entropy
normative isomorphism

open systems
primary stakeholders
progressive mechanization
progressive segregation
secondary stakeholders
self-regulation
supply-side stakeholder
system boundaries
systems thinking
voluntary stakeholder

ORGANIZATIONS AS OPEN SYSTEMS

In Chapter 2, we looked at a few definitions of organizations and described the significant attributes applicable to most organizations. We also discussed the different classifications of organizations, helping us to understand the differences among various classes of organizations. The foregoing descriptions of organizations provide a beginning understanding of organizations.

Students should take note of the word *systems* in the subtitle of this text. The term *system* is descriptive of the complex interrelationships among elements within an organization. Studying sport delivery systems is consistent with the views of several authors who have suggested that an organization can be perceived as an *open system* (as in Bowman & Jarrett, 1996; Immegart & Pilecki, 1973; Katz & Kahn, 1966; Robbins, 1990; Waring, 1996). Accordingly, this chapter outlines the concept of a system and its relevance to sport management. The advantages of viewing organizations as open systems **(systems thinking)** are also explained.

According to Black and Porter (2000), "a *system* refers to an interconnected set of elements that have orderly interactions that form a unitary whole" (p. 57). The notion of interactions is further explained by Morecroft, Sanchez, and Heene (2002) when they state that "the essential meaning of *interactions* between system elements, however, is that a change in one system element causes, induces, or otherwise leads to a change in one or more other system elements. . . . This *interdependence* of the elements is therefore a defining characteristic of a system" (pp. 7–8). In Ritchie-Dunham and Rabbino's (2001) view, "systems thinking is about seeing, understanding, and working with 'the whole.' It focuses more on the relationships that link the parts of the whole than on the parts themselves" (p. 5).

The human body provides a good illustration of a system as defined above. It is composed of different parts (head, legs, eyes, heart, and so on) that are put together in such a way as to constitute a meaningful whole. Each of the parts has its own attributes or qualities, but what makes the human body a system is the interrelationships among the parts, and the specific qualities that result from these interrelationships. This is clearly illustrated when a short, mesomorphic body type is contrasted with a tall, ectomorphic body type. These two specific body types contribute to potential for excellence in specific activities. The contrast between the body types lies not only in the differences in the attributes (parts), but also in the qualities of the relationships among those parts.

A wooden table can also be viewed as a system. Four legs and a top, constructed in a particular way, make up the system of a table. The different configurations in which these parts can be put together make for different systems of tables. In similar ways, almost everything can be conceived of as a system.

There is, however, one fundamental difference between the human body and the table as systems. The human body shivers when exposed to cold, and it perspires in reaction to heat. The human body consumes oxygen from the air it breathes, and it disposes of carbon dioxide. These reactions to environmental conditions, and the exchange of energy with the environment, do not take place to the same extent in the case of a table. Thus, the human body can be thought of as an **open system** (relatively open to the influences of the environment in which it lives), while the table can be thought of as a closed system (relatively impervious to the environment).

The systems view of organizations draws out the basic elements common to all organizations, the relationships among these elements, and their interactions with the environment. Organizations are open systems in that they influence and are influenced by the social, cultural, and economic conditions of the community in which they operate. They depend on society for their resources, and, in exchange, they provide products or services for that society. For example, a university receives from the society or government the funds and facilities necessary for its survival and growth. In return, the university provides a service to the society by educating its youth. A professional sport franchise depends on the community for facilities, media coverage, corporate support, and attendance at its events. In return, the franchise provides entertainment for the public, generates a certain degree of economic activity, and brings prestige and publicity to the community.

Sidebar

The designation of the human body as relatively open and the table as relatively closed is deliberate. The notions of "openness" and "closedness" should be viewed as two ends of a continuum, and the systems can be located at different points on that continuum. That is, some systems will be relatively more open (or closed) than others. In the preceding example, environmental influences will have an effect on the table, which, as a result, will decay over a period of time. However, when compared to the environmental influences on the human body, the table lies near the "closed" end of the continuum while the body is near the other extreme. Note also the possibility that the subsystems of a system may vary in the degree to which they are open or closed. Thus, the skeletal subsystem is relatively more closed than the circulatory system. Similar differences are likely to be found among the units of an organization.

PROPERTIES OF ORGANIZATIONS AS OPEN SYSTEMS

he view of organizations as open systems can be further clarified by examining some of the relevant system properties. The two that seem most pertinent here are boundaries and environments.

Subsystems and Boundaries

Every system (except the very smallest) has subsystems that can be conceived of as systems in themselves. For example, the circulatory system is a subsystem of the human body and is itself a complete system consisting of the heart, arteries, veins, capillaries in the muscles, alveoli in the lungs, and so on.

Similarly, a college athletic department consists of the administrators, the support staff, the various teams, the facilities, and equipment. A team that is a subsystem in the athletic department is also a system in itself from another perspective. It is composed of the coach, the athletes, the team's facilities and equipment, and so on. Consider a large fitness club. Each of its programs such as fitness evaluation, aerobics, aquatics, and strength training is a subsystem. And each one of these programs consists of its own subsystems of specialized activities, equipment and facilities, and personnel.

While the idea of a system and subsystems is quite direct and clear, the notion of a system boundary is less so. The reason for this is that humans as analysts or managers must decide on what elements should be included in a system of interest. Moreover, humans are limited in their ability to analyze and manage. Thus, while in a sense everything is connected to everything else in this world, human analysis leads to the exclusion of a number of things and people only remotely related to the system in question. As Khandwalla (1977) stated, "it is because of our ability to fail to see many weak relationships that we are at all able to perceive 'systems'" (p. 224).

A good example of this problem lies in sport sciences. All the subsystems of the human body are integrally interrelated. However, an exercise physiologist tends to focus on the cardiovascular and muscular systems; a scholar in biomechanics emphasizes the skeletal and muscular systems and the mechanical laws that govern their action; a sport or exercise psychologist may be concerned with the personality and cognitive dynamics of individuals. Each of these scholars has set the boundaries of the system under investigation, but each also recognizes that the system is integrally linked to a suprasystem—the human.

In the case of organizations, the boundary of the system is also critical. For a city recreation department, the system would consist of all the arenas and playgrounds, the staff, and the participants. On the other hand, for an arena manager, the system would be delimited to such things as the building itself, the heating and refrigeration units, the electrical and plumbing arrangements, the employees, and the policies and procedures that regulate the management of the arena. **System boundaries**, then, are arbitrarily set to suit specific purposes, and anything and everything outside the selected boundaries is considered the focal system's environment.

External Environment

In any discussion of the properties of an organization as an open system, it is important to consider the external environment. Naylor (1999) defines an organization's **environment** as "all those elements that lie outside its boundary with which it interacts" (p. 61). As shown in Exhibit 3.1, the environment is usually subdivided into two categories: (1) the *task* or *operating environment*

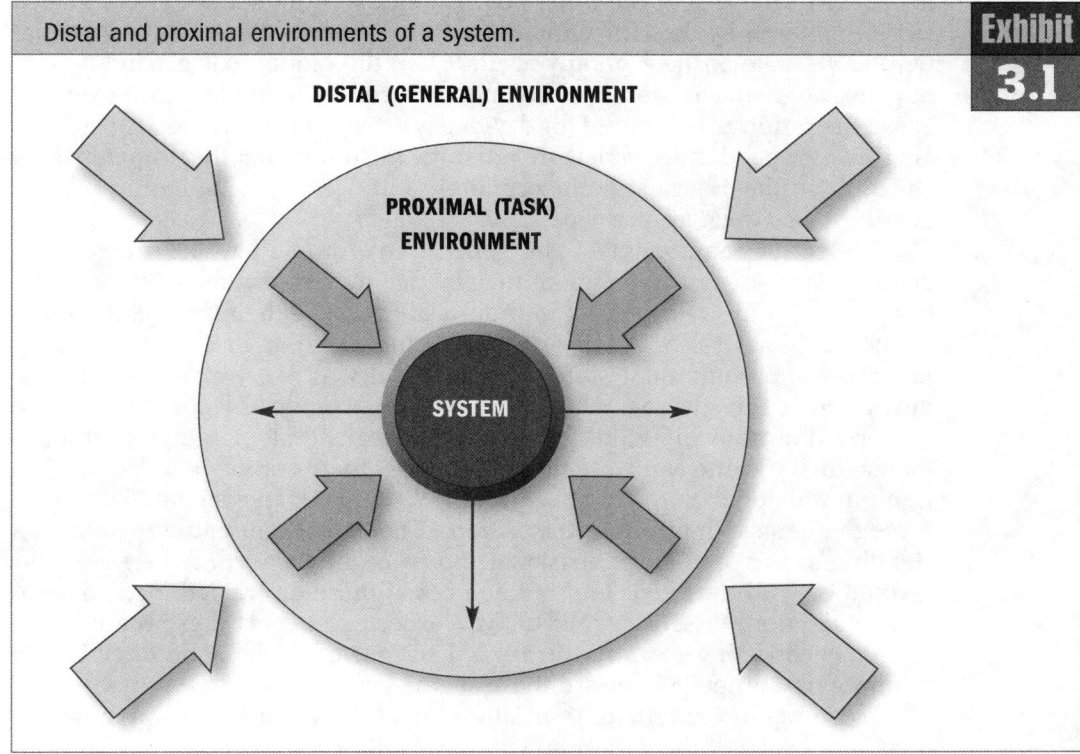

Exhibit 3.1 Distal and proximal environments of a system.

(also called the *proximal environment*), and (2) the *general environment* (also called the *distal environment*). Some of the elements in the environment are more clearly related to the system and influence it more directly. These elements make up what is referred to as the *task* (or *proximal*) environment. The other elements constitute the *general* (or *distal*) environment. Thus, for a profit-oriented tennis club, the task environment would include its competitors and the attitude of the community in which it operates. The general environment might include the television coverage of major tournaments that could positively influence the community's attitudes toward tennis. This, in turn, could increase the demand for the club's services. Note that the distinction between task and general environment refers to proximity not in geography but in tasks. For instance, the task environment for the Ohio State University football team would include the affairs of the University of Minnesota football team even though it is hundreds of miles away from Columbus, Ohio. However, the softball program of the Columbus City Recreation Department would not be within the task environment of the Buckeye football team.

Key Elements of the General Environment

There are several ways of grouping the elements in the general environment (see Pierce & Dunham, 1990; Slack, 1997; Wehrich & Koontz, 1993). The following scheme is drawn from Certo (1992): "The environmental elements may be grouped into (a) *economic component,* (b) *social component,* (c) *political component,* (d) *legal component,* and (e) *technology component.*" The economic component for a fitness club, for example, would include the rates of wages paid to labor (fitness and aerobic instructors), availability of labor (trained instructors), the cost of the fitness equipment, and the market prices for the services offered by the club. Another critical issue in the economic component is the state of the economy itself. When the economy is expanding and incomes are rising, customers have more discretionary funds (funds over and above the minimum required for day-to-day expenses). Therefore, consumers are likely to spend more on leisure pursuits, including membership in fitness clubs. If, on the other hand, the economy is in decline, consumers are likely to cut back on such leisure expenses.

The social component of the general environment would include the demography, or characteristics, of the population. For instance, if the population is aging—as is happening in industrial nations—the fitness club's operations would have to be modified to attract and maintain its clients by adding programs and equipment suited to older adults. It is estimated that in the next three or four decades, the majority of the American labor force will be comprised of nonwhites and females. This means that a large proportion of the national income will go to these diverse segments of the population. This trend in the population will affect how sports organizations could best serve these segments. For example the National Football League could maintain its standing as the premier professional sports league in North America only if it could cater to the needs and preferences of these diversified income earners. In addition, the NFL would also be expected to court these market segments by educating them in the art and science of football and directing its promotional campaigns toward these segments.

According to Certo (1992), social values also have an impact on organizations. For instance, the American emphasis on competition and excellence in sports is not shared by all nations. At the same time, the emphasis Americans place on sports has been intensifying over the past few decades. In line with this trend, sport organizations have changed. Media enterprises are tuned into sports, and other commercial enterprises look at sports, sports competitions, and sport organizations from more of a marketing perspective.

The political component includes the extent to which democracy and free trade are practiced in a country, the influence (or interference) of political parties in the affairs of industry and commerce, and the ability of labor unions to affect organizational practices. Closely related to the political component is the legal component, which refers to the laws and rules of the land. For example, both the American and Canadian governments have legislated against sweatshop conditions in the workplace, as seen in the Occupational Safety and Health Act of 1970. Every sport organization needs to understand the legislated requirements and abide by them (for example, by paying at least the minimum wages and maintaining the specified range of temperature in the workplace).

The technology component refers to the technology associated with the production of a firm's goods and services. The introduction of artificial turf had a great impact on how professional franchises and intercollegiate athletics departments operated. Every fitness club and strength-training program would be affected if manufacturing firms were to come up with a series of new exercise equipment scientifically proven to be more effective. And of course firms in the sport management industry continue to be affected by and take advantage of Internet and World Wide Web innovations, particularly in marketing and promoting products.

Sidebar

It was once believed that government agencies do not react to environmental pressures and requirements to the extent private organizations do. Today, however, government agencies do adopt certain business practices as a result of economic, political, and social pressures, including building alliances and linkages with other organizations, both profit and nonprofit, in the private sector. Thibault, Frisby, and Kikulis (1999) showed this to be the case with three local government agencies in British Columbia providing leisure services, including fitness and sport services. They found that all three government agencies had built linkages with schools and nonprofit organizations in the past. In recent years, they have also begun to build such linkages with profit-oriented organizations. This illustrates that no organization can be impervious to its environment.

Key Elements of the Task Environment

The task or operating environment includes those elements that have a more direct and immediate effect on the organization. The introduction of a scientifically improved exercise machine stems from the general or distal environment affecting all fitness clubs all over the country. In contrast, if a nearby fitness club buys these new machines, it has an immediate and direct effect on the focal club. Thus, the fitness club in the vicinity and its operation would be considered within the task or operating environment of the focal club. Similarly, the national economy is part of the general environment that could affect attendance at sporting events all over the country. By the same token, a

specific professional sport franchise could be affected by the economy of the region and city in which it is located. Thus, the regional economy is an element in the operating environment. Another example occurs when a university athletic department has to cope with the competition posed when a new professional sport franchise is awarded to the city.

A major concern of management of a sport organization is to understand clearly the task or operating environment, the opportunities it offers, and the constraints it places on the organization. The success of the organization is a function of the extent to which it capitalizes on the opportunities and satisfies the demands placed on it. Certo (1992) breaks down the operating environment into:

- *customer component* (those who buy the organization's goods and services, such as the spectators at a professional sporting event, customers of a golf course, clients of an aerobics class, or students in a sport management program)
- *competition component* (all other individuals or organizations that produce the same type of services and goods and compete for the same customers or clients, such as other professional sport franchises, golf courses, and fitness clubs in the vicinity)
- *labor component* (availability of suitable employees, their demands, and their general attitude toward the professional sports club, golf course, or fitness club under consideration)
- *supplier component* (all the individuals and organizations that supply the equipment and other needed resources for the professional sports team, golf course, or fitness club)

Internal Environment

The concept of environment is also applicable to the internal operations of the organization. Consider, for example, two professional sport franchises in football. In one, the primary owner may take part extensively in the recruitment, training, and deployment of the players. In contrast, the primary owner in the other franchise may leave these affairs in the hands of the manager and coach. The two clubs may also differ in the extent and manner of planning that takes place, the arrangement of the relationships among the units and employees of the organization, the leadership provided, and the ways in which individuals or units are evaluated and rewarded. These are topics to be covered in later chapters. At this point, just note that top managers create the internal environment through their specific policies and procedures. The reactions of the employees (both positive and negative) and their adherence to these policies also contribute to the creation of the internal environment.

In Exhibit 3.1, the arrows that go outward from the system indicate the organization's efforts to influence its environment. For example, a professional sport franchise may embark on a public relations project to convince the

An organization, like any other living system, is also characterized by subsystems—each interacting with its own task and general environments. However, it is up to the decision makers to define the system's boundaries to suit their specific purposes.

residents of a city that the franchise can enhance the economic and social profile of the city. The lobby groups function essentially to influence the relevant environments of the organizations they represent.

PROCESSES IN OPEN SYSTEMS

he view of organizations as open systems can also be clarified by examining the processes of systems. The processes that are particularly pertinent in this regard are *negative entropy* (which is reflected in the processes of self-regulation, progressive segregation, progressive mechanization) and *equifinality* and *multifinality*.

Negative Entropy

Entropy is the tendency of a system toward disorder and decay. However, open systems such as organizations can prolong the length of their life and enhance their quality by constantly evolving and adapting to environmental conditions. Such an attempt to reverse the entropic process is called **negative entropy**. As Immegart and Pilecki (1973) noted:

> The open system has great control over its existence and destiny; it can choose whether or not to fight entropy or to maximize its existence. All living or open systems exist for a finite period in time/space. Few, indeed, have infinite lives. However, the duration and quality of life for the open system is, in large measure, in its own hands. (pp. 44–45)

The implication here is that the management of an organization must understand that unless it takes positive steps to adapt to the changing conditions, the entropic process cannot be arrested. Thus, a department of sport management must constantly scrutinize its program of activities (the courses offered) and change or upgrade them to suit environmental exigencies. In the case of a commercial golf course, the entropic process can be seen in the physical decay of the fairways and greens, the parking lots, the clubhouse, the restaurant, and the pro shop. The maintenance and upkeep of these facilities is, in fact, a process of arresting this decay—negative entropy. This concept applies not only to physical facilities but also to managerial activities. The measures to arrest the decay (i.e., the entropy) can take several forms. The more significant measures are *self-regulation, progressive segregation,* and *progressive mechanization*.

Self-Regulation

The notion that open systems/organizations tend to reverse the process of decay implies that these systems do, in fact, regulate their own activities. Just as the human body perspires to reduce the adverse effects of heat, organizations also react to fluctuations and disturbances in their environment. Such **self-regulation** may consist of changes in personnel, organizational structure, or internal processes. When a university athletic department fires a coach and hires a new one, it is regulating itself in order to arrest the presumed decline in its status. Attempts to modernize the reservation procedures at a golf course would also be a form of self-regulation. In addition, the management may train the employees in the use of the new computer and software. Similarly, a fitness club may send its fitness specialists to clinics in exercise physiology or fitness testing as a means of keeping up to date with emergent technology. These types of self-regulatory activities are aimed at stopping the decline and ensuring the growth of the organization.

In addition, these regulatory adaptations and adjustments maintain the system in a state of dynamic equilibrium. That is, the subsystems of an organization must be in harmony with each other, and the organization as a whole must be in tune with environmental influences and pressures. Thus, changes in our previous examples (the curriculum of a department of sport management, reservation procedures in the golf club, or exercise testing in a fitness club) must be consistent not only with the expertise of the members, but also with the requirements of the society. Subsequent changes in the environment necessitate suitable alterations in the system, which in turn result in a new state of equilibrium.

Progressive Segregation

One of the regulatory processes of a system is its tendency to subdivide its subsystems into functional and specialized units and to order them in a hierarchy. Immegart and Pilecki (1973) comment on this process:

> At a basic level, this is the tendency of an open system to determine what subsystems it will formally create, what subsystems it will use to process work, the nature and order of subsystem activity, and the priority of subsystem duties and obligations within the overall system perspective. (pp. 43–44)

The national sport organizations (NSOs) in several countries, in response to pressures to improve their operations and produce world-class athletes, have established special units to identify and develop athletic talent and to promote excellence in their respective sports. These units are differentiated from other units such as those that deal with promotion of the sport in the community and training of volunteer referees and coaches. This is an example of **progressive segregation.** A golf club as it grows in size and attendance may create and segregate the units that deal with (a) tournaments, (b) golfing for youth, adults, and seniors, (c) membership and reservations, (d) ancillary services such as parking, child care, restaurant, and so on. Similarly, segregation of the aerobics, aquatics, and strength-training units in a fitness club is commonplace.

This progressive segregation provides for greater specialization and regulation of work. Note that the process of creation and segregation of subsystems can take many different forms. The question of which units need to be created or segregated in a golf or fitness club must be addressed only in the context of that club and its unique circumstances.

Progressive Mechanization

As the system grows and the number of subsystems with specialized functions increases, the system faces the problem of coordinating all of its activities. Managers achieve such coordination by stipulating a set of procedures and regulations for each subsystem regarding what to do and when and how it should be done. These procedural and regulatory arrangements develop from the perspective of total system coordination. A large fitness club that offers facilities and instructions in a number of fitness activities (such as swimming, weight training, and aerobics) will tend to specify rules and procedures for each of these units so that the total effort can be coordinated and productive. On a larger scale, the National Collegiate Athletic Association (NCAA) offers another example of **progressive mechanization**. In order to coordinate and control intercollegiate athletics in the United States, the NCAA has instituted rules and regulations, such as recruiting and eligibility rules, and has created special units to monitor compliance to these rules (Departments of Legislative Services and of Enforcement and Appeals). To the extent that these rules and procedures are comprehensive, the tasks within the units tend to become more and more mechanical and routine.

Equifinality and Multifinality

Equifinality refers to the idea that two systems that initially start from different positions can end up at the same final position (Gresov & Drazin, 1997; Reeves, Duncan, & Ginter, 2003). It is "the idea that an objective—a final result or desired state—can be achieved in different ways by following different routes" (Roth, 2002, p. 14). That is, any two systems can be distinguished on the basis of the number and nature of their subsystems, and the particular internal processes within each system. However, either of the systems can be equally effective. For example, two football teams might be contrasted on the basis of their coaches' authoritarian versus participative orientation. Both teams could be effective provided that in each team the types of players and their preferences were consistent with the coach's orientation. If players under an authoritarian coach preferred to be told what, when, and how they should do things, then that team would be internally consistent and, therefore, could be effective. Similarly, if the players under the participative coach were more autonomous and preferred to make their own decisions in the course of play, then they would be consistent with their coach's orientation and, thus, could be as effective as the first team. As this example suggests, the ability of differing organizations to achieve similar ends depends on the subsystems and their processes being consistent with each other and with the task environments.

> **In Brief**
>
> Organizations tend to avoid decline by self-regulating their subsystems, creating specialized units, and instituting rules and regulations. Organizations with different resources and processes can achieve the same ends if the resources and processes are consistent with each other.

As another example, the former Soviet Union was competitive with the United States in international sport competitions. Yet the two countries differed in their economic strength and in the process of identifying and grooming athletic talents. The two systems began with different economic resources, adopted different processes, and yet arrived at the same point of international supremacy in athletics. Similarly, two fitness clubs (or two golf clubs) may differ in the number and type of segregated subsystems and the extent and character of the rules they have instituted. Yet they may both be successful or unsuccessful.

Multifinality is "the idea that similar initial conditions can lead to different final states" (Roth, 2002, p. 14). For example, most universities structure their intercollegiate athletic departments in similar ways and institute similar processes to achieve their objectives. They are also governed by the rules and regulations of a common umbrella organization, the NCAA. Despite such similarities in system attributes, not all athletic departments achieve their objectives in a given period of time. In fact, a particular university athletic department may not perform at the same level from year to year. We can find this phenomenon of multifinality in other spheres of the sport industry such as recreation units, fitness clubs, professional franchises, and so forth.

In sum, the concepts of equifinality and multifinality simply assert that "managers must reject the 'one right way' concept because there are several ways in which an organization can succeed, just as there are several ways that lead to failure" (Reeves et al., 2003, p. 41). Each organization is unique; what is important is to ensure that the subsystems and their processes are consistent with each other and with the task requirements.

ORGANIZATIONS AS SYSTEMS OF INPUTS–THROUGHPUTS–OUTPUTS AND FEEDBACK

We noted earlier that an open system is in an exchange relationship with its environment. The system receives the necessary inputs (the resources) from the environment and processes these inputs into certain outputs (the finished products) for the benefit of the environment. A conceptualization of a system consisting of **inputs, throughputs, and outputs** and two feedback loops is illustrated in Exhibit 3.2.

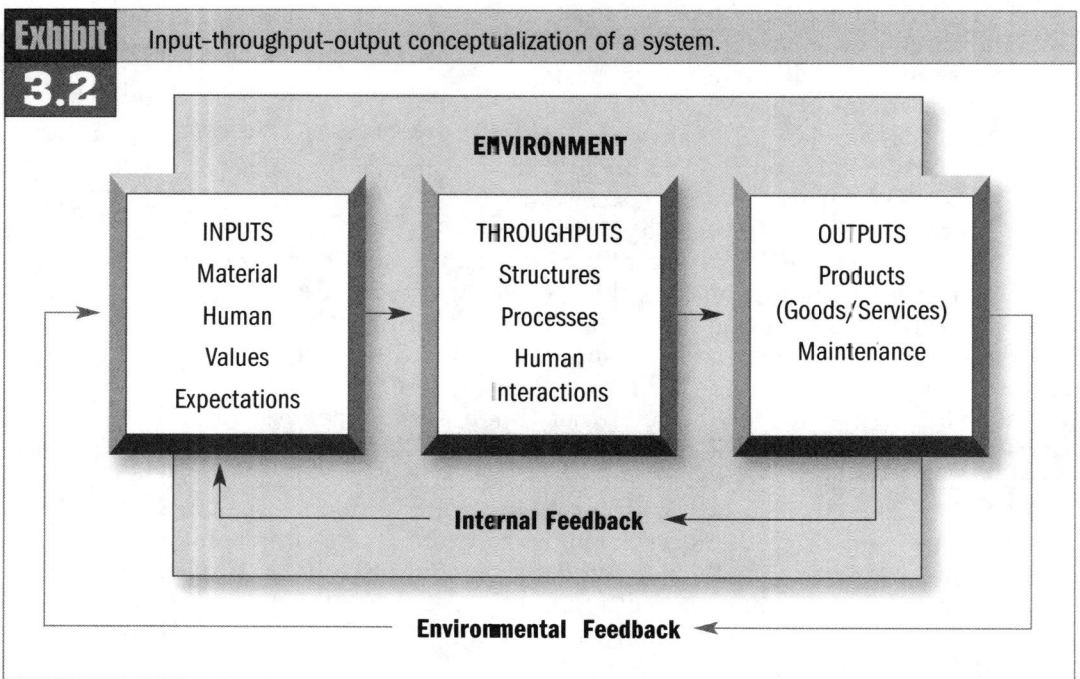

Exhibit 3.2 Input-throughput-output conceptualization of a system.

Inputs

The inputs or resources that flow into a system are many and varied. First, the organization needs material resources in the form of money, facilities, equipment, supplies, and raw material. Human resources in the form of professional and nonprofessional employees are also needed. The personal characteristics of those individuals coming into the organization define, to a large extent, the nature of an organization and set the tone for its operations. Although departments of sport management in neighboring universities may have identical goals and structures, the way they operate may vary because their professors and students (the inputs) may differ in many respects.

While the organization actively seeks to secure the needed resources, the environment also imposes some demands and expectations on the organization. Societal values, norms, and expectations constrain the organization to operate in specific ways. For example, individual needs and desires are paramount in North American society, whereas group requirements override individual requirements in Japanese society. Accordingly, the structures of organizations and their managerial processes are different in the two cultures.

Throughputs

The throughputs in a system are all the processes instituted by the organization to convert or transform the inputs/resources into desirable outputs such as goods or services. The processes of planning, organizing, leading, and evaluating these processes (to be discussed in greater detail in later chapters) form part of the throughput. The specification of the means and ways of carrying out the organization's production activities, the structure of authority and control, and the system of rewards within the organization are significant facets of throughput. The essence of good management is to make these throughput processes congruent with the attitudes, beliefs, skills, role orientations, and group affiliations of the employees in the organization. We already noted that the curriculum design in a department of sport management should be consistent with the expertise of the faculty members, the needs of the students, and the requirements of the larger society. Similarly, the processes employed by golf or fitness clubs would need to take into account the expertise of the employees, preferences of the clients, legal requirements, and societal expectations.

Outputs

The outputs of an organization can be neatly classified as product outputs and maintenance outputs. The products may be goods, as in sporting goods produced by a manufacturing firm, and/or services. (See Chapter 2 for a description of various types of sport services.) The outputs (products) of an organization should be acceptable to the environment. Milstein and Belasco (1973) emphasized this when they pointed out that:

> the system is as dependent upon environmental acceptance of its outputs or products as it is upon environmental resource inputs. In fact, the relationship between the two dependencies—resource needs and output acceptance—is direct, the one affecting the other, with systems thruput processes being the intervening variables. (p. 81)

Sidebar

"You have probably experienced some of the unintended but nonetheless unwanted effects of other people's work procedures: accounting 'systems,' monitoring 'systems,' payroll 'systems,' stock control 'systems,' and so on. Essentially, such procedures take ingredients (inputs) through a procedure (process) which is expected to convert them into useful products (outputs). . . . This simple 'sausage-machine' view of a system is sometimes called a 'black-box model'—the details of the process are regarded as relatively unimportant and remain hidden in a notional 'black box.'

The input–process–output principle is essential to all systems, but it is rather weak on its own and can encourage a false sense of confidence about successful outcomes. Systematic effort alone does not guarantee success. A systematic arrangement requires a lot more before it can be called a system." (Waring, 1996, p. 19)

Thus, a municipal recreation department can get the necessary resources (inputs) from the community only if its recreation services (outputs) are desired and consumed by the public. For example, the department will be able to get council approval for the construction of a new roller hockey rink only if there is a demand for it. As another example, an athletic department can get donations and public support only if it is run efficiently according to the educational goals of the university, and if it has a winning tradition in selected sports. To get the resources it needs it must satisfy the needs and expectations of the local community.

Apart from producing goods and services, the organization is also concerned with its own survival and growth. Therefore, the satisfaction of the employees and the ability of the organization and its members to cope with and adapt to external influences are critical to the maintenance of the organization, its growth, and its viability. When a fitness club institutes new technology and trains its employees in that technology, it is adapting to external influences. Employee satisfaction is even more critical to sport organizations that for the most part provide one form of sport service or another. Studies have shown that the extent of employee satisfaction is reflected in customer perceived quality of services. If the aerobic instructors or the fitness leaders are dissatisfied with their work, their supervisors, or their club, such dissatisfaction will be reflected in how they deliver the service and how they treat their clients. These aspects constitute what can be referred to as *maintenance* outputs. These maintenance outputs of an organization are as critical as the actual products of the organization.

Feedback

As Exhibit 3.2 illustrates, the system contains two feedback loops. One of these is internal to the organization; the other channel connects the organization to the environment. Organizational feedback provides an indication of the degree to which the organization has achieved or is achieving its objectives. Any shortfall in the attainment of objectives, as well as deviations from the originally specified patterns of operation, would require modifications in the inputs or throughputs. One of the concerns of the director of a city recreation department is the efficient operation of the areas under his jurisdiction. Periodic inspections and reports provide the feedback that is the basis for corrective action.

The second feedback loop helps to keep the organizational products (the outputs) in tune with the environmental needs. The acceptability of organizational products is contingent upon both the quality of the product and the needs of the environment. As the needs of the environment change, so must the organizational outputs. For example, at one time, institutions offering degree programs in physical education emphasized teacher training because of the great demand for physical education teachers. Environmental needs changed, however. Thus, the content and structure of many of these institutions also changed. Now, these institutions have diversified their programs under different names to include exercise physiology, sport and exercise psychology, sport sociology, sport management, and other specializations. The growth of educational programs in sport management shows one way that universities adapt to environmental needs.

From a systems perspective, organizations receive resources from society (input) and convert those resources (throughput) into products for the society (output).

Another important feature of this environmental feedback loop is that it also provides information on the sources for needed inputs and the means to those sources. If an organization is not actively seeking information about its boundary conditions and adapting to changes in its environment, it may not be able to dispense its products and, in turn, may not be able to secure resources. Thus, the boundary-spanning activity becomes critical to the organization. For example, the success of the city recreation department lies in its ability to recruit volunteer and part-time help to run its various programs. Success also depends upon the department's continued search for information relating to the likes and dislikes of the public with respect to the programs offered. Thus, the director of the recreation department and specified individuals within it must be in constant touch with the community.

THE SYSTEMS APPROACH IN OVERVIEW

A systems view of organizations is very useful for portraying the social, cultural, and economic forces that impinge upon the organization; the people and the interplay of their personal characteristics; the internal processes of authority, control, and task activities; and the dynamic interactions among all these variables. On the other hand, a systems view is also exceedingly complex. Because there are a number of variables in a system and their interactions are diverse, a systems approach does not permit detailed specifications for the optimal relationships among these variables. Neither does it suggest a managerial approach to a given configuration of system variables.

> In systems theory, or systems thinking, a system is merely a way of thinking about, or understanding, any dynamic process, whether the dynamic process is riding a bicycle, or a process, or an organization, or a job, or a machine, or any other entity we care to think of which involves a dynamic process. (Cusins, 1994, p. 19)

The systems approach *does* provide a framework for the analysis of an organization or a subsystem within it. The manager must first define the boundaries of the system of interest by including the relevant elements and identifying the forces in the task environment. The throughput processes within the system also must be clearly spelled out. Next, any inconsistencies must be identified with a view to correcting the problem or improving the performance of the unit. When any action is taken, the effect of such action on other subsystems and on the whole system must be examined. Bowman and Jarrett (1996) note:

> [The systems view] of what is an organization is comprehensive, sufficiently inclusive and robust as a test of reality. It covers the rational, emotional and political aspects of organizational life yet provides a baseline to explore organizational relationships in a systematic and organized manner, without losing some of the complexity. (p. 7)

Thus, a systems approach emphasizes the gestalt, or total, view of the organization while at the same time it provides opportunities to focus on well-defined subsystems for the purposes of analysis and action. Accordingly, we will refer to the systems approach in discussing the managerial processes in subsequent chapters.

ENVIRONMENTAL INFLUENCES ON ORGANIZATIONS

In discussing the systems theory, we placed a great emphasis on the notion of the environment in which an organization is embedded. We noted that the environment consists of both internal and external segments. The internal environment includes the goals, structures, and processes of the organization, the employees, and the leaders and supervisors. The external environment consists of suppliers, clients or customers, other organizations competing for the resources or to sell their products, government agencies, political groups, social activists, and so forth. The importance and impact of the organizational environment has led to the articulation of three different theoretical frameworks for understanding environmental dynamics. They are (1) stakeholder theory, (2) institutional theory, and (3) resource dependence theory.

Stakeholder Theory

In discussing the environment of an organization, several factors, such as economic and technological components, have been described as part of the environment. These factors are largely inanimate in the sense that they refer to organizations and political, social, or legal systems. Bearing in mind that these systems are created and directed by people, we can look at an organization's environment in such a way as to include various groups of stakeholders. The term *stakeholder* is a derivative of the word *stake*. The stake, which is "a pointed piece of wood" (*Webster's Ninth New Collegiate Dictionary*, 1986), has been traditionally used to mark off a field or territory to be claimed, and hence the usage of the phrase "to stake a claim." In the context of organizations and their management, *stakeholders* are defined as "persons or groups that have or claim ownership, rights, or interests in a corporation and its activities, past, present, or future" (Clarkson, 1995, p. 106). Freeman (1984) defines a stakeholder as "any group or individual who can affect or is affected by the achievement of the organization's objectives" (p. 46).

Clarkson (1995) notes that stakeholder rights and interests stem from stakeholders' interactions with the focal organization. For instance, the police who are involved in directing the traffic for a professional sport competition have a

Sidebar

Another example of stakeholder influence on an organization occurred in 2003/2004 when the Louisiana State University (LSU) football team was declared the national champion by the Bowl Championship Series (BCS) while the Associated Press Poll declared the University of Southern California (USC) team the national champions. Many were disconcerted with the notion of two national champions. The computer manufacturer Gateway Inc. jumped into the fray and offered $30 million in scholarship money if a game between LSU and USC would be played to declare a single national champion. The NCCA reacted to this offer as shown in the following press release:

> NASHVILLE, TENNESSEE—Gateway Computers has it wrong about who will make the decision regarding postseason football in Division I-A. The decision will not be made by the NCAA staff. It will be made by college presidents in Division I-A. Many of those presidents have not been supportive of a playoff. Coaches are not supportive of a playoff.
>
> Anyone who believes that higher education would jump at a cynical publicity stunt are [sic] mistaken and missing the point. This is exactly the type of inappropriate intrusion of commercialism that I warned the membership of yesterday in my speech to the NCAA Convention. It puts all the emphasis on intercollegiate athletics as entertainment and erodes the critical concept that the welfare of the student-athlete is paramount.
>
> —Myles Brand, NCAA President

Note the NCAA view of this offer as a "publicity stunt," an "intrusion of commercialism," and "athletics as entertainment." The statement appears to be not so consistent with the actual practices of the NCAA and member institutions. Many athletic departments (e.g., the Ohio State University Athletic Department) do proclaim that their goals include providing entertainment for the community and generating publicity for the university, and the NCAA garners millions of dollars by letting the media cover the NCAA basketball tournaments (a commercial practice).

---

stake in how and when the franchise schedules its competitions. Those who are affected by the organization's actions can also be considered stakeholders.

Consider the case of Rush Limbaugh, the radio talk-show personality. As a football commentator with ESPN at the beginning of the 2003 NFL season, he remarked that the performance of the Philadelphia Eagles quarterback Donavan McNabb did not merit the attention and accolades he received from the media. In Limbaugh's words,

> I think what we've had here is a little social concern in the NFL. The media has been very desirous that a black quarterback do well. . . . There is a little hope invested in McNabb, and he got a lot of credit for the performance of this team that he didn't deserve. The defense carried this team. (ESPN, 2003)

His suggestion that the media bestowed attention and praise on Donavan because he was black created a furor among the players, the owners, the fans, and the media personnel. These are the stakeholders in close proximity to the ESPN and NFL. But Limbaugh's comment also invoked harsh criticism from other groups, such as politicians and church leaders, who were not as closely aligned with the NFL and ESPN. At that point in time, they became critical stakeholders (although transitory) of ESPN.

Clarkson (1995) notes that the interests of some stakeholders may be strictly moral. In the case of Limbaugh's remarks, the reactions of players, owners, fans, and media personnel can be seen as responses to a direct attack on them. However, many people not belonging to these groups also expressed a revulsion against such behavior. These reactions were largely based on moral grounds. Another example of stakeholders reacting on moral grounds is groups who have expressed morally based concerns about sweatshop conditions under which some products are made.

Classifications of Stakeholders

Stakeholders can be individuals or groups of people who share similar interests, claims, or rights. Such groups might be composed of the athletes, the coaches, the spectators, the media people, the alumni, or the employees of the athletic department. We can identify similar groups of stakeholders in any sport organization—for example, the shareholders and player agents in the case of a professional sport franchise, or community organizations or taxpayer groups in the case of a city recreation department. These various stakeholders can be classified as voluntary and involuntary stakeholders, primary and secondary stakeholders, and demand-side and supply-side stakeholders.

Voluntary and involuntary stakeholders. The foregoing example of various stakeholders reacting to an action by an organization (i.e., ESPN) or a member of an organization (i.e., Rush Limbaugh) illustrates the distinction between *voluntary* and *involuntary* stakeholders. The players, the media personnel, the coaches, and the teams themselves are in close proximity, and they have a direct stake in the operation of ESPN. In contrast, the politicians and social activists who reacted to Limbaugh's comment do not have any close association with ESPN. Thus, the former set are **voluntary stakeholders** who engage in creating and distributing the products of ESPN. The latter groups are **involuntary stakeholders** who are indirectly and unknowingly involved with the organization's outcomes or results (Clarkson, 1995).

As another example, consider a riot breaking out after a home team loses a critical game against a rival. Much damage is done to the properties of the athletic department and the university. The fans may suffer from loss of property or bodily injuries, and the students and faculty may also suffer from the loss of prestige for the university. But these groups are voluntary stakeholders in the sense that they wanted to be part of the organization and its proceedings. In addition, they stand to gain from the athletic department and the performance of its teams. In contrast, the homeowners outside the university boundaries who suffer may not be fans of the team or students or faculty of the university. Such groups are labeled involuntary stakeholders because they tend to be affected by whatever happens in the organizational context despite not having chosen the association.

Primary and secondary stakeholder groups. According to Clarkson (1995), stakeholders can also be classified as primary and secondary stakeholders based on the relative contributions they make for the survival and growth of the organization. A **primary stakeholder** group is one "without whose continuing participation the corporation cannot survive as a going concern" (Clarkson, 1995, p. 106). For instance, the players of a professional sport league are a primary stakeholder group because the league cannot exist without their participation. By the same token, the employees and coaches of a university athletic department are its primary stakeholder groups because the department cannot offer its programs without them. Imagine for a moment that the spectators at university football games refuse to be civil and orderly during the contest. By disrupting the event, they become a significant stakeholder group. The significance of spectators as a stakeholder group is very much understood by soccer leagues in Europe and South America, where violence among spectators has disrupted the operations of the leagues. Similarly, the lawmakers and people of communities that provide the stadiums and arenas are primary stakeholder groups for professional sport franchises. In sum, a sport organization is very dependent on the cooperation and participation of its primary stakeholders.

Secondary stakeholder groups are those that do not directly interact with the focal organization but that can affect or be affected by the focal organization (Clarkson, 1995). We already noted that stakeholder groups had an impact on ESPN because of Limbaugh's comments. Several of the groups did not have any direct transactions with ESPN, yet they were able to mobilize public opinion against ESPN and thereby influence its decisions. Similarly, citizen groups that complain about student behavior on their streets after a football game are not directly involved with the athletic department. From this perspective they are not primary stakeholders, and yet their influence is great enough for the department and the university to take actions to address their concerns. Thus, they constitute a secondary stakeholder group. From a different perspective, Donaldson and Preston (1995) note that "stakeholders are identified by their interest in the corporation and not necessarily by whether the corporation has any corresponding functional interest in the stakeholders." These authors also note that an organization must be concerned with and learn to manage all stakeholder groups because the interests of these groups have merit.

Demand-side and supply-side stakeholders. Ben-Ner and Gui (1993) provided yet another classification of stakeholders. Referring to nonprofit organizations, they made a distinction between demand-side stakeholders and supply-side stakeholders. **Demand-side stakeholders** include all those who consume the products of an organization. The payment for these products may be from the consumers themselves, as in the case of members of a local YMCA paying for the use of the weight room or the services of a yoga instructor. The payment could also be made by a sponsor, as in the case of a local

> **In Brief**
>
> Persons and groups that have an interest or a right in an organization are labeled its stakeholders. Primary stakeholders are those whose participation is necessary for the growth and survival of the organization. Secondary stakeholders do not directly interact with the organization but do have an influence on it.

business sponsoring a youth sports camp. The **supply-side stakeholders** are all those individuals, groups, or organizations that facilitate the production and distribution of the focal organization's products. The volunteer coaches and officials of a youth sport league are supply-side stakeholders. The municipal council financing the recreation department and the school district subsidizing athletic programs would also be supply-side stakeholders.

Managing Stakeholders

Note that the conception of an organization faced with multiple constituencies has been in vogue for several decades. However, the emphasis on management of stakeholders as a strategic issue has taken root only recently. An important component of effective stakeholder management is to gain a clear understanding of stakeholder perceptions and preferences.

In the context of intercollegiate athletics, the study of the values and preferences of specific stakeholder groups, such as students, student–athletes, alumni, faculty and athletic program employees, media, the community, and local businesses, has been the focus of several recent investigations (see Putler & Wolfe, 1999; Wolfe & Putler, 2002; Trail & Chelladurai, 2000). Putler and Wolfe investigated the perceptions of six different stakeholders of intercollegiate athletics: students, prospective students, student–athletes, alumni, faculty, and athletic program employees. They found that members of these stakeholder groups fell into four distinct groups with unique priorities: athletic program revenue, winning, education, and ethics. Interestingly, the pattern in which the respondents endorsed these priorities did not parallel their membership in the stakeholder groups. This means that members within a single stakeholder group may differ widely in the priorities they place on organizational goals and processes.

Trail and Chelladurai (2000) investigated the extent to which two stakeholder groups of intercollegiate athletics (faculty and students) differed in the importance they attached to 10 selected goals and their approval of 11 selected processes within intercollegiate athletics. They found that the subgroups as defined by faculty–student status and gender differed significantly in the relative importance they placed on various intercollegiate athletic goals, as well as in their approval of the different processes of intercollegiate athletics. (These goals and processes are further explained in Chapter 5, in which we examine the concept of organizational goals.) All subgroups were congruent in rating development goals (that is, those focused on development of athletes) as more important than performance goals (those focused on winning and generating revenue). Similarly, the groups endorsed developmental processes at a higher level than performance processes. Notably, the females of the study were more concerned with the process of creating gender equality and the goal of a diverse culture.

Salience of Stakeholders

It is one thing to identify the various stakeholders and to categorize them as voluntary or involuntary, primary or secondary, and demand-side or supply-side. But it is different and more difficult to rank them in terms of their salience or criticalness to the organization. For instance, a fitness club depends on the managers who maintain the facility and equipment as well as the exercise physiologists and fitness leaders who prescribe and provide the services for the clients. Both groups are easily categorized as either primary or voluntary stakeholders. But which one of the two groups is more critical to the club than the other? That is, how does an organization with several stakeholder groups with varying interests, demands, and expectations decide whose interests or demands are critical to the organization? In other words, how does one decide on the relative *salience* of the various stakeholders? Mitchell, Agle, and Wood (1997) noted that the stakeholders can be distinguished on the basis of three significant attributes—power, legitimacy, and urgency.

Power. Stakeholders may differ in the power they hold over the focal organization, which reflects their capacity to influence the organization. For example, contributors of large donations may have greater influence over an athletic department than those who contribute smaller amounts. Because media controls the avenues of publicity (both positive and negative) for the institution, the media personnel possess greater power over the athletic department than does an alumni or fan club in a neighboring small town.

Legitimacy. The legitimacy of a stakeholder is based on contractual or legal obligations, as well as moral interests in the harms and benefits that an organization creates (Mitchell et al., 1997). Thus, every entity that has a business contract with the athletic department (e.g., the contract to sell one brand of beverage in the stadium) has legitimacy of the claims that the contract permits. As another example, the claims of student-athletes for academic support from the athletic department will be far more legitimate than such claims from the general student body. Recall the concept of prime beneficiary. That is, every organization exists primarily for the benefit of a particular group. In the present case, the athletes are the prime beneficiaries; therefore, their claims on the athletic department are more legitimate than are those of other students.

Apart from legal titles and rights and contractual obligations, legitimacy may also stem from moral grounds and value-based beliefs. For example, every university athletic department takes extraordinary measures to control crowd behavior within and outside of the university boundaries. The concern with what happens outside its own boundaries is based more on moral grounds than on any legal or contractual obligations. By the same token, the university's neighboring residents do have a legitimate claim that the university safeguard their persons and property.

Urgency. Urgency refers to the speed with which a claim by a stakeholder group should be attended to. Consider the athletes involved in a competition and the spectators watching the contest. Consider also the athletic trainers and the medical staff on the sidelines. The athletes' claims on the services of these medical staff are far more legitimate than those of any of the spectators. Yet, if a spectator shows symptoms of a heart attack, the medical staff would certainly jump into action and drop their work on an athlete's minor injury to help the spectator. That is the notion of urgency: it implies that the claims of some stakeholders may be more pressing than those of others, irrespective of their power or legitimacy. Mitchell and colleagues (1997) hold that power and legitimacy are the core attributes that could be used to identify a stakeholder group. They also note that stakeholder power to influence the organization may or may not be legitimate and that the impact of power or legitimacy is a function of the urgency of the claims of a stakeholder group.

An important point Mitchell and colleagues (1997) make is that power, legitimacy, and urgency are not mutually exclusive. Instead, they interact with each other. A powerful stakeholder may have an urgent and at the same time legitimate claim. For instance, let us assume that a television network has a legal contract with a university athletic department to televise its football games, with a stipulation that the network has the final say in the starting time of the game on a given day. Let us also assume that the network approaches the athletic department just a week before a game with a request to change the starting time of the game because of its own scheduling problems. The television network is a powerful stakeholder because it helps the athletic department generate revenue. The claim is also legitimate, because it is within the limits of the contract. In addition, the claim has urgency, because the network has to know the response immediately so that it can proceed with other arrangements.

Institutional Theory

Institutional theory may be seen as another extension of systems theory. The basic premise of institutional theory is that just as individuals try to respond to significant others and behave in ways that are consistent with the orientations and expectations of significant others, organizations also seek legitimacy or approval from their respective environments. That is, institutional theory postulates that every organization is influenced by the institution of similar organizations and by its social system (Scott & Meyer, 1994). An organization gains the legitimacy it seeks by strong association with similar other organizations and by adopting structures and processes similar to those of other organizations. For example, the legitimacy of a fitness club is enhanced when it becomes a member of an industry association, accepts the mission of the association, and abides by the association's code of ethics. Constant interactions with other fitness clubs and other agencies promoting fitness (e.g., an exercise physiology lab in a university setting) would further the legitimacy of the fitness club.

Institutional Isomorphism

A significant proposition of institutional theory is that an organization tends to imitate the other organizations in the institutional sphere. For example, a university athletic department is likely to be very similar to other athletic departments in the same conference in terms of the mission and values it espouses, structures and processes it adopts, the kinds of services it offers, and its interactions with external agents. The process of organizations becoming similar to each other is called **institutional isomorphism** (DiMaggio & Powell, 1983, 1991; Scott, 2001). DiMaggio and Powell (1983) suggested that three different forces may lead to isomorphism—coercive, mimetic, and normative isomorphism.

Coercive isomorphism. **Coercive isomorphism** occurs when external political and social influences direct organizations to behave in similar ways. For instance, the governments in many countries provide a large portion of the budgets of their respective national sport governing bodies. In conjunction with the financial support, the governments stipulate that the sport governing bodies adopt specific structures and processes. When these organizations adopt these structures and processes, they become isomorphic (alike). This is the effect of the coercion of the government through its funding procedures (see, e.g., Silk & Amis, 2000c; Slack & Hinings, 1994). In the American con-

> ### Sidebar: Government Involvement
>
> The extent of government involvement in promoting and governing sport is highest in France among western countries (Camy, 2004). According to Camy, France holds the view that star athletes are the representatives of the nation and, therefore, they need the support of the nation and its government. In line with this perspective, the French government has enacted a law to bring sport within its purview and has enacted several other laws to promote and regulate sport within its borders. Further, the Ministry of Sports employs 6,000 civil servants of whom 1,600 are assigned to work for the governing bodies of various sports. The governments of Canada, the United Kingdom, and Australia do get involved in sport but not to the same extent as the government of France. The former limit their involvement to providing funds to sport governing bodies for specific projects but refrain from managing the organizations or embedding government employees in them as is done in France.

text, the NCAA as the apex body of the intercollegiate athletic network imposes certain demands and constraints on all member institutions. Consider all the rules and regulations concerning critical operations in athletics such as recruitment, number of practices and games, number of scholarships, and academic requirements. These rules cause member athletic departments to become similar in orientation as well as operations.

Mimetic isomorphism. A second force that may be operative is **mimetic isomorphism**. As noted before, organizations may imitate other organizations and become similar to them in their quest for legitimacy and support from their environments. Sport teams are famous for copying the strategies and tactics of other, successful teams. Intercollegiate athletic departments adopt the managerial and marketing practices of other athletic departments in order to legitimize their own operations and gain support from their own stakeholders. Also, when an organization is not certain about its actions and its future, it is likely to imitate others to reduce the uncertainty. Consider, for example, the colors of automobiles produced by different companies. If five colors are available in a given year for a given make, it is likely that you will find different shades of the same five colors in other makes, too. Because every manufacturer is not sure which colors will gain popularity among consumers, they all avoid the risk due to uncertainty by picking shades of the same colors.

Normative isomorphism. The third force is **normative**, in the sense that all organizations behave similarly because of the value and belief systems of decision makers. It is likely that the decision makers or managers have been trained and educated in institutions advocating similar business strategies and tactics. For example, the MBA programs of most universities display very similar curricula, and the students are exposed to textbooks of the same kind. Despite the disparity in reputation of universities, graduating MBAs across the nation (indeed around the world) are likely to have cultivated very similar value and belief systems regarding what should be done and how. This simi-

larity in values and beliefs will be reflected in the structures and processes the graduates institute in their respective organizations. This would also be the case with sport management graduates, who tend to be exposed to similar curricula and literature. External agencies, such as the professional associations, may advocate similar professional practices, which are likely to be adopted across many organizations. Further, managers tend to be transferred from one organization to another, and they are likely to carry their previous practices with them to their new institutions.

In the context of sport organizations, Danylchuk and Chelladurai (1999) found that the national sport governing bodies in Canada tended to become similar in structural and procedural properties. They attributed this tendency to institutional forces as outlined above. Silk and Amis (2000) have shown that telecasts of sporting events in different countries (e.g., Indonesia) are subjected to institutional pressure to conform to production practices elsewhere. In contrast, Cunningham and Ashley (2001) found considerable variation in the structural properties of the NCAA athletic programs. They concluded that environmental pressures may not be as dominant as suggested by institutional theory. In other words, their results support the notion of equifinality discussed above.

The third theoretical framework for articulating environmental influences on organizations is resource dependence theory.

Resource Dependence Theory

Readers will recall that the systems view of organizations holds that the organization is in an exchange relationship with its environment. In other words, the system imports its resources from the environment and exports its outputs to the environment. The notion that an organization is dependent on other entities in its environment for its resources is the basis of *resource dependence theory*. The basic thrust of the theory is that because the organization depends on other entities in the environment for its resources (e.g., land, labor, capital, information), those entities gain power over the focal organization (Knoke, 2001). For example, the media is the major source for all publicity for a university athletic department and is a conduit for all information from the department to the public. Hence, the media has some power over the athletic department. Individuals who have invested in a private profit-oriented fitness club have some power over the club and its managers. A city recreation department is beholden to the elected politicians because they influence the budget allocations to the department.

The power differential between two organizations is conditioned by (a) the importance of a resource to an organization, (b) control by another party (i.e., other organization or group) over the resource, and (c) a lack of other alternatives for securing that resource (Knoke, 2001). Given the above, it follows that the dependence relationship between any two organizations is fluid and can change with alterations in one or more of the conditions listed above. For instance, the dependence of the United States on foreign countries for the oil it consumes can be drastically altered if major oil fields are found in U.S. territories, if solar energy can be more efficiently harnessed, or if wind-based energy generation becomes widespread and efficient. In a similar manner, the dependence of a sports club on local businesses and the local municipality for its resources (i.e., finances and facilities) can change if a wealthy person bequeaths a large sum of money to the club.

The significance of stakeholder influence and management of stakeholders will be illustrated at various points in the following chapters.

SUMMARY

In this chapter, we described an organization as an open system—that is, a set of interrelated parts making up an integrated whole. After defining the concept of a system, we looked at the concepts of subsystems and their boundaries, and we related the concepts to an organization. We described in detail the types and significant elements of the environment of a system or organization. We discussed the applicability of the processes of a system (negative entropy, self-regulation, progressive segregation, progressive mechanization, and equifinality and multifinality) in relation to an organization. This chapter also presented the input–throughput–output conceptualization of a system, and how the same perspective applies to organizations. We saw how the systems approach provides a framework for the analysis of an organization or its units and gives us a handy way of thinking about the organization, its units, and its processes. The final segment of the chapter dealt with environmental influences on organizations and three theories regarding an organization's relationship with its environment.

> **Sidebar**
>
> "A fundamental exchange principle is that actor A becomes dependent on actor B to the extent B controls a resource or behavior highly valued by A, which A can neither do without nor obtain elsewhere. Hence to acquire that vital resource, A must comply with the exchange conditions that B imposes, particularly by paying whatever price B demands. In any exchange relationship, A's dependence is inverse to B's power: the more A depends on B for an essential resource, the greater is B's power to control A's actions. These basic resource imbalance principles apply to social exchanges across many levels of analysis, ranging from small work groups to giant international corporations to national governments." (Knoke, 2001, pp. 54-55)

DEVELOPING YOUR PERSPECTIVES

1. Choose an organization you are familiar with and identify the subsystems in it. Discuss the bases on which the subsystems of that organization can be defined.
2. Bearing in mind the same organization, describe it in terms of its inputs, throughputs, and outputs.
3. How would you describe the organization's environment? What elements would you include in the environment, and how would you classify those elements?
4. Explain who would be the stakeholders of the organization you have chosen, and why.
5. Identify the organizations on which a focal organization depends for its resources.
6. Explain your organization's similarities to other organizations delivering the same kind of services.

References

Ben-Ner, A., & Gui, B. (1993). Nonprofit organizations in the mixed economy: A demand and supply analysis. In A. Ben-Ner & B. Gui (Eds.), *The nonprofit sector in the mixed economy* (pp. 27–58). Ann Arbor: The University of Michigan Press.

Black, J. S., & Porter, L. W. (2000). *Management: Meeting new challenges.* Upper Saddle River, NJ: Prentice Hall.

Bowman, C., & Jarrett, M. G. (1996). *Management in practice: A framework for managing organizational change* (3rd ed.). Oxford, U.K.: Butterworth-Heinemann.

Camy, J. (2004). Configurations of national sports systems in the E.U. countries: Their impact on training in the sports sector. Paper presented at the 12th Congress of the European Association of Sport Management. Ghent, Belgium. September 22–25, 2004.

Certo, S. C. (1992). *Modern management: Quality, ethics, and the global environment* (5th ed.). Boston: Allyn and Bacon.

Clarkson, M. B. E. (1995). A stakeholder framework for analyzing and evaluating corporate social performance. *Academy of Management Review, 20,* 92–117.

Cunningham, G. B., & Ashley, F. B. (2001). Isomorphic tendencies in NCAA athletic departments: The use of competing theories and advancement of theory. *Sport Management Review, 4,* 47–63.

Cusins, P. (1994). Understanding quality through systems thinking. *The TQM Magazine, 6,* 19–27.

Danylchuk, K. E., & Chelladurai, P. (1999). The nature of managerial work in Canadian intercollegiate athletics. *Journal of Sport Management, 13,* 148–166.

DiMaggio, P., & Powell, W. (1983). The iron cage revisited: Institutional isomorphism and collective rationality in organizational fields. *American Sociological Review, 48,* 147–160.

DiMaggio, P., & Powell, W. (1991). Introduction. In W. Powell & P. DiMaggio (Eds.), *The new institutionalism* (pp. 1–38). Chicago: University of Chicago Press.

Donaldson, T., & Preston, L. E. (1995). The stakeholder theory of the corporation: Concepts, evidence, and implications. *Academy of Management Review, 20,* 65–91.

ESPN (Thursday, October 2, 2003). Limbaugh resigns from NFL show. Retrieved January 4, 2004 from http://espn.go.com/gen/news/2003/1001/1628537.html.

Freeman, E.R. (1984). *Strategic management: A stakeholder approach.* Marshfield, MA: Pitman.

Gresov, C., & Drazin, R. (1997). Equifinality: functional equivalence in organizational design. *Academy of Management Review, 22,* 403–428.

Immegart, G. L., & Pilecki, F. J. (1973). *An introduction to systems for the educational administrator.* Reading, MA: Addison-Wesley.

Katz, D., & Kahn, R. L. (1966). *The social psychology of organizations.* New York: John Wiley.

Khandwalla, P. N. (1977). *The design of organizations.* New York: Harcourt Brace Jovanovich.

Knoke, D. (2001). *Changing organizations: Business networks in the new political economy.* Boulder, CO: Westview Press.

Milstein, M. M., & Belasco, J. A. (1973). *Educational administration and the behavioral sciences: A systems perspective.* Boston: Allyn and Bacon.

Mitchell, R., Agle, B., & Wood, D. (1997). Toward a theory of stakeholder identification and salience: Defining the principle of who and what really counts. *Academy of Management Review, 22* (4), 853–886.

Morecroft, J., Sanchez, R., & Heene, A. (2002). Integrating systems thinking and competence concepts in a new view of resources, capabilities, and management processes. In J. Morecroft, R. Sanchez, & A. Heene (Eds.), *Systems perspectives on resources, capabilities, and management processes* (pp. 3–16). Amsterdam: Pergamon.

Naylor, J. (1999). *Management.* London: Financial Times Management.

NCAA (2000). NCAA statement regarding Gateway's offer to underwrite a postseason football game between Louisiana State University and the University of Southern California. Retrieved January 14, 2004 from http://www.ncaa.org/

Pierce, J. L., & Dunham, R. B. (1990). *Managing.* Glenview, IL: Scott, Foresman/Little Brown Higher Education.

Principles of stakeholder management. (January 2, 2000). The Clarkson Centre for Business Ethics, Joseph L. Rotman School of Management, University of Toronto. [On-line]. Available: http://mgmt.utoronto.ca/~stake/principles.htm.

Putler, D. S., & Wolfe, R. A. (1999). Perceptions of intercollegiate athletic programs: Priorities and tradeoffs. *Sociology of Sport Journal, 16*, 301–325.

Reeves, T. C., Duncan, W. J., & Ginter, P. M. (2003). Strategic configurations in health services organizations. *Journal of Business Research, 56* (1), 31–43.

Ritchie-Dunham, J. L., & Rabbino, H. T. (2001). *Managing from clarity: Identifying, aligning, and leveraging strategic resources.* Chichester, NY: John Wiley & Sons.

Robbins, S. P. (1990). *Organization theory: Structure, design, and applications* (3rd ed.). Englewood Cliffs, NJ: Prentice Hall.

Robbins, S. P. (1997). *Managing today!* Upper Saddle River, NJ: Prentice Hall.

Roth, W. (2002). Business ethics: Grounded in systems thinking. *Journal of Organizational Excellence, 21* (3), 3–16.

Scott, R., & Meyer, J. (1994). *Institutional environments and organizations: Structural complexity and individualism.* Thousand Oaks, CA: Sage.

Scott, W. R. (2001). *Institutions and organizations.* Thousand Oaks, CA: Sage.

Silk, M. L., & Amis, J. (2000). Institutional pressures and the production of televised sport. *Journal of Sport Management, 14*, 267–292.

Slack, T. R. (1997). *Understanding sport organizations: The application of organization theory.* Champaign, IL: Human Kinetics.

Slack, T., & Hinings, C. R. (1994). Institutional pressures and isomorphic change: An empirical test. *Organization Studies, 15*, 803–827.

Thibault, L., Frisby, W., & Kikulis, L. M. (1999). Interorganizational linkages in the delivery of local leisure services in Canada: Responding to economic, political and social pressures. *Managing Leisure, 4*, 125–141.

Trail, G., & Chelladurai, P. (2000). Perceptions of goals and processes of intercollegiate athletics: A case study. *Journal of Sport Management, 14*, 154–178.

Waring, A. (1996). *Practical systems thinking.* London: International Thomson Business Press.

Webster's Ninth New Collegiate Dictionary (1986).

Wehrich, H., & Koontz, H. (1993). *Management: A global perspective.* New York: McGraw-Hill.

Wolfe, R. A., & Putler, D. S. (2002). How tight are the ties that bind stakeholder groups? *Organization Science, 13*, 64–80.

Wolfe, R. A., & Putler, D. S. (1999). *Addressing homogeneity of interests within stakeholder groups: Current practice, empirical assessment, and implications.* Unpublished manuscript. The University of British Columbia.

CHAPTER 4

Meaning of Management

ANAGE YOUR LEARNING

After completing this chapter you should be able to:

- Understand the general meaning of management.
- Explain the functions of management, including planning, organizing, leading, and evaluating.
- Discuss the distinctions among technical, human, and conceptual skills.
- Explain the 10 roles of a manager and the relationships among them.
- Explain what is meant by the "universal nature of management."

STRATEGIC CONCEPTS

decisional roles
evaluating
informational roles
interpersonal roles
leading
management

managerial roles
organizing
planning
technical, human, and conceptual skills

MANAGEMENT DEFINED

ll of us have a general idea of what the term *management* means. Some of us may think of the field of study called management. Others may think of a group of people at the top of an organization who guide the affairs of that organization, and still others may think of the actual processes of managing the organization. While all three meanings are commonly employed, this chapter focuses on the third meaning—that is, the chapter is devoted to defining and describing management as the act of managing, by which we are referring to the functions and activities of managers. Let us begin with some of the numerous definitions of **management**:

> A manager is "someone who gets work done through other people by initiating and directing action . . . makes decisions time and time again about what work has to be done, how it has to be done, and who has to do it." (Keuning, 1998, p. 8)

> "The term *management* refers to the process of co-ordinating and integrating work activities so that they are completed efficiently and effectively with and through other people." (Robbins, Coulter, & Stuart-Kotze, 2003, p. 5)

"Management is a form of work that involves coordinating an organization's resources—land, labor, and capital—toward accomplishing organizational objectives." (Rue & Byars, 1997, p. 4)

"Management is the process of designing and maintaining an environment in which individuals, working together in groups, efficiently accomplish selected aims." (Wehrich & Koontz, 1993, p. 4)

"Management is partly the process of getting things done through people; and partly the creative and energetic combination of scarce resources into effective and profitable activities and the combination of the skill and talents of the individuals concerned with doing this." (Pettinger, 1997, p. 1)

The foregoing definitions highlight three common elements that management is concerned with. They are (a) the goals/objectives to be achieved, (b) with limited resources, and (c) with and through people. Management's fundamental task is to coordinate these three elements so that the goals will be achieved. Readers will note that the above description of management as a process parallels the definition of sport management as a field provided in Chapter 1. Sport management was defined as "a field concerned with the coordination of limited human and material resources, relevant technologies, and situational contingencies for the efficient production and exchange of sport services."

Robbins, Coulter, and Stuart-Kotze (2003) draw two other implications from their definition of management. The first one is that management is concerned with effectiveness in achieving the goals. The second, equally critical implication is that management is concerned with efficiency. Efficiency refers to maximizing the benefits for a given cost (limited resources). Insofar as resources are limited, it is important that managers attempt to get the most out of those resources—that is, minimize the inputs and maximize the outputs. We will deal with these two concepts—effectiveness and efficiency—in greater detail in later chapters.

An emphasis on the importance of goals and people dominated the earliest scholarly work in the area of management. For example, in 1911, Taylor proposed that all work could be analyzed scientifically, and that one best way could be determined for its execution. He also suggested that incentive pay schemes—that is, basing salary on how much is produced—could be used to ensure that employees followed this one best way. Such an analysis of work entails time and motion studies and the design of appropriate workstations and equipment. This classical approach to the design of work, known as scientific management, still pervades business and industry in all developed nations. In the domain of sport and physical activity, teachers and coaches speak of the best way to execute a skill or implement a strategy. There is a constant endeavor to design new tools and equipment (fiberglass poles for vaulting, new rackets made of different materials for tennis and badminton).

> **In Brief**
>
> Management is the process of achieving organizational goals with and through other people within the constraints of limited resources.

In contrast to Taylor's exclusive focus on work, in 1933 Mayo emphasized the human element in the organization. His research led him to suggest that people are not cogs in a machine, and that the satisfaction of personal needs and desires is a prerequisite to productivity. This swing toward the human aspects of management, referred to as the human relations movement, has contributed greatly to the development of managerial thought. However, like the scientific management approach, the human relations movement has been the object of criticism because it also focuses exclusively on only one main element in the management process. Not surprisingly, as modern definitions of management would suggest, recent approaches to management emphasize both the work and the people. In these approaches, it is still important, as Taylor noted, to design the work for efficiency (how best to store the equipment in a locker room, set up the reservation system, or organize the fitness testing of several clients). At the same time, however, managers should consider the issue of individual differences in ability, attitudes, and preferences in designing jobs and assigning them to employees. Who is best suited to manage the locker room? What is the preference of the reservation clerks? How will the clients react? In addition, the structure and processes that coordinate the various jobs and the people performing them should also be consistent with the human dimensions. Thus, this approach, referred to as the behavioral movement, is concerned with the work, the people, and the processes that bring them together.

THE FUNCTIONS OF MANAGEMENT

We can gain a clearer grasp of the concept of management by exploring what functions are necessary for managers to perform. These functions were described by Fayol in 1916 in his book *General and Industrial Management* (Fayol, 1949). Fayol saw management as composed of planning, organizing, commanding, coordinating, and controlling. Considerable discussion has ensued around the functions of management since Fayol presented his list. As a result, the number and types of functions have undergone changes. From the perspective of modern sport management, four functions are worth emphasizing: planning, organizing, leading, and evaluating.

Planning

Planning involves setting the goals for the organization and its members, and specifying the activities, or programs, through which to achieve those goals. Robbins (1976) points out:

> Because it bridges the gap from where we are to where we want to be, it is the most basic of the four functions. Further, because planning requires determination in advance of action, decision making occurs throughout the function. However, decision making alone is not planning. (p. 16)

In the process of planning, the manager needs to identify the constraints within which the organization must operate. For instance, the goals set for the organization and the means selected to achieve them should be within the financial capabilities of the organization, and at the same time they should be acceptable to the society

In Brief

Planning includes setting goals within constraints, selecting activities to achieve the goals, and establishing policies and procedures to carry out those activities.

in which the organization operates. Planning also entails forecasting the future. In setting up a private fitness club, the manager or owner must be concerned not only with the current market but also with the future potential of the market, as well as probable trends in the activity preferences of the population. Similarly, when a professional sport league wants to expand and sanction new franchises in specific cities, it has to consider the financial strength of the backers of the franchise, the support from the city and the surrounding community, and the potential for growth in the market.

An organization generally announces its area(s) of business, its general aims to serve the customers/clients, and its social responsibility in a mission statement. Mission statements are general in nature and reflect the long-term orientation of the organization. The mission statement indicates to clients what is to be expected of the organization and its members. Once the specific goals for the immediate future and the means of achieving them have been identified, these must be formally stated in the form of policies, procedures, methods, standards, and rules. The purpose of such formal statements is to outline clearly to the members of the organization what is to be done and how.

> **Sidebar**
>
> A comprehensive list of managerial functions would include planning, organizing, staffing, directing, coordinating, reporting, and budgeting (POSDCORB). Some of these functions can be considered aspects of the four functions emphasized: planning, organizing, leading, and evaluating (POLE). For instance, budgeting is one aspect of planning, and staffing can be considered a part of the organizing function. Similarly, coordinating is ensured through the organizing and leading functions. For this reason, and because the concern in this book is with macro issues in sport management, this text deals only with the four main functions.

Consider the example of a head coach of a university football team. He sets the goals for his team in terms of a championship or a certain number of wins. In doing so, he takes into account constraints such as the finances, the quality of players, and the opposition. Further, the means adopted to achieve the goals must be within the rules of the sport, the league, and the university, and they must be consistent with societal expectations. The coach then states these goals and the means to the goals in the form of strategies and tactics to be adopted. The plan may encompass the whole season or even beyond (a long-range plan), or it may pertain only to the first few games (a short-range plan).

The total planning process is often subdivided and a specific distinctive label then attached to the various components—policy setting, strategy formulation, and so on. In this text, we will use the general term, *planning*, to cover all of the different components.

Organizing

The second function of management, **organizing**, involves breaking down the total work specified in the planning process into specific jobs, and then establishing a formal relationship among these jobs and among the individuals assigned to carry them out. Whereas the planning process specifies *what* should be done and how, the organizing process elaborates on *who* should do it.

Organizing involves the management of not only each individual employee, but of the employees in a group. In every large organization, managers

formally create and designate groups as separate departments or units. This grouping, or departmentation as it is also called, is a critical component of the organizing process.

After the creation of jobs and units, the task of assigning the right people to do the right job becomes important. All the efforts that have gone into the earlier steps are to no avail if the staffing procedures are inefficient or ineffective. In fact, a number of theorists place such great importance on this step that they treat it as a separate function.

Another essential element in the organizing process is specifying the methods for coordinating the activities of the many individuals involved. We achieve this by establishing a formal hierarchy of authority specifying the chain of command within the organization. Every organization except the very smallest prepares an organizational chart showing the relationships among individuals and departments within the organization.

> **In Brief**
> Organizing involves creating jobs, grouping them, establishing relationships among them, and establishing a formal authority structure.

For example, a football coach must assign the available players to the offensive, defensive, and special squad. Within each squad, the appropriate individual must fill each position. Further, each individual must be told what is expected in every situation. The playbook is a planning document and serves as a coordinative mechanism. Another mode of coordination is the development of a hierarchy of authority consisting of the head coach, assistant coaches, specialty coaches, offensive and defensive captains, and the quarterback.

Leading

The third function of management, **leading**, has been defined as "a process in which leader and followers interact in a way that enables the leader to influence the actions of the followers in a non-coercive way, towards the achievement of certain aims or objectives" (Rollinson, 2002, p. 357). While the planning and organizing functions set the stage for the work activities to be carried out, the leading function deals with influencing or motivating individual members to carry out their specific assignments efficiently.

In order to be an effective leader, the manager must have a working knowledge of the motivational processes of individuals—their needs and dispositions as well as the situational elements that help or hinder motivation. Because leading focuses on the interactions and reciprocal influence among the manager, the subordinates, and the situation, and because differences among individuals are numerous and complex, some have suggested that this is the most difficult and critical of the managerial functions. For example, Likert (1967) states that "managing the human component is the central and most important task because all else depends on how well it is done" (p. 1).

> **In Brief**
> Leading is the process of influencing members to achieve organizational goals. It is an interpersonal process in which the manager and member(s) interact directly.

Going back to the example of a football team, when the coach and his assistants encourage the players individually or in groups toward greater effort, or when they compliment them for good performance, they are engaged in the leading function—that is, motivation. Pep talks and the various motivational posters in a locker room are examples of techniques used by coaches as leaders or motivators.

Evaluating

Finally, a manager must be concerned with assessing the degree to which the organization as a whole, as well as the various units and individuals comprising it, have accomplished what they set out to do. This is the **evaluation** function. Evaluation provides the manager with the feedback necessary to take corrective action when organizational performance does not match expectations.

The evaluation process involves measuring performance and comparing that performance to standards set in the planning process. If performance does not meet established standards, the manager may lower the organizational expectations if they are judged to be unrealistic. On the other hand, changes in the organizational structure, communication patterns, the type of leadership, or the reward systems may bring about the desired level of performance. In order to determine the proper course of action, evaluation is essential. Also note that evaluation must be carried out at strategic points from the initiation of a program of activities to the conclusion of those activities.

In Brief

Evaluation is measuring performance of individuals, units, and the total organization and comparing it to the standards set in the planning process.

When the football coach views a game film or scrutinizes the statistics of a game, he is carrying out the evaluating function. The feedback he gains from his own personal observation and from the recorded details provides a basis for refining or redesigning the strategies and tactics to be used in future games.

The above discussion of the four managerial functions may imply that they are necessarily carried out in the sequence in which they have been described. This, however, is far from the case. Although such sequencing of the managerial functions is possible when setting up a new organization or starting an independent project, it is more realistic to view these as ongoing processes occurring simultaneously at times and sequentially at other times. Note also that these functions are not independent of each other. For example, the feedback from the evaluation function can affect goal setting (the planning function), the distribution of particular activities to specific individuals (the organizing function), and leadership behavior (the leading function).

The reference to coaching may seem out of place. However, as noted in Chapter 2, if sport teams are organizations in their own right, then the coaches of the teams can be compared to managers and leaders. In fact, the leader of a baseball team is called a "manager." That many outstanding coaches (e.g., Lasorda and O'Reilly) are invited to speak to groups of managers or to conduct motivational seminars is proof that coaching is closely related to management. Robbins (1997) had this to say about coaching and management:

> Today's manager is increasingly more like a coach than a boss. Coaches don't play the game. They create a climate in which their players can excel. They define the overall objectives, set expectations, define the boundaries of each player's role, ensure that players are properly trained and have the

resources they need to perform their roles, attempt to enlarge each player's capabilities, offer inspiration and motivation, and evaluate results. Contemporary managers look much more like coaches than bosses as they guide, listen to, encourage, and motivate their employees. (pp. 42-43)

In giving advice to chief executives on coaching their subordinate managers, Waldroop and Butler (1996) have this to say:

> Let us be clear: Good coaching is simply good management. It requires many of the same skills that are critical to effective management, such as keen powers of observation, sensible judgement, and an ability to take appropriate action. Similarly, the goal of coaching is the goal of good management: to make the most of an organization's valuable resources. (p. 111)

THE SKILLS OF MANAGEMENT

The concept of management can be understood not only by looking at the four managerial functions of planning, organizing, leading, and evaluating, but also by determining the skills necessary to carry out these functions effectively. Katz (1974) takes this approach. He proposed that three main types of skills—*technical, human,* and *conceptual*—are necessary for management. Katz also placed each of these skills within a three-tier hierarchy, with technical skills being the most fundamental, followed by human skills and then by conceptual skills at the top.

Katz developed his three classes of managerial skills as a counter to the traditional view that managers are born, not made. Although he originally maintained that all these skills could be developed independently of inborn traits, he later modified his position and noted that conceptual skill cannot be easily developed after adolescence.

Technical Skills

According to Katz (1974) **technical skills** involve "an understanding of and proficiency in a specific kind of activity, particularly one involving methods, procedures or techniques" (p. 91). Katz sees technical skill as specific to that area of specialization in which the organization is engaged. For example, the technical skills associated with manufacturing tennis rackets may not be relevant to running a fitness club. However, some technical skills are transferable across organizations. Because every organization must manage its finances efficiently, budgeting and accounting skills are necessary in all types of organizations.

The technical skills required of a manager of a fitness club include a working knowledge and experience in the use of the equipment (such as various weight training machines and bicycle ergometers); an understanding of the physiological effects of exercise and the interrelationships of exercise, diet, and body composition; expertise in exercise testing and exercise prescription; and so on. The manager also needs to be proficient in accounting, legal liability, and other concerns related to operating a fitness club. Similarly, a facility manager in a large university athletic department should be familiar with the technologies associated with the ice rink, the maintenance of playing fields, and such other technical aspects of the facilities she manages.

Human Skills

As the term would suggest, the human skills of managers center on their interactions with people. Katz (1974) emphasized this point when he defined **human skill** as the:

> executive's ability to work effectively as a group member and to build a cooperative effort within the team he [she] leads. As *technical* skill is primarily concerned with working with "things" (processes or physical objects), so *human* skill is primarily concerned with working with people. The skill is demonstrated in the way the individual perceives (and recognizes the perceptions of) his [her] superiors, equals, and subordinates, and in the way he [she] behaves subsequently. (p. 91)

The human skills of a fitness club manager would show in the effectiveness of his interactions with the customers and the other employees of the organization (instructors, medical specialists, and caretakers). As another example, the director of a university intramural recreation department needs good human skills to interact effectively with the participating students and staff, the employees of the department, the heads of other departments, and the university administrators. Clearly, because there is much more variety and variability among human beings than among processes or physical objects, human skill is of a higher order than technical skill.

Conceptual Skills

The highest, most complex type of skill in the hierarchy is **conceptual skill**. Katz defined it as the:

> ability to see the enterprise as a whole; it includes recognizing how the various functions of the organization depend on one another, and how changes in any one part affect all the other; and it extends to visualizing the relationship of the individual business to the industry, the community, and the political, social, and economic forces of the nation as a whole. (p. 93)

For the manager of a fitness club, this definition of conceptual skills implies that she must be capable of perceiving the organization as a gestalt, or whole, and be cognizant of the effects of every managerial decision on the total organization and its various parts. The manager should be aware that a decision to buy more costly equipment might reduce the funds available for part-time help, which in turn may affect the morale of the full-time employees. Further, it also implies that the manager must be concerned with the relative emphasis to be placed on the various goals of the club (such as whether to increase the number of customers or enhance the quality of the service to be provided).

Finally, Zeigler (1979) proposes that two more skill categories should be added to the three proposed by Katz (1974)—conjoined skills and personal skills. Conjoined skills are a mixture of Katz's technical, human, and conceptual skills. Zeigler's inclusion of this as a combined category is meaningful because an effective manager needs to be proficient in all

In Brief

To be an effective manager, one needs to possess technical skills (an understanding of the methods, procedures, and techniques), human skills (interpersonal skills), and conceptual skills (the ability to see the organization as a whole).

> **Sidebar**
>
> Quarterman (1998) collated from the literature the following skills necessary for transformational leadership:
>
> - **Empowerment skills**—sharing power, promoting others' development, and realizing that visions are achieved by teams
> - **Visioning skills**—using persuasion and inducing individuals and groups to achieve visions
> - **Self-understanding skills**—being aware of one's strengths, weaknesses, wants, and needs
> - **Value congruence skills**—understanding and teaching the organization's guiding beliefs and values
> - **Anticipatory skills**—developing and utilizing foresight and strategies consistent with the changing environment
> - **Intuitive skills**—utilizing "gut feelings" and "hunches" in decision making and problem solving
>
> The concept and features of transformational leadership are discussed in Chapter 11.

three skills. Personal skills refer to the ability to manage personal time efficiently, organize and articulate personal thoughts, and keep abreast of current events and innovations, along with other attributes that make a good manager.

Along similar lines, Klemp and McClelland (1986) suggest that successful managers are characterized by three sets of competencies—intellectual competencies, influence, and self-confidence. Intellectual competencies consist of seeing implications and consequences, analyzing causal relationships, seeking information from multiple sources, and making plans and strategies to achieve goals. They also include understanding how parts fit together and identifying and interpreting patterns of events. The next set, influence competencies, includes desiring to persuade people, directing them to do things in specific ways, effectively interacting with groups to influence outcomes, letting key members be part of decisions, setting a personal example, and using symbols for group identity. The final competency is self-confidence, which is seeing oneself as the prime mover and the most capable person to get the job done.

THE ROLES OF A MANAGER

The discussion of both managerial functions and managerial skills contributes to a picture of the manager as a person who is concerned with and has ample time, scope, and ability to carry out these functions. It also implies that the manager is not likely to be involved in routine and mundane activities. This is far from the case, as a number of researchers have clearly shown (see Carlson, 1979; Guest, 1956; Mintzberg, 1975; Stewart, 1967).

Mintzberg (1975), whose research is considered the most definitive of its kind, concluded that the classical descriptions of managerial jobs are myths. He found that instead of being reflective and systematic planners, managers "work at an unrelenting pace . . . their activities are characterized by brevity, and discontinuity, and . . . they are strongly oriented to action and dislike reflective activities" (p. 50). He also found that contrary to general impressions, "managerial work involves performing a number of regular duties including ritual and ceremony, negotiations, and processing of soft information that links the organization with its environment" (p. 51). He also found that instead of relying on formal information systems, "managers strongly favor the verbal media—namely, telephone calls and meetings" (p. 51).

Rather than adopting the classical descriptions of management, Mintzberg suggests that management can best be described in terms of the roles managers play in their day-to-day activities. Ten **managerial roles** were identified within three broad categories: interpersonal roles, informational roles, and decisional roles. These are illustrated in Exhibit 4.1.

> Before we made the study, I always thought of a chief executive as the conductor of an orchestra, standing aloof on his platform. Now I am in some respects inclined to see him [her] as the puppet in a puppetshow with hundreds of people pulling the strings and forcing him [her] to act in one way or another.
>
> **CARLSON,** *1979, p. 52*

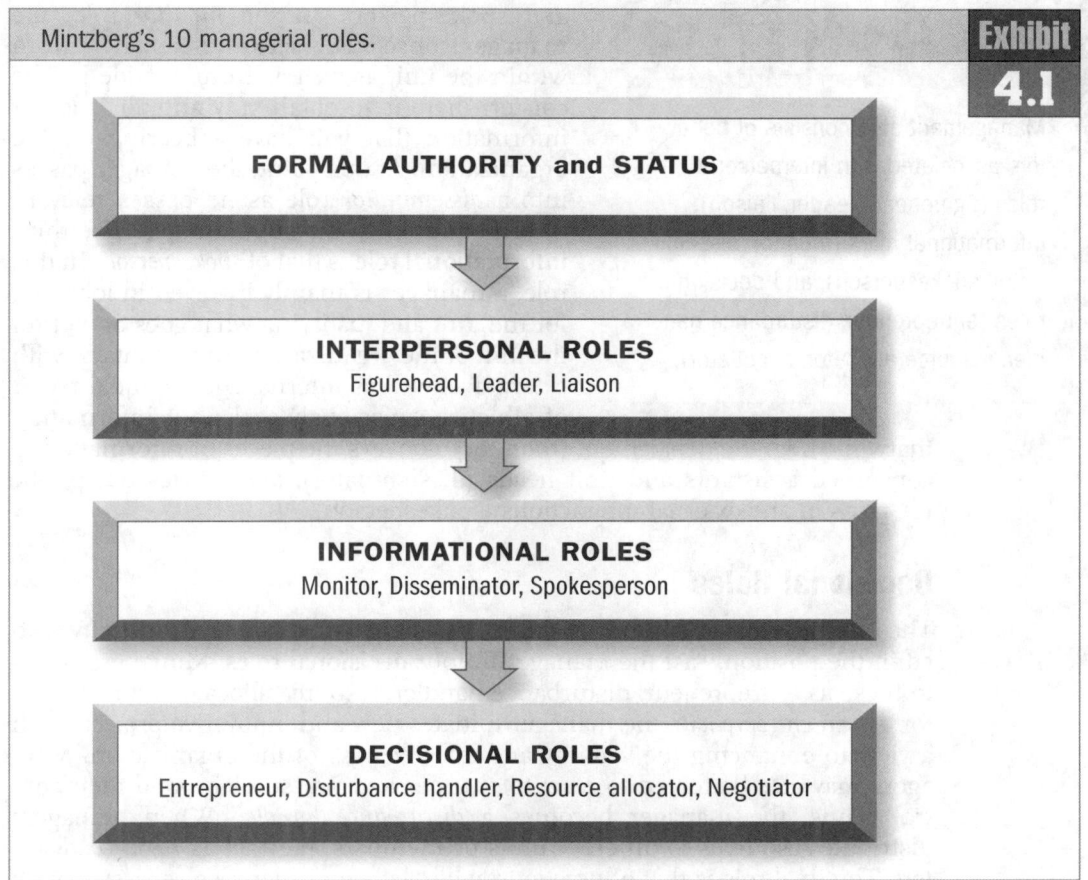

Exhibit 4.1 Mintzberg's 10 managerial roles.

FORMAL AUTHORITY and STATUS

INTERPERSONAL ROLES
Figurehead, Leader, Liaison

INFORMATIONAL ROLES
Monitor, Disseminator, Spokesperson

DECISIONAL ROLES
Entrepreneur, Disturbance handler, Resource allocator, Negotiator

Adapted and reprinted by permission of *Harvard Business Review.* From "The Manager's Job: Folklore and Fact," by H. Mintzberg, July–August, 1975, p. 55. Copyright © 1975 by the Harvard Business School Publishing Corporation; all rights reserved.

Interpersonal Roles

The formal position of manager involves three separate **interpersonal roles:** figurehead, leader, and liaison. The *figurehead* role involves ceremonial duties in which the manager represents the organization in public functions. This role is particularly important in larger organizations. In the *leader* role, of course, the manager supervises and motivates subordinates, while the *liaison* role involves the establishment and maintenance of contacts outside the department, unit, or group. Examples of the interpersonal roles in operation occur when the director of an athletic department addresses a meeting to honor sport persons in the community (figurehead); talks to her assistants individually or collectively about the importance of generating more donations (leader); or meets with other departmental heads, the president of the university, or other administrators (liaison).

Informational Roles

The interpersonal contacts emerging from the three interpersonal roles enable managers to become the nerve-centers of their groups because of the amount of information that flows through them. This informational base leads the manager to become a monitor, disseminator, and spokesperson. In the *monitor* role, the manager consciously seeks information from within the unit as well as from outside it. The concern here is to obtain any and all kinds of information that will have a bearing on the organization. At this point, the manager passes into a *disseminator* role as he passes relevant information on to his subordinates. The third **informational role** is that of *spokesperson*. In this role, a manager is mainly involved in lobbying for the unit and justifying what goes on within the unit or the organization. In all contacts with external as well as internal agents, the director of athletics consciously seeks out information that will affect the department (monitor), conveys the pieces of information to concerned assistants and unit heads (disseminator), and carries out public relations in any external interactions (spokesperson).

> **In Brief**
>
> Management also consists of behaviors associated with interpersonal roles (figurehead, leader, liaison), informational roles (monitor, disseminator, spokesperson), and decisional roles (entrepreneur, disturbance handler, resource allocator, negotiator).

Decisional Roles

The interpersonal and informational roles, along with the formal authority vested in the position, cast the manager in four **decisional roles.** Mintzberg refers to these as entrepreneur, disturbance handler, resource allocator, and negotiator. As an *entrepreneur*, the manager initiates new and innovative projects with a view to enhancing the viability and effectiveness of the organization. Managers may also be forced to react to changes and pressures beyond their control. Thus, the manager becomes a *disturbance handler*. When managers distribute resources to different units or members, they act as *resource allocators*. The final role is that of *negotiator*, whereby a manager resolves issues with employees and outsiders. The athletic director acts as (a) an entrepreneur when adding a new sport or program to the existing ones; (b) a disturbance handler when designating an interim coach if the regular coach leaves the university for any reason; (c) a resource allocator when allotting budgets to various units and teams; and (d) a negotiator when resolving disputes among coaches or players.

Mintzberg (1975) has stated that these roles are inseparable and that every manager needs to be effective in all 10. He acknowledges, however, that "to say that the ten roles form a gestalt is not to say that all managers give equal attention to each role" (p. 59). Further, Mintzberg describes the inaccuracy of traditional descriptions of managerial work—a view he illustrates by contrasting the folklore about management with the facts (see Exhibit 4.2).

Countering Mintzberg's claims, Carroll and Gillen (1987) argue that observing a manager in action does not provide a clear grasp of the total work she does because (a) managerial work is largely mental and therefore cannot be observed, (b) mental time is different from physical time, and (c) the activity of the brain during the mental time, including the thought trials, can be enormous and efficient. They go on to say that in any interaction with subordinates, peers, and superiors, the manager gets not only basic information but also attitudinal and emotional clues that are critical for decision making. Finally, Carroll and Gillen suggest that managers have their own mental agenda, and they use all the pieces of information they get to revise and implement that agenda. We may add that the supposedly soft information the manager gets through verbal communications may be based on hard data. The manager's subordinates may have worked long on a large set of data before passing on this information to the boss in a distilled and simple format. For the observer, it is soft information, but in truth it is based on hard data.

Exhibit 4.2

Mintzberg's management folklore and facts.

FOLKLORE	FACT
The manager is a reflective, systematic planner.	Study after study has shown that managers work at an unrelenting pace, that their activities are characterized by brevity, variety, and discontinuity, and that they are strongly oriented to action and dislike reflective activities.
The effective manager has no regular duties to perform.	In addition to handling exceptions, managerial work involves performing a number of regular duties, including ritual and ceremony, negotiations, and processing of soft information that links the organization with its environment.
The senior manager needs aggregated information, which a formal management information system best provides.	Managers strongly favor the verbal media—namely, telephone calls and meetings.
Management is, or at least is quickly becoming, a science and profession.	The managers' programs—to schedule time, process information, make decisions, and so on—remain locked deep inside their brains.

Adapted and reprinted by permission of *Harvard Business Review*. From "The Manager's Job: Folklore and Fact," by H. Mintzberg, July–August, 1975, p. 55. Copyright © 1975 by the Harvard Business School Publishing Corporation; all rights reserved.

Managerial Roles and Managerial Levels

Although identifying and describing the various managerial roles is essential, determining which roles are more critical to which level of management is also important. Note that Mintzberg's work was based on his observation of the chief executive officers (CEOs) of five large corporations, and, therefore, his classification may not be relevant to lower levels of management. In a more recent study of managerial jobs, Kraut, Pedigo, McKenna, and Dunnette (1989) identified seven critical managerial roles that are differentially important to three levels of management—first-line supervisors, middle managers, and executives. Their findings show that the managers in their study rated certain roles as more critical for each of the three levels of management (see Exhibit 4.3).

Managerial Roles in Athletic Contexts

Mintzberg's (1975) scheme of managerial roles has been the basis for the investigation of a manager's job in some athletic contexts. Quarterman (1994) used Mintzberg's model of managerial roles to examine the different managerial roles played by athletic conference commissioners in carrying out their job-related responsibilities. Quarterman saw collegiate athletic conference commissioners as the highest ranked managers in the conference setting. They belong to the cadre of top-level managers because they are responsible for the organization and conduct of athletic competitions in their conference. In addition, the commissioners monitor and supervise the activities of other units dealing with compliance, game officials, public relations, and other vital activities of the conference.

Quarterman's (1994) respondents, 63 intercollegiate athletic conference commissioners from all three divisions of the NCAA, rated the importance of the 10 roles. The results show that these commissioners considered the roles of disseminator, liaison, disturbance handler, and monitor as the four most important roles, in that order. According to Quarterman's findings, the major functions of a commissioner are

1. communicating relevant information to member institutions and subordinate managers within the conference office (the disseminator role);

Exhibit 4.3 Managerial levels and importance of managerial tasks.

MANAGEMENT LEVEL	MAJOR THRUST	MANAGERIAL TASKS
First-Line Supervisor (e.g., Stadium Manager)	Supervising individuals	1. Managing individual performance 2. Instructing subordinates
Middle Manager (e.g., Assistant Athletic Director)	Linking groups	1. Planning and resource allocation 2. Coordinating interdependent groups 3. Managing group performance
Executive (e.g., Athletic Director)	Monitoring the business environment	1. Monitoring the environment 2. Linking the organization with the environment

2. interacting with presidents and athletic directors of member institutions and the NCAA (the liaison role);
3. resolving conflicts among member institutions (disturbance handler role);
4. monitoring the environment for useful information (the monitor role).

These results make sense when we take into account that a commissioner's major responsibility is to organize and conduct the competitions within the conference. The actual preparation of the teams for the competitions, and the costs of such preparation, are left to the individual institutions. Thus, the roles of leader, entrepreneur, spokesperson, figurehead, negotiator, and resource allocator were not rated as high as the former four roles. In fact, resource allocator was rated the least important.

Danylchuk and Chelladurai (1999) examined the total managerial work (including the managerial activities of assistant athletic directors and staff) in a university athletic department in Canada. Expanding on Mintzberg's conceptual scheme, they proposed 19 managerial activities associated with an intercollegiate athletic department. They sought to assess (a) the importance of, (b) the time devoted to, and (c) the percentage responsibility for each of those activities. Athletic directors of 37 Canadian universities perceived financial management, leadership, policy making, disturbance handling, revenue generation, and concern for athletes as the most important and most time-consuming activities. In essence, these athletic directors considered the roles of resource allocator (financial management and revenue generation), leader and entrepreneur (policy making), and disturbance handler to be the most important. Given the financial constraints faced by Canadian university athletic departments, not surprisingly the directors emphasized resource management (both securing and distributing the resources) as most important. This contrasts with Quarterman's finding that the commissioners of athletic conferences in the United States rated this the least important of the 10 roles. If we were to ask the U.S. athletic directors the same questions, they would probably rate resource allocation among the most important roles. These findings collectively suggest that the relative significance of Mintzberg's managerial roles vary from one context to another.

The athletic directors in Danylchuk and Chelladurai's (1999) study reported that they were largely responsible for the more important tasks, with average responsibility of 55 percent. The average responsibility assigned to assistant directors was 29.5 percent, and this limited responsibility was significantly but inversely related to the importance of the tasks. This finding substantiates Mintzberg's claim that managerial work involves a number of regular duties.

THE MANAGEMENT PROCESS IN OVERVIEW

The descriptions of management as a set of functions, skills, and roles are simply different perspectives on the same phenomenon. As such, the functions, skills, and roles are highly interrelated (Robbins & Stuart-Kotze, 1992; Rue & Byars, 1997). An examination of the 10 roles of management and the three skills of management reveals considerable overlap among these and the four functions of management (see Exhibit 4.4). For example, Katz's three managerial skills can

Exhibit 4.4 Correspondence among managerial functions, skills, and roles.

MANAGERIAL FUNCTIONS	MANAGERIAL SKILLS	MANAGERIAL ROLES
Planning		Monitor
		Disseminator
		Entrepreneur
	Conceptual	
		Disturbance handler
Organizing		Resource allocator
		Negotiator
Leading	Human	Leader
Evaluating	Technical	Spokesperson
		Liaison
		Figurehead

easily be synthesized with the four managerial functions: the planning and organizing functions entail a great amount of conceptual skill, whereas the leading function presupposes higher levels of human skill. Finally, technical skill is more closely associated with the evaluation phase of management.

In a similar vein, there is also considerable overlap among Mintzberg's 10 roles and the four managerial functions. For example, a manager's decisions in the roles of entrepreneur and resource allocator are based on the information gained in the role of monitor, and these are, in fact, the essential elements of the planning function. The manager sets the priority of objectives and selects the appropriate means only after securing all the relevant information. Resources are then distributed on the basis of the priority of objectives. As Rue and Byars (1997) noted,

> All three approaches to examine the management process look at the process from a different perspective. All have their merits. But in the final analysis, a successful manager must (1) understand the work that is to be performed (the managerial functions); (2) understand the organized set of behaviors to be performed (the managerial roles); and (3) master the skills involved in performing the job (managerial skills). (p. 10)

In Brief

Management consists of planning, organizing, leading, and evaluating, which require conceptual, human, and technical skills. In performing these functions, the manager fills interpersonal, informational, and decisional roles.

THE UNIVERSAL NATURE OF THE MANAGEMENT PROCESS

Anyone who has any experience with various organizations as an employee or as a customer or client is aware that organizations differ dramatically from one another in size, complexity, products, objectives, and so on. Thus, it seems common sense to state that they cannot all be managed in the same way. Nevertheless, Robbins, Coulter, and Stuart-Kotze (2003) speak of *universality of management*. In their words, "we can say with absolute certainty that management is needed in all types and sizes of organizations, at all organizational levels, in all organizational work areas, and in all organizations, no matter in what country they're located" (p. 15). This assertion means that all organizations, without reference to their shape or size, or their goals and purposes, or their cultural context, need to be managed. Simply stated, management in any type of organization consists of planning, organizing, leading, and evaluating, and these processes are universal across all organizations. This does not mean, however, that the methods and consequences of any of the four functions will not differ from one organization to another. By the same token, the significance of each of these functions and the extent to which a manager emphasizes one function over another depend on the hierarchical level at which the manager operates. For instance, the commissioner of a professional sports league will spend more time on strategic planning for the entire enterprise than will the supervisor of interns in the marketing department. The supervisor, on the other hand, is likely to be more engaged in the leading function than the commissioner.

To see how organizations may differ, consider the organizing function. It involves breaking down the total work into specific jobs and then grouping those jobs into meaningful units or departments. This function is made simpler in smaller organizations with limited activities and fewer members. Thus, a fitness consulting firm with three partners or employees is less complex from an organizational perspective than a department of athletics with 100 employees distributed over four or five levels of administration. The critical point, however, is not whether the organizing function is simple or complicated, but that it is essential in both organizations. The effectiveness of the small fitness consulting firm depends as much as the large athletic department on how work is distributed among the members and how well their activities are controlled and coordinated.

From a slightly different perspective, many organizations that carry out identical programs or produce identical products can be organized differently. For example, many governments are involved in promoting sport and recreation. However, some governments have a separate ministry for sport and recreation; some have placed this unit within the ministry (or department) of health, and some others within the ministry (or department) of education. In yet another example, considerable differences exist in the way different universities structure their units responsible for sport management or athletics. Similarly, the structure and processes of interscholastic athletics vary from one state to another in the United States.

The previous examples illustrate that while the consequences of the organizing process may be different, the process of organizing is universal across all organizations. In short, all four of the managerial functions—planning, organizing, leading, and evaluating—must be carried out if an organization is to be effective. Only the decisions made under each process are unique to and contingent upon the specific circumstances of the organization and the manager's orientation. In later chapters, we will explore similarities and differences among sport organizations, and how they facilitate or constrain the managerial processes.

Sidebar

It is not uncommon for people to distinguish between management and marketing based on the idea that management is concerned with production while marketing is concerned with the exchange of products. This is far from the truth. As you will understand from reading this chapter, the concept of management refers to coordination of people, their activities, and limited resources to achieve goals and objectives. A goal of a sport enterprise could be to produce an excellent team and stage exciting sports competitions. Similarly, another goal of the same enterprise would be to sell all the seats in the stadium and secure sponsorships for its programs. The enterprise may set up two units to achieve these objectives. Each unit may consist of several positions hierarchically organized, and these positions would carry out different activities. Further, each unit may be allotted a certain budget. If the units are to achieve their respective objectives, their resources, activities, and people need to be coordinated properly. And that is management. So it is more meaningful to consider management as a process applicable to both production and marketing.

A related debate is whether production or marketing is more important to an organization. Obviously, production and marketing are highly interrelated, and both are critical to an organization. You cannot market anything if it is not produced, and there is no point in producing anything if it cannot be marketed. Despite this, marketing is considered more critical in many types of organizations, and rightly so. Why is this so? We can identify several differences between the two functions that make marketing more critical for an organization.

First, the production function is internal to the organization, while marketing is externally oriented. The production of an excellent team in our example is carried out within the organization. The coaches and the facility and event managers are employees of the organization. The athletes are employees, students, or members of the organization, depending on whether it is a professional franchise, scholastic institution, or sports club. In contrast, marketing is externally oriented in the sense that the spectators and the sponsors are external to the organization. This distinction leads to the difference in the relative control the organization has in the production versus the marketing of its products. The people, processes, and resources involved in production are under the control of the organization, whereas the spectators or sponsors are independent of the organization. Thus, it is easier to manage the production function than it is to manage the marketing function. We can also argue that the technology associated with the production of an excellent team is, relatively speaking, better known and better mastered (e.g., coaching, event management, and facility management) than the technology associated with marketing (e.g., consumer psychology/behavior).

A final distinction is that the production function involves the expenditure of resources while the marketing function involves the acquisition of such resources. In many types of organization, the units that deal with elements in the external environment or secure the necessary resources are likely to have greater power and influence. Accordingly, marketing is likely to be accorded greater status than production in most sport organizations. However, those units that produce products that are excellent and most sought after by the public, such as the football and basketball programs in Division I universities, are likely to have clout equal to if not greater than that of marketing.

SUMMARY

This chapter describes the concept of management—the process of achieving organizational goals with and through other people, given limited resources. Management was described from three different perspectives: managerial functions, managerial skills, and managerial roles. Managerial functions include planning, organizing, leading, and evaluating. To carry out these functions, managers need to have three kinds of skills: conceptual, human, and technical. Management was also described as consisting of interpersonal roles (the roles of figurehead, leader, and liaison), informational roles (the roles of monitor, disseminator, and spokesperson), and decisional roles (the roles of entrepreneur, disturbance handler, resource allocator, and negotiator). These three perspectives complement each other in describing management in detail. We also discussed the idea that management is a universal process.

In Chapter 1, we defined sport management as the coordination of limited human and material resources, relevant technologies, and situational contingencies for the efficient production and exchange of sport services (refer to Exhibit 1.5). The four functions of management as outlined above, in fact, are aimed at coordination of the activities of organizational units and their members (see Exhibit 4.5). The goals set and the activities chosen to achieve those goals in the planning process, the creation of organizational units and hiring of the right people to run those units, the guidance and coaching provided in the leading function, and the evaluations of individual-, unit-, and organizational-level performances all aim at coordination. Accordingly, we will elaborate further on these four functions in the next chapters.

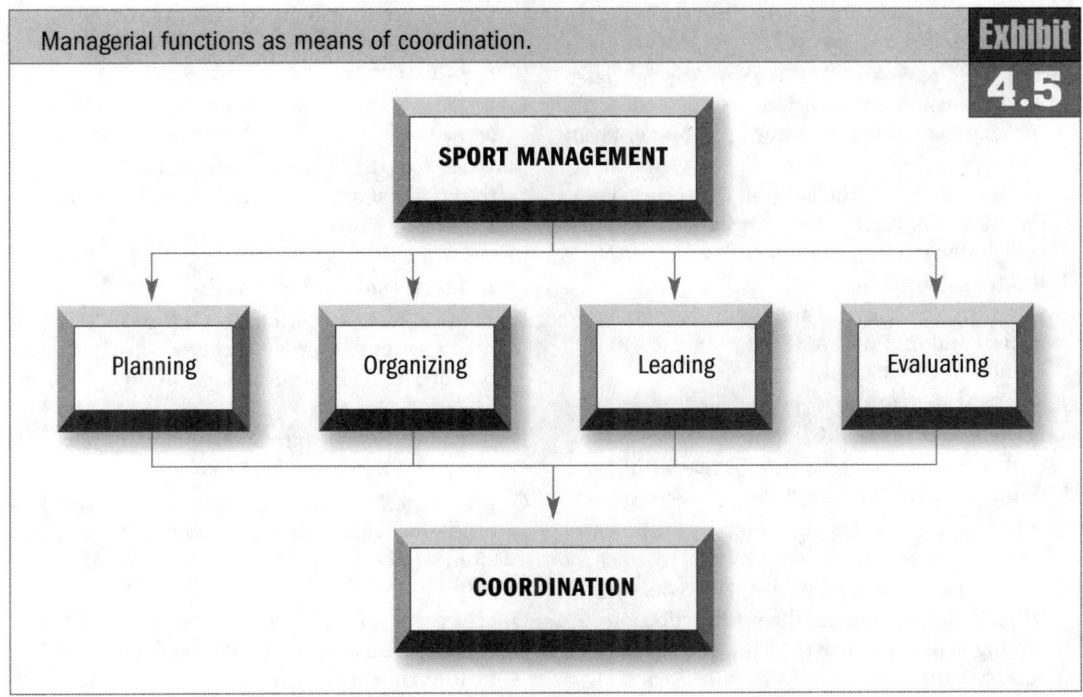

Exhibit 4.5 Managerial functions as means of coordination.

Developing Your Perspectives

1. Compare any two sport organizations in terms of the relative importance of the four functions.
2. Select a large sport organization (for example, a Division I athletic department) and discuss how, and to what degree, the various levels of managers are involved in the four managerial functions.
3. In the organization you choose, which of the technical, human, and conceptual skills are relatively more important to which levels of management?
4. What does the head of your unit or department actually do in a typical day? How is his or her time apportioned among the 10 managerial roles described by Mintzberg?
5. Compare the daily activities of the coach of an athletic team to those of the athletic director. Discuss the differences in their roles and in the time they spend in each of the roles.

References

Barrow, J. C. (1977). The variables of leadership: A review and conceptual framework. *Academy of Management Review, 2*, 231–251.

Carlson, S. (1979). *Executive behavior: A study of the workload and the working methods of managing directors.* New York: Arno Press. (Original work published in 1951).

Carroll, S. J., & Gillen, D. J. (1987). Are the classical management functions useful in describing managerial work? *Academy of Management Review, 12*, 38–51.

Danylchuk, K. E., & Chelladurai, P. (1999). The nature of managerial work in Canadian intercollegiate athletics. *Journal of Sport Management, 13*, 148–166.

Fayol, H. (1949). *General and industrial management.* London: Pitman. (First published in French in 1916).

Guest, R. H. (1956). Of time and the foremen. *Personnel, 32*, 478–486.

Katz, R. L. (1974). Skills of an effective administrator. *Harvard Business Review, 52*, 90–102.

Keuning, D. (1998). *Management: A contemporary approach.* London: Pitman.

Klemp, G. O., Jr., & McClelland, D. C. (1986). What characterizes intelligent functioning among senior managers? In R. J. Sternberg & R. K. Wagner (Eds.), *Practical intelligence: Nature and origins of competence in the everyday world* (pp. 31–50). New York: Cambridge University Press.

Kraut, A. I., Pedigo, P. R., McKenna, D. D., & Dunnette, M. D. (1989). The role of the manager: What's really important in different management jobs. *The Academy of Management Executive, 3*, 286–293.

Likert, R. (1967). *The human organization, its management and value.* New York: McGraw-Hill.

Mayo, E. (1933). *The human problems of an industrial civilization.* Cambridge, MA: Harvard University Press.

Mintzberg, H. (1975). The manager's job: Folklore and fact. *Harvard Business Review, 53*, 49–61.

Parkhouse, B. L., & Ulrich, D. O. (1979). Sport management as a potential cross-discipline: A paradigm for theoretical application. *Quest, 31*, 264–276.

Pettinger, R. (1997). *Introduction to management* (2nd ed.). London: Macmillan.

Quarterman, J. (1994). Managerial role profiles of intercollegiate athletic conference commissioners. *Journal of Sport Management, 8*, 129–139.

Quarterman, J. (1998). An assessment of the perception of management and leadership skills by intercollegiate athletics conference commissioners. *Journal of Sport Management, 12,* 146–164.

Robbins, S. P. (1976). *The administrative process: Integrating theory and practice.* Englewood Cliffs, NJ: Prentice Hall.

Robbins, S. P. (1997). *Managing today!* Upper Saddle River, NJ: Prentice Hall.

Robbins, S. P., Coulter, M., & Stuart-Kotze, R. (2003). *Management* (7th ed.). Toronto: Prentice Hall.

Robbins, S. P., & Stuart-Kotze, R. (1992). *Management: Concepts and applications* (Canadian 2nd ed.) Scarborough, ON: Prentice Hall Canada.

Rollinson, D. (2002). *Organisational behaviour and analysis: An integrated approach* (2nd ed.). Harlow: Financial Times Prentice Hall.

Rue, L. W., & Byars, L. L. (1997). *Management: Skills and application* (8th ed.). Boston: Irwin/McGraw-Hill.

Soucie, D. G. (1982). Management theory and practice. In E. F. Zeigler (Ed.), *Physical education and sport: An introduction* (pp. 190–212). Philadelphia: Lea & Febiger.

Stewart, R. (1967). *Managers and their jobs.* New York: Macmillan.

Taylor, F. W. (1911). *The principles of scientific management.* New York: Harper & Bros.

Waldroop, J., & Butler, T. (1996). The executive as coach. *Harvard Business Review, 74* (6), 11–117.

Wehrich, H., & Koontz, H. (1993). *Management: A global perspective* (10th ed.). New York: McGraw-Hill.

Zeigler, E. F. (1979). Elements of a competency based approach to management development: A preliminary analysis. Paper read at the Convention of the Canadian Association for Health, Physical Education and Recreation. Winnipeg, Manitoba.

Zeigler, E. F., & Bowie, G. W. (1983). *Management competency development in sport and physical education.* Philadelphia: Lea & Febiger.

CHAPTER 5

Planning

MANAGE YOUR LEARNING

After completing this chapter you should be able to:

- Understand the steps in the process of planning.
- Explain the significance of the various steps in the planning process.
- Define and describe strategic management.
- Understand the significance of mission statements.
- Explain tactical/operational plans.
- See the relationship between planning and budgeting.
- Explain how goals can be constraints.
- Explain the significance of information in planning and discuss the methods used to gather information.
- Understand the need for planning without goals or directional planning.

STRATEGIC CONCEPTS

alternative	means and ends
brainstorming	mission statement
budgeting	nominal group technique
constraint	planning
Delphi technique	real/operative goal
directional planning	stated/official goal
forecasting	strategic planning
goal	tactical/operational planning

THE PLANNING FUNCTION

In the first four chapters, we described the field of sport management (Chapter 1), the concept of organizations (Chapter 2), organizations as open systems (Chapter 3), and the act of management (Chapter 4).

The previous chapters set the stage for an in-depth discussion of management itself. As we noted in Chapter 4, management can be described from several different perspectives. The approach of this book is to describe and discuss management as a set of functions: planning, organizing, leading, and evaluating. This chapter is devoted to the function of planning. We begin with a definition of planning and go on to describe the steps in the planning process.

Then, we explore the distinctions between strategic planning and operational planning. Following this is a description of the elements of a good mission statement—an integral part of strategic management. Then, after contrasting long-range planning with short-term planning, we look at the issues surrounding organizational goals. The chapter concludes with a discussion of directional planning as a viable option for managers and organizations.

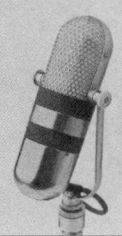

KEY DEFINITIONS In the previous chapters, we defined sport management as the coordination of resources (human and material), relevant technologies, and situational contingencies for the efficient production and exchange of sport services. We defined an organization as consisting of people whose specialized activities are coordinated to achieve specified goals. Management is the specialized activity of coordinating the activities of others, and limited resources, toward efficiently achieving the goals.

DEFINITION OF PLANNING

While all of the four managerial functions referred to in Chapter 4—planning, organizing, leading, and evaluating—are integrally linked, the planning function must precede the others. Let us therefore look at how some authors define **planning**:

Planning, then, is essentially a decision making process that focuses on the future of the organization and how it will get where it wants to go. (Black & Porter, 2000, p. 174)

Planning is the process of deciding what objectives to pursue during a future time period and what to do to achieve those objectives. It is the primary management function and is inherent in everything the manager does. (Rue & Byars, 1992, p. 150)

Planning encompasses defining an organization's goals, establishing an overall strategy for achieving those goals, and developing a hierarchy of plans to integrate and coordinate activities. It is concerned, then, with *ends* (what is to be done) as well as with *means* (how it is to be done). (Robbins, 1997, p. 130)

Planning is the systematic preparation and attuning of decisions aimed at the realizing of goals in the future. Planning precedes the action. (Keuning, 1998, p. 480)

Planning is the process of setting the objectives of an organization and the means for their achievement. (Naylor, 1999, p. 270)

These definitions suggest that planning is concerned with establishing goals for the organization and identifying the activities and programs to achieve those goals. There is also the underlying notion that planning precedes other managerial activities. This process of deciding on what is to be achieved and how it should be done involves several steps, which we will now examine.

STEPS IN THE PLANNING PROCESS

We can use the framework illustrated in Exhibit 5.1 to help define and discuss the total planning process. In the model, planning is composed of the stages of specifying goals, identifying opportunities, identifying constraints, generating alternatives, establishing performance criteria, evaluating alternatives, selecting an alternative, and presenting the plan document. First of all, note that the specification of organizational goals takes place along with identification of opportunities and constraints, even though they are discussed sequentially.

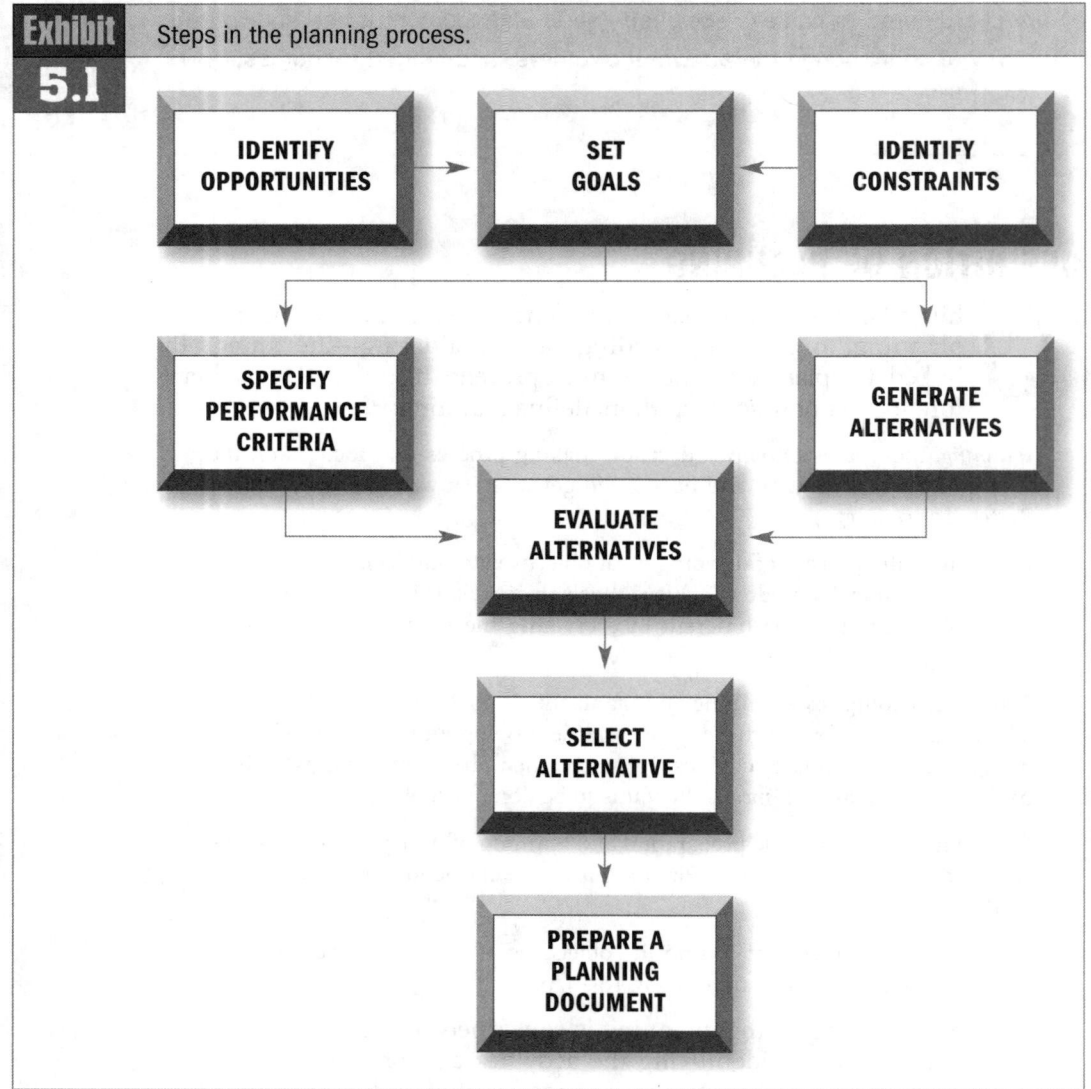

Exhibit 5.1 Steps in the planning process.

Specifying Goals

As we noted earlier, the first step in the planning process is to set out the **goals** for the organization. An organization may have more than one goal, and these may relate to profitability, growth, market share, productivity/efficiency, leadership, client satisfaction, or social awareness (Pettinger, 1997; Robbins, 1997; Rosen, 1995; Rue & Byars, 1992). We will now describe these various goals.

Profitability refers to the fact that a profit-oriented sports organization may aim at securing a specified number of dollars as its profits. Alternatively, it may seek a certain percentage of its capital outlay as profits. Thus, a fitness firm may aim for a profit of $10,000 or a 15-percent return on its capital outlay. Most professional sport organizations are likely to have profitability as the primary goal, and they run their business with that motive firmly in mind. However, this is not to deny that some professional sport franchises may tolerate monetary losses in favor of other benefits such as tax shelter and prestige.

Another goal might be related to *growth* of the organization—growth in terms of profits, total revenue, market share, number of employees, or the number of products or activities. The growth concept is equally relevant to both profit and nonprofit organizations. For instance, a department of sport management may seek to increase its number of faculty members and the number of courses it offers. One growth objective of organizations such as Branada Sports Communications' "Streetball" in Canada and the National Basketball Association's "Hoop-It-Up" in the United States is to stage their three-on-three basketball tournaments in a growing number of cities. Profit-oriented fitness clubs may view the increase in number of clients as a sign of growth. By the same token, they may also seek to grow by opening new centers in different locations in the same city or in a different city. Because size is often equated with status, it is not uncommon for nonprofit organizations to emphasize growth as their primary objective. For the YMCA, growth may be measured by enrollments in its various physical activities programs.

Market share refers to the fact that some organizations may have the securing of a certain share of the market as their goal. In fact, relative market share has been used as a measure of effectiveness in many comparative studies of organizations. Even universities tend to have as an objective the recruitment of a certain percentage of the total student population. Businesses providing fitness and sports services also compete for a larger percentage of the market in their geographical area. Sporting goods manufacturers such as Wilson and Nike are also sure to work toward gaining a larger share of the market.

The concept of *productivity/efficiency* refers to the maximization of the output relative to a given input. While all organizations are concerned with efficiency, it becomes a singular concern in times of crisis. For example, educational institutions have recently been forced to consider efficiency in their operations as a result of dwindling financial resources. The practices of downsizing and restructuring are often a part of efforts to enhance productivity by paring down the labor force and getting rid of inefficient operations. When a professional sport franchise attempts to trade a high-salaried athlete, it could be for the purpose of reducing expenses and thereby becoming more efficient. Of course, it is assumed that the franchise will perform as well without the star player. Similarly, a fitness club may drop a program for a special group, such as seniors, because the program is not profitable—that is, the program costs more than its revenue. In a similar manner, a profit-oriented golf club may reduce the number of employees in order to become more efficient. In these examples, the organization may already be successful in other respects (such as making a profit), but not necessarily efficient.

Organizations may also aspire to *leadership in the market* in terms of the products they produce or the methods of production. For example, many computer companies compete to produce new and innovative products, both hardware and software. Universities and departments of sport management also take pride in offering new and more relevant courses or programs, and in being known as leaders in the educational domain. University athletic departments also strive to be leaders in the country in terms of number of sports supported, extent and quality of facilities, athlete assistance programs, and so on. Also, sporting goods manufacturers compete with each other to be leaders in introducing new and improved products such as footwear and protective equipment.

Client satisfaction also may be an important objective sought by an organization. Such satisfaction is, of course, primarily contingent upon whether the products (goods or services) are of sufficiently high quality. Rigorous quality control measures, procurement of high-quality raw materials, and improvement of production processes are indicative of the importance that sporting goods manufacturers place on this objective. In the case of a fitness club, for instance, efforts to keep the premises and equipment clean, to respond quickly to clients' requests, and to establish a congenial atmosphere are all aimed at satisfying customers. Golf courses make every effort to satisfy their patrons, including making sure that they do not have to wait too long for their turn to play.

Many organizations may also set goals in terms of *social awareness*—being socially responsible and responsive. For example, Nike's "Just Do It" slogan was born out of social awareness insofar as it encourages people to get physically active. The actions of municipal recreation departments to improve safety features in playgrounds or the actions of a professional sport franchise in controlling the crowd could be a function of social awareness as well as the desire to avoid legal liability. In fact, you could say that risk management must be primarily a social responsibility.

Most nonprofit organizations are guided by their awareness of societal needs. The Red Cross and the Salvation Army are two examples in which social awareness is the main guide for action. Schools and universities are also sensitive to the fact that their contributions are to society as a whole and not just to the current roster of students. One of the purposes of any intercollegiate athletic department is to ensure that athletes obtain a quality education so that they can become useful citizens.

It is neither necessary nor practical for an organization to limit its goals to any one of the above areas. In fact, most organizations have multiple goals. (The concept of multiple goals and the effect on rational planning are discussed in a later section of this chapter.) However, specification of one or more goals should be undertaken only after thoroughly considering the opportunities available to, and the constraints faced by, the organization.

Identifying Opportunities

The choice of organizational goals depends on the opportunities available in the organization's environment. For instance, a fitness club may find that many senior citizens have moved into its locality. This suddenly presents an opportunity for the club to start a fitness program for seniors. A charitable organization may find that it cannot maintain and run its recreational facility for lack of funds. This may provide an opportunity for a commercial sport enterprise or the city recreation department to take over the facility. The National Collegiate Athletic Association (NCAA) expectation that all university athletic departments should attempt to achieve gender equity may prove to be an opportunity for a university to start new programs for women. Generally, the opportunities are a function of economic, social, cultural, demographic, environmental, political, legal, technological, and competitive trends (David, 1997).

Opportunities may also arise out of conditions internal to the organization. For example, a fitness club may be building a reserve fund for use in case of emergencies. Over the years, the fund may have exceeded the planned-for level of emergency. In such a case, the club has the opportunity to invest the excess money in additional facilities, equipment, or programs. Similarly, the employees of the fitness club may have gained additional certifications that will enable the club to offer more programs that require such certification.

Identifying Constraints

The third stage in the planning process involves identifying **constraints** (see Exhibit 5.1). While an organization may fancy a number of goals, some of them may not be attainable owing to specific constraints. These constraints may be in the form of limited resources—finances, time, or personnel. Thus, a fitness club may wish to expand its program of offerings but be unable to do so because of limited capital or staff. Additional constraints may also be placed on an organization by virtue of societal norms, government regulations, or competition from other organizations. A firm specializing in representing athletes, for example, is constrained by legal requirements in several states.

We noted earlier that the NCAA's expectation regarding gender equity could be an opportunity for some university athletic departments. By the same token, it could be a constraint on a university considering adding one more men's sport. As is the case with opportunities, constraints may stem from environmental influences such as regulations by the government or inter-organizational networks. For instance, a university athletic department must consider the financial rules of the Internal Revenue Service and the regulations of the NCAA regarding amateur status in its recruiting efforts. (Unlike a pro sports franchise, it cannot simply outbid other schools competing for a talented player.) Another example of environmental constraints is the existence of competition in the market. For example, a fitness club may not be able to extend its operations to another locality because another fitness enterprise is already there. Geography, climate, and physical resources can impede the implementation of a plan. For example, a plan for the development of ice hockey could not be easily implemented in a tropical country because of the hot climatic conditions.

Constraints may also be internally generated. For instance, while many university athletic departments are quite willing to hold gender equity as a goal, they may be constrained in implementing it owing to a scarcity of funds. As another example, a fitness firm may not be able to offer fitness appraisal as one of its services because the available expertise and equipment may not meet the technological standards, and it does not have the capital to acquire

SWOT and the Tennis Club

The three stages of identifying opportunities, identifying constraints, and setting goals as outlined in the text involve environmental analyses and internal evaluations. Our discussion implied that such analyses would show the strengths and weaknesses of the organization in question. These analyses are popularly known by the acronym SWOT: Strengths, Weaknesses, Opportunities, and Threats (Pettinger, 1997; Robbins, 1997; Rosen, 1995). Consider, for example, Dan Jackson, a former member of the tennis team of the local university in a mid-size city who wants to start his own tennis club. As shown in the accompanying figure, the strengths include the owner's tennis expertise. (He was an outstanding player trained by expert coaches.) Jackson is very knowledgeable in tennis instruction and coaching, and could prove to be an outstanding pro. Further, former teammates have agreed to help out with the tennis club. Both Jackson and the teammates are well known in and around the city, having won several tournaments and championships as members of the local university team. Jackson has continued to play competitive tennis with some success.

The weaknesses are the lack of expertise and experience in running a business. Jackson majored in social work, and none of the teammates has any background in business. Further, there is the lack of initial capital necessary to start up a business. Jackson would have to rely on well-wishers and banks to provide such capital. However, there is some indication that such capital might be forthcoming.

The following are the opportunities. The city is one of the fastest-growing cities in the region. It can boast of an average family income above the median for the region. In addition, the citizens are known to be highly involved in sport and physical activity. These factors indicate that there are likely to be enough customers who would be willing to pay to join a tennis club. If the facility could be located near the university, it would be easier and perhaps more successful in targeting the students for membership. Furthermore, the city itself is promoting new businesses by offering sizable incentives.

As for threats, the city's two existing fitness clubs are planning to expand into tennis operations. If they do, they would pose a severe competition for clients. There may not be enough customers to sustain all three tennis enterprises.

With a careful consideration of this situation's strengths, weaknesses, opportunities, and threats (SWOT), Jackson will be able to make a decision regarding whether to start the business. This process is illustrated in the following figure.

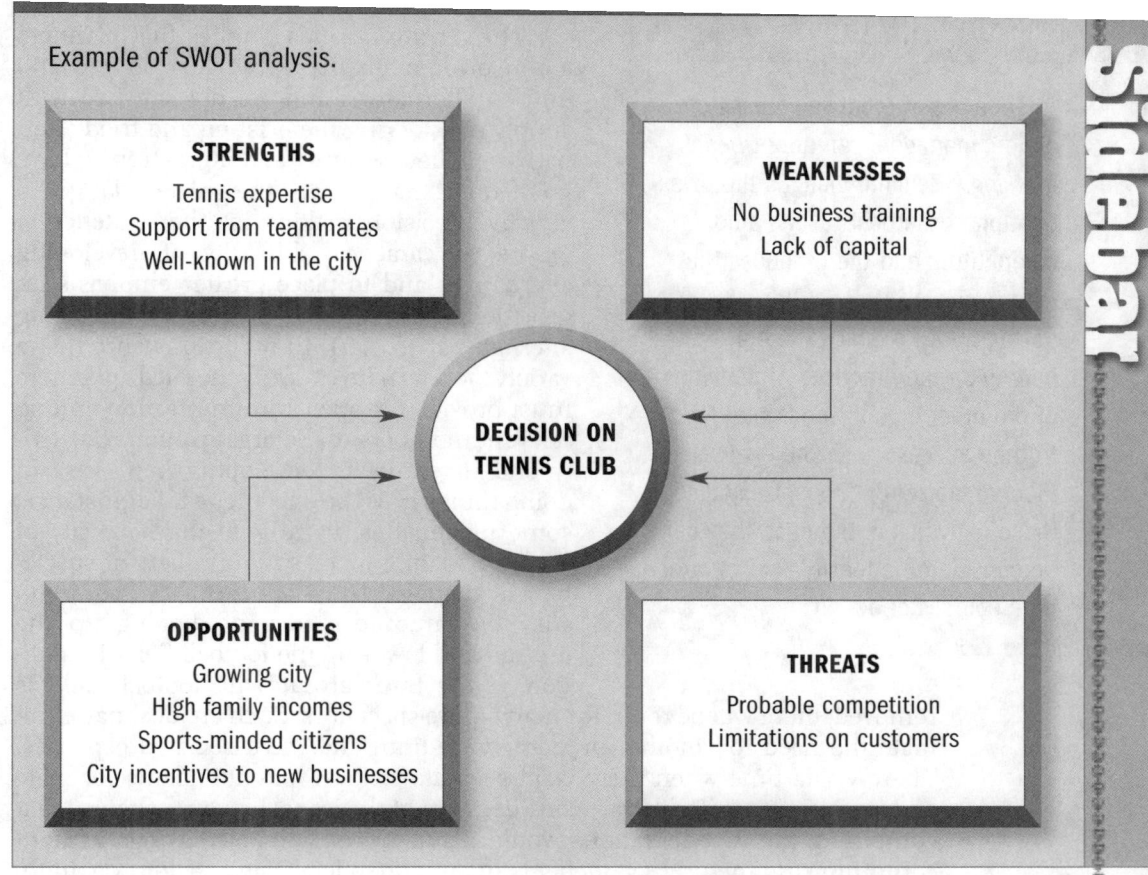

Example of SWOT analysis.

the needed equipment. A sport marketing firm wishing to expand its operations to include events management may not be able to do so because its employees do not have the necessary training or experience, and hiring people with such expertise may be too expensive for the firm.

In the foregoing analysis of opportunities and constraints, we noted that these can be a function of both internal and external (or environmental) conditions. The emphasis on environmental conditions takes us back to the notion of organizations as open systems, as discussed in Chapter 3. That is, any plan to be successful needs to be formulated so that it is aligned with the organization's environment. Stated another way, planners must hold a systems view of the organization, taking into consideration the external environment as well as the internal conditions in setting goals for the organization. A review of all the opportunities and constraints in the environment would show which of the desired goals are within reach and which are not feasible.

Generating Alternate Courses of Action

After specifying the goals, two sets of activities must be carried out independently: generation of **alternative** courses of action for achieving the specified

> **Sidebar**
>
> To generate alternative courses of action, managers can adopt *benchmarking*. "Benchmarking is the investigation of the best results among competitors and the practices that lead to those results" (Black & Porter, 2000, p. 181). The emphasis here is on the practices or activities of the other organizations that lead to their successes. To the extent the focal organization has not engaged in those activities in the past, they can be considered a feasible set of alternate courses of action.

goals, and the establishment of criteria to evaluate these alternatives with a view to selecting the best ones (see Exhibit 5.1).

The term *generation* implies that planners are involved in an attempt to develop new and untried alternatives and are not satisfied with simply considering the existing and tried alternatives. Filley, House, and Kerr (1976) have pointed out that perhaps the greatest danger to effective decision making is "the tendency to ignore the practical difficulty of developing alternatives and to place greater emphasis on goal definition and the process of weighting alternatives" (p. 431). In order to ensure that a variety of alternatives are generated, planners must provide for open communication among relevant members of the organization. Creativity and ingenuity in developing new ways of doing things must be encouraged. For instance, some universities, faced with the necessity of accommodating increasing numbers of spectators in their football stadiums, have come up with the innovative idea of digging up the ground and lowering the football field. In addition, if the track around the football field is removed, there will be room for many more spectators. Such an idea may eliminate the need for another brand-new stadium and the associated expenses. There was a time when there were separate locker room attendants for male and female clients. Deliberate consideration of the issue, however, showed that combining the two operations would result in considerable savings without compromising the privacy of clients of either gender. That decision was innovative at the time. In a similar manner, some fitness and tennis clubs have located the operations of the locker room attendant and the receptionist in the same room with a portable screen between them. A client checks in with the receptionist, who faces the entrance. After checking in, the client walks around the corner of the room to the locker room attendant, located at a point before the entrance to the locker room. While there is nothing spectacular about this arrangement, there is the advantage of having one individual attend to both the operations during the times of the day when the flow of customers is low—a simple, innovative way of saving labor costs.

Establishing Performance Criteria to Evaluate Alternatives

After alternatives have been generated, it remains to select the best one. In order to do so, there must be guidelines, or performance criteria (see Exhibit 5.1). These evaluative criteria must be established independently from the process by which the alternatives were generated. Otherwise, there is a tendency to fit the evaluative performance criteria to a preferred alternative, and the resulting choice might not be optimal. These performance criteria may be useful in evaluating the alternatives:

1. relative cost and associated benefits of each alternative (efficiency)

2. alternative's potential contribution to more than one goal
3. ease of implementation
4. ease of measurement
5. conformity to societal norms and government sanctions
6. availability of personnel with requisite ability to implement the alternative
7. other similar factors

For instance, a city may decide to build an arena to attract professional basketball and hockey teams. The decision is based on consideration of several factors such as the economic activity the arena will generate, the pride and prestige a professional team would bring to the city, the costs associated with building the arena, and the reaction (positive and negative) of the citizens. The city has two options on where to build the arena: in the core of downtown or on the periphery of downtown where two major highways intersect. The downtown option is more expensive primarily because of the real estate cost. In addition, it will create huge traffic problems. On the positive side, building the arena downtown is consistent with the city's determination to revitalize its core.

The other option—building the arena out of the downtown area—is attractive because of the reduced costs for the real estate. In addition, it will not create any significant traffic congestion in the vicinity of the arena. However, the arena in that location will not contribute much to the downtown revitalization project. The costs, the traffic congestion, and the contribution to more than one goal (the revitalization project) are just a few examples of criteria the decision makers can use in evaluating the two options. Once again, the idea of a systems view comes into play. The analyses of internal and external environments and the organization's strengths and weaknesses will indicate which of the alternatives is more feasible as well as more acceptable to the environment.

Evaluating Alternatives

The evaluation of alternatives follows the establishment of performance criteria and the generation of alternative courses of action (see Exhibit 5.1). This process involves the comparison of alternatives to the performance criteria. It might be solely computational in nature if the established performance criteria are all quantitative ones. Under these circumstances, there is no need for the planners to make any judgment decisions. For example, in planning for the transportation of a football team for a bowl game, the athletic department may have several alternatives. Because each alternative will have clear quantifiable data on the expenses, time lost, and other criteria, it is easy to evaluate these alternatives and choose the best one according to the set performance criteria. For a more critical decision, consider again the case of the city considering building its arena either in the downtown area or outside it. We said that the real estate cost would be much lower outside the downtown area, so if the only criterion were the cost, then the decision would be clear: build outside the downtown area. These are examples of quantitative criteria applied to planning.

However, in most instances the performance and measurement criteria are qualitative in nature. When this is the case, greater care must be taken to be as objective as possible in evaluating each of the alternatives on the selected performance criteria. Any variability in such assessment could falsely indicate one alternative's superiority over the others. A case in point is the hiring of a football coach. Many of the selection criteria, such as years of experience and past performance records of the candidates, are quantifiable; therefore, it is easy to evaluate and compare the candidates. On the other hand, other selection criteria, such as disposition, interpersonal skills, values, and ethics, are qualitative in nature. For instance, a candidate's capacity to interact effectively with the players, administrators, other coaches, and the media is a function of personality and interpersonal skills. Similarly, whether a candidate shares the values of the organization in promoting the welfare of the athletes, and whether the candidate will refrain from violating the letter and spirit of the NCAA rules, are based on her own values and ethical standards. These are not as easily measured as years of experience or a win/loss record. Therefore, the evaluation of the pool of candidates on these criteria becomes problematic, and the selectors have to use their best judgment. In the case of the city building an arena, consider that two different designs for the exterior of the arena have been presented. While cost may be one criterion in the selection of one design over the other, there is also the criterion of aesthetics. Does one design present a more tasteful, elegant, and pleasing appearance? As this criterion is qualitative in nature, decisions made in this regard will be more subjective than objective.

> **In Brief**
>
> The critical steps in the planning process are specifying goals after identifying the constraints, generating alternatives to achieve those goals, and evaluating these alternatives on previously stated criteria.

Selecting an Alternative

Selection of an alternative as outlined in Exhibit 5.1 is technical and routine in nature. That is, the alternative with the highest rating on the evaluative criteria is selected automatically as the means to a given goal. If two or more alternatives are given the same highest rating, the choice can be made simply by tossing a coin! The simplicity of this step emphasizes the fact that serious thought, careful deliberations, and necessary computations need to have gone into the previous steps of the planning process. A common fallacy is to equate this final step with the entire planning process. For example, when the hiring of a football coach is announced, the public and the media tend to say that the university has made a decision. This simple statement masks the time and effort spent in the painstaking processes of searching, recruiting, and evaluating several coaches. Similarly, when the city officials announce the chosen site or design for the arena, they are deemed to have made the decision at that moment, but this decision followed discussions and debates, media scrutiny, polls taken, and political struggles in and out of the city council that were all part of the decision-making process.

The Plan Document

As the final step in the planning process, the administrators must draw up a document for the benefit of all members of the organization (see Exhibit 5.1). This document should specify (a) the goals being sought; (b) the activities to be carried out to achieve those goals; (c) the initiatives of the management in this regard; (d) the corresponding responsibilities of the members or units; (e) the standards to be maintained; (f) the methods and measures of performance; and (g) the controls to be exercised at various levels to ensure conformance to the plan.

STRATEGIC PLANNING

So far we have discussed the dynamics of the planning process and several guidelines to make it more effective. Note that the scope of planning, the time frame for it, and the rigor with which it is formulated will all vary with the type of problem addressed and the organizational level at which the planning occurs. The planning that occurs at the top level of management is called strategic planning (David, 1997; Rosen, 1995). Interestingly, "the term *strategy* is derived from the Greek word *strategos,* which means 'a general.' In ancient times, it meant the art and science of managing military forces to victory" (Megginson, Mosley, & Pietri, 1992, p. 197). The idea here is that whatever planning occurs at the highest levels is strategic in the sense that it affects the whole organization and its future. Such strategic planning encompasses all the units within the organization and their operations. **Strategic planning** is sometimes called strategic management and is defined as:

> that part of the management process concerned with achieving an overall integration of an organization's internal divisions, while simultaneously integrating the organization with its external environment. (Pierce & Dunham, 1990, p. 170)

To Black and Porter (2000), the first step in strategic planning is to determine the *strategic intent,* which is an expression of "what the organization ultimately wants to be and do" (p. 197). For example, the National Football League (NFL) can have the intent of being the most popular league around the world and of having several competitive divisions in various countries all culminating in a final world championship, as with the World Cup of soccer. With this strategic intent in mind, the NFL may begin to operate in different continents as it does in Europe. Black and Porter (2000) suggest that strategic intent is the heart of strategic planning or management. Thus, strategic planning includes "those activities that involve defining the organization's mission, setting its objectives, and developing strategies to enable it to operate successfully in its environment" (Megginson et al., 1992, p. 197).

The emphases in the above definitions are twofold. First, strategic planning (or strategic management) involves the entire organization and its units. Second, strategic planning is concerned with matching the organization with the external environment. In other words, those who are involved with strategic planning must take into account the opportunities available in the larger environment and the obstacles and constraints (including competition) posed by the environment. Strategic planning addresses the challenge of exploiting the opportunities while at the same time overcoming the obstacles.

Once a strategic decision is made, other planning activities follow. For example, the strategic decision to build an arena is followed by planning by the architects, builders, facility managers, marketing units, concert managers, and others.

Sidebar: Strategic Planning on a Smaller Scale

Strategic planning does not necessarily involve huge sums of money. When students choose one university over another, they have done strategic planning. When two or more entrepreneurs decide to form a company to get into the golf business instead of real estate, they have done strategic planning. If they decide to construct a new golf course instead of buying an existing one, they have made a strategic decision. Similarly, when a fitness club extends its operations to provide tennis facilities and services, the decision is born of strategic planning.

Strategic planning differs from other forms of planning because it:

1. involves decision by top management
2. requires allocation of large amounts of resources
3. has significant long-term effects
4. focuses on the organization's interactions with the external environment

Of course, such planning should take into account the internal strengths and weaknesses of the organization itself. In other words, although strategic planning focuses primarily on environmental contingencies, it cannot be effective if it does not consider the resources available within the organization.

On occasion, the effects of strategic planning/management may be quite drastic. For instance, consider the efforts by many corporate managers to downsize their enterprises, while some other executives take the path of acquisitions and diversification. These differing strategic processes are undertaken only after careful analysis of the opportunities and obstacles posed by the external environment and an audit of internal dynamics and the resources, strengths, and weaknesses of the organization.

When an entrepreneur holding a franchise in one sport in one city bids for a franchise in a new league in another sport in another city, such a move is said to be strategic. It should involve an extensive analysis of several factors, including the growth in the popularity of the sport, the sporting tradition of the city and the community surrounding it, and even the viability of the new league.

In another example, a university athletic department has to decide whether to renovate and extend the existing arena or build a new one. This strategic decision involves many factors—the cost of each alternative, inputs from various contributors, and the long-term viability of the old arena. If a new arena is built, there is the opportunity to name it after a person or organization and thereby secure a large donation for the building. On the other hand, it is possible that the public and funding agencies such as the state government may question the wisdom of having two arenas in one university. The decision makers may also consider renting the new facility for entertainment purposes, such as concerts, to offset the cost of maintaining the arena. Then again, others may question the notion of the university getting into the entertainment business. These are just two examples of opposing forces operating in the environment. Decision makers have the formidable task of weighing all these factors and making the most appropriate strategic decision—one that will have a long-lasting effect on the department and the university.*

---

*The Ohio State University faced a decision of this type and did, in fact, build the new Schottenstein Center instead of renovating the old St. Johns Arena.

A professional sport club moving from one city to another, a city replacing its old arena with a new one, and the National Basketball Association (NBA) starting the Women's NBA (WNBA) are other examples of strategic planning. These are impressive decisions, chiefly because of the millions (if not billions) of dollars involved. In fact, Noll and Zimbalist (1997) estimate that more than $7 billion will be spent on new sport facilities by the year 2006. The Ohio State University will have spent nearly $500 million on new sport and recreation facilities during the decade ending in 2005. These kinds of expenses reflect strategic planning. Thus, "strategy is the art and science of combining the many resources available to achieve the best match between an organization and its environment" (Pierce & Dunham, 1990, p. 170).

What is important to note is that the decision to build a new arena is not a random act. It follows from the global approach and strategic direction taken by the athletic department and the university administrators. That direction may include becoming a leader in university athletics, being known for its athletic and academic achievements, and being acknowledged for its facilities as well. From this perspective, building a new arena is one step toward attaining national prominence. Thus, we see that setting and articulating the mission for the organization is critical to strategic management.

In Brief

Strategic planning focuses on the direction the total organization and its units will take over the long run. Such planning takes place at the top levels of the organization and covers a long time frame. More important, it links the organization with its environment.

Mission and Mission Statement

According to Pearce and David (1987), a **mission statement** (a) sets a business apart; (b) reveals an organization's product or service, markets, customers, and philosophy; (c) provides the foundation for priorities, strategies, plans, and work assignments including managerial jobs and structures; and (d) specifies the fundamental reason why an organization exists.

According to Pearce and David (1987), a mission statement should include the following eight specific elements:

1. Specification of key elements in the company philosophy
2. Identification of the company's self-concept
3. Identification of the company's desired public image
4. Specification of target customers and markets
5. Identification of principal products/services
6. Specification of geographic domain
7. Identification of core technologies
8. Expression of commitment to survival/growth/profitability

The mission statements of The Ohio State University's Department of Athletics and Department of Recreational Sports are shown in Exhibit 5.2. Exhibit 5.3 shows the mission statements of Major League Soccer and Nike. A perusal of these mission statements shows that they follow the relevant guidelines proposed by Pearce and David (1987). Note that they are general but at the same time specific about the direction in which the enterprises want to move, the tar-

Exhibit 5.2 Mission statements of the athletic and recreation departments of The Ohio State University.

THE OHIO STATE UNIVERSITY

DEPARTMENT OF ATHLETICS

Mission Statement

The OSUDA supports the University mission by providing student athletes with exceptional educational and athletic opportunities. We commit to national leadership, excellence and the highest ethical standards in intercollegiate athletics. We will sustain a strong financial and community base of support by presenting outstanding intercollegiate athletic teams which provide quality entertainment and positive public identity for the university.

DEPARTMENT OF RECREATIONAL SPORTS

Mission Statement

We are committed to providing the finest programs, services, facilities, and equipment to enrich the University learning experience. We also want to foster a lifetime appreciation of wellness and recreational sports and activities among our students, faculty, and staff.

Used with permission of the Department of Athletics and the Department of Recreational Sports, The Ohio State University.

Exhibit 5.3 Examples of mission statements from businesses.

MISSION STATEMENT OF MAJOR LEAGUE SOCCER (MLS)

"To create a profitable Division I professional outdoor soccer league with players and teams that are competitive on an international level, and to provide affordable family entertainment. MLS brings the spirit, passion and intensity of the world's most popular sport to the United States.

"On the field of play, two of MLS' main goals are to encourage attacking and entertaining soccer with dynamic players and coaches, and to assist and improve the performance of U.S. soccer teams in competition on an international scale for club, national and youth sides."

Major League Soccer, www.mlsnet.com

MISSION STATEMENT OF NIKE

To lead in corporate citizenship through proactive programs that reflect caring for the world family of Nike, our teammates, our consumers, and those who provide services to Nike. On the labor front, Nike ensures "policies, practices and programs affecting the lives and well-being of people making Nike products around the world." On the global community, Nike states, "Giving back to the community isn't part of what we do—it's part of who we are." On the environment, Nike states, "We have the ambition, technology, and opportunity to protect the environment—so we do."

Responsibilities, www.nikebiz.com/social/index.shtml

MLS statement courtesy of Major League Soccer L.L.C. All rights reserved. NIKE is a trademark of Nike, Inc. and its affiliates. Used by permission.

get populations they want to serve, and the products they will deliver. Because it is free from details, "[the] mission statement has breadth of scope; it provides for the generation and consideration of a range of alternative objectives and strategies because it does not unduly stifle management" (p. 109). In sum, a mission statement and strategic plan make the organization more systematic, direct its efforts to specific objectives, and reduce guesswork for the managers.

TACTICAL/OPERATIONAL PLANNING

The description of strategic planning highlights its significant attributes: (a) a long-term plan, (b) devised by top level managers, (c) involving considerable outlay of resources, and (d) affecting the entire organization. This description implies that other forms of planning need to follow the strategic plan. These plans are called **tactical or operational plans.**

In general, the implementation of the grand strategy outlined in the strategic plan is the responsibility of several units of the organization. Thus, each unit will develop its own plan, which includes the goals for the unit and the activities that unit will engage in to achieve its goals. In essence, the strategic goal is broken down into smaller goals and restricted sets of activities specific to each unit. If a unit contains subunits, then the subunits will have their own goals and plans. This phenomenon of every set of goals acting as a means to the achievement of goals at a higher level is referred to as a chain of **means and ends.**

Suppose the strategic goal of a certain professional sport franchise is to increase rate of return on investment, achieve 5 percent growth in gross revenue, and provide excellent entertainment to customers. The attainment of this overall goal is possible only if the various units in the organization improve their operations (units dealing with player personnel, ticketing operations, marketing, event management, public relations, finance, administration, and so on). That is, each unit will set its own goals to be consistent with the overall strategic goal and will identify a set of activities to achieve its specific goals. For example, the administrator of player personnel could set the goal of forming an outstanding team with charismatic performers in the pursuit of winning championships and providing quality entertainment. At the same time, the administrator will also be concerned about containing costs because the strategic goal aims for increasing rate of return. One way of doing this is to become more efficient by reducing operating costs. Similarly, the marketing unit may set its goal to raise more money through securing more corporate advertisements and selling luxury boxes and seat licenses while curtailing its own operating costs. The event managers could set their goal to make their operations more efficient, smooth, and user-friendly to customers. In a similar manner, every unit within the organization would set its goals to reflect the strategic goal, with a view to attainment of the strategic goal.

But these goals of individual units are only means to the goals of the larger organization, that is, the professional franchise. Thus, a goal for a lower level is a means for the achievement of a goal at a higher level. Fink, Jenks, and Willits (1983) clarify this notion of a means–ends chain as follows:

> Two characteristics of such means to a final goal are noteworthy. The means themselves constitute ends (goals). . . . Thus, each major goal of an organization is the beginning of a chain of goals and sub-goals, in which each sub-goal

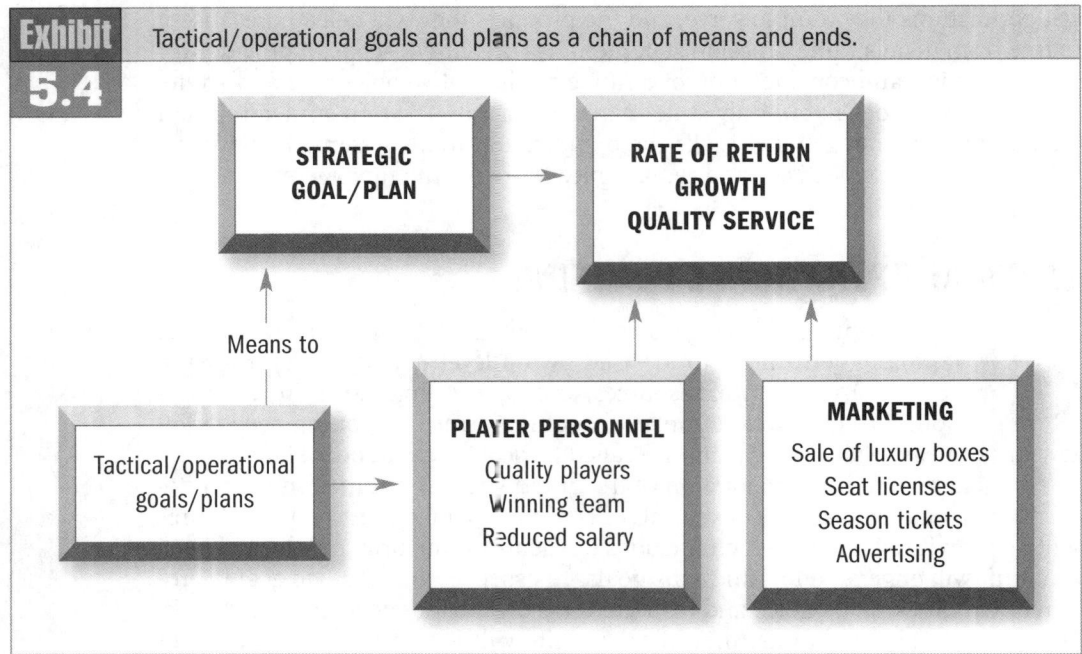

Exhibit 5.4 Tactical/operational goals and plans as a chain of means and ends.

is a means to a larger goal. Second, each sub-goal tends to be more concrete and tangible than the related goal. (p. 22)

This view of goals and subgoals as a chain of means and ends is illustrated in Exhibit 5.4.

Each unit prepares its own tactical and operational plans to achieve its goals. Traditionally, tactical goals and plans refer to those at middle levels of management, and operational goals and plans to the subunits within each unit. In other words, the strategic plan is devised at the top management level, the tactical goals at the middle management level, and the operational goals at the first-line supervisory level. However, as most sport organizations are not characterized by three levels of management, the tactical and operational plans are likely to be combined into one, as shown in Exhibit 5.4.

PLANNING AND BUDGETING

Although it is customary to discuss budgeting as a managerial process separate from planning, the two functions are integrally linked. When an objective is identified and suitable alternatives selected based on some evaluative criteria, those alternatives must be funded so that they can be carried out. As Robbins (1997) states, "A budget is a numerical plan for allocating resources to specific activities" (p. 166). Insofar as these activities have been specified in the planning process, **budgeting** is actually a reflection of the plan in monetary terms. Therefore, the allocation of funds to specific activities becomes a simple technical/clerical detail because the cost of a chosen alternative will have been worked out before it was chosen. That is, all of the preliminary steps associated with budgeting have been carried out in the planning process.

Sidebar

Consider the case of the professional sports franchise referred to earlier. It needs to organize and conduct a certain number of home games in a year. In the initial year of operation, the organization and event managers will have gone through elaborate planning. Then, after a few games, the activities and processes of event management will have become routine—the plan that was originally prepared and revised during the first few games will be good enough for the next set of games. In fact, with some minor adjustments, it may be sufficient for the next few seasons. Thus, the plan becomes a *standing plan*.

In contrast, sport organizations may undertake a one-time project, which it is not likely to repeat in the near future. A good example is a U.S. city hosting the Olympics (summer or winter). Of course, the Organizing Committee will have begun its planning at least 10 years in advance of the Olympics. Such planning will involve the International Olympic Committee (IOC), the U.S. Olympic Committee (USOC), federal and state governments, the media, and other stakeholders. This elaborate plan, involving so much effort and resources, will be put to use only once in the foreseeable future. Such plans are called *single-use plans*. Single-use plans are not restricted to large undertakings such as the Olympics. A small city recreation department may undertake to stage the state championships in some sporting events. A fitness club may embark on a unique promotional campaign without the intention of repeating it in the future.

Haggerty and Paton (1984) distinguished between two forms of budgeting: the incremental approach and the rational–comprehensive approach. In its most basic form, *incremental budgeting* exists when decision makers look at the total amount of money available and distribute it to various activities, programs, or departments based on precedent. This could take the form of a fixed percentage of increase or decrease for every unit based on previous budget(s). Haggerty and Paton (1984) point out that:

> The incremental approach does not require much information concerning what programs are actually doing, nor the manner in which budget units spend dollars. Rather, the focus is on percentage (or dollar) increments or decrements from the previous year or historical base. (p. 6)

An implication of the incremental approach is that the decision makers are satisfied with the status quo in terms of the objectives sought, the programs instituted to achieve those objectives, and the degree to which those objectives were reached in the previous budget year. It is also conceivable that the decision makers may adopt the incremental budgeting approach in order to avoid conflicts with the units. Thus, the incremental approach to budgeting resembles the planning process, even though serious thought and discussion have not been invested in the identification of objectives and the generation and evaluation of alternatives.

The *rational–comprehensive budgeting* approach forms a marked contrast to the incremental approach. One rational–comprehensive budgeting technique is known as the Planning–Programming–Budgeting System (PPBS). As the

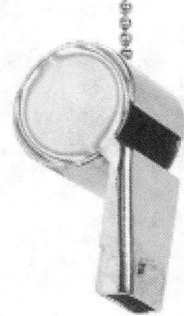

Budgeting is nothing more than planning translated into sums of money. Money is the only common denominator into which all activities in the organization can be translated. This is because planning must always have a financial aspect: budgeting is a logical consequence of planning. Just like planning, budgeting has an active character.

KEUNING, *1998, p. 486*

name of the technique suggests, this is actually a planning process in a different guise. The steps involved in PPBS also highlight this fact.

"Planning," in PPBS, involves defining the objectives to be accomplished; "programming" entails designing various alternative programs to accomplish these objectives; and "budgeting" involves funding some of these programs and eliminating others based on the evaluative information on the various programs (Gannon, 1977). A detailed description of a program is provided in Chapter 12. Briefly, a program is a collection of activities aimed at achieving specified goals. Thus, the steps in PPBS are exactly the same as the steps in the planning process outlined earlier. In sum, PPBS and other similar budgetary systems are, in fact, planning techniques. However, some authors find it convenient to deal with budgeting as a separate topic because other related financial issues (like accounting) can also be considered along with budgeting.

In summary, from an organizational point of view, sport managers must always attempt to be rational in their planning and other critical decisions. That is, they must try to generate as many alternatives as are feasible, evaluate them on previously specified criteria, and select the best alternative(s) to achieve the desired ends. In short, they must strive to be rational in their approach. This, however, is not always the case. Two factors limiting rationality in the planning process are problems that arise in the determination of organizational goals and problems that arise from a lack of information. These are examined in the two major sections that follow.

RATIONAL PLANNING AND ORGANIZATIONAL GOALS

n episode from Lewis Carroll's (1969, p. 160) *Alice's Adventures in Wonderland* is quoted in several management science textbooks to illustrate the significance of goals for an organization:

Alice: "Would you tell me, please, which way I ought to go from here?"

Cat: "That depends a great deal on where you want to get to."

Alice: "I don't much care where—"

Cat: "Then it doesn't matter which way you go."

Goals provide the direction and the source of motivation for the behavior of the organization's members. Goals also determine the standards for performance and evaluation. From the earlier description of the planning process, it would appear that planning cannot proceed without goal specification. "Thus, goals and objectives permeate the whole management process, providing an underpinning for planning efforts, direction, motivation, and control" (Richards, 1978, pp. 8–9). Given the importance of goals in organizational activities, examining some of the issues raised about goals/objectives in management literature is beneficial.

Perrow (1961) has made a distinction between the official goals and the operative goals of an organization. Modern authors label this distinction as stated (official) goals and real (operative) goals (see Robbins, 1997). Because this distinction is so critical in the operation of any organization, it is elaborated in the following sections.

Stated Goals

Perrow (1961) stated that "Official goals are the general purposes of the organization as put forth in the charter, annual reports, public statements by key executives and other authoritative pronouncements" (p. 855). To Robbins (1997), **stated goals** "are official announcements of what an organization says—and what it wants various constituencies to believe—are its objectives. However, they are often conflicting and excessively influenced by what society believes organizations *should* do" (p. 149). For example, the type of statement likely to be found in the official pronouncement of a university is "the purpose of intercollegiate athletics is to provide an opportunity for the pursuit of excellence in physical activity." But, as Perrow (1961) pointed out:

> Official goals are purposely vague and general and do not indicate two major factors which influence organizational behavior: the host of decisions that must be made among alternative ways of achieving official goals, and the priority of multiple goals and the many unofficial goals pursued by groups within the organization. (p. 855)

For example, the global statement of "pursuit of excellence" as the purpose of intercollegiate athletics does not provide any clue as to whether a large number of sports will be fostered or excellence in a few sports will be emphasized.

Genesis of Stated Goals

If goals are to provide the direction and motivation for the behavior of the organization and its members, they must be concise, clear, and specific. Further, if there are several goals, they should be consistent with each other in order to provide a unified thrust for the organization. However, in many organizations, the formal goals are stated in vague and global terms. Such global statements are necessary to accommodate the desires and preferences of those associated with the organization, both internally and externally.

From a systems perspective (as noted in Chapter 3), the organization is in an exchange relationship with the environment. The organization is dependent upon various subgroups in the environment for its inputs and for the disposition of its outputs. In order for such a relationship to continue to exist, the organization must meet the goals that those subgroups hold for the organization. As Hasenfeld (1983) states:

> Human service organizations must also respond to multiple goals assigned or ascribed to them by various publics and constituencies. . . . An organization may face different publics composed of other human service organizations, interest groups, legislative bodies, and professional associations, all having some stake in the organization and its services. An organization, in turn, may be dependent on these publics for resources, legitimation, and social support, and must, therefore, take their interests into account—interests that may be incompatible or in conflict with each other. (pp. 90–91)

> **To Recap**
>
> **STAKEHOLDERS** In Chapter 3, stakeholders were defined as individuals or groups that have a stake in the organization (some rights or interests). A group of stakeholders, such as the athletes, coaches, spectators, media people, alumni, or the employees of the athletic department, may share similar interests, claims, or rights. These stakeholder groups can be classified as **primary** stakeholder groups, whose participation in the organization and its affairs are necessary for organizational survival. In contrast, the **secondary** stakeholder groups are not necessary for the organization, although they could influence the affairs of the organization.

In the case of an intercollegiate athletic program, for example, the alumni, the faculty, the students, other universities, and other sport organizations are some of the stakeholders that would expect the organization to pursue specific goals. The administrators, the coaches, and the athletes are some of the internal groups with different expectations for the athletic program. If all of these goals are taken together, some may conflict with others. For instance, promotion of all sports versus pursuit of excellence in specific sports is an example of conflicting goals sought by two different groups. Insofar as an organization cannot afford to alienate any of the groups with conflicting orientations and preferences, it tends to proclaim its goals in general and vague terms. As noted before, most athletic programs state their goal as "the provision of opportunities for students to pursue excellence in sports." No subgroup can take exception to such a broad and all-encompassing goal statement. Thus, general goal statements are abstractions distilled from the demands of the external and internal environments (Hall, 1996). Perrow (1961) also suggests that stated goals serve the purpose of legitimizing the organization in the societal context and thus, of securing the necessary resources.

> Formal goal statements are "a fiction produced by an organization to account for, explain, or rationalize its existence to particular audiences rather than . . . valid and reliable indicators of purpose."
>
> **WARRINER,** 1965, p. 141

Real Goals

Although the stated goals are an attempt to justify the existence of the organization and the support extended to it, they do not provide the focus and direction that they are purported to provide. However, stating broad goals allows the key administrators the opportunity to emphasize specific subdomains within these broad goals. For example, under the rubric of pursuit of excellence, one intercollegiate athletic program may support the popular sports while another may support some of the less popular international sports. These contrasting orientations and thrusts are the **real goals** pursued by the organizations. Perrow (1961) describes them as follows:

> **Sidebar**
>
> In a study of NCAA Division IA, IAA, IAAA, and III university presidents' perspectives on athletic department goals, McGuire and Trail (2002) found that all Division I presidents placed greater importance on the goals of entertainment, financial security, visibility and prestige, and winning than Division III presidents did. These differences do reflect the policies and practices of the Division I athletic departments, which emphasize recruiting outstanding athletes, paying high salaries to coaches of major sports, building bigger and better facilities, and organizing major events. They also found that presidents of all divisions included in the study were less satisfied (relative to the importance they attached) with the extent to which the athletic departments achieved the developmental goals of academic achievement, social moral development, culture of diversity, careers, and health/fitness. These latter results are encouraging in that the presidents are aware that these developmental goals are not achieved to the same extent as the performance goals. Such awareness should move them to take actions to rectify the deficiencies.

> Operative goals designate the ends sought through the actual operating policies of the organization; they tell us what the organization is actually trying to do, regardless of what the official goals say are the aims. (p. 855)

We have already referred to two contrasting real goals in intercollegiate athletics—support of locally popular sports versus support of international sports. If various intercollegiate athletic programs are analyzed, it is possible to identify a number of real goals. Chelladurai, Inglis, and Danylchuk (1984) identified nine real goals of university athletic programs in the Canadian context. More recently, Trail and Chelladurai (2000) investigated the importance attached to 10 goals of intercollegiate athletics by faculty and students of one Midwestern university. They further divided the 10 goals into those focusing on the development of the athletes (developmental goals) and those focusing on the performance of the teams that provide entertainment, generate revenue, and bring prestige and visibility to the university (performance goals). As shown in Exhibit 5.5, both schemes are quite similar, although the labeling of the goals differs.

Note the features of the real goals shown in Exhibit 5.5. First, all of them are contained in the official goal of pursuit of excellence in physical activity. That is, each of the real goals does not in any way violate the general thrust of the stated goal. Exhibit 5.6 illustrates this relationship between the stated (official) goal and the real (operative) goals within it.

While some of the real goals are complementary to each other, others are in conflict. In general, the goals classified as performance-oriented goals are complementary to each other. For example, insofar as providing entertainment, enhancing prestige, and creating good public relations are all a function of winning teams, they are complementary to each other—that is, an emphasis on any one of the objectives would result in the enhancement of the other two objectives. On the other hand, transmission of culture and national sport

Exhibit 5.5 Two lists of goals of intercollegiate athletics.

CHELLADURAI ET AL. (1984) LIST OF GOALS	TRAIL & CHELLADURAI (2000) LIST OF GOALS
DEVELOPMENTAL GOALS	
Athletes' Personal Growth: Promotion of athletes' personal growth and health (physical, mental, and emotional)	Academic Achievement: Academic progress and achievement of athletes
Career Opportunities: Provision of those athletic experiences that will increase career opportunities for the athletes	Health/Fitness: Health and physical well-being of athletes
	Social/Moral Citizenship: Development of athletes into social, moral, and ethical citizens
	Careers: Career development and growth of athletes
	Culture of Diversity: Racial, ethnic, and gender equality, and respect for diversity
PERFORMANCE GOALS	
Achieved Excellence: To support those athletes performing at a high level of excellence	Winning: Conference and national championships, winning record, and victories over traditional rivals
Entertainment: To provide a source of entertainment for the student body, faculty/staff, alumni, and community	Entertainment: Entertainment for university, local, regional, and national communities
Financial: To generate revenue for the university	Visibility and Prestige: Positive public identity, national image, and prestige for the university
Public Relations: To enhance university–community relations	Financial Security: Revenue generation, financial self-sufficiency, and financial surplus
Prestige: To enhance the prestige of the university	National Sport Development: Excellent performances of athletes in Olympic and international sports/competitions
National Sport Development: To contribute to national sport development and performance in the international context	
Transmission of Culture: To transmit the culture and tradition of the university and community	

Exhibit 5.6 Official and operative goals in intercollegiate athletics.

OFFICIAL GOAL

OPERATIVE GOALS

PURSUIT OF EXCELLENCE IN SPORTS
- Entertainment
- Finanical
- Public Relations
- University Prestige
- Athletes' Careers
- Athletes' Personal Growth
- Community Solidarity
- Transmission of Culture
- Promotion of Olympic Sports

development may be in conflict with each other. To be more explicit, if transmission of culture implies support of locally popular sports such as football, and if national sport development suggests support for internationally played sports, then these are obviously in conflict. That is, a greater emphasis on one objective could mean reduction in the other (given that resources are limited). The nature of complementary and conflicting goals is illustrated in Exhibit 5.7.

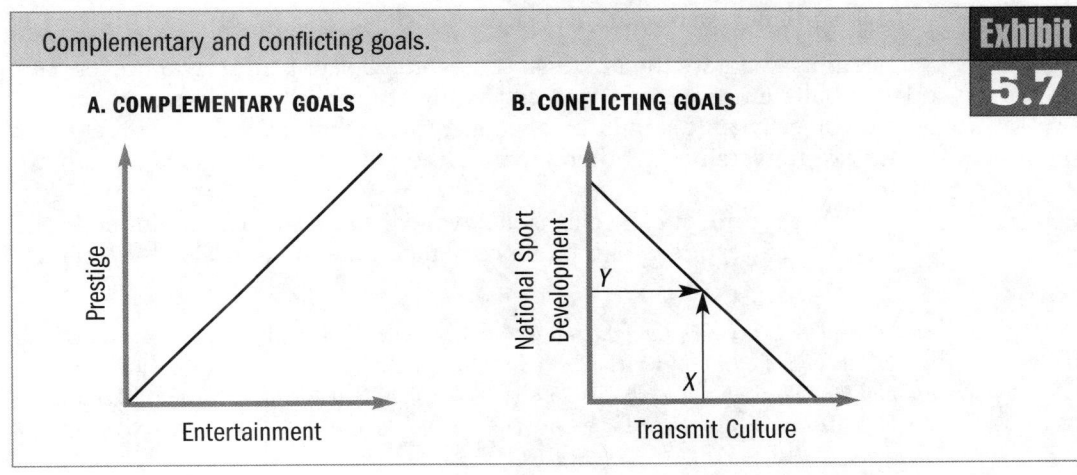

Exhibit 5.7 Complementary and conflicting goals.

A. COMPLEMENTARY GOALS — Prestige vs. Entertainment

B. CONFLICTING GOALS — National Sport Development vs. Transmit Culture

PLANNING 145

Sidebar: Intercollegiate Athletics in America and Olympic Sports

Despite the relatively lower support for Olympic sports compared to the support for locally popular sports such as football, basketball, and baseball, athletes from the NCAA schools won 85 of the 103 medals won by Americans at the 2004 Athens Olympics. Nevertheless, both the U.S. Olympic Committee and the NCAA have been concerned with the decline of Olympic sports on the collegiate scene. For example, only 61 Division I and 17 Division I universities support women's and men's gymnastics respectively. Further, men's sports such as fencing (supported by only 21 universities), rifle (27 universities), volleyball (23 universities), water polo (21 universities), and wrestling (85 universities) are considered to be high-risk. The USOC and the NCAA set up a 15-member task force in May 2004 to study and recommend ways to raise money, manage, and market these sports.

Source: *Columbus Dispatch,* Monday, January 10, 2005.

The third feature of real goals is that decisions on the competing values represented by the goals "influence the nature of the organization, and distinguish it from another with an identical official goal" (Perrow, 1961, p. 856). This was brought out in a study of the operative goals of intercollegiate athletics in Canadian universities (Chelladurai & Danylchuk, 1984). Using the list of operative goals developed by Chelladurai, Inglis, and Danylchuk (1984), the authors found that those athletic administrators in Canadian universities who emphasized public relations, prestige, entertainment, national sport development, and/or financial objectives tended to favor athletic scholarships and unrestrained recruitment of athletes.*

> To elaborate, the objectives of enhancing the image of the university, generating revenue, and satisfying the entertainment needs of the fans can all be achieved through a winning team. One way of producing the winning team is to recruit the best available talent by offering athletic scholarships and other perks as inducements. (Chelladurai & Danylchuk, 1984, p. 40)

Exhibit 5.8 shows the processes that could be adopted by two universities differentially emphasizing two contrasting real objectives—educational and athletic objectives. It should be apparent from Exhibit 5.8 that the real goals of the two universities set them apart, although the official goals of both are the same.

Another feature of real goals is that while the official goals are found in the charter, annual reports, and pronouncements of the top officials of the organi-

---

*Intercollegiate athletics in Canada and the United States differ on two counts: Most Canadian universities do not offer athletic scholarships. When offered, the scholarships are very few in number, and the dollar value of a scholarship is much less than in the United States. Further, recruiting of athletes is rather restricted when compared to recruiting in the United States. Many Canadian coaches prefer the American model, as shown by the above research.

> **Exhibit 5.8**
> Contrasts in real goals and processes.
>
> **STATED OBJECTIVE FOR UNIVERSITIES A AND B**
> "Provide Educational and Athletic Opportunities for Student-Athletes"
>
> | | UNIVERSITY A | UNIVERSITY B |
> |---|---|---|
> | **Real Objectives** | Student development/growth | Entertainment/University prestige |
> | **Processes** | Less focus on winning | More focus on winning |
> | | Developing students | Recruiting athletes/athletic scholarships as incentives |
> | | Treating athletes as students | Special treatment of athletes |
> | | Teaching the spirit of rules | Flouting the spirit of rules (e.g., teaching good fouls, four-corner offense) |

zation, the real goals can be inferred only through a scrutiny of the decisions made in key areas such as budgeting and personnel. For example, the objectives of entertainment, publicity, and so on were not stated explicitly by universities in the past. On the contrary, many scholars have proscribed such objectives in the educational context. For example, Mathews (1974) emphasized that the success of an intercollegiate athletic program should not be gauged by the prestige it brings to the university, the revenue it generates, or the entertainment it provides. If, however, the actual decisions relating to budget allocations and staffing procedures were analyzed, it would quickly become evident that many universities are pursuing the objectives of entertainment, prestige, and public relations.

Take the case of a university that proclaims that "all sports are equal." However, when it spends considerable time and effort to recruit and hire a coach at a high salary for one or two selected sports while for some other sport it is quick to hire a part-time coach at a nominal salary, it is clear that some sports are more "equal" than others. For the favored sports, the athletic department would identify all possible candidates for the coaching position, scrupulously evaluate each one, rank them all, and try to recruit them in the order of their ranking. For the less favored sports, the department would not go through the search and selection process as rigorously, and would be satisfied in simply choosing the top candidate from the pool of applicants. That is, in one case the department attempts to maximize its opportunity to get the best candidate, while in the other case it is satisfied with the available candidate. These two different processes of maximizing and satisficing will be discussed in greater detail in the next chapter.

As early as 1979, Broyles and Hay provided an alternate view of the objectives of intercollegiate athletics. They were quite explicit in stating that the prime objective of intercollegiate athletic programs is to satisfy the entertainment needs of fans. Starting with this premise, the authors proceeded to outline logically the processes that create entertainment value. These processes include recruitment of athletes, athletic scholarships, high-quality coaching, emphasis on those sports with entertainment value, and so on.

Along similar lines, Chelladurai and Danylchuk (1984) argued that entertainment and prestige are legitimate objectives for a university athletic program because they benefit the institution and the student body respectively. If universities and their units publicize their various academic and non-academic programs (employment rate of students, research grants secured, facilities, etc.) with a view to enhancing prestige, then they can also use intercollegiate athletics as a vehicle for prestige. Similarly, if universities arrange plays, music festivals, and other entertainment events, then it could be argued that intercollegiate athletics, recognized as an integral part of the total educational process, can also be used for the same purposes.

Today many universities in the United States emphasize entertainment, prestige, and publicity as legitimate goals of intercollegiate athletics. However, they state these as secondary to the goals oriented toward the development of student–athletes. Once again, a scrutiny of the decisions made by administrators and coaches might lead us to question the primacy of student–athlete development. This has been the focus of criticism by several authors who suggest that educational or developmental goals are not promoted to the same extent as performance goals (see Andre & James, 1991; Bailey & Littleton, 1991; Sperber, 2000). In Telander's (1989) view, coaches are primarily interested in winning, athletic administrators in revenue generation, and university presidents in prestige for the university. Thus, even today the stated goals of athletic departments may not reflect what the departments in fact are pursuing.

Genesis of Real Goals

It has been stated that organizations do not have goals; only the individuals in the organization have goals. This is particularly true in the case of the real goals that are set by the top administrators of the organization. While external agents such as resource providers, clients, and governments largely influence the choice of the real goals, internal groups and administrators also exercise their influence in the choice of these goals. The conflict over these real goals leads to the formation of coalitions among groups and individuals (Cyert & March, 1963; Rosen, 1995). According to Hasenfeld (1983),

Stated goals are broader statements, whereas real goals are the actual goals sought by the organization. Stated goals are general in order to accommodate the preferences of several constituents of the organization. They also tend to encompass all real goals, even if some of the real goals conflict with each other.

> Typically, these negotiations are marked by the emergence of various coalitions whose members can agree on a common set of goals for the organization, and thus can pool their resources to influence the organizational decision making in their direction. The relative power of each coalition is determined by the total amount of resources needed by the organization that it can control and mobilize. The most powerful among them will be the dominant coalition. The negotiations and compromises among the members of the dominant coalition will determine the nature of the organizational [real] goals. (p. 96)

A coalition exists when the alumni of a university or college and the businesses in the local community band together to influence the goals and processes of the intercollegiate athletic program. Their dominance over the program is mainly due to the control they exercise over the resources needed by the program or the university.

This does not mean, however, that the administrators will entirely disregard the preferences of others. Administrators, and members as well, respect precedents. Insofar as the conflicting orientations have been supported in the past, administrators will likely continue to cater to those orientations. It is also possible to satisfy sequentially the conflicting preferences. (However, in those instances where the organization is blessed with abundant resources, the conflicting goals can be simultaneously satisfied.) These factors permit the administrators to pursue their operative goals in a steady manner.

Goals and Constraints

The fact that two conflicting goals cannot be maximally pursued with limited resources led Eilon (1971) to suggest that goals may also be perceived as constraints. In Exhibit 5.7, for example, it is apparent that if one goal, such as transmission of culture, is to be secured to a minimum level (as indicated by point X on the horizontal axis), it acts as a constraint on the other goal (national sport development). That is, National Sport Development cannot be pursued beyond point Y on the vertical axis. This notion of one goal acting as a constraint on another is valid only under the condition of limited resources—but, of course, the fact of limited resources is one of the main reasons for setting up an organization and emphasizing its management in the first place.

Eilon (1971) pointed out that, from a different perspective, the constraints "may be regarded as an expression of management's desire to have minimum attainments or levels of performance with respect to various criteria [goals]. *All constraints are, therefore, expressions of goals*" (p. 295).

Thus, when the athletic department declares its support for a minimum number of women's sports, it imposes on itself a constraint as well as proclaims a goal. The present emphasis on gender equity in American intercollegiate athletics is perceived as a constraint by some and a goal by others, although in fact it is both.

In summary, two goal-related factors reduce the rationality of the planning process. First, ambiguity in the statement of official goals (and the inherent instability of the operative goals) does not permit rational planning over a period of time. Second, conflicts among the goals of an organization can make one goal a constraint on another.

Rational Planning and Information Gathering

Another factor that limits the rationality and effectiveness of the planning process is paucity of information. While information (or the lack of it) bears directly on any decision, its impact is more pronounced in (a) forecasting the future, and (b) generating or developing alternative solutions, both of which are essential steps in the planning process. These two sub-processes of planning require a special type of skill and knowledge base.

Forecasting

Planning, by definition, deals with the future. That is, specific programs or activities are instituted in the expectation that they will lead to some desired

Sidebar

In contrasting forecasting the future with enacting a planned future, Priesmeyer (1992) had this to say:

"[A] meteorologist studies the weather—its temperature, its wind speed and direction, its pressure and humidity. He studies the advancing fronts and cloud formations, and from this information, from this pattern of the past and present, he forecasts the future.... He reports what he believes will be, knowing that no one can influence what actually happens. The meteorologist's forecast is a prediction.

"[In contrast,] consider an athlete who is committed to running a mile in six minutes. Each day she takes a morning jog. She adjusts her diet to build strength and lose weight. She joins a health club near work so she has a place to exercise during lunch each day. She talks about running with others who run. She buys new running shoes. She challenges herself by entering local charity events in which she runs with hundreds of others. Eventually—and perhaps quite soon—she reaches and surpasses her goal of running the mile in six minutes.... In her case, the future is defined by her and her willingness to make all the changes necessary to attain a goal. She had a vision of how she wanted the future to be; your best forecast would be her vision. The runner's forecast is a goal, a vision." (pp. 123-124)

outcomes at a future point in time. In addition, the plan itself, or parts of it, will be implemented in the future. Morden (1993) noted that:

> An enterprise cannot plan ahead without making forecasts, and it cannot make forecasts without having some kind of plan to act as a framework for the forecasting process. The process of **forecasting** attempts to produce a picture of the kind of *future environment* in which enterprise plans and activities are likely to be implemented. It makes assumptions about the future conditions that are likely to determine the success of these plans. And it attempts to predict the outcome from the implementation of these plans. (p. 54)

These expectations are based on some assumptions regarding the state of affairs in the future. Although the future cannot be perfectly predicted, individuals (whether they are administrators or not) do make some assumptions about the future in almost every activity in which they engage. For instance, if children make plans to play soccer the next afternoon, they assume that it will not rain during that time period. Such a forecast may be based on the weather reports, or intuition or even a belief in luck. Since children's soccer is not a significant spectator event, the presence or absence of rain is relatively unimportant. However, if the event being planned is a World Cup championship (i.e., the world championships in soccer) several years in the future, the accuracy of the forecast is critical. In this case, the planners must look into the forecasts, records of rainfall in previous years, the texture and drainage of the playing fields, and their durability in rainy conditions. The forecasts should also include details about economic, political, and social conditions that might prevail at the time of the world championships. All of these factors

could affect the successful conduct of the World Cup. Thus, planners must make every effort to gather all available information and tap all possible sources. This, in effect, is forecasting.

One focus of forecasting may be to determine the demand for the products of the organization. In this focus, the purposes of forecasting are to "predict future *demand* for the organization's goods or services; future *trends* in demand; future *changes* in these trends; and the *magnitude* of change in the trends" (Gannon, 1977, p. 119). An entrepreneur who plans to start a commercial golf course needs to forecast the number of people who will play golf on the course, whether the customer base will increase or decrease over time, and whether the changes in demand will be substantial. Similarly, prior to constructing a new facility, a city recreation department must forecast the demand for the facility.

Forecasting may also be concerned with (a) predicting the outcome of a future event and (b) the timing of a future event (Rue & Byars, 1992). When the decision is being made to build a new arena, the senior athletic administrators will be concerned about the final cost of the arena. That is, given that the arena will be built (a definite event), the outcome (the final cost) needs to be forecast. Similarly, the administrators will be interested in when the construction of the arena will be completed and ready for events (event timing forecast).

The importance as well as the difficulty of forecasting increases with the planning time frame. That is, forecasting tomorrow's weather is much easier than forecasting the weather two years in advance. Using past trends and present situations to predict tomorrow's conditions is an uncertain enterprise, as seen in the plight of educational institutions. In all long-range plans, enrollment figures must be forecast. These figures depend on population trends, the job market, and the orientation of new generations toward higher education. History abounds with instances in which the forecasts of educational institutions were far from the real occurrences.

> A trend is a trend. The question is when will it bend? Will it climb higher and higher, or eventually expire, and come to an untimely end?
>
> **CHAIRNCROSS,** *quoted in Dessler, 1979, p. 57*

Planners can profitably use many of the reports published by government agencies and other private research organizations. There are numerous statistical reports relating to the gross national product (GNP), other leading indicators of economic growth, population trends, and so on. Planners may also gather information by polling relevant individuals. For instance, the director of a city recreation department can poll the residents of the city concerning their preferences for activities or programs for the future. The director can also ask the city administrators about future trends in the budgetary allocations for recreation.

Planners can profitably employ spreadsheet computer programs to facilitate their forecasting efforts. For instance, a fitness club can use a spreadsheet to project membership three years hence by using (a) the historical average of membership patterns and (b) the capacity of the club to serve the clients. Similarly, a golf course can use spreadsheets to project its revenues by using the data on (a) membership patterns, (b) membership fees, (c) rates of participation by members and nonmembers, and (d) greens fees for members and nonmembers.

Forecasting by Experts

Planners may also consult with experts in the field to help them in the formulation of forecasts. Two specific techniques used to capitalize on the skills of experts are the nominal group technique and the Delphi technique (see Exhibit 5.9).

Nominal group technique. In the **nominal group technique**, approximately eight to ten experts are brought together in a structured format. After receiving the question or the problem of interest, the members are allowed to think about the issue for a short period of time. Following this, each expert presents his or her ideas in consecutive order. After all the experts have presented their ideas, limited interaction is permitted. Following this, each expert ranks the ideas on the basis of the probability of their occurrence. The average of these rankings is then accepted as the forecast for that particular question. In the nominal group technique, it is important that all of the ideas are given equal importance. Therefore, a secretary or moderator must be present not only to record the proceedings but also to ensure that every idea is given equal time and attention.

Delphi technique. The general concept underlying the **Delphi technique** is the same as in the nominal group technique. In the Delphi technique, however, experts arrive at a consensus without ever meeting together to discuss the issue in question—that is, the opinions of experts are sought individually. The anonymity of the participants is crucial for the process. Typically, a problem such as "Will men's soccer or women's basketball enjoy greater success as a professional sport in North America?" is mailed to experts, who respond in writing with their opinions. A summary of these opinions is prepared and sent back to

Exhibit 5.9 Nominal group technique versus Delphi technique.

NOMINAL GROUP TECHNIQUE

Involves a meeting of experts

Experts think about an issue or questions, present ideas to the group, and then interact with each other

Experts rank the ideas on the basis of probability of their occurrence

Average of the rankings is accepted as the forecast

All ideas are given equal time and attention

Requires the presence of a secretary or moderator

DELPHI TECHNIQUE

Experts do not meet; they remain anonymous

Experts are presented with an issue or a question and respond in writing

Summary of opinions is prepared and sent back to experts

Experts revise their opinions based on the summary

Process is repeated as often as needed

Final report summarizing the opinions is submitted to top management

Sidebar

The nominal group, Delphi, and brainstorming methods discussed in this section have been used to generate information on varied matters. The following are a few examples from our field.

- Richman, Hardy, and Rosenfeld (1989) employed the brainstorming method with a group of coaches and sport psychologists to identify strategies coaches and sport psychologists could implement to affect the type and level of social support provided to student-athletes.
- Hammersley and Tynon (1998) employed the Delphi technique to identify the core job competencies required for entry-level jobs in resort and commercial recreation.
- Li, Song, and Hancock (1997) used the Delphi method to forecast labor demand in the facility management industry. Their experts felt that job opportunities in that industry were promising.
- Whyte (1992) had 19 administrators and 17 scholars of leisure participate in his Delphi study. They reported five key trends in local government recreation and park administration that needed immediate action. These trends were deteriorating infrastructure, increasing crime, declining budgets, increasing competition for tax dollars, and public sector debt.
- Branch and Crow (1994) involved a group of Division I athletic administrators in a Delphi study of future trends in intercollegiate athletics that would change the landscape of collegiate athletics.
- Lambrecht (1991) employed the Delphi technique with nine prominent sport management educators to identify pertinent content for preparation of sport club managers.

each expert, and the experts are then allowed to revise their estimates based on this feedback. This entire process may be repeated a number of times. Those experts whose estimates deviate from the average are asked to justify their position. A final report summarizing the opinions of the group is then submitted to top management. One problem associated with this technique lies in accurately describing the problem to the experts (Byars, 1987). Another problem is to interpret the opinions of the experts and to summarize them accurately.

Gannon (1977) has suggested that organizations should update their forecast when new information about the future becomes available. An organization might draw up a five-year plan only to find that after a year, new evidence reveals that the earlier forecasts were not accurate. Therefore, a new set of forecasts is required. Also, of course, the five-year plan will have to be redrawn to agree with the new forecast. This is not an unusual scenario. Many organizations draw up a three-year or five-year plan, *but they do it every year*. During the periodic planning phases, the original forecasts, budget estimates, and other vital parameters of planning are revised on the basis of new information available to the planners.

Generation of Alternatives

While forecasting requires expert knowledge about past historical data, trends, and the future, alternative generation requires innovative ability and creativity. Alternative generation is perhaps the most critical step in planning, and therefore, management must attempt to harness the creative abilities of relevant members during this stage of the planning process.

Brainstorming. One technique that has been used successfully to encourage and marshal the creativity and ingenuity of members is **brainstorming**. Osborn (1953), who developed this technique, suggested that the brain is used to "storm" a creative problem in the same fashion that commandos might audaciously attack a fortress. The brainstorming process calls for relevant members to come together and think of solutions or alternatives for a particular problem. Members present their ideas one at a time. A significant guideline of this process is that no one is permitted to evaluate the ideas as they are presented (Byars, 1987). This enables individuals to come up with a variety of ideas without fear of being ridiculed or criticized. A basic premise in brainstorming is that it is important to encourage a large number of different ideas even if they seem improbable, preposterous, or foolish. In Osborn's view, it is much more difficult to come up with new ideas than it is to evaluate them.

Another crucial aspect of the brainstorming process is that members are allowed to "hitchhike" on the ideas of others. That is, after hearing one member's idea, others may be able to improve on it or combine two or more ideas to make a better idea. Some members may be better hitchhikers than originators of ideas, and planners must capitalize on both types of talent.

In Brief

Information is important in all decision making, particularly about future trends and available alternatives. The nominal group and Delphi techniques are useful in forecasting future trends, whereas brainstorming is most useful in generating alternatives.

DIRECTIONAL PLANNING

In the conventional view of planning, the first step in the process involves setting specific, concise, and clear goals. Given the clarity and specificity of the goals, the plan itself will be quite clear and specific in its details. However, as Robbins (1997) notes, at times such planning becomes too rigid and "locks people and organizational units into specific goals with specific time periods" (p. 132). Moreover, formal plans cannot adequately deal with the constantly changing environment. Given these issues, it has been suggested that plans should be flexible.

In a similar vein, McCaskey (1974) proposed another mode of planning whereby:

> the planner or planners identify a domain and direction. *Domain* is the area in which the organization or individual will work. The *direction* is the actor's tendencies, the favored styles of perceiving and doing. Instead of specifying concrete, measurable goals, the planners work more from who they are and what they like to do. (p. 283)

McCaskey suggested that in those cases where the organization cannot spell out specific goals, it should set the domain for its activities and let the organization members move ahead in that domain according to their preferred ways of acting. It is quite conceivable that as the organization moves it will discover goals.

For example, a private profit-oriented firm might decide that its domain is the fitness area. The proprietor would then lease some exercise equipment and set up a fitness center. This initial business activity could be based on the proprietor's personal expertise and experience in fitness activities. After a period of time, the proprietor may note that customers are bored with the monotonous and tedious workouts. Based on this observation, the proprietor may open up a few racquetball courts with a view to providing variety for the customers. In the course of time, the firm might expand to include a tennis court, badminton court, sauna, pool, and possibly even an area for food and liquor (products not directly related to fitness). In the end, the firm might turn out to be in the recreation business rather than the fitness business.

Another example is that of a Swiss watch company that started out manufacturing watches for the general public but ended up producing high-priced watches for the very rich. The chairman of the company is reported to have denied that his company was in the watch business. He insisted that it was in the "luxury" business. Some university athletic departments in the United States are capitalizing on the entertainment opportunities offered by their teams as well as their facilities. The preceding examples illustrate McCaskey's suggestion that new goals can be discovered and highlighted after the organization begins operating in a particular domain.

McCaskey emphasized the flexibility that **directional planning** offers. The specific goals sought are determined only after interaction with environmental forces—an approach that is consistent with the systems view of organizations (see Chapter 3). Planning in this manner permits planners to capitalize on unexpected opportunities and adapt to new constraints that may arise after the organization has entered a domain.

Although McCaskey has advocated a general directional approach to planning (whereby a domain and direction are initially identified), he has also acknowledged that planning with specific goals is appropriate under certain conditions. According to McCaskey, planning with goals is more suitable when:

1. planners want to narrow the focus so that the efforts of members will converge
2. the environment of the organization is stable and predictable
3. there are severe time and resource limitations that call for programming of activities
4. members prefer well-defined conditions for their work

Similarly, planning without goals (directional planning) is appropriate when:

1. the organization has just come into existence
2. the environment is unpredictable
3. members cannot build enough trust or agreement to decide on a common goal

Directional Planning and Stated Goals

Note that the distinction between planning with goals and directional planning (planning without goals) is conceptually similar to Perrow's (1961) notion of dichotomizing goals into stated versus real goals. Stated goals are couched in very broad, general terms, and thus they serve to outline a general domain for organizational activity.

On the other hand, the choice of real goals is a reflection of the specific thrust of the organization at a given point in time. Thus, real goals may shift with changes in administrators, personnel, or environmental conditions. This is directly comparable to the flexibility afforded by directional planning. The overlapping of these two conceptual schemes is illustrated in Exhibit 5.10. In this example, the real goals are within the domain agreed upon for intercollegiate athletics. Also, although the shifts in focus are drastic, the organizational efforts remain within the general domain.

Directional Planning and Information

One of the main reasons for directional planning is that planners seldom have all the necessary information to permit them to be specific about their goals. In directional planning, it is possible to work around the scarcity of information and to proceed in the general domain or direction. In the course of time, as new information becomes available, planners can become more specific in their goal setting.

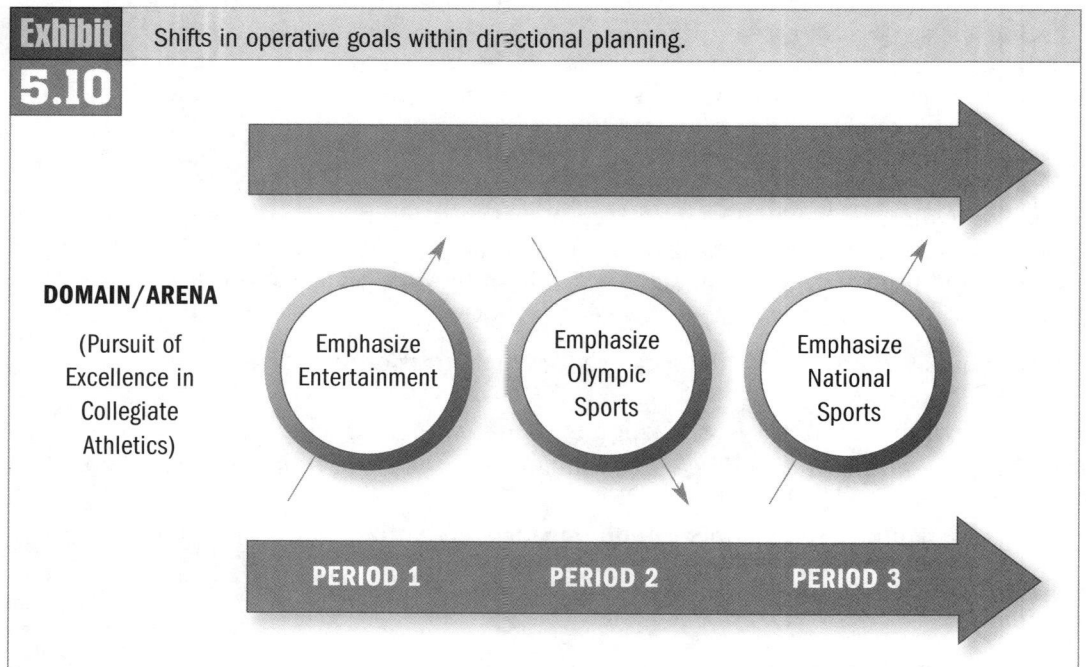

Exhibit 5.10 Shifts in operative goals within directional planning.

SUMMARY

In this chapter, we defined the planning process as the specification of goals to be achieved and the activities to be carried out to achieve those goals. We described the steps in the planning process—identifying constraints, generating alternatives, and evaluating those alternatives. We distinguished between strategic plans and tactical plans and looked at budgeting as it relates to planning, and at the types of budgeting processes. We explored the differences between, and genesis of, stated goals and real goals. Having noted the crucial importance of information and forecasting to decision making, we explored several methods of seeking information: nominal group technique, Delphi technique, and brainstorming. Finally, the need for directional planning—planning without specific goals—as an alternate mode of planning was explained.

DEVELOPING YOUR PERSPECTIVES

1. What real (operative) goals are emphasized in your intercollegiate athletic program or school? Explain the basis of your opinion.

2. Discuss the environmental factors, including stakeholder groups, that influence the goals of your intercollegiate athletic program. Is there a dominant coalition among these stakeholder groups? How does this coalition achieve dominance over others?

3. Consider the mission statements of Major League Soccer and the Nike Corporation provided in Exhibit 5.3. Discuss the extent to which these mission statements reflect what these organizations are actually doing.

4. Consider all the programs, processes, and decisions of the athletic department in your university, and identify those that reflect each of the eight components of a mission statement. Are there any programs, processes, or decisions that do not fit into the mission statement? Are all the programs, processes, and decisions consistent with each other?

5. Discuss the relevance of (a) planning with specific goals and (b) planning without specific goals to any two or three sport organizations you are familiar with.

6. Give examples of problem situations in which the nominal group technique, Delphi method, and brainstorming could be used.

References

Andre, J., & James, D. N. (Eds.) (1991). *Rethinking college athletics*. Philadelphia: Temple University Press.

Bailey, W. S., & Littleton, T. D. (1991). *Athletics and academe*. New York: Macmillan.

Black, J. S., & Porter, L. W. (2000). *Management: Meeting new challenges*. Upper Saddle River, NJ: Prentice Hall.

Branch, D., & Crow, R. B. (1994). Intercollegiate athletics: Back to the future. *Sport Marketing Quarterly, 3* (3), 13–21.

Broyles, J. F., & Hay, R. D. (1979). *Administration of athletic programs: A managerial approach*. Englewood Cliffs, NJ: Prentice Hall.

Byars, L. L. (1987). *Strategic management: Planning and implementation*. New York: Harper & Row.

Carroll, L. (1969). *Alice's adventures in wonderland*. In D. Rackin (Ed.), *Alice's adventures in wonderland: A critical handbook*. Belmont, CA: Wadsworth.

Chairncross, A. (1975). Quoted in Thomas E. Milne, *Business for forecasting: A managerial approach*. London: Longman.

Chelladurai, P., & Danylchuk, K. E. (1984). Operative goals of intercollegiate athletics: Perceptions of athletic administrators. *Canadian Journal of Applied Sport Sciences, 9*, 33–41.

Chelladurai, P., Inglis, S. E., & Danylchuk, K. E. (1984). Priorities in intercollegiate athletics: Development of a scale. *Research Quarterly for Exercise and Sport, 55*, 74–79.

Cyert, R. M., & March, J. G. (1963). *The behavioral theory of the firm*. Englewood Cliffs, NJ: Prentice Hall.

David, F. R. (1997). *Concepts of strategic management*. Upper Saddle River, NJ: Prentice Hall.

Dessler, G. (1979). *Management fundamentals: A framework*. Reston, VA: Reston Publishing.

Eilon, S. (1971). Goals and constraints. *Journal of Management Studies, 8*, 292–303.

Filley, A. C., House, R. J., & Kerr, S. (1976). *Managerial process and organizational behavior*. Glenview, IL: Scott, Foresman.

Fink, L. F., Jenks, R. S., & Willits, R. D. (1983). *Designing and managing organizations*. Homewood, IL: Richard D. Irwin.

Gannon, M. J. (1977). *Management: An organizational perspective*. Boston: Little, Brown.

Haggerty, T. R., & Paton, G. A. (1984). *Financial management of sport-related organizations*. Champaign, IL: Stipes.

Hall, R. H. (1996). *Organizations: Structure, processes, and outcomes* (6th ed.). Englewood Cliffs, NJ: Prentice Hall.

Hammersley, C. H., & Tynon, J. F. (1998). Job competency analysis of entry-level resort and commercial recreation. *Journal of Applied Recreation Research, 23* (3), 225–241.

Hasenfeld, Y. (1983). *Human service organizations*. Englewood Cliffs, NJ: Prentice Hall.

Keuning, D. (1998). *Management: A contemporary approach*. London: Pitman.

Lambrecht, K. W. (1991). A study of curricular preparation needs for sport club managers. *Journal of Sport Management, 5*, 47–57.

Li, M., Song, C., & Hancock, D. (1997). The Delphi technique in labor demand forecasting: A case in the public assembly facility industry. *International Sport Journal, 1* (1), 96–107.

Major League Soccer (On Line). Objectives. Available at www.mlsnet.com.

Mathews, A. W. (1974). *Athletics in Canadian universities: The report of the AUCC/CIAU study of athletic programs in Canadian universities*. Ottawa: Association of Universities and Colleges of Canada.

McCaskey, M. B. (1974). A contingency approach to planning: Planning with goals and planning without goals. *Academy of Management Journal, 17*, 281–291.

McGuire, R., & Trail, G. (2002). Satisfaction and importance of athletic department goals: The views of university presidents. *International Journal of Sport Management, 3*, 53–73.

Megginson, L. C., Mosley, D. C., & Pietri, P. H., Jr. (1992). *Management: Concepts and applications* (4th ed.). New York: HarperCollins.

Morden, A. R. (1993). *Business strategy and planning*. London: McGraw-Hill.

Naylor, J. (1999). *Management*. London: Financial Times/Pitman.

Noll, R. G., & Zimbalist, A. (1997). Sports, jobs, and taxes: The real connection. In R. G. Noll & A. Zimbalist (Eds.), *Sports, jobs & taxes: The economic impact sports teams and stadiums*. Washington, DC: Brookings Institution Press.

Osborn, A. F. (1953). *Applied imagination.* New York: Charles Scribner's Sons.

Pearce, J. A., II, & David, F. (1987). Corporate mission statement: The bottom line. *The Academy of Management Executive, 1* (2), 109–116.

Perrow, C. (1961). The analysis of goals in complex organizations. *American Sociological Review, 26,* 854–865.

Pettinger, R. (1997). *Introduction to management* (2nd ed.). London: Macmillan Business.

Pierce, J. L., & Dunham, R. B. (1990). *Managing.* Glenview, IL: Scott, Foresman/Little, Brown.

Priesmeyer, H. R. (1992). *Organizations and chaos: Defining the methods of nonlinear management.* Westport, CT: Quorum Books.

Responsibilities. (On Line). Available at www.nikebiz.com/social/index.shtml.

Richards, M. D. (1978). *Organizational goal structures.* St. Paul, MN: West.

Richman, J. M., Hardy, C. J., & Rosenfeld, L. B. (1989). Strategies for enhancing social support networks in sport: A brainstorming experience. *Journal of Applied Sport Psychology, 1* (2), 150–159.

Robbins, S. P. (1976). *The administrative process: Integrating theory and practice.* Englewood Cliffs, NJ: Prentice Hall.

Robbins, S. P. (1997). *Managing today!* Upper Saddle River, NJ: Prentice Hall.

Robbins, S. P., & Stuart-Kotze, R. (1990). *Management: Concepts and applications.* Scarborough, ON: Prentice Hall Canada.

Rosen, R. (1995). *Strategic management: An introduction.* London: Pitman.

Rue, L. W., & Byars, L. L. (1992). *Management: Skills and application* (6th ed.). Homewood, IL: Irwin.

Sperber, M. (2000). *Beer and circus: How big-time college sports is crippling undergraduate education.* New York: Henry Holt.

Telander, R. (1989). *The hundred yard lie: The corruption of college football and what we can do to stop it.* New York: Simon and Schuster.

Trail, G., & Chelladurai, P. (2000). Perceptions of goals and processes of intercollegiate athletics: A case study. *Journal of Sport Management, 14,* 154–178.

Warriner, C. K. (1965). The problem of organizational purpose. *The Sociological Quarterly, 6,* 139–146.

Whyte, D. N. B. (1992). Key trends and issues impacting local government recreation and park administration in the 1990s: A focus for strategic management and research. *Journal of Park and Recreation Administration, 10* (3), 89–106.

CHAPTER 6

Managerial Decision Making

MANAGE YOUR LEARNING

After completing this chapter you should be able to:

- Understand the significance of decision making in management.
- Define the steps in decision making.
- Explain the programmability and significance of decisions.
- Explain the rationality of decisions as related to the means and goals.
- Discuss the differences between the economic person, administrative person, and implicit favorite models of decision making.
- Explain the advantages and disadvantages of member participation in decision making.
- Understand the varying degrees of participation by members.
- Know the critical attributes of a problem situation that determine the appropriate level of participation by members.

STRATEGIC CONCEPTS

administrative person model
alternative
bounded rationality
economic person model
framing the problem
implicit favorite model

nonprogrammed decision
opportunity
participative decision making
problem
programmed decision
significance of decision

THE SIGNIFICANCE OF DECISION MAKING

The last chapter was devoted to the managerial function of planning. A look at the different steps in the planning process shows us that planners make decisions at every step of the planning process. For instance, in the first step of goal setting, the planners might have several choices, but they select one or more of them as the goals and then set priorities among these selected goals. Even constraints require decisions, and the planners must decide which of the constraints are more critical than the others. Similarly, the environment may offer several opportunities, which the planners must narrow down to just a few. In all these ways decision making is critical to planning.

Decision making, defined as the process of making a choice from among alternatives, underlies all managerial activities—not just planning. In fact, Nobel laureate H. A. Simon (1977) equates decision making with management. As he points out:

> The task of "deciding" pervades the entire administrative organization quite as much as does the task of "doing"—indeed, it is integrally tied up with the latter. A general theory of administration [management] must include principles of organization that will insure correct decision-making, just as it must include principles that will insure effective action. (p. 1)

The city council has to make a decision on constructing a $100-million arena. The player personnel management unit in a professional franchise needs to decide which players to draft and which ones to trade. The management committee of the YMCA has to decide whether to extend the building to make way for more exercise and dance rooms. A fitness club manager has to decide who will be in charge of the weight room and who will lead the aerobics classes. The marketing director of a university athletic department has to choose a printing firm to print the promotional materials. The assistant to the director of a city recreation department has to decide how to reorganize the office. The locker room attendant has to decide if a particular client should be given a towel. The receptionist in a tennis club has to decide if he can reserve a court for a client at a particular time and date. These are all examples of decisions made in sport organizations. In one sense, every action by every member and unit in an organization is based on a decision some person or group has made. From this perspective, we can say that an organization is a forum for making decisions. In the same vein, we can also say that managers are there *only* to make decisions.

To Recap

MANAGERIAL ROLES Recall that we discussed Mintzberg's 10 managerial roles in Chapter 4. In every one of these roles, the manager must make decisions. The significance of those decisions is much more pronounced in the last four roles. As entrepreneur, the manager has to choose new projects for implementation to ensure the viability and growth of the organization. That is, the manager conceives of effective ways to capitalize on the opportunities offered by the environment. In the role of disturbance handler, the manager has to decide how to respond to changes in the environment. As resource allocator, she also makes critical decisions on which individual or unit will get what resources. Finally, as negotiator, the manager has to make decisions in resolving the problems and conflicts that arise within the organization. In both the disturbance handler and negotiator roles, the manager is solving problems that abound in organizations. In fact, there would not be much need for managers if there were no problems.

OPPORTUNITIES AND PROBLEMS

Opportunities and problems as perceived by the manager present the occasions for making decisions. An **opportunity** is a situation that, when acted upon, could benefit the organization in such areas as profitability, productivity, and growth. For instance, assume that the aerobics instructor in a fitness club has become qualified as a nutritionist. The manager can see this as an opportunity to begin nutrition counseling as a new service to the clients. When a city gets the state government's permission to annex neighboring farmland, the recreation managers can see an opportunity to create a new state-of-the-art recreation complex.

A **problem** is a situation that reduces or could reduce the effectiveness of the organization, or a situation that disrupts operations. For instance, two aerobics instructors in conflict argue constantly in front of clients. Such an occurrence does not project a good image of the club and reduces the quality of the services offered by the club. In another example, consider the aerobics instructor who has just been certified as a nutrition counselor. We noted that this could be an opportunity for the club to introduce nutrition counseling as an additional service. From a different perspective, it could also pose a problem if the instructor decides to leave the club for another, better-paying job. A different kind of problem occurs when the heat pump in the building breaks down, disrupting the operations for a while. All of these situations call for decision making, either to seize the opportunities or solve the problems.

Because of the central place of decision making in management, sport managers need to have a comprehensive understanding of the process of managerial decision making and the difficulties associated with it. Accordingly, we will explore the process of decision making in the following sections. Then, we examine the distinction between two broad classes of decisions—programmed decisions and nonprogrammed decisions. Following this, we discuss the issue of rationality in decision making and learn to distinguish between the *ethical* and *factual* content of a decision. Finally, we look at different models of decision making that reflect varying degrees of rationality.

STEPS IN DECISION MAKING

Exhibit 6.1 shows the steps in decision making. Note the resemblance between this exhibit and Exhibit 5.1. This exists because planning is a special aspect of decision making.

Problem Statement/Framing the Problem

As shown in Exhibit 6.1, the first step in decision making is to define the goal to be achieved or the problem to be solved. Managers must be clear about the problem they are trying to solve. If the problem is not clearly defined and clarified, the subsequent steps will be futile. Managers need to look into the nature of the problem, the frequency of it, its causes, and the elements involved in the problem (people, place, or things). Based on this analysis, they must then state the problem in unambiguous terms.

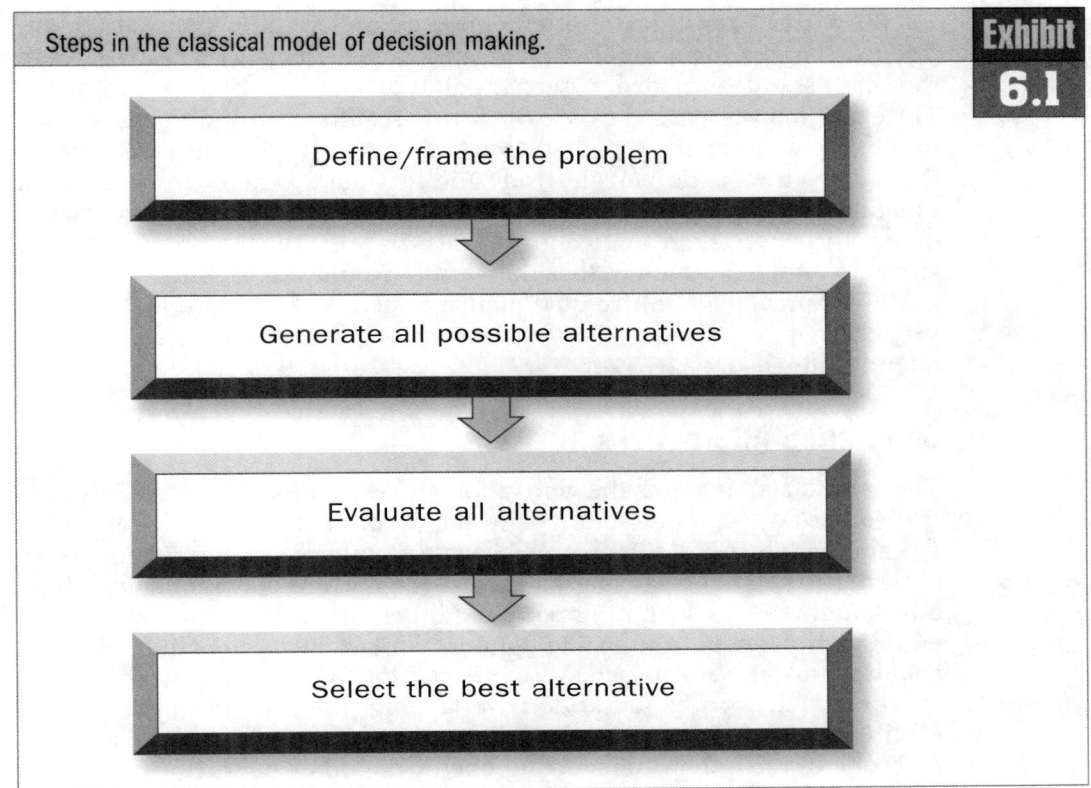

Exhibit 6.1 Steps in the classical model of decision making.

This first step is also called **framing the problem.** Variations in defining the same problem could lead to different and often meaningless solutions. For example, suppose you are the major partner in a tennis club in a mid-size city. Your business is not doing as well as expected, because of the existence of another tennis club close to your club. In fact, your club has become a losing proposition. You are at the point of letting go some of your employees in an attempt to reduce costs. Just as you are getting ready to downsize, you learn that your competitor is going out of business and would like to sell his club to you. You would like to capitalize on this opportunity, but you have to get the approval of your partners. You can frame the situation in two different ways:

Frame 1. If we buy the other club, there is a 100 percent chance that we can retain 10 of our 15 employees, and there is a 75 percent chance that we will be making a profit.

Frame 2. If we buy the other club, there is a 100 percent chance that we will have to let go 5 of our 15 employees, and there is a 25 percent chance of us losing money.

Although both frames contain the same information, the partners may be more inclined toward the acquisition of the other tennis club in the first frame but less likely in the second frame, because the second frame is negative in its tone. A more comprehensive frame would combine and synthesize both frames and present a holistic picture. For example, it would emphasize the positive outlook for making a profit (75 percent chance) while also pointing out the negative impact of letting go five of 15 employees.

Black and Porter (2000) offer a good example of the effects of the differences in framing a problem. It relates to the Challenger disaster when the space shuttle exploded 72 seconds after its launch on January 18, 1986. The explosion was caused by a leaky O-ring seal that became worse because of the cold weather. Prior to that launch, NASA asked engineers to confirm that a launch was 100 percent ready and that there would be no risk at all in launching the shuttle. But because this launch had already been delayed once, NASA was keen to go ahead. Thus, in this case the engineers were asked to "prove absolutely that the shuttle would fail. . . . the engineers could not provide definitive quantitative evidence of a failure that had not yet occurred . . ." (Black & Porter, 2000, p. 313) and the shuttle was subsequently launched.

Generating Alternatives

The second step involves the generation and evaluation of possible **alternative** courses of action or solutions to the problem. In the earlier example, the alternatives for the tennis club owners could be to (a) downsize, (b) acquire the neighboring club, (c) expand the current operations to include a restaurant and a swimming pool, or (d) get out of the business altogether. If the problem is arguing and fighting aerobics instructors, the solutions could be to (a) have a face-to-face discussion with both instructors, (b) schedule their work hours at non-overlapping times, (c) fire instructor A, (d) fire instructor B, or (e) fire both instructors. If the fitness club has more than one branch, then transferring one or the other instructor to another branch is another alternative. The point is that all possible alternatives must be explored.

Evaluating Alternatives

The third step in decision making is to evaluate all the alternatives generated in the second step. Such evaluation must be based on meaningful criteria. In the case of the tennis club, the cost of each alternative, the risk involved in each, and expected payoff of each are some of the criteria that could be employed in evaluating the alternatives. The concern for retaining the employees versus making profits could also come into play at this step. The fourth and final step in decision making is to select and implement the alternative that was rated the best based on the selected criteria.

PROGRAMMABILITY AND SIGNIFICANCE OF DECISIONS

The foregoing description of the decision process is applicable to all kinds of decisions faced by managers. However, the extent to which a manager would spend effort and time over a decision is based on two issues: (a) the programmability of the decision and (b) the significance of the decision. Earlier in the chapter, we posed several decision situations in sport management. Let us take three of those examples to illustrate these two issues.

Programmed and Nonprogrammed Decisions

The first case is the locker room attendant giving out towels to clients. This is a repetitive action in that the attendant gives out hundreds of towels every day. Because of the repetitive nature, the decision to hand out a towel becomes routine. Further, the decision criteria are also simple and straightforward. For instance, the attendant has to check (a) if the client is a member of the club, and (b) if he or she has paid for the towel service. Because clubs usually have a card or token to indicate these, the attendant's decision process is even more simplified. This kind of decision is called a programmed decision. A **programmed decision** is one made by applying decision rules in response to recurring situations or problems.

On the other hand, take the case of the player personnel unit of a professional club deciding whom to draft and whom to trade. This is much more complex than handing out towels. The decision makers must consider the current status of the team in terms of team performance, team composition, salary total for the team, and attributes of individual players (performance capabilities, physical and psychological profiles); the dollar amount management is willing to invest in players; and what is offered in return for a trade. Because the players in the pool change every year and because the order of pick changes every year, the decision makers cannot set specific decision rules or criteria that can be applied from year to year. That is, these decisions cannot be programmed in advance, as in the case for the towel service. Instead, the decision makers have to come up with decision rules specific to that year of draft. These are nonprogrammed decisions. A **nonprogrammed decision** is one made in a situation that is unique and poorly defined.

Typically, a manager is faced with a series of both programmed decisions and nonprogrammed decisions. Because of time pressures and because it is easier to attend to programmed decisions than to nonprogrammed decisions, managers usually focus more on clearing the programmed decisions and let the more complex and important decisions take a back seat (Black & Porter, 2000). An effective manager would set aside the necessary time to focus exclusively on the complex decisions without being sidetracked by programmed decisions.

Significance of Decisions

The extent to which a manager focuses on a particular decision is also a function of the significance of the problem and the consequences of making a specific decision. In the above example, the programmed decision of the locker room attendant is not as significant as the decision made on drafting players. Any errors made in the locker room are not going to have grave consequences for the club; the loss of a few towels or the use of the service by a few ineligible clients is not going to affect the bottom line of the club to any extent. On the other hand, the nonprogrammed decision of drafting a player is a significant one having severe consequences for the club. Consider, for example, drafting a player for a professional franchise. The cost of drafting a player is of great consequence in that it takes away the resources available for drafting other players or carrying out other needed projects for the franchise. This issue becomes even more pronounced when the franchise approaches the salary cap imposed by the league. In addition, the decision to draft a high-ranking player also has long-term consequences. For instance, National Basketball Associa-

Sidebar

We noted that the drafting of the NBA player has long-term consequences in terms of structuring the operations around that player. This tendency, known as *escalating commitment*, means that the managers commit themselves more and more to the earlier decision even though it may not yield the desired results. It is "the tendency for decision makers to persist with failing courses of action" (Brockner, 1992, p. 39). That is, "The fact that resources have already been committed to such a player leads to a situation where escalation might arise: rather than decrease the player's court time based on poor performance, a team may over-use a player relative to his value if a large previous commitment has been made" (Camerer & Weber, 1999, p. 61). This tendency to be committed to decisions could be based on self-justification, meaning an unwillingness to admit past incorrect decisions (Arkers & Blumer, 1985; Brockner, 1992). In order to avoid admitting a faulty decision, managers may allocate more resources to that course of action. The escalating commitment to the drafting of the player could also be based on the expectancy that additional resource allocations (in terms of playing time, drafting of other players to complement the talents of the drafted player, and so on) will lead to better results (Brockner, 1992, p. 40). Matsuoka and Chelladurai (2000) use this perspective to explain sports fans' continued commitment to a team. Unwilling to admit that their attachment to an unsuccessful team was futile and incorrect, fans may devote more resources in terms of money, effort, and time to the team, and thus become more attached to it. Also, fans of that team may expect that it will do better in the future, and based on that expectation, they continue to support the team.

---

tion (NBA) basketball players who were high-ranking draft picks tend to play more minutes, stay longer in the league, and have a lower likelihood of being traded than is justified by their performance (see Staw & Hoang, 1995; Camerer & Weber, 1999). Thus, many other future decisions will be based on the previous decision to draft that player, extending the significance of drafting that player beyond just the salary and bonuses paid to him.

While the relationship between programmability and the **significance of a decision** is true in many cases, it does not extend to all situations. Consider space flights, for example. The countdown to the final takeoff is almost totally programmed through highly sophisticated computer software and hardware. In fact, the computers are even programmed to scrub a flight under certain circumstances. Event management at a large university is another example. Most of the decisions (traffic routes, traffic signals, who can go where, and so on) are programmed to a great extent. These decisions are critically important despite the fact that they are programmed. As another example, take the case of a football coach who emphasizes set plays. He has programmed specific plays for specific circumstances, and he has given specific responsibilities to every player and drilled them in their specific responsibilities—programmed them to act in specific ways. These decisions are as significant as those made by any other coach who works without programming plays.

RATIONALITY IN DECISION MAKING

The rationality of decisions is an issue that has been debated at length. What is rationality? How rational are the decisions made by individuals and organizations? Can someone be fully rational in all decisions? We will discuss these and other questions in the following sections.

A decision is said to be rational when the best means are selected to achieve a given end. Note that rationality refers to the *selection of the best means* to achieve a goal and *not to the selection of the goal* itself. Thus, if an individual wishes to own a car primarily as a means of transportation, then the purchase of an inexpensive, efficient model would represent a rational decision. On the other hand, if that same individual purchased a Rolls Royce, the decision would not be rational. A second individual might wish to achieve status and prestige through car ownership. Thus, if this individual purchased a Rolls Royce, the decision would be rational. In short, the purchase is a means to an end, and consequently, purchase of the Rolls Royce may or may not be rational depending on the end (goal) sought.

Simon (1976, 1977) made a distinction between the ethical content of a decision and the factual content. The ethical content refers to the decision maker's beliefs of "what ought to be," and thus it reflects the goal that an administrator may pursue. However, the choice of that goal cannot be proved to be "true" or "false." For instance, in the example of the purchase of the car, the decision maker's preference for owning a car merely as a means of transport versus owning a car for status and prestige cannot be disputed as correct or incorrect. However, the factual content of an economy car versus a Rolls Royce can establish the decision as logical or illogical. That is, given the primary goal (transportation versus prestige), we can demonstrate that the decision to buy one car instead of the other was logical.

> **In Brief**
>
> Rationality in planning refers to generating many alternatives and choosing the best one to achieve a goal. It does not refer to the goal itself.

Simon points out that the concept of rationality can be strictly applied only to the factual elements of a decision and not to its ethical components. For example, if the athletic department has a goal of achieving national standing in one sport and then decides to hire a specific coach because he is available at a lower salary, the decision would not be considered rational. If, on the other hand, minimizing expenses in order to balance the budget was the main objective, then the decision to hire a less expensive coach would be rational. Note that the choice of the goal (attaining national status versus balancing the budget) cannot be subjected to the test of rationality because it is based on beliefs and values. On the other hand, the choice of a coach can be judged rational or not based on the extent to which it relates to the specified objective.

The idea that rationality refers to the choice of *best* means to a given goal implies that several alternative means would be considered and evaluated against specified criteria. This comprehensive and rigorous process of comparing several alternatives and selecting the best is labeled the *economic person model* of decision making.

Sidebar

Bill Morgan, a renowned sport philosopher, counters the position that the notion of rationality applies only to the means and not ends. He argues as follows:

"Proponents of ends-based rationality take proponents of means-based rationality (commonly referred to as instrumental reason) to task for getting things exactly backwards. They argue that carefully selecting the most efficient means to achieve our ends is only rational if the ends sought are of value, are worthy of pursuit in the first place. Hence, only a reflective assessment of the value of ends can tell us if our actions are rational. To this, enthusiasts of instrumental reason typically insist either that ends are incapable of rational assessment because they merely register those things that we want and desire, our subjective preferences, or that ends are givens, things that are so obvious and apparent they require no critical scrutiny. But these responses leave much to be desired. First, whereas it is true that sport organizations sometimes justify their actions by claims like we are only giving people what they want, we shouldn't take them at their word here. It is always open to question whether people really want these things or not, or simply seek them because they have no other good alternatives. Further, it is always open to question whether people should get what they want, since sometimes what they want should be denied them for moral, social, or other overriding reasons. For much the same reason, it is doubtful that the ends sought by sport organizations are as obvious or as uncontroversial as their members think. We can see this by asking straightforwardly what are the ends of such organizations: to realize the value of their private owners?, to protect the financial goals of their shareholders?, to ensure the athletes and teams they work for win?, to make the community in which they are located proud? None of these ends are so unambiguous, none are so clearly separable from the others, and none are so clearly private or public goals that it is immediately clear, meaning without further rational deliberation, how or even whether we should try to accomplish them. What is clear, however, is that in both this case, in which ends are reduced to givens, and the previous one, in which ends are reduced to preferences, the only way we can be sure we are acting rationally is to subject our ends to careful scrutiny." (Personal communication, February 2, 2004)

Economic Person Model

In the **economic person model**, or classical model, the decision maker wishes to maximize the benefits and minimize the costs (Simon, 1977). In the attempt to maximize the benefits, the decision maker will rigorously follow the steps outlined in Exhibit 6.1. This is the ideal model of rationality. It is *prescriptive* in the sense that it details what ought to be done. The economic person model, is based on certain fundamental assumptions. Naylor (1999, p. 349) notes these:

1. Objectives are clear and agreed.
2. Problems are clearly defined.

3. The manager seeks and gains full information on all possible alternatives before making any choice.
4. The criteria for evaluation can be unambiguously drawn from the objectives and problem definition.
5. Decision makers will make logical decisions to satisfy objectives as well as possible.

Although the economic person model has an inherent appeal, problems do arise because human capacity is rather limited (Schermerhorn, Hunt, & Osborn, 1997). Recognizing these human limitations, Simon (1957) introduced the key notion of bounded rationality.

ECONOMIC PERSON MODEL OF DECISION MAKING
The first step is to define clearly the objective to be achieved or the problem to be solved. The second step is to generate all possible alternatives to achieve the objective or solve the problem. In the third step, the decision maker evaluates all the alternatives generated. Finally, the alternative judged to be the best based on the evaluation in the previous step is selected.

Bounded Rationality

As we noted earlier, rationality implies that managers gather all the necessary information, identify all possible alternatives, evaluate each one carefully, and select the best one. In Simon's view, this is simply impossible. First, organizational problems are so complex that it is not possible to collect all the information needed. In fact, the manager may not know all the factors that contribute to the problem and therefore cannot collect the relevant information. Moreover, not all the possible choices will be known and/or evaluated. In addition, as human capacity is limited, managers may not be able to process the available information. Thus, despite the manager's best intentions, she can exercise only **bounded rationality**. That is, the rationality of the decision is bounded by the complexity of the problem, the lack of information, and the limits on human capacity.

Administrative Person Model

Based on his notion of bounded rationality, Simon (1945, 1977) proposed an alternate model of decision making that is based on assumptions contrary to those of the economic person model. His **administrative person model** is *descriptive* in that it describes how managers actually make decisions. As we have noted, decision makers are inherently limited in terms of their knowledge and capacity to evaluate all possible alternatives. Given such limitations, it is not possible to maximize a decision as the economic person model would suggest. Therefore, the decision maker is prepared to "satisfice" rather than maximize. The term *satisfice* was coined by Simon from the two words *satisfy* and *suffice*. It means that the decision maker is willing to accept an alternative that is minimally sufficient in meeting the goal. In the model of the administrative person, a decision maker specifies evaluative criteria that are minimally acceptable. Then a few alternatives are evaluated against these criteria, and the first alternative that meets the criteria is selected. Thus, a decision is made with the least cost of search. The next alternative to come along might have been far superior to the one selected, but the decision maker is not concerned with this possibility. The manager is satisfied with the choice that has been made because it is sufficient for the purpose. Exhibit 6.2 illustrates this process of decision making.

The critical distinction between the economic and administrative models of decision making is that the economic person lists and evaluates all possible alternatives before selecting the best one, whereas the administrative person evaluates the alternatives one at a time and selects the first alternative that is satisfactory/sufficient. According to Simon, the decisions of the administrative person are characterized by "bounded rationality," which he describes as follows:

> The individual can be rational in terms of the organization's goals only to the extent that he is *able* to pursue a course of action, he has a correct conception of the *goal* of the action, and he is correctly *informed* about the conditions surrounding his action. Within the boundaries laid down by these factors his choices are rational-goal oriented. (Simon, 1976, p. 241)

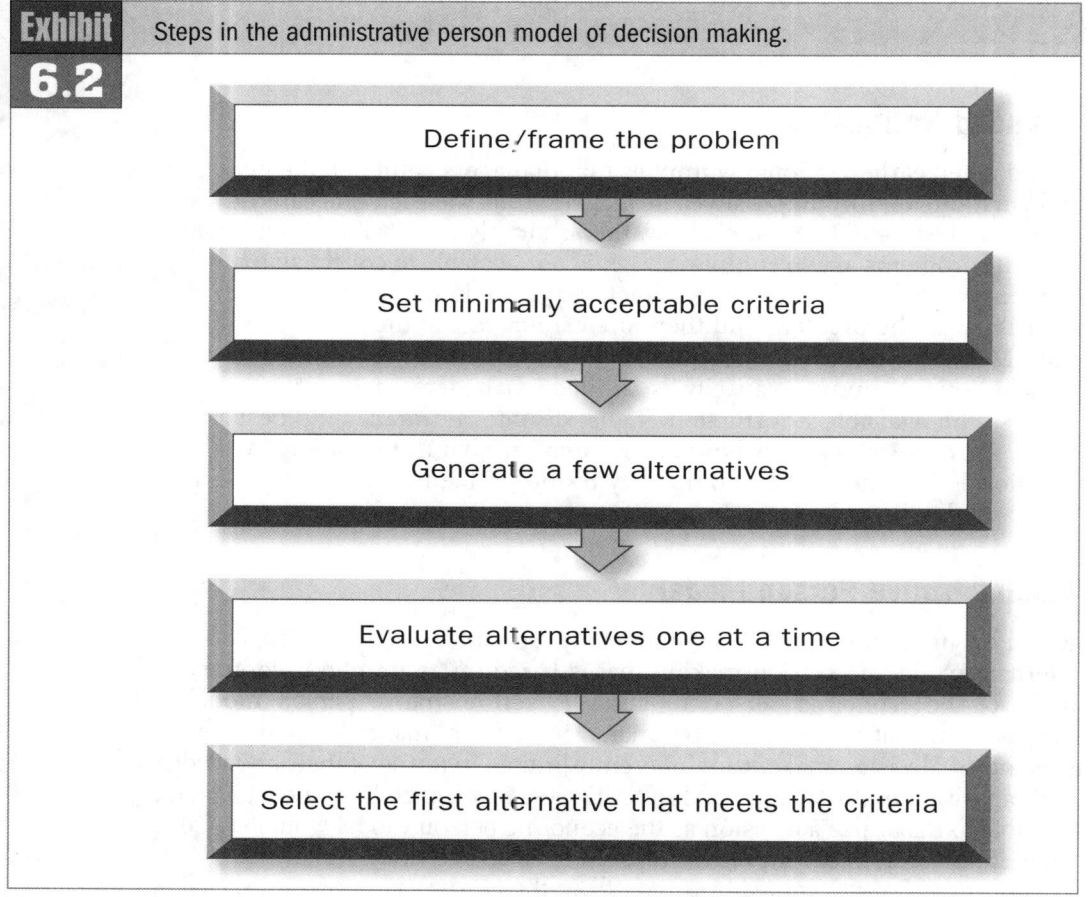

Exhibit 6.2 Steps in the administrative person model of decision making.

- Define/frame the problem
- Set minimally acceptable criteria
- Generate a few alternatives
- Evaluate alternatives one at a time
- Select the first alternative that meets the criteria

Simon also used the term *subjective rationality* (as opposed to objective rationality) to refer to decisions made with little information about the alternatives and their consequences. Insofar as a decision maker has made the best choice with the available information, he is said to be rational—but only subjectively. The objectively rational decision—the decision made with all the necessary information available—could prove to be an entirely different one. Thus, in Simon's (1976) view,

> The need for an administrative theory resides in the fact that there *are* practical limits to human rationality, and that these limits are not static, but depend upon the organizational environment in which the individual's decision takes place. The task of administration is to design this environment so that the individual will approach as close as practicable to rationality (judged in terms of the organization's goals) in his decisions. (pp. 240–241)

Both models of decision making are relevant to management. In situations critical to an organization's growth or survival (as in the planning process), managers must try to use the model of the economic person. In not-so-critical situations such as buying a water cooler for the office, the model of the administrative person is adequate. In decisions regarding the transportation for the football team or the hiring of a coach, the managers may lean toward "satisficing" (the administrative person model) in the transportation issue and toward "maximizing" (the economic person model) in hiring a coach.

Note that even satisficing—arriving at something that is merely sufficient and satisfactory—can be rational, if the decision maker's objective is to minimize the cost of the search and the decision situation is not highly critical to the organization's functioning. The critical thrust of the administrative person model is the notion of satisficing based on the concept of bounded rationality. That is, managers tend to satisfice because they do not have the information or capacity to maximize the benefits. On the other hand, managers could be rational in deliberately choosing to satisfice rather than maximize. For example, the marketing manager who is seeking a printing firm may choose the first firm that meets his minimal criteria (a certain cost, a certain quality of output, and commitment to deadlines). The manager may satisfice in this case because the decision is not that critical and the additional benefits one may get through maximizing may not be worth the time and effort of the manager and the department. Viewed from this perspective (minimizing cost in less critical decisions), satisficing may indeed be a maximizing strategy.

In Brief

In critical issues, managers may have to maximize in making decisions by evaluating a large number of feasible alternatives. They may "satisfice" in less critical issues by selecting the first alternative that meets the minimal criteria.

Implicit Favorite Model

Another model of decision making, the **implicit favorite model**, was proposed by Soelberg (1967). In this model, while searching for a number of alternatives, the decision maker develops a preference for one alternative early in the search. Soelberg refers to this alternative as the implicit favorite. The subsequent search for alternatives and their evaluation is aimed at confirming the suitability of the implicit favorite. As Filley, House, and Kerr (1976) noted:

> The final decision process is one of *decision confirmation*. The decision maker will not enter into this period until one of the alternatives discovered thus far can be identified as an *implicit favorite*. In other words, decision making during the confirmation stage is an exercise in prejudice—in rationalization rather than in rationality. The decision maker ensures during the confirmation phase that the implicit favorite will indeed turn out to be the "right" choice. (p. 122)

Confirmation of the implicit favorite is achieved by selecting evaluative criteria that, when applied to the other alternatives, automatically result in their elimination.

Athletes choosing from among a number of universities that have similar scholarship offers, programs, facilities, and opportunities often adopt an implicit favorite approach. They make a choice early and then examine alternative universities as a means of confirming their initial selection. Similarly, when an organization has a preference for a particular individual and then places an advertisement for the position with job specifications that only the preferred candidate can meet, it is following the implicit favorite model. Exhibit 6.3 illustrates this process.

The implicit favorite model may be employed by individuals in making personal decisions like buying a car or going to a particular college or university, but managers need to be very careful in using the model in an organizational context. The implicit favorite model may be acceptable and may prove func-

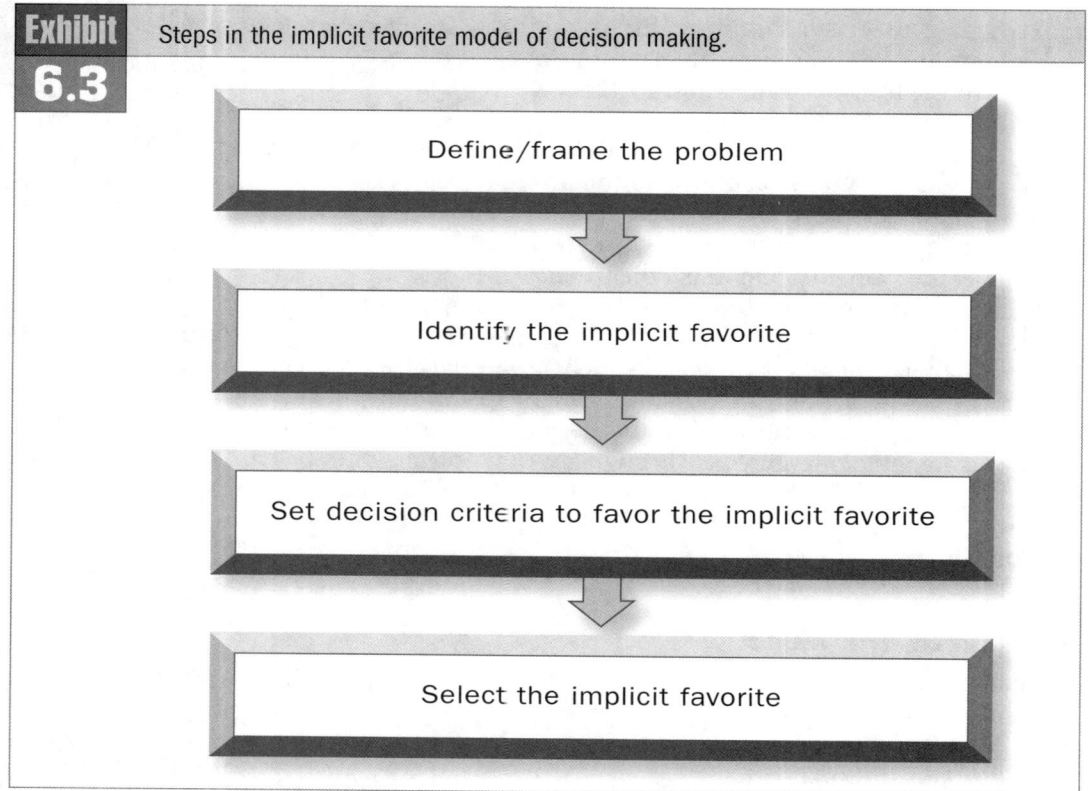

Exhibit 6.3 Steps in the implicit favorite model of decision making.

Sidebar

The foregoing models of decision making, whether prescriptive or descriptive, alert us to the biases that can creep into the decision-making process and thus reduce the effectiveness of the decision. Vecchio (2003) refers to six kinds of biases that might influence a decision. First is the *availability bias*, which refers to the availability of relevant information through one's memory or perception. Such information could be limited and misleading, thus leading to a faulty decision. Consider, for example, a marketing manager of a large fitness club who neglects to target the Mexican American population based on his memory of 20 years ago when that segment of the population was rather small. Current statistics seem to suggest that it constitutes a large enough segment to warrant the attention of marketers. In short, a manager's readily available knowledge may be limited and dated.

The second bias, *representativeness bias*, stems from the tendency of decision makers to rely on their sense that one person (or object or event) resembles another and lump them together in making judgments. Suppose, for example, a friend of the athletic director points to a tall and muscular African American and suggests that the athletic director may want to consider her for a job in the department. The athletic director (just like you and me) is likely to see the features of the applicant as similar to those of excellent athletes and would tend to judge her as qualified based on assuming she is an athlete. It could turn out, however, that the applicant was never an athlete but instead an outstanding lawyer or accountant.

The *implicit favorite bias* is the tendency of a decision maker to justify the choice of an alternative without realizing that it was his preference in the first place. Another bias is the *loss-aversion bias*, where the decision maker tends to avoid alternatives that run the risk of a loss. That is, such a person would go with the "sure bets." The *selective perception bias* is the tendency for a decision maker to interpret the available information selectively. For instance, a manager of a golf course, having recruited a groundskeeper, might have positive impressions of that person. That positive expectation could be reflected in the subsequent performance evaluation of the groundskeeper.

Finally, the *personal experience bias* is the influence of one's personal experiences to cloud judgment. For instance, if the son of an event manager of a local professional franchise had a negative encounter with a group of high school students, that experience may influence the manager to think that all high school students engage in unruly behavior.

tional in decisions relating to buying equipment, supplies, and other decisions not involving humans. For instance, a manager and her assistants may decide to buy one brand of lawn mowers because she has a liking for that mower. However, the model should not be used in any decisions involving humans, such as hiring, training, and promotions. For instance, although buying a lawn mower may be influenced by the implicit favorite model, hiring those who would use the lawn mower cannot be based on that model. For one thing, there are laws and government regulations that prohibit such practices. Second, it would be unwise and unethical to shut out other candidates merely because the manager

favors one individual based on characteristics irrelevant to the job in question. The risk of falling into the traps of the implicit favorite model can be avoided if, and only if, the setting of the evaluation criteria is done independently of, and concurrently with, the generation and search for alternatives.

We can draw one important guideline from the implicit favorite model. According to the model, once the decision maker has identified the implicit favorite, the subsequent processes are said to be geared to *confirm* the favorite choice. Good managers can use the same processes in an attempt to *disconfirm* the favorite choice. That is, even though the favorite is chosen based on some meaningful criteria, such criteria tend to pose the choice in a good light. The problem here is that the process tends to overlook another equally qualified candidate or alternative. In order to guard against making a mistake, the decision maker may purposely attempt to evaluate the favorite on other criteria that might show its weaknesses. If in this process the candidate or alternative is not discredited or disconfirmed, then the decision maker can be more confident of the choice.

DECISION MAKING AS A SOCIAL PROCESS

The foregoing models of decision making are cognitive processes. But there is another equally important aspect of decision making—the social process. The social process of decision making refers to the degree to which members of a group are allowed to participate in decision making and the varying degrees of influence the members have on the decisions. Thus, the social process of decision making may vary from strictly autocratic decision making by the manager to varying degrees of participation by members (consultation with one or a few members, consultation with all members, group decision making, or delegation). These variations have been called the *decision styles* of the manager (Chelladurai & Haggerty, 1978).

Because member involvement in decision making is a major concern in management, let us look at the social processes of decision making in greater detail. We are all familiar with descriptions of some leaders and managers as autocratic and others as democratic. For example, coaches of sport teams in general are said to be autocratic (see Ogilvie & Tutko, 1966). It is also often suggested that one's personality predisposes that person to be autocratic (see Hendry, 1968). A different perspective holds that instead of viewing individuals as autocratic or democratic, we must view the situation as calling for autocratic or democratic decisions (Vroom & Yetton, 1973). In this view, being autocratic is in itself neither evil nor immoral. For instance, when a parent decides autocratically that the preschooler should go to bed, the parent is genuinely concerned about the welfare of the child and is deemed to be making an optimal, albeit autocratic, decision. On the other hand, we would expect a parent to permit a teenager to engage in discussions and participate in the decision regarding the choice of a university for higher education. The difference between the preschooler's and the teenager's capacity to par-

Decision making as a cognitive process involves an analysis of the problem, generation of alternative solutions, and choice of the optimal solution to the problem. Decision making as a social process is concerned with the extent of member participation given varying problem attributes.

ticipate meaningfully in decisions calls for different social processes of decision making. From the human resource management perspective, it is critical that a manager be aware of the benefits and drawbacks of **participative decision making** and the appropriate degrees of participation under varying circumstances.

Advantages of Participative Decision Making

The benefits of allowing members to participate in decision making can be summarized as (a) higher rationality of the decisions, (b) better understanding of the decisions, (c) broader ownership of the decisions, and (d) better execution of the decisions. The rationality of a decision depends on the amount of available information relevant to the problem on hand. Readers will recall from Chapter 5 that the nominal group and Delphi techniques involve experts to forecast the future. Similarly, brainstorming is a process in which members engage in generating alternatives. The basic principle behind those methods is that there is more information and insight in a group than in an individual. This wider and deeper base of information and expertise can assist the manager in clarifying the problem and in identifying and evaluating alternative solutions to the problem. Consider, for example, a marketing unit in a large fitness and recreation club or a university athletic department. The employees of the marketing unit would look at a problem from different perspectives and with different insights stemming from their varied backgrounds and experiences. By the same token, they would also have different pieces of information about the problem. Thus, the unit as a collective would have more information than any individual. Let us assume that the fitness club or the athletic department would like to market its programs to different segments of the local population including the elderly and women. The seniors and women in the marketing unit are likely to have some pertinent information on how to reach these two segments. This information combined with the marketing expertise of the entire group is likely to result in a comprehensive marketing plan. The idea that people of diverse backgrounds have different contributions to make is explored further in Chapter 14, on management of diversity.

An equally important benefit of participative decisions is that they enable members to comprehend more clearly the problem and its solution. Because employees of the marketing unit in the above example participated in decisions concerning the marketing strategies, they gained a better understanding of the rationale behind those decisions. They are therefore better equipped to implement the strategies. In addition, when members participate in decision making, they feel it is "their" decision and thereby develop a sense of ownership in the decision. Such a sense of ownership in the decision motivates them to execute the strategies more efficiently and effectively. All of these advantages contribute to the success of the decisions made. This view is supported by Nutt's (2002) finding that while over half of the decisions made by organizations failed, 80 percent of the decisions where significant members participated in the decisions succeeded.

An additional advantage of participation in decision making relates to development of individual employees. Participation in decision making makes the members more knowledgeable and capable of analyzing problems and their attributes, and of evaluating options. These experiences are critical to individuals' personal growth and development, which in turn enhances the human resources of the organization.

Disadvantages of Participative Decision Making

We must also be aware of some of the drawbacks of participative decisions. The obvious problem is that participative decisions take time. Have you ever seen a basketball coach engage in participative decisions during timeouts? There simply is not enough time for discussion and participation during a timeout. Also, it is possible that the leader may have more information than the group as a whole. In our previous example of the marketing unit of a fitness club, we made an implicit assumption that the employees offered different sets of knowledge and experience. This is not necessarily true in all circumstances. Consider the case where the fitness club or the athletic department hires an experienced marketing manager and five or six raw graduates for the marketing unit. If the new graduates do not possess the relevant knowledge and experience, participative decision making would simply be "pooling of ignorance" (Chelladurai, 1985), and may not lead to higher quality decisions.

Another significant factor influencing the effectiveness of participative decisions is the extent to which the group is integrated. If a group is poorly integrated and is marked by conflicts among cliques within the group, the leader should be very careful in engaging that group in participative decisions. In our example of the marketing unit, it is possible that its members could have formed cliques (e.g., along gender lines or on another basis), and the cliques could have developed animosity toward each other. In such a case, the leader of the marketing unit should be wary of engaging these members in participative decision making.

> **In Brief**
>
> Participative decision making capitalizes on the abilities and knowledge of the members, which results in better decisions. In addition, a participative process creates a better understanding of the problem and the solution, and ensures the acceptance of a decision. Disadvantages of group decision making include the cost of time it takes to make decisions, possible "pooling of ignorance," and the possibility of group conflicts arising out of differences in preferred solutions to a problem.

Decision Styles

We noted earlier that the social process of decision making refers to the *degree* to which members participate in decision making. The degree of participation leads to the suggestion that participation in decision making may take several forms. For instance, the manager of the marketing unit may make a decision by herself. In this case, there would be no participation by members. This form of decision making is usually labeled *autocratic decision*. At the other extreme, the marketing manager may engage all his members in making a decision. Such decision making is known as a *group* or *participative* decision.

Thirty years ago, Vroom and his associates (Vroom & Jago, 1978, 1988; Vroom & Yetton, 1973) embarked on a concerted effort to study the social processes of making decisions. The cumulative results of this extensive and intensive research were summarized by Vroom (2000, 2003). Basically, Vroom's model includes five social processes in making a decision. They are described in Exhibit 6.4. Chelladurai and his associates (Chelladurai, 1993; Chelladurai & Arnott, 1985; Chelladurai & Haggerty, 1978; Chelladurai, Haggerty, & Baxter, 1989; Chelladurai & Quek, 1995) have labeled these varying degrees of participation as *decision styles*.

Note that in Exhibit 6.4, the last two procedures (Facilitate and Delegate) are participative decisions, whereas in the other three procedures (Decide, Consult Individually, and Consult Group) the leader is the sole decision maker. However, the influence of members in the decision progressively increases from "Decide" procedure to "Delegate." In fact, Vroom (2000) provides a rating of member influence on each of the decision styles (on a 10-point scale) by 40 specialists. These are shown in the rightmost column of Exhibit 6.4.

Problem Attributes

The issue now centers on the extent to which group members are allowed to influence the decisions, and in what situations. In other words, which of the decision styles would be appropriate under which conditions? Vroom (2000, 2003) suggested that every situation could be described in terms of seven attributes. That is, each problem situation may be characterized by varying degrees of the attributes described below.

1. *Decision significance:* the extent to which the decision in question is important to the project or the organization. In our example of a marketing unit, the choice of a marketing strategy is a more significant decision, since it impacts a company's sales and growth, than the purchase of a table for the conference room. This distinction is analogous to the distinction between maximizing and satisficing processes discussed earlier. It is suggested that

Exhibit 6.4 Decision styles and their descriptions.

DECISION STYLE	DESCRIPTION	MEMBERS' INFLUENCE (10-point scale)
1. Decide	The leader makes the decision based on available information, and announces it.	0
2. Consult individually	The leader explains the problem to members individually, gets their feedback, and then makes the decision.	3
3. Consult group	The leader explains the problem to the group as a whole, gets their feedback, and then makes the decision.	5
4. Facilitate	The leader explains the problem to the group, sets the limits to the decision, and attempts to get the members to concur on a decision. Leader's influence is minimal.	7
5. Delegate	The leader permits the group to make a decision within certain limits. The group defines the problem and its characteristics, generates alternative solutions, and decides on one or more of the alternatives.	10

Reprinted from *Leadership and Decision-Making,* by Victor H. Vroom and Philip W. Yetton, by permission of the University of Pittsburgh Press. © 1973 by University of Pittsburgh Press.

the greater the significance, the greater the need for participation by members because they bring in more information and insights.

2. *Importance of commitment:* members' commitment to the decision. If members will be called upon to implement the decision diligently (e.g., the selected marketing strategy), their commitment to the chosen strategy becomes critical. As noted earlier, such commitment can be secured by having the members participate in making the decision, thus creating in them a sense of ownership of the decision. In other cases, a manager or her immediate assistants may execute the decision without the involvement of the members (for example, interacting with the media). The higher the requirement of member commitment, the higher the need for member participation.

3. *Leader's expertise:* the amount and quality of information, knowledge, and expertise the leader has in relation to the problem at hand. When the leader does not have all the information, it is prudent for him to get members involved in decision making. On the other hand, group decision making may not be worth the time and effort involved when the leader has all the information.

4. *Likelihood of commitment:* the degree to which members will be committed to a decision even when the leader makes the decision by herself. Earlier we suggested that members' commitment can be secured through engaging them in making the decision. If the leader is well respected and liked, it is possible that members may be committed to a decision made by the leader. In such a case, participation in decision making may not be necessary.

5. *Group support for objectives:* the extent to which members of the group accept and support the goals and objectives of the group and organization. If they all share the group goals, they can be expected to participate diligently in making an optimal decision. If, however, some members have divergent perceptions of what the group goals should be, their participation may not be whole-hearted. In such a case, participative decision making would likely be futile. In the example of the marketing unit, some members may believe that the organization or the unit should concentrate on satisfying the existing customer base instead of attempting to expand its market. If so, their participation in the choice of strategies for expansion may not be worthwhile. The lower the goal congruence among members, the lower the need for group decisions.

6. *Group expertise:* the amount and quality of information and expertise the members have relative to the problem at hand. A basic premise for participative decision making is that there is more information in the group. However, as noted above, in certain circumstances the members may lack the necessary information or experience to contribute to group decision making. Therefore, engaging them in group decisions would not be fruitful.

7. *Team competence:* the ability of the members to work together on the problem and come up with a solution. It is expected that the members get along as a group and have learned to interact with each other and participate effectively in decision making. If, in contrast, the group is characterized by internal cliques and conflicts, members' self-interest is likely to interfere with effective decision making and lower the competence of the team to make good decisions.

Vroom and his associates also took into account the leader's concern with the time it takes to make decisions on the one hand and, on the other hand, her desire to develop the subordinates' cognitive abilities to analyze problems and evaluate alternatives. There may be occasions where the leader does not

> **Sidebar**
>
> Chelladurai (1993) cautioned against confounding the decision style adopted by a person in a given situation with the mannerisms and affectations of that person. For instance, consider a football coach who presents his playbook for the season to the quarterback with the apparently menacing command: "This is your bible. You better master it." In contrast, another coach may present his playbook with a smile and the comment: "Here is the playbook I drew up during the summer. You may get a kick out of reading it." The obvious difference in their mannerisms should not be allowed to mask the fact that both coaches autocratically decided on the plays.
>
> Chelladurai (1993) also suggests that we should not be misguided by "window-dressing." That is, a person may project herself as very democratic by letting members make decisions in trivial matters. For instance, a basketball coach may allow his players to choose the starting five for a game. How does that make the coach more democratic when he substitutes those players at the first whistle? The coach has just created a façade of democratic leadership.

have much time to engage the members in decision making, as in the case of a timeout during a basketball game. Even when there are no such constraints, the leader needs to balance the labor costs associated with the time it takes to make participative decisions with the developmental benefits of participation. Thus, the leader may engage in less participative decision styles if there are concerns about time and more participative styles if the developmental benefits outweigh the concern with time.

It should be noted that the above attributes can be categorized on the basis of whether they relate to the problem per se, to the leader, or to the members in juxtaposition with the problem. Thus, the attribute of decision significance refers to the problem itself. Leader's expertise refers to the leader's information relevant to the problem. The remaining attributes pertain to the group members, their interrelationships, and their relationship to the leader and the problem.

As Vroom and Yetton (1973) pointed out, "the quality of the decision is dependent not only on the information and expertise of those participating in it, but also on their disposition to use their information in the service of the goal stated in the problem" (p. 29). In reading the above attributes, you will recognize that some of the attributes refer to members' information and expertise while some others relate to their willingness to participate meaningfully in making decisions. The effects of problem attributes on the choice of decision styles are summarized in Exhibit 6.5.

A consistent finding from the 25-year research on the model proposed by Vroom and his associates is that the influence of situational attributes on a manager's decision style choices dwarfs the influence of individual difference (i.e., personal) factors (Vroom, 2000). A similar trend appeared in an athletic context. Chelladurai and his associates (Chelladurai & Arnott, 1985; Chelladurai, Haggerty, & Baxter, 1989; Chelladurai & Quek, 1995) investigated basketball players' preferences for a particular decision style under various problems that were defined by selected problem attributes—quality requirement, coach's information, players' information, problem structure, and team integration.

Exhibit 6.5 Relationships between problem attributes and subordinate participation in decision making.

WHEN THIS PROBLEM ATTRIBUTE IS HIGH . . .	MEMBER PARTICIPATION IS
Decision significance	High
Importance of commitment	High
Leader expertise	Low
Likelihood of commitment	Low
Group support	High
Group expertise	High
Team competence	High

Adapted from P. Chelladurai, *Human Resource Management in Sport and Recreation*, p. 178, figure 10.3. © 1999 by Packianathan Chelladurai. Reprinted with permission from Human Kinetics (Champaign, IL). Data from Vroom & Jago, 1988.

High and low levels of these attributes were built into differing scenarios or problem situations. Basketball players at the university and high school levels were asked to indicate which one of the decision styles they would prefer their coach to employ. Results indicated that a vast majority of the players agreed that their coaches should make the decision with or without consultation with the players. Further, the results showed that the problem attributes built into the scenarios had three to four times more influence on decision style preferences than individual differences did. That is, the players' preferences for specific decision styles varied with the type of situation.

In overview, an analysis of the specific attributes of a particular problem would assist the leader on deciding on a specific decision style. It is important that the leader take into consideration all the attributes in totality instead of focusing on just one or two attributes. Along with viewing the problem attributes in a comprehensive manner, managers must also consider four possible outcomes of a given decision style—(a) quality of the decision that is consistent with organizational goals, (b) the extent to which subordinates understand and accept the decision, (c) the cost in terms of time, and (d) the development of group members (Vroom, 2003).

From this perspective, deciding on the social process to be employed in decision making itself is a cognitive process. The ideas presented here represent a logical and rational framework with which managers may analyze problem situations and select an appropriate decision style. Also, this framework minimizes the importance of a manager's personal characteristics, including personality, as determinants of decision style choices.

Vroom (2000) noted that over the 25-year research period, there has been a shift in managers' choice of decision styles to relatively more participative

In Brief

While a leader would be better off allowing his members to participate in decision making, the extent to which such participation should occur is a function of the attributes of the problem, including the characteristics of individual members and the group. A leader should evaluate these attributes and choose the most appropriate decision style in a given problem situation.

There has always been a strong push to *democratize* the organization. Increasing participation by workers in making decisions on organizational policies and processes has been advocated either on the ground that it is the moral or right thing to do or that such an approach would lead to a more committed workforce and thus to better organizational performance. Yet the practice of democracy in organizations has never kept pace with the rhetoric for democracy. Kerr (2004) points to the fallacy of two assumptions behind the push for democracy. First is the assumption that the *political* democracy as we know it in the United States and other Western countries can be translated into *organizational* democracy. The second assumption is that such organizational democracy would be the best method of governance and decision making in all organizational settings.

Kerr (2004) notes that (a) organizations are not the same as societies where democracy is practiced, (b) managers are not elected as is the case with representatives to legislative bodies, and (c) the roles and responsibilities of employees are not the same as those of citizens. The critical democratic characteristics of accountability to the governed, equal rights of participation, free exchange of information, and representation of the governed are not relevant to or even existent in organizations. That is, while the elected in a political democracy are accountable to the governed (i.e., the electorate), managers are accountable to the owners and not the employees. In a political democracy, equal participation is guaranteed by law, while such participation is controlled by management in an organization.

As for free exchange of information, the electorate in a democracy has unconstrained access to almost all information, whereas such access and exchange is controlled by management in an organization. Finally, representation of the people in a democracy is guaranteed through the electoral process; such representation is incidental in an organization. It must also be noted that the legitimacy of those who govern in a society is derived from the democratic process, whereas such legitimacy in an organization stems from the legal ownership of the organization. For all these reasons, democracy has not taken root in organizations.

> The "problem" with organizational democracy is that it is not a trivial or superficial adjustment. . . . It requires a fundamental redistribution of responsibility, authority, power, and resources that affects every member of the organization and the relationships between them. It is also not an easy system to live with once established. In place of straightforward commands and controls, every interaction is a potential negotiation, every decision a potential political moment. (Kerr, 2004, p. 93)

Kerr (2004) also suggests that the democratic process in an organization can be successful only if (a) the process would enhance the work of the organization, (b) the workforce has the talent and attitude to engage in the process, (c) the cost and risk of changing to a democratic process would be minimal, and (d) the upper management is prepared for and committed to democratic values and practices.

processes. He speculates that this shift reflects (a) the higher rates of change in and increased complexity of the environment, (b) a move toward flatter organizational structures, (c) improved information technology, and (d) a more highly educated and sophisticated labor force. He also noted that women managers tended to be more participative than men. Finally, he noted that managers at higher levels of the organization tended to be more participative than those at lower levels.

SUMMARY

The emphasis in this chapter was on decision making as a significant component of management. The importance of stating and framing the problem (or opportunity) clearly was highlighted. We noted that the way a problem is framed can influence subsequent decisions on the problem. As in the planning process, we recognized the need to generate alternative solutions and evaluate those alternatives. We identified the differences between a programmed decision and a nonprogrammed decision, and the relationship between a decision's programmability and its significance. We noted that the classical model of decision making is aimed at being rational; however, managers are bounded in their rationality owing to the lack of information and their own inability to digest all the information. We discussed Simon's concept of bounded rationality and the three models of decision making—economic person, administrative person, and implicit favorite. We discussed the concepts of maximizing and "satisficing" and the appropriateness of each to different problems. Finally, we looked at decision making as a social process, the advantages and disadvantages of participative decision making, and problem attributes.

DEVELOPING YOUR PERSPECTIVES

1. Explain the steps in decision making and its significance to a sports manager.
2. Consider a sport organization you are familiar with. Give examples of the opportunities and problems that the manager may have to decide on.
3. Which of the examples you gave would involve programmed decisions and which nonprogrammed decisions? Explain.
4. Describe what you think would be the short-term and long-term consequences of the decisions you listed in #2.
5. What is meant by rationality of a decision? Describe a decision made by a sport manager that, in your opinion, was not rational. Explain.
6. Explain the concepts *maximizing* and *satisficing*. Give examples in which a manager should maximize or satisfice.
7. Recall a situation where you were involved in participative decision making. Describe the situation in terms of the problem attributes explained in the chapter. Was the group effective in making a decision? What were the strengths and weaknesses of the group in making the decision?

References

Arkers, H. R., & Blumer, C. (1985). The psychology of sunk cost. *Organizational Behavior and Human Decision Processes, 35*, 124–140.

Black, J. S., & Porter, L. W. (2000). *Management: Meeting new challenges.* Upper Saddle River, NJ: Prentice Hall.

Brockner, J. (1992). The escalation of commitment to a failing course of action: Toward theoretical progress. *Academy of Management Review, 17* (1), 39–61.

Camerer, C. F., & Weber, R. A. (1999). The econometrics and behavioral economics of escalation of commitment: A re-examination of Staw and Hoang's NBA data. *Journal of Economic Behavior and Organization, 39*, 59–82.

Chelladurai, P. (1985). *Sport management: Macro perspectives.* London, Canada: Sports Dynamics.

Chelladurai, P. (1993). Styles of decision making in coaching. In J.M. Williams (Ed.), *Applied sport psychology: Personal growth to peak performance* (2nd ed., pp. 99–109). Palo Alto, CA: Mayfield.

Chelladurai, P., & Arnott, M. (1985). Decision styles in coaching: Preferences of basketball players. *Research Quarterly for Exercise and Sport, 56* (1), 15–24.

Chelladurai, P., & Doherty, A. (1998). Styles of decision making in coaching. In J. M. Williams (Ed.), *Applied sport psychology: Personal growth to peak performance* (3rd ed., pp. 115–126). Mountain View, CA: Mayfield.

Chelladurai, P. & Haggerty, T. R. (1978). A normative model of decision styles in coaching. *Athletic Administrator, 13*, 6–9.

Chelladurai, P., Haggerty, T. R., & Baxter, P. R. (1989). Decision style choices of university basketball coaches and players. *Journal of Sport and Exercise Psychology, 11*, 201–215.

Chelladurai, P., & Quek, C. B. (1995). Situational and personality effects on the decision style choices of high school basketball coaches. *Journal of Sport Behavior, 18* (2), 91–108.

Filley, A.C., House, R.J., & Kerr, S. (1976). *Managerial process and organizational behavior.* Glenview, IL: Scott, Foresman.

Hendry, L.B. (1968). A personality study of highly successful and "ideal" swimming coaches. *Research Quarterly, 40*, 299–305.

Kerr, J. L. (2004). The limits of organizational democracy. *Academy of Management Executive, 18* (3), 81–95.

Matsuoka, H., & Chelladurai, P. (2000). *Components of psychological attachment to sport teams.* Unpublished manuscript. The Ohio State University.

Morden, A. R. (1993). *Business strategy and planning.* London: McGraw-Hill.

Morden, T. (1996). *Principles of management.* London: McGraw-Hill.

Morgan, B. (2004). Personal communication. February 2.

Naylor, J. (1999). *Management.* London: Financial Times Management.

Nutt, P. C. (2002). *Why decisions fail: Avoiding the blunders and traps that lead to debacles.* Williston, VT: Berrett-Koehler.

Ogilvie, B.C., & Tutko, T.A. (1966). *Problem athletes and how to control them.* London: Pelham Books.

Priesmeyer, H. R. (1992). *Organizations and chaos: Defining the methods of nonlinear management.* Westport, CT: Quorum Books.

Schermerhorn, J.R., Hunt, J.G., & Osborn, R.N. (1997). *Organizational behavior* (6th ed.). New York: John Wiley & Sons.

Simon, H. A. (1945). *Administrative behavior.* New York: Macmillan.

Simon, H. A. (1957). *Models of man.* New York: John Wiley.

Simon, H. A. (1976). *Administrative behavior: A study of decision-making processes in administrative organizations.* New York: Free Press.

Simon, H. A. (1977). *The new science of managerial decision making.* Englewood Cliffs, NJ: Prentice Hall.

Soelberg, P. (1967). Unprogrammed decision making. *Industrial Management Review, 8*, 19–29.

Staw, B. M., & Hoang, H. (1995). Sunk costs in the NBA: Why draft order affects playing time and survival in professional basketball. *Administrative Science Quarterly, 40*, 474–494.

Vecchio, R.P. (2003). *Organizational behavior: Core concepts.* Mason, OH: Thompson/South-Western.

Vroom, V. H. (1959). Some personality determinants of the effects of participation. *Journal of Abnormal and Social Psychology, 59*, 322–327.

Vroom, V. H. (2000). Leadership and the decision-making process. *Organizational Dynamics, 28* (4), 82–94.

Vroom, V. H. (2002). Leadership and the decision making process. *Organizational Dynamics, 28* (4), 82–94.

Vroom, V. H. (2003). Educating managers for decision making and leadership. *Management Decision, 41* (10), 968–978.

Vroom, V. H., & Jago, A. G. (1978). On the validity of the Vroom–Yetton model. *Journal of Applied Psychology, 63,* 151–162.

Vroom, V. H., & Jago, A. G. (1988). *The new leadership: Managing participation in organizations.* Upper Saddle River, NJ: Prentice Hall.

Vroom, V. H., & Yetton, R. N. (1973). *Leadership and decision-making.* Pittsburgh: University of Pittsburgh Press.

CHAPTER 7

Principles of Organizing

MANAGE YOUR LEARNING

After completing this chapter you should be able to:

- Describe the classical principles of organizing.
- List the tenets of a bureaucracy.
- Discuss the relevance of bureaucracy and its tenets to sport organizations.
- Describe the dysfunctional aspects of bureaucracy.
- Explain the place of bureaucracy in a democracy, and how the two complement each other.

STRATEGIC CONCEPTS

abstract rules	impersonality
bureaucracy	span of control
bureaucracy in sport organizations	specialization
democracy	stability
departmentation	technical competence
division of labor	unity of command
hierarchical authority structure	

ORGANIZING DEFINED

In Chapter 5, we described the planning function. The fundamental tasks accomplished in that function are the identification and clarification of goals to be pursued, and the specification of activities and programs to achieve those goals. In essence, the sum of these activities and programs constitutes the total work to be accomplished. For instance, a commercial fitness club may set as its goal a 5 percent increase in the number of its clients. This simple goal stated in a straightforward manner belies the host of activities to be engaged in by the employees. First, there is the concern with increasing the quality of services offered, which will involve all employees—instructors in weight training, aerobics, swimming, and tennis; receptionists; locker room attendants; and day care supervisors. Second, there is the concern with improving efficiency in scheduling the activities and instructors. This may also entail rearranging the equipment and activity spaces. Marketing of the improved services will be another area that needs attention. These are just a few examples of how a simple goal generates a host of activities to be completed.

Once the goals have been specified and the courses of action to achieve those goals have been selected (that is, after the planning process has been completed), it is necessary to divide the total work into specific jobs, assign these jobs to individuals, and coordinate the activities of these individuals toward the achievement of the organizational goals. This is the process of organizing. Some of the definitions of organizing are:

> The arrangement of people and tasks to accomplish the goals of the organization. (Fink, Jenks, & Willits, 1983, p. 46)

> The process of establishing orderly uses of all resources in the organization. (Certo, 1992, p. 257)

> Organizing is (1) the identification and classification of required activities, (2) the grouping of activities necessary to attain objectives, (3) the assignment of each grouping to a manager with the authority (delegation) necessary to supervise it, and (4) the provision for coordination horizontally (on the same or similar organizational level) and vertically (for example, corporate headquarters, division, and department) in the organization structure. (Weihrich & Koontz, 1993, p. 244)

In essence, then, the organizing process results in an organizational structure that specifies the relationships among tasks and among the people who perform them. These definitions imply that:

- there is division of labor in the sense that different people are asked to carry out different activities (ticketing personnel, marketing personnel, and event management personnel in a professional sport franchise), and
- there is a hierarchy in the sense that some positions are placed in supervisory roles over other persons or positions (ticketing manager, marketing manager, event manager, and the general manager, who supervises the other managerial positions in a professional sport franchise).

Such a structure is expected to maximize the use of all available resources within the organization. As Hall (1996, p. 49) noted, the organizational structure serves three basic functions: to (a) produce organizational outputs and achieve organizational goals, (b) minimize and regulate individual variations from organizational requirements, and (c) define which positions will exercise power over other positions, and how. Hall also notes that organization structure defines the flow of information needed for effective decision making.

> Every organized human activity—from the making of pottery to the placing of a man on the moon—gives rise to two fundamental and opposing requirements: the division of labor into various tasks to be performed and the coordination of those tasks to accomplish the activity. The structure of an organization can be defined simply as the total of the ways in which its labor is divided into distinct tasks and then its coordination achieved among tasks.
>
> **MINTZBERG,** *1989, pp. 100–101*

The fundamental purpose of organizing (and the resultant organization structure) is to establish a means of coordination. You will recall that sport management was defined as the coordination of the activities in the production and marketing of sport services. You also saw that the managerial functions of planning, organizing, leading, and evaluating are the means of such coordination. The focus here is on organizational structure as a coordinating mechanism. The structure enables coordination through systematically allocating diverse tasks, creating specified means of cooperation among people and units, establishing channels of communication among people and units, and allocating decision-making powers to those people or positions most qualified to make the decisions (Filley, House, & Kerr, 1976). In the following sections, the various principles of organizing are outlined. Because these principles have been in vogue for several decades, they are called the *classical* principles. The fact that management scholars and many management textbooks hold to these principles attests to their veracity and utility.

CLASSICAL PRINCIPLES

The classical principles that have been the cornerstones of organizing include specialization, span of control, departmentation, unity of command, and responsibility and authority.

Specialization

Specialization refers to the notion that individuals in an organization perform tasks that are narrow in scope. Specialization calls for each person to perform, as far as possible, one function. For an extreme example, consider the assembly line in a factory, where one individual's task may be reduced to merely fixing a bolt on the product. The idea is germane to all kinds of organizations. For example, a fitness club may employ specialists in weight training, aerobics, swimming, tennis, exercise physiology, nutrition, accounting, marketing, and so on. Similarly, a professional sport franchise may have specialists in media relations, marketing, sport law, accounting, and so on. Sport management degree programs in many universities have professors specializing in sport marketing, sport finance, sport law, organization theory, human resource management, and facility and event management.

Specialization may be necessary because one person does not have the time, energy, or knowledge to carry out a number of tasks associated with an organization. An added advantage of specialization is that it allows for those with the knowledge and ability to perform skilled tasks, and those without the competency to perform the unskilled tasks.

Specialization contributes to efficiency in the following specific ways:

1. Specialization in a limited number of tasks increases the skill or ability to perform those functions.
2. Specialization eliminates the time spent in putting away tools and equipment from one step and preparing for another.
3. Specialization facilitates the training of workers. It is easier and more effective to train individuals in a restricted number of specific and routine tasks than an array of different tasks.

Span of Control

Span of control refers to the number of people, units, and operations that a manager can control effectively and efficiently in a given time period. Research generally supports the suggestion that the span of control should be narrow at the top level of management (a ratio of approximately four subordinates to one manager) and wide at the lower levels (a ratio of approximately eight or more subordinates to one manager). Research also suggests that seven is the optimum number of subordinates a manager should supervise. However, Fink and his colleagues (1983) have outlined a series of factors that will affect the actual span of control in an organization or unit. These include the type of work done, the competence of the employee, the competence of the supervisor, the relationship between the employee and supervisor, and the pressure for production.

Type of work done. If the employees are engaged in similar and routine tasks, then it is possible for one manager to supervise a large number. For example, in a professional sport franchise, an individual may be able to supervise effectively a number of ticket takers for a game because they are all involved in similar tasks (checking the tickets and directing the spectators to their location). If, however, the tasks of the employees are complex and changing, then a narrower span of control is necessary. For example, the marketing personnel for that professional franchise would be performing relatively more complex tasks than the ticket takers. In addition, if they were all involved in tackling different segments of the market, they would be dealing with different sets of customer information and differing opportunities and barriers. One supervisor cannot effectively deal with this complexity. Therefore, such a situation would call for a narrow span of control.

Competence/expertise of the person doing the job. If employees are well trained and dedicated to their respective jobs, then close supervision is not necessary. Therefore, the span of control can be wider. For instance, if the subordinates of a marketing director in a university athletic department have good training in marketing, have experience in sport marketing, and are committed to their tasks, it will not be necessary for the director to spend as much time and energy in supervising them. Thus, she can supervise more employees. On the other hand, if the employees are new to the organization and to the field of marketing, and to sport marketing in particular, the director will have to spend more time giving them guidance and direction. Therefore, the manager can effectively supervise fewer employees. Similarly, greater supervision and therefore a narrower span of control are required where workers are indifferent to their task.

Competence/expertise of the supervisor. A more competent and technically qualified supervisor is able to supervise a greater number of subordinates than a less qualified and less skilled supervisor. Consider the case of two directors of sport marketing. If one is well versed in sport marketing, has had considerable experience in supervising other marketing professionals, has been with the present organization for a number of years, and is familiar with the client groups of the organization, he can supervise a greater number of employees. In contrast, a newly hired marketing manager with less experience needs time to become familiar with the new organization, its client groups, and the employees themselves. Hence, she may not have the time and energy to supervise as many employees as the first director.

Relationship between the supervisor and employees. In situations where there is respect for the supervisor and for the legitimacy of the supervisor's role, and a warm interpersonal relationship is present between supervisor and employees, a wider span of control is feasible. As we will note in a later chapter on leadership, respect and liking for the manager can motivate employees to carry out their responsibilities in order not to let the manager down. With such good rapport, the manager may be able to supervise more employees than when such feelings are absent. For example, a director of marketing in a professional sport franchise may be highly respected for her successes in marketing the franchise and generating revenues for the franchise. In addition, the employees and colleagues may personally like the director. Under those circumstances, she can supervise relatively more employees than if such respect and liking were not there.

Pressure for production. If there is pressure on the organization to produce more or better-quality goods or services, then the organization must impose greater control and supervision over its employees, which in turn leads to a narrower span of control.

In Brief

Span of control refers to the number of people, units, and operations under the control of a manager. The width of the span is influenced by the type of work, the competence of the employees and the supervisor, the relationship between them, and the pressure for production.

Note that a narrower span of control implies greater control and more supervision, while a wider span entails less supervision and less control. Therefore, whenever it is deemed necessary to exert greater control over the subordinates and their tasks, the number of subordinates under a manager is reduced.

When an organization institutes a narrow span of control in its mode of operation, the result is a greater number of levels in the hierarchy. On the other hand, if an organization adopts a wider span of control, there will be fewer levels in the hierarchy. The former situation results in a "tall" structure, the latter, a "flat" structure. Suppose that there are 12 employees working under one marketing director. That is, there are only two levels of hierarchy in the marketing unit—the director level and the employee level—resulting in a flat structure. Now, for some reason, the organization finds it necessary to supervise these 12 employees more closely to improve the efficiency and quality of the marketing operations. Accordingly, the decision is made to promote two of the senior employees to the rank of assistant directors of marketing. This arrangement results in a narrow span of control in the unit. First, the director will now supervise only the two assistant directors instead of the 12 employees. Second, each of the two assistant directors will supervise only five employees. In addition, the reorganization has created one more level of hierarchy in the unit, as shown in Exhibit 7.1, making the structure "taller" than before.

Departmentation

The principle of span of control leads to the concept of departmentation. That is, "since no one person can administer an unlimited number of subordinates, it is necessary to group activities into some homogeneous formation" (Robbins, 1976, p. 222). This process of forming homogeneous groupings is called **departmentation**. There are two broad types of departmentation.

Exhibit 7.1

Flat and tall structures.

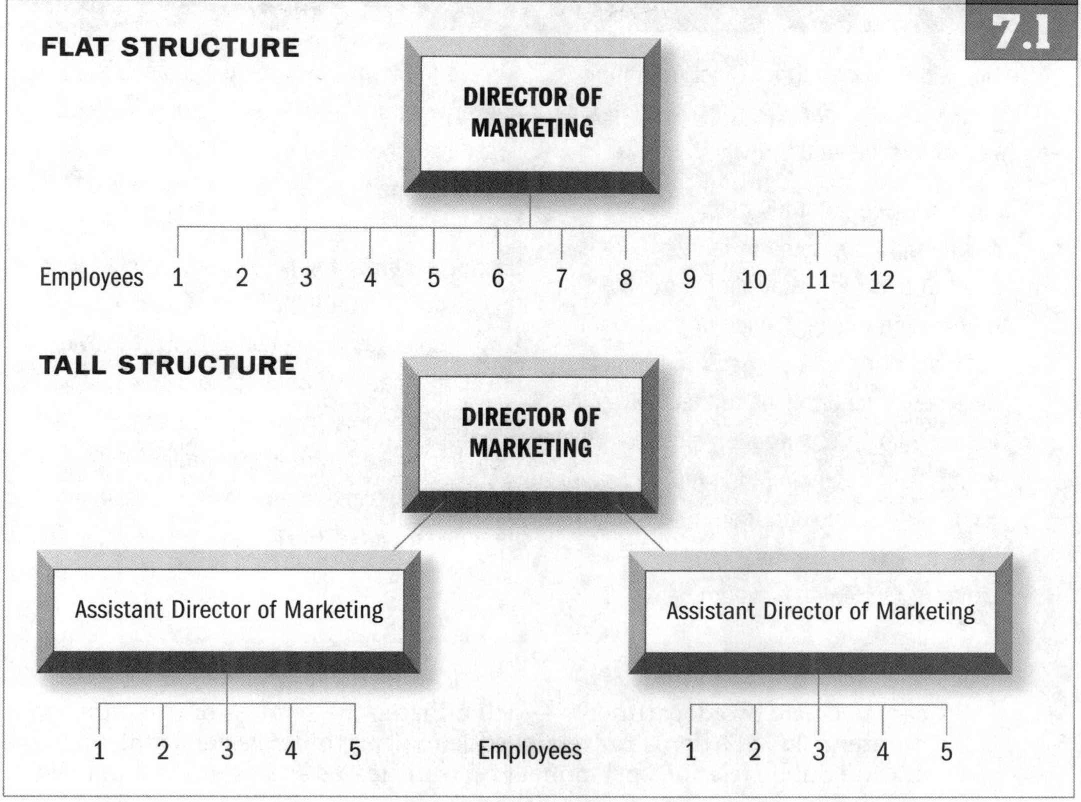

FLAT STRUCTURE

DIRECTOR OF MARKETING

Employees 1 2 3 4 5 6 7 8 9 10 11 12

TALL STRUCTURE

DIRECTOR OF MARKETING

Assistant Director of Marketing   Assistant Director of Marketing

1 2 3 4 5   Employees   1 2 3 4 5

Process-oriented or functional. This grouping is based on the concept of specialization. That is, individuals performing the same functions, or in positions involving similar skills, expertise, and resources, are grouped into a department. A ticketing department in a professional sport franchise, an accounting department in a large fitness club, and a sport management department in a university are examples of departmentation according to specialized functions.

Product- or goal-oriented. This way of grouping is basically a division of the organization according to different products, different geographical areas, different customer types, or different projects. In this type of departmentation, each unit consists of members with different specialized skills performing different functions. Consider a profit-oriented fitness club that has expanded its business to different geographical areas. Each geographical unit must hire people with various skills to perform the necessary functions. Similarly, when the firm decides to cater to two different sets of customers, such as those who seek general conditioning and those who prepare for athletic competitions, it may be neces-

In Brief

Departmentation is forming homogeneous groupings of tasks based on either the functions they perform (functional departmentation) or the products they produce (product departmentation).

Sidebar

R. J. Herbold (2004), former Chief Operating Officer of Microsoft, had this to say on intercepartmental rivalries and turf wars:

> "Over the course of my thirty-six years in business, I have come to realize there is a set of behaviors that people exhibit that remind me very much of the feudal fiefdoms of the Middle Ages. Individuals and groups tend to isolate themselves from the larger organization, and worry more about defending their turf and protecting the status quo than in moving the organization forward. I call such behavior the Fiefdom syndrome" (p. 1).

He found this syndrome in organizations in every sector (private, profit, nonprofit, public, educational, etc.). Noting that the behaviors associated with fiefdom go against common sense and innovation, and lead to destructive turf wars, he also said that "it's not that people who exhibit fiefdom tendencies are mischievous or unethical. These behaviors are simply natural human tendencies that emerge as people try to exercise control over their workplace environment, protect their domain, and avoid change that might upset the present order" (p. 1).

sary to create two departments—each utilizing the services of personnel with different skills. When a university athletic department assigns athletic trainers and public relations personnel to specific teams and expects them to work under the supervision of the coaches or managers of the respective teams, it is following goal-oriented departmentation.

A number of advantages and disadvantages are associated with the two forms of departmentation. Functional departmentation provides for the development of subspecialties (a division of labor within a specialty); advancement in the specialty; supervision by a specialist; professional contagion (the opportunity to learn from professional colleagues and to be motivated by them); efficient and maximum use of resources (that is, the use of existing personnel or equipment to the maximum extent before additions are made); and satisfaction with work (members of functional departments are more satisfied with their work than members of goal-oriented departments). For instance, employees of a marketing department in a sport enterprise have the opportunity to specialize in promotions, advertising, sponsorship, and other subdomains of marketing. At the same time, they have the opportunity to advance within the department. They also get to work with people who have training and expertise in the same specialty and to be supervised by a specialist in marketing, and thus learn from all these interactions.

On the negative side, functional departmentation leads to difficulties in coordinating and scheduling the activities of different units. Also, functional structures lead to conflict and competition between departments due to differences in professional orientations of the personnel. That is, the professional goals of the members in the department, rather than the goals of the organization, may be the dominating force. For instance, the marketing department, the event management unit, and other functionally specialized units in an organization providing spectator services may be in conflict with each other for two reasons: First, they compete with each other for resources as well as for the status and prestige accorded to each unit within the organization. Second, the conflicts (or at least lack of harmony) may be a function of their differing ways of looking at problems and arriving at solutions.

In a goal- or product-oriented department, the glue that binds the members is the goal of the project and its customers. Therefore, each of the units and its members are more focused on their respective customers and the requirements of the project or goal. Also, in such departmentation, personnel of different specialized skills function under one manager, resulting in greater coordination and less conflict among members. However, goal-oriented departmentation is less efficient in the sense that skills and equipment are duplicated and are not fully utilized. Further, since supervision by a specialist is denied to most of the members, they may feel isolated—particularly if there are no others in the same specialty within the department. That is, the opportunities for learning and professional growth are reduced.

Matrix. *Matrix* structure is another form of departmentation that attempts to gain the advantages of both the functional and goal-oriented modes of departmentation. A matrix organization is simply the imposition of one structure over the other. In Exhibit 7.2, members of an athletic department of a university belonging to a particular functional specialization are grouped together as a functional unit. At the same time, each individual member belongs to a goal-oriented

Exhibit 7.2 Matrix structure for a department of athletics and for a fitness center.

DEPARTMENT OF ATHLETICS	Project Grouping (Programs)			
Functional Grouping	Football	Basketball	Hockey	Gymnastics
Athletic Training				
Marketing				
Public Relations				
Academic Counseling				

FITNESS CENTER	Location Grouping		
Functional Grouping	Location A	Location B	Location C
Aerobics			
Weight Training			
Swimming			

unit—that is, a team. This allows for greater and more efficient coordination in a team's activities while, at the same time, providing a "home base" for each member. In a similar manner, a fitness club with two or more locations within a city may decide to adopt the matrix structure. In this scheme, there will be functional units such as aerobics, weight training, swimming, and so on, each under the supervision of a functional specialist. At the same time, members of the functional units are assigned to different branches supervised by the club manager. The matrix structure has one serious drawback: each member is supervised by two different managers—a violation of the principle of *unity of command,* which is discussed below.

> **In Brief**
>
> The matrix structure is a combination of process- and product-oriented departmentation in which an individual reports to a functional unit as well as a product unit.

Unity of Command

Unity of command is similar to the Biblical principle "No one can serve two masters." The principle of **unity of command** means that each member of the organization should follow the orders of only one supervisor and be accountable only to that supervisor. This serves to protect against the possibility that conflicting commands will be given by different superiors. While the unity of command concept is useful in highly structured organizations such as a government bureaucracy, it is likely to be disregarded in more modern, complex forms of organizational structure such as the matrix organization. In such structures, an employee may be expected to follow the advice and suggestions of more than one person rather than to comply strictly with the directives of one supervisor. The athletic trainer in a university athletic department, for example, may be asked to serve under both the supervisors of the athletic training units catering to the football and basketball teams. Similarly, a marketing specialist may serve under the supervisor of marketing for the athletic teams as well as the supervisor of marketing for the large arena.

Responsibility and Authority

The classical principle of responsibility with equal authority states that an employee must be given the necessary authority to carry out an assigned responsibility. It is readily apparent that individuals cannot carry out their duties if they do not have the authority to make decisions relating to their tasks. Thus, a manager put in charge of a sporting event must have the authority to decide on the traffic and security measures necessary to carry out the responsibility effectively and efficiently. This notion of authority equaling responsibility becomes critical in the case of those who have to monitor and control the activities of subordinates. For instance, the event manager has to monitor and control the activities of many individuals prior to and during a competition. That means that the manager should have the authority to assign

> **In Brief**
>
> Unity of command states that a worker should be placed under the command of a single supervisor. Another principle states that those who have a responsibility must have the authority to carry out the responsibility.

different people to different tasks, ask them to perform certain duties, correct them when they are not doing things correctly, and reward (or punish) them for their performances. In the absence of such authority, the manager cannot be held responsible if the subordinates do not carry out their duties effectively.

In summary, the principles of specialization, span of control, departmentation, unity of command, and responsibility and authority are intended to enable the organization to function efficiently and with a minimum of friction. Almost all organizations embrace these principles to varying degrees.

BUREAUCRACY

Bureaucrats have been likened to cockroaches. The reasoning is, like cockroaches, they are everywhere; like cockroaches, they don't seem to serve any useful purpose; and like cockroaches, they seem to defy all attempts at their extinction. (Watch Donald Brittain's documentary *Paperland: The Bureaucrat Observed*—the sourse of this comparison—for a savagely funny criticism of bureaucrats.)

This description sums up the negative attitude of anybody who has come up against a bureaucracy. Nevertheless, despite all criticisms, bureaucratic organizations are dominant in all nations, whether democratic or totalitarian, rich or poor, large or small. Professional sport clubs, commercial fitness clubs, city recreation departments, national sport governing bodies, and international sport federations are all patterned as bureaucracies. Even the departments of intercollegiate athletics and recreational sports in American universities are organized as bureaucracies. As Perrow (1972) points out, a **bureaucracy** is

> a form of organization superior to all others we know or can hope to afford in the near and middle future; the chances of doing away with it or changing it are probably nonexistent in the West in this century. Thus it is crucial to understand it and appreciate it. (p. 7)

Tenets of a Bureaucracy

Although bureaucracy has been practiced in some form or another since ancient times, the analysis and discussion of the phenomenon has gained momentum only since the beginning of the 20th century. Classical theorists like Taylor and Fayol emphasized some of the characteristics of a bureaucratic organization, but it was left to Max Weber, a German sociologist, to coin the term *bureaucracy* and write extensively on the concept in the early part of the 19th century. In his writings, Weber (1947) emphasized that an organization, if it is to operate rationally and efficiently, must be structured to include certain fundamental characteristics. His bureaucratic tenets, or principles, are described below. Note that some of these tenets are the same as or similar to the classical principles of organizations detailed earlier.

- **Division of labor.** In any organization, the total work must be broken down into simple, well-defined tasks, and these tasks must be distributed to members as official duties.
- **Hierarchical authority structure.** The positions in an organization are arranged in a hierarchical authority structure, meaning that progressively increasing authority is vested at each successively higher level.

The concepts of division of labor and hierarchy of authority are usually represented in an organizational chart. Exhibit 7.3 shows a typical organizational chart for a professional baseball team. The horizontal row of five boxes represents the division of labor into player personnel, scouting, public relations, ticket operations, and finance and administration. The vertical arrangement of the boxes shows the hierarchy of authority within the organization, beginning with the chief executive officer (CEO) and extending down to the directors of marketing and operations, the controller, and the information systems manager. You should note that there may be other employees below the lowest shown in Exhibit 7.3.

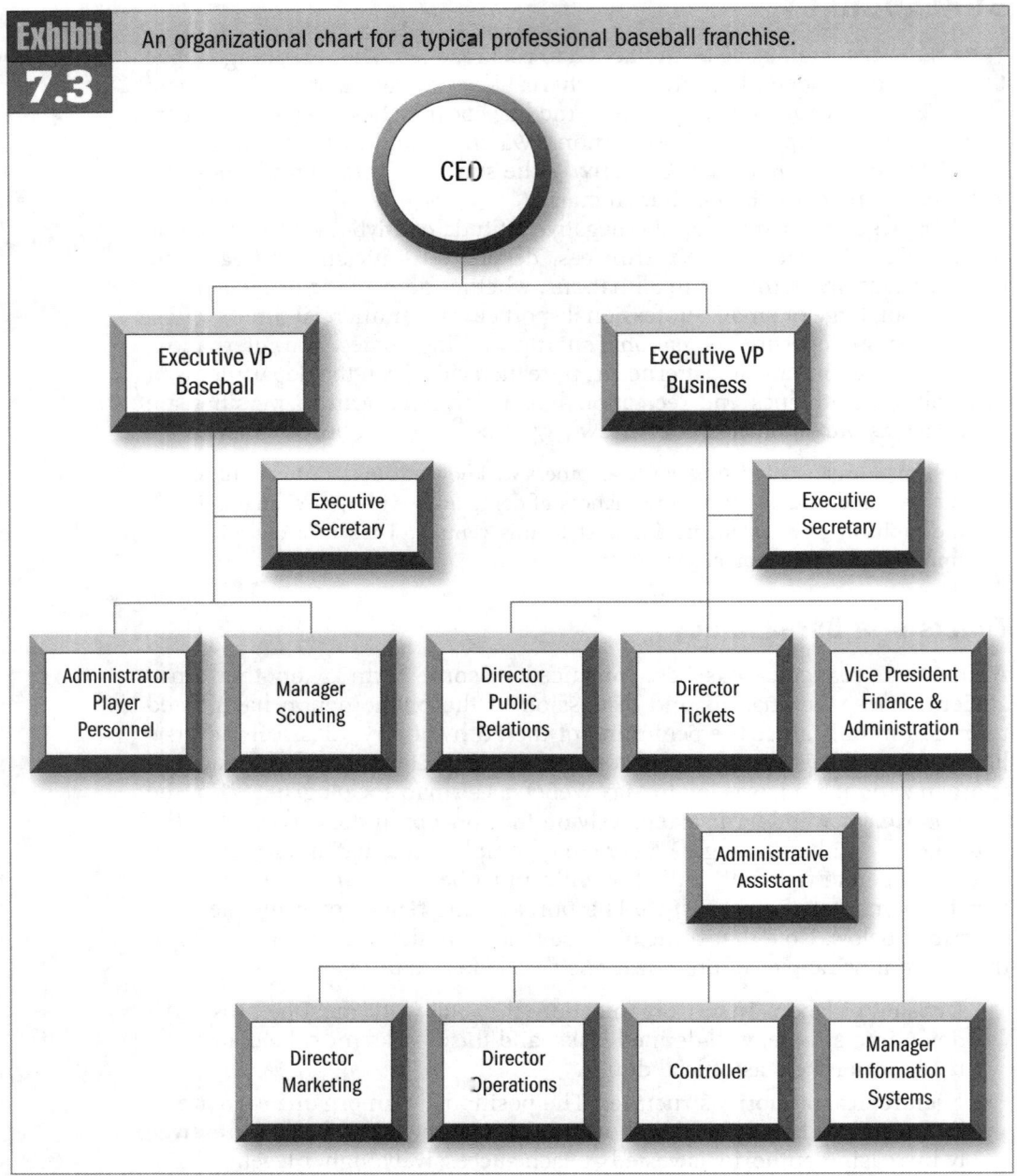

Exhibit 7.3 An organizational chart for a typical professional baseball franchise.

198 CHAPTER 7

- **A system of abstract rules.** This principle refers to the fact that an organization will specify a set of rules to regulate what is to be done, by whom, for whom, and under what conditions.
- **Impersonality.** Bureaucracies also exhibit impersonality, the notion that employees of an organization must deal with clients/customers, subordinates, and superiors on the same categorical basis without any personal, emotional, or social considerations.
- **Technical competence.** In a bureaucracy, employees should be hired and promoted on the basis of their technical competence relevant to a particular office or position in the organization.

Criticisms of Bureaucracy

It is worth noting that Weber was describing an "ideal" construct. As is most often the case, the ideal is never reached. This has resulted in some serious criticisms being leveled against bureaucracy and its prescriptions.

The major criticism against the creation of a *division of labor* is that each individual's job is reduced to a monotonous and degrading routine. The reduced content of the job leads, in turn, to decreased initiative, creativity, and motivation. The resulting boredom and frustration have been known to reduce the productivity of the workers. Thus, a division of labor that produces expertise and, through it, efficiency, can also lead to boredom and inefficiency. For example, the work in a ticketing operation could be divided into attending the phone, recording written requests, keeping track of tickets issued, and so on. If such division of work were done carefully, it would no doubt increase the efficiency of the operations. On the other hand, those who carry out these divided pieces of work are likely to be bored and frustrated with the routine.

Another tenet of bureaucracy to come under fire is *departmentation*—the division of labor at the unit level. This creates interdepartmental rivalry, which in turn leads to the displacement of organizational goals. That is, each department sets and pursues its own goals without reference to the wider organizational goals.

A serious drawback to *hierarchy of authority* is that the communication flow ultimately becomes inconsistent with the workflow. Two employees handling the case of a client may belong to two different authority units. Although they are closely connected to the case and may work in close proximity to each other, they cannot work together to make official decisions. Instead, each must communicate through a different superior, and this indirect path of communication leads to delays in the work process. Consider, for example, the case of a client who is eligible for tickets in a specific location in the football stadium because she has made a donation or paid for an advertisement in the stadium. The ticketing clerk is not aware of the client's status, but the employee in the marketing department knows the details. The most prudent and efficient thing is for the two employees to confer and issue the ticket to the client. However, if the bureaucratic principle of hierarchy of authority is strictly and blindly followed, then the two employees cannot consult with each other but must go through their respective bosses. In such a case, the operation becomes inefficient and the client is annoyed by the "red tape."

The bureaucratic tenet of *abstract rules* has drawn the severest criticisms. First, quite often the rules become outdated and out of tune with current conditions. For instance, a Canadian university athletic department used to have

Sidebar

The term *bureaucratization* refers to the processes of division of labor, specialization, routinization of jobs controlled by rules, and hierarchy of authority. The concept "Taylorism," named after its main proponent, Frederick Taylor, refers to assessing the time taken and motions involved in a job and identifying the "best" way (i.e., most efficient use of time and motion) to carry out that job.

Ritzer (1997) discussed the *McDonaldization* of the workplace. The term, derived from the fast-food giant McDonald's, refers to the application of the production principles and processes of the fast-food industry to other workplaces. The process is based on:

- *Efficiency*, which is assured when the best means is chosen to achieve a particular goal.
- *Calculability*, which is attained by quantifying everything the worker does (e.g., time and motions involved in a task).
- *Predictability*, by making sure that the products and services are the same every time they are produced.
- *Control*, whereby the behaviors of both workers *and* customers are guided by the technology of the production process.
- *Irrationality of rationality*, where the above rational processes lead to an irrational outcome, particularly the dehumanization of the people involved.

Ritzer (1997) noted that the process is an offshoot of earlier approaches such as bureaucracy and scientific management. He contended that the process of McDonaldization creates "McJobs," which:

- involve simple tasks designed for efficiency
- are simplified
- are predictable (e.g., in terms of work done and interactions with customers)
- are controlled by nonhuman technologies
- are dehumanized.

Ritzer (1997) noted that McJobs are tightly scripted. In his words, "McDonaldized jobs tend to be characterized by *both* routinized actions (for example, McDonald's hamburgers are to be put down on the grill moving from left to right, six rows of six patties, and the burgers are to be flipped beginning with the third row, with the first two rows to be flipped last) and scripted interactions (examples include, 'May I help you?'; 'Would you like a dessert to go with your meal?'; 'Have a nice day!')."

Readers should recognize that both bureaucratization and McDonaldization are designed to increase efficiency and consistency in the operations. Both also involve impersonal interactions with customers. Although McDonald's employees are trained to be courteous to the customer, they are also trained to be consistent in how they deal with individual customers.

separate arrangements (separate location and gender-based personnel) for the distribution of towels and equipment for male and female students. When the manager of the program wanted to change the rules, there was some resistance among other administrators and clients. When the rule was first established (who knows when!), it might have been consistent with the social norms of the day. The norms, however, changed far more quickly than the rule did.

A second criticism of abstract rules concerns the application of appropriate rules. In handling a particular incident or subject, a bureaucrat must first place it into the proper category. Moreover, errors in categorization may result in inappropriate treatment in some cases. It is not uncommon for fitness clubs to have unique and separate rules for different classes of clients. The simplest example is differential rates for seniors, students, and children. The employee dealing with a particular client first has to place the client in the proper category and then charge the rate applicable to that category. An error made in categorizing the client can result in the application of inappropriate rules.

Third, the existence of rules effectively sets the minimum acceptable level of performance for employees. This reduces the initiative of the workers, who tend to conform strictly to the rules. The result is that rules that were intended to serve only as a means to an end are treated as the ends themselves.

Finally, strict reliance on rules makes employees rigid in their interactions with clients. This rigidity produces tension between employees and clients which, in turn, leads the employees to adhere even more closely to the rules. This phenomenon is reflected in the phrase "throwing the book at you." For instance, consider a locker room attendant who refuses a towel or some equipment to a regular client who has left her identity card with another official. The attendant is within the rules in refusing the request. However, his reliance on the rule only, and not on the knowledge that the person before him is a regular client with a valid excuse, makes him too rigid. Such rigidity is likely to lead to resentment and friction in future interactions.

The bureaucratic notion of *impersonality* overlooks the community of humans inside and outside the organization. Critics of the impersonality of a bureaucracy have argued that it is not realistic to expect employees to suppress all their interpersonal feelings and attitudes.

Technical competence is generally accepted as a requisite for organizational efficiency and effectiveness. However, bureaucracies tend to promote individuals to higher positions on the basis of seniority, not competence. Although seniority often reflects experience and accrued knowledge at various lower-level positions, promotion on the basis of seniority alone denies the gifted and bright the opportunity to move up the hierarchy. Also, it could be argued that in some bureaucracies "twenty years' experience is one year's experience twenty times over."

Despite these criticisms, many organization theorists support the ideas of Weber and endorse the view that the bureaucracy should be the dominant mode of structuring large and complex organizations. Perrow (1972) has gone even further, suggesting that "the sins generally attributed to bureaucracy are either not sins at all or are consequences of the failure to bureaucratize sufficiently" (p. 6). On the other hand, Perrow also acknowledges that the "ideal" form of a bureaucracy is never realized. One of the reasons for this is that members of the organization "track all kinds of mud from the rest of their lives with them into the organization, and they have all kinds of interests that are independent of the organization" (p. 5). Another reason is that people "are only indifferently intelligent, prescient, all-knowing, and energetic. All organizations must be designed for the 'average' person one is likely to find in each position, not the superman" (p. 5).

Perrow also pointed out that a bureaucracy is structured to be stable in order to be efficient. In the case of governments, the **stability** requirement may be the most critical criterion. One paradox, however, is that if the stability requirement is achieved, the bureaucracy becomes impervious to changes in the environment. In turn, this results in the development of so-called red tape and inefficiency. Government bureaucracies are often strongly criticized for their stability and the red tape and inefficiency that result. However, it is important to remember that the stability of a bureaucracy is the very thing that provides some form of consistency during periods of rapid and dramatic change (democratic or revolutionary) in the government. Stability may also be needed in nongovernmental organizations. Consider a new chief executive officer taking charge of a university athletic department or a professional franchise. The new CEO may be considering drastic changes to transform the organization into a better and more efficient organization. However, she needs time to study the situation and identify the areas in which changes in the structure and processes can occur. Until such time, the organization needs to be stable in carrying out its traditional activities, such as ticketing, marketing, and event management, without disruption. The existing bureaucracy (division of labor, hierarchy of authority, rules and procedures, and so on) provides stability until the CEO initiates organizational changes.

Bureaucracy in a Democracy

It has been argued that the emphasis placed on the establishment of a hierarchy, and the discipline and obedience to superiors that are necessary components of a bureaucracy, are antithetical to the democratic notions of equality, freedom of choice, and dissent. If this is the case, how can a bureaucracy be tolerated and allowed to grow in a democracy?

Blau (1956) resolved this issue by outlining the contrasting purposes and processes of a democracy and a bureaucracy. The purpose of a **democracy** is to identify commonly agreed social objectives. The process of identifying these goals occurs through freedom of expression and dissent. Based on these differing expressions, the electorate and lawmakers can make an informed decision.

In contrast, the purpose of a bureaucracy is to achieve specified goals. Its concern is with the determination and implementation of efficient ways of achieving those goals. To achieve efficiency, rules and procedures must be specified, and an authority structure instituted to ensure adherence to the rules. Also, members must exhibit disciplined compliance to the rules and obedience to authority. Thus, as Blau (1956) pointed out:

> Bureaucratic and democratic structures can be distinguished, then, on the basis of the dominant organizing principle: efficiency or freedom of dissent. Each of these principles is suited for one purpose and not the other. When people set themselves the task of determining the social objectives that represent the interests of most of them, the crucial problem is to provide an opportunity for all conflicting viewpoints to be heard. In contrast, when the task is the achievement of given social objectives the essential problem to be solved is to discover the efficient, not the popular, means for doing so. Democratic values require not only that social goals be determined by majority decision,

but also that they be implemented through the most effective methods available, that is, by establishing organizations that are bureaucratically rather than democratically governed. The existence, therefore, of such bureaucracies does not violate democratic values. (p. 107)

The contrasting objectives and processes of a democracy and a bureaucracy are illustrated in Exhibit 7.4.

Although theorists like Perrow and Blau have supported the concept of bureaucracy, they have also pointed out the threat posed by large bureaucracies. Because of their control over vast amounts of resources (people and money), large bureaucracies have the power to influence democratic processes. In fact, their tendency to perpetuate themselves and to increase their power leads them to interfere in the affairs of the democracy. For instance, the lobbying efforts of government agencies (such as the Pentagon in the United States) or the attempts of large corporations and industries such as tobacco to influence the decision-making processes of democratically elected bodies are just a few examples. Perrow (1972) provided a caution when he noted that

> it is also crucial to understand not only how it [bureaucracy] mobilizes social resources for desirable ends, but also how it inevitably concentrates those forces in the hands of a few who are prone to use them for ends we do not approve of, for ends we are generally not aware of, and more frightening still, for ends we are led to accept because we are not in a position to conceive alternative ones. (p. 7)

In overview, it seems reasonable to suggest that a bureaucracy in a democracy is "value neutral"—that is, the positive and negative consequences are produced by humans in bureaucracies and not by bureaucracy itself.

In Brief

Democracy's purpose is identifying majority goals, while bureaucracy's purpose is achieving those goals. In order to identify majority goals, democracy permits debates and dissension. In contrast, bureaucracy emphasizes obedience and compliance in order to achieve the goals set for it efficiently.

Exhibit 7.4 Purposes and processes of a democracy and a bureaucracy.

	DEMOCRACY	BUREAUCRACY
PURPOSE	Identify majority goals ▼	Achieve majority goals ▼
CONCERN	Informed opinion ▼	Efficiency ▼
PROCESS	Freedom of expression Discussion Dissent	Disciplined obedience Compliance to procedures and authority

Bureaucracy in Sport Organizations

We have discussed the concept of bureaucracy at length for two main reasons. First, modern society is controlled to a greater and greater extent by bureaucracies (the government, large corporations, universities, hospitals, unions, political parties, and so on). Thus, all individuals need to have an understanding and appreciation of the principles underlying bureaucratic structures. Second, although the concept of bureaucracy appears to be more relevant to large organizations, the elements that make a bureaucracy rational and efficient can also be profitably applied to smaller organizations. For example (see Exhibit 7.5), football teams are clearly characterized by a division of labor (offensive and defensive units, and the specializations within each); a hierarchy (the chief coach, assistant coach, coaches for specialized units, the captain, quarterback); impersonality in selection, utilization, and rewarding of athletes; and technical competence on the part of the coaches and players. Further, rules are numerous in football—from the rules of the sport to league rules to team rules that even control the athlete's life away from the field. What is most significant is that these rules are closely followed by the players. There is perhaps no better example of members' willing compliance and obedience to the rules and authority of a bureaucracy.

Frisby (1983) noted that a number of authors

> have bemoaned the loss of personal autonomy on the part of the participants and volunteers, the intrusion of the law and government into the arena of sport, and the usurpation of expressive values by instrumental values as sport has become more bureaucratic in nature. (p. 80)

These concerns that the fundamental elements of sport are lost with bureaucratization are somewhat analogous to the concerns expressed about bureaucracy as it relates to a democracy. In the latter context, Blau (1956) argued that the contrasting purposes of a democracy and a bureaucracy necessitate as well as justify different processes—freedom of expression and dissent in a democracy versus compliance and obedience in a bureaucracy. Similarly, an examination of the purposes of competitive and recreational sports reveals that they are radically different, and, consequently, the process within each differs. In this regard, Keating (1964) has distinguished between *athletics,* whose purpose is pursuit of excellence, and *sport,* whose purpose is maximizing pleasure for contestants:

> In essence, sport is a kind of diversion which has for its immediate and direct end fun, pleasure and delight and which is dominated by a spirit of modera-

Exhibit 7.5 Bureaucracy in sport organizations.

FOOTBALL TEAM
- Division of labor into offensive and defensive units and specialization within units
- Hierarchy of chief coach, assistant coaches, special teams coaches, captain, quarterback, etc.
- Impersonality in selection, use, and rewarding of athletes
- Technical competence of coaches and players
- Numerous rules, including sport rules, league rules, team rules, with member compliance and obedience to rules

tion and generosity. Athletics, on the other hand, is essentially competitive activity which has for its end victory in the contest and which is characterized by a spirit of dedication, sacrifice, and intensity. (p. 28)

If the differences between recreational sport (which is concerned with the pursuit of pleasure) and athletics or competitive sport (which is concerned with the pursuit of excellence) are taken into account, then it is only logical to expect that the two endeavors will be structured differently. Recreational sport should be loosely structured; competitive sport, bureaucratically structured.

The relevance of bureaucratic concepts to national sport organizations is illustrated by Frisby's (1983) study of those organizations in Canada. She found that those national sport organizations that were more bureaucratic were also more effective in terms of both goal attainment and resource acquisition.

SUMMARY

This chapter outlined the classical principles of specialization, span of control, departmentation (both functional and product), unity of command, and responsibility and authority. We discussed the organizational form known as bureaucracy, including its tenets of division of labor, hierarchy of authority, system of abstract rules, impersonality, and technical competence, and we looked at various criticisms of these tenets. We noted that, despite these criticisms, bureaucracy is the best form for managing organizations. The role of bureaucracy in achieving the goals set by the democracy was explained, and we noted the contradictory processes of dialogue, debate, and dissension in a democracy on the one hand and obedience to authority and compliance to rules in a bureaucracy. We saw how the differing processes are consistent with the respective purposes of democracy (identifying majority goals) and bureaucracy (achieving those goals efficiently). Finally, we discussed the relevance of bureaucracy for sport organizations.

DEVELOPING YOUR PERSPECTIVES

1. Recall a job you have had. Describe the extent to which it was specialized. Did that specialized work contribute to efficiency of the organization? Did it allow you to become an expert in the task? Did it contribute to your personal growth?

2. Describe a significant experience you have had with a bureaucracy in terms of both the positive and negative aspects of that experience.

3. To what degree are the programs (graduate, undergraduate, athletic, intramural) in your university or college bureaucratized? What changes, if any, would you make in the administrative structure of these programs? Why?

4. Which of the bureaucratic tenets do you favor? Why? Which ones do you dislike? Why?

5. Consider two or three sport management jobs you are familiar with. Describe the extent to which each of them has been or could be McDonaldized.

References

Blau, P. M. (1956). *Bureaucracy in modern society.* New York: Random House.

Certo, S. C. (1992). *Modern management: Quality, ethics, and the global environment* (5th ed.). Boston: Allyn and Bacon.

Chelladurai, P. (1976). A composite production model for the degree programs in institutions of physical education. *CAHPER Journal, 42,* 30–35.

Filley, A. C., House, R. J., & Kerr, S. (1976). *Managerial process and organizational behavior.* Glenview, IL: Scott, Foresman.

Fink, S. L., Jenks, R. S., & Willits, R. D. (1983). *Designing and managing organizations.* Homewood, IL: Richard D. Irwin.

Frisby, W. M. (1983). *The organizational structure and effectiveness of Canadian national sport governing bodies.* Unpublished doctoral dissertation, University of Waterloo, Waterloo, Canada.

Hall, R. H. (1996). *Organizations: Structures, processes, and outcomes* (6th ed.). Englewood Cliffs, NJ: Prentice Hall.

Herbold, R.J. (2004). *The fiefdom syndrome.* New York: CURRENCY/Doubleday.

Keating, J. W. (1964). Sportsmanship as a moral category. *Ethics, 75,* 25–35.

Maraghy, D. R. (1998). Event management: A practical approach. In H. Appenzeller (Ed.), *Risk management in sport: Issues and strategies.* Durham, NC: Carolina Academic Press.

Mintzberg, H. (1989). *Mintzberg on management: Inside our strange world of organization.* New York: The Free Press.

Perrow, C. (1972). *Complex organizations: A critical essay.* Glenview, IL: Scott, Foresman.

Ritzer, G. (1997). McJobs. http://icdl.uncg.edu/ft/051199-05.html. Retrieved October 15, 2003.

Robbins, S. P. (1976). *The administrative process: Integrating theory and practice.* Englewood Cliffs, NJ: Prentice Hall.

Sofer, S. (1972). *Organizations in theory and practice.* New York: Basic Books.

Vroom, V. H., & Jago, A. G. (1988). *The new leadership: Participation in organizations.* Upper Saddle River, NJ: Prentice Hall.

Weber, M. (1947). *The theory of social and economic organization.* (Translated by A. M. Henderson and T. Parsons). New York: Oxford University Press.

Weihrich, H., & Koontz, H. (1993). *Management: A global perspective* (10th ed.). New York: McGraw-Hill.

CHAPTER 8

System-Based Organizing

MANAGE YOUR LEARNING

After completing this chapter you should be able to:

- Explain the need to view organizations from a systems perspective and design them to be responsive to environmental conditions.
- Understand the concepts of differentiation and integration of organizational units, and explain why organizations need to undertake both simultaneously.
- Discuss the methods of integrating differentiated units.
- Explain the applicability to sport organizations of Thompson's idea of insulating the technical core.
- Understand the significance of boundary-spanning units.
- Discuss Parsons' notions of vertical differentiation of the institutional, managerial, and technical subsystems.
- Explain the role of the technical core in service organizations in boundary-spanning activities.
- Describe the five types of network organizations and identify their purposes.

STRATEGIC CONCEPTS

authority
authority structure
boundary-spanning unit
differentiation
environmental influences
external network
functional power
institutional subsystem
integration

internal network
interorganizational network
managerial subsystem
network organization
operational unit
professional services
systems perspective
technical core

ORGANIZING: OPEN SYSTEMS PERSPECTIVES

In the previous chapter, after describing the classical principles of organizing, we made a lengthy investigation of bureaucracy as an organizational form. Although the bureaucratic form has its strengths, we also noted several criticisms of it. One of the strengths, as well as a weakness, is the fact that it is slow to change. Although that slowness may be a virtue in terms of the stability it offers, it also underscores the closed nature of a bureaucracy as an organizational system. In the bureaucratic view, the organizational goals are assumed to be clear and fixed, and the organization and its processes are designed to be efficient in all internal operations. However, in its drive for efficiency, a bureaucracy tends to ignore the **environmental influences.**

Organizations do not operate in a vacuum. Fundamentally, an organization is an instrument of society, and, consequently, it has a primary responsibility to society and its needs. For instance, a university athletic department is there to promote the pursuit of excellence among its students and to provide entertainment for the university population and the community. Therefore, it needs to be aware of the needs and preferences of the student–athletes, the students at large, the faculty, and the community. In addition, it has to compete with the athletic departments of other universities in order to create good entertainment and bring prestige to the university. Thus, it needs to monitor what is happening in other universities and the National Collegiate Athletic Association (NCAA), and to be open to changing its own operations. In addition, the athletic department must be responsive to stakeholder groups and their demands. Similarly, a city recreation department has to be attuned to taxpayers who are at the same time the benefactors and beneficiaries of its operations. Because societal needs change, it is essential for any organization to monitor the changes and adapt in order to function effectively in meeting the needs of society.

From a different perspective, organizations are self-serving in that they pursue their own goals. For instance, a profit-oriented sports organization such as a professional sport franchise is there to make a profit for the owners. Insofar as the clients or customers are the source of such profits, the organization must be attuned to the needs and preferences of those clients and customers. Also, the organization can make a profit only if it competes effectively with other organizations providing the same products or services (another sport franchise or other entertainment enterprise). Thus, a professional sport franchise must recruit outstanding athletes in order to present a winning team and quality entertainment to the public. If its products are not acceptable to the public, the franchise will eventually go out of business. In addition, the professional franchise must also ensure that the athletes do not violate the moral and ethical standards of society (for example, by illegal drug use). The professional sport franchise needs to change its managerial practices if and when the ethical and moral standards of society change. Otherwise, it could eventually be forced out of business.

The sponsors and the advertisers are also a source of income, and therefore the franchise must deal with them effectively. As media coverage is essential for the franchise, the media's demands and requirements must be addressed. Finally, the franchise must also be aware of and follow government regulations and guidelines. Considering that all sources of profit and constraints to profits are part of the organization's environment, the franchise must adapt and change with the changes in the environment in order to survive. Similar arguments can be advanced in the case of other profit-oriented sport enterprises such as a commercial fitness club, a golf course, a sport law consulting firm, a player agency, or a footwear and apparel company.

The idea of environment and the need to monitor and adapt to changes within it are implied in some of the topics covered so far. For instance, in Chapter 4, we found that the conceptual skills needed for effective management must include an awareness of the relationship of the organization to the industry, the community, and the political, social, and economic forces of the nation as a whole (Katz, 1974). Similarly, three of the 10 managerial roles described by Mintzberg (1975) in Chapter 4 deal specifically with environmental conditions. In the monitor role, the manager monitors the environment for information on the opportunities and constraints affecting the organization. In the entrepreneur role, the manager seizes upon the opportunities offered by the environment and embarks on new projects. Finally, in the disturbance handler role, the manager deals with problems posed by the environment. Similarly, the planning function discussed in Chapter 5 rests heavily on identifying opportunities and constraints in setting goals for the organization. This sensitivity to the demands of the environment forms the basis for the approach taken by many theorists in designing organizations. In the following sections, we will look at the approaches taken by three of these theorists—Lawrence and Lorsch (1967), Thompson (1967), and Parsons (1960).

> **To Recap**
>
> **OPEN SYSTEMS** In Chapter 3, organizations were described as open systems. A system is a set of interrelated parts organized in such a way as to make a recognizable whole (Robbins, 1997; Waring, 1996). The attribute that makes an organization an open system is its need to interact and be consistent with its environment. Some parts of the environment are closely linked to the organization's goals and tasks (such as other fitness enterprises in the locality of a fitness club). Other parts are more remotely connected to the local fitness club (for example, the research that goes on in physiology labs on the efficacy of different exercise regimens). Note that an organization is dependent upon the environment for its resources as well as the disposal of its outputs; therefore, it is imperative that an organization be attuned to the vagaries of the environment. Insofar as an organization has to interact with the various elements or agents in its environment, it must be structured in such a way as to make that interaction possible and effective.

The Lawrence and Lorsch Model

Lawrence and Lorsch (1967) did research on manufacturing organizations. Their basic premise was that a manufacturing organization is divided into three major subsystems: sales, production, and research and development. Each of these subsystems must deal with different segments of the environment—market, technical–economic, and scientific sub-environments respectively.

The three subsystems differ with respect to three elements: (1) the rate at which their respective sub-environments change, (2) the relative amounts of information they have about their environments, and (3) the feedback they receive from the environment. These three elements constitute what Lawrence and Lorsch called "certainty of the environment." According to these authors, the relative certainty of the environment faced by the subsystems creates two specific problems for the organization—differentiation and integration.

Differentiation

Differentiation occurs when an organization is divided into units according to environmental exigencies, and those units are then staffed with people of the appropriate aptitude and skills. Note that the concept of differentiation is not identical to the concept of departmentation. According to the classical and bureaucratic approaches, departmentation occurs when an organization is divided into units that are concerned with specific functions or purposes. The internal structure within the various units is similar and is characterized by hierarchy of authority and rules and regulations.

Differentiation, on the other hand, according to Lawrence and Lorsch, is the division of labor based on differing environmental conditions. Because each unit is required to interact with different segments of the environment (and these segments differ in terms of certainty, feedback, and rate of change), each organizational unit must be organized differently to enable it to cope with the particular sub-environment and its requirements. A further necessary condition for differentiation is that the members of a unit possess those specific talents and aptitudes that match the demands of the environment. For instance, a sales agent for a manufacturing company needs to interact with reluctant customers and convince them of the benefits of buying the company's products. On the other hand, the purchasing agent for the company often has to resist attempts by sales agents of other companies who want to sell their products to the focal company. Thus, the sales agent and the purchasing agent need different persuasive and analytical skills in responding to their respective environments.

Integration

Lawrence and Lorsch pointed out that while differentiation is relatively easy to implement, integrating the subunits into a meaningful and effective whole is a problem. Because differentiated units have different structures and follow different operating procedures (and, more important, the members of these units have different training and orientations), the task of **integration** is more difficult than the task of differentiation. It is possible for organizations to achieve the difficult task of integration by creating liaison or integrator roles, by making interactions across groupings mandatory, by promoting joint responsibilities for common goals, by developing task forces or committees with joint memberships, and by holding meetings to foster understanding among different groups.

Although the Lawrence and Lorsch model was developed for business firms and industries, the concepts of differentiation and integration are also useful in the context of sport organizations. This is certainly the case in the

> **In Brief**
>
> Differentiation refers to structuring organizational units in specific ways to meet the environmental requirements of each, and to staffing the units with personnel who possess the necessary skills and aptitudes. Integration refers to the ways in which the differentiated units are brought together to cooperate with each other in the pursuit of organizational goals.

Sidebar

Following is a case of differing perspectives on how to structure an intercollegiate athletic department and its departments. At The Ohio State University, the units (a) providing academic support to student-athletes (named Student-Athlete Support Services at OSU), (b) investigating rule violations (i.e., the Compliance Office at OSU), and (c) interacting with boosters and alumni were all housed in the same administrative department under the supervision of the athletic director. This organization makes sense if the focus of analysis is the athletic department. That is, coordination and integration of units within intercollegiate athletics is improved by this arrangement. However, when the university faced problems with rule violations and academic integrity, the president and the athletic director decided to restructure the department to place the academic support services under the supervision of the Office of the Provost and the Compliance unit in the Office of Legal Affairs. Although the interaction with boosters and alumni remained under the athletic director's supervision, it was mandated that all correspondence to these groups and other donors was to emphasize the rules governing their activities and there was to be greater vigilance of those activities. This reorganization makes sense from the perspective of the university as the focus of analysis. That is, the units that ensure academics are emphasized and the rules followed in intercollegiate athletics are assigned to university units specializing in those two areas. At the least, this restructuring should eliminate the perceptions that rule violators and rule enforcers are colluding with each other.

organization of programs of intercollegiate athletics, recreational sport, and sport management in a university. In some universities, sport management is placed under the department of athletics. Coaches, administrators, and sport management faculty members are familiar with the long-standing discussions, arguments, and debates that revolve around questions of control, jurisdiction, and responsibility. These discussions become particularly heated when intercollegiate athletic programs deviate (or are perceived to deviate) from the fundamental educational mandate of the university. Unfortunately, however, these discussions do not often address fundamental organizational issues relating to the goals of each program, the environments they have to deal with, or the required internal structures and processes within each program.

If the concept of differentiation is applied to a university, the three programs might be organized according to the structure illustrated in Exhibit 8.1. Given that each of the three programs has different sets of goals and that they interact with different environments, they would be allowed to adopt structures and processes appropriate to their situation (differentiation). The concept of differentiation also requires that those members involved in the three programs have different talents and skills. Faculty members in the sport management program must have the academic talents to teach a large number of students and to design and follow a specified curriculum, as well as the talents needed for conducting research. Similarly, administrators and personnel

Exhibit 8.1

Lawrence and Lorsch's concepts of differentiation and integration applied to intercollegiate athletics, recreational sports, and sport management.

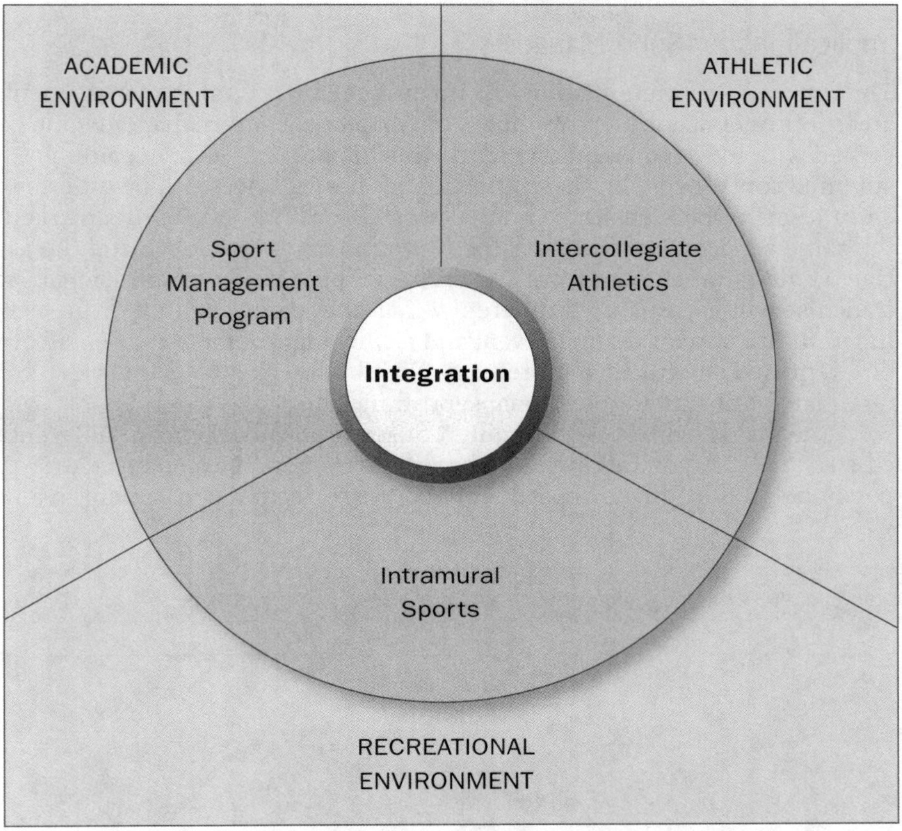

ACADEMIC ENVIRONMENT
ATHLETIC ENVIRONMENT
Sport Management Program
Intercollegiate Athletics
Integration
Intramural Sports
RECREATIONAL ENVIRONMENT

in the athletic and recreational sport programs must have the necessary managerial talents and skills.

While the academic, intramural, and athletic programs are easily segregated, integrating them into a meaningful whole in the pursuit of larger organizational goals requires careful thought and conscious effort. Integration is achieved differently in different universities. One obvious method is to place one of these programs in a superior position to the other programs and then to assign it the responsibility and the authority to coordinate the activities of all programs. In some instances, an attempt has been made to achieve integration through policy statements and rules and procedures, but these have been only partially successful. It has proved more effective to bring the managers of the three programs together in face-to-face encounters so that they may confront each other over any contentious issues, typically in the form of a committee that meets periodically. This process of direct communication and confrontation has been found to be an effective integrative mechanism.

Another factor that can contribute to the integration of the three programs is to employ individuals who have responsibilities spread across two or more programs. Thus, a professor might teach an undergraduate course and also coach a university team. In this situation, faculty members are expected to develop an understanding of the requirements, constraints, and values of the two programs, and thereby to integrate their activities across both.

Implications for Sport Managers

The concepts of differentiation and integration are critical to management of any sport organization. As we noted in Chapter 1, sport management is concerned with the production and marketing of sport services. Accordingly, the subunits concerned with the production of these services will be differentiated in terms of both structure and personnel from those subunits marketing the same services. For instance, the unit producing excellence and the associated entertainment (the team and the coaching staff) in a professional sport franchise will be structured differently than the marketing unit or the ticketing unit. In a similar manner, event and facility management may entail other differentiated structures and processes. Exhibit 8.2 illustrates this view of differentiated units in a professional sport franchise.

Note that the production of different services will also entail differentiated structures. A good example is the differentiation between structures and personnel in the athletic department and the recreation department in a uni-

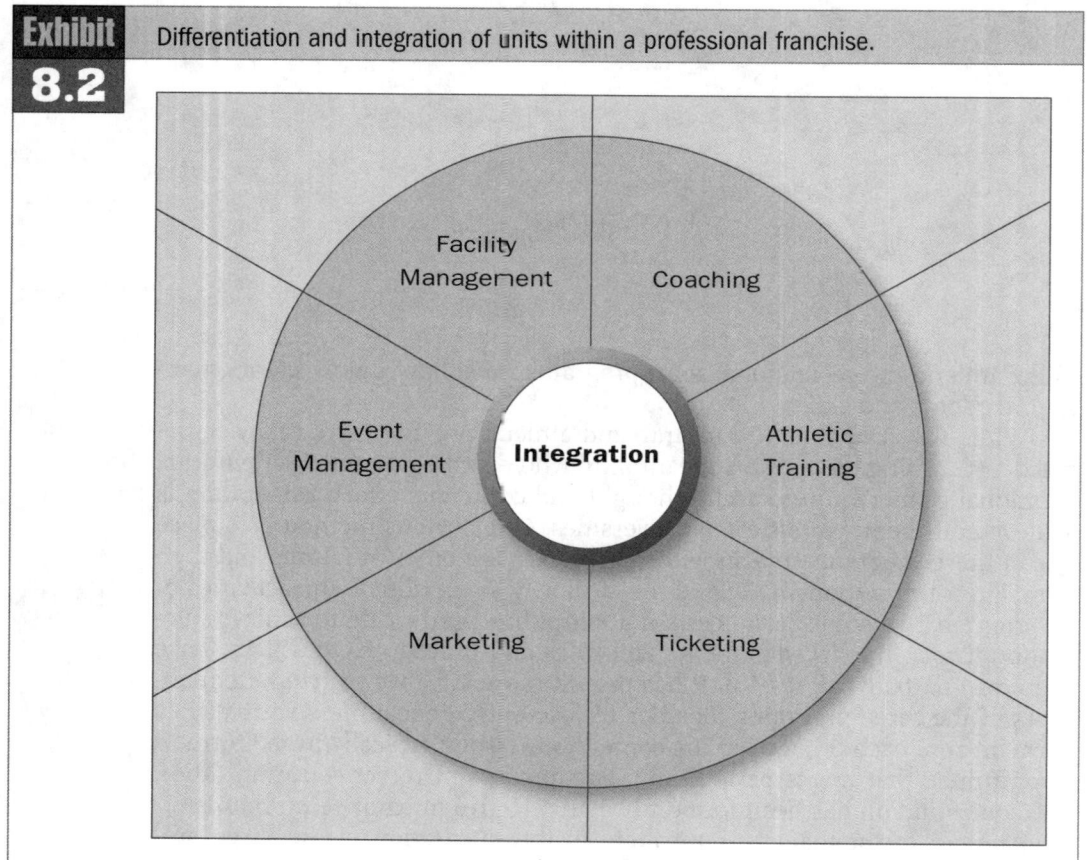

Exhibit 8.2 Differentiation and integration of units within a professional franchise.

versity. Because the athletic department is concerned with producing excellence and entertainment, whereas the recreation department's focus is on participant services, the expectations of their respective stakeholders are different. For instance, the public and the media will be very critical of the athletic department if the athletic teams are not performing well. Because such a situation is likely to reflect on the image of the university, the university authorities will also be concerned. In contrast, such negative consequences are not likely when specific units within the recreation department are not performing well. Accordingly, the structures, processes, and personnel of the two departments will differ from each other.

As another example, consider a sport marketing firm that offers its services to (a) professional sport franchises, (b) commercial fitness clubs, and (c) city recreation departments. Business is booming, and the firm finds it necessary to create specialized units to deal with each of these three segments of its customers. In a sense, this is a response to the need to differentiate its offerings. Accordingly, different structures and processes must be put in place in each unit so that each can deal effectively with the particular set of customers and the environment it faces. In addition, the firm is likely to place personnel in each unit with the necessary skills, training, and orientation to deal effectively with the specific set of customers and the competitive environment the unit faces. This would amount to the application of the Lawrence and Lorsch model.

The Thompson Model

Thompson (1967) endorsed the Lawrence and Lorsch view that an organization should be subdivided into units on the basis of the segments of the environment with which they interact. Those units that have direct contact with the external environment are called the *boundary-spanning units*. In addition, Thompson, along the lines of Parsons (1960) (discussed later in the chapter), endorsed the view that organizations must attempt to seal off one of the units—the *technical core*—from environmental uncertainties.

Technical Core

Technical core refers to the unit that is most directly concerned with the production of goods or services. The assembly line in an automobile factory, the classrooms in a high school, and an athletic team in an intercollegiate athletic program are some examples of the technical core in their respective organizations. Consider an aerobics class in a fitness club. The aerobics instructor, the clients, the music, and the room where the class is conducted constitute one part of the technical core of the fitness club—the part associated with the production of the aerobics service. The weight training instructor, the clients, and the equipment in the weight room would be another part of the technical core of the fitness club.

Thompson argued that if the technical core is to be efficient, it must be able to work in a stable environment in terms of a steady flow of resources (inputs), prompt disposal of its products (outputs), and minimal interference from other units and organizations. That is, the technical core must be able to focus on its fundamental task of producing goods or services without being distracted by environmental concerns such as securing resources and disposing of products. Note that the notion of disposing of products is more germane to manufacturing organizations where the production and consumption (buying) of the product are separated. We noted in Chapter 1 that a service is produced and consumed simultaneously. In the previous example of the fitness club, the production and consumption of the aerobic service (the participant service) are simultaneous. Despite this difference between producing a good and producing a service, the idea of a stable environment for the production is equally applicable to both goods and services. For instance, the efficiency and quality of the aerobics class cannot be assured if the instructor is distracted by the malfunctioning public address system or worried about how to get rid of the used towels.

Boundary-Spanning Units

Environmental stability is provided by what Thompson (1967) calls the **boundary-spanning units:**

> Organizations subject to rationality norms seek to isolate their technical cores from environmental influences by establishing boundary-spanning units to buffer or level environmental fluctuations. These responsibilities help determine the structure of input and output units. (p. 67)

In business and industry, units dealing with marketing, purchasing, legal affairs, and public relations interact with their respective task environments in their specific ways, and in so doing secure the resources needed for the technical core, dispose of its outputs, and thereby create a relatively stable environment for the technical core.

The teacher, students, and classroom in a university sport management course constitute the technical core. The classroom is where the fundamental function of a university (i.e., teaching) is carried out. For the teacher and the students to carry on their respective tasks of teaching and learning, they must be protected from disturbances that could arise from outside the immediate classroom situation. The buffer between the technical core and outer environment is composed of the dean, program chairpersons, and other administrative officers within the faculty; members of the registrar's office; employees in the physical plant, reservation office, and time-tabling office; the president; and other members of the upper management of the university.

Typically, these buffer agents handle the admission of the students to the university, the general program of studies, entrance requirements into the particular course, the scheduling of classes and exams, reservation of classrooms, and so on. The major concerns of the teacher are to teach the course according to the prepared course outline and to evaluate the students. The students, after they have selected the course, are concerned only with learning. Scholarships, bursaries, and student loans are also a buffering mechanism in the sense that they permit students to concentrate on their studies rather than spend time trying to earn money for upkeep.

On a wider scale, the top officials of the university interact with groups in the environment, such as government or private corporations, in order to secure the necessary resources for the university. One of their main functions is to smooth out fluctuations imposed by disturbances in the general (distal) environment.

Implications for Sport Managers

The relevance of the Thompson model to sport organizations can be highlighted through one or two examples. The operation of a university athletic team illustrates the notion of insulating the technical core from environmental disturbances. As shown in Exhibit 8.3, the athletic team (including the athletes and coaches) is the technical core. The boundary-spanning units are the athletic department, university administration, the physical plant, and the university board of governors. Because the athletic team must strive for excellence in the sport and attempt to win as many games as possible, its major focus must be on training and preparation. All factors and influences that might detract from this exclusive focus must be blocked out. Athletic departments do this, in part, by providing athletic scholarships in order to relieve athletes of concerns for their upkeep. Some universities used to have separate dormitories for athletes in order to filter out the "distracting influences" of other students. In some universities, special classes or instructors are provided so that activities (practices and games) are not affected by regularly scheduled classes. While many educators question such practices in a university setting, it cannot be denied that those institutions that adopt these strategies—provide a buffer between the technical core and the outer environment—are able to nurture, develop, and produce the best athletic talent.

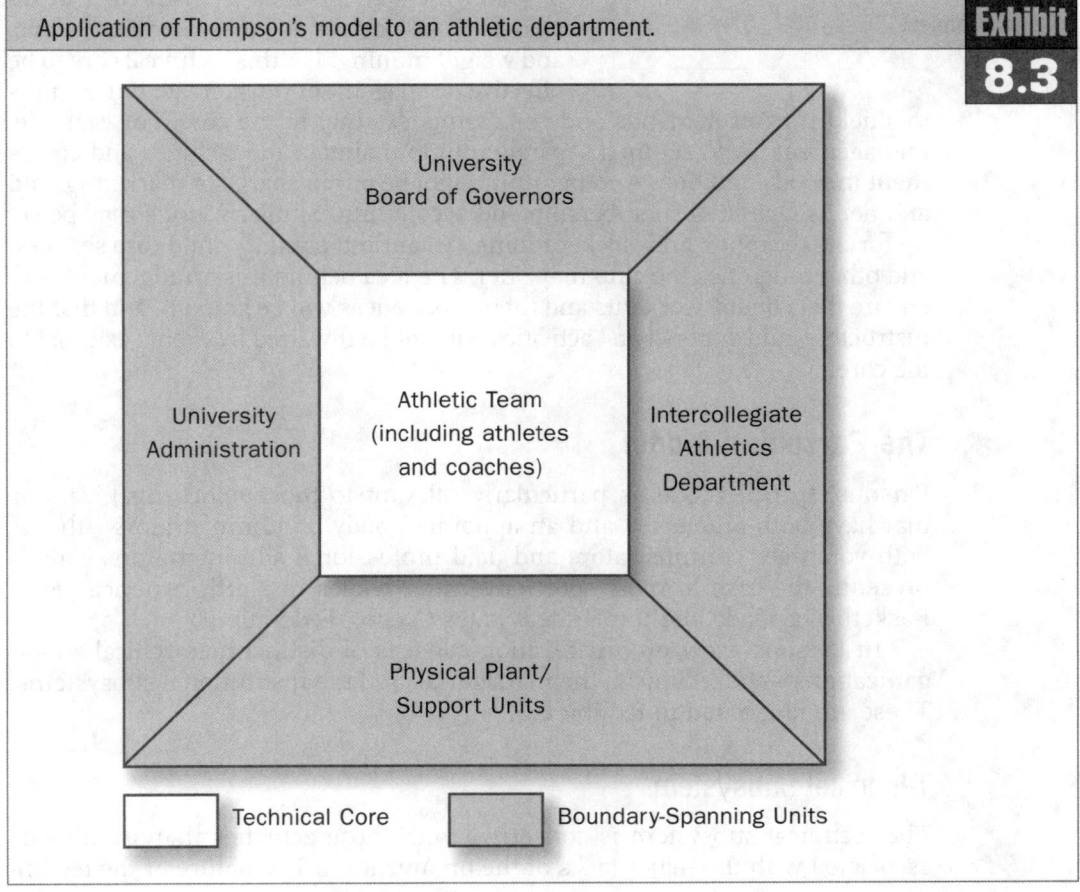

Exhibit 8.3 Application of Thompson's model to an athletic department.

In addition, the athletic department, through its various subunits such as academic counseling, facility management, event management, marketing, and ticketing, acts as a boundary-spanning unit and insulates the athletic teams from environmental influences. By being the buffers between the athletic teams and the environment, these units facilitate the smooth functioning of the university teams.

This concept of insulating the athletes from environmental influences is also evident in the manner in which the communist bloc countries used to prepare their athletes. Good athletes were recruited and employed by a factory or a government agency such as the army. Typically, the coaches were also employees of the organization. Salaries for the athletes were equivalent to the athletic scholarships provided by a North American university. Instead of reporting for regular work, the athletes reported for athletic practices. The work requirements were rescheduled to fit the athletic schedule, just as is the case in some North American universities. Thus, both cases illustrate Thompson's idea of insulating the technical core.

The idea of insulating the technical core can be extended to any sport organization that is large enough to have different subunits to carry out different functions. Consider a large fitness club. The technical core for the club is composed of the supervisors and instructors of fitness activities such as aquatics, aerobics, tennis, and weight training. For this technical core to be effective, management must create buffer units to shield it from demands and constraints external to the core. For example, management could set up a separate unit to maintain the facilities and equipment in good condition. Another unit might be put in charge of marketing, and another in charge of membership and accounting. Similarly, units may be set up for the reception area, locker rooms, restaurant, parking, child care services, and other amenities the club may offer. The idea behind this arrangement is to ensure that clients' workouts and their experiences will be smooth, and that the instructors' and supervisors' activities will not be thwarted by events external to the core.

In Brief

It is important that the units involved in the production of organizational outputs be insulated by boundary-spanning units from environmental disturbances.

The Parsonian Model

Parsons' (1960) model is particularly relevant to those sport organizations that have both an elected and an appointed body of administrators—that is both volunteer administrators and paid professional administrators. This is presently the case in most sport governing bodies in North America (as in Basketball Canada and the United States Cycling Federation).

In Parsons' view, an organization consists of distinct hierarchical suborganizations—the technical, the managerial, and the institutional subsystems. These are illustrated in Exhibit 8.4.

Technical Subsystem

The technical subsystem is concerned with those activities that are directly associated with the major tasks of the organization. The nature of the techni-

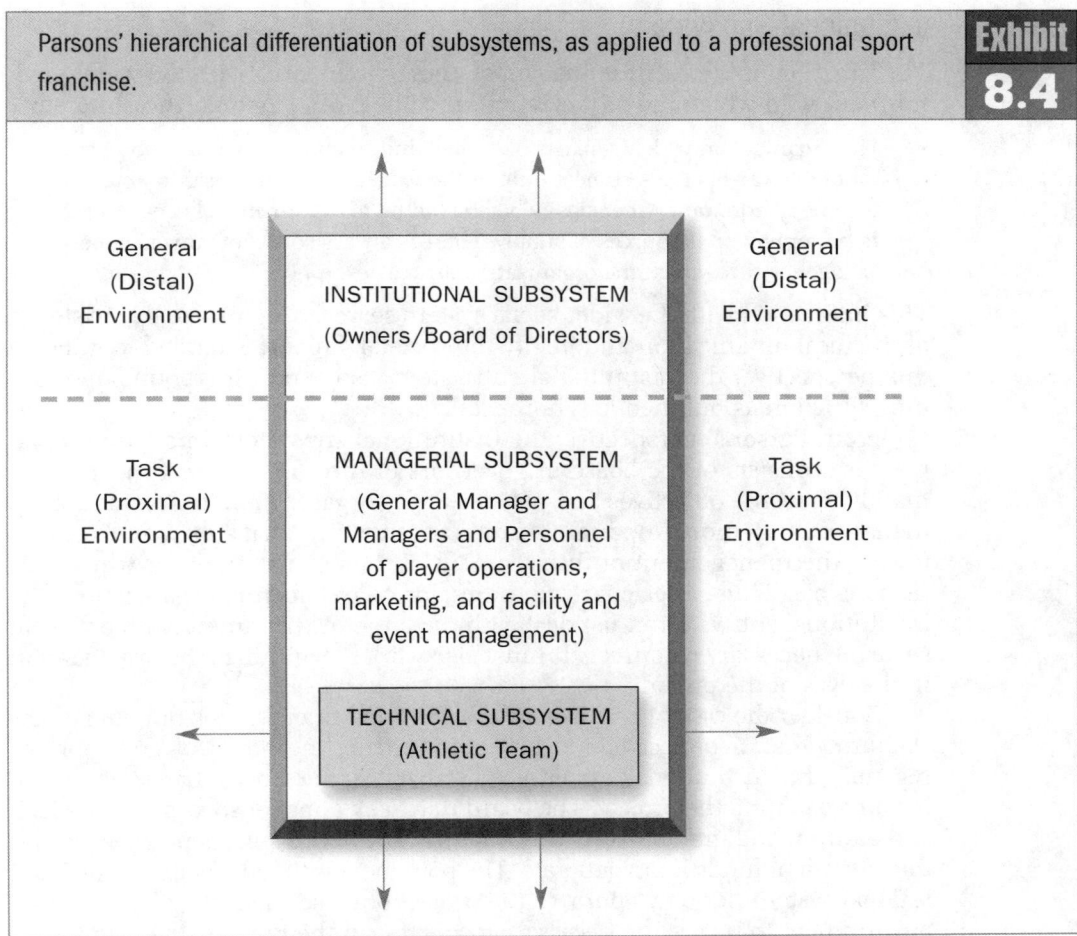

Exhibit 8.4 Parsons' hierarchical differentiation of subsystems, as applied to a professional sport franchise.

cal task and the processes involved define its fundamental requirements. This is identical to Thompson's concept of technical core discussed earlier.

Managerial Subsystem

The **managerial subsystem** is a higher-order system that both administers and serves the technical system. Parsons (1960) attributed two major areas of responsibility to the managerial subsystem:

> The primary one is to mediate between the technical organization and those who use its "products"—the "customers," pupils or whoever. The second is to procure the resources necessary for carrying out the technical functions (i.e., financial resources, personnel and physical facilities). (p. 62)

Thus, the managerial subsystem carries out part of the boundary-spanning functions included in Thompson's model. In the case of a professional sport franchise, the general manager and the managers and personnel of player operations, marketing, and facility and event management would constitute the managerial subsystem. This subsystem is the buffer insulating the team and its coaches from environmental disturbances.

Institutional Subsystem

The function of the **institutional subsystem** is to interact with the wider environment with which the organization must deal. As Parsons (1960) noted:

> The organization which consists of both technical and managerial suborganizations never operates subject only to the exigencies of disposal to and procurement from other agencies (which stand on an approximately equal level) as customers or as sources of supply. There is always some "organized superior" agency with which the organization articulates. (p. 63)

This interaction with the wider social system serves to legitimize the existence of the focal organization and justify the societal support extended to it. From this perspective, the institutional subsystem also serves the boundary-spanning function as outlined by Thompson.

From Parsons' perspective, the institutional subsystem in a typical organization consists of the board of governors or directors. Their functions are mainly to set the objectives and policies of the organization, to recruit the top managers, and, more important, to direct the institutional subsystem's efforts toward the management of that segment of the environment for which it is responsible. Thus, after charting the major course for the organization, the institutional subsystem must deal with the larger environment with a view to securing necessary resources. It must also work to legitimize the organization in the eyes of the public.

Consider the case of a university athletic department that is building a new stadium. First, a project has to be authorized by the board of governors or regents (the institutional system). Then, the same board has to find the resources to fund the project. The board may seek donations from corporations and alumni, and grants from governments. The board's influence determines the amount of funds it can generate. The point here is that the board as the institutional system not only approves the project but also interacts with the wider environment to secure the necessary resources. In the process, the board legitimizes not only the project but also the athletic department as a whole.

Comparison of the Thompson and Parsons Models

Numerous similarities exist between Thompson's model and Parsons' model. This is not surprising since Thompson's model is partly derived from Parsons'. Both models acknowledge the need to seal off the technical core from environmental influences and to create boundary-spanning units. However, there is a difference in how the two models distribute the boundary-spanning activities to the various subsystems. In Thompson's model, various departments are expected to deal with various segments of the environment. For example, the purchasing department interacts with suppliers, while the sales department interacts with customers. In the case of a fitness club, the marketing unit will be dealing largely with the media and advertising people in marketing the services offered by the club. The unit in charge of facilities will interact with suppliers and technicians associated with such needs as plumbing, air conditioning, and so on. In the case of a professional sport franchise, the event managers interact with the local police, city government, and the media. On the other hand, player personnel units deal with other teams, player agents, and scouts. In contrast, in Parsons' model, the total environment is subdivided into proximal (or task) and distal (general) environments (see Chapter 3). Parsons proposed that the responsibilities for these two segments of the environment be split by hierarchical levels. That is, while the managerial subsystem must deal with the immediate task environment (including customers and suppliers), the institutional subsystem must interact with the larger segment of the environment (the society at large). As we noted, the board of governors of a university, after approving a new stadium, embarks on securing resources from the general environment. The athletic department itself also engages in securing funds, but only by marketing luxury seating and seat licenses to the fans and spectators and advertising space to commercial interests, and by engaging in other activities involving elements in the task environment.

> **To Recap**
>
> **TASK AND GENERAL ENVIRONMENTS** We noted in Chapter 3 that an organization as an open system interacts with elements that lie outside its boundaries. Those elements that affect the organization more directly, and with which the organization interacts constantly, belong to the *task* (or *proximal*) environment. The other elements that impact the organization indirectly are labeled the *general* (or *distal*) environment. The organization does not interact with the elements in the general environment as often as it does with the elements in the task environment.

Parsons further argues that although the hierarchy places the institutional subsystem above the managerial system (which is, in turn, above the technical subsystem), there must be a clear break in the simple continuity of the **authority structure.** The two interfaces (that between the institutional and managerial subsystems, and that between the managerial and technical subsystems) must be designed in such a way that one subsystem does not interfere with the functioning of the other two subsystems. That is, "the institutionalization of these relations must typically take a form where the relative independence of each is protected" (Parsons, 1960, p. 69).

Parsons' concept of differentiation along hierarchical levels also is very meaningful in the context of sport organizations. Take the case of a university athletic department. The board of directors, as the institutional system, may have considerable power over its athletic department, yet it refrains from engaging in the internal affairs of the department. That is left solely to the athletic director and her immediate subordinates—the managerial subsystem. In fact, the athletic director and her managerial subsystem should resist any attempt by the board or its members to engage in the internal affairs of the technical core—that is, in how the coaches coach their respective teams.

With sport governing bodies, generally a board of governors (or directors) is elected and charged with the promotion and development of a sport. It represents the institutional subsystem for the organization. This board is responsible for hiring the executive director (ED) for the organization. The board also approves projects, such as sending the national team for an international competition or setting up a training center, and budgets for those projects. An equal-

Sidebar

The last two chapters focused on how organizations are structured in terms of roles, responsibilities, and coordination and control. In Chapter 7, we discussed some of the classical principles of structuring an organization and one of the dominant forms of organizational structure: bureaucracy and its tenets. In this chapter, we have looked at organizational structure from a systems perspective, and emphasized the notions of differentiation and integration.

Readers should be aware of other concepts associated with organizational structure. For instance, Slack and his associates (e.g., Amis, Slack, & Berrett, 1995; Kikulis, Slack, & Hinings, 1995; Slack, 1997; Thibault, Slack, & Hinings, 1991) employed the notions of *complexity, formalization,* and *centralization* in their studies of sport organizations. *Complexity* refers to the various ways in which the units within an organization are differentiated (Slack, 1997). It includes horizontal, vertical, and spatial (that is, geographical) differentiation. Horizontal and vertical differentiation are similar to the concepts of differentiation discussed in this chapter. Spatial differentiation refers to different units being located in different geographical locations. The higher the various types of differentiation, the higher the complexity of that organization, and the higher the difficulty of managing it (Slack, 1997).

Formalization refers to the extent to which "mechanisms such as rules and regulations, job descriptions, and policies and procedures govern the operation of a sport organization" (Slack, 1997, p. 49). *Centralization* refers to whether authority to make critical decisions resides in the top-level positions (centralized decision making) or is distributed to lower-level positions in the organization (decentralized decision making). A bureaucracy, as discussed in the last chapter, tends to be high on both formalization and centralization.

ly important, if not more important, function of the board is to interact with the general environment and generate resources for the organization. The ED and his immediate assistants constitute the managerial subsystem, which is responsible for hiring the national coaches (with the approval of the board) and for supervising the day-to-day operations of his subordinates. A critical function of the ED is to market the organization's programs and seek revenues from the proximal (task) environment. In addition, the ED facilitates the technical core by serving as liaison with external agents such as other national sport organizations, agencies that control facilities, government agencies, and travel agencies.

The national team, which consists of the athletes, the coach, and the assistants, represents the technical core. Since the coach has been hired or appointed (put in charge of the technical core) on the basis of expertise, the entire operation of the team should be left to her discretion. If Parsons' prescriptions are followed, the technical core (the coach and athletes) will be allowed to carry out its activities without undue influence from the managerial subsystem or the institutional subsystem. The coach should be allowed to select the athletes for the national team and decide on the training regimen and the competitive schedule. She should also be free to take disciplinary actions in the case of any rule violations.

This ideal of Parsons is followed mostly in university athletics in the United States and Canada. Unfortunately, the principles are often flouted among sport governing bodies. For example, individuals who are elected to the board of directors are often former athletes or club representatives. Thus, all their skills, capacities, and orientations may be most strongly related to the internal operations of the organization, such as the selection and operation of the national team. Conversely, they may not have the capacity or inclination to deal with external groups. When this is the case, it is not surprising to see considerable confusion and conflict in the management of the team. Even in the case of professional teams, owners are known to interfere with the affairs of the technical core (the team and the coaches).

Technical Core in Service Organizations

Both Thompson and Parsons argue that the technical core of an organization must be insulated from environmental disturbances, but their models overlooked one significant factor relating to service organizations—the interface between the customer and the employee. Chapter 1 emphasized that the customer–employee interface differentiates service organizations from organizations that produce goods. Whereas the notion of insulating the technical core is most meaningful and practical in organizations producing goods, it may not be appropriate or practical in the case of service organizations. This is certainly the case in those organizations that depend on their employees to seek and recruit more customers from among a larger population. In many service organizations, employees who belong to the technical core (which, according to theory, should be insulated) are expected to interact with the public in the provision of their services and in the recruitment of more customers. Consider, for example, the intramural department in a university. Its major purpose is to provide recreational opportunities for all the students on the campus. Consequently, it organizes various competitions and instructional classes in as many activities as possible. The task of managing these various programs is left to paid or volunteer leaders. These are, in essence, the employees who provide the services. However, their effectiveness is related not only to their ability to provide quality service but also to their ability to interact with and recruit from the student population. That is, the boundary-spanning activities relating to both current and prospective customers are left to the technical core employees. Thus, the notion of insulating the technical core appears to be irrelevant in the context of the intramural department and other similar service organizations. From another perspective, though, it is apparent that the departmental chairpersons and their assistants do in fact shield the technical core from some environmental segments. For example, in matters relating to other academic departments, the board of governors, the physical plant, and so on, the managerial system acts as a buffer.

Let us return to the example of a fitness club. Being that the instructors' clients are part of the larger environment, the instructors, in one sense, are dealing with the external environment. In their efforts to promote their program and to recruit more clients, they are almost certain to interact with people outside the technical core and the fitness club itself. In a similar manner, a coach of a professional team or university team may interact with other

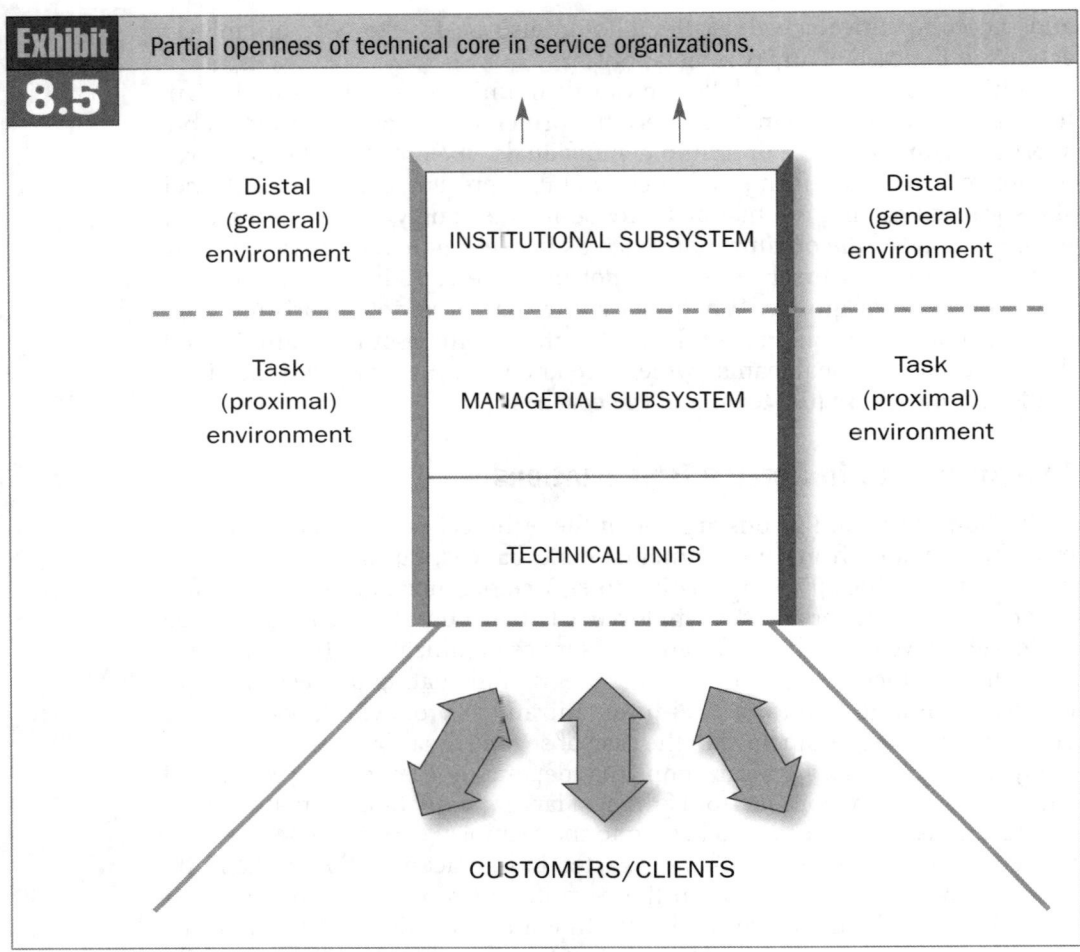

Exhibit 8.5 Partial openness of technical core in service organizations.

coaches, players, and scouts with a view to recruiting the best athletes for the team. Thus, the boundary between the instructors or coaches (the technical core) and the environment need to be permeable. This partial insulation from some segments of the environment and openness to relevant publics in the immediate task environment is illustrated in Exhibit 8.5.

AUTHORITY STRUCTURE IN SERVICE ORGANIZATIONS

We have seen that the conventional notions of a hierarchy of authority may not be meaningful in the context of service organizations, particularly professional and human service organizations (see Chapter 1). As we noted, the raw material for a professional/human service organization is primarily knowledge and information. The processing of that information is the fundamental task of the employees. Insofar as customers are unique, and the problems that they bring to the interface are also highly variable, the customer–employee interface in a **professional service** organization operates in a highly unpredictable environment. Also, because professional employees possess expertise and have direct access to relevant information, they must be given the freedom and authority to make decisions regarding the type of services that should be offered, how these should be produced, and how the services should be delivered.

Noting the unique properties of professional service organizations, Mills, Hall, Leidecker, and Margulies (1983) proposed a structural model for these organizations—the flexiform (see Exhibit 8.6). The essence of the flexiform model is that the **operational units** (which are conceptually similar to the technical subsystem discussed earlier) and the administrative core (the managerial subsystem) are loosely coupled to each other.

The operational units are those involving the professionals and their customers. Each unit may consist of one professional or a team of professionals interacting with their customers. For example, each professor and her students in a department of sport management would constitute an operational unit. The exercise physiologist and his clients in a fitness club, and the team and its coach in an athletic department are other examples of operational units in their respective organizations.

According to Mills and colleagues (1983), these operational units "need to be basically self-contained, relatively autonomous units and essentially to operate as mini-companies; the service is being produced and delivered concurrently" (p. 125). Thus, a professor is given the autonomy and responsibility to design and teach a course, and to decide on the evaluation system to be used. Further, the professor is also authorized to deal with each student according to the student's needs and abilities. This would also be the case with coaches of athletic teams, who have the autonomy and authority to select the athletes and train them in the strategies and tactics they (the coaches) selected.

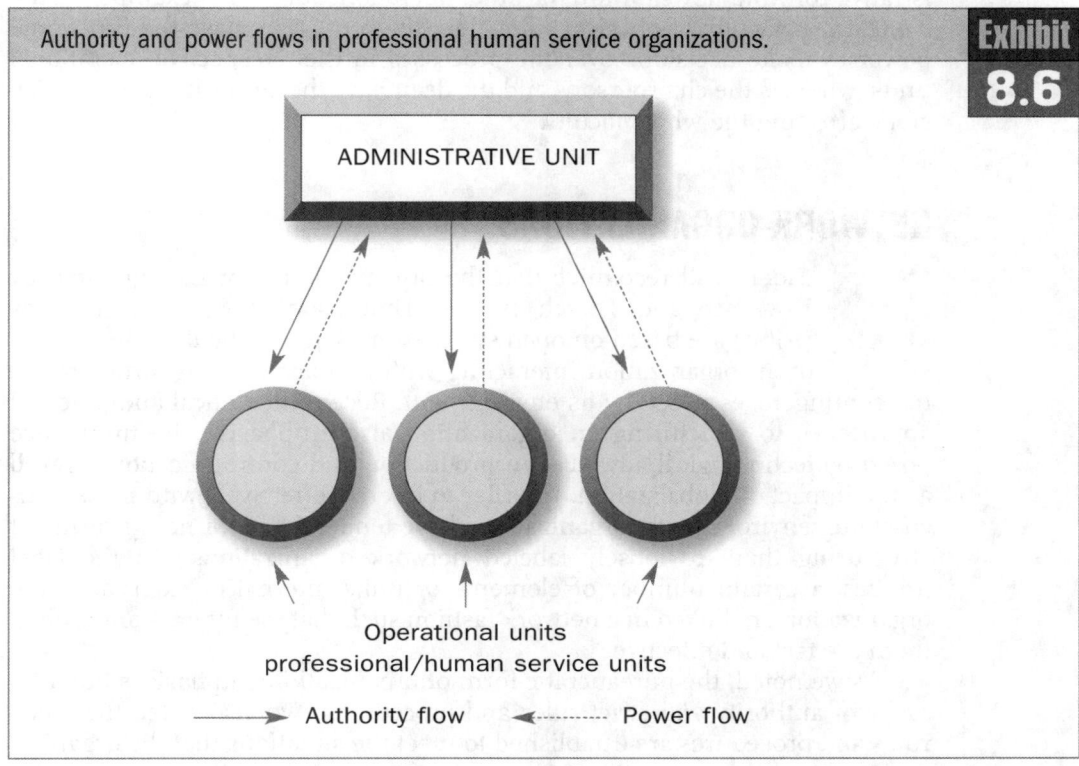

Exhibit 8.6 Authority and power flows in professional human service organizations.

Mills and colleagues (1983) point out that the functions of the administrative core include setting broad policies, controlling the boundary conditions, linking and coordinating the activities of the operational units, and systematizing routine activities. In the example of the department of sport management, the chair, the dean, and the business managers, if any, form the management team. Their function is to mediate and coordinate among the various professors and their operational units (the courses or groups of courses and various research laboratories).

The idea of loosely coupled systems in the flexiform model stems from the distinction between authority and functional power (Mills et al., 1983). The concept of authority, as perceived by Mills and colleagues, is conceptually similar to the concept of bureaucratic authority as perceived by Weber (1947). It refers to the right of superiors to make decisions that affect all subordinates of the organization. In the case of a department of sport management, the dean and other administrators have the authority to decide on the budget allocations to the professors and their labs, and on their teaching assignments. In contrast, functional power emerges from the expertise of the professional, and the exigencies of the situations they face. Thus, as we noted before, each of the professors in the department of sport management has the functional power to decide on the course content and methods of teaching and evaluation.

Simply stated, **authority** relates to decisions that affect all units (or most of them), and it resides in the administrative core. **Functional power** relates to what happens within individual units, and it stems from the expertise residing in the units. In the flexiform model (see Exhibit 8.6), functional power is greatest at the operational unit level. It decreases as it moves toward the administrative core at the center. Conversely, authority resides in the administrative core and flows toward the outer operational units. For example, in the context of a faculty of physical education, the professors have the functional power to make decisions over the processes in their respective operational units, whereas the chairpersons and the dean have the authority to make decisions affecting the whole faculty.

NETWORK ORGANIZATIONS

Readers will recognize that the organizational forms suggested by Lawrence and Lorsch (1967), Thompson (1967), and Parsons (1960) are based on open systems thinking, particularly the notion of an organization interacting with and adapting its structures to the contingencies posed by its environment. Recent theoretical and practical approaches to structuring an organization also emphasize the turbulence posed by technological advances in production and communication, as well as the impact of globalization. In order to interact effectively with these ever-changing environments, organizations have tended to adopt newer forms of structuring that are loosely labeled **network organizations**. As the label implies, a certain number of elements or units internal or external to the organization are linked in a network fashion such that the interactions among them are fast and effective.

As we noted, the bureaucratic form of organization emphasizes the hierarchy of authority and strict rules and procedures. We also noted that such rules and procedures are established to meet the situations that the organization or its employees face. That is appropriate if those situations are finite and known—that is, if the environment is stable. However, if the environment changes fast and in unpredictable ways, one cannot set rules and regulations for every contingency. Hence the idea of networking those units that will be affected. In a network, its members are allowed to interact with each other to make decisions as they see fit to meet the environmental challenges or opportunities they face.

Several authors (e.g., Birkinshaw, 2000; Hall, 1996; Kanter & Myers, 1991; Knoke, 2001; Miles & Snow, 1996) have discussed the emergence of various forms of networked organizations. This discussion follows Birkinshaw (2000) in classifying network forms of organization into *internal* and *external* networks. An **internal network** involves actors within the organization interacting with each other to solve problems or to innovate new methods and techniques. Such interactions may be in response to internal issues or external events. An **external network** involves one or more internal units interacting with units external to the organization. Such interactions may be to facilitate the work processes within the organization or to outsource processes. Internal and external networks are described below, followed by a discussion of a third form of network—interorganizational—particularly relevant in sport management.

Internal Networks

As noted, internal networks may be formed to address the work processes within the organization or to respond to events occurring outside the organization.

Internal Networks for Work Processes

In a traditional organization, specialized work units are hierarchically organized, and the communications among them are channeled through the hierarchical ranks. We noted that such arrangements can lead to delays and distortions in communication and that the communication flow can be inconsistent with the workflow. Another problem with centralized decision making is that the decision makers at the top may not be aware of or understand the demands of the work carried out at the front line (see criticisms of bureaucracy in Chapter 7). To alleviate these problems, many organizations have adopted the network form of organization as shown in Exhibit 8.7.

The first notable feature of this form is the absence of a strict formal hierarchy like that of traditional organizations. In other words, the communication channels are more lateral instead of vertical; every unit or employee interacts with any other unit or person as the situation warrants. Consider the case of an arena used by several teams. It is conventional for someone in authority to schedule the practices and games for the teams using the arena. It is also conventional to have a unit in charge of managing the facility and another unit to manage the events (i.e., the competitions). It is also not uncommon to have other units take care of the electrical, heating, ventilation, and similar systems. In a traditional organization, a clear hierarchy and communication channels would be established to coordinate the activities. In a network organization, the units or persons would be permitted and encouraged to communicate among themselves to solve problem(s) they may face. For instance, suppose the volleyball coach wants to switch the practice time

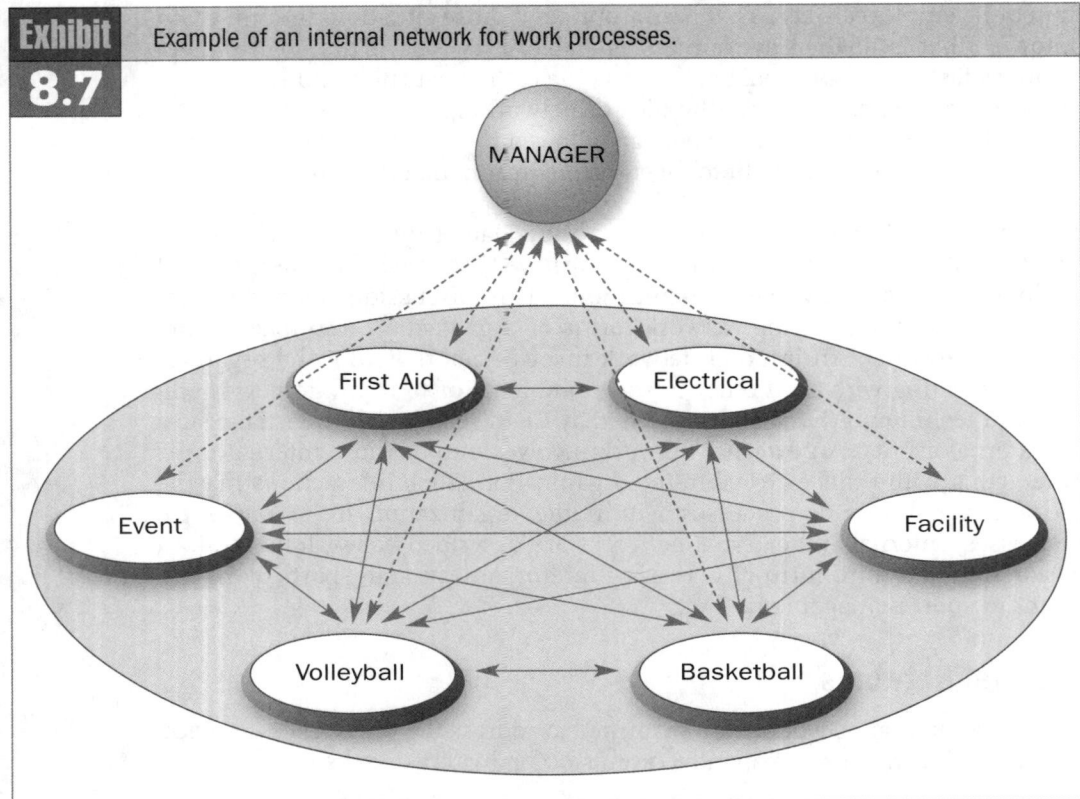

Exhibit 8.7 Example of an internal network for work processes.

with the basketball coach for the next day. In a conventional organization, the volleyball coach would have to submit the request to a superior (e.g., the associate athletic director in charge of volleyball), who would, in turn, communicate formally with the associate director in charge of basketball and others in charge of facility management and first-aid services. In a networked organization, the volleyball coach would directly request the basketball coach for a change in the practice time. If the basketball coach accedes to the request, the volleyball coach would then inform the event and facility managers and those who provide first-aid services. In this example, the network arrangement facilitates smooth and speedy internal workflow.

Internal Networks for External Events

Another form of internal network organization permits the units to interact with each other to react collectively to an external and unexpected event. Exhibit 8.8 illustrates this arrangement: here, Units 1, 5, and 6 jointly react to external Event 1, and Units 2, 3, and 4 interact to counter Event 2. Which units will interact will depend on the nature of the event. Examples from athletic contests abound. The special teams in football (i.e., the offense, defense, punt-return, etc.) are made up of athletes with specialized skills to tackle specific problems. Basketball, hockey, and volleyball coaches shuffle their lineups to counter the strategies of their opponents.

Consider the case where the development officer of an intercollegiate athletic department learns through hearsay that a former member of the uni-

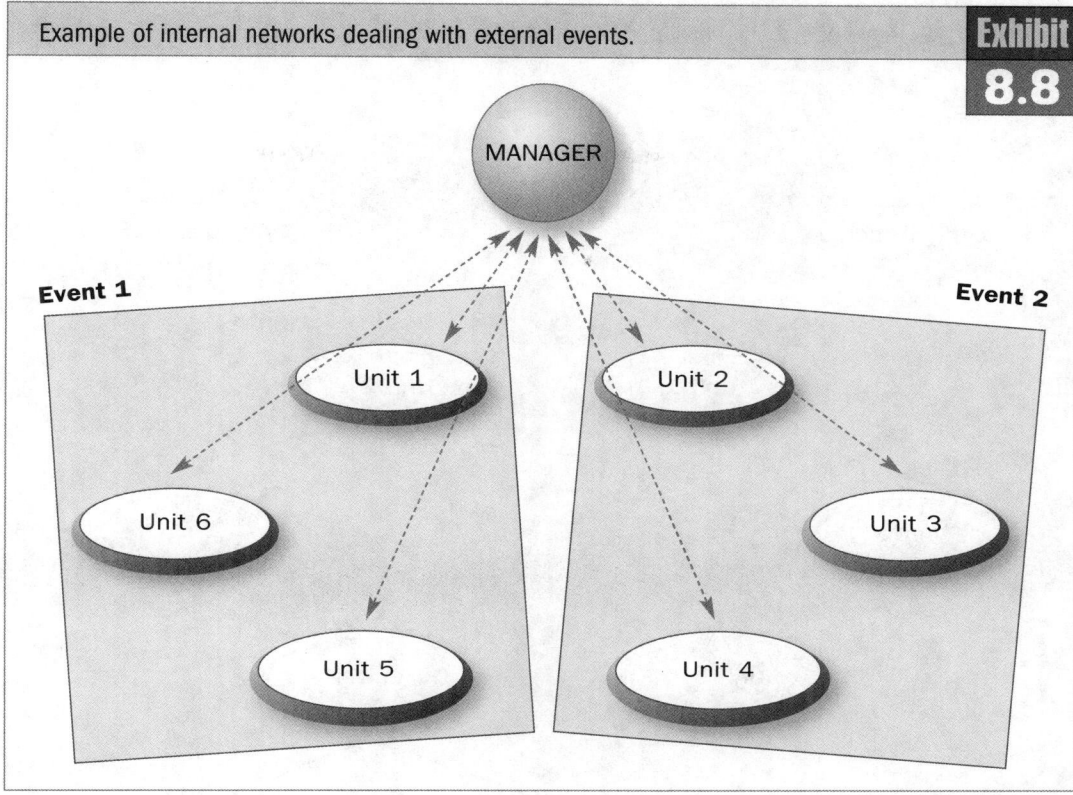

Exhibit 8.8 Example of internal networks dealing with external events.

versity's swim team is considering dispersion of some of her considerable wealth to charities. The development officer would enlist several people, including the president, the athletic director, the senior women's administrator, the swim coaches (current and former), and the members of the women's swimming team, in an effort to solicit substantial donations from the former swimmer. For another example, consider a riot that breaks out on the campus after a football game. The units within the university in charge of security, traffic, physical plant, and fire prevention, as well as other emergency units, would interact with each other to handle and control the riot. If necessary, these units will also be empowered to interact with external agencies, such as the city police and fire departments. The idea here is that these units interact with each other directly instead of going through the president or the board of governors.

External Networks

External networks may be formed to facilitate processes within the organization, or they may be formed to outsource these processes.

External Networks Facilitating Internal Processes

It is becoming increasingly necessary for the units within a given sport organization to interact with other organizations in the environment to facilitate internal processes (see Exhibit 8.9). Earlier in the chapter, we referred to units

Exhibit 8.9 Example of external network facilitating internal processes.

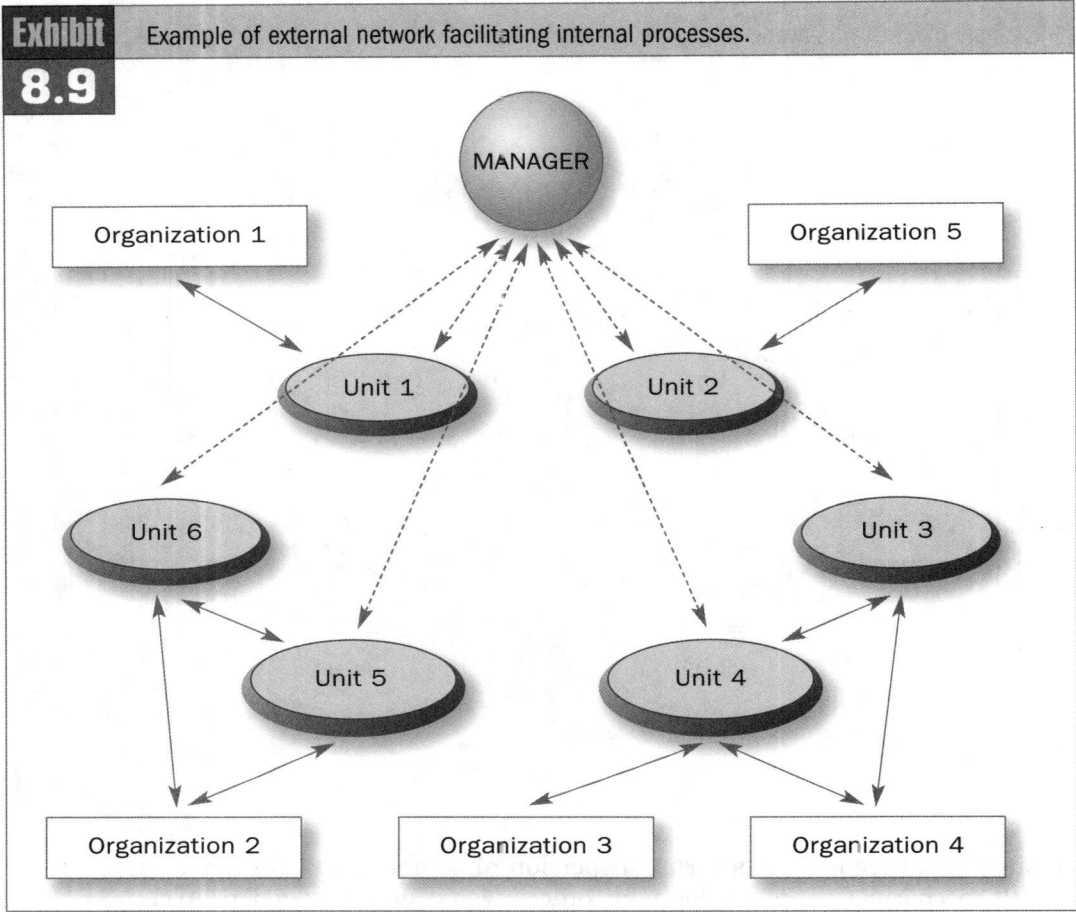

such as the marketing and development departments as boundary-spanning units (i.e., the boundary between the organization and its environment). If the marketing department wants to distribute a flier to fans, it can directly contact and negotiate a contract with an organization specializing in the design and printing of fliers. Similarly, the event management unit would be permitted to contact the local police department and make traffic and security arrangements. The marketing unit in a large fitness club would be free to interact directly with the local newspaper regarding advertisements for the club. The units within a city recreation department promoting sport and recreation programs would be at liberty to contact local high schools, labor unions, associations of retirees, and other agencies to publicize their programs.

External Networks for Outsourcing

Another type of external network is formed when an organization decides to let another organization take on production or marketing functions. For example, the focal organization may buy its supplies from other organizations, may contract out the manufacturing function (i.e., the conversion of the supplies into its products) to other organizations, and may enlist the services of retailers to sell the products.

This idea is catching on in the case of maintaining a facility and organizing the events in that facility. SMG (2004) is an example of an external agency managing the arenas and facilities of other organizations. As of October 2004, SMG managed seven stadiums, with more than 422,000 seats; five stadiums were the home field for NFL teams. SMG claims that it managed the stadium for the Super Bowls of 2002, 2004, and 2005. SMG stadiums also hosted Major League Baseball and NCAA collegiate sporting events. SMG also managed 69 arenas across the United States, Canada, and Europe. As a firm specializing in arena and stadium management, SMG has accumulated the knowledge and competencies necessary for efficiency and effectiveness. Thus, the owners and tenants of these arenas and stadiums find it worthwhile to pay SMG for its services in managing the facilities.

As another example of outsourcing, BKB Services (BKB Services, 2004) is a firm specializing in organizing and conducting road races, triathlons, and Nordic events. Their services include (a) creating a management plan and timeline for brand-new recreational sporting events, (b) managing recreational sporting events, (c) providing event management and timing services for convention special events, (d) assisting with media contacts, direct-mail, and email campaigns, and (e) helping with brochure production and placement.

Readers should note that in the networked organizational forms described above, the top management still has hierarchical authority over all operations of the organization. It is just that the lower-level units are given the flexibility and authority to manage day-to-day operations and coordinate horizontal workflows. It must also be understood that these modes of organizing have evolved over time.

Interorganizational Networks

One other form of network organization is very relevant to sport management—the **interorganizational network.** This network is made up of "legally independent, autonomous, interdependent organizations with converging, but also diverging, interests and characteristics, which are connected with each other through interactive, reciprocal exchange relations" (Van Gils, 1998, p. 92). The member organizations engage in a common set of activities and demonstrate a pattern of interrelationships to attain collective and individual goals and resolve problems that arise among them (Hall, 1996). The NCAA in the United States and the Canadian Interuniversity Sport (CIS) are interorganizational networks that link member organizations (i.e., university athletic departments) producing the same services with similar goals and operating in comparable organizational contexts. That is, they (a) possess different characteristics, (b) compete with each other in various sports (i.e., have divergent interests), and (c) collaborate with each other to regulate their own activities and promote intercollegiate sport (i.e., have convergent interests).

In one form of interorganizational networks, the member organizations create an external agency to (a) facilitate collective decision making, (b) monitor the members' behaviors, and (c) coordinate and direct members' efforts toward common goals. The central agency is given the power to make decisions that bind the member organizations and to impose sanctions when a member organization violates its rules (Park, 1996). This form of interorga-

Sidebar

Following is a scenario (illustrated in Exhibit 8.10) to ponder. Let us assume that a wealthy individual buys a franchise in an expanded National Football League. She decides to outsource almost every activity fundamental to the operation of the franchise. The owner may decide to sign a contract with a university (e.g., Oklahoma State University) for the use of its stadium for all the team's home games. The university athletic department may undertake to maintain the facility as well as manage every game for the new franchise. Such an arrangement would be tantamount to outsourcing the functions of facility and event management. It is also possible to outsource the functions of promotions, marketing, ticketing, security, and other essential functions to the university itself or to agencies like SMG. Then there are the most important functions: forming the team and coaching the team during practices and games. The owner is contemplating outsourcing even those functions to an external enterprise.

Can we conceive of an outstanding coach forming a business enterprise consisting of himself plus assistant coaches, trainers, recruiting staff, and other essential personnel associated with coaching? Many business consulting firms and detective agencies operate this way with specialists under their employ. If there were such an athletic coaching enterprise, the new franchise owner could outsource the coaching function to that enterprise. With all these functions outsourced, the owner needs to have just a few professional assistants to help with the overall supervision of the franchise. Discuss the feasibility of this scenario.

While there are firms that specialize in managing stadiums and organizing competitions, there is no firm that specializes in forming and coaching teams. But the concept is not far off from current practices. Consider the coaches of NCAA Division I football and basketball teams. Their services are contracted for huge sums of salary for a certain number of years. They are permitted to hire their own assistant coaches and support staff. They are in full charge of which players they will recruit and whom they will play in a given game. If the team performs well over the period of the contract, the contract may be extended. If not, the contract may not be renewed. The coach may be fired even before the end of the contract, if the team is not faring well. When a new coach is hired, the coach brings her own lawyers and accountants to make sure that the contract and its provisions are in order and to safeguard her interests. From this perspective, the coaches of NCAA Division I football and basketball teams are in fact private enterprises without being formally and legally incorporated as businesses. And the process of hiring and firing a coach resembles outsourcing in many respects.

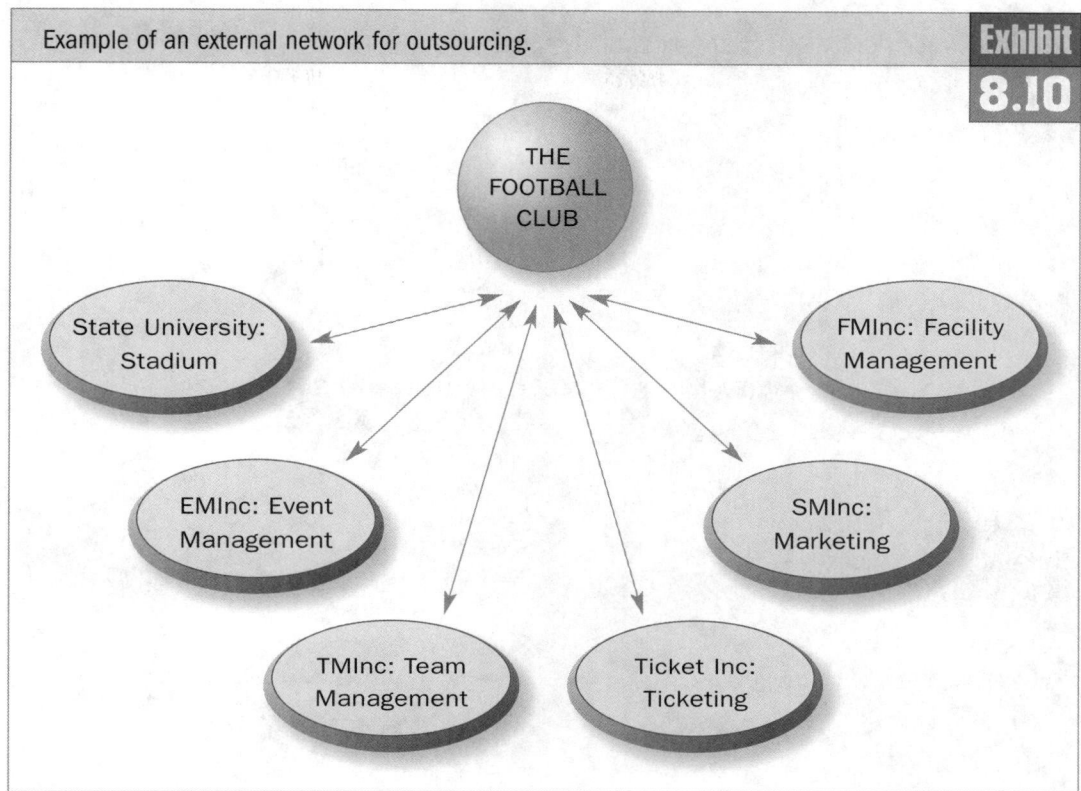

Example of an external network for outsourcing.

Exhibit 8.10

nizational network is illustrated in Exhibit 8.11, with the NCAA as the apex organization of the network. In the case of the NCAA, the member institutions granted the NCAA regulatory authority in 1952 that gave the NCAA "the right to control the athletic programs through rule-making and sanctions" (Stern, 1979, p. 247). It serves as the private regulatory network and coordinates the intercollegiate activities through surveillance and sanctioning (Stern, 1981). In fact, the NCAA has become a powerful control agent capable of punishing member schools for violating its rules (particularly recruiting rules) and providing a growing number of valued resources and services, including financial rewards and legitimacy (Knoke, 2001).

The National Basketball Association (NBA) and other professional sport organizations (e.g., National Football League, National Hockey League) are also interorganizational networks. The International Olympic Committee and the international sport federations such as FIFA (football) and FIBA (basketball) are interorganizational networks at the global level. At the national level, the national Olympic committees and the national sport federations such as the United States Cycling Federation fall under this category. Units of these organizations at the regional and state levels would also fall under the category of interorganizational networks. Similarly, state high school athletic associations and their national counterpart, the National Federation of State High School Associations, as well as various national youth sport organizations such as the American Youth Soccer Organization, are interorganizational networks.

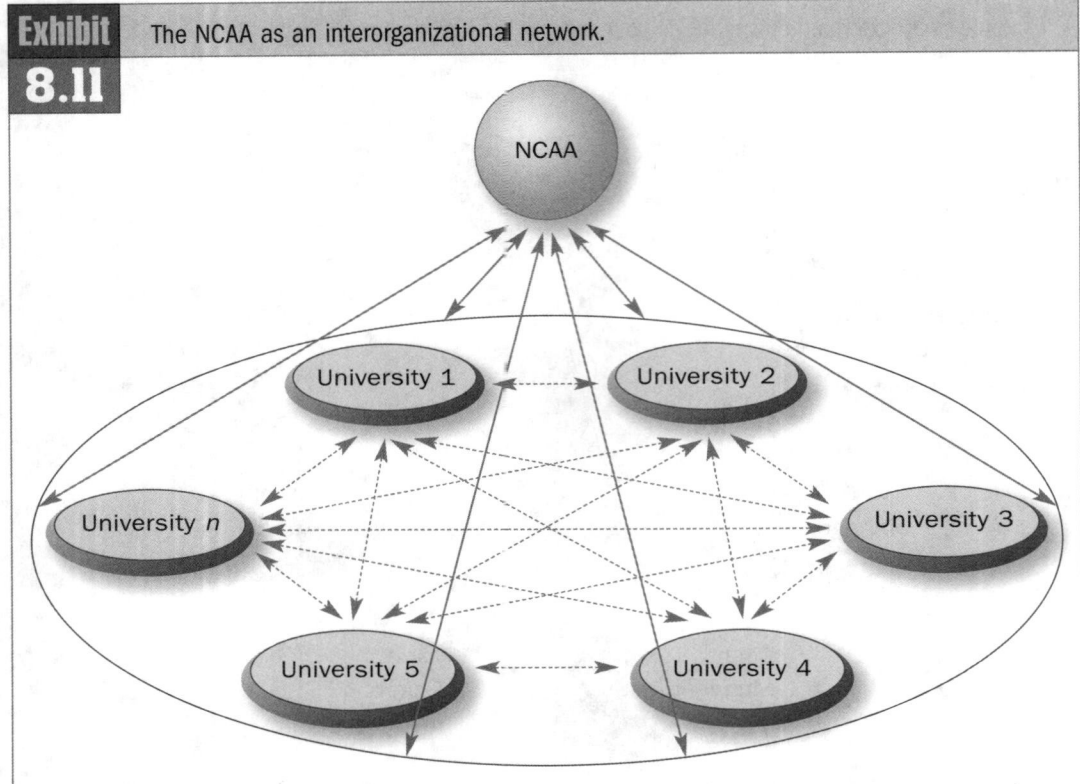

Exhibit 8.11 The NCAA as an interorganizational network.

Network Functions

Interorganizational networks create greater access to resources for member organizations and help to increase the financial performance of members (Human & Provan, 1997). Further, an interorganizational network is expected to

1. facilitate innovation and sharing of knowledge and learning among member institutions (Goes & Park, 1997; Kraatz, 1998)
2. reduce variety and uncertainty in transactions (Park, 1996)
3. economize the costs of information gathering and dissemination (Kraatz, 1998; Park, 1996)
4. coordinate the interdependent activities among member institutions (Provan, 1983)

Network functions in professional sport. In the context of professional sport, Gerrard (2003) identifies three basic functions of a professional sport league: (1) administrative, (2) sporting, and (3) financial. The administrative function entails the planning and conduct of a schedule of sporting contests and a tournament structure, as well as instituting and policing the rules of the game. As for sporting viability, the league's responsibility is to maintain the interests of the spectators and sponsors in the league. This is often accomplished by "ensuring uncertainty of outcome through competitive balance brought about by revenue redistribution, salary caps and/or restrictions on player mobility" (p. 219). Finally, a professional sport league may institute measures to ensure the financial viability of the league and its teams, which may involve restrictions on the bargaining power of players in the labor market and "limiting the number of franchises such that the demand from big-market cities for franchises exceeds the available supply" (p. 219).

Network functions in the NCAA. The purposes and services of the NCAA (2004a, 2004b) are shown in Exhibit 8.12. Readers will note that these purposes and services reflect the network functions described above. The establishing and monitoring of eligibility rules, publishing rules of play governing intercollegiate athletics, and organizing and conducting regional and national athletics events are examples of critical network functions of the NCAA that bind its members and coordinate their activities.

Exhibit 8.12 The purposes and services of the National Collegiate Athletic Association.

The National Collegiate Athletic Association's purposes are:

- To initiate, stimulate and improve intercollegiate athletics programs for student–athletes and to promote and develop educational leadership, physical fitness, athletics excellence and athletics participation as a recreational pursuit.
- To uphold the principle of institutional control of, and responsibility for, all intercollegiate sports in conformity with the constitution and bylaws of the Association.
- To encourage its members to adopt eligibility rules to comply with satisfactory standards of scholarship, sportsmanship and amateurism.
- To formulate, copyright and publish rules of play governing intercollegiate athletics.
- To preserve intercollegiate athletics records.
- To supervise the conduct of, and to establish eligibility standards for, regional and national athletics events under the auspices of the Association.
- To legislate, through bylaws or by resolutions of a Convention, upon any subject of general concern to the members related to the administration of intercollegiate athletics.
- To study in general all phases of competitive intercollegiate athletics and establish standards whereby the colleges and universities of the United States can maintain their athletics programs on a high level.

The NCAA serves as a governance and administrative structure through which its members:

- Enact legislation to deal with athletics problems when the problems spread across regional lines and when member institutions conclude that national action is needed.
- Interpret legislation adopted by the membership.
- Combine to represent intercollegiate athletics in legislative and regulatory matters on the state and Federal levels. This involvement includes such areas as Federal taxes affecting college athletics, antibribery and gambling laws, television, international competition, and Federal aid to education affecting sports and physical education.

(continued)

Exhibit 8.12 Continued.

- Provide financial assistance and other help to groups that are interested in promoting and advancing intercollegiate athletics.
- Promote their championship events and all intercollegiate athletics through planned activities of the NCAA national office. In addition to general public relations activities, the Association publishes The *NCAA News* and dozens of other publications on behalf of its members.
- Compile and distribute football, basketball, baseball, ice hockey, men's and women's lacrosse, and women's softball and volleyball statistics. Regular-season records are maintained in women's volleyball, football and basketball; championships records are maintained in all sports in which the members sponsor NCAA championship competition.
- Maintain committees to write and interpret playing rules in 13 sports.
- Conduct research as a way to find solutions to athletics problems. These efforts include surveys about academics, television, postseason events, athletics and recreational facilities, sports injuries and safety, recruiting, financial aid, playing seasons, the cost of intercollegiate athletics, and the effects of participation on the student–athlete.
- Annually produce, in conjunction with NCAA Productions, special programs for television along with television coverage of NCAA championships not carried by a national network. This operation includes a library of films and videotapes of more than 100 titles available for purchase and rental, plus the NCAA Television News Service, which supplies information to television and cable networks.
- Maintain a compliance services program that assists members in conducting institutional self-studies through a central resource clearinghouse and counseling agency to answer questions about intercollegiate athletics and athletics administration.
- Administer insurance programs, including a lifetime catastrophic injury insurance program, to ensure that member institutions can provide protection for student-athletes during competition, practice and travel. The Association also arranges disability insurance protection for elite student-athletes.
- Promote and participate in international sports planning and competition through membership in the U.S. Olympic Committee, USA Basketball, the United States Collegiate Sports Council, The Athletics Congress (track and field), the U.S. Volleyball Association, and the U.S. Baseball, Gymnastics and Wrestling Federations.
- Sanction postseason competition and certify certain noncollegiate contests to protect their institutional interests and those of their student-athletes.
- Support several community service programs, including NYSP (National Youth Sports Program), and offer Youth Education through Sports (YES) Clinics at numerous NCAA championship locations.
- Administer national and international marketing and licensing programs to enhance intercollegiate athletics and to expand youth development programs.

Source: NCAA (2004a, 2004b). Reprinted with permission.

SUMMARY

This chapter began with a critique of Weber's (1947) bureaucracy (described in the previous chapter) as a closed system. We saw that organizations need to be open to the influences of the greater environment. Accordingly, the chapter presented three different models of organizing based on the **systems perspective.** We explored the concepts of differentiation and integration proposed in the Lawrence and Lorsch (1967) model. Following this was a description of the Thompson (1967) model, which focused on the concept of insulating the technical core of an organization via its boundary-spanning units. The third model covered in the chapter was that of Parsons (1960), with its three hierarchically arranged subsystems—technical subsystem, managerial subsystem, and institutional subsystem. We then looked at the relevance of these models to different kinds of sport organizations and examined the distinction between the authority flowing from the administrative unit and the power flowing from the professional (operational) units. Finally, we discussed the various network structures that are becoming popular.

DEVELOPING YOUR PERSPECTIVES

1. Select one sport organization of your choice (other than a university athletic team), and define and describe its environment. Explain the influences of different elements in the environment.

2. Describe the extent to which your organization's units are differentiated. Explain how integration among the differentiated units is achieved.

3. Considering the same organization, describe its "technical core." To what extent is that technical core protected from the external environment? How is this insulation of the technical core achieved?

4. Identify an organization characterized by Parsons' three levels of subsystems—technical subsystem, managerial subsystem, and institutional subsystem. Explain the extent to which Parsons' perspectives are reflected in that organization.

5. Explain the concepts of authority flow and power flow. How relevant are these concepts to the various types of sport organizations?

References

Amis, J., Slack, T., & Berrett, T. (1995). The structural antecedents of conflict in national sport organizations. *Leisure Studies, 14,* 1–16.

Birkinshaw, J. (2000). Network relationships inside and outside the firm, and the development of capabilities. In J. Birkinshaw & P. Hagstrom (Eds.), *The flexible firm: Capability management in network organizations* (pp. 4–17). Oxford, UK: Oxford University Press.

BKB Services (2004). www.bkbltd.com/about.htm. Retrieved on October 13, 2004.

Gerrard, B. (2003). Editorial introduction: Efficiency in professional sports leagues. *European Sport Management Quarterly, 3,* 219–220.

Goes, J. B., & Park, S. H. (1997). Interorganizational links and innovation: The case of hospital services. *The Academy of Management Journal, 40,* 673–696.

Hall, R. H. (1996). *Organizations: Structures, processes, and outcomes* (6th ed.). Englewood Cliffs, NJ: Prentice Hall.

Human, S. E., & Provan, K. G. (1997). An emergent theory of structure and outcomes in small-firm strategic manufacturing networks. *The Academy of Management Journal, 40*, 368–403.

Kanter, R. S., & Myers, P. S. (1991). Interorganizational bonds and intraorganizational behavior: How alliances and partnerships change the organizations forming them. In A. Etzioni & P. R. Lawrence (Eds.), *Socioeconomics: Toward a new synthesis* (pp. 329–344). Armonk, NY: M.E. Sharpe.

Katz, R. L. (1974). Skills of an effective administrator. *Harvard Business Review, 52*, 90–102.

Kikulis, L., Slack, T., & Hinings, C. R. (1995). Does decision making make a difference?: Patterns of change within Canadian national sport organizations. *Journal of Sport Management, 9*, 273–299.

Knoke, D. (2001). *Changing organizations: Business networks in the new political economy.* Boulder, CO: Westview Press.

Kraatz, M. (1998). Learning by association? Interorganizational networks and adaptation to environmental change. *Academy of Management Journal, 41*, 621–643.

Lawrence, P. R., & Lorsch, J. W. (1967). Differentiation and integration in complex organizations. *Administrative Science Quarterly, 12*, 1–47.

Miles, R. E., & Snow, C. C. (1996). Twenty-first century careers. In M. B. Arthur & D. M. Rousseau (Eds.), *The boundaryless career: A new employment principle for a new organizational era* (pp. 97–115). New York: Oxford University Press.

Mills, P. K., Hall, J. L., Leidecker, J. K., & Margulies, N. (1983). Flexiform: A model for professional service organizations. *Academy of Management Review, 8*, 118–131.

Mintzberg, H. (1975). The manager's job: Folklore and fact. *Harvard Business Review, 53*, 49–61.

NCAA (2004a). NCAA Purposes. www.ncaa.org/about/purposes.html. Retrieved October 17, 2004.

NCAA (2004b). NCAA Services. www.ncaa.org/about/services.html. Retrieved October 17, 2004.

Park, S. H. (1996). Managing an interorganizational network: A framework of the institutional mechanism for network control. *Organization Studies, 17*, 795–824.

Parsons, T. (1960). *Structure and process in modern societies.* New York: The Free Press of Glencoe.

Provan, K. G. (1983). The federation as an interorganizational linkage network. *Academy of Management Review, 8*, 79–89.

Robbins, S. P. (1997). *Managing today!* Upper Saddle River, NJ: Prentice Hall.

Slack, T. (1997). *Understanding sport organizations: The application of organization theory.* Champaign, IL: Human Kinetics.

SMG (2004). www.smgworld.com. Retrieved on October 13, 2004.

Stern, R. N. (1979). The development of an interorganizational network: The case of intercollegiate athletics. *Administrative Science Quarterly, 24*, 242–266.

Stern, R. N. (1981). Competitive influences on the interorganizational regulation of college athletics. *Administrative Science Quarterly, 26*, 15–31.

Thibault, L., Slack, T., & Hinings, C. R. (1991). Professionalism, structures and systems: The impact of professional staff on voluntary sport organizations. *International Review for the Sociology of Sport, 26*, 83–99.

Thompson, J. D. (1967). *Organizations in action.* New York: McGraw-Hill.

Van Gils, M. R. (1998). Interorganizational networks. In P. J. D. Drenth, H. Thierry, & C. J. de Wolff (Eds.), *Organizational psychology.* Volume 4 of *Handbook of organizational psychology* (2nd ed.). Hove, East Sussex: Psychology Press.

Waring, A. (1996) *Practical systems thinking.* London: International Thomson Business Press.

Weber, M. (1947). *The theory of social and economic organization.* (Translated by A. M. Henderson and T. Parsons). New York: Oxford University Press.

CHAPTER 9

Motivational Basis of Leading

MANAGE YOUR LEARNING

After completing this chapter you should be able to:

- Explain the importance of individual motivation in managing sport delivery systems.
- Distinguish between need-based and process-based theories of motivation.
- Explain the hierarchy of needs proposed by Maslow (1943).
- Understand the two-factor theory of Herzberg (1968) and explain the effects of motivators and hygiene factors.
- Explain how individuals' preferences for specific rewards and perceptions of the probability of receiving the rewards result in motivated behavior.
- Describe the concept of equity of rewards as judged by individuals.
- Explain the concepts of justice and fairness in the workplace.
- Develop a comprehensive framework to incorporate the various perspectives on motivation.

STRATEGIC CONCEPTS

abilities and traits	instrumentality
content and context of work	intrinsic and extrinsic rewards
critical incident method	job enrichment
effort–performance relationship	love needs
effort–reward probability	motivator
esteem needs	need
expectancy	outcomes
hierarchy of needs	physiological needs
hygiene factors	role perception
individual motivation	safety and security needs
inequity	self-actualization
inputs	valence

LEADING AND MOTIVATING

After defining the goals for the organization and specifying the ways of achieving those goals (planning), then clarifying who should do what (organizing), it becomes necessary for managers to motivate their subordinates to carry out their assignments so that the goals can be achieved (leading). While the planning and organizing functions require more of the technical and conceptual skills, the leading function is based on the human skills (see Chapter 4). Also, whereas the planning and organizing functions can be carried out without a great deal of interpersonal interaction with members, the leading function entails considerable face-to-face interactions with members—either collectively or individually. If managers are to be effective as leaders, they should have a clear understanding of how individuals are motivated and what factors influence motivation. While insights into member motivation can be gained through personal experience, it is also useful to consider the theories of motivation that have been advanced for an organizational context. This chapter presents some of the more relevant theories of work motivation.

Note that, because human behavior is highly variable and individual differences in terms of needs and personality are numerous, none of the theories discussed in this chapter can serve as a single framework to be applied in all circumstances. However, an understanding of these theories does provide the manager with a gestalt view of the intricacies and complexities of human motivation, as well as insight into the appropriateness of the theories to specific situations. Moreover, although the various theories have a more direct bearing on the leading function, their relevance to the planning, organizing, and evaluating functions is also important.

MOTIVATION DEFINED

What is motivation in the context of leading? According to Schermerhorn, Hunt, and Osborn (1997), motivation "refers to forces within an individual that account for the level, direction, and persistence of effort expended at work" (p. 87). In a similar manner, Saal and Knight (1995) view motivation as energizing, directing, and sustaining particular behaviors. According to Kanfer (1992), "motivation is frequently described in work settings by referring to what a person does (direction), how hard a person works (intensity), and how long a person works (persistence)" (p. 78). Finally, according to Pinder (1998), "*work motivation* is a set of energetic forces that originates both within as well as beyond an individual's being, to initiate work-related behaviour, and to determine its form, direction, intensity, and duration" (p. 11).

The above definitions point to five critical elements of **individual motivation:** (a) forces within the individual, (b) the energy for actions/behaviors, (c) direction of such behaviors, (d) intensity of those behaviors, and (e) persistence of the behaviors. The forces refer to the needs, drives, and motives to be satisfied. The energy is the activation of the individual to pursue satisfaction, while direction implies the specific goals an individual is seeking. Intensity refers to the magnitude of determination to achieve the goal, and persistence refers to an individual's continued effort to achieve the goal.

As with many concepts in organizational psychology, there are several theories of motivation in the workplace. These theories generally fall into two broad classes—content theories and process theories (see Exhibit 9.1). Some theories focus on the **needs** within individuals that provide the motivational energy. When needs are unsatisfied, the individual experiences a tension and is motivated to engage in some activity to satisfy them. That is,

In Brief

Motivation is reflected in the level and direction of the effort an individual puts forth and the extent to which he or she persists with that effort.

Exhibit 9.1 Classes of motivational theories.

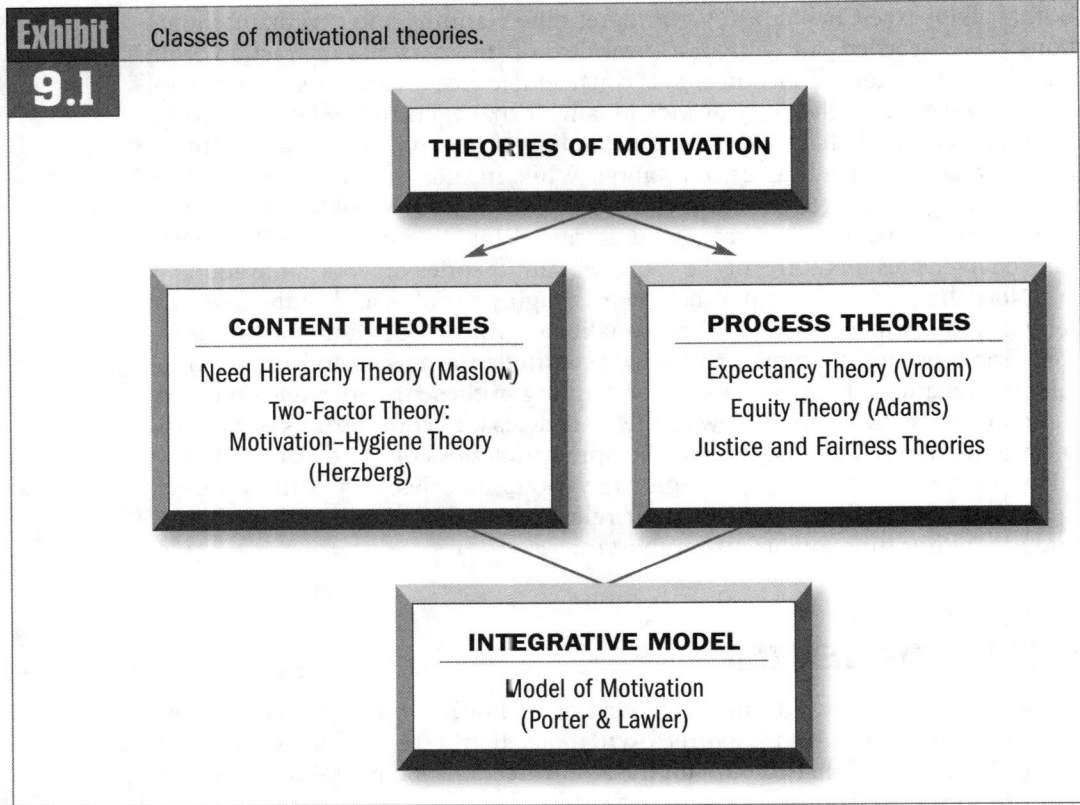

these theories address the issue of *what* motivates individuals. Thus, they are called *content* theories. In the following sections, we will explore the following content-based theories: Maslow's (1943) need hierarchy theory and Herzberg's (1968) motivation–hygiene theory.

While the issue of what motivates an individual is critical, it is also important to understand *how* and *why* individuals choose one form of behavior over another in their efforts to satisfy their needs or desires. The process that individuals go through in selecting one course of action over another is the focus of the second set of theories of motivation. Accordingly, they are called *process* theories of motivation. The process theories considered in this text are Vroom's (1964) expectancy theory, Adams' (1963) equity theory, and the recently articulated justice and fairness theories. The final theory discussed in the text is Porter and Lawler's (1968) model of motivation, a framework that integrates both the need-based and process theories.

NEED-BASED (OR CONTENT) THEORIES

The general paradigm for motivational theories based on needs is that when a need is deprived, the individual is aroused and driven to seek sources for the satisfaction of that need, and to take some action to achieve satisfaction. The need-based theories are also called content theories because they indicate what (content) motivates individuals to engage in specific behaviors.

> Commenting on the relationships among motivation, behavior, and performance, Kanfer (1992) noted that "the constructs of motivation subsume the determinants and processes underlying the development of intentions, choice behaviors, and volitional activities. The products of these motivational processes are the individual's overt and/or covert behaviors. In contrast, performance in organizational psychology typically refers to an evaluation of the individual's behaviors. For example, a salesperson motivated to perform his or her job well may make many customer contacts and still perform poorly according to a criterion based only on sales volume. Performance theory differs from motivation theory in that prediction of performance requires consideration of additional factors, including individual differences in variables such as abilities and task comprehension, and environmental factors such as situational constraints and task demands" (p. 80).

Although we can assume that needs underlie every action, there is some question about which of the numerous needs is most important in the determination of behavior. Does one need take precedence over another when two needs are deprived? Does one class of needs predominate in influencing behavior? These are the types of questions addressed by the various content theories of motivation.

The Need Hierarchy Theory

The essence of Maslow's (1943) need hierarchy theory lies in its specification of five classes of needs that are ordered in a hierarchy of prepotency (i.e., power or force). After stating that only unsatisfied needs are the basis of behavior and that satisfied needs lose their potency to instigate behavior, Maslow argued that people focus on meeting their basic needs and then move up the scale of the **hierarchy of needs** when the lower-order (prepotent) needs are satisfied. Maslow proposed five categories of needs in order of importance to the individual: physiological, safety and security, love and belonging, esteem, and self-actualization needs.

- **Physiological needs** relate to the more fundamental and biological requirements of a human being, such as food and shelter and the need to avoid pain. From an organizational perspective, then, the employee must be provided with sufficient financial rewards (such as salary and bonus) to ensure that the physiological needs are satisfied.

- **Safety and security needs** refer to an individual's preference for "a safe, orderly, predictable, organized world, which he can count on, and in which unexpected, unmanageable or other dangerous things do not happen" (Maslow, 1943, p. 378). In an organizational context, job security, health coverage, and retirement schemes are related to security needs, while safe working conditions, precautions against accidents, and other such organizational efforts are aimed at satisfying the safety needs of employees.

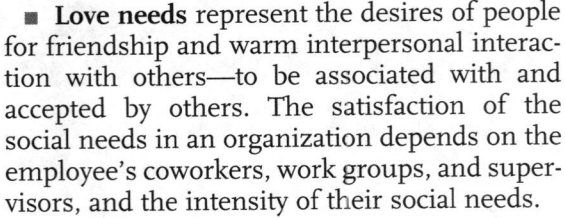

Sidebar

"Needs and the drive to fulfill them are two of the cornerstones of motivation. Although some common needs can be identified, the intensity of these needs, their priority, and therefore the impact they have on behavior can be different between people of different cultures and even between individuals within a culture. Understanding your own needs can be an important step in selecting appropriate jobs or careers; understanding the needs of others can be critical in your attempts to motivate and influence them." (Steers & Black, 1994, p. 156)

- **Love needs** represent the desires of people for friendship and warm interpersonal interaction with others—to be associated with and accepted by others. The satisfaction of the social needs in an organization depends on the employee's coworkers, work groups, and supervisors, and the intensity of their social needs.

- **Esteem needs** are considered to be higher-order needs that relate to a person's desire to be recognized by others and to have status among them. According to Maslow, the esteem needs include a desire for strength, achievement, adequacy, confidence (self-esteem), recognition, and respect (esteem) from others. The title and status accorded to individuals in an organization, and the respect with which they are treated by peers, are the kinds of factors that cater to esteem needs.

- **Self-actualization** lies at the highest level in Maslow's hierarchy. Individuals operating at this level endeavor to be what they can be. According to Maslow, people who have satisfied their self-actualization need will provide the fullest and healthiest creativity. He also acknowledged that such people are the exceptions rather than the rule—that is, most people do not progress up the ladder to the level of self-actualization.

The relevance of the need for self-actualization is not as clear as the other classes of needs for two reasons. First, individuals reach that stage, if at all, in the hierarchy of needs very late in their life. Second, individuals at that stage transcend the realities of organizational life, and are likely to be impervious to managerial actions. However, the idea of a self-actualizing person is attractive in itself. In fact, some advertisers have exploited the idea in creating catchy slogans for their clients. For instance, the U.S. Army's recruiting slogan "Be all you can be" connotes self-actualization.

One important component of Maslow's theory is often overlooked. Conventionally, the deprivation of a need is seen as the driving force, and scant attention is given to the effects of gratification of that need. In Maslow's theory, gratification of a need is as important as deprivation, because gratification releases the organism from one set of needs and activates another set. The process of the deprivation of a need dominating the individual and its gratification activating the next higher level need is illustrated in Exhibit 9.2.

The notion of the hierarchy of the prepotency of needs is illustrated in the following example. A recent sport management graduate might be offered a position in a distant location. In order of priority (prepotency), the grad-

In Brief

In Maslow's view, human needs can be hierarchically organized into physiological, safety and security, love, esteem, and self-actualization needs. The hierarchy is based on their relative prepotency (or power) to motivate the individual.

Exhibit 9.2 Maslow's need hierarchy theory applied to a sport management graduate's future employment.

HIERARCHY OF PREPOTENCY

SELF-ACTUALIZATION
(Challenging tasks, involving innovation and creativity)

Activation

Satisfaction
ESTEEM NEEDS
(Promotion and salary increases)
Deprivation

Activation

Satisfaction
LOVE AND SOCIAL NEEDS
(Types of coworkers and neighbors)
Deprivation

Activation

Satisfaction
SAFETY AND SECURITY NEEDS
(Job security, safety of prospective residential area and working conditions)
Deprivation

Activation

Satisfaction
PHYSIOLOGICAL NEEDS
(Salary and availability of housing)
Deprivation

MOTIVATIONAL BASIS OF LEADING

uate will be concerned with (a) salary and availability of housing (physiological needs); (b) job security, safety of the prospective residential area and the working conditions, including equipment (safety and security needs); and (c) type of coworkers and neighbors, including their personalities and their interpersonal orientation (social needs). After visits and interviews, the graduate might be reasonably confident that these needs will be satisfied, and consequently, she will accept the job and work hard at it. After a period of time, her superiors might recognize her effective performance and reward her with a promotion and an increase in salary (esteem needs). The graduate will be highly satisfied and will continue to work diligently and obtain the rewards and recognition associated with good performance. After a number of years, however, a sense of restlessness might develop. The graduate might feel that her personal abilities and personality require a different and more challenging task, involving innovation and creativity (self-actualizing needs). Therefore, the graduate might leave the present job and seek a different kind of job. If need be, she might start a business or undertake further education in the same or some other field to be qualified for a more challenging job. It is also possible that the graduate may decide on starting her own business in fitness, sponsorship, player agency, or consulting in marketing.

> **In Brief**
>
> Individual differences in personality and experience might affect the hierarchy. Some people may be fixated at one level, whereas others may renounce a higher level of needs. It is also not necessary for one level of needs to be completely satisfied before the next level is activated.

It is common to designate the esteem and self-actualization needs as *higher-order needs* or *growth needs*, and the physiological, safety/security, and love needs as *lower-order needs* or *deficiency needs* (see Steers & Black, 1994).

Maslow viewed the classification of the needs as general in nature. However, he was the first to acknowledge that individual differences in personality and experience might make the hierarchy of needs irrelevant in some cases. For instance, individuals who have been deprived of a lower-order need for any length of time might either "fixate" at that level even after gratification of that need, or they might "renounce" that need and focus on a higher need. It is also possible that for some individuals, self-esteem might become prepotent even before the satisfaction of the love and social needs. In innately creative people, creativity could supercede all other needs, whereas in some others, "the level of aspiration may be permanently deadened or lowered. That is to say, the less prepotent goals may be lost, and may disappear forever, so that the person who has experienced life at a very low level, i.e., chronic unemployment, may continue to be satisfied for the rest of his life if only he can get enough food" (Maslow, 1943, p. 386).

Maslow also emphasized that the notion of a hierarchy of needs does not imply that one set of needs has to be fulfilled completely before another set becomes potent. In fact, "a more realistic description of the hierarchy would be in terms of decreasing percentages of satisfaction as we go up the hierarchy of prepotency" (Maslow, 1943, p. 388). That is, the average person experiences greater percentages of satisfaction of the lower-order needs (physiological, security, and love needs) while much smaller percentages of the higher-order needs are satisfied.

Limitations of Need Hierarchy Theory

One major limitation of Maslow's theory is that it cannot be adequately tested. Because individuals progress through the hierarchy of needs one at a time, it could take a lifetime for some individuals to reach the highest level, self-actualization. Thus, it becomes inconvenient, if not impossible, to test the theory, because data would have to be collected over the lifetime of subjects.

A second limitation of the theory is associated with difficulties in measurement. There is also a possibility that one set of behaviors could result in the satisfaction of more than one set of needs. For example, when a faculty member engages in research and produces quality publications, it might result in the award of tenure (security), recognition by colleagues (esteem), and a sense of achievement and growth (self-actualization). There is no acceptable way of determining which of these was prepotent.

Implications for Sport Managers

Although the theory is not readily subject to empirical research, it does have an intuitive appeal, particularly from a managerial perspective in terms of the emphasis placed on needs. The theory's simple and useful classes of a wide range of needs provide a basis for instituting reward systems and for judging their effectiveness. For example, a sport organization aims its salary increases at satisfying physiological needs. When a sport organization undertakes to provide for medical or life insurance, or pays into the employees' pension fund, it is catering to safety and security needs. The picnics and celebrations organized by a sport organization address the love and social needs of its employees. The titles bestowed on employees (Assistant to the Associate Athletic Director, Coordinator of Aerobics, Manager of Facilities), and the privileges offered to specific employees (larger offices, offices with windows or carpeting, keys to the executive washroom) satisfy some of the esteem needs. The attraction the theory holds for managers is that, to a large extent, they are in control of the monetary and material resources that they can manipulate to satisfy all of the classes of needs in the hierarchy except the self-actualization need.

The Two-Factor Theory: Motivation–Hygiene Theory

Whereas Maslow felt that even the lower-order needs could serve as motivators when they were deprived, Herzberg and associates (Herzberg, Mausner, & Snyderman, 1959; Herzberg, 1968) contended that the two sets of needs (higher-order and lower-order needs) are associated with satisfaction and dissatisfaction differentially. In contrast to the common view that satisfaction and dissatisfaction are two polar extremes on one continuum, Herzberg considered them to be on two separate continua. Herzberg (1968) explained that:

> The factors involved in producing job satisfaction (and motivation) are separate and distinct from the factors that lead to job dissatisfaction. Since separate factors need to be considered, depending on whether job satisfaction or job dissatisfaction is being examined, it follows that these two feelings are not opposites of each other. The opposite of job satisfaction is not job dissatisfaction, rather *no* job satisfaction; and, similarly, the opposite of job dissatisfaction is not job satisfaction, but *no* job dissatisfaction. (p. 56)

The fundamental postulate of the theory is that only higher-order needs affect satisfaction, and the lower-order needs are associated with dissatisfaction. As a consequence, Herzberg's theory is called a two-factor (or dual factor) theory. To understand the theory better, it is useful to examine how it evolved.

In their analysis of previous research results, Herzberg and his colleagues could not find any consistent results relating needs to motivation. They also felt that the available research supported the conclusion that different classes of needs are differentially associated with satisfaction or motivation. To test this proposition, they interviewed and administered a semi-structured questionnaire to approximately 200 engineers and accountants. The questionnaire required the respondents to think back to one incident in their work that made them feel extremely happy and satisfied, and to another incident that left them feeling extremely unhappy and dissatisfied. They were also asked to indicate what effects these feelings of happiness and unhappiness had had on their subsequent work, and how long these feelings lasted. The authors then analyzed the content of the responses and identified 16 factors as the causes of satisfaction or dissatisfaction. The data analysis showed that one set of factors, called the satisfiers or **motivators**, showed up more often in reference to satisfaction than to dissatisfaction. Another set, called the dissatisfiers or **hygienes**, showed up more often in incidents of dissatisfaction than of satisfaction. As mentioned previously, all of the satisfiers or motivators were related to higher-order needs, and the dissatisfiers were associated with lower-order needs. Exhibit 9.3 presents the composite of the results of this and 12 subsequent research studies.

One set of job factors, called motivators, relate to the content of the job; whereas the second set, called hygienes, relate to the context of the job. Motivators influence satisfaction, whereas hygienes influence dissatisfaction.

The most important product of Herzberg's work was the finding that the motivators (or growth factors) were all related to the **content** of the work itself, while the hygiene factors were all related to the **context** in which the work was carried out. The content factors are achievement, recognition for achievement, the work itself, responsibility, and growth or advancement. The contextual factors are company policy and administration, supervision, interpersonal relationships, working conditions, salary, status, and security.

On the basis of his research findings, Herzberg concluded that management must be concerned with eliminating dissatisfaction by improving the hygiene factors—providing adequate salary and wages, ensuring good working conditions, and having meaningful company policies and quality supervision. He also pointed out that these hygiene factors alone do not result in motivated or satisfied workers. Management must also change jobs in order to provide for the psychological growth of employees.

Implications for Sport Managers

The two-factor theory has relevance for sport management contexts also. For instance, a manager of a commercial golf course needs to ensure that her employees are well paid in relation to the labor market. In addition, the manager should make the working conditions (lighting, ventilation, office furniture, and so on) adequate. Equally important, the manager's supervision of

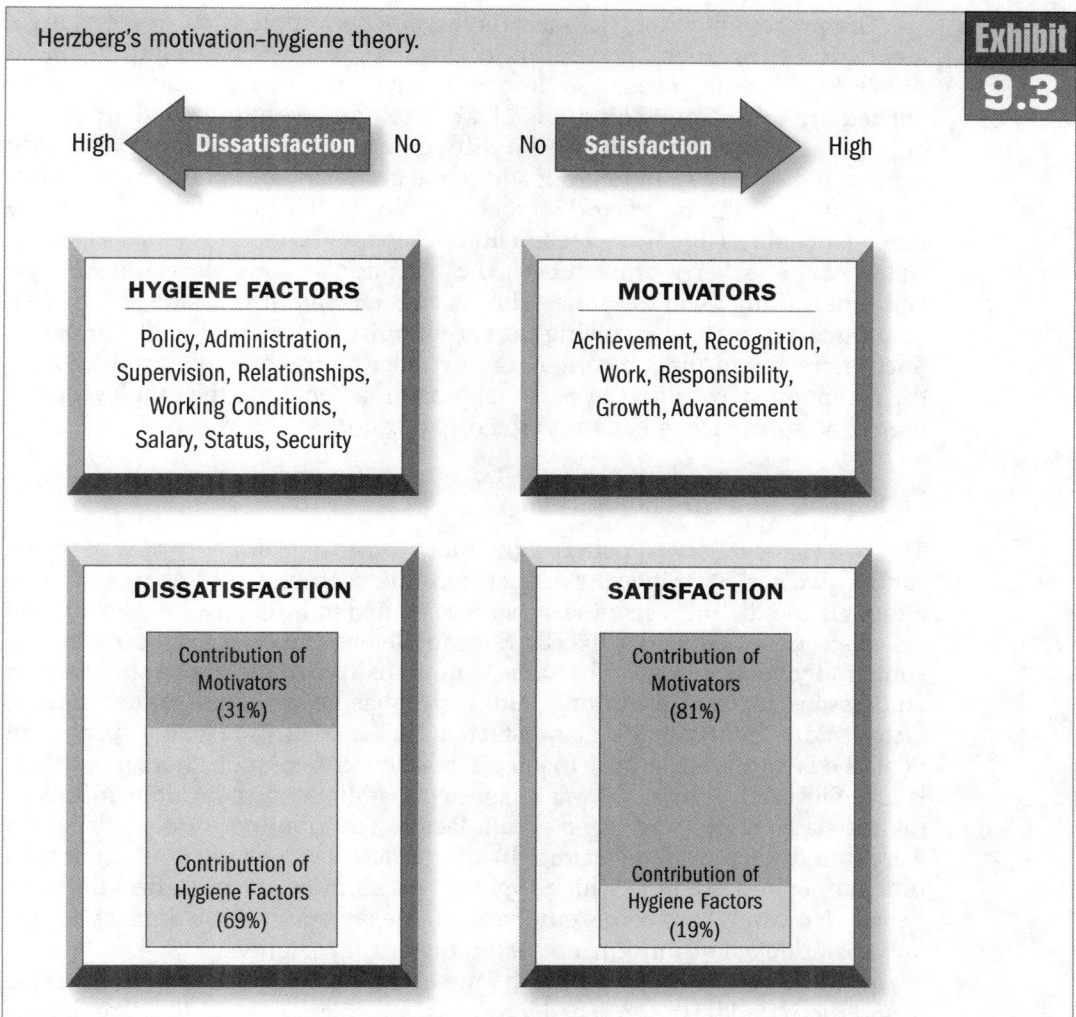

Exhibit 9.3 Herzberg's motivation–hygiene theory.

Source: Adapted and reprinted by permission of *Harvard Business Review*. From "One more time: How do you motivate people?" by F. Herzberg, Jan.–Feb., 1968. Copyright © 1968 by the Harvard Business School Publishing Corporation; all rights reserved.

the employees should be fair, and the interactions among the employees need to be warm and pleasant. Deficiencies in one or more of these hygiene factors would cause dissatisfaction among the employees. Cumulatively, they can cause great dissatisfaction and lowered morale. Therefore, the manager should take every effort in making sure these hygiene factors are maintained at acceptable levels. However, when the manager succeeds in ensuring adequate levels of these factors, only the dissatisfaction among employees disappears—greater motivation and higher performance do not miraculously result. According to Herzberg's two-factor theory, only the job and its content can provide the motivational force. That is, only when the job offers responsibility, a sense of achievement, and opportunities for growth and advancement will the employees be motivated. Accordingly, the manager should progressively increase the challenge and responsibility for the employees in their respective jobs.

The process of job enrichment is the practical application of Herzberg's theory. **Job enrichment,** or vertical job loading, involves redesigning jobs to satisfy higher-order needs. Some of the ways in which this can be accomplished are to assign whole units of work to employees (rather than having different employees responsible for different segments), to remove or reduce control and supervision, to grant additional authority, and to increase the difficulty of the tasks assigned (Herzberg, 1968). In the case of a golf club, the manager could assign more responsibilities to the receptionist (such as supervision of the locker rooms) and let the receptionist make decisions on how and when things will be done. The manager could also assign more challenging tasks, such as involving the receptionist in a promotional campaign. Such increases in the job content are expected to increase the motivation of the receptionist, resulting in personal growth (a benefit to the employee) and higher performance (a benefit to the organization).

Limitations of Two-Factor Theory

The two-factor theory is, perhaps, the most controversial theory of work motivation. Two serious criticisms detract from the usefulness of this theory. First, although two distinct sets of factors are assumed to influence satisfaction and dissatisfaction, Herzberg's data do not completely support this assumption. In some individuals, many of the same conditions contribute to both satisfaction and dissatisfaction. For example, although it has been suggested that hygiene factors alone influence job dissatisfaction, in Herzberg's research, 31 percent of all the factors contributing to job dissatisfaction were motivators (see Exhibit 9.3). Similarly, although it was suggested that the motivators alone influence job satisfaction, 19 percent of all the factors contributing to job satisfaction were found to be hygiene factors. In short, there are individual differences in the manner and extent to which hygiene and motivator factors affect different people. However, Herzberg's emphasis on the generality of the impact of each factor overlooked or minimized such individual differences.

In our example of the golf club, one of the receptionists may be attracted to and motivated by the enriched job. Thus her experience would fall under the 81 percent of motivators on the right side of Exhibit 9.3. In contrast, another receptionist may be more interested in and motivated by an increase in salary, and less appreciative of the enriched job. In fact, the receptionist could be dissatisfied with the enriched job because it is beyond his abilities. Thus, the second receptionist would fall under both the 19 percent of hygiene factors on the right-hand side and the 31 percent of the motivators on the left side of Exhibit 9.3. The implication for the manager is that while the theory offers some guidelines on enriching the jobs she supervises, the use of those guidelines should be consistent with individual differences and preferences. Accordingly, the golf club manager would attempt to enrich the job for the first receptionist and refrain from doing so in the case of the second receptionist.

The second criticism relates to the methodology used by Herzberg and his associates. The respondents were asked to recall incidents in which they felt satisfied or dissatisfied—an approach known as the **critical incident method.** However, when individuals are asked to recall incidents and express their reactions to them, they tend to attribute all the positive or happy events to their own efforts and achievements. Conversely, all negative outcomes are assigned to some external agent like company policy, supervision, and so on.

This is a defensive mechanism individuals use to protect their image and self-esteem. As Vroom (1964) stated:

> Persons may be more likely to attribute the causes of satisfaction to their own achievements and accomplishments on the job. On the other hand, they may be more likely to attribute their dissatisfaction not to personal inadequacies or deficiencies, but to factors in the work environment, i.e., obstacles presented by company policies or supervision. (p. 129)

Studies that attempted to use other methods found that Herzberg's theory was not supported by the results (see Dunnette, Campbell, & Hakel, 1967; Hulin & Smith, 1967). Consequently, it has been suggested that the two-factor theory is limited by the method used to develop it.

The motivators in the two-factor theory are similar to Maslow's higher-order needs. However, this is where the similarity ends. As we noted previously, while Maslow contended that even lower-order needs can motivate workers, Herzberg stated that only factors intrinsic to the job can serve as motivators.

Implication of Need-Based Theories for Sport Managers

Despite the differences, the need-based theories have one general implication for management—that management should be concerned with making work meaningful for the workers. This viewpoint contrasts with the classical and bureaucratic approaches, which emphasized the fractionation of work (resulting in narrow routine and monotonous jobs) to ensure efficiency and productivity (see Chapter 7 for discussion of classical principles). Also, earlier approaches that emphasized uniformity and consistency of operations tended to impose restrictive rules and procedures that governed the activities of the workers. These two aspects of the classical approach to management are not conducive to the pursuit or fulfillment of higher-order needs. Thus, the need-based theories of motivation discussed above—particularly the job enrichment recommended by Herzberg—are in sharp contrast to the classical approach to job design.

The upshot of the need theories for sport managers is that managers must balance the concern for efficiency on the one hand with the interest in providing growth opportunities for employees on the other. The efficiency concern can lead to simplifying jobs and making them routine, whereas concern for employee growth and motivation can lead to job enrichment. These are the golf club manager's choices when he decides whether to keep the job of the receptionist simple as it is now or improve the content of the job by adding more responsibility and autonomy.

The difficulty in designing jobs to meet the needs of individuals while maintaining efficiency is real. The happy fact is, however, that not all individuals are motivated by higher-order needs and higher skills. Those who do not seek fulfillment of higher-order needs and those who do not have the skills necessary for enriched jobs can be assigned relatively more simple and routine tasks. Accordingly, the manager of the golf club in the previous example may assign the simpler task of receptionist to an employee who prefers to be involved in such simple tasks. By the same token, she may assign the relatively more enriched jobs to those who seek such jobs and have the ability to carry out those tasks. In fact, this rationale should be the basis of promotions and upgrading of jobs.

PROCESS THEORIES

As we noted earlier, the content theories are concerned with the factors that motivate the worker—personal factors like individual needs and organizational factors like task assignment and rewards. However, they do not explain how individuals choose one behavior from the several available to them. The process theories of motivation deal with the individual's evaluation and choice of certain courses of action, and how other factors influence the results of such courses of action. In the following sections we will look at three process models of motivation—Vroom's expectancy theory, Adams' equity theory, and Porter and Lawler's model of motivation. These three models are considered to be most relevant to organizations.

Vroom's Expectancy Theory

The main postulate of expectancy theory is that individuals evaluate the various courses of action that are available to them and choose the one that they expect to lead to the outcomes they prefer. Vroom's expectancy theory incorporates four major variables (or concepts)—valence, outcome (or result), expectancy, and instrumentality.

Valence

An individual's preferences for particular outcomes is referred to as **valence.** If a particular result is very strongly preferred (for example, a trade from one team to another in professional baseball), then the valence for the result will approach the value of +1. If, on the other hand, an outcome is strongly detested (as in, say, a transfer to a distant locality), then the valence will approach −1. According to the theory, the actual valence for the trade is based on the relative weighting of the positive and negative aspects of that result. Thus, if a trade is a valued outcome, but it entails a transfer to another place that is negatively valued, the degree to which the trade is preferred is indicated by the average value of the two outcomes (the trade and the transfer). When an individual is indifferent to a particular outcome, the valence is considered to be zero. Other terms that can be used to refer to the "valence" concept are *incentives, rewards,* and *utility.*

Outcomes

Outcomes or results refer to the consequences of a given act. For instance, an employee's promotion is an outcome. But this promotion is only a consequence of the employee's having achieved certain performance standards set by the organization. Thus, there are two sets of outcomes or results that stem from the efforts of the employee. Vroom calls these the first-level and second-level outcomes. The first-level outcome refers to the performance standards achieved by the employee; the second-level outcome refers to the rewards for that performance. Note that the first-level outcome is what the organization expects (productivity), while the second-level outcomes are what the employee desires (promotion, a pay increase).

Expectancy

Expectancy is the probability estimate that effort will lead to the first-level outcome or result—the performance standards set out by the organization. If, in the above example, the employee believed that his efforts would result in superior performance, then the expectancy would approach the value of +1. If, however, the employee felt that his capacities were not sufficient to reach that level of performance, then the expectancy would approach the value of zero. Note that expectancy refers to the individual's *perception* of the probability that effort will lead to a standard of performance.

Instrumentality

The individual's estimate of the relationship between first-level results and second-level results is called **instrumentality**. If the employee in the above example believed that performing at a high level would automatically result in promotion, then instrumentality would approach the value of +1. If, however, he believed that promotion was based only on seniority and not on performance, then instrumentality would drop to zero. In contrast to expectancy (perceived probability), instrumentality reflects the individual's perception that there is a good relationship between first-level and second-level outcomes. Expectancy connects individual effort to first-level outcomes, whereas instrumentality links the first- and second-level results. A coach might have a strong belief that if she recruits heavily her team will be successful (expectancy). She might also hold the strong belief that if her team is successful, she will receive a pay increase (instrumentality).

Interplay of Concepts

The relationships among the preceding variables or concepts are illustrated in Exhibit 9.4. It is assumed in Vroom's expectancy theory that the force (equat-

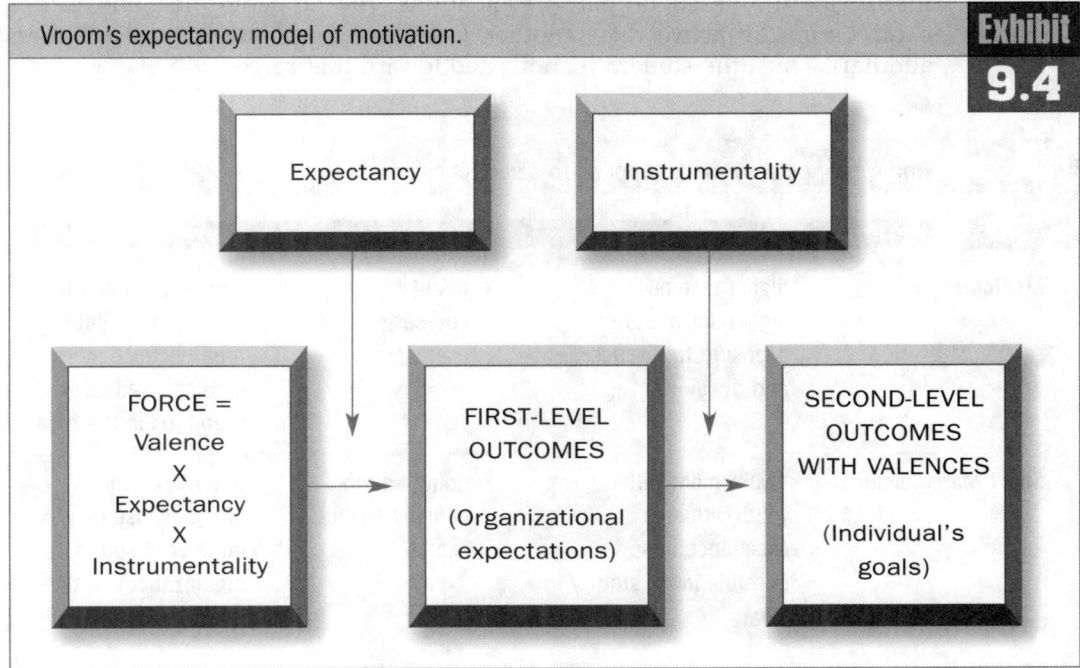

Exhibit 9.4 Vroom's expectancy model of motivation.

ed here with motivation) with which an individual engages in an activity depends on the valence or attraction for the outcomes (rewards or incentives the organization has to offer), the expectancy that the effort will result in a certain level of performance, and the instrumentality of performance in the attainment of those rewards.

This interplay among the factors of Vroom's theory can be expressed as follows:

$$\text{Force} = \text{Valence} \times \text{Expectancy} \times \text{Instrumentality}$$

In this equation, the values for all of the variables on the right-hand side of the equation must be positive (and not equal to zero) if the force is to be positive (that is, if the individual is to be motivated). In simpler terms, if an individual dislikes an outcome (the promotion), the valence will be negative and there will be no motivation toward that outcome. If anything, behavior aimed at *avoiding* that outcome will be motivated. Similarly, both expectancy and instrumentality must be nonzero. That is, the individual must believe that effort will ultimately result in the preferred rewards.

Consider a student contemplating a future career (see Exhibit 9.5). The career could be in any of several professional areas such as engineering, law, medicine, education, sport management, and so on. The student is likely to choose one of these areas based on the rewards and satisfactions (the positive outcomes in Vroom's model) that each professional area is expected to offer. A career in medicine is likely to yield more income and a higher social status. On the other hand, a career in sport management is likely to offer the satisfaction of being involved with youth and excellence in sport, whereas medicine often deals with disease and decay. A student is likely to evaluate both the positive outcomes (higher salary and status in medicine, and exposure to youth and excellence in sport management) and negative outcomes (exposure to disease and decay in medicine, and, perhaps, lower status or salary in sport management). Based on these evaluations, the student finds one career choice more attractive than another (one career has greater valence than another). Thus, the student is motivated toward that career.

Exhibit 9.5 Vroom's expectancy model applied to career choice.

	FORCE =	VALENCE *(expected outcome)* X	EXPECTANCY X	INSTRUMENTALITY
Medicine:		+ higher income + higher social status − exposure to disease and decay	− doing well in courses, taking exams	− limited potential for jobs in immediate area because more medical graduates than jobs in the area
Sport Management:		+ involvement with youth/athletes + excellence in sport − possible lower status/salary	+ doing well in courses, taking exams	+ potential for jobs high because of number of sports organizations in the area

However, the student must also evaluate the likelihood of achieving that career. For instance, a student may believe that he does not have the orientation and potential to succeed in a professional career (doing well in the courses and passing the entrance examinations). If so, the student is likely to shun that career even though it is attractive from several other perspectives. This assessment corresponds to the expectancy estimates in Vroom's model.

A final evaluation the student is likely to make is the extent to which her performance in professional preparation will actually lead to getting a good job in that career. For instance, a student may like the prospects of working with youth and excellence in intercollegiate athletics or professional sports (high valence) and may be convinced that she can do very well in the professional preparation for a career in those areas (high expectancy). However, she may believe that getting a good job in one of those areas is not a given owing to the limited number of jobs or discriminatory practices in hiring (low instrumentality). In such a case, the student may not choose to enter that career. This process of computing or estimating valence, expectancy, and instrumentality is the essential thrust of Vroom's expectancy model of motivation.

We used the example of a student's choice of a career because many readers of this text are likely to be in the process of making just such choices. However, the model is relevant to any job context in any sport organization. For instance, the degree of effort an employee puts into a job could be based on such calculations. In the discussion of bureaucracy (see Chapter 7), we saw that the extensive rules and regulations of a bureaucracy may actually set the minimum standards for performance. Furthermore, bureaucracies also tend to promote employees based on seniority rather than performance. If these are the convictions of an employee in a bureaucracy, that person is not motivated to put in extra effort. On the other hand, an employee in a private profit-oriented sport enterprise may perceive the organization as rewarding employees only on performance and firing those who do not perform adequately. With such perceptions, the employee is likely to put a lot of effort into his job.

> **In Brief**
>
> The three significant concepts in Vroom's model are (a) valence (one's preferences for specific outcomes), (b) expectancy (one's estimate that effort will lead to achievement of organizational expectations), and (c) instrumentality (one's estimate that performance of what the organization expects will lead to personal rewards). The interplay of these three elements determines motivation.

Implications for Sport Managers

The practical implication of Vroom's model is that a sport organization and its managers can intervene in the process of individual motivation. For instance, an individual may believe that she does not have the ability to carry out a particular task or project (say, a promotional campaign for a fitness club), and, therefore, she may not be willing to take on the task or project (that is, she may have low expectancy). On the other hand, the manager knows the requirements of the task better and also knows that the employee can perform well in the task. It is the duty of the manager to convince the employee of this fact, provide background or training the employee may feel she is lacking, and motivate the employee to undertake the job. That is, the manager needs to help the employee revise her expectancy estimate.

Similarly, the employee may not be convinced that successful performance in the task is likely to lead to any additional rewards. Once again, the manager can clarify the relationship between level of performance in the project and the associated rewards and outcomes. Thus, the manager corrects the employee's misperceptions of instrumentality. From this perspective, Vroom's model is very useful in managing the motivational process of employees. In fact, a very popular theory of leadership—the path–goal theory of leadership—is based on the concepts of Vroom's model. That theory will be explained in the next chapter.

In overview, Vroom's model outlines relevant variables associated with motivated behavior, and their interrelationships. More important, through the introduction of concepts such as valence, expectancy, and instrumentality, Vroom's model helps to account for individual differences in motivated behavior. However, an assumption implicit in the model is that individuals always behave in a rational manner. This is simply not the case. As was already noted in Chapter 6, individuals often do not have the capacity or time to go through all the complicated calculations.

Adams' Theory of Inequity

Although the content theories of Maslow and Herzberg emphasize the concept of satisfaction, they are simplistic in their assumption that when a need is fulfilled, satisfaction automatically follows. From an organizational perspective, this is not necessarily true. For instance, when an individual gets a raise in pay, does it automatically lead to satisfaction? Or does the person compare the raise to some standard and then experience satisfaction or dissatisfaction?

For instance, it is not enough for a student to receive a B grade in a course. The student compares the grade to what other students receive. Similarly, a raise of $1,000 in salary does not provide happiness for an assistant director of marketing in a professional sport franchise if the other assistant director received $1,100. The important point in both of these examples is that the absolute amount does not have a bearing on the estimation of equity; it is the relative amount that is critical.

Input/Outcome Balance

According to Adams (1963, 1977) the individual's internalized standard could be simply a comparison between personal effort **(inputs)** and the rewards of that effort (outcomes). For example, if someone makes great sacrifices in an effort to lose weight but loses only two pounds in six months, the individual could have a feeling of inequity. The assistant director of marketing in the preceding example may be dissatisfied because the salary increase is not commensurate with all the time and effort he has put into the job. This feeling results from a simple comparison of personal cost versus personal benefit. In an organizational context, however, the cost–benefit comparison extends to referent others in the organization. That is, the assistant director compares the personal cost–benefit ratio to the cost–benefit ratio of other(s) in the work group, as indicated below:

Personal Benefits (Outcomes)	Other's Benefits (Outcomes)
$1,000	$1,100

Compared to

Personal Costs (Inputs)	Other's Costs (Inputs)
45 hr work week	40 hr work week
Extensive travel/time away from family	Minimal local travel

Adams' theory is anchored on this comparison to a referent other(s). As he noted:

> Inequity exists for *Person* [italics added] whenever he perceives that the ratio of his outcomes to inputs and the ratio of *Other's* [italics added] outcomes to Other's inputs are unequal. (Adams, 1977, p. 113)

The *other* in Adams' theory could be a subordinate, a supervisor, a coworker, or an employee in another comparable organization or occupation. It is also possible for an individual to compare the input/outcome balance of a current situation to that experienced in a previous one.

The concept of *inputs* in Adams' theory refers to the personal contributions for which the individual expects to receive a reward. Some of the factors that a person may consider as inputs are: intelligence, education and training, experience and seniority, personal appearance or attractiveness, health, and effort on the job. *Outcomes* in an organizational context include pay, seniority and other fringe benefits, working conditions (including status and perquisites), and the psychological or intrinsic rewards of the job. Outcomes may also be negative, as in the case of poor working conditions. Thus, the theory of **inequity** is based on an individual's perception of the balance between personal outcomes (benefits) and inputs (costs) relative to the outcomes and inputs of others.

> **In Brief**
>
> According to Adams (1977), individuals tend to compare their outcomes and their inputs to the outcomes and inputs of comparable others. If the comparison is equal, there is equity. If not, the individual experiences inequity and resultant tensions.

Implications for Sport Managers

There are three possible results of such comparisons—equity, inequity unfavorable to the individual (a referent other's cost–benefit ratio is greater), and inequity favorable to the individual (the individual's cost–benefit ratio is greater). A person who perceives inequity and feels the tension and discomfort associated with such inequity may attempt to restore equity (or reduce the inequity) in a number of ways. Obviously, the person may attempt to alter the values of any of the four elements of the inequity formula—personal outcomes, personal inputs, others' outcomes, and others' inputs. The most frequently used strategy is to attempt to increase personal outcomes. Thus, an individual is most likely to approach the employer and ask for more pay, greater benefits, and so on. If that approach fails, the individual may attempt to increase personal outcomes by putting in a greater number of hours or producing better-quality work. It is also possible, of course, to reduce the feeling of inequity by reducing personal inputs through decreased productivity or increased absenteeism. Inequity could also be reduced by reducing others' outcomes or inputs. However, the individual may be constrained from adopting this strategy. Others' outcomes, such as pay and promotion, are most likely to be determined by superiors, and others' inputs are most strongly influenced by the other individuals themselves. More important, a strategy that focuses on others' inputs or outcomes may not be psychologically acceptable to the person. Very few students go to a professor and ask that the grade of another student be reduced. Also, very few students destroy another student's class notes.

Although the possibility exists that inequity in favor of the individual may occur (for example, someone receives a higher pay raise than is deserved), that individual may not express a feeling of inequity as often (or as strongly) as when perceiving inequity of the opposite type. However, feelings of discomfort and guilt could arise. If this is the case, the individual is likely to put in greater efforts in an attempt to justify the rewards received.

Apart from manipulating personal outcomes and inputs, there are other ways of reducing inequity. Adams suggested that individuals might alter their perceptions of personal and others' outcomes and inputs in such a manner that equity is perceptually restored. Alternatively, a person may change the referent other of comparison. Thus, a sport marketer might believe that she had a productive year and, therefore, deserves a high merit increase. However, this perception could change if she were to know the actual accomplishments of others. Another possibility is that the sport marketer could leave the current organization and join another organization.

It is clear from the foregoing that a sport manager can intervene in restoring equity perceptions among his employees. First, as equity perceptions are fundamentally based on relative performances of individuals, managers must ensure that their evaluation of employee performance is fair and accurate. Any errors in this area will naturally lead to inequity in the distribution of rewards. Thus, performance evaluation is a significant area of human resource management. Second, distribution of rewards or resources must also be equitable—that is, equal rewards for equal performance or contributions. Managers must take care to avoid any personal biases or preferences in such decisions. Third, as feelings of inequity in most cases are based on inadequate information or misperceptions, managers should publicize all the bases and rules of distribution of rewards. Being secretive about performance evaluations and distribution of rewards is a sure means of creating misperceptions and subsequent feelings of inequity. We further discuss this issue below under the heading "Justice and Fairness Theories."

Although Adams considered his theory relevant to any situation of social exchange (husband and wife, partners in tennis, and so on), he used the organizational context as the backdrop for its development, and most of the examples listed in his writings relate to organizations and their members. The significance of the Adams theory lies in the fact that organizational reward systems are considered meaningful and effective only insofar as they create a sense of equity among the members of the organization. This notion is further elaborated in the Porter and Lawler model of motivation discussed later in this chapter.

Note here that the emphasis so far has been on the outcomes for individual members, such as pay and promotions. The concept of fairness and equity, however, extends as well to distribution of resources among groups and units within the organization. For instance, allocation of additional resources to specific teams is frequently a point of perceived unfairness by other teams. Similarly, improved office space for units such as marketing and event management may become the focus of perceived unfairness.

Justice and Fairness Theories

Our discussion of Adams' theory of inequity focused on an individual's reactions to the perceived fairness of outcomes for that individual alone. An extension of this view would hold that members of an organization value and seek fairness in all employee–employer exchanges (Kanfer, 1992). For example, an employee in a sport organization may perceive that some of his colleagues are not dealt with fairly in pay raises or promotions. If these perceptions are strong and they lead to negative feelings, the focal employee may become disenchanted with the organization and its practices as much as when he himself is affected by such unfairness. These feelings may lead to lowered motivation.

Distributive Justice versus Procedural Justice

In our discussions so far the emphasis has been on the outcomes to individuals or units—that is, the concern is with the distribution of available resources to individuals or groups. This aspect of justice and fairness is known as *distributive* justice or fairness. Another aspect to the concept of justice deals with the procedures that determine how resources are distributed. While a person may fundamentally be concerned with her personal outcomes, she may also be concerned with the rules and procedures that determine the distribution of outcomes to members of the group or units of the organization. This aspect of justice is called *procedural* justice and refers to the degree to which those affected by allocations of resources or rewards perceive them to have been made according to fair methods and guidelines (Niehoff & Moorman, 1993).

Procedural justice refers to means, or *how* various ends, or content or consequences (distributive justice), are attained (Folger & Greenberg, 1985). Thus, procedural justice is an intermediary stage that is instrumental in the attainment of distributive justice. However, procedures may have equal if not more weight than the actual outcomes in perceptions of justice (Folger & Greenberg, 1985). For example, employees of a sport marketing firm may perceive organizational justice when the criteria for evaluating their performance and the processes of such evaluation are clear and just, even though the actual salary increases they received were less than expected.

In their attempts to ensure procedural justice, sport managers should strive to formulate procedures that adhere to the following rules outlined by Leventhal (1980):

- *Consistency* specifies that allocation procedures should be consistent across persons, and over time. For instance, managers cannot use performance as the basis of allocation for one or more employees and seniority for another set of employees.
- *Bias suppression* implies that decision makers should not let self-interest or biases affect the allocation process. Recall the implicit favorite model of decision making (see Chapter 6). A manager in a city recreation department would be succumbing to this process if he gives a higher

salary increase to an employee because the manager likes the employee's athletic prowess. That would not be bias suppression!
- *Accuracy* means that all allocation decisions must be based on accurate information.
- *Representativeness* refers to making the allocation process representative of the concerns of all recipients. It is conceivable that a sport manager might decide on the allocation procedures based on input from her favorite subordinates, whereas the rest of the employees may prefer some other allocation rules. In such case, the allocation process chosen by the manager would not be representative.
- *Ethicality* requires that allocations adhere to prevailing ethical and moral standards of the community.
- *Correctibility* acknowledges that decision makers may unintentionally violate one or more of the foregoing rules and err in making allocations. According to this rule, it should be possible for allocation decisions to be modified and the errors corrected. One tactic a sport manager may adopt is to set aside a certain amount of rewards or resources in order to correct any errors. If the manager distributes all the rewards in the first place, he will find it difficult to correct any errors that might have been made.

Interactional Justice

Yet another aspect of justice, known as *interactional justice*, refers to the manner in which the distribution of outcomes is explained to recipients, and to the procedures employed in such distribution (Bies & Moag, 1986; Bies & Shapiro, 1987; Greenberg, 1990; Tyler & Bies, 1990). The focus here is on communication about the outcomes and procedures. Any insufficient or erroneous communication would be seen as unjust. By the same token, a lack of respect, concern, pleasantness, and warmth in such communications will also be seen as unjust. For instance, when an athletic director tells a subordinate in an abrupt and coarse manner that "that's the way it's done here," he is violating both aspects of interactional justice. First, no explanation is given in that communication. Second, the communication is abrupt and coarse, without showing any respect or concern for the employee.

Implications for Sport Managers

The concept of organizational justice (including distributive, procedural, and interactional aspects of justice) has two important implications for sport managers. First, any violation of organizational justice may lead to legal ramifications. That is, the affected employees may seek legal redress through litigation or other means. It is not uncommon for organizations to set up a procedure for the employee to appeal the decision made by a manager. Equally important is the idea that the affected employees, and even those that are not affected, are likely to see the organization and its managers as unjust. These feelings may influence the employees to change their attitudes and behaviors toward the organization. In other words, such perceived injustice may reduce employees' motivation to work hard and achieve organizational goals. Thus sport managers must understand that the concepts of equity and justice are pervasive in their organizations. Almost every decision they make is subject to standards of equity and fairness.

AN INTEGRATIVE FRAMEWORK: THE PORTER AND LAWLER MODEL OF MOTIVATION

You will note that each of the various theories of motivation discussed thus far deals with significant but limited aspects of human motivation. Each theory provides some insights for the sport manager that will facilitate appropriate organizational practices. However, reliance on one single theory may not be a prudent approach for a manager. Instead, managers should attempt to develop a mental model of how motivation works and how it can be enhanced in an organizational context. With this in view, we now describe a motivational model that represents an attempt to synthesize the significant elements of other theories.

The model of motivation proposed by Porter and Lawler (1968) is an extension and elaboration of Vroom's expectancy theory, as well as a synthesis of the content and process theories discussed previously. The model is schematically represented in Exhibit 9.6. To facilitate discussion of the model, numbers have been placed in the boxes in Exhibit 9.6.

Effort (Box 3), which is equivalent to the force concept in Vroom's model, refers to the motivation behind an individual's effort in the work context. That is, the degree of effort expended is a reflection of an individual's motivational state. This motivation is a function of the value that the individual attaches to the possible rewards (Box 1) and the individual's perception of the probability that effort will result in reward (Box 2). It should be apparent that "value of rewards" and "perceived effort–reward probability" are equivalent to Vroom's concepts of "valence" and "expectancy" respectively. The effort expended results in a certain level of performance (Box 6). Performance in this context refers to what is expected of the employee by the organization. That is, individuals may have their own standards of performance, but in an organization performance is measured in terms of organizational standards, rules, expectations, and so on. Thus, an employee of a city recreation department assigned the task of organizing competitions would be expected to do an adequate job in soliciting participants, forming teams, drawing up a schedule of competitions, reserving facilities, and supervising the conduct of the tournament. The individual could do an outstanding job of coaching various community volleyball clubs, but this would be irrelevant to the assigned job and of minimal value to the city recreation department.

Effort–Performance Relationship

One of the significant contributions of the Porter and Lawler model is to highlight the complexity of the **effort–performance relationship.** Effort does not always lead directly to good performance. For effective performance to occur, an individual must have the necessary **abilities and traits** (Box 4). Thus, a player who is five feet in height (a trait) cannot adequately perform in the position of basketball center. Similarly, a person who is seven feet tall would also be ineffective as a basketball center without previous training (ability). From a managerial perspective, any employee can perform ade-

> **In Brief**
>
> With sufficient effort an individual can perform adequately in the assigned job, but only if that individual has the necessary abilities and a clear understanding of the role. Without a correct perception of the role, the individual may be wasting time and energy in unrelated activities.

Exhibit 9.6 Porter and Lawler model of motivation.

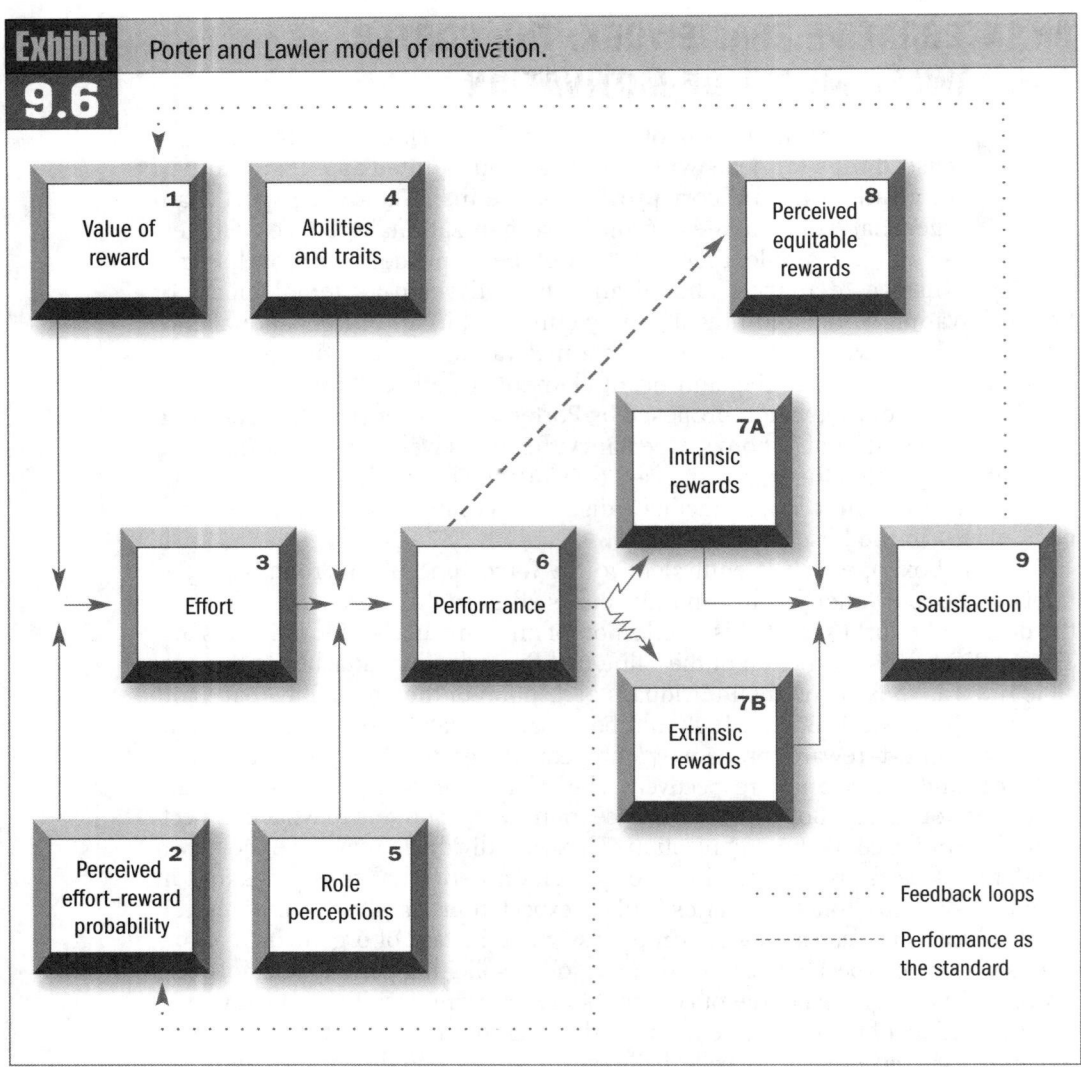

Used by permission from L. W. Porter and E. E. Lawler, 1968, *Managerial attitudes and performance.* (Homewood, IL: Richard D. Irwin. Library of Congress Catalog Card No. 67-29148.)

quately in a job only if the employee has the necessary abilities and traits to carry out the job. For example, the employee of the city recreation department could organize competitions effectively if she is adept at forming teams and drawing up schedules, and if she possesses the interpersonal and communicative skills for recruiting participants and volunteers. Similarly, a fitness instructor can be successful only if he has the necessary physical abilities (e.g., muscular endurance, cardiovascular stamina, and flexibility). Similarly, the instructor would be expected to possess a positive attitude toward the clients, as well as patience and concern for them. Note that whereas abilities are transient and trainable qualities, traits are enduring and stable characteristics.

Another factor that affects the effort–performance relationship is the accuracy of the individual's **role perception** (Box 5). Each employee must have a complete understanding of what activities are necessary and how these activities should be carried out. Thus, the marketing director in an athletic department spends time and effort identifying potential sponsors, contacting them, and persuading them to sponsor events organized by the department. As another example, a coach or fitness trainer does not involve marathon runners in the same type of training as weight lifters.

Performance–Reward Relationship

If the individual has the necessary abilities and traits and perceives her role correctly, it is reasonable to expect that she will achieve an acceptable level of performance (acceptable in terms of organizational expectations). Such a performance will result in certain rewards. Intrinsic rewards (Box 7A) relate to the higher-order needs of the individual. These rewards are personally derived from the accomplishments. That is, the individual receives a sense of achievement and experiences growth on the successful completion of a challenging task. In contrast to the intrinsic rewards that are personally derived, the extrinsic rewards (Box 7B) are administered by external agents (such as the supervisors). These rewards are the equivalent of Herzberg's hygiene factors and Maslow's lower-order needs. They are usually reflected in factors such as salary increases and promotions. The fact that the intrinsic rewards relate directly to personal performance is indicated by the solid connecting line in Exhibit 9.6. The criteria on which extrinsic rewards are distributed may not be related to performance. Thus, in Exhibit 9.6 a wavy line connects performance with extrinsic rewards. As an example, promotion could be based on seniority, not on performance. Likewise, salary increases could be fixed for every employee; relative performance may not be taken into account.

> **In Brief**
>
> Work rewards can be intrinsic, such as sense of achievement, or extrinsic, such as pay and bonus. Intrinsic rewards are mediated by the individual, whereas extrinsic rewards are administered by agents such as the supervisor.

Reward–Satisfaction Relationship

The receipt of rewards should lead to satisfaction (Box 9 in Exhibit 9.6). However, the relationship between receipt of rewards and satisfaction depends on the individual's perception of whether the rewards were equitable (Box 8). Thus, the Porter and Lawler theory incorporates constructs from Adams' theory of inequity.

It should be pointed out that the relative performances of self and coworkers have a significant effect on how equity is perceived. Individuals who believe that they have performed well tend to emphasize performance as a standard for equity of rewards rather than the cost–benefit comparisons suggested by Adams' theory. An NBA player is not as concerned about the effort he put in to get to the NBA (or the effort put in during the season) as he is about receiving a salary comparable to

> **In Brief**
>
> Some individuals who perceive their performances to be superior to those of others may emphasize performance as the criterion for equity, rather than comparing cost–benefit ratios.

other players whose performance contributions are similar. Thus, the importance of performance in one's determination of equity of rewards is illustrated by the dashed line going straight between performance (Box 6) and perceived equitable rewards (Box 8). Also note that the perceived equity of rewards does not affect the relationship between intrinsic rewards and satisfaction, because this relationship is internally experienced.

Feedback Loops

Finally, Exhibit 9.6 shows two feedback loops—one leading from satisfaction back to value of reward, and the other leading from the relationship between performance and rewards back to perceived **effort–reward probability**. The first feedback loop reflects the fact that the receipt of rewards affects the values attached to those rewards. In the case of **extrinsic rewards** such as pay, the value attached by employees to these rewards is likely to be lowered as more and more of them are received. Thus, an athlete who receives a high salary is less likely to emphasize salary increases as much as an athlete on the low end of the pay scale. This view is consistent with both the Maslow and Herzberg theories. They suggest that the lower-order needs, once satisfied, cease to be motivators. However, Porter and Lawler acknowledged that the satisfaction derived from the **intrinsic rewards** is likely to lead the individual to value these rewards more.

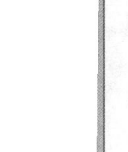

In Brief

The value that a person attaches to intrinsic rewards increases as more of them are received, whereas the value a person places on extrinsic rewards decreases as more of them are received. In addition, a person's belief that effort will lead to rewards is affected by organizational practices.

The second loop relates to the employee's perception of the probability that his efforts will result in the rewards sought. If a baseball organization habitually promotes its managers on the basis of seniority, the perceived relationships of effort–performance–promotion will be weakened. That is, an individual desiring promotion might not be motivated to work hard, owing to her perception that the best way to get a promotion is to get old. Thus, as Porter and Lawler point out, organizational practices have a great influence in determining the perceived connection between performance and rewards.

In overview, the Porter and Lawler model of work motivation is comprehensive enough to include the concepts of Maslow's need hierarchy theory, Herzberg's two-factor theory, Vroom's expectancy theory, and Adams' theory of inequity. Accordingly, the implications of the model are cumulative with respect to each of the other theories included in the model.

MOTIVATION IN SPORT ORGANIZATIONS

The practical implication of the need theories, particularly Herzberg's motivation–hygiene theory, is that the job must be designed in such a way that it triggers as well as satisfies the higher-order needs of the worker. As stated previously, however, the principles behind job enrichment run counter to bureaucratic prescriptions. For instance, on the one hand, the principle of job enrichment leads to the suggestion that a person must be given "a complete natural unit of work." On the other hand, the bureaucratic concept of division of labor suggests that the job should be broken down into smaller units. Similarly, removing controls over employees and giving them additional authority (techniques of enriching a job) are contrary to the bureaucratic principles of division of labor and hierarchy of authority respectively.

We noted in Chapter 7 that concerns for rationality and efficiency, and for uniformity and consistency in organizational activities are the basis for the bureaucratic way of structuring jobs. On the other hand, individual needs are the basis for the practice of promoting job enrichment. These two apparently contradictory approaches to the design of jobs can be reconciled if individual differences in needs, and their relative strengths, are taken into account. As noted before, individuals with a strong desire for achievement, responsibility, and recognition can be given enriched jobs, while those who are low on those needs can be assigned to fractionated and routine jobs.

In addition, organizations differ in their purposes and processes, as well as in their environmental conditions. Such differences can also facilitate the matching of jobs, individuals, and organizational characteristics.

Professional Service versus Consumer Service Organizations

The categorization of sport organizations into professional service organizations and consumer service organizations (see Chapter 1) provides a basis for recommendations relating to the matchup of jobs, individuals, and organizational characteristics. We saw that professional service and consumer service organizations differ in the types of services they provide. Professional services are nonstandardized in the sense that they are individualized to suit the needs of customers and their unique problems. Thus, a professional employee is required to use personal expertise and knowledge to solve the problem. If help from professional colleagues or associations is needed, it is still the employee's prerogative to seek that help. That is, the professional employee has almost complete autonomy and control. In addition, a job in a professional service organization has greater task significance attached to it than a job in a consumer service organization. Furthermore, it possesses greater variety and variability and involves whole units of work. From this perspective, jobs in professional service organizations are "enriched." Mills, Hall, Leidecker, and Margulies (1983) emphasized this notion when they proposed the flexiform model for the organization of a professional service organization (see Chapter 8). Examples of these types of organizations include a sport marketing firm with different experts dealing with different groups of clients; a sport law firm with lawyers specializing in different fields of law; and a university athletic department, in which the coaches are the professionals involved.

The services in a consumer service organization are usually standardized in the sense that they involve minimal information processing by employees, and they are governed by rules and procedures to a much greater extent than is the case in professional service organizations (see Chapters 1 and 2). Thus, the employees in consumer service organizations do not experience autonomy and responsibility to the same extent as employees of professional service organizations. Furthermore, their jobs are also lower on task significance, variety, and variability, and they tend to be more specialized and routine in nature.

The foregoing discussion leads us to conclude that there is great potential for enriching the jobs in consumer service organizations—but is this feasible or practical? This question must be answered from two perspectives—the perspective of the employee and the perspective of the organization.

If the perspective of the employee is considered, it is obvious that an attempt must be made to match the person and the job. That is, job enrichment is meaningful only to the extent that the strength of the employee's growth need warrants such enrichment, and to the extent that the employee is capable of handling an enriched job. In the absence of either or both of these conditions, job enrichment will not have the desired effect of motivating the individual. In fact, it could be damaging to the individual's self-esteem if he fails to deal effectively with the enriched job because of a lack of expertise and ability.

If the organizational perspective is considered, job enrichment is feasible in a consumer service organization, provided that the organization is relatively small with few employees. In the initial stages of growth, it would be possible, and indeed desirable, to permit employees autonomy and freedom to be individualistic in providing services to customers. As the organization grows and expands, however, there is an increase in services to a large number of customers. The need for standardization then increases, and with it the need for more rules and procedures for the guidance of employees. Given a choice between cost-effectiveness and job enrichment, a profit-oriented consumer service organization will choose cost-effectiveness. An organization responsible for the management of a professional sport arena must have a standard protocol for its ticket sellers. That protocol may be monotonous and boring, but it will also be cost-effective.

The resolution of the dilemma concerning whether to emphasize uniformity and consistency or a job enrichment protocol lies in the staffing procedures. Managers of consumer service organizations must determine the extent to which they can afford job enrichment, and then must attempt to recruit individuals whose needs and abilities match the characteristics of the target jobs that they offer.

Even in situations where it is feasible and practical to redesign a job for enrichment purposes, a manager may not have the authority to do so. For example, a middle line manager in a large organization may not be permitted to alter a job description that was drawn up by superiors. This problem is more acute in those organizations that are bureaucratically organized. A supervisor of ticket sellers, to use the previous example, may not have the liberty to alter the protocol set by the director of operations. This does not, however, preclude the manager from exercising a leadership function by intervening in the motivational process. This issue is discussed in the next chapter.

Volunteer Organizations

The notion of matching individual needs to the job is more pertinent to volunteers in organizations. That is, those who join an organization as employees might be prepared to accept a job and its requirements for economic reasons; the satisfaction of other needs may be relatively less important. Volunteers, by definition, do not seek economic benefits through their membership in an organization. A volunteer might join an organization for several reasons—learning and growing, helping others, cultivating friendships, using present skills and learning new skills, gaining work experience, repaying a debt to society, and using leisure time more effectively.

Although it is true that the volunteer organization and the services it provides may be innately attractive to volunteers, their continued membership and commitment to the organization largely depend on the type of work assignment they receive as well as the satisfaction they derive from it. For example, when a community association requests assistance to organize a basketball league, to handle registration and organize a schedule, and to coach the teams, several members of the community might volunteer. The total organizational effort must be broken down into specific units of work. In turn, this work must be assigned to the volunteers. Some of the work units, such as coaching a team, are high on autonomy, responsibility, significance, variety, and so on. Others, such as answering the telephone during registration, are simple and routine. It is likely that the coaches will find their work more rewarding than the registration agents.

From a different perspective, some volunteers are high on the need for growth and power. They desire more complex and challenging tasks, like coaching a team. Others prefer to handle the simpler and more routine tasks. The proper matching of these individuals with the right type of work is the task of the manager. When there is a good fit between the task demands and the personal needs of the volunteers, the volunteers feel satisfied and are likely to continue to participate. When there is a mismatch, however, the experience is frustrating for the volunteer. Individuals who have a high need for growth find the simple tasks meaningless and unfulfilling. Conversely, individuals who are low on the growth need find the more complex jobs frustrating and stressful. To decrease the likelihood of a mismatch, managers of volunteer organizations should draw up job descriptions for all the activities to be carried out. Then, the volunteers can better choose the activity they prefer.

In overview, the need-based or content theories support the suggestion that jobs must be enriched so that workers find them challenging and satisfying—so that they can fulfill higher-order needs. However, job enrichment is not practical in certain kinds of organizations (such as a profit-oriented consumer service organization). Also, any attempt to redesign jobs must take into account the needs and desires of the members. It is unreasonable to assume that all employees will actively seek the satisfaction of higher-order needs in the workplace. This notion of person–task fit is most applicable to volunteer organizations.

SUMMARY

Our discussion of theories of motivation emphasized the motivational basis of the leading function. The "content" theories of motivation include Maslow's need hierarchy theory and Herzberg's two-factor theory. We discussed Maslow's conception of prepotency (the force in effect) for his hierarchical ordering of human needs, and then clarified the various classes of needs. Then we looked at Herzberg's two-factor theory. Herzberg's distinction between hygiene factors and motivators and their effects on individual motivation were clarified.

We noted that, whereas the content theories discuss external factors that motivate individuals, the process theories deal with the internal processes that motivate individuals. The "process" theories covered in the chapter are Vroom's expectancy theory, Adams' theory of inequity, justice and fairness theories, and Porter and Lawler's model of motivation. Vroom's concepts of valence, expectancy, and instrumentality were explained; then we went on to discuss the concept of inequity (or equity) as espoused by Adams and the motivational impact of perceived inequity. Porter and Lawler's model of motivation provided an integrating framework for the relationships between motivation and performance, between performance and reward, and between reward and satisfaction. Finally, we discussed the implications of these theories for sport managers.

DEVELOPING YOUR PERSPECTIVES

1. Consider a few people you know well. With respect to Maslow's need hierarchy theory, can you identify the level at which one of them is operating? Explain how you make those assessments.

2. From your experience as a student or an athlete, recall a situation in which you felt the happiest (or most satisfied). Narrate the sequence of events that led to this high feeling. How long did this feeling last? How did it affect your subsequent work, interpersonal relations, and your well-being? Similarly, recall an incident when you felt most unhappy (or most dissatisfied), and describe it along the same lines. Does your experience support Herzberg's two-factor theory? Explain.

3. You have your own career aspirations, and you are striving hard to reach those aspirations. Discuss your motivation from the perspective of Vroom's expectancy theory.

4. In your experience as either a paid or volunteer worker, did you ever feel that inequity was affecting you or your coworkers? If so, narrate the incident and explain how equity could have been restored.

5. Porter and Lawler's model suggests that motivation or effort is a function of the value one attaches to the rewards attainable through such efforts. Considering your own career aspirations, what are the rewards you expect in that career?

References

Adams, J. S. (1963). Toward an understanding of inequity. *Journal of Abnormal Social Psychology, 67,* 422–436.

Adams, J. S. (1977). Inequity in social exchange. In B. M. Staw (Ed.), *Psychological foundations of organizational behavior.* Santa Monica, CA: Goodyear.

Bies, R. J., & Moag, J. S. (1986). Interactional justice: Communication criteria of fairness. In R. J. Lewicki, B. H. Sheppard, & M. H. Bazerman (Eds.), *Research on negotiations in organizations* (Volume 1, pp. 43–55). Greenwich, CT: JAI Press.

Bies, R. J., & Shapiro, D. L. (1987). Interactional fairness judgements: The influence of causal accounts. *Social Justice Research, 1,* 199–218.

Dunnette, M. D., Campbell, J. P., & Hakel, M. D. (1967). Factors contributing to job satisfaction and job dissatisfaction in six occupational groups. *Organizational Behavior and Human Performance, 2,* 143–174.

Folger, R., & Greenberg, J. (1985). Procedural justice: An interpretive analysis of personnel systems. In K. M. Rowland & G. R. Ferris (Eds.), *Research in personnel and human resource management* (Volume 3, pp. 141–183). Greenwich, CT: JAI Press.

Greenberg, J. (1990). Organizational justice: Yesterday, today, and tomorrow. *Journal of Management, 16,* 399–432.

Hackman, J. R., & Oldham, G. R. (1980). *Work design.* Reading, MA: Addison-Wesley.

Herzberg, F. (1968). One more time: How do you motivate people? *Harvard Business Review,* January–February, 53–62.

Herzberg, F., Mausner, B., & Snyderman, B. B. (1959). *The motivation to work.* New York: John Wiley & Sons.

Hoy, W. K., & Miskel, C. G. (1982). *Educational administration: Theory, research, and practice.* New York: Random House.

Hulin, C. L., & Smith, P. A. (1967). An empirical investigation of two implications of the two-factor theory of job satisfaction. *Journal of Applied Psychology, 51,* 396–402.

Kanfer, R. (1992). Motivation theory and industrial and organizational psychology. In M. D. Dunnette & L. M. Hough (Eds.), *Handbook of industrial and organizational psychology* (2nd ed., pp. 75–170). Palo Alto: Consulting Psychologist's Press.

Leventhal, G. S. (1980). What should be done with equity theory? New approaches to the study of fairness in social relationships. In K. J. Gergen, M. S. Greenberg, & R. H. Willis (Eds.), *Social exchange: Advances in theory and research* (pp. 27–55). New York: Plenum.

Maslow, A. H. (1943). A theory of human motivation. *Psychological Review, 50,* 370–396.

Mills, P. K., Hall, J. L., Leidecker, J. K., & Margulies, N. (1983). Flexiform: A model for professional service organizations. *Academy of Management Review, 8,* 118–131.

Niehoff, B. P., & Moorman, R. H. (1993). Justice as a mediator of the relationship between methods of monitoring and organizational citizenship behavior. *Academy of Management Journal, 36,* 527–556.

Pinder, C. C. (1998). *Motivation in work organizations.* Upper Saddle River, NJ: Prentice Hall.

Porter, L. W., & Lawler, E. E. (1968). *Managerial attitudes and performance.* Homewood, IL: Richard D. Irwin.

Saal, F. E., & Knight, P. A. (1995). *Industrial and organizational psychology: Science and practice* (2nd ed.). Pacific Grove, CA: Brooks/Cole.

Schermerhorn, J. R., Hunt, J. G., & Osborn, R. N. (1997). *Organizational behavior* (6th ed.). New York: John Wiley & Sons.

Shaw, S., & Hoeber, L. (2003). "A strong man is direct and a direct woman is a bitch": Gendered discourse and their influence on employment roles in sport organizations. *Journal of Sport Management, 17,* 347–375.

Steers, R. M., & Black, J. S. (1994). *Organizational behavior* (5th ed.). New York: Harper-Collins College Publishers.

Tyler, T. R., & Bies, R. J. (1990). Beyond formal procedures: The interpersonal context of procedural justice. In J. S. Carroll (Ed.), *Applied social psychology and organizational settings* (pp. 77–88). Hillsdale, NJ: Erlbaum.

Vroom, V. H. (1964). *Work and motivation.* New York: John Wiley & Sons.

CHAPTER 10

Behavioral Process of Leading

MANAGE YOUR LEARNING

After completing this chapter you should be able to:

- Define leadership.
- Describe the behavioral and situational approaches to leadership.
- Discuss the focuses of the contingency model and the path–goal theory of leadership effectiveness.

STRATEGIC CONCEPTS

achievement-oriented behavior
adaptive behavior
behavioral approach
consideration
contingency model
employee orientation
environmental factors
influence
initiating structure
instrumental behavior
leader–member relations
leadership
leadership style
least preferred coworker
managerial motivation
member factors
need for achievement
need for affiliation
need for power
organizational set
participative behavior
path–goal theory
position power
production orientation
reactive behavior
situational approach
situational favorableness
supportive behavior
task structure
trait approach

THE LEADING FUNCTION

he concept of leadership can be viewed from two perspectives. In the etymological sense, a leader is a person who actually goes ahead of the group to show the way. Thus, in early military history, a captain would lead the charge or attack for the brigade that followed. In other contexts, individuals such as Winston Churchill, Mohandas Gandhi, Martin Luther King, Jr., or Nelson Mandela would initiate some action based on personal convictions. Others would follow in their footsteps, either because they were convinced of the causes espoused by these leaders or because they were attracted by their personal qualities. The essence of this type of leadership is that the leaders not only initiate a movement or activity but also spearhead it by engaging in it directly.

> **To Recap**
>
> **PLANNING AND DECISION MAKING** The previous few chapters focused on two significant management functions. Chapters 5 and 6 outlined in detail the processes of planning and decision making. The next two chapters were concerned with the function of organizing, from a classical as well as a systems perspective. The essence of the planning function is to specify the goals to be achieved and the activities undertaken to achieve those goals. In the organizing function, managers divide the total work of carrying out the organizational activities into specific jobs, which they then assign to specific individuals. In order to coordinate the jobs and the individuals performing the jobs, managers establish a hierarchy of authority and create procedures and rules governing the activities of the employees and their supervisors. Thus, the two functions set the stage for what is to be done, how it is to be done, and by whom. In the final analysis, the success of the planning and organizing functions depends on how well the "who"—the employees of the organization—carry out their assigned functions. Therefore, managers need to influence and motivate their employees. Chapter 9 looked at several theories that help us to understand the complexity of human motivation. That discussion prepared us for an in-depth examination of the process of leadership—the focus of this chapter.

From an organizational perspective, however, leadership is just one of the functions of a manager who is placed in charge of a group and its activities and is, in turn, guided by superiors and organizational factors. The process of such leadership in this context does not require the leader to be out in front or working alongside the members, or even to be chosen by the members. Rather, it is the organization that has decided upon the members and their leader. This form of organizational leadership is the focus in the sections that follow.

The specification of goals, the identification of the courses of action to achieve those goals, the assignment of individuals and positions to carry out the specific activities, and the appointment of managers to coordinate those activities all happen in the processes of planning and organizing. When these functions have been handled, it becomes the manager's responsibility to ensure that members carry out their assigned responsibilities. This function is leadership.

LEADERSHIP DEFINED

Consider the following definitions of leadership in the organizational context:

> Effective leadership involves exerting influence in a way that achieves the organization's goals by enhancing the productivity and satisfaction of the work force. (Johns, 1988, p. 309)

Leadership is a process that includes influencing the task objectives and strategies of a group or organization, influencing people in the organization to implement the strategies and achieve the objectives, influencing group maintenance and identification, and influencing the culture of organizations. (Yukl & Van Fleet, 1992, p. 149)

Leadership is social influence in an organizational setting, the effects of which are relevant to, or have an impact upon, the achievement of organizational goals. (Saal & Knight, 1995, p. 321)

Tosi and Mero (2003) define leadership as "a form of organizationally based problem-solving that attempts to achieve organizational goals by influencing the action of others." (p. 248)

In Ivancevich and Matteson's (2002) view, leadership is "the process of influencing others to facilitate the attainment of organizationally relevant goals." (p. 425)

According to the above definitions, a leader would:

- ensure that members fulfill the requirements of the organization and achieve organizational goals
- increase members' capacity for production
- enhance members' satisfaction
- shape organizational objectives (by setting new objectives or altering old ones)
- maintain the group and organizational culture.

Thus, leadership pervades not only at the individual level but also at the group and organizational level.

All of the definitions of **leadership** given embody three significant elements: (a) leadership is a behavioral process; (b) it is interpersonal in nature; and (c) it is aimed at influencing and motivating members toward group or organizational goals. That is the notion of influencing others is a significant component of leadership. In fact, Hollander and Julian (1969) have suggested that the two terms *leadership* and *influence* are synonymous. Furthermore, the process of **influence** is, in its very essence, interpersonal in nature. This requirement distinguishes the leading function from the other functions of a manager. In other words, whereas the planning, organizing, and evaluating functions can be largely carried out without significant interaction, the leading function requires interpersonal contact between a manager and the members.

In Brief

All definitions of leadership emphasize that it is a behavioral process aimed at influencing members to work toward achieving the group's goals.

The definitions presented above also specify that leadership is a behavioral process that emphasizes what the leader *does* rather than what the leader *is*. Although there is general consensus on this issue, the dialogue continues as to whether what the leader *does* is a function of what the leader *is*, or whether *doing* and *being* are independent factors. This dialogue is reflected in the various theories of leadership, which fall into three main categories: those that deal with the traits of leaders (the **trait approach**); those that deal with the behaviors of leaders (the **behavioral approach**); and those that deal with the leaders' traits or behaviors in a specific situational context, taking into account the characteristics of both the members and the organization (the **situational approach**).

THE TRAIT APPROACH

Early leadership researchers attempted to identify a finite set of personal characteristics that distinguish good leaders. The characteristics studied included physical traits such as height, weight, age, and appearance; mental traits such as intelligence; personality traits such as aggressiveness, dominance, extroversion, self-esteem, achievement motive, and task orientation; social background characteristics such as education and socioeconomic status; and social or interpersonal skills. However, these research efforts did not yield any consistent findings—no universal set of traits characterized effective leaders. Understandably, the general trait approach to the study of leadership fell into disfavor. Further, as Szilagyi and Wallace (1980) point out, this general trait approach was concerned with the *emergence* of leaders and not their *effectiveness*.

THE BEHAVIORAL APPROACH

The futility of the trait approach led researchers to focus on what a leader actually does to contribute to group performance and satisfaction. The most notable among these efforts were the major research programs conducted at the Ohio State University and the University of Michigan. The contributions of these scholars are discussed below.

Ohio State Studies

A major thrust in the Ohio State studies was to identify and describe leadership behaviors relevant to the organizational context. To this end, an important Ohio State study identified a large number of leader activities and classified them into nine categories (Hemphill & Coons, 1957). Subsequent research, however, concluded that it would be difficult to use nine dimensions of leader behavior effectively, some of which were highly intercorrelated. Thus, the nine were collapsed to yield four dimensions of leader behavior (Halpin & Winer, 1957). Further research indicated that even these four behaviors could be condensed into two broad categories—consideration and initiating structure (Halpin & Winer, 1957).

Consideration is defined as leader behavior that reflects a leader's concern for members' well-being and concern for warm and friendly relations within the group. **Initiating structure** is defined as leader behavior that reflects a leader's concern for clarifying the roles for both the leader and the members and a concern for effective performance of the group's tasks. According to the Ohio State scholars, it is possible for a leader to be described as high on both dimensions, low on both, or high on one and low on the other. Thus, a leader's style can be located in one of the quadrants in Exhibit 10.1. In a study of NCAA Division I athletic directors, Branch (1990) found that the more successful athletic directors were perceived to be high on initiating structure and low on consideration. Thus, they would fall into quadrant 4 in Exhibit 10.1.

Exhibit 10.1 The Ohio State leadership styles.

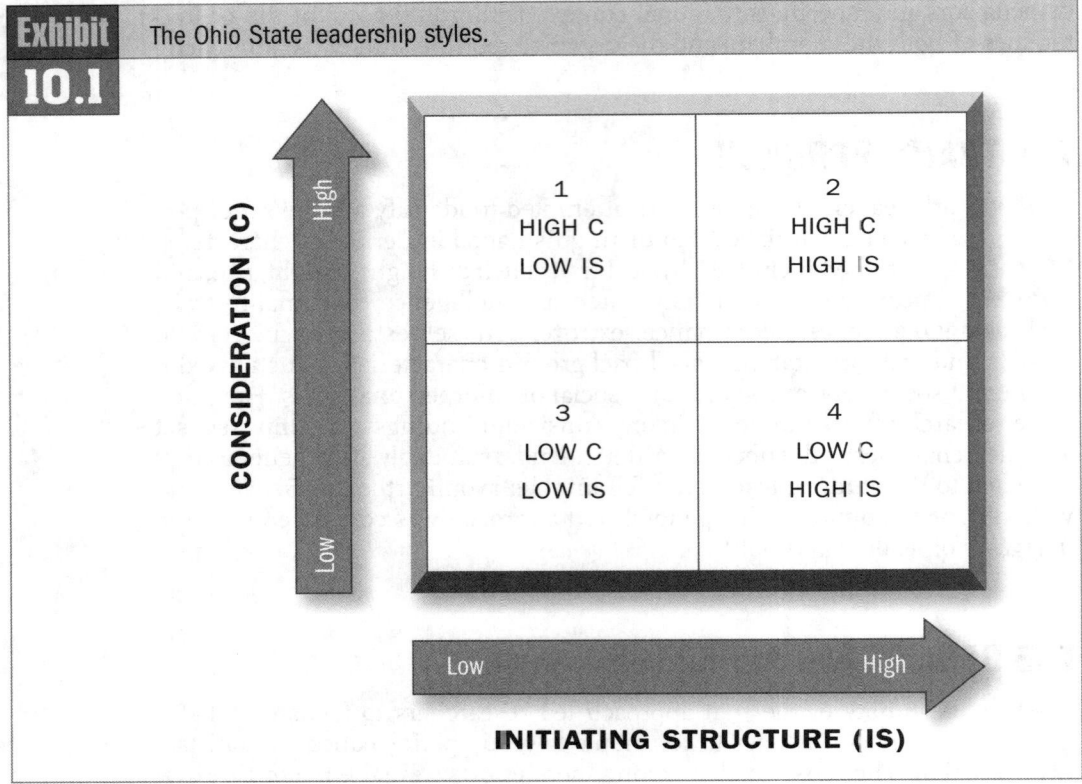

Although there was a general expectation that leaders falling in quadrant 2—those that exhibit high levels of both consideration and initiating structure—would be most effective, research results did not support this position. This lack of support was mainly attributed to the fact that the Ohio scholars did not consider the situational elements that can interact with the behaviors of a leader to influence effectiveness.

Michigan Studies

Scholars at the University of Michigan were also concerned with the description of leader behaviors (Katz, Maccoby, & Morse, 1950; Katz, Maccoby, Gurin, & Floor, 1951). In a manner identical to the Ohio State researchers, the Michigan group also identified two styles of leader behavior—an employee orientation or employee-centered leadership style, and a production orientation or job-centered leadership style. The **employee orientation** dimension reflects the degree to which a leader is concerned with the human relations aspect of the job. On the other hand, the **production orientation** dimension reflects the degree to which the leader is concerned with the technical aspects of the job and productivity.

The Michigan team found that emphasis on either one of the dimensions resulted in increased productivity to almost the same extent. However, they also observed that a production orientation caused a greater degree of employee resentment, dissatisfaction, turnover, and absenteeism (Morse & Reimer, 1956). The positive and detrimental effects of production orientation are shown in Exhibit 10.2. Note that the Michigan studies, which were carried out

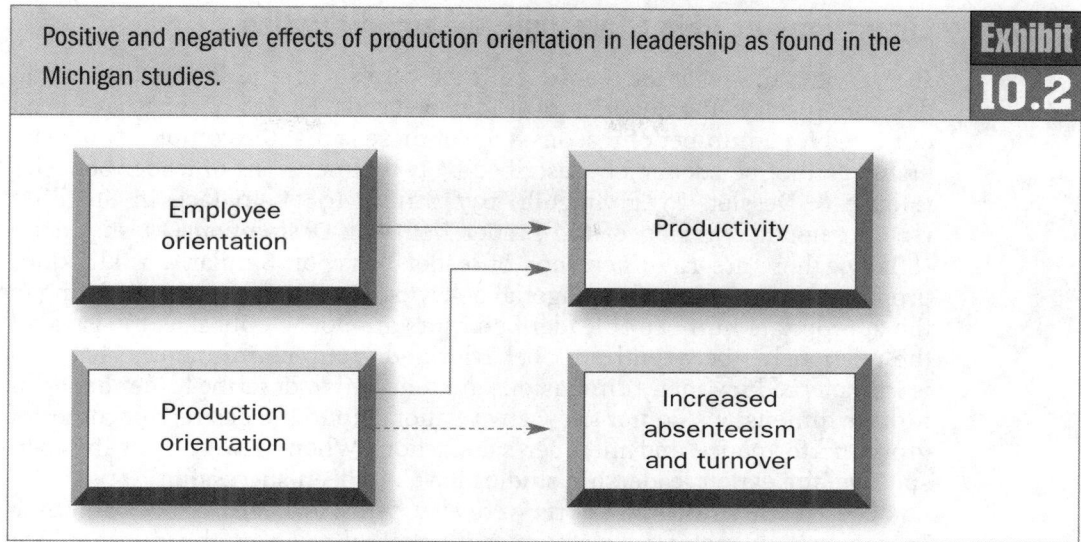

Exhibit 10.2 Positive and negative effects of production orientation in leadership as found in the Michigan studies.

concurrently with but independently of the Ohio State studies, yielded conceptually similar dimensions of leader behavior.

In 1966, Bowers and Seashore of the University of Michigan, in an effort to synthesize the results of earlier research involving both the Michigan and Ohio State descriptions of leader behavior, proposed a four-dimensional description of leader behavior. As shown in Exhibit 10.3, their four dimensions included support, interaction facilitation, goal emphasis, and work facilitation. *Support* refers to behaviors that enhance a subordinate's feelings of personal worth and importance; *interaction facilitation* refers to behaviors that foster close and mutually satisfying relationships within the group; *goal emphasis* refers to behaviors that emphasize the group's goals and their attainment; and *work facilitation* refers to behaviors that facilitate goal attainment by coordinating group activities and providing technical guidance. The scales to measure these four dimensions of leader behavior are found in *Survey of Organizations* (Taylor & Bowers, 1972).

Exhibit 10.3 Bowers and Seashore's (1966) four dimensions of leader behavior.

DIMENSION OF LEADER BEHAVIOR	DESCRIPTION
Support	Behaviors aimed at increasing subordinates' sense of self-worth
Interaction Facilitation	Behaviors to create good and productive interpersonal relationships in the group
Goal Emphasis	Behaviors aimed at subordinates' concern with group goals and their attainment
Work Facilitation	Behaviors aimed at coordinating group activities and providing technical guidance

Limitations of Ohio State and Michigan Studies

In overview, these earlier research efforts were successful in identifying and describing relevant categories of leader behavior. However, they have been criticized for a number of reasons. One of these is that the complexity of leadership cannot be adequately described by two dimensions of leader behavior (House & Dessler, 1974; Stogdill, 1974; Yukl, 1981). In fact, in Stogdill's (1974) extended version of the Leader Behavior Description Questionnaire (LBDQ), there are 12 dimensions of leader behavior. Similarly, Yukl (1989) proposed 11 categories of managerial behavior. However, questions relating to the appropriate number of leader behaviors are not as critical as the issue of the relationship between leader behavior and group performance. That is, it is immaterial how many dimensions are required to describe leader behavior if these dimensions do not show any relationship to the desired outcomes of group performance and member satisfaction. When viewed from this perspective, the earlier leadership studies have not been successful.

These earlier research efforts were also criticized because they confounded the *style* of making a decision with the *substance* of the decision. For instance, in the LBDQ, the subscale that assesses initiating structure contains items that reflect the degree to which a leader uses an autocratic manner to make decisions. Similarly, the consideration subscale includes items that reflect the degree to which the leader possesses a participative orientation. Several authors (see Chelladurai, 1993; House & Dessler, 1974; House & Mitchell, 1974; Sheridan, Downey, & Slocum, 1975; Yukl, 1971, 1981) have argued that the decision-making aspects of leadership (autocratic, participative, delegative, and so on) should be viewed in isolation from other aspects (task oriented versus person oriented). In this regard, House and Mitchell (1974) distinguished among participative behavior (behavior that allows members to participate in decision making), instrumental behavior (behavior that serves to control and coordinate activities), achievement-oriented behavior (behavior that sets challenging goals and serves to express confidence in subordinates), and supportive behavior (behavior concerned with the welfare of the members and the creation of a pleasant work environment). Similarly, in Yukl's (1981) scale, *decision participation* measures "the extent to which a leader consults with subordinates and otherwise allows them to influence his or her decisions" (p. 122).

Finally, a third general criticism of the Ohio State and Michigan studies is that they do not assess the specific dimensions of leader behavior appropriate to specific contexts (House & Dessler, 1974; Sheridan, Downey, & Slocum, 1975; Yukl, 1971). That is, certain leader behaviors might be effective in certain situations and ineffective in others. The situational theories of leadership address this issue.

SITUATIONAL THEORIES OF LEADERSHIP

Although the descriptions developed via the trait and behavioral approaches were very good, these descriptions unfortunately did not specify under what circumstances a given trait or behavior would lead to group performance. That is, the traits or behaviors were not linked to differences in situations. The theories described in the following sections take into account the differences in organizational contexts and leadership situations in suggesting which particular trait or behavior would be appropriate.

In Chapter 3, organizations were described as open systems, and a system was defined as a set of parts put together in such a way as to make up a whole. An open system reacts to and interacts with its environment to secure the resources it needs and to dispose of its products. In extending the system perspective to leadership, we can say that the leadership system consists of the leader, the members, and the organizational context in which they operate. The theories that view leadership from this perspective have generally tended to emphasize one of these elements more than the others. The following sections deal, in order, with the theories that focus on:

1. the leader—Fiedler's (1967) contingency model of leadership and McClelland and Burnham's (1976) theory of managerial motivation
2. the members—House's (1971) path–goal theory of leadership
3. the organization—Osborn and Hunt's (1975) adaptive–reactive theory of leadership

In the next chapter, we examine the contemporary theories relating to transformational leadership (Bass, 1985, 1990) and leader–member exchange. Finally, the multidimensional model of leadership (Chelladurai, 1978, 1993), a synthesis of the above theories, is presented in the next chapter as an integrative framework.

The Contingency Model of Leadership Effectiveness

The impetus toward situational approaches to leadership was first provided by Fiedler (1954, 1967, 1973). His **contingency model** of leadership effectiveness proposes (a) that a leader's style (task orientation versus employee or interpersonal orientation) is a relatively stable personality characteristic; (b) that the situation in which the leader operates may be more or less favorable to the leader (that is, favorable in the leader's exercise of influence over the subordinates); and (c) that leadership effectiveness is contingent upon the fit between the leader's style and the situational favorableness.

Leadership Style

Leadership style refers to the tendency of an individual to emphasize task accomplishment (task orientation) or interpersonal relations (employee orientation) in a task situation. For instance, a fitness club manager may be concerned with efficiency, productivity, and profitability in operating the club. She would express this concern (task orientation) by closely monitoring the activities of the employees and directing them on what should be done and how it should be done. On the other hand, the manager of another fitness club may be more concerned with the employees and their welfare. This manager would express this employee orientation by making the working conditions better for the employees, by being flexible in scheduling their assignments, and in general by being more supportive of the employees and the group.

Fiedler (1967) introduced a unique method for assessing leadership style. The respondent is asked to recall a **least preferred coworker** (LPC)—that is, a person the respondent has had the greatest amount of difficulty working with in the past. The respondent is then asked to evaluate that least preferred coworker on a scale that consists of 16 to 20 items (depending on the form used) that are bipolar adjectives. The following are three sample items from the scale:

Pleasant . . 8 7 6 5 4 3 2 1 . . Unpleasant

Tense . . . . 1 2 3 4 5 6 7 8 . . Relaxed

Efficient . . 8 7 6 5 4 3 2 1 . . Inefficient

An individual's score on this *LPC scale* is considered to reflect the individual's leadership style. In Fiedler's (1967) view:

> We visualize the high-LPC individual (who perceives his least preferred coworker in a relatively favorable manner) as a person who derives his major satisfaction from successful interpersonal relationships, while the low-LPC person (who describes his LPC in very unfavorable terms) derives his major satisfaction from task performance. (p. 45)

Thus, the basic motivation of the high-LPC is primarily toward the development of warm and friendly interpersonal relations with subordinates, whereas the basic motivation of the low-LPC is primarily toward task accomplishment. In a later revision of the theory, Fiedler (1972) suggested that the LPC score represents a two-level (primary and secondary) motivational system. That is, the primary orientation of the high-LPC is toward interpersonal relations. When that is achieved, the high-LPC leader focuses on task accomplishment (secondary motivation). On the other hand, the low-LPC focuses first on task accomplishment, and when that goal is reached or is about to be reached, the focus may shift to fostering warm interpersonal relations.

Situational Favorableness

Situational favorableness reflects the degree to which the situation permits or facilitates the exercise of influence by the leader. According to Fiedler, three elements in the situation affect its favorableness: leader–member relations, task structure, and power position of the leader.

Leader–member relations refers to the degree to which the members like and respect the leader. Thus, the friendlier the members are, the easier it is for the leader to exert influence. Consider the case of the managers of the two fitness clubs in the previous example. Irrespective of whether one is task-oriented or employee-oriented, the manager's attempts to influence the subordinates will be easier if those subordinates like the manager and are friendly with her. With such feelings, the employees may not mind the manager's attempts at influence and will be willing to express their liking and friendship by following the manager's directions or requests. Thus, the manager is in a favorable situation. If, on the other hand, the subordinates do not like or respect the leader, the manager's attempts to influence the subordinates may fall on deaf ears. They are likely to see such managerial action as domineering in the case of the task-oriented leader and manipulative in the case of the employee-oriented leader. This would be an unfavorable situation for the leader. Fiedler viewed leader–member relations as the most important element contributing to the favorableness of the situation.

The second element in the situation affecting favorableness for the leader is the **task structure** itself. According to Fiedler, the more structured the task is, the more it contributes to situational favorableness. Task situations can vary in terms of goal clarity (the degree to which the requirements of the group are clearly defined), goal-path multiplicity (the degree to which there are different paths to accomplish the task), decision verifiability (the extent to which the outcomes of decisions can be easily evaluated), and solution multiplicity (the degree to which a number of correct solutions are possible). In the contingency model, the task of the group is considered to contribute to situational favorableness if the goals are clearly defined, if there are limited procedures to accomplish the task, if the output of the group can be easily measured, and if there is only one possible standard by which to evaluate performance. Take the case of the directors of two intercollegiate athletics departments. Let us assume that the two major goals of the first athletic department are winning more games and more championships, and generating more revenue. The goals of the second athletic department are to increase opportunities for students to pursue excellence in sport and to provide quality services in terms of coaching, facilities, and support services. Of the two athletic departments, the goals of the first department are clearer, the paths to the attainment of those goals are relatively more limited, the outcomes of decisions can be more easily evaluated, and the number of correct solutions is limited. Hence, in Fiedler's model, the situation in the first athletic department is more favorable to the leader than it is in the second department. That is, the more structured the group task is, the easier it is for the leader to influence the group.

The **position power** of the leader, the final element of situational favorableness, reflects the authority invested in the leader's position and the degree of control he has over rewards and sanctions. For instance, the president and the athletic council of the university may curtail the power of the athletic director by requiring their approval for every decision. In addition, they may decide on salary raises for the coaches, as well as on punishing the coaches for violations. Under these conditions, the athletic director holds no power. According to Fiedler's model, this is an unfavorable situation for the leader because the position does not have the potential to influence the members.

Contingency Effects

Fiedler's research showed that task-oriented leaders (low-LPC) were more effective in situations very high or very low in favorableness. On the other hand, employee- (relations) oriented leaders (high-LPC) were more effective in moderately favorable situations. These contingent relationships between leader's style and situational favorableness are illustrated in Exhibit 10.4. The figure illustrates how situations can fall along a favorableness continuum. At one end, the most favorable situations are found: leader–member relations are good, task structure is high, and the leader power position is strong. At the other end are the most unfavorable situations—leader–member relations are poor, the task is unstructured, and the leader power position is weak.

Implications for Sport Managers

One implication of Fiedler's theory is that any leadership style can be effective provided it is matched with the situation and its favorableness. Sport seems to be an area where the situation might be most favorable to the leader

Exhibit 10.4 Fiedler's contingency model of leadership.

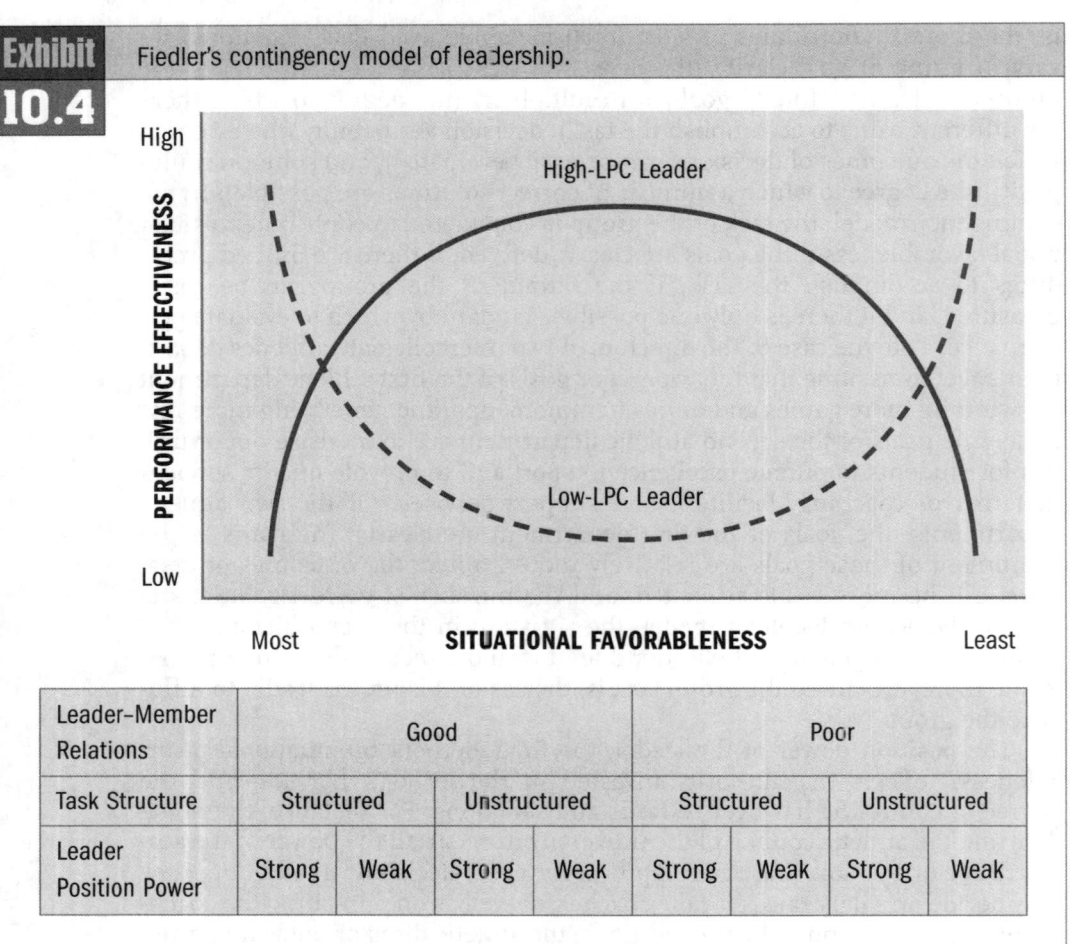

Source: Adapted with permission from Fiedler (1967).

(see Exhibit 10.5). Athletics is generally a voluntary activity. That is, individuals freely choose to participate. Quite often, athletes also have a choice of team (and, consequently, a choice of coach). Also, both the coach and the athletes share the organizational goal of pursuit of excellence. And finally, the processes by which to achieve that goal are also clearly understood and accepted by all members of the organization. As a result, the three elements—the leader, the member, and the situation—are in congruence with each other. Consequently, the situation is very favorable for the exercise of influence by the coach (an autocratic coach could be very effective). In short, Fiedler's proposal, that task-oriented and autocratic leaders are most effective in highly favorable situations, is reasonable in an athletic setting. In fact, a number of studies have found that coaches do tend to be generally autocratic and task-oriented in their leadership style (see Hendry, 1968, 1969; Ogilvie & Tutko, 1966). Interestingly, Chelladurai and his associates found that athletes in Canadian universities preferred their coaches to be relatively more autocratic than participative in decision making (Chelladurai & Turner, in press).

The reference to the athletic team is provided to illustrate the extreme favorableness of the situation for a leader. A similar situation might be avail-

> **Exhibit 10.5** Fiedler's model and sport (Chelladurai & Doherty, 1998).
>
> **HIGH CONGRUENCE IN LEADER/MEMBERSHIP/SITUATION**
> - Voluntary activity
> - Choice of team/coach
> - Common goal of pursuit of excellence in sport
> - Process of achieving goal understood and accepted by members
>
> **HIGH SITUATIONAL FAVORABLENESS**
> - Autocratic task-oriented leadership style
> - Athletes' preference for autocratic rather than participative decision making

able in the case of an entrepreneur who has just started a business such as a fitness club, a marketing agency, or an event management consulting firm. Assume that she has hired a few of her closest, most trustworthy friends as employees of the firm. Thus, for the moment, there are good leader–member relations within the group. If the entrepreneur has set specific and clear goals, has identified the activities to achieve those goals, and has articulated them well to the employees, there is goal clarity. Thus, the task is highly structured and makes the situation more favorable for the leader. Finally, the position power is quite high because the entrepreneur is the sole owner of the business and the chief boss of the operation. Hence, she has considerable power over the employees. Collectively, these elements of the situation make it extremely favorable for the entrepreneur. However, instances of extreme favorableness of the leadership situation are rare in general business and industry as well as in sport management. By and large, sport managers are likely to be operating in only moderately favorable situations.

Another implication of Fiedler's model is that since leadership style is a stable personality characteristic, it is easier to change the situation than to change leadership style. For example, when the leaders and members of a marketing group of a professional sport franchise are not getting along well, top management may change the composition of the marketing unit (that is, fire, hire, or transfer members) in order to improve leader–member relations. They may also change the leader if necessary. Alternatively, top management may change the task structure of the unit by increasing or decreasing the extent of rules and procedures for engaging in specific marketing activities and reporting the results. Finally, top management may give more power to, or take away power from, the leader. By altering these elements, top management can change the favorableness of the situation to be consistent with the leader's task or interpersonal orientation. In Fiedler's view, this approach is much more practical and productive than trying to change the orientation (personality) of the leader.

This perspective of the theory also provides a practical guideline for aspiring managers/leaders. That is, the theory provides a basis for individuals to assess their own leadership style, evaluate the various positions of leadership open to them, and then choose a position in which the situation's favorableness matches their personal leadership style.

Criticisms of Fiedler's Theory

Fiedler's contingency model has been extensively tested in various organizational contexts. It is not surprising that the research by Fiedler and his associates was supportive of the theory, because the theory itself was built on that research. However, subsequent research by others has brought out some limitations of the theory. One issue pertains to the question of what the LPC scale actually measures. Initially it was viewed as a measure of personality, but a subsequent interpretation advanced by Fiedler (1973) determined that it measures a hierarchy of goals (task accomplishment versus interpersonal relations). Larson and Rowland (1974) suggested that the LPC measures the cognitive complexity of the individual—that is, the extent to which an individual can process and assimilate numerous and complex bits of information.

Somewhat related to the aforementioned issue is the question of stability in a leader's orientation. Fiedler's model does not allow for the possibility of a shift in LPC scores owing to experience with different groups. Also, in the model, task orientation and interpersonal orientation are treated as extremes on a single continuum. The possibility that a leader could be high on both orientations is not considered in the theory.

Another limitation is that the theory overlooks the possibility that the manager's leadership style could actually change the situational characteristics. For example, a leader might be operating under the condition of poor leader–member relations. If the leader is a high-LPC (relations-oriented) leader, then his activities will tend to improve leader–member relations, and over time, the situation will become more favorable.

Another comment on the theory relates to the issue of either task or relations orientation versus style of decision making. That is, according to the theory, a task-oriented leader is autocratic in arriving at a decision, and a relations-oriented leader is democratic. As noted in the earlier discussion of descriptions of leader behavior, the assumption that a task (or relations) orientation is associated with a particular style of decision making is unjustified.

It is also questionable whether situations representing the extreme ends of the favorableness continuum (see Exhibit 10.4) are common in organizations. The least favorable situation on this continuum represents a chaotic situation that could not continue to exist for any length of time. Similarly, the most favorable situation on this continuum represents utopia.

In overview, despite the criticisms, Fiedler's contingency model was the first attempt to view leadership from a situational perspective. Fiedler emphasized the need to analyze the leadership style as well as the situational characteristics. Although the meaning of the LPC score is questionable, the theory has highlighted the significance of (a) a leader's personality and orientations, and (b) the fit between the leader and the situation.

McClelland's Model of Managerial Motivation

A second model that focuses on a leader's traits is that of McClelland and his associates (McClelland, 1961, 1975; McClelland & Burnham, 1976; McClelland & Winter, 1969). McClelland's well-known work dealt with the human needs of affiliation, achievement, and power, and how they influence human behavior in general. His major contribution to research on **managerial motivation** was to show that the needs for affiliation, achievement, and power have specific relevance to the organizational context. More specifically, McClelland and his associates demonstrated that the need for power is more critical to managerial effectiveness than the other two needs. Exhibit 10.6 summarizes this model.

Need for Affiliation

The **need for affiliation** refers to the desire to be liked and accepted by the group. According to McClelland and Burnham, the affiliation motive is least important to successful management. In fact, they suggest that it can even be detrimental to successful management. Managers with a high need for affiliation might tend to compromise on various rules in order to satisfy individual needs. For instance, an event manager, in his eagerness to be accepted by specific employees, may be a little lenient with them when they are late for work. While the individual recipients may enjoy this preferential treatment, other members of the organization will consider these practices unfair, thus lowering the morale of the group.

Need for Achievement

The **need for achievement** refers to "the desire to do something better or more efficiently than it has been done before" (McClelland & Burnham, 1976, p. 100). Individuals who have a high level of this need prefer a task that is moderately difficult rather than one that is too difficult or too easy. These same individuals also prefer rapid, specific feedback on how well they are doing. In addition, because achievement-motivated people try to improve their personal performance, they tend to do things themselves.

These characteristics would benefit the owner/manager of an individual business or small firm. Thus, as Yukl (1981) pointed out, "the dominant motive for successful entrepreneurial managers appears to be need for achievement. Of course, success depends on the manager's ability as well as his motivation" (p. 79). When sport management graduates start their own businesses (for example, a pro shop, a fitness club, or a player agency), they are often in the position of having to do everything themselves, from sales to marketing to accounting. These new business owners will have a greater chance of being successful if they are highly achievement-oriented versus if they are low on that motive.

Exhibit 10.6 McClelland's model of managerial motivation.

EFFECTS OF	SMALL ENTREPRENEURIAL ORGANIZATIONS	LARGE ORGANIZATIONS
Need for Affiliation	Irrelevant	Detrimental
Need for Achievement	Beneficial	Detrimental
Need for Power: Personal Power Socialized Power	Beneficial Irrelevant	Detrimental Necessary and beneficial

The perseverance, dedication, and work ethic that are characteristic of achievement-motivated people have led many theorists and practitioners to suggest that the need for achievement should be the dominant prerequisite for *all* successful managers. However, this is not necessarily the case in larger organizations where what the manager personally does is less important than what the subordinates do. As McClelland and Burnham (1976) suggested, "the manager's job seems to call more for someone who can influence people than for someone who does things better on his own. In motivational terms, then, we might expect the successful manager to have a greater 'need for power' than need to achieve" (p. 101).

Need for Power

Need for power refers to "a desire to have impact, to be strong and influential" (McClelland & Burnham, 1976, p. 103). For example, the success of a departmental director of intercollegiate athletics or recreational sports is likely to be based on the degree to which he has influenced the members toward greater effort and achievement rather than on what he has personally accomplished. A director's willingness and ability to influence members is far more important than personal achievements. Similarly, the general manager of a professional sport franchise is responsible for many different activities. It stands to reason that the general manager cannot carry out all those activities personally. Therefore, the success of the general manager depends on how well her subordinates carry out their assignments. Thus, the general manager needs to be high on the need for power so that she will be more oriented toward influencing her subordinates to carry out the tasks. On the other hand, the general manager should be relatively lower on the need for achievement in order to avoid the tendency to carry out the tasks by herself. In contrast, we noted earlier that in the case of the fitness entrepreneur, the need for achievement is most important.

McClelland and Burnham (1976) observed that the need for power must be moderated by a concern for the organization and the subordinates: "Above all, the good manager's power is not oriented toward personal aggrandizement but toward the institution which he or she serves. . . . This is the 'socialized' face of power as distinguished from the concern for personal power" (p. 103). Again, a comparison among a college dean, a city recreation director, and an entrepreneur helps to clarify the distinction between "socialized power" and "personalized power." The successful dean must exhibit controlled and socialized power. Similarly, the director of a city recreation department should direct his attempts at influencing the subordinates toward attainment of organizational goals and the welfare of the community rather than to attainment of personal glory and power. In the case of the entrepreneur, personal goals and organizational interests coincide and few others, if any, are involved in the operation of the firm. Therefore, the personalized power motive may not be detrimental to the success of the firm. Consolidating the power, gaining control over the agenda of operation, and making more profit are all consistent with the notion of an entrepreneurial firm.

McClelland's emphasis on the power motive appears to be in opposition to a conventional "people orientation" and to the traditional reluctance to utilize an authoritarian form of management. McClelland and Burnham (1976), however, have argued that:

The bogeyman of authoritarianism has in fact been wrongly used to downplay the importance of power in management. After all, management is an influence game. Some proponents of democratic management seem to have forgotten this fact, urging managers to be primarily concerned with people's human needs rather than with helping them to get things done. (pp. 104–105)

McClelland and Burnham (1976) noted that the presence of a power motive in management does not preclude the possibility that the manager can also adopt a democratic style. In fact, their research showed that successful managers were those who possessed a high need for power and a high concern for the organization, and who used a democratic managerial style. Subordinates under these types of managers possessed a high sense of responsibility and perceived a high degree of organizational clarity and team spirit (McClelland & Burnham, 1976). Chapter 6 described the advantages of member participation in decision making.

> **To Recap**
>
> Participation in decision making leads to (a) a greater understanding of the problem and its solutions by the members; (b) a belief that the problem is their own and the choice of a solution is their decision; leading to (c) the effective execution of the decision.

Given these advantages, the manager who wants to influence the members to perform well in their jobs should include the members in making decisions that affect them and their jobs. McClelland and Burnham concluded that:

> Oddly enough, the good manager in a large company does not have a high need for achievement . . . although there must be plenty of that motive somewhere in his organization. The top managers . . . have a high need for power and an interest in influencing others, both greater than their interest in being liked by people. The manager's concern for power should be socialized—controlled so that the institution as a whole, not only the individual, benefits. (p. 109)

Note that the above conclusion pertains to managers of large organizations, such as a Division I athletic department or the NCAA. As we noted before, in the case of small firms and entrepreneurs, the achievement motive and personalized power motive might not adversely affect managerial effectiveness.

Comparing Fiedler's and McClelland's Views

In overview, the two approaches described above—Fiedler's contingency model of leadership effectiveness and McClelland's view of managerial motivation—emphasize the importance of specific personal traits of the leader. Although Fiedler's task orientation and McClelland's power motivation appear to be similar to the extent that both focus on task accomplishment, they differ in one significant aspect. While Fiedler's task-oriented leader is autocratic by definition, McClelland's power-motivated manager may also express the power motive in democratic ways. This difference notwithstanding, both Fiedler and McClelland have highlighted the significance of personal traits for effective leadership.

The Path–Goal Theory of Leader Effectiveness

Both Fiedler's contingency model of leadership and McClelland's model of managerial motivation emphasize the traits of the leaders. If the leader's traits and attributes are critical to the leadership phenomenon, then the traits and attributes of the members are also critical. Members and their attributes are the focus of the **path–goal theory** of leader effectiveness. The theory was first proposed by Evans (1970) and later expanded upon by House and his associates (House, 1971; House & Dessler, 1974; House & Mitchell, 1974). House (1971) succinctly outlined the essence of the theory:

> The motivational function of the leader consists of increasing personal payoffs to subordinates for work-goal attainment, and making the path to these pay-offs easier to travel by clarifying it, reducing road blocks and pitfalls, and increasing the opportunities for personal satisfaction en route. (p. 323)

Because the theory focuses on members' personal goals and their perceptions of the organizational goals, and the most effective paths to these goals, it is called the path–goal theory of leader effectiveness. That is, the theory attempts to specify how leadership should clarify the paths of members to the desired goals and rewards.

On the simplest level, every worker can be assumed to be seeking more monetary rewards from the organization. The leader can help the member by linking his personal goal to the incentive plans of the organization. In doing so, the leader would also identify the specific activities and performance levels necessary for receiving those incentives. In addition, the leader would also attempt to train the member in those tasks and remove any barriers that might hinder him from achieving the required performance level. In a similar manner, the director of the marketing department of an athletic enterprise can help her subordinates attain their personal objective of a promotion by suggesting the performance standards the employees need to achieve in order to be considered for promotion (such as securing a certain number of sponsorships or a certain dollar amount of sponsorships, and proposing and implementing innovative marketing strategies). In addition, the leader would also help the employees reach those standards by, for example, introducing them to prospective sponsors and training them in the art of making a presentation.

Leader Behaviors Related to the Path–Goal Theory

As we noted in the discussion of the classification of leader behavior, four classes of leader behavior are taken into account in the path–goal theory: instrumental behavior, supportive behavior, participative behavior, and achievement-oriented behavior (House & Mitchell, 1974). **Instrumental behavior** is similar to the traditional initiating structure dimension discussed earlier. It is leader behavior that serves to clarify for members what is expected. It also involves leader behaviors associated with planning and coordinating. **Supportive behavior** reflects the concern of the leader for the welfare of the members and for a warm and friendly environment in the workplace. Thus, this dimension is very similar to the consideration dimension from the Ohio State studies. **Participative behavior** reflects the degree to which a leader shares information with members and allows the members to participate in decision making. Finally, **achievement-oriented behavior** reflects the degree to which the manager sets challenging goals, expects good performance, and expresses confidence in the members. The path–goal theory, in essence, suggests that the extent to which the leader engages in these behaviors is a function of the situation that leader faces. These situational differences are described below.

Propositions of the Path–Goal Theory

The path–goal theory is composed of two basic propositions: The first is that the leader's function is a supplemental one, and the second is that the motivational effect of leadership is a function of the situation.

Leadership function as supplemental. A leader's behavior will have an impact on member motivation and effort only to the extent that such behavior is seen as an immediate source of rewards and satisfaction, or as a path to future rewards and satisfaction. For example, when a supervisor of youth sports programs compliments a student–volunteer on a job well done, the behavior is an immediate reward and is likely to motivate the student to do even more. The supervisor may also teach and train the student in managing the programs and engage the student in some managerial activities. These behaviors serve to enhance the student's experience and expertise, which in turn will serve the student well in his search for a job in the recreation field. Thus, the supervisor's behaviors are a source of future rewards. Also, the leader's function supplements other factors that might contribute to member motivation, and those that might be supportive of the individual. In our example of the student–volunteer, other workers may provide the same kind of support, positive feedback, and training to the student. In addition, the clients of the programs may also express their gratitude for the work done by the student. Under these circumstances, the supervisor's supportive and instrumental behaviors may become redundant. In other words, leadership is most necessary when there is a lack of motivation in the organizational context in which the members operate.

Motivation as a function of the situation. The second proposition of the path–goal theory is that the motivational effect of leadership is a function of the situation, which in turn is composed of the members and the environmental pressures and demands.

According to the theory, the personality and perceived ability of members **(member factors)** affect the degree to which they prefer or react to specific forms of leader behavior. For instance, subordinates with a high need for affiliation prefer supportive leadership behaviors, while subordinates with a high need for achievement would prefer achievement-oriented leadership behaviors (House & Dessler, 1974). Similarly, a member who has a high perception of personal ability would prefer less instrumental leadership behavior (and in fact, would react negatively to such behavior).

Consider two different scenarios for the student–volunteer in the youth sports program. If the student is highly achievement-oriented and has less need for affiliation, he is likely to be more motivated by the supervisor's help in enhancing the student's managerial competencies than by the supervisor's warm and friendly manner. In contrast, the competence-enhancing behaviors of the supervisor may not have much motivational impact if the student is not oriented toward achievement in that area.

Environmental factors are reflected in the nature of the task, the primary work group, and the organizational set. Tasks may vary in the degree to which they are routine or variable, the extent to which they are interdependent, and the degree to which they are inherently satisfying. Insofar as the leader's role is supplemental, the leader's behavior should vary according to the demands of the task. Thus, instrumental behavior is more appropriate when the task is a variable one than when it is a routine one. Similarly, interdependent tasks require a greater degree of coordination than independent tasks, and, therefore, a leader's efforts at coordination (one aspect of instrumental behavior) will be more appreciated in interdependent tasks than in independent tasks. In support of these propositions, Chelladurai and Carron (1982) found that athletes in interdependent sports (team sports) and athletes in variable sports (such as basketball) preferred more training and instruction (instrumental behavior) than athletes in independent sports and nonvariable sports (such as track and field). In short, the degree to which a leader's behavior will be acceptable to the members, and the degree to which that behavior will have a motivational impact, depend on the nature of the task.

The nature of the work group also influences the degree to which specific leader behaviors are necessary and relevant. For example, in a close-knit work group, senior members may provide the necessary guidance and coaching to junior members. In such a case, a leader's instrumental behavior is redundant. Similarly, supportive behaviors are unnecessary because the cohesive group would fulfill that need. As noted earlier, the student–volunteer in the youth sports program may be surrounded by a group of paid and volunteer workers who are close-knit and cohesive. That work group may be quite warm and friendly toward the student and may help the student gain experience and expertise. Thus, the work group makes unnecessary the supervisor's behavior in these directions.

The final element in the situation is the **organizational set**. That is, the goals of the organization, the rules and procedures laid down, and other organizational practices serve to determine the need for and the effects of leader behavior. Thus, when an organization has extensive rules and procedures for each member concerning how to carry out assigned tasks, the leader's instrumental behavior becomes unnecessary.

Path–Goal Theory and Individual Motivation

The path–goal theory of leadership can be better understood if it is viewed from the perspective of individual motivation. In fact, the path–goal theory is largely based on the expectancy theory of individual motivation. You will recall that the notion of expectancy is built into the Porter and Lawler model of motivation described in Chapter 9.

To facilitate an understanding of the relationship between the path–goal theory of leadership and individual motivation, Chelladurai (1981) presented a modified version of the Porter and Lawler (1968) model of motivation and discussed the relevance of the various dimensions of coaching/leader behavior (see Exhibit 10.7) to the motivational process.

As Exhibit 10.7 shows, motivation (effort in Porter and Lawler's terminology) will lead to performance, which in turn will lead to the reward. The

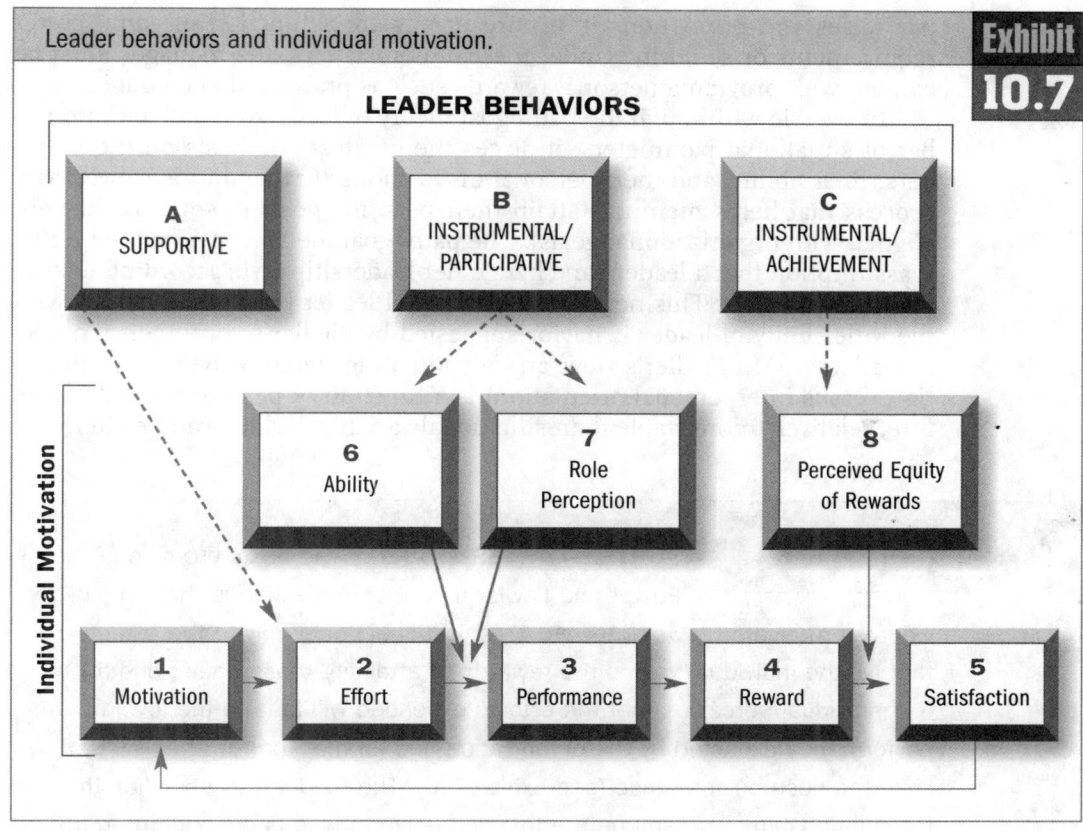

Exhibit 10.7 Leader behaviors and individual motivation.

effort–performance relationship (Box 2 to Box 3) is moderated by the member's ability (Box 6) and the accuracy of the perception of her role (Box 7). Finally, the reward–satisfaction relationship (Box 4 to Box 5) is influenced by the member's perception of the equity of the rewards (Box 8).

Based on this framework of individual motivation, it is possible to identify the points along the motivation–performance–satisfaction sequence where the leader should intervene in an attempt to enhance the motivational state of the individual. First, the value an individual attaches to intrinsic rewards is heightened when the leader sets challenging goals and expresses confidence in the member's capacity to attain those goals (achievement-oriented behavior, Box C). Supportive behavior (Box A) makes the effort phase enjoyable and frees it from any interpersonal frictions. Instrumental leader behavior (Box B) is beneficial when it leads to the development of the member's ability and when it serves to clarify role expectations. Thus, instrumental behavior strengthens the relationship between effort and performance. Participative behavior contributes to a member's role clarity as well as to feelings of involvement in decisions. Both of these effects of participative behavior enhance role performance. Finally, the equitable distribution of a leader's personal rewards (that is, equal rewards for equal performance) leads to a sense of equitability among the members.

The emphasis on personal rewards is deliberate. In small organizations, the manager may have considerable control over the rewards offered by the organization. In contrast, in larger organizations, the manager may not have a great deal of input into the determination of individual rewards. For example, pay raises and promotions in a bureaucracy are a function of some preset requirements or seniority. Under these circumstances, the manager must be content with providing personal rewards such as praise and encouragement.

In overview, although the path–goal theory of leadership includes a number of situational parameters, it places the greatest emphasis on the members, their ability, and their personal dispositions. Leadership is viewed as a process that helps members attain their personal goals (insofar as they are aligned with organizational goals). The path–goal theory contains the implicit assumption that a leader can change her leadership style according to situational exigencies. This notion of flexibility of leader behavior contrasts with the inflexibility of leader behavior suggested by Fiedler's contingency model of leadership. In Fiedler's view, an individual's leadership style (task orientation versus interpersonal orientation) is a function of personality and, therefore, relatively more stable than situational variables, which can be altered.

To Recap

PORTER–LAWLER MODEL The basic premise of the Porter and Lawler model of motivation is that an individual is motivated to work toward organizational goals only to the extent that (a) the individual values the rewards of attaining those goals; and (b) the individual perceives that the efforts expended will lead to the level of performance expected by the organization and (c) that the rewards will be linked to such performance (see Exhibit 9.6). The model also specifies that the relationship between one's effort and performance is dependent on the individual's having the necessary abilities and traits and on his or her correct perception of the job responsibilities. Finally, the linkages between performance and rewards and the resultant satisfaction are a function of organizational practices in tying rewards to performance and distributing the rewards equitably based on relative performances of the members.

Implications of Path–Goal Theory: Substitutes for Leadership

We noted that one of the propositions of the path–goal theory is that the leader's function is only supplemental. That is, the leader is expected to provide guidance and coaching, to structure activities for the members, and to provide social support only to the extent that these are lacking in the work environment. This means that whatever function the leader must perform may be partially accounted for by other factors in the environment. Kerr and Jermier (1978) have listed a number of such factors, which they refer to as *substitutes for leadership*. The most significant ones are the members' characteristics, their professional orientation and affiliation, the nature of their task and the work group, and the organizational structure (including the policies and procedures).

The significance of member characteristics and the nature of the task was discussed earlier in this chapter in connection with House's path–goal theory of leadership. The work group (or peer group) can also serve as a substitute for the leader. For example, a new student at a college or university receives assistance during the orientation period from classmates. Similarly, in work situations, fellow employees provide the necessary guidance and coaching to help a new employee or volunteer carry out assignments. More important, the work group also provides the social support necessary when both personal and organizational problems arise.

> **In Brief**
>
> In cases where there are numerous substitutes for leadership, a manager's attempts to influence members must be minimal; otherwise, there is the risk that the leadership will be viewed as interference.

If the organizational policies and procedures are elaborate and if they clearly specify what the employee should do, and how, and under what circumstances (as is the case in bureaucracies), then the leader's instrumental behavior becomes redundant. The employee simply has to follow the rules. As we noted earlier, within consumer service organizations, the concern for the standardization of services results in a tendency to fractionate jobs and to specify extensive rules. For example, the ticketing section in a university athletic department may specify extensive rules and procedures to handle requests for tickets and their allocation. Because of the specificity of these rules and regulations, a supervisor's instrumental behavior tends to be redundant. However, since these service tasks are relatively routine and monotonous, the supervisor must attempt to create a warm climate and establish good interpersonal relationships within the group. Thus, the leader's supportive behavior is important.

In professional or human service organizations, the professional orientation of the members and their relationships with other professionals serve as substitutes for leadership. Professional orientation ensures that members are committed to providing a quality service. For instance, medical personnel and athletic trainers in university athletic departments (or exercise physiologists in fitness clubs) are expected to abide by their professional standards of providing quality service to their clients. Further, their respective professional associations set standards of performance for their professions, and members internalize these standards. In addition, periodic meetings of peers and professional publications also provide some guidance and incentives for greater productivity. Given this orientation within professional services, it is unnecessary for the managers of these organizations to attempt to influence the members.

The Adaptive–Reactive Theory

Osborn and Hunt (1975) noted that the variables of the larger organizational system have an impact on both the leader and members and, therefore, must be treated as separate classes of contingency variables. One class of variables in the organizational system, called *macro variables,* includes unit size, level of technology, and formal structure of the organization. A second class of contingency variables, called *micro variables,* includes the task itself and differences among individual members. On the basis of these two classes of variables that influence a leader, Osborn and Hunt dichotomized leader behavior into *adaptive behavior* and *reactive behavior.* (See Exhibit 10.8.)

> **To Recap**
>
> **FIEDLER AND HOUSE** The major focus of Fiedler's contingency theory is on the leader and his personality and leadership style. In contrast, House's path–goal theory of leadership emphasizes the members and their needs, preferences, and abilities. Although both Fiedler and House included organizational variables among the situational elements in their respective theories, their treatment of organizational requirements is superficial. In Fiedler's contingency model of leadership, the situation includes the variables of leader–member relations (whether members respect and like the leader or not), task structure (whether the task is simple and routine or complex), and the position power of the leader (the extent to which the leader has power to reward and punish members). The elements of task structure and power position can be seen as organizational variables. Similarly, House's path–goal theory of leadership includes as situational elements member characteristics (personality, preferences, and abilities), the nature of the task (routine or variable and independent or interdependent), the nature of the work group (friendly and cohesive or not), and the organizational set (goals, extent of rules and procedures, and so on).

Adaptive Behavior

Adaptive behavior refers to the degree to which the leader adapts to the requirements of the organizational system (macro variables). That is, the nature of the organization and its processes demand or constrain leader behavior in specific ways. A football team and a badminton team provide a good example from sport. First, the football team is larger than the badminton team (unit size). Second, football consists of highly differentiated and specialized positions, whereas badminton does not. Therefore, the control and coordination exerted and the guidance provided are necessarily different for a coach of a badminton team with four players who perform independently for the most part, versus the coach of a football team with 100 players who perform specialized tasks in interaction with each other.

As another example, consider the differences in the constraints and demands faced by a director of NCAA Division I athletic programs, where performance expectations and attained excellence are high, versus a director in a Division III program where both the excellence and the expectations for such excellence are relatively low. Thus, unit size and level of technology contribute to a need for different formal structures (the size of the coaching staff in football, and the hierarchy and differentiation among the coaching staff in Division I and III institutions). These, in turn, contribute to the emergence of different leader behaviors.

Reactive Behavior

Reactive behavior refers to leader behaviors in reaction to member preferences and the differences among the tasks performed by the members. In

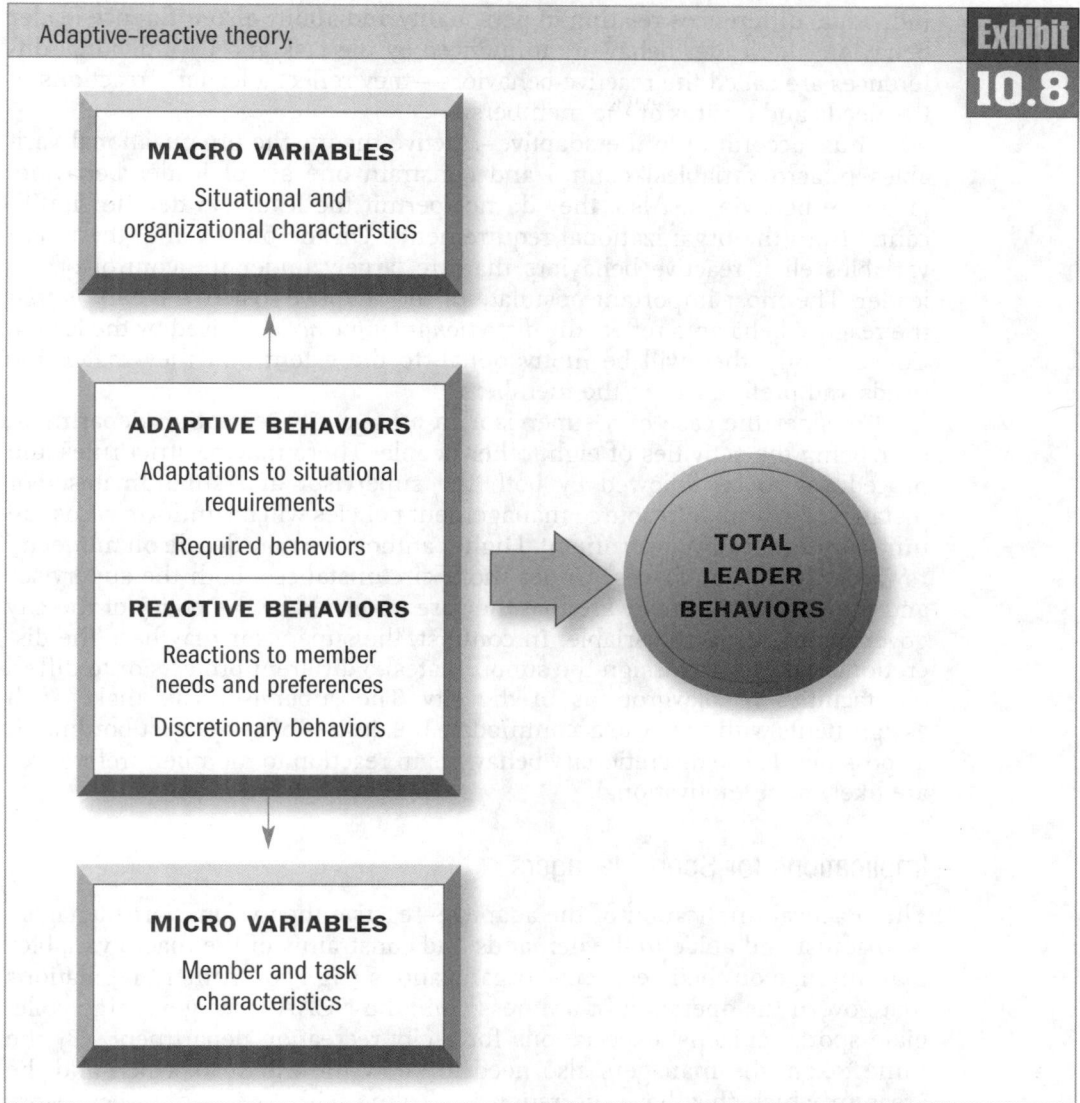

Exhibit 10.8 Adaptive-reactive theory.

Osborn and Hunt's theory, the nature of the task and individual differences are called the micro variables. You will recall that House's path–goal theory also includes the nature of the task and individual differences as elements in the situation, which also included organizational characteristics. Osborn and Hunt separate the larger organizational variables (the macro variables) and the individual and task differences (the micro variables). The contrast between football and badminton again serves to illustrate the significance of the nature of the task. While the individual tasks in football involve relatively more large muscle groups, badminton tasks involve relatively finer movements. Also, while football is an interdependent sport, badminton is an independent sport. These differences, in turn, influence leader behavior.

For example, talking loudly or shouting by a football coach might positively affect the players and the team. But such behaviors would be detrimental to the performance of the badminton players. It was already noted that individual differences relating to personality and ability also influence leader behavior. The leader behaviors influenced by the task and by individual differences are called the reactive behaviors—they reflect a leader's reactions to the needs and desires of the members.

Thus, according to the adaptive–reactive theory, the organizational variables (macro variables) control and constrain one set of leader behaviors (adaptive behaviors). Also, they do not permit the leader to deviate significantly from the organizational requirements. On the other hand, the micro variables elicit reactive behaviors that are largely under the control of the leader. The most important postulate of the adaptive–reactive theory is that the reactive behaviors reflect the *discretionary influence* exercised by the leader. Consequently, they will be motivational, to the extent that they match the needs and preferences of the members.

Consider the case of a supervisor in a large city recreation department overseeing the activities of eight other people. There may be strict rules and procedures to be followed by both the supervisor and subordinates. For instance, the human resource management policies will be uniform across all units within the city government. Higher authorities may decide on monetary rewards for all employees. Under those circumstances, both the supervisor and the employees are aware that they are governed by the policy of the city government, a macro variable. In contrast, the supervisor may have the discretionary powers to assign the subordinates to different projects or to different facilities or playgrounds in the city. The supervisor can make such assignments with a view to accommodate the desires of as many subordinates as possible. These discretionary behaviors in reaction to member preferences are likely to be motivational.

Implications for Sport Managers

The practical implication of the adaptive–reactive theory for sport managers is to adjust and abide to the demands and constraints of the macro variables that impinge on their respective organizations (e.g., government regulations that govern the operation of a fitness club, the NCAA rules governing collegiate sports, citizens' expectations for a city recreation department). By the same token, the managers also need to know the extent to which and the areas in which they have discretion in dealing with their employees. More important, they need to learn to make the best use of their limited discretionary behavior in motivating their subordinates.

SUMMARY

This chapter described various theories of leadership categorized under the trait, behavioral, and situational approaches to the study of leadership. The chapter described the various dimensions of leader behavior developed by scholars at Ohio State University (consideration and initiating structure) and the University of Michigan (employee orientation and production orientation). Following this was a description of Fiedler's contingency model of leader effectiveness, with the emphasis on a match between leadership style as a personality characteristic (task orientation versus interpersonal orientation) and situational favorableness (defined by leader–member relations, task structure, and position power). We discussed the implications of Fiedler's model and the criticisms against it. Then we examined McClelland's view that the need for power in a manager is more critical than the needs for affiliation or achievement. House's path–goal theory stated that the leader's role is to increase the members' personal payoffs for their efforts and to make the path to those payoffs easier. Leadership was seen as a supplemental role providing instrumental, supportive, and achievement-oriented behaviors. The effects of these behaviors were said to be dependent on environmental factors, including member characteristics and the nature of the task. We looked at the implications of the path–goal theory and the notion of substitutes for leadership. Finally, the adaptive–reactive theory of leadership placed the emphasis on environmental demands and constraints.

DEVELOPING YOUR PERSPECTIVES

1. Are you relatively more task-oriented or relations-oriented? What is the basis of your self-perception?
2. In the case of an athletic team, what factors serve as "substitutes for leadership"?
3. It has been suggested that sport is generally an autocratic situation. Do you agree or disagree with this position? Why?

References

Barrow, J. C. (1977). The variables of leadership: A review and conceptual framework. *Academy of Management Review, 2*, 231–251.

Bass, B. M. (1985). *Leadership and performance beyond expectations*. New York: The Free Press.

Bass, B.M. (1990). From transactional to transformational leadership: Learning to share the vision. *Organizational Dynamics, 18* (3), 19–31.

Bowers, D. G., & Seashore, S. E. (1966). Predicting organizational effectiveness with a four-factor theory of leadership. *Administrative Science Quarterly, 11*, 238–263.

Branch, D., Jr. (1990). Athletic director leader behavior as a predictor of intercollegiate athletic organizational effectiveness. *Journal of Sport Management, 4*, 161–173.

Chelladurai, P. (1981). The coach as motivator and chameleon of leadership styles. *Science Periodical on Research and Technology in Sport*. Ottawa: Coaching Association of Canada.

Chelladurai, P. (1993). Leadership. In R. N. Singer, M. Murphey, & L. K. Tennant (Eds.), *Handbook of research on sport psychology* (pp. 647–671). New York: Macmillan.

Chelladurai, P., & Carron, A. V. (1978). *Leadership*. Ottawa: Canadian Association for Health, Physical Education, and Recreation.

Chelladurai, P., & Carron, A. V. (1982). Task characteristics and individual differences and their relationship to preferred leadership in sports. *Psychology of motor behavior and sport—1982: Abstracts*. College Park, MD: North American Society for the Psychology of Sport and Physical Activity.

Chelladurai, P., & Doherty, A. (1998). Styles of decision making in coaching. In J. M. Williams (Ed.), *Applied sport psychology: Personal growth to peak performance* (3rd ed., pp. 115–126). Mountain View, CA: Mayfield.

Chelladurai, P., & Turner, B. (in press). Styles of decision making in coaching. In J. M. Williams (Ed.), *Applied sport psychology: Personal growth to peak performance* (5th ed.). Mountain View, CA: Mayfield.

Evans, M. G. (1970). The effects of supervisory behavior on the path–goal relationships. *Organizational Behavior and Human Performance, 5*, 277–298.

Fiedler, F. E. (1954). Assumed similarity measures as predictors of team effectiveness. *Journal of Abnormal and Social Psychology, 49*, 381–388.

Fiedler, F. E. (1967). *A theory of leadership effectiveness.* New York: McGraw-Hill.

Fiedler, F.E. (1972). How do you make leaders more effective? New answers to an old puzzle. *Organizational Dynamics, 1* (2), 3–18.

Fiedler, F. E. (1973). Personality and situational determinants of leader behavior. In E. A. Fleishman & J. G. Hunt (Eds.), *Current developments in the study of leadership*. Carbondale, IL: Southern Illinois University Press.

Halpin, A. W., & Winer, B. J. (1957). A factorial study of the leader behavior description. In R. M. Stogdill & A. E. Coons (Eds.), *Leader behavior: Its description and measurement.* Columbus, OH: The Ohio State University.

Hemphill, J. K., & Coons, A. E. (1957). Development of the Leader Behavior Description Questionnaire. In R. M. Stogdill & A. E. Coons (Eds.), *Leader behavior: Its description and measurement.* Columbus, OH: The Ohio State University.

Hendry, L. B. (1968). The assessment of personality traits in the coach–swimmer relationship and a preliminary examination of the "father-figure" stereotype. *Research Quarterly, 39*, 543–551.

Hendry, L. B. (1969). A personality study of highly successful and "ideal" swimming coaches. *Research Quarterly, 40*, 299–305.

Hollander, E. P., & Julian, J. W. (1969). Contemporary trends in the analysis of leadership processes. *Psychological Bulletin, 71*, 387–397.

House, R. J. (1971). A path–goal theory of leader effectiveness. *Administrative Science Quarterly, 16*, 321–338.

House, R. J., & Dessler, G. (1974). The path–goal theory of leadership: Some post hoc and a priori tests. In J. G. Hunt & L. L. Larson (Eds.), *Contingency approaches to leadership*. Carbondale, IL: Southern Illinois University Press.

House, R. J., & Mitchell, T. R. (1974). Path–goal theory of leadership. *Journal of Contemporary Business, 3*, 81–97.

Ivancevich, J. M., & Matteson, M. T. (2002). *Organizational behavior and management* (6th ed.). Boston: McGraw-Hill Irwin.

Johns, G. (1988). *Organizational behavior: Understanding life at work* (2nd ed.). Glenview, IL: Scott, Forsman.

Katz, D., Maccoby, N., Gurin, G., & Floor, L. (1951). *Productivity, supervision, and morale among railroad workers.* Ann Arbor, MI: University of Michigan.

Katz, D., Maccoby, N., & Morse, N. (1950). *Productivity, supervision and morale in an office situation.* Ann Arbor, MI: University of Michigan.

Kerr, S., & Jermier, J. M. (1978). Substitutes for leadership: Their meaning and measurement. *Organizational Behavior and Human Performance, 22*, 375–403.

Larson, L. L., & Rowland, K. (1974). Leadership style and cognitive complexity. *Academy of Management Journal, 17*, 36–45.

McClelland, D. C. (1961). *The achieving society.* New York: Van Nostrand.

McClelland, D. C. (1975). *Power: The inner experience.* New York: Irvington.

McClelland, D. C., & Burnham, D. H. (1976). Power is the great motivator. *Harvard Business Review, 54*, 100–110.

McClelland, D. C., & Winter, D. (1969). *Motivating economic achievement.* New York: The Free Press.

Morse, N. C., & Reimer, E. (1956). The experimental change of a major organizational variable. *Journal of Abnormal and Social Psychology, 51*, 120–129.

Ogilvie, B. C., & Tutko, T. A. (1966). *Problem athletes and how to handle them.* London: Pelham Books.

Osborn, R. N., & Hunt, J. G. (1975). An adaptive-reactive theory of leadership: The role of macro variables in leadership research. In J. G. Hunt & L. L. Larson (Eds.), *Leadership frontiers.* Kent, OH: Kent State University.

Porter, L. W., & Lawler, E. E. (1968). *Managerial attitudes and performance.* Homewood, IL: Richard D. Irwin.

Saal, F. E., & Knight, P. A. (1995). *Industrial/organizational psychology: Science and practice* (2nd ed.). Pacific Grove, CA: Brooks/Cole.

Sheridan, J. E., Downey, H. K., & Slocum, J. W. (1975). Testing causal relationships of House's path–goal theory of leadership effectiveness. In J. G. Hunt & L. L. Larson (Eds.), *Leadership frontiers.* Kent, OH: Kent State University.

Stogdill, R.M. (1974). *Handbook of leadership.* New York: Free Press.

Szilagyi, A. D., & Wallace, M. J. (1980). *Organizational behavior and performance*. Santa Monica, CA: Goodyear.

Taylor, J. C., & Bowers, D. G. (1972). *Survey of organizations: A machine-scored standardized questionnaire instrument*. Ann Arbor, MI: Institute for Social Research, The University of Michigan.

Tosi, H. L., & Mero, N. P. (2003). *The fundamentals of organizational behavior: What managers need to know*. Malden, MA: Blackwell Publishing.

Yukl, G. A. (1971). Toward a behavioral theory of leadership. *Organizational Behavior and Human Performance, 6*, 414–440.

Yukl, G. A. (1981). *Leadership in organizations*. Englewood Cliffs, NJ: Prentice Hall.

Yukl, G. A (1989). *Leadership in organizations* (2nd ed.). Englewood Cliffs, NJ: Prentice Hall.

Yukl, G. A., & Van Fleet, D. D. (1992). Theory and research on leadership in organizations. In M. D. Dunnette & L. M. Hough (Eds.), *Handbook of industrial and organizational psychology* (2nd ed., pp. 147–197). Palo Alto, CA: Consulting Psychologists Press.

CHAPTER 11

Contemporary Approaches to Leadership

MANAGE YOUR LEARNING

After completing this chapter you should be able to:

- Explain the multidimensional model of leadership, its components, and the relationships among these components.
- Distinguish between transactional and transformational leadership, and their effects.
- Define charismatic leadership.

STRATEGIC CONCEPTS

actual leader behavior	punctuated equilibrium
charismatic leadership	required leader behavior
congruence	satisfaction
performance	transactional leadership
preferred leader behavior	transformational leadership

In recent years, there has been a great concern with the transformation of organizations. We see around us frantic efforts to change the structure and processes of all forms of organizations. Such efforts are variously called downsizing, right-sizing, re-engineering, restructuring, and refocusing. Any restructuring or repositioning of organizations requires strong leadership at the top. Those who guide their organizations to transform into innovative and profitable enterprises are called *transformational leaders*. Along with the pace of change, the study of these leaders and transformational leadership has also intensified in the past two decades.

EVOLUTION OF CONTEMPORARY THEORIES OF LEADERSHIP

The criticisms of existing theories of leadership are twofold. First, the leader is purported to act within the constraints imposed by the situation (see Exhibit 11.1). The dichotomy of adaptive and reactive leader behavior proposed by Osborn and Hunt (1975) suggests that the leader can only adapt to the situation and react to member preferences. This view reflects Stewart's (1982) demands–constraints and choices theory, which states that a leader's discretionary behavior is circumscribed by the demands and constraints in her environment. Stewart (1982) suggested that in any organizational context, the manager/leader will be faced with certain

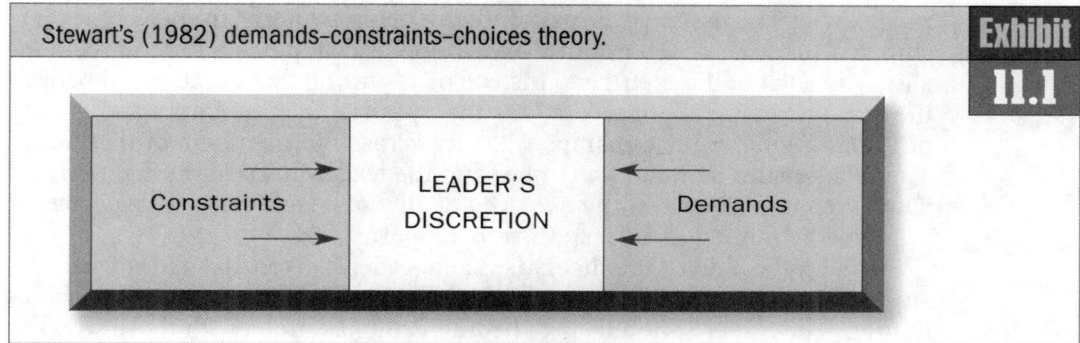

Exhibit 11.1 Stewart's (1982) demands–constraints–choices theory.

demands and constraints imposed on the position. Demands are those activities expected of a leader in a given situation that he must fulfill to be accepted by the group or organization. Constraints set the limits within which the leader can act. In other words, the leader is prohibited from acting in the domain beyond the boundaries set by the constraints. According to Stewart (1982), the area between demands and constraints of the situation represents the choices a leader has. Stewart's demands–constraints–choices theory is illustrated in Exhibit 11.1. A significant portion of the demands and constraints stems from the members themselves. Thus, the leader needs to transact with members individually and collectively to have them perform their duties. Such transactions involve the leader in providing some resources, including leader approval and support, in return for members' efforts toward the attainment of organizational goals.

The second focus of criticisms against the leadership theories described so far is the transactional nature of leadership as portrayed by the theories. For example, Osborn and Hunt's adaptive–reactive theory implicitly acknowledges this aspect when it states that the leader needs to react to members' needs and preferences. Chelladurai's (1978, 1993, 1999) model (to be discussed later in the chapter) also suggests that the leader's actual behaviors need to be consistent with the style of leadership preferred by members. The transactions with the members in general involve the leaders offering rewards to members, who in turn comply with leaders' directions and suggestions. The transaction may also take the form of punishment or threat of punishment in order to elicit the desired behavior or performance from the members.

TRANSACTIONAL THEORY

he theories mentioned earlier imply the transactional nature of leadership; therefore, they are rightfully called **transactional leadership** theories. One prominent transactional theory is the leader–member exchange (LMX) theory.

Leader–Member Exchange Theory

When it was proposed in the 1970s, the leader–member exchange theory was known as the vertical dyadic linkage (VDL) model (see Dansereau, Cashman, & Graen, 1973; Dansereau, Graen, & Haga, 1975; Graen, 1976; Graen & Cashman, 1975). The essential thrust of the model is that effectiveness of leadership is a function of the extent to which the leader builds a unique relationship with each of the members. Instead of assuming that a leader will behave the same way with all members, this theory posits that the forms and quality of leader–member relationships will vary across the members of the group. The relationship between a member and the leader is based on the interpersonal exchanges between the two. The quality of such a relationship is characterized by mutual trust, respect, and support.

The implication of the theory is that a leader is likely to bestow trust and support on those individuals the leader values as contributors to group functioning. The leader is not likely to be interacting as much with those who are seen as less valuable to the group. This differential treatment of members is likely to lead to the formation of an *in-group,* whose members have high-quality exchange relationships with the leader. The other members form the *out-group.* Exhibit 11.2 illustrates these differential leader–member exchanges.

The in-group members will tend to assume more responsibility and contribute more to the group. In turn, their performances will also be evaluated higher than those of out-group members, and these factors would lead to higher commitment and satisfaction of in-group members (Basu & Green, 1997; Duchon, Green, & Taber, 1986). Note that the relationships noted above are circular in nature. That is, the leader identifies a few members as valuable and

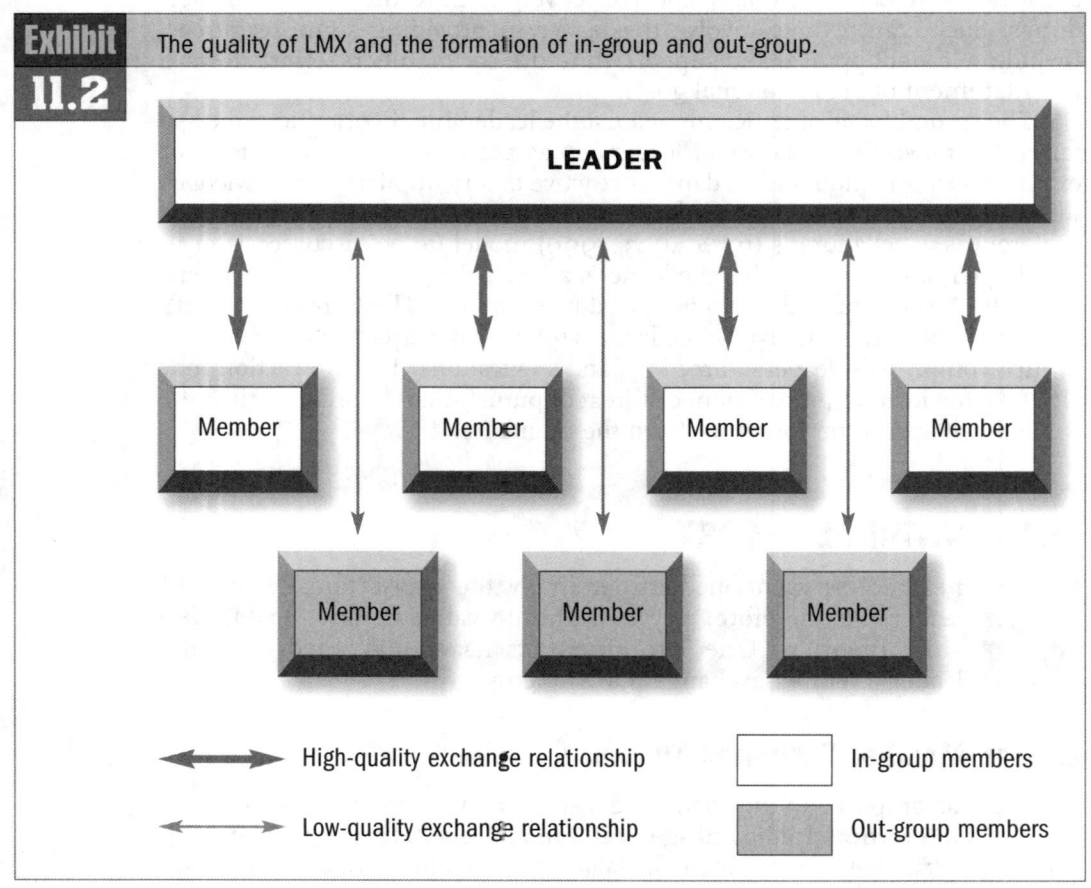

Exhibit 11.2 The quality of LMX and the formation of in-group and out-group.

treats them with trust and respect. This will lead those members to reciprocate by taking on more responsibility to relieve the leader, perform better, and contribute more to the group. With such high performance and contributions, they are, in turn, likely to be evaluated higher than the others. More important, the leader is going to value them even more and further enhance his relationship with them. Note that the LMX theory is also transactional in nature—it involves the exchange of mutual feelings of trust, support, and performance.

Transactional versus Transformational Leadership

Transactional leadership is not, in itself, a bad thing. In fact, it may even be a fruitful approach when the environment of the work group is somewhat stable and when both the leader and members are satisfied with the work group's purposes and processes. Moreover, it is assumed that members with a stable set of needs and desires will engage in transactions with the leader in order to benefit themselves, the leader, and the organization. Thus, transactional leadership can be effective in maintaining the status quo in terms of productivity and effectiveness. However, transactional leadership is not seen as very useful when an organization has to change in response to changes in the environment.

Transformational leadership, on the other hand, is defined as "the process of influencing major changes in the attitudes and assumptions of organization members (organizational culture) and building commitment for major changes in the organization's objectives and strategies" (Yukl & Van Fleet, 1992, p. 174). According to this definition, the transformation occurs at three levels: (a) changes in organizational objectives and strategies; (b) member commitment to the new set of goals and strategies; and (c) changes in the assumptions and attitudes of members. This shift in conceptualizing leadership has been spearheaded by different groups of scholars, each with their own unique perspectives. Bass and his associates (Bass, 1985, 1990, 1997; Bass & Avolio, 1993) used the terms *transformational* and *transactional* to label the two different aspects of leadership as defined above. They view these aspects as independent dimensions, meaning that a leader can be both transformational and transactional. Conger and Kanungo (1987, 1988, 1998) used the term *charismatic* to refer to leadership that is concerned with larger issues, as opposed to that concerned with daily routine and maintenance activities. A third approach is that of House and his associates (see House, 1977; House & Howell, 1992; House & Podsakoff, 1994; House & Shamir, 1993), who view charisma as a characteristic attributed to a transformational leader. Although there are differences among the theories, they also share a considerable overlap in their concepts and the relationships they espouse.

TRANSFORMATIONAL LEADERSHIP

The basis for transformational leadership is a general discontent with the status quo. Transformational leaders are concerned with creating a new vision and order for the organization. In the process of changing the total organization, a transformational leader (a) articulates the vision, (b) convinces the members of the viability of the vision, and (c) expresses confidence in their capacity to achieve that vision. Transformational leadership involves the arousal of members' higher-order needs, which in turn elevates the level of effort beyond expectations (Bass, 1985; Conger & Kanungo, 1987). It also entails empowering the members to engage in innovative and creative ways to achieve the stated vision. It is important to note that transformational leadership involves a new vision—an alternative to the status quo. In fact, the terms *transformational* and *visionary* are used interchangeably to describe this form of leadership. Exhibit 11.3 shows the contrasts between transformational and transactional leadership.

The labels *transformational leadership* and *visionary leadership* have been used to refer to essentially the same thing. Because the critical focus of transformational leadership is the vision, it is also appropriate to label it visionary leadership. Bennis (1984) uses the label *visionary leadership* and suggests that it calls for competency in four different areas: (1) *Management of attention* is garnering the attention of the followers to the vision that the leader has espoused. (2) *Management of meaning* is clarifying for the members what the vision means for them and for the organization, and how their activities would contribute to attaining that vision. (3) *Management of trust* is creating a sense of trust among the followers that the leader is honest and trustworthy and deserves to be followed. (4) Finally, *management of self* is understanding and accepting one's own strengths and weaknesses, acknowledging that risk and failure are part of visionary leadership. In a later work, Bennis (1997) observes that effective leaders of groups (a) provide the direction for the members and signify to them the importance of what they do, (b) generate trust among the group members including the leader, (c) make resolute but sometimes risky decisions, and (d) stimulate hope among the members that their efforts will be successful.

Readers will note that both Bass (1985) and Bennis (1984, 1997) refer to the same essential components even though they use different terms. Weese (1995), a sport management scholar from Canada, illustrates this perspective

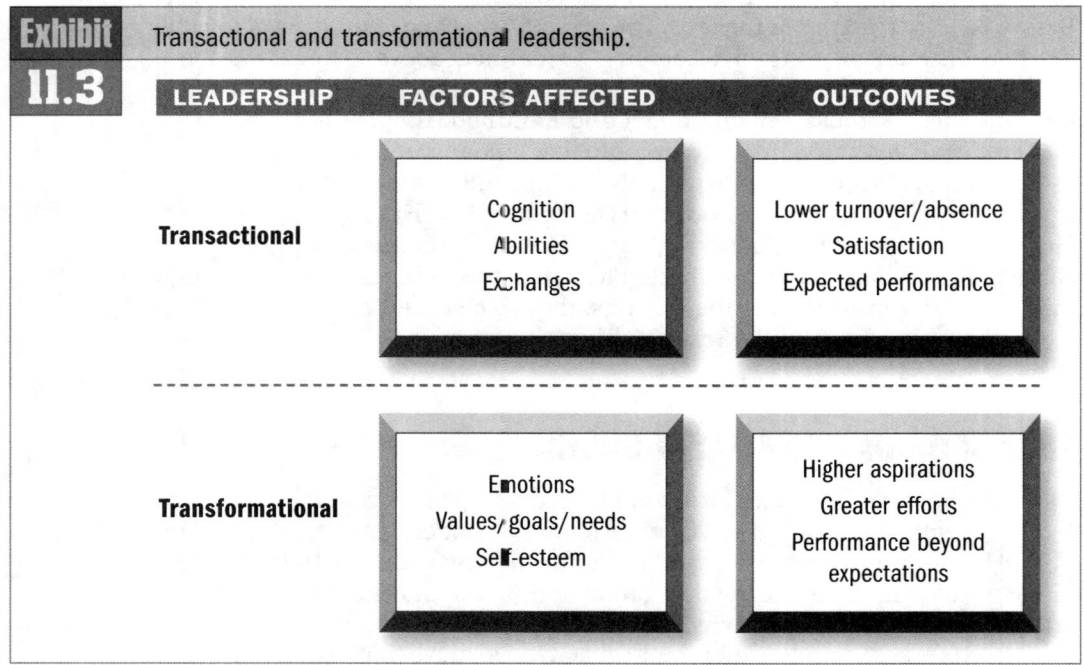

Exhibit 11.3 Transactional and transformational leadership.

LEADERSHIP	FACTORS AFFECTED	OUTCOMES
Transactional	Cognition Abilities Exchanges	Lower turnover/absence Satisfaction Expected performance
Transformational	Emotions Values/goals/needs Self-esteem	Higher aspirations Greater efforts Performance beyond expectations

> **Sidebar**
>
> In Bass's (1985) view, transformational leadership is composed of (a) charismatic leadership, meaning "the faith and respect in the leader and the inspiration and encouragement provided by his or her presence" (p. 209); (b) intellectual stimulation, defined as "the arousal and change in followers of problem awareness and problem solving, of thought and imagination, and of beliefs and values, rather than arousal and change in immediate action" (p. 99); and (c) individualized consideration, referring to treating each subordinate "differently according to each subordinate's needs and capabilities" (p. 82). Bass (1985) also developed the scale called the Multifactor Leadership Questionnaire (MLQ) to measure these three dimensions of transformational leadership.

when he combines the works of Bass (1985), Bennis (1984), and Shaskin (1986) to propose a five-component model of leadership. He labels it the *Five "C" model* because the labels of the five components begin with a "c." The five components are (1) *credible character*—being perceived as trustworthy and reliable; (2) *compelling vision*—proposing a convincing vision that creates a focus for action by followers; (3) *charismatic communicator*—communicating through effective speech patterns and nonverbal actions thereby creating a sense of charisma; (4) *contagious enthusiasm*—expressing an enthusiasm for the vision, the organization, and the members that like a contagion instills similar enthusiasm among the members; and (5) *culture builder*—cultivating a culture (i.e., dominant beliefs, values, and attitudes) that is consistent with the articulated vision. Most recently, Rafferty and Griffin (2004), have developed a scale to measure five dimensions of transformational leadership. These five dimensions, described in Exhibit 11.4, parallel the description provided above.

We noted earlier that transformational leaders tend to empower their subordinates. This idea of empowering leadership has been the focus of a recent study by Arnold, Arad, Rhoades, and Drasgow (2000). They developed a measure named *Empowering Leadership Questionnaire* (ELQ) that measures five dimensions of leadership focused on empowering subordinates. These dimensions are described in Exhibit 11.5.

In many of the descriptions of transformational leadership, there is the implication that such leadership begins with the chief executive officer of an organization, and that it begins to filter down to lower levels through the empowerment of successive levels of subordinates. At the social and political level, renowned transformational leaders such as Mahatma Gandhi of India and Nelson Mandela of South Africa could not have achieved what they did without the active cooperation of their immediate followers.

> **In Brief**
>
> Transactional leadership involves members' contributions in exchange for rewards from the leader in maintaining the status quo. In contrast, a transformational leader strives to change the goals and processes, to incite the higher-order needs of the followers, and to exhibit confidence in their capacity.

Exhibit 11.4 Dimensions of transformational leadership.

DIMENSION	DESCRIPTION
1. Vision	"The expression of an idealized picture of the future based around organizational values." (p. 332)
2. Inspirational communication	"The expression of positive and encouraging messages about the organization, and statements that build motivation and confidence." (p. 332)
3. Supportive leadership	"Expressing concern for followers and taking account of their individual needs." (p. 333)
4. Intellectual stimulation	"Enhancing employees' interest in and awareness of problems, and increasing their ability to think about problems in new ways." (p. 333)
5. Personal recognition	"The provision of rewards such as praise and acknowledgement of effort for achievement of specified goals." (p. 334)

Source: Rafferty and Griffin (2004).

Exhibit 11.5 Dimensions of empowerment leadership.

DIMENSION	DESCRIPTION
1. Leading by example	Setting high standards for own behavior, working hard to maintain that standard, and setting an example of good behavior.
2. Participative decision making	Encouraging and listening to group's ideas and suggestions, and giving members a chance to voice their concerns.
3. Coaching	Providing help to members to improve performance, encouraging members to share ideas and to work together, and supporting group members.
4. Informing	Explaining organization's goals, policies, rules, decisions, and how the group fits into the organization.
5. Showing concern/ interacting with the team	Caring about members' personal problems, their well-being, treating members as equals, and getting along well with the members.

Source: Arnold & colleagues (2000).

Within the context of sport organizations and sport management, several transformational leaders are recognized. Just to name a few, leaders like professors Earl F. Zeigler and James G. Mason were instrumental in transforming the field of administration of physical education and athletics into what is now the scholarly and professional field known as sport management. While the women's movement was taking hold in society at large, it was Dr. Donna Lopiano who spearheaded the formation of the Women's Sports Foundation to promote women in sport and bring long overdue recognition and status to

> **Sidebar**
>
> A transformational leader encourages followers to develop their own leadership abilities. That is, the transformational leader serves as a role model for subordinates to follow and stimulates them to be effective leaders. This notion of the "cascading" effects of transformational leadership was tested by Kent and Chelladurai (2000) in the context of intercollegiate athletics. They assessed the perceptions of 75 third-tier employees of a large university athletic department regarding (a) the transformational leadership exhibited by the athletic director, (b) the quality of their relationship with their immediate supervisor (i.e., leader–member exchange), and (c) their commitment to the organization (organizational commitment) and their citizenship behaviors within the organization (organizational citizenship). Their results showed that perceived transformational leadership at the athletic director level was reflected in the quality of leader–member exchange between the second level supervisors and their subordinates. In addition, both transformational leadership at the top and quality of leader–member exchange at the middle level contributed to employee commitment to the department and increased citizenship behavior. Thus, the notion of "cascading" effects of leadership was supported in this study.
>
> In another study, Kent and Chelladurai (2001) investigated the effects of transformational leadership and leader–member exchange on organizational commitment of 283 third-tier employees of a state parks and recreation department. These employees' perceptions of transformational leadership of the executive chief of the department and the quality of leader–member exchange with their immediate supervisor were significantly correlated, which again supports the notion of the cascading effects of transformational leadership. They also found that both transformational leadership and leader–member exchange had cumulative and unique effects on employee commitment to the organization. This latter result suggests that leadership provided by managers at different levels of an organization is critical in cultivating organizational commitment.

women's sport. The Women's Sports Foundation has become a model for similar organizations promoting the causes of women in sport around the world. On the commercial side, Philip Knight has become a legendary figure because of the success of his Nike enterprise. His Excellency Juan Antonio Samaranch is credited with transforming the International Olympic Committee (IOC) and the Olympics itself into the multi-billion-dollar enterprise it is today.

The notion of transformational leadership need not, however, be confined to large organizations with several levels of hierarchical structure. Smaller organizations with fewer levels of management and fewer members can also be the focus of transformational leadership. For instance, Doherty and Danylchuk (1996) found that coaches of intercollegiate athletics in Ontario, Canada, perceived their athletic directors to be more transformational than transactional in their behaviors. This perceived transformational leadership was associated with coaches' increased satisfaction and extra effort. Another typical example is that of a coach of an athletic team who transforms her team

from a perennial doormat into a winning team. Such a coach begins with sowing discontent with the current image of the team, then articulates a vision of the team performing in a winning fashion and convinces the members that the vision is attainable and that they have the abilities to be a winning team. The only difference between the transformational leadership of a CEO of a large corporation and that of the coach is that the coach does not have to deal with several layers of managers. Instead, he interacts with the members directly.

We must note that not all organizations need to be subjected to transformation, nor does an organization need to be transformed all the time. Transformation entails upheaval and turmoil, and that cannot be a permanent state. The organization has to find its equilibrium soon so that it can continue to achieve its designated goals. Some authors have called the transition from transformation to equilibrium the **punctuated equilibrium** (e.g., Miller & Friesen, 1984). Transactional leadership is said to be more relevant to the steady-state or equilibrium stage. This does not mean that transactional leadership would be content with the current level of effectiveness or efficiency of the organization. Transactional leadership could indeed be focused on continuously improving the performance of the organization. In fact, Moore (2004) notes that three kinds of leader are needed—transformational leader, steady-state leader, and evolutionary leader. The *transformational leader* is one charging in from the outside with a great discontent with the status quo and little patience with it and those who support it, and who turns the place inside-out. The *steady-state leader* is usually an insider who knows how things are done around the organization and who is focused on regrouping and rebuilding the organization after the upheaval of the transformational process. Finally, the *evolutionary leader,* who may also be from within the organization, is not content with the steady state and focuses on steady improvement in organizational performance.

CHARISMATIC LEADERSHIP

A term that is often used in conjunction with transformational leadership is *charismatic leadership*. Although the two terms have been used synonymously in some contexts, it is useful to consider them as distinct concepts. Yukl and Van Fleet (1992) noted that **charismatic leadership:**

> refers to the follower perception that a leader possesses a divinely inspired gift and is somehow unique and larger than life. . . . they [followers] also idolize or worship the leader as a superhuman hero or spiritual figure. . . . Thus, with charismatic leadership, the focus is on an individual leader rather than on a leadership process that may be shared among multiple leaders. (p. 174)

In this view, charisma is something the leader is purported to have that enables her to transform the group or organization. Thus, charisma is a set of laudable attributes of the leader, as well as a set of beliefs the members have about the leader. From this perspective, charisma is a personal resource, which leaders exploit successfully in transforming their organizations and their members. Note that charisma is an attributional phenomenon—it involves attributions made by the followers regarding the extraordinary abilities of the leader.

Such strong and positive attributions are the source of power that facilitates greater acceptance of the leader's pronouncements and the willingness to abide by his dictates and directions. The great followings enjoyed by leaders like Mahatma Gandhi, Nelson Mandela, Martin Luther King, Jr., and John F. Kennedy were partly based on the significance of the causes they promoted, partly on the sacrifices they made, and partly on the beliefs the followers held about superhuman qualities of those leaders. In the context of sports, the success of Vince Lombardi, the legendary football coach, was said to be partly a function of his charisma. While the respect bestowed on Michael Jordan by his peers was largely based on his playing prowess, it was also based on his charisma. On the commercial side, the charisma of Philip Knight, the CEO of Nike Corporation, is said to be a significant factor in the success of the corporation.

Charisma refers to perceptions of members that the leader possesses some extraordinary gifts and talents.

AN INTEGRATIVE FRAMEWORK: THE MULTIDIMENSIONAL MODEL OF LEADERSHIP

The multidimensional model of leadership (Chelladurai, 1978, 1993, 1999) is an attempt to synthesize and reconcile existing theories of leadership. A schematic illustration of the model is presented in Exhibit 11.6.

Essentially, the model focuses on three states of leader behavior: required, preferred, and actual. The antecedent variables that determine these leader behaviors are classified as situational characteristics, member characteristics, and leader characteristics. In the model, required leader behavior is largely determined by situational characteristics, and the preferred leader behavior is a function of member characteristics. The actual leader behavior is influenced by leader characteristics, required leader behavior, and leader behavior preferred by the members. The consequences (outcome variables) in the model are group performance and member satisfaction.

Required Leader Behavior

Required leader behavior refers to what the leader needs to do as well as what the leader is not permitted to do. Note that the notion of required leader behavior as defined by the demands and constraints on leader behavior reflects Stewart's demands–constraints–choices theory and is the same as Osborn and Hunt's (1975) adaptive behavior (adaptations to the macro variables). For instance, a commissioner of a professional sports league is confronted with many demands and constraints from different groups. Beginning with the need to satisfy the contrasting and at times conflicting needs and preferences of the club owners and the players' union, the commissioner also must deal with the demands of the media, the sponsors, and other stakeholders. While the commissioner may have some freedom in how she satisfies the interests of the different stakeholders, clearly they cannot be overlooked—hence the notion of required leader behavior. Add to these demands the constraints imposed on the commissioner, such as government rules and regulations, legal and accounting requirements, and the contracts entered into by the league as a whole and by its member clubs. Thus, a por-

Exhibit 11.6 Multidimensional model of leadership.

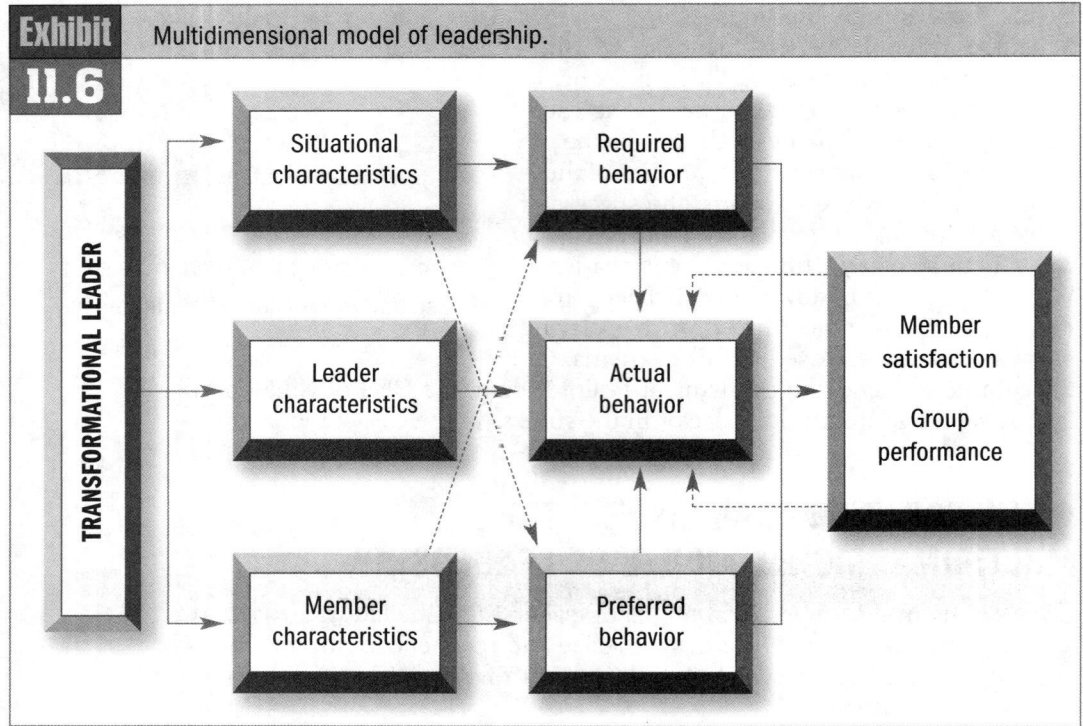

From Chelladurai, P., "Leadership," in R. N. Singer, M. Murphy, & L. K. Tennant, Eds., *Handbook of research on sport psychology*, pp. 647–671. © 1993 by The International Society of Sport Psychology. Used by permission of Gale Group.

tion of the commissioner's behavior is required in terms of what has to be done (prescriptions) and what cannot be done (proscriptions).

Situational Characteristics

What are those situational elements (demands and constraints) that have such strong influence on leader behavior? As noted earlier, Osborn and Hunt (1975) named these situational characteristics *macro variables*. As shown in Exhibit 11.7, Osborn and Hunt identified the size of the group, its technology, and its formal structure as some of the macro variables. In addition to these, the multidimensional model also includes other situational characteristics that influence and control leader behavior:

- the task of the group
- the organizational goals
- the norms of a particular social setting
- the nature of the group.

Since the construct of leadership refers to a group, it is necessary to consider leader behavior in terms of group tasks, processes, and performance. For example, in a university department of sport or recreation management, different units (or groups) may be involved in the performance of different tasks (such as undergraduate or graduate programs in marketing or organizational behavior). Similarly, for each athletic team in a university, the group task becomes a part of the situation.

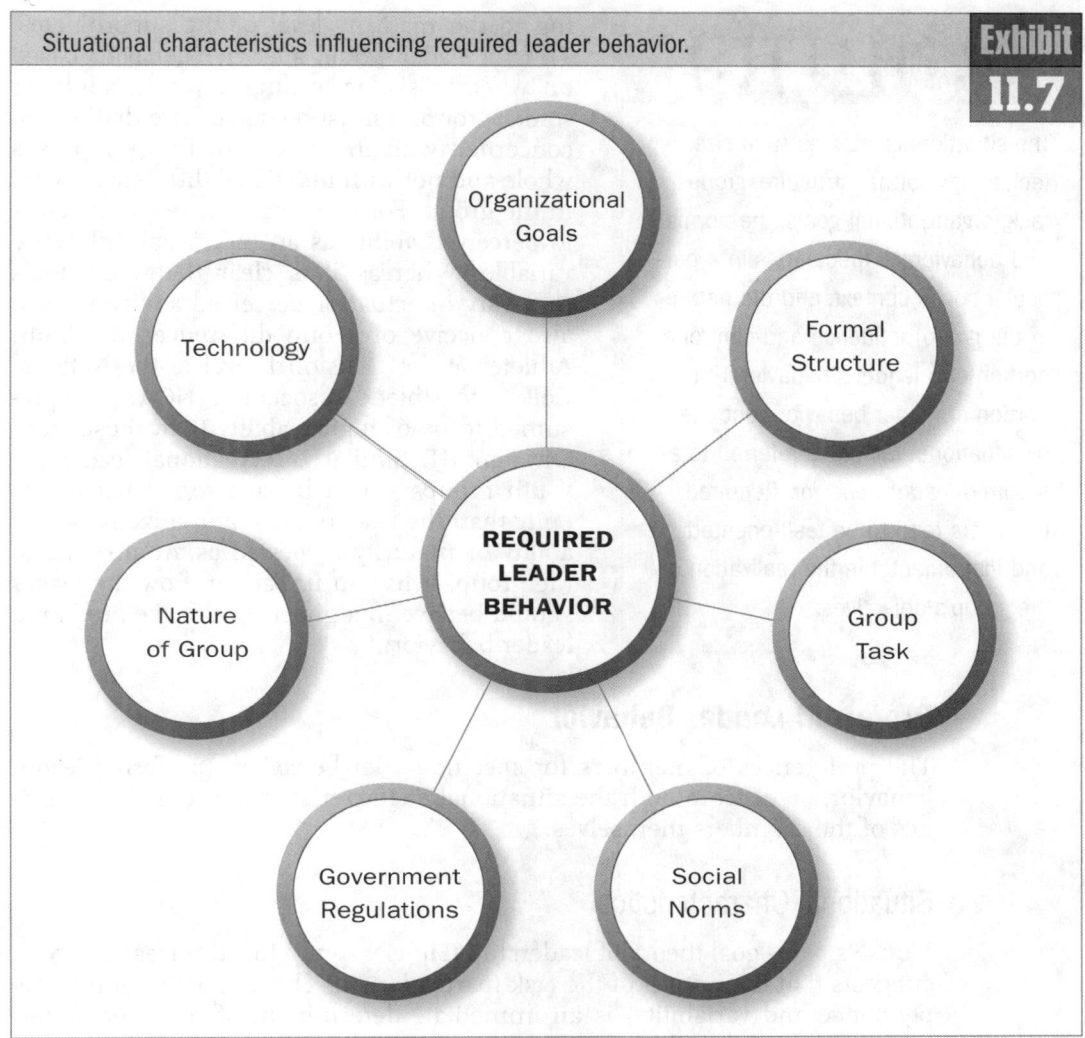

Exhibit 11.7 Situational characteristics influencing required leader behavior.

Organizational goals also affect the total group, including the leader. For instance, the relative emphasis placed on quality versus quantity in a production firm affects both the manager's and the employees' behavior. In the athletic field, the differing goal orientations of professional and educational athletics lead to different behavioral expectations for the coaches and athletes.

The norms and codes of conduct prevalent (or emerging) in a given social setting form a significant set of situational factors that impinge on leadership. Contrast, for instance, the social norms surrounding a coach with those surrounding a manager of a city recreation department. The social norms of the athletic setting permit a coach to yell and scream at the players, whereas such behaviors are proscribed in the case of the manager.

Chelladurai (1993, 1999) argued that the nature of the group as a whole also influences that segment of leader behavior required in a situation. For instance, the differences in orientations between volunteers and professionals will impose different demands on the leader. As another example, Hersey and Blanchard (1969, 1977) argued that leaders should vary their behaviors accord-

In Brief

The situational variables (unit size, technology, formal structure, group task, organizational goals, the norms and behavioral expectations in a particular social context, and the nature of the group) influence and control a portion of a leader's behavior. That portion of leader behavior controlled by situational factors is referred to as *required leader behavior*. Required behaviors tend to be task-oriented and instrumental in the realization of the group's objectives.

ing to the maturity level of the subordinates. Thus, a leader would alter her behavior based on whether she is leading a youth, adult, or senior group. It must be noted here that we are concerned with the nature of the group as a whole and not with individual differences within the group. For instance, House (1971) refers to perceived ability as an individual difference variable. Whereas it is clear that individuals may vary in actual or perceived ability, we can also conceive of group differences in ability. Athletes at the Division I level of the National Collegiate Athletic Association (NCAA) are presumed to be of higher ability than those from Division III. Similarly, recreational leaders of youth groups would behave somewhat differently than the leaders of senior citizens. When ability or maturity is viewed as an attribute of the group, it has an impact on how the leader should behave in a given context (i.e., required leader behavior).

Preferred Leader Behavior

The preferences of members for specific leader behaviors **(preferred leader behavior)** stem from both the situational characteristics and the characteristics of the members themselves.

Situational Characteristics

House's path–goal theory of leadership (House, 1971; House & Dessler, 1974) suggests that the impact of the task (particularly its characteristics of interdependence and variability) is an immediate determinant of member preferences. We noted earlier that the situational characteristics of group size, group task, technology, organizational goals, formal structure, social norms, and government regulations place some constraints and demands on the leader. The same situational characteristics also influence member preferences for specific forms of leader behavior. Therefore, the members' preferences for certain forms of leader behavior will reflect the influences of the situation (Bass, 1985; House, 1971; Yukl, 1989; Yukl & Van Fleet, 1992). In our example of a supervisor and employees of a city recreation department, we noted that the supervisor needs to abide by the organizational requirement that all salary decisions will be made at a higher level. To the extent this requirement is also known to the subordinates, they would not expect or prefer the supervisor to increase their salary.

Member Characteristics

Individual differences influence members' preferences for particular leader behaviors. For example, the effect of task-relevant ability is highlighted in the path–goal theory (House, 1971; House & Dessler, 1974). Similarly, a number of personality traits such as need for affiliation and need for achievement influence members' preferences for different leader behaviors. Lorsch and Morse (1974) and Morse (1976) found that an individual's attitude toward authority affects his reactions to different types of supervision. For instance, those who have a high regard and respect for authority may not mind close supervision from a manager, whereas those who do not have the same positive attitude toward authority may resent close supervision. Cognitive complexity, which refers to the way individuals process information, also helps to determine the preference for structuring behavior from the leader (Wynne & Hunsaker, 1975). Those who can manage in complex and ambiguous work situations may not need much guidance from the supervisor. On the other hand, those who have a lower capacity to handle complex situations may prefer the supervisor telling them what to do, when, and how. Authoritarianism and the need for independence affect the degree to which members prefer their leader to use participation in decision making (Vroom, 1959). Those high in achievement motivation prefer the leader to provide challenge, responsibility, and feedback (McClelland, 1961). The interpersonal needs (need for affiliation, succor, and so on) of members also affect their preferences for specific leader behaviors.

In Brief

Although all members operate under the influence of the same situational characteristics, their preferences for specific forms of leader behavior may vary. These variations are a function of member characteristics including ability, expertise, and personality.

Actual Leader Behavior

The third, and obviously the most central, state of leader behavior is **actual leader behavior**—that is, how a leader behaves in any given situation. Two of the determinants of actual leader behavior are the requirements of the situation (i.e., required leader behavior as discussed above) and the preferences of members (i.e., preferred leader behavior). As discussed previously, Stewart (1982) pointed out that the leader needs to abide by the demands and constraints of the situation in which she operates. Osborn and Hunt (1975) divided actual leader behavior into adaptive behaviors (adaptations to situational requirements) and reactive behaviors (reactions to member preferences). How a leader adapts to the demands and constraints of the situation and reacts to member preferences is also a function of the leader's personal characteristics—in particular, personality and ability. That is, two leaders facing the same situational contingencies and member preferences may not behave similarly because of differences in their personalities and abilities.

Leader Characteristics

Significant leader characteristics include ability, knowledge, experience, and personality. We noted earlier that the leader's personality (task orientation versus people orientation) is the central focus of Fiedler's (1967) contingency model of leadership. Also, McClelland and Burnham (1976) isolated the needs for power, achievement, and affiliation as the most significant in the organizational context, particularly with reference to leaders or managers.

The ability of the leader is made up of two components. One of these is the leader's specific knowledge and expertise concerning various aspects of the group task and the processes necessary for the attainment of the group's goals. This specific ability will vary with different leadership positions. In a city recreation department, knowledge of all the complex rules and regulations governing the activities of the group represents this type of ability. In a university athletic department, a comprehension of the recruiting, eligibility, and league rules is likewise specific to the group task and processes.

The second component of ability includes the leader's capacity to conceptualize the organization as a whole, to analyze the complexities of a problem, and to persuade subordinates about the efficiency of a particular approach. This is a general ability that is transferable across situations. For instance, the director of the city recreation department would be expected to comprehend the place of the department and its activities in the overall scheme of city governance, the politics in and around the department, the way other city recreation departments are being run, the emerging trends in recreation and sport, and other large issues that will impact the department in both the short and long run. Similarly, an understanding of the environment of the university athletic department, the relative influence of various stakeholders (such as faculty, students, alumni, local business, and media), trends in the local entertainment market, and the innovations carried out in other universities transcend the immediate concerns of running the specific department. These general abilities of the recreation and athletic director are relevant in many top managerial positions in other organizational contexts.

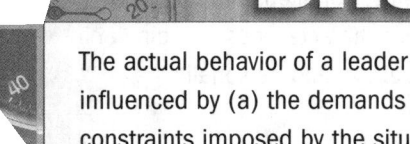

The actual behavior of a leader is influenced by (a) the demands and constraints imposed by the situation, (b) the preferences of the members under the leader's charge, and (c) the leader's own personal characteristics.

Performance and Satisfaction

The consequences included in the multidimensional model are **performance** and **satisfaction** (see Exhibit 11.6). The degree to which the three states of leader behavior are **congruent** (that is, that the actual behavior is consistent with both the preferred and required behaviors) is said to influence performance and satisfaction. Thus, any of the states of leader behavior could be a limiting factor.

For instance, the manager of a firm specializing in organizing and conducting sports events needs to abide by the rules and ordinances of the city where the event takes place. In addition, the manager has to follow legal requirements in running the event. The manager also has to accept the demands and constraints of the parent body that sanctions the event (for example, the Special Olympics). If the manager's behaviors deviate from the requirements (the required behavior), she may jeopardize the standing of the firm. By the same token, the employees of the firm should not prefer that their manager flout the situational requirements. In other words, member preferences should be consistent with situational requirements. From a different perspective, the manager must try to satisfy as much as possible the members' legitimate preferences (actual behavior). Members' motivation to perform well and their satisfaction with their leader as well as with their work will be reduced if the manager continually disregards their needs and desires.

In the multidimensional model, the leaders are assumed to be flexible and capable of altering their behavior according to changing conditions. This perspective is consistent with the position taken by many scholars and researchers. If a leader finds that his behavior has not resulted in increased performance by the group, the leader is likely to alter the actual behavior with a view to enhance productivity (for example, the coach may spend more time and effort in training and instructing the players). By the same token, if the leader finds that the group is not cohesive and integrated, he could begin emphasizing those aspects of his own behavior that would foster warm interpersonal relations within the group.

Transformational Leadership Within the Multidimensional Model

The final component of the model (shown at the left of Exhibit 11.6) links the notion of transformational leadership to the elements of transactional leadership within the model. That is, a transformational leader attempts to alter the situational and member characteristics. Transformational leadership involves a new vision, meaning a new and higher set of goals, and innovative and creative ways of achieving those loftier goals. In creating and stating this vision, the transformational leader may also change the value system guiding the organization. She also implies that perceived barriers to goal attainment are surmountable. Thus, the transformational leader alters the situational characteristics to some degree. As we noted, required behavior is a function of situational characteristics, including organizational goals, the values subscribed to by the organization, and the traditions of the organization.

Equally important to transformational leadership is its focus on members. Insofar as the members can only actualize the vision espoused by the leader, it is important to convince the members of the goodness and viability of the vision. While the transformational leader tells the members that they have the ability to achieve those goals, he also expresses great confidence that the members and the organization will achieve the vision. In this sense, the transformational leader alters member characteristics in terms of their values, aspirations, and confidence in their abilities to reach the goal. In turn, these changes in member characteristics will affect their preferences for leadership and make them consistent with the new vision and order.

In the process of transforming all members, the transformational leader has to rely on immediate subordinates (that is, second level managers). Thus, it is necessary for the transformational leader also to influence her immediate subordinates in terms of their acceptance of the vision, their belief in the attainability of the vision, their aspirations, and their self-esteem.

> **In Brief**
>
> A critical proposition of the multidimensional model of leadership is that the performance of a group and the satisfaction of its members will be enhanced if there is congruence among three states of leader behavior: (a) the leader behavior required by the situational demands and constraints, (b) the leader behavior preferred by the members, and (c) the actual behavior of the leader.

In overview, the multidimensional model takes into account the characteristics of the situation, the leader, and the members, and conceptualizes three states of leader behavior—required, preferred, and actual. The degree of congruence among these three states of leader behavior is related to group performance and member satisfaction. A portion of the leader's behavior is dictated by situational and member characteristics. However, that portion of behavior at the discretion of the leader is expected to have greater impact on member motivation and satisfaction. Thus, leadership plays a significant role in effective management of human resources.

SUMMARY

This chapter focused on contemporary theories of leadership. We first looked at the contemporary theories of transformational leadership, charismatic leadership, and leader–member exchanges. Whereas earlier theories were concerned with the transactions between a leader and the members, transformational leadership is said to be focused on transforming both the organization (including its goals and vision) and its members. The leader–member exchange theory was described as focused on cultivating quality relationships between a leader and each of the members. We examined Osborn and Hunt's distinction between macro and micro variables and their impacts on leadership. Finally, we studied the multidimensional model of leadership, described as a framework integrating the earlier approaches of Fiedler, House, Osborn, and Hunt.

DEVELOPING YOUR PERSPECTIVES

1. Recall one of your work experiences (either part-time or full-time). Describe the leadership provided by your supervisor in terms of one of the leadership theories discussed in the chapter.

2. From your experiences in groups with formal leaders, recall a group where there was an in-group and an out-group. Contrast the specific relationships the leader had with members of the in-group versus members of the out-group. How did these relationships affect the total group and its effectiveness?

3. Based on your work experiences (either full-time or part-time), identify a leader who was transformational. Explain in detail the specific actions the leader took that transformed the situation. Were the members also transformed? Give details of the changes in members as well as in the total group as a result of the transformational leadership.

References

Arnold, J. A., Arad, S., Rhoades, J. A., & Drasgow, F. (2000). The Empowering Leadership Questionnaire: The construction and validation of a new scale for measuring leader behaviors. *Journal of Organizational Behavior, 21,* 249–269.

Bass, B. M. (1985). *Leadership and performance beyond expectations.* New York: The Free Press.

Bass, B. M. (1990). *Bass and Stogdill's handbook of leadership.* New York: The Free Press.

Bass, B. M. (1997). Does the transactional-transformational leadership paradigm transcend organizational and national boundaries? *American Psychologist, 52,* 130–139.

Bass, B. M., & Avolio, B. (1993). Transformational leadership: A response to critiques. In M. M. Chemers & R. Ayman (Eds.), *Leadership theory and research perspectives and directions* (pp. 49–80). New York: Academic Press.

Basu, R., & Green, S. G. (1997). Leader–member exchange and transformational leadership: An empirical examination of innovative behaviors in leader–member dyads. *Journal of Applied Social Psychology, 27* (6), 477–499.

Bennis, W. (1997). *Organizing genius: The secrets of creative collaboration.* Reading, MA: Addison-Wesley.

Bennis, W. B. (1984). Good managers and good leaders. *Across the Board, 21* (10), 7–11.

Chelladurai, P. (1978). *A contingency model of leadership in athletics.* Unpublished doctoral dissertation. University of Waterloo, Waterloo, Canada.

Chelladurai, P. (1993). Leadership. In R. N. Singer, M. Murphey, & L. K. Tennant (Eds.), *Handbook of research on sport psychology* (pp. 647–671). New York: Macmillan.

Chelladurai, P. (1999) *Human resource management in sport and recreation.* Champaign, IL: Human Kinetics.

Conger, J. A., & Kanungo, R. N. (1987). Toward a behavioral theory of charismatic leadership in organizational settings. *Academy of Management Review, 12,* 637–647.

Conger, J. A., & Kanungo, R. N. (Eds.). (1988). *Charismatic leadership: The elusive factor in organizational effectiveness.* San Francisco: Jossey-Bass.

Conger, J. A., & Kanungo, R. N. (1998). *Charismatic leadership in organizations.* Thousand Oaks, CA: Sage Publications.

Dansereau, F., Cashman, J., & Graen, G. (1973). Instrumentality theory and equity theory as complementary approaches in predicting the relationship of leadership and turnover among managers. *Organizational Behavior and Human Performance, 10,* 184–200.

Dansereau, F., Graen, G., & Haga, B. A. (1975). A vertical-dyad linkage approach to leadership within formal organizations: A longitudinal investigation of the role making process. *Organizational Behavior and Human Performance, 13,* 46–78.

Doherty, A. J., & Danylchuk, K. E. (1996). Transformational and transactional leadership in interuniversity athletics management. *Journal of Sport Management, 10,* 292–309.

Duchon, D., Green, S. G., & Taber, T. D. (1986). Vertical dyad linkage: A longitudinal assessment of antecedents, measures, and consequences. *Journal of Applied Psychology, 71,* 56–60.

Fiedler, F. E. (1967). *A theory of leadership effectiveness.* New York: McGraw-Hill.

Graen, G. (1976). Role making processes within complex organizations. In M. D. Dunnette (Ed.), *Handbook of industrial and organizational psychology* (pp. 1201–1245). Chicago: Rand-McNally.

Graen, G., & Cashman, J. F. (1975). A role making model of leadership in formal organizations: A developmental approach. In J. G. Hunt & L. L. Larson (Eds.), *Leadership frontiers* (pp. 181–185). Kent, OH: Kent State University Press.

Hersey, P., & Blanchard, K. H. (1969). Life cycle theory of leadership. *Training and Development Journal, May,* 26–34.

Hersey, P., & Blanchard, K. H. (1977). *Management of organizational behavior.* Englewood Cliffs, NJ: Prentice Hall.

House, R. J. (1971). A path–goal theory of leader effectiveness. *Administrative Science Quarterly, 16,* 321–338.

House, R. J. (1977). A 1976 theory of charismatic leadership. In J. G. Hunt & L. L. Larson (Eds.), *Leadership: The cutting edge.* Carbondale, IL: Southern Illinois University Press.

House, R. J., & Dessler, G. (1974). The path–goal theory of leadership: Some post hoc and a priori tests. In J. G. Hunt & L. L. Larson (Eds.), *Contingency approaches to leadership.* Carbondale, IL: Southern Illinois University Press.

House, R. J., & Howell, J. M. (1992). Personality and charismatic leadership. *Leadership Quarterly, 3* (2), 81–108.

House, R. J., & Podsakoff, P. M. (1994). Leadership effectiveness: Past perspectives and future directions for research. In J. Greenberg (Ed.), *Organizational behavior: State of the science,* pp. 135–153. Hillsdale: Lawrence Erlbaum Associates.

House, R. J., & Shamir, B. (1993). Toward the integration of transformational, charismatic, and visionary theories. In M. Chemers & R. Ayman (Eds.), *Leadership theory and research perspectives and directions* (pp. 579–594). Orlando, FL: Academic Press.

Kent, A., & Chelladurai, P. (2001). Cascading effects of transformational leadership on organizational commitment and citizenship behavior: A case study in intercollegiate athletics. *Journal of Sport Management, 15,* 135–159.

Kent, A., & Chelladurai, P. (2000). *The differential effects of multiple sources of leadership on employee reactions in a state parks and recreation department.* Unpublished manuscript. Tallahassee, FL: The Florida State University.

Lorsch, J. W., & Morse, J. J. (1974). *Organizations and their members: A contingency approach.* New York: Harper and Row.

McClelland, D. C. (1961). *The achieving society.* New York: Van Nostrand.

McClelland, D. C., & Burnham, D. H. (1976). Power is the great motivator. *Harvard Business Review, 54,* 100–110.

Miller, D., & Friesen, P. (1984). *Organizations: A quantum view.* Englewood Cliffs, NJ: Prentice Hall.

Moore, K. (2004). An evolution in leaders. *Globe and Mail* (Friday, February 6, 2004), C 1 and 6. Toronto, Canada.

Morse, J. J. (1976). Person–job congruence and individual adjustment and development. *Human Relations, 28,* 841–861.

Osborn, R. N., & Hunt, J. G. (1975). An adaptive-reactive theory of leadership: The role of macro variables in leadership research. In J. G. Hunt & L. L. Larson (Eds.), *Leadership frontiers.* Kent, OH: Kent State University.

Rafferty, A.E., & Griffin, M.A. (2004). Dimensions of transformational leadership: Conceptual and empirical extensions. *The Leadership Quarterly, 15,* 329–354.

Shaskin, M. (1986). True vision in leadership. *Training and Development Journal, 40* (5), 58–61.

Stewart, R. (1982). The relevance of some studies of managerial work and behavior to leadership research. In J. G. Hunt, U. Sekaran, & C. Schriesheim (Eds.), *Leadership: Beyond establishment views* (pp. 11–30). Carbondale, IL: Southern Illinois University Press.

Vroom, V. H. (1959). Some personality determinants of the effects of participation. *Journal of Abnormal and Social Psychology, 59,* 322–327.

Weese, W. J. (1995). A synthesis of leadership theory and a prelude to the Five "C" Model. *The European Journal of Sport Management, 2* (1), 59–71.

Wynne, B. E., & Hunsaker, P. L. (1975). A human information-processing approach to the study of leadership. In J. G. Hunt & L. L. Larson (Eds.), *Leadership frontiers.* Kent, OH: Kent State University.

Yukl, G. A. (1989). *Leadership in organizations* (2nd ed.). Englewood Cliffs, NJ: Prentice Hall.

Yukl, G. A., & Van Fleet, D. D. (1992). Theory and research on leadership in organizations. In M. D. Dunnette & L. M. Hough (Eds.), *Handbook of industrial and organizational psychology* (2nd ed., pp. 147–197). Palo Alto, CA: Consulting Psychologist's Press.

CHAPTER 12

Program Evaluation

ANAGE YOUR LEARNING

After completing this chapter you should be able to:

- Distinguish the performances at individual, unit, and organization levels.
- Understand the relationships between planning and programming.
- Define and describe a program and its components from a systems perspective.
- Distinguish between the outputs and impacts of a program.
- Describe the different types of programs.
- Define program evaluation, its purposes, and its processes.
- Understand the differences among various standards applied to programs.

STRATEGIC CONCEPTS

client satisfaction	program
cost–benefit analysis	program evaluation
cost-effectiveness	program logic
impact	program profile
meeting objectives	public and nonprofit programs
output	social intervention
performance appraisal	socioeconomic evaluation
planning	standards of evaluation
professional judgment	

EVALUATION DEFINED

he previous chapters have been devoted to describing the managerial processes of planning, organizing, and leading. The identification of desired goals and the selection of activities and programs to achieve those goals are the essence of the planning process as outlined in Chapters 5 and 6. Grouping the activities into meaningful units, establishing appropriate rules and regulations to govern and coordinate these units, and hiring and assigning the right people to the right jobs are part of the organizing process, which we discussed in Chapters 7 and 8. The leading function aims at motivating and influencing the members toward organizational goals (see Chapters 9, 10, and 11). All of the time and effort that the managers spend on these processes is expected to lead to some specified results. Now comes the equally critical function of evaluating, whereby the organization and its units are judged on the basis of their achievements.

Individual-, Unit-, and Organizational-Level Performances

As shown in Exhibit 12.1, there are three major categories to be considered in the evaluation stage: performances at the individual, unit, and organizational levels. The first concern pertains to performances of individual employees. The analysis focuses on finding out if every employee has completed effectively the tasks assigned to that individual. This issue is fundamental to all of management because the whole enterprise is ultimately dependent for its success on the members and their performances.

The assessment or evaluation of the work of individual employees is called **performance appraisal** and is an integral part of the field known as human resource management. The importance of performance appraisal is such that many organizations have separate departments to address this issue. This topic is dealt with extensively in Chelladurai (1999) *Human Resource Management in Sport and Recreation*. Briefly, performance appraisal has two purposes. First is the developmental purpose, whereby managers (a) appraise individual performances; (b) identify strengths and weaknesses; (c) discuss with the member any areas where improvements can be made; and (d) determine how to overcome the barriers, if any, to enhancing performance. The second is the evaluative purpose, by which the performances of all employees are appraised on some common and standard criteria and then compared with each other, and the resulting comparisons are used to distribute organizational rewards (promotion, merit pay, bonus, and so on).

From a macro perspective, managers must also be concerned with how well the different units are doing and how effective the total organization is. Even when individuals in an organization carry out their assigned tasks effectively, the units within an organization and the total organization may not be achieving the goals specified for them. We can identify several reasons for the

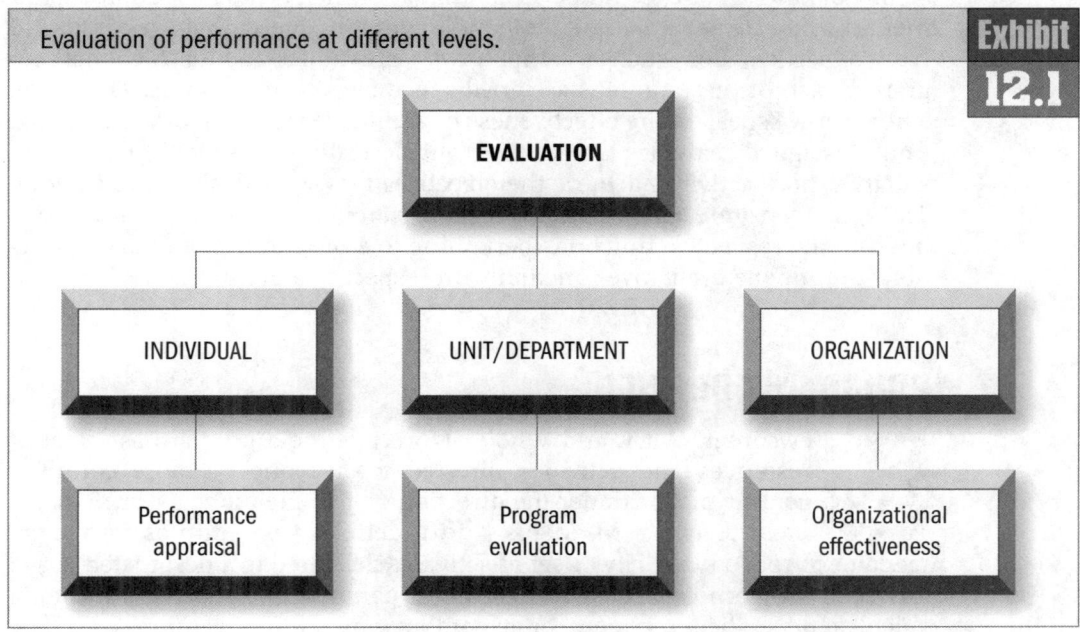

Exhibit 12.1 Evaluation of performance at different levels.

lack of correspondence between employee-level performance and unit- or organizational-level performance. The unit- or organizational-level goals may have been too high or inappropriate in the first place. For example, a promotional program aimed at recruiting 200 new customers for a fitness/health club may not achieve that goal despite the best efforts of the employees, simply because the goal is too high. Or it could be because severe constraints have been overlooked in the planning stage, such as the inaccessibility of the club's location. The environment may have changed since the inception of the plan. For example, a new fitness/health enterprise that recently opened nearby may have attracted would-be customers. The failure could also be because the chosen activities for the promotional campaign were inappropriate or because there was poor coordination among the employees involved in the promotion. Therefore, it is important that assessment of unit- and organizational-level performance be evaluated independently of the appraisal of individual performances, as shown in Exhibit 12.1. This chapter deals with the evaluation of unit-level performance (or programs), and Chapter 13 deals with organizational-level performance.

> **In Brief**
>
> Evaluating is one of the four major functions of management. It involves evaluating the performance of (a) individuals (performance appraisal), (b) individual programs (program evaluation), and (c) the total organization (organizational effectiveness).

Organizational Units and Programs

Very often each of the units in an organization is created to carry out a specific set of activities. For instance, the specific activities carried out by event management, facility management, or ticketing units (or departments) in a university athletic department or a professional sport franchise are sufficiently distinct from each other. In a similar manner, a city recreation department may create separate units to handle different age groups, genders, and types of participation, such as competitive, recreational, and instructional programs. Each of these units is assigned specific tasks or activities. Therefore, whenever we speak of the effectiveness of a unit, we really mean whether that unit's assigned activities are carried out according to specifications, and whether those activities achieve the objectives they were designed to achieve. The terms *program management, program planning,* and *program evaluation* indicate the respective functions pertaining to a program. The following sections outline the evaluative function with respect to a program.

PROGRAMS DEFINED

Newcomer, Hatry, and Wholey (1994) define a **program** as "a set of resources and activities directed toward one or more common goals, typically under the direction of a single manager or management team" (p. 3). Myers (1999) defines a program as "any organized or purposeful activity or set of activities delivered to a designated target group. A program can consist of a class, a pamphlet or booklet, a poster, a video, a prescribed regimen, or a combination of interventions" (p. 10).

According to these definitions, those activities attempting to achieve a specific goal or a set of goals are grouped together as a program. For instance, a youth sports program aimed at fostering sports participation among teenagers may consist of several activities, such as scheduled daily or weekly instructional, competitive, or recreational sessions.

In addition, it is also conventional for the group of activities associated with a program to be assigned to one unit or department rather than being spread across different units. Locating an entire program and its activities in one unit makes for better coordination and control of those activities. This does not mean that each unit will be restricted to only one program. For instance, the city recreation department may offer programs such as adult sports, youth sports, hobby and art workshops, and park maintenance. It is also essential to conceive of a program as a distinct entity from the unit that runs the program.

Another element common to all programs is that some resources (human, material, and monetary) are allocated to a given program. It is conventional for a university athletic department to speak of its sports teams as programs (football program, men's and women's basketball programs, and so on). It is also conventional to allocate certain resources to each of these programs. In addition to the facilities and support services assigned to each one, a certain dollar amount is also allocated. You will recall that such allocation of resources is referred to as program budgeting (see Chapter 5).

Planning and Programming

Owen (1993) states that a program is "a manifestation of the planning process. . . . [and that] program development means converting value choices into concrete directions for action by choosing from among alternatives and allocating resources to achieve defined goals" (p. 5). The foregoing description of a program parallels that of **planning** and goals discussed in Chapter 5. The notable difference is that the objectives of a program are narrow, with a limited number of activities, and that a program is usually targeted toward a specific client group (as in a youth sport program).

To Recap

PLANNING AND BUDGETING In Chapter 5, we noted that planning includes budgeting—the allocation of resources to various activities chosen to achieve the desired ends. We also noted that organizations need to take a rational, comprehensive approach to planning. Such an approach would entail assessing the importance of the various programs (or activities) and their effectiveness in contributing to organizational goals. We noted that this is the essence of the budgeting technique known as the Planning–Programming–Budgeting System (PPBS). Thus, the process of program evaluation discussed in this chapter feeds back into the planning and budgeting processes described earlier.

Programs versus Projects

We must distinguish between a program and a project. A program is a set of activities carried out on a continuing basis. For example, the coaching and associated activities provided for an athletic team in an educational setting are a program because these activities are carried out every year on a continuous basis. Similarly, the organization and conduct of competitions in one or more sports by a university recreation department is a program, for it is done on a continuous basis. In contrast, an athletic department may decide for the first time to conduct coaching clinics in various sports for the benefit of high school coaches in the region. Because it is being carried out for the first time, it is a project. Similarly, a city recreation department may begin a project of sports competitions for wheelchair athletes. Just as in a program, a set of resources will be expended on specified activities for the benefit of the target group(s) in the preceding two examples.

> **In Brief**
>
> A program and a project, while similar in most respects, exhibit one significant difference. A program is repeated on a continuing basis, whereas a project is a one-shot affair. However, a project may be later converted into a regular program.

What distinguishes a project from a program is that the project is carried out for the first time without any prior intention to continue it in the coming years. However, after the initial run of the project, the administrators may find that it was successful and of great benefit to everyone concerned. At this point the managers may decide to continue with the project every year. When that happens, the project becomes a program. Apart from this difference, a program and a project are planned and executed in similar ways. Therefore, the following sections are applicable to both programs and projects.

Public and Nonprofit Programs

The terms *program* and *program evaluation* are more often used in the context of public and nonprofit organizations than in the business context. We are all familiar with the welfare programs, drug education programs, and highway maintenance programs of the federal, state, and city governments. These types of **public and nonprofit programs** are often aimed at improving the conditions of targeted groups and thereby benefiting the society at large.

In a similar manner, the International Olympic Committee (IOC) and its administrators may embark on a specific program to improve sport performance around the world. The IOC would select certain developing countries and embark on a program of activities (training coaches and athletes, educating administrators, and so on). Along similar lines, sport governing bodies offer coaching programs to teach the skills of the sport; the knowledge associated with that sport, such as its history, psycho-physical requirements, and rules; sportsmanship; and respect for rules, officials, and opponents.

The National Collegiate Athletic Association (NCAA) may institute a program to educate prospective university athletes about various regulations, the rights and responsibilities of athletes, and the dangers of drug use and gambling. The NCAA activities within this program may include publication of material for athletes and administrators. In addition, the NCAA created the

NCAA Foundation as a nonprofit, tax-exempt corporation in 1988, which was reconstituted in 2002 as NCAA Leadership Advisory Board (NCAA, 2002). The board's purpose is "to generate and award funds in support of programs that enable student–athletes to participate fully in the college community, to achieve successful academic and athletics experiences, and to prepare to be effective citizens and productive contributors to society" (NCAA, 1999). In pursuit of this mission, the organization initiated several programs such as:

- degree completion awards
- CHOICES (an alcohol education program)
- Life Skills (an academic and personal development program)
- Winning for Life (scholarships in the sciences)
- sports journalism scholarships.

The NCAA has also instituted programs to promote opportunities for women and minorities. Its Women's Enhancement Program offers:

- ten annual postgraduate scholarships of $6,000 each for females accepted into sport administration or related programs
- one-year internships at the NCAA national office for female college graduates
- a vita bank for women interested in pursuing a career in intercollegiate athletics.

NCAA's Ethnic Minority Enhancement Program is very similar to the Women's Enhancement Program; it offers 10 scholarships of $6,000 each to qualified applicants in order to increase the pool of qualified minority candidates for coaching and administrative positions in intercollegiate athletics. The program also offers internships at its national office and maintains a minority vita bank.

One of the most popular programs of the Government of Canada is its funding of the agency called PARTICIPACTION, which advocates an active lifestyle through its innovative slogans and advertisements. In the United States, the mandate of the President's Council on Physical Fitness and Sports (PCPFS) is promoting "the benefits of sports, fitness, and physical activity and motivating all Americans to become and stay active and fit. . . . [with] a special focus on the nation's youth, encouraging them to lay the foundation for an active, healthy adult life" (President's Council on Physical Fitness and Sports, 1999). One of the programs under this broader mission is the President's Challenge of the Youth Physical Fitness Program. The program is to promote physical fitness among youth by challenging them to achieve specific levels of performance in five selected activities (curl-ups, mile run/walk, shuttle run, pull-ups, and V-sit reach), and offering four different awards for attaining those levels (President's, National, Participant, and Health–Fitness Awards). The activities include publicizing the challenge, enlisting the services of physical education teachers in promoting the program and conducting the tests, and the actual presentation of the awards.

On the local level, city recreation departments maintain the parks or play fields as a consumer service for their communities. That is, citizens can visit these parks and use them as they please, but within the rules and regulations. These departments may also develop playgrounds and arenas, and organize recreational or competitive activities for the benefit of the members of the community.

Programs in the Commercial/Profit Sector

The concepts of a program and of program evaluation are equally relevant to every kind of organization, including commercial, profit-oriented organizations. A public or media relations program in, for example, a professional sport franchise may consist of several activities (e.g., media relations, advertising, lobbying), all of which are expected to achieve a positive public image for the franchise. Consider the National Basketball Association (NBA)'s "I love this game" campaign to promote the game of basketball and the NBA itself. Similarly Nike's "Just do it" campaign may also be considered a program with specific objectives and an allotment of resources.

A sponsorship, defined as "a cash and/or in-kind fee paid to a property (typically in sports, arts, entertainment, or causes) in return for access to the exploitable commercial potential associated with that property" (IEG, Inc., 1999) is a program in itself. When a commercial enterprise hires a fitness expert and allocates space and dollars to offer on-site exercise classes for its employees with a view to reduce absenteeism, this is called a program (Myers, 1999). It has specific objectives, the activities in the program are identified, and it has been assigned certain resources.

Programs in Small Organizations

Many of the foregoing examples of programs are drawn from large and rich organizations (both profit and nonprofit) and may involve large sums of money, impact a vast number of people, and cover a large territory. Because of their large size and scope, such programs are often in the news, and the public, politicians, and commentators debate over the purposes and outcomes of these programs.

Programs and program evaluation are just as relevant to smaller organizations. For instance, the intramural department in a small university may engage in a program designed to encourage greater participation by the students, staff, and faculty of the university. As another example, consider the owner of a fitness club in a small city. Concerned with the low membership in the club, she may engage in a marketing program to boost the club's image in terms of its parking and other amenities, the layout of the facilities and equipment, and the qualifications of its exercise leaders. Each of the above examples is a program by itself, and evaluation of each would shed some light on where improvements could be made, which of them could be made more cost-effective, and how each could be made attractive to prospective customers.

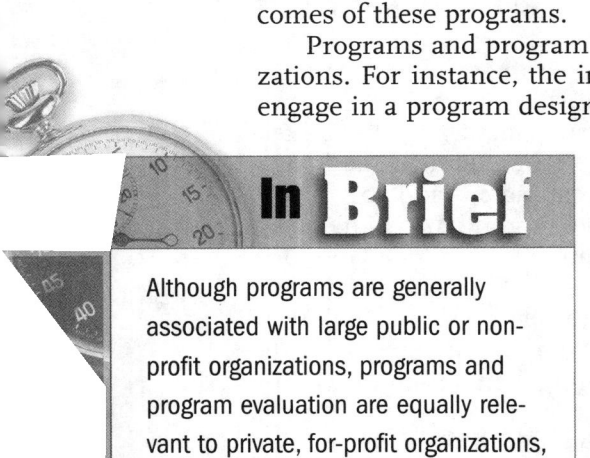

In Brief

Although programs are generally associated with large public or nonprofit organizations, programs and program evaluation are equally relevant to private, for-profit organizations, and small enterprises.

The efforts and funding that go into a program may be much smaller than in the programs of larger organizations. However, those small amounts of money may be huge when considered as a percentage of the overall budgets of these units. The point here is that if substantial effort and money go into a program, then it is incumbent upon the managers to verify whether the program achieves what it is supposed to achieve.

PROGRAMS FROM A SYSTEMS PERSPECTIVE

It is important to note that the definitions of a program cited so far highlight (a) resources, (b) activities, (c) and outputs. As shown in Exhibit 12.2, these elements resemble the input, throughput, and output of a system, described in Chapter 3. Resources refer to the dollars, the labor (number of employees, number of hours they spend on the program), and other inputs allocated to the program. For instance, the resources of the football, volleyball, and cross-country programs of a university athletic department can be compared on the basis of the budgets allotted to each, the number of full- and part-time coaches, and the effort and expenditure of maintaining the practice and competition facilities.

The activities are the major tasks undertaken to achieve the purposes of the program. These activities also include the arrangement of positions and powers among the program's personnel. As noted in Chapters 7 and 8, this refers to the distribution of responsibilities and authority, and to the methods of coordination of the activities of the members assigned to the program. For example, the American Sport Education Program is involved in developing multilevel curricular programs and offering courses for coaches (called SportCoach), for sport administrators (SportDirector), and for parents (SportParent). Similarly, the coach education program undertaken by the Coaching Association of Canada includes the preparation and production of instructional material, different levels of coaching classes, and various methods of assessment of trainees. These activities are often carried out with the collaboration of national and provincial sport governing bodies, educational institutions, and local recreation departments. These activities are governed by a hierarchically arranged system composed of a director, several assistant direc-

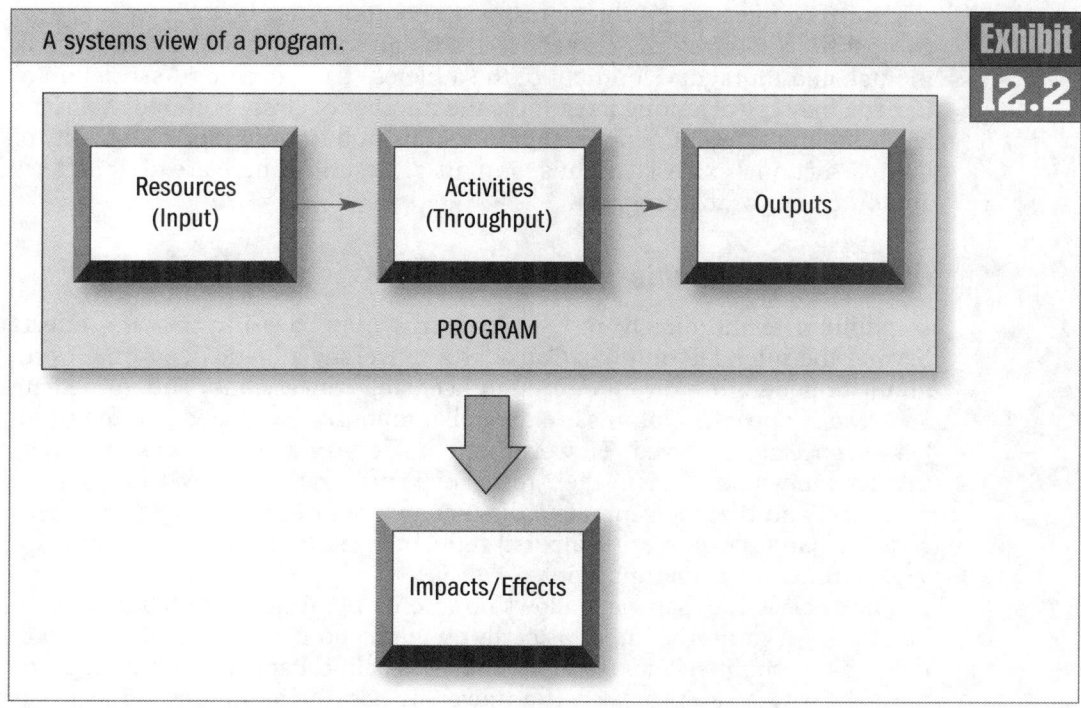

Exhibit 12.2 A systems view of a program.

Sidebar

Speaking of the economic impact of scalpers, Spindler (2003) likens them to parasites that get their nourishment (i.e., profit) by hitching on to the event produced by another organization. But unlike most natural parasites that derive their nourishment from the host organism without being of any use to the host, scalpers are seen as serving the host by increasing ticket-producing firms' revenues. "Scalpers, as market specialists, may increase ticket-producing firms' revenues, and the ticket market, when scalpers are relatively limited in number" (Spindler, 2003, p. 694). Further, "producing firms will indeed benefit from higher revenues if scalpers exist because the latter will contribute to initial demand by extracting more surplus from the ultimate consumers. In this, scalpers are just like other market makers, or middlemen, who intercede between producer and consumer" (p. 695). Swofford (2003) views the scalper as the speculator with a lower cost of marketing with a higher risk. The scalpers' activities create more exchange in the market place. Thus, there is a symbiotic relationship between the producing firm and the scalper where the producer benefits from the existence of the scalper, the scalper benefits from reselling the product, and the customers benefit from the opportunity to buy the tickets.

---

tors, regional coordinators, and many more instructors throughout Canada. From a systems perspective, these are the throughput processes.

The **outputs** are the intended (and sometimes unintended) results of the program. In the case of athletic teams, the outputs may be the percentage of competitions won by the respective teams and the physical, psychological, mental, and moral development of the athletes. The Coaching Association of Canada may count among its outputs the number of classes offered at various levels and in different regions, the sales of its publications, and the quality of the instructional materials. Thus, outputs as described here are direct effects and outcomes of the program.

Outputs and Impacts

In addition to the direct outputs, programs may have **impacts** and effects beyond the intended outputs. Consider a university athletic department program for generating revenue through licensing concessions. The immediate and readily apparent outputs are the dollar amounts generated and the number of spectators served. However, the holders of these concessions may invest money and labor in their respective enterprises (to buy and sell their products) and thereby generate a distinct sphere of economic activity. These activities (and those of the scalpers!) reflect the significant impact a program may have on the economic front.

If the athletic department allows nonprofit organizations to sell their products during a game, the impact is partly on the economic side and, more important, on the public relations side as well. The political and social impact of the program may be even greater. If a university has a winning football team, its

public image may be greatly improved; recruitment of quality students becomes easier; influence with the lawmakers increases; and solidarity with the local and regional community, the media, and alumni across the nation is vastly enhanced. In the case of the Coaching Association of Canada, the impact is evidenced by the quality of coaching offered by its trainees and by the quality of the experience of participants in youth sport across the country.

Programs as Social Interventions

From a different perspective, almost all the programs of public (government) and nonprofit organizations may be considered as **social interventions** (Owen 1993). This means that these organizations may initiate and execute programs for the benefit of society in general and a specific client group in particular (such as the programs of the Red Cross, Salvation Army, and educational institutions, and the welfare programs of the federal, state, and city governments). The concept of intervention implies that a need exists that must be addressed or satisfied—that is, a need exists to improve some neglected or deficient aspect in the society.

Note that the idea of social intervention need not be restricted to public and nonprofit organizations. Some commercial enterprises may devise and undertake specific programs to solve a problem for the society or a segment of the society. Profit-oriented enterprises may initiate programs to encourage greater participation in sport and physical activity. For example, programs such as street basketball, three-player basketball, charity runs, and walkathons may be organized by profit-oriented firms to promote participation in these activities. To the extent these programs are aimed at changing the behavior of the community in pursuit of fitness and health, they may be considered social interventions. However, this does not negate the fact that when commercial enterprises engage in programming to the good of society, they usually do so as a public relations strategy to promote themselves and their products. In fact, the promotion and sponsorship of many sport events are primarily business propositions from the companies' perspective. For our purposes here, however, they are still programs of social intervention.

PROGRAM EVALUATION

ow that we have defined and described programs and their types, let us look at **program evaluation** itself. According to Newcomer, Hatry, and Wholey (1994),

> *Program evaluation* is the systematic assessment of program results and, to the extent feasible, systematic assessment of the extent to which the program caused those results. . . . [It also] includes process evaluations which assess the extent to which a program has been implemented as intended, even when such evaluation does not assess the longer-term results of the program implementation. (p. 3)

Program evaluation is also a "review and assessment of . . . the adequacy of its objectives, its design and its results both intended and unintended" (Treasury Board of Canada, 1981, p. 19). Three significant questions are

Sidebar

In outlining the importance of program evaluation for exercise leaders, Myers (1999) noted that it is critical "whether you work or intend to work in the fitness or health club sector, the corporate sector, the clinical sector, the community sector, the public health sector, or as an independent entrepreneur. In today's competitive fitness market, commercial facilities and personal trainers must position themselves or find their niche in their market place. Nonprofit exercise programs similarly want to attract and keep clients, deliver high quality services that meet client expectations, maximize client benefits, and minimize adverse effects such as injuries. Evaluation shows how well you are doing in each area and provides direction for improving your services" (p. xiii). The essential points here are that (a) program and program evaluation are meaningful in every type of organization, including individually owned enterprises; (b) a program may involve recruiting and retaining clients and/or providing quality services and other benefits to clients; and (c) every one of these programs can be evaluated.

addressed in this description of program evaluation. First, the concern may lie with whether the program has achieved its goals or reached the intended outcomes. The second question is whether the activities were carried out in accordance with specifications. If the activities deviated from what was planned one cannot necessarily expect the program to achieve its objective. Even when the processes are in order, and even when the objectives are achieved, a third question remains: Were the objectives achieved because of the program and its activities or because of something else? For instance, an ice-cream company may experience increased sales in the three months following its marketing program, but that increase could be a function of changing weather conditions. That is, if the marketing campaign was launched in February and March and if the increase in sales came about in June and July, was it an effect of the marketing efforts, or was it an effect of the summer heat? In a similar manner, any increase in participation in outdoor sports activities during spring and summer in Canada and the northern United States cannot be solely attributed to promotional efforts by sport organizations.

Finally, an underlying theme in any program evaluation is to verify if the program should exist at all given its cost relative to its impact on the public. In many cases the costs associated with a program may exceed the value of the outcomes and benefits of that program. The issue of estimating benefits is a difficult one and will be discussed later in the chapter. In addition to the **cost–benefit analysis**, there is the question of whether alternate programs could achieve the same results with less cost. For example, a national government may decide on improving the performance level of its athletes. It may institute several programs to achieve this end such as:

- financial aid to cover the training and competition expenses of top athletes
- scholarships so that the athletes can enroll in institutions with strong athletic traditions
- grants to educational institutions, enabling them to nurture and foster athletic talent
- government-financed sport schools/colleges to recruit top talents and train them in both academics and athletics.

Evaluation of these programs would show which ones are more effective in achieving the goal (producing international-caliber athletes) and which ones are **cost-effective** (low-cost in relation to what they achieve). On a smaller scale, a city in one of the southern states might consider building an ice rink to serve the local public. A fundamental question is whether there will be enough participants to justify the cost of the ice rink. Another question would be whether people's desire to experience skating can be satisfied more cost-effectively through other means, such as an in-line skating rink.

Purposes of Program Evaluation

The many reasons given by scholars for why organizations and their management engage in periodic program evaluations (e.g., Affholter, 1994; Farley, 1984; Kestner, 1996; Royse & Thyer, 1996; Scheirer, 1994; Wholey, 1981) can be summarized as

- accountability/credibility
- improved performance
- cost-effectiveness
- safety of participants
- breadth of programs
- accessibility of programs.

Because many sport organizations are third-sector organizations (see Chapter 2) funded by government agencies or by donations and membership fees, they are accountable to those who provide the resources. Therefore, it is imperative that they justify their operations by demonstrating that their programs are effective and are achieving the ends sought. Program evaluations will provide data and results to support the claims and lend credibility to an organization and its programs.

Program evaluations also show which aspects of a program are weak, and how even a successful program can be improved. A concomitant benefit is the identification of measures that could make a program more cost-effective. That is, the evaluation will show how the available resources can best be used to improve the performance of the program.

The next three benefits are quite relevant to sport and recreation programs. Kestner (1996) points out that evaluation of a sport program can identify the factors that may jeopardize the safety of the participants in the program. An equally important consideration is to verify if the programs are sufficiently broad to include many segments of the community, and if those programs are easily accessible to all members. The major thrust of Title IX is to ensure that athletic programs are broad enough to cater to the needs of women. The NCAA Women's Enhancement Program and the Ethnic Minority Enhancement Program, described earlier, were initiated to increase opportunities for women and minorities in intercollegiate athletics.

> **In Brief**
>
> Program evaluation will show if (a) the goals of the program are achieved, (b) the activities are carried out as planned, and (c) the program can be justified.

In sum, proper evaluation of a program can (a) provide information to the administrators for more informed decision making; (b) clarify the program and its logic for its users, service providers, and administrators; and (c) offer advance information for any proposed new program (Owen, 1993). Through such an evaluation, the manager will also gain confidence not only in organizational performance but also in his own abilities, including the ability to conduct successful evaluations.

Program Profile

A useful way to begin the evaluation of a program is to draw up a **program profile** (Owen, 1993). Such a profile is actually a description of the program, including background information, the structure and processes of the program, and expected outcomes and impacts. The background information should outline the genesis of and reasons for creating the program, its scope and objectives, the population it serves or the market it targets, and the amount of resources assigned to the program.

The profile should also describe:

- the activities chosen for the delivery of the program and the interrelationships among them
- the personnel involved in the program
- the distribution of responsibilities and authority among the personnel (who does what, who is responsible for what, and who reports to whom).

The final section of a program profile should describe the expected outcomes and the impact of those outcomes.

The advantages of drawing up a program profile are twofold. First, the evaluator gains some insight into the logic of the program. **Program logic** refers to the interrelatedness among the objectives, activities, personnel, structure, and expected outcomes of the program. The connections among these factors must be based on correct reasoning. If the evaluator finds any inconsistencies in the logic of the program, this would suggest redesigning the program to eliminate the flaws in the logic.

The second benefit of a program profile is that it distinguishes the structural and process attributes of the program from the expected outcomes. That is, the focus of evaluation could be on (a) whether the program was implemented as it was designed or (b) whether the program achieved what it was supposed to achieve. A program profile makes it easier to focus on evaluating the processes, the outcomes, or both. In essence, a program profile shows if (a) the goals and objectives of the program are meaningful and attainable, (b) the links between ends and means are strong, and (c) the cause–effect relationships within the program are sound (Wholey, 1981).

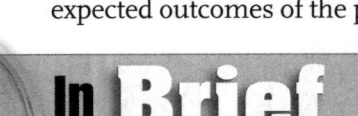

In Brief

A program profile outlines the genesis of the program and its goals, the resources assigned to it, the activities to be carried out, and the expected outcomes. It also highlights the relationships among the goals, resources, processes, and outcomes.

Standards of Evaluation

Earlier, in discussing the purposes of program evaluation, we identified the benefits of such evaluation. While that discussion established the reasons for evaluating programs, it is also critical to decide on the standards by which a

> **Sidebar**
>
> In discussing the measurement of the impact of sponsorship, Horn and Baker (1999) suggest the following questions be asked:
>
> 1. What was the business objective? Was it increased sales, volumes, shares, or prices?
> 2. What was the target audience? Was it customers, key accounts, vendors, financial institutions, investors, community and civic organizations, or employees?
> 3. What was the desired action on the part of the audience? Was it trial of a new brand, in-home consumption of a brand, change in beliefs about or perceptions of a brand?
> 4. What did happen? How far did the desired actions go?
> 5. What were the reasons for the results, either good or bad?
> 6. What have we learned from the experience, and what will we do better next time?

program will be judged to be effective **(standards of evaluation).** For instance, if a person clears 6 feet in the high jump, how do we judge that performance? What standards should we apply in making that judgment? The standards could be others' performances, the individual's own resources (height), the training time and expenses, or the goals that were set earlier (for example, the goal of clearing 5'9" versus 6'3"). Thus the final determination about the high jumper's performance depends on the standards we choose to apply. The same issue often comes up in program evaluation. Theobald (1987) provided a historical account of the various standards that have been used in evaluating leisure programs and services. These are described in the following sections.

Meeting Objectives

A program by definition is intended to achieve certain objectives; therefore, a program's effectiveness can best be judged by the extent to which it **meets the objectives.** This is obviously a straightforward and logical approach. For instance, marketing efforts to boost attendance at volleyball games can be judged to be effective or not by the increase in the number of spectators. A sponsorship program can be evaluated on the basis of whether the program has met the commercial objectives of increased awareness of and positive attitudes toward the sponsor or its products; increased sales of the products; and media exposure due to sponsorship relative to the cost of equivalent advertising space or time (IEG, Inc., 1999). Similarly, the NCAA's gender equity initiatives and associated programs described earlier can be judged to be effective based on the degree to which they attain their objectives.

In fact, the NCAA has conducted five gender equity studies, in 1991, 1996, 1998, 2000, and 2002, with a view to evaluate its initiatives in this regard. The specific outcomes assessed include the proportion of female athletes in the three divisions of competitions, proportion of scholarship dollars offered to females, proportion of operating expenses for women's programs, proportion of recruiting expenses for women's programs, and comparative budgets for salaries of coaches and assistant coaches. Cedric W. Dempsey, the then NCAA president, noted that while the NCAA has made some progress (about 9 percent improvement in women's participation), it still needs to do a lot more to increase women's participation and the resources devoted to women's sports (NCAA, 1999). Despite the moderate gains, women's athletic programs continue to lag behind men's programs.

However, the attainment of objectives cannot be adequately measured in all cases. Take, for example, a program of instruction and guidance to cultivate sportsmanship, citizenship, or awareness about drug abuse. It will be very hard to judge whether the athletes have in fact changed their attitudes and behavior because of the program. In such cases, the standard of achieving the objectives may not be so meaningful.

Standards Set by Experts

In many instances, experts from among scholars and practitioners may decide that if a program is to be effective in achieving its stated purposes, it must include certain processes and be structured in specific ways. For example, expert scholars from the North American Society for Sport Management (NASSM) and the National Association for Sport and Physical Education (NASPE) have specified minimum standards for degree programs in sport management. The standards with reference to the number and type of courses offered and the number of professors involved in the degree programs at the bachelor's, master's, and doctoral levels are outlined in Exhibit 12.3.

Any college or university with degree programs in sport management may apply to NASSM/NASPE for certification as a recognized degree program. After careful scrutiny of the course offerings, their content, and the number of professors involved, and purposeful visitations and interviews, NASSM/NASPE may extend certification to the university. This is generally the case with many educational programs. The colleges or universities themselves also have their own structures and procedures for sanctioning a degree program or a course. In the example of the guidance program for athletes cited above, it is a common practice for a group of experts to judge what should be included in the program, how it should be delivered, and who should do it.

Professional Judgment

Another standard of evaluation is **professional judgment**. That is, one or more professionals may be asked to determine whether a program is effective. In making their judgments, they will focus more on the outcomes than on the structure and processes of the program. This is in contrast to the "standard of norms" cited above, in which the focus is on the processes and not on the outcomes. In the example of sport management degree programs, experts may look at the knowledge gained by the students of a degree program or at their job placements. Experts may also observe the behavior of athletes in an athletic department's guidance program to judge whether the program was successful.

One of the objectives of the Kamloops Women's Action Project in the Canadian province of British Columbia is to enhance recreation opportunities for those living in poverty (Frisby, 1998). Accordingly, the organization offers three different programs at no cost: Self-Defense, Fun and Games for Moms & Preschoolers, and Fun & Friendly Fitness. The project has laid out several ways of evaluating the success of these programs. One of these ways is for leaders and experts to visit the

Exhibit 12.3 The 2000 NASSM/NASPE guidelines for sport management degree programs.

DEGREE	CRITICAL MASS CURRICULUM	REQUIRED CONTENT AREAS	NUMBER OF FACULTY
Bachelor's	20% of the total course work (exclusive of field experience credit) required for the bachelor's degree should be sport management courses offered in the home unit.	Socio-Cultural Dimensions in Sport Management and Leadership in Sport Ethics in Sport Management Marketing in Sport Communication in Sport Budget and Finance in Sport Legal Aspects of Sport Economics in Sport Governance in Sport Field Experience in Sport Management	Two
Master's	50% of the total course work (exclusive of field experience credit) required for the master's degree should be sport management courses offered in the home unit.	Socio-Cultural Context of Sport Management and Leadership in Sport Ethics in Sport Management Marketing in Sport Public Relations in Sport Financial Management in Sport Legal Aspects of Sport Research in Sport Field Experience in Sport Management	Two (Three for both bachelor's and master's degrees)
Doctoral	50% of the total course work (exclusive of field experience credit) required for the doctoral degree should be sport management courses offered in the home unit.	*All the above experiences plus:* Research Foundations Sport Management Theory in an area of specialization Advanced Cognate Area Field Experiences	Two for doctoral and three for master's
All Combined			Five

centers where these programs are offered. These leaders/experts observe the interactions (including facial expressions and body gestures) among the participants, instructors, and volunteers; listen to their casual comments; and note any conflicts or issues that may arise. Judgments about the program based on these observations would be labeled professional judgments.

Socioeconomic Evaluation

Some programs are instituted to serve the public at large equitably. For instance, a city recreation department may embark on enhancing its recreational facilities and its sports programs to the public. Any judgment of the program's effectiveness should consider whether the extensions of the facilities and services were related to the needs of all the different communities. For example, the population density and the social and economic status of the communities within the city reflect the needs of those communities. Thus, if the recreation department has distributed its facilities and services in relation to these needs, the program may be judged to be effective. This is called **socioeconomic evaluation**.

Accessibility and Safety

When a program is established for the benefit of the public or a segment of it, it is important that the program be accessible to all those who are entitled to those services. An obvious example is that it is now law that the facilities of a university be accessible to persons with disabilities. In the university where I teach, professors are required to state at the beginning of their course outlines that alternate formats of the course outline are available on request for those whose vision is impaired. In addition, the safety standards for the equipment and facilities in a fitness club or a weight training room in an athletic department, for example, are important in evaluating the respective programs.

> A cost-effectiveness analysis does not produce a 'bottom line' number, with benefits exceeding costs or costs exceeding benefits. If a program costs $1 million and produces 10 units of outcome X, 12 units of outcome Y, and 20 units of outcome Z, how is the evaluator to make a judgment concerning the cost-effectiveness of the program? The question for the decision maker is whether the outcomes produced are worth the $1 million expenditure.
>
> KEE, 1994, p. 459

Cost–Benefit

A standard often applied to programs is the cost–benefit analysis. The essence of this standard is that the benefits accruing from a program should exceed the costs of the program. We noted earlier the example of a program of licensing concessions as a means of generating revenue for an intercollegiate athletic program. This program certainly will cost some money in terms of building the concessions and maintaining them, administration and staffing, and legal fees in monitoring and enforcing the licensing agreements. If the revenues do not exceed the costs, then the program is judged to be ineffective. This is a straightforward business proposition. However, a monetary value cannot be assigned to the outcomes of many programs. Take the case of the drug education program of the NCAA. Assuming that the program costs $500,000, what value do we place on the redemption of a person from drug abuse? What value do we place on a life saved? When strict monetary values cannot be assigned to a benefit or outcome, a cost–benefit analysis would be inappropriate.

Cost-Effectiveness

In the above example of the drug education program, we said that we cannot place a dollar value on recovery from drug abuse (or a life saved), and, therefore, cost–benefit analysis would be meaningless. True enough, but it cannot be denied that the program may indeed redeem a certain number of athletes from drug abuse. For instance, if the incidence of drug abuse has fallen to 50 from 100 in recent years, we can confidently say that the program was successful even though its costs were high. Here our concern lies with the number of athletes who have given up drugs and not with the dollar value of "not using drugs." That is, the program was effective in the sense it helped 50 athletes give up drug use. If another program can be shown to save the same number of athletes from drug use at a cost of only $250,000, then the second program would be more cost-effective.

There is currently a debate over the privatization of the educational system. In most of the discussions, the arguments focus on how much it would cost per graduating student (cost-effectiveness discussions). The number of students graduating is compared to the costs. In such arguments, the quality of education takes a backseat, not because people are uninterested in quality, but because it is hard to judge quality and to put a dollar value on it.

To extend the argument to intercollegiate athletics, how can we judge whether a program of study tables and tutoring is effective? Judgment is usually made on the basis of number of athletes graduating. While everybody may be truly concerned with the quality of education received by the athletes, there is no effort to evaluate the quality. The issue is simply whether an alternate program would result in the same or better graduation rates at a lower cost.

Can we calculate the monetary benefits of a parks and playground program of a city recreation department? Theobald (1987) refers to the economic equivalency index (EEI), which is calculated as follows:

EEI = number of participants
x hours of participation
x minimum wage

From a different perspective, we could argue that the value derived through the above formula could be treated as a cost incurred by the participants rather than a benefit to them.

Client Satisfaction

A final, and perhaps the most important, standard that can be applied to a program is **client satisfaction**. If a program is carried out for the benefit of specific groups, then it stands to reason that those clients should be the ultimate arbiters of the program. This is the central argument offered by proponents of total quality management and service quality management (see Goetsch, 1994; Schneider & Bowen, 1995; Zeithaml, Parasuraman, & Berry, 1990).

In the context of sport, Chelladurai and Riemer (1997) and Riemer and Chelladurai (1998) have argued that the success of intercollegiate athletics should be based on the satisfaction of athletes in various facets of their experience in athletics, mainly because the athletes are the prime beneficiaries or clients of intercollegiate athletics. The evaluators of a program could develop a survey to gauge clients' reactions to specific attributes of a program. This was the approach taken by Riemer and Chelladurai in developing the Athlete Satisfaction Questionnaire (ASQ). The ASQ has 56 items to measure 15 facets of athlete satisfaction. Examples of the items and their facets include: How the team works to be the best (team's task contribution), competencies of the medical personnel (medical personnel), the extent to which all team members are ethical (team ethics), the funding provided to a team (budget), the training received from the coach (training and instruction), and the academic support services provided (academic support services).

Such information can also be gathered through well-designed interviews with selected clients. We might assemble a group of clients together and let them discuss the various attributes of a program. This latter technique, known as the focus group, would identify the benefits from the clients' viewpoint. It would also reveal which of the processes or activities of the program are seen to be efficient and useful, and which are not. For instance, the city recreation department, in evaluating its sports program for wheelchair athletes, may assemble some of the participants for a focus group session. In such a session, participants will describe what they enjoyed about the program and what they disliked about it. They may also be encouraged to suggest new elements that might be added to the program and what elements might be eliminated. Such free discussions among clients would yield valuable insights into the program and its effectiveness. Of course, such discussions need to be moderated by someone well versed in focus group techniques.

Thus, evaluators have a choice of means of assessing clients' reactions to a program and its attributes.

SUMMARY

This chapter emphasized the significance of evaluating an organization's programs of activities. After defining a program as a set of resources and activities designed to achieve a narrow set of goals, we contrasted performance appraisal (evaluation of individual performance) with organizational effectiveness (evaluation of organizational performance). We noted that the concepts of program and program evaluation are applicable to all organizations—public and private, profit and nonprofit, large and small. A program was also described as a system in itself, consisting of inputs, throughputs, and outputs. After this, the chapter outlined the purposes of program evaluation and described the standards that can be employed to evaluate programs. These included meeting objectives, standards set by experts, professional judgment, socioeconomic evaluation, accessibility and safety, cost–benefit evaluation, and cost-effectiveness.

DEVELOPING YOUR PERSPECTIVES

1. Identify a sport-related program you are familiar with, and describe its profile in terms of its objectives, activities, finances, and outcomes.
2. Referring to the program you have described, discuss the logic of the program (cause–effect and means/ends relationships).
3. Can you place a monetary value on the benefits of the program? Explain.
4. Bearing in mind the distinction between cost–benefit evaluation and cost-effectiveness evaluation, identify sport-related programs that could be subjected to either of these evaluations.
5. Consider the economic equivalency index (EEI) suggested by Theobald (1987). Discuss its merits from the perspective of program evaluation.
6. What are your reactions to the guidelines for sport management degree programs outlined in Exhibit 12.3? Do you agree with the standards? Why? What other standards would you suggest? Why? Do we need a certification program?

References

Affholter, D. P. (1994). Outcome monitoring. In J. S. Wholey, H. P. Hatry, & K. E. Newcomer (Eds.), *Handbook of practical program evaluation* (pp. 96–118). San Francisco: Jossey-Bass.

Chelladurai, P. (1999). *Human resource management in sport and recreation.* Champaign, IL: Human Kinetics.

Chelladurai, P., & Riemer, H. A. (1997). A classification of facets of athlete satisfaction. *Journal of Sport Management, 11,* 133–159.

Farley, M. (1984). Program evaluation as political tool. *Journal of Physical Education, Recreation, and Dance,* 64–67.

Frisby, W. (1998). *Leisure access: Enhancing recreation opportunities for those living in poverty.* Vancouver, BC: British Columbia Health Research Foundation.

Goetsch, D. L. (1994). *Introduction to total quality: Quality, productivity, competitiveness.* New York: Macmillan.

Horn, M., & Baker, K. (1999). Measuring the impact of sponsorship. *International Journal of Sport Marketing and Sponsorship, 3* (1), 296–301.

IEG, Inc. (1999). *IEG's Complete Guide to Sponsorship.* Chicago: Author.

Kee, J. E. (1994). Benefit–cost analysis in program evaluation. In J. S. Wholey, H. P. Hatry, & K. E. Newcomer (Eds.), *Handbook of practical program evaluation* (pp. 456–491). San Francisco: Jossey-Bass.

Kestner, J. L. (1996). *Program evaluation for sport directors.* Champaign, IL: Human Kinetics.

Myers, A. M. (1999). *Program evaluation for exercise leaders.* Champaign, IL: Human Kinetics.

NCAA (2002). www.ncaa.org/news/2002/20020401/active/3907n03.html. Retrieved on November 2, 2004.

NCAA (1999). www.ncaa.org/edout. Retrieved on November 1, 1999.

Newcomer, K. E., Hatry, H. P., & Wholey, J. S. (1994). Meeting the need for practical evaluation approaches: An introduction. In J. S. Wholey, H. P. Hatry, & K. E. Newcomer (Eds.), *Handbook of practical program evaluation* (pp. 1–10). San Francisco: Jossey-Bass.

Owen, J. M. (1993). *Program evaluation: Forms and approaches.* St. Leonards, NSW, Australia: Allen & Unwin.

President's Council on Physical Fitness and Sports. (November 1, 1999) [On-line]. Available: www.indiana.edu/~~preschal.

Riemer, H. A., & Chelladurai, P. (1998). Development of athlete satisfaction questionnaire (ASQ). *Journal of Sport and Exercise Psychology, 20,* 127–156.

Royse, D., & Thyer, B. A. (1996). *Program Evaluation: An Introduction.* Chicago: Nelson-Hall.

Scheirer, M. A. (1994). Designing and using process evaluation. In J. S. Wholey, H. P. Hatry, & K. E. Newcomer (Eds.), *Handbook of practical program evaluation* (pp. 40–68). San Francisco: Jossey-Bass.

Schneider, B., & Bowen, D. E. (1995). *Winning the service game.* Boston: Harvard Business School Press.

Spindler, Z.A. (2003). How "parasites" serve their host: A graphical analysis of of "scalping." *Public Finance Review, 31* (6), 694–699.

Swofford, J.L. (2003). A graphical analysis of "scalping": A reply. *Public Finance Review, 31* (6), 700–704.

Theobald, W. (1987). Historical antecedents of evaluation in leisure programs and services. *Journal of Park and Recreation Administration, V,* 1–8.

Treasury Board of Canada–Comptroller General (May 1981). *Guide on the program evaluation function.* Ottawa, ON: Minister of Supply and Services Canada.

Wholey, J. S. (September, 1981). Using evaluations to improve program performance. *The Bureaucrat, 20* (2), 55–59.

Zeithaml, V. A., Parasuraman, A., & Berry, L. L. (1990). *Delivering service quality: Balancing customer perceptions and expectations.* New York: Free Press.

CHAPTER 13

Organizational Effectiveness

MANAGE YOUR LEARNING

After completing this chapter you should be able to:

- Explain the concept of organizational effectiveness and the complexities associated with it.
- Distinguish between the multidimensional and the multiple-perspectives aspects of organizational effectiveness.
- Explain the differences and the relationships among the goals, system resource, and process models of organizational effectiveness.
- Understand the relationships between values and organizational effectiveness.
- Discuss the issue of the primacy of multiple perspectives of organizational effectiveness.
- Debate the utility of the "prime beneficiary" approach to organizational effectiveness.

STRATEGIC CONCEPTS

competing values
evolutionary perspective
goals model
human relations model
internal process model
multidimensionality
multiple constituencies
multiple perspectives
open system model

organizational effectiveness
organizational paradox
power perspective
prime beneficiary
process model
rational goal model
relativistic perspective
social justice perspective
system resource model

As was pointed out in Chapter 4, evaluating is defined as the process of assessing the degree to which the organization as a whole and various units and individuals have accomplished what they set out to do. It was also pointed out that the four managerial functions—planning, organizing, leading, and evaluating—must be considered as ongoing processes that are intricately intertwined with each other. Thus, the planning process sets the stage for organizational initiatives while the evaluating function provides the rationale for the revision or reorganization of organizational activities. From this perspective, evaluating is critical to the management of any organization.

Evaluating, as defined above, is a broad concept encompassing the organization as a whole, the units within it, and its members. Theorists and practitioners have traditionally distinguished between the evaluation of the organization and its units—organizational effectiveness and program evaluation—and evaluation of individual performances—performance evaluation. Since this text is concerned with macro issues relating to sport and recreation organizations, only the concepts of program evaluation and organizational effectiveness are examined. We studied program evaluation in the last chapter, and now we will look at organizational effectiveness.

It is important to note that although the successes of the various programs may contribute to the effectiveness of the total organization, organizational effectiveness is a larger concept. As Herman and Renz (1999) noted, "an organization is not the sum of its parts or functions. It is possible to assess the effectiveness of a program or the use of service volunteers in an organization; however, such assessments do not necessarily reveal much about overall organizational effectiveness" (p. 108).

> **To Recap**
>
> **PROGRAM EVALUATION** As noted in Chapter 12, those activities intended to achieve a specific goal or set of goals are grouped together as a program. Evaluation of a program consists of determining whether (a) the program has achieved its goals, (b) the activities were carried out in accordance with specifications, and (c) the objectives were achieved because of the program and its activities or because of something else.

EFFECTIVENESS AND EFFICIENCY

The terms *effectiveness* and *efficiency* are often used interchangeably. However, from an organizational perspective, they are quite different (see Etzioni, 1964; Ostroff & Schmitt, 1993; Steers & Black, 1994). As Steers and Black (1994) noted, "*Effectiveness* is the extent to which operative goals can be attained; *efficiency* is the cost/benefit ratio incurred in the pursuit of those goals" (p. 330). An example from the athletic field serves to illustrate this distinction. A 6-foot-tall individual might clear 6 feet in the high jump while a 5-foot, 6-inch-tall individual might clear 5 feet, 10 inches. The taller individual is more effective because she cleared 2 inches more than the other person. However, the shorter individual is more efficient because the height cleared (goal achieved) was greater in relation to personal height (resources).

For another example, consider two comparable sport marketing firms A and B. Both had set the goal of making a $200,000 profit in a year. If Firm A makes the $200,000 and Firm B makes only $175,000, Firm A would be considered more effective because it attained its goal or because it made more profit than Firm B. However, when we consider that Firm A invested $2 million dollars while Firm B invested only $1.5 million, we can make a different judgment. Because Firm B had a better rate of return on its capital than Firm A, Firm B would be considered more efficient than Firm A. These two evaluations are illustrated in Exhibit 13.1. Thus, *effectiveness* and *efficiency* are distinct concepts, and we should avoid the tendency to use them synonymously.

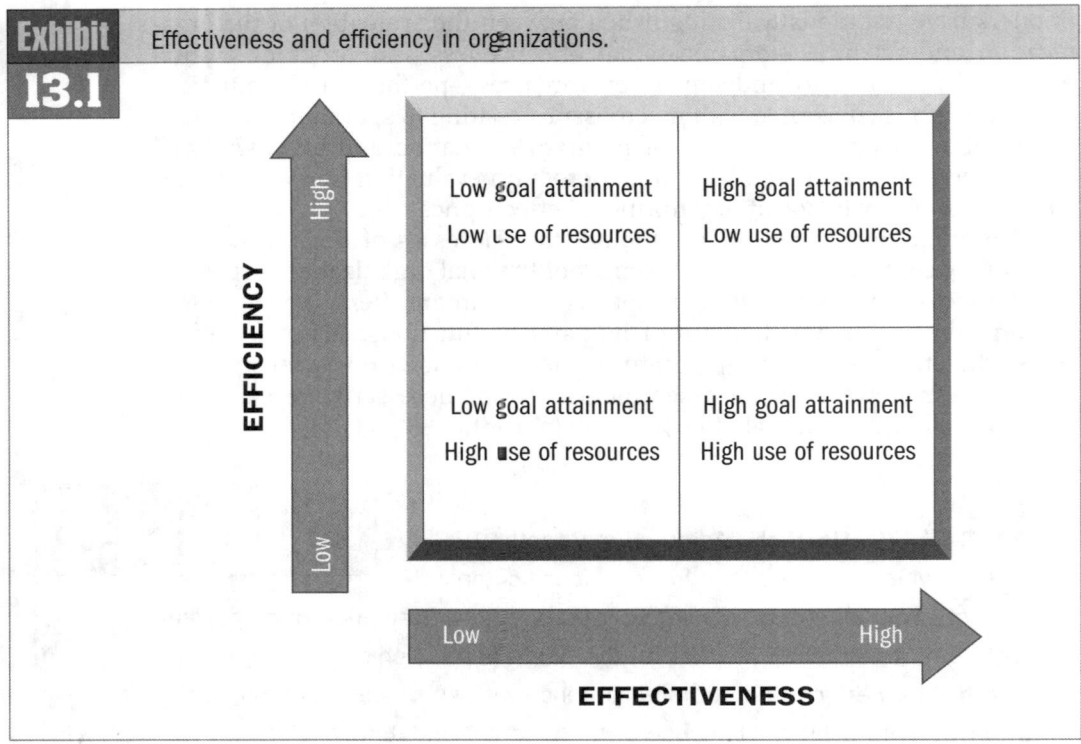

Exhibit 13.1 Effectiveness and efficiency in organizations.

It is, however, conceivable that an organization may set efficiency itself as a goal. For example, a university athletic department, concerned with revenue generation, may embark on a campaign of seeking donations. At the same time, it may also set a second goal of reducing its expenses while keeping the same levels of service and performance. The latter effort is aimed at making operations more efficient. If the department becomes more efficient, then it will be considered to be effective insofar as that objective is concerned. Many profit-oriented organizations are oriented toward efficiency in order to maximize their profits. For our purposes here, it is useful to consider the two concepts—effectiveness and efficiency—as separate entities while treating the attainment of efficiency as a measure of effectiveness (if indeed that was the goal of the organization).

In Brief

Effectiveness refers to the attainment of a goal, whereas efficiency refers to the ratio of cost to benefits of achieving the goal. Organizations may set efficiency as a goal in itself.

ORGANIZATIONAL EFFECTIVENESS: THE ULTIMATE CONCERN

Organizational effectiveness is the ultimate dependent variable in any organizational analysis. Organizations, as noted earlier, are social entities that set out to achieve certain purposes. All of the managerial functions and processes discussed in the preceding

> **Sidebar**
>
> Robbins and Coulter (1996) defined management as "the process of getting activities completed efficiently and effectively with and through other people" (p. 8). They expanded on this definition by saying, "Efficiency is a vital part of management. It refers to the relationship between inputs and outputs. If you can get more output from the given inputs, you have increased efficiency. Similarly, if you can get the same output from less input, you also have increased efficiency. Since managers deal with input resources that are scarce—mainly people, money, and equipment—they are concerned with the efficient use of these resources. Management, therefore, is concerned with minimizing resource costs. Efficiency is often referred to as 'doing things right.'
>
> "However, it is not enough simply to be efficient. Management is also concerned with getting activities completed; that is, it seeks effectiveness. When managers achieve their organization's goals, we say they are effective. Effectiveness can be described as 'doing the right things.' So efficiency is concerned with means and effectiveness with ends." (p. 8)

chapters are aimed at reaching the specified ends. Thus, whether those purposes are achieved or not is critical to the analysis of an organization and its management. That is why both scholars and practitioners consider organizational effectiveness the bottom-line concern of all managerial activities.

Despite its importance, organizational effectiveness is, perhaps, the most controversial and complex concept in management. A number of authors have studied organizational effectiveness from different perspectives and with different criteria (see Campbell, 1977; Robbins, 1990; Steers, 1975; Steers & Black, 1994). Some have used a single criterion of effectiveness while others have used multiple criteria. Some have approached the problem from a normative perspective (what *ought to be*). This perspective simply reflects the theoretical expectations for an organization. Other authors have taken a descriptive approach (what *is*).

Thus, as summaries of the literature suggest, the effectiveness concept has proved to be imprecise—there is no consensus on its definition or, therefore, on its measurement (e.g., Campbell, 1977; Molnar & Rogers, 1976; Robbins, 1990; Steers, 1975; Steers & Black, 1994). It is possible, however, to reconcile the various theoretical orientations toward organizational effectiveness and produce a gestalt view of the construct. This is the approach adopted in this book.

Specifically, the five significant models of organizational effectiveness—the *goals model*, the *system resource model*, the *process model*, the *multiple constituency model*, and the *competing values approach*—are examined within the general framework of a systems perspective. (Chapter 3 contains a lengthy discussion of the systems view of organizations.) To facilitate the discussion of the first four models, the input–throughput–output model of a system is reproduced in Exhibit 13.2. The figure also shows how the various models of effectiveness relate to the specific elements of the input–throughput–output cycle of an open system.

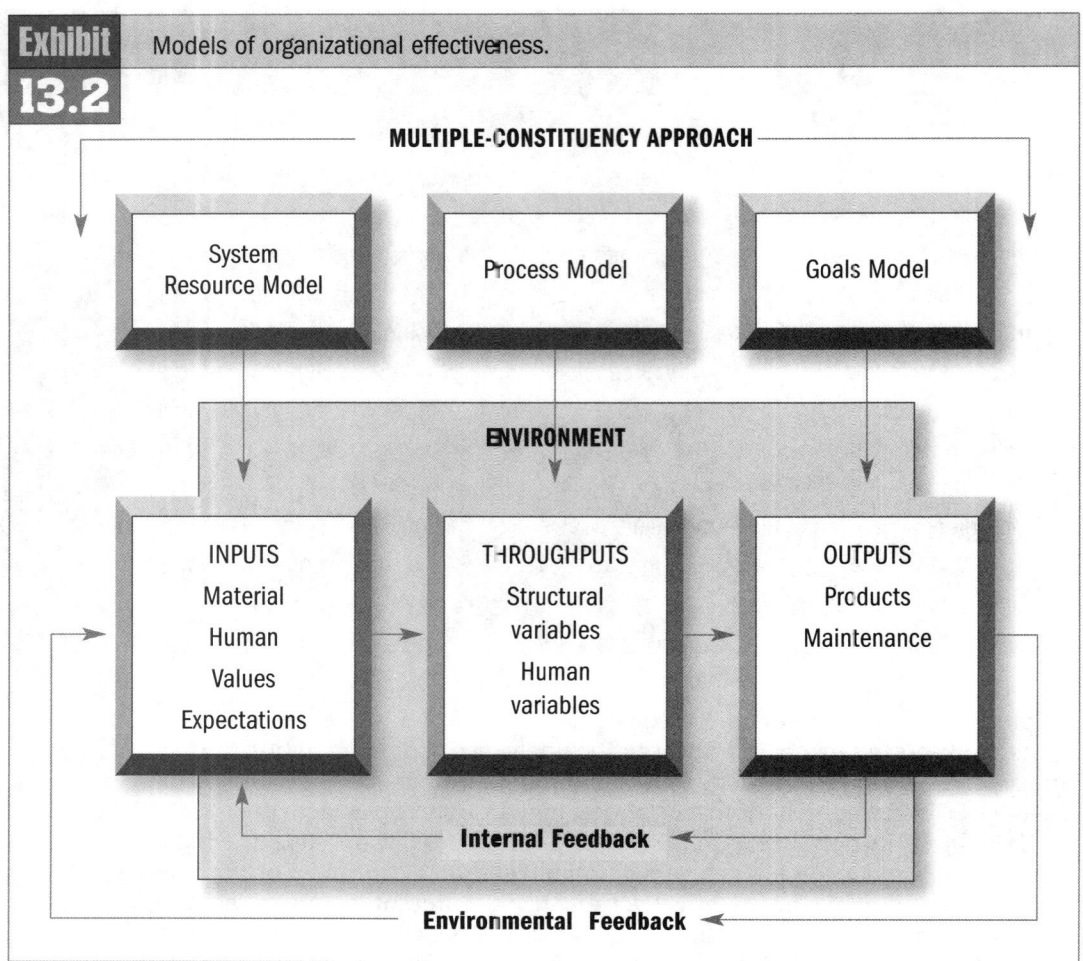

Exhibit 13.2 Models of organizational effectiveness.

GOALS MODEL

The most fundamental approach to the study of organizational effectiveness is suggested in the description provided above. In the **goals model**, effectiveness is the degree to which an organization has achieved its goals (Etzioni, 1964; Price, 1972). Implicit in this definition is the assumption that because organizations exist to achieve some specific purpose, an organization's effectiveness is a function of the degree to which it has achieved those goals. Thus, if a fitness firm has established making a specific amount of profit as its goal, and by the end of the year it has made that profit, it can be described as an effective organization.

Similarly, a national sport governing body might set a goal that its national team will be ranked in the top 10 in the world within a two-year period. If the team is only ranked 15th at the end of that period, it can be considered an ineffective organization. Many university athletic departments set the goal for their teams to finish the season in the top half of their respective leagues. A team (and the entire department) will be considered effective if it reaches that plateau and ineffective if it does not.

Two underlying conditions for the goals model of effectiveness become evident from the examples given above. The first is that a goal must be identifiable. In the two examples, the goals were the set amount of profit for the fitness firm and the world ranking for the sport governing body. The second condition is that organizational performance must be clearly measurable. Thus, there is no difficulty in measuring the profit made by the fitness firm or the world ranking attained by the sport governing body. In other words, in the two examples, the criteria of effectiveness are crystallized (goals are clear and precise), and they are also observable and measurable (Hasenfeld, 1983). While the goals model is intuitively appealing, the two conditions behind the model—clarity of goals and measurement of goal attainment—may not be valid for all types of organizations.

Need for Clear Goals

As we noted in Chapter 5, many organizations tend to proclaim their goals in broad, global terms. That is, their goals are designed to delineate a domain of activity, and their charters and official notifications are formulated to rationalize their existence and to justify support from the larger community (Perrow, 1961). However, global statements (official goals in Perrow's terminology) do not provide a focus for organizational analysis. In other words, if you did not specify where you wanted to go in the first place, how can you know whether you have arrived?

Price (1972), while acknowledging the difficulty of identifying organizational goals, suggested that there are ways to overcome this limitation. For example, he felt that it is possible to identify the real, or operative, goals of the organization by focusing on the major decision makers. Their statements and their decisions regarding major organizational processes (like budgeting and staffing) should reveal the organization's priorities. Price also argued that the actual activities of the organization and its members will clearly reveal what goals are sought by the organization. We noted in Chapter 5 that operative goals can be identified through an analysis of organizational processes and the decisions relating to them. For example, when a university athletic department fires a coach after a losing season without considering his accomplishments in other aspects of coaching, it can be inferred that winning is important to that department despite all protestations to the contrary.

Although Price's proposals have some merit, there are problems in their implementation. For example, Price's assumption that there will be consensus among the major decision makers on the goals for an organization may not be true in all cases (see Lawrence & Lorsch, 1967; Robbins, 1990; Steers & Black, 1994). Also, as we noted in Chapter 5, an organization's operative goals may not remain stable over time. Insofar as the major decision makers may have fluctuating preferences, and insofar as their power to influence decisions is subject to change (this reflects the notion of dominance of coalitions referred to in Chapter 6), the operative goals of an organization also might shift. Thus, it might not be possible to obtain the clarity and focus necessary to apply the goals model.

Many organizations pursue multiple goals, and this factor also limits the utility of a goals model approach for the analysis of organizational effectiveness. For instance, the sport governing body of the previous example might have two goals—to increase the number of its registered clubs and to improve its world ranking. These two goals are reflected in the two programs usually referred to as mass sport and elite sport. Prior to assessing the relative goal attainment of the organization, it would be necessary to know the relative weight attached to each goal (that is, the relative importance of the two programs).

The problem of multiple goals is further complicated by the fact that some organizational goals can be in conflict with each other (see Chapter 5). When this is the case, the attainment of one goal may contribute to a failure to attain the second. That is, the organization would be effective in terms of one goal but would be ineffective in terms of the conflicting goal. For example, in the case of an intercollegiate athletic program, the goal of promoting a large number of sports and the goal of winning national championships in many sports might not be attainable simultaneously within the context of budgeting constraints. This issue of multiple and conflicting goals is not addressed by the goals model.

Need for Measurable Goals

The second assumption of the goals model is that the outcomes of the organization can be measured and compared against the priority established for the goals. However, objectively measuring outputs (i.e., goal attainment) is a problem in service organizations. For example, many university athletic departments state that one of their goals is to develop their athletes to be worthy citizens. It should be obvious that it is not possible to determine with any validity the degree to which this goal is attained or approached. Similarly, the university as a whole may have as its goal, "the education of youth." Again, this goal is not easily quantifiable. In the same vein, a sport governing body (say, that of soccer) may set as one of its goals the cultivation of an appreciation for the sport among the public. The attainment of this goal is not easily measurable.

To the extent goals are intangible and their attainment is not easily measured, the goals model appears to have little utility. This issue extends to services in general because they are intangible, and, therefore, the quality of services cannot be easily ascertained. Thus, the problem of measuring outputs is acute in all service organizations, particularly in professional service organizations.

Substitution of Surrogate Measures

Given the difficulty of measuring intangible goals, it is not uncommon for organizations to use some quantitative measures as indicators of qualitative outcomes. For example, quantitative measures such as the number of graduating students or students' scores on standardized tests are often used by educational institutions as indicators of their effectiveness. In our own context, the percentage of graduating athletes is often used as a measure of the effectiveness of university athletic departments.

As Hoy and Miskel (1982) point out, assessing school (or athletic department) effectiveness through such measures is based more on expediency than on theory. That is, such quantitative measures are readily available and easily understood by those who demand "accountability" by the schools or departments. Although such measures are significant by themselves, they may not indicate effectiveness in terms of educating the youth. For example, the number of students graduating might be simply a reflection of lower standards. Standardized tests measuring cognitive skills are just that. They do not measure criteria in the affective domain, like "motivation, creativity, self-confidence, and aspirations—all of which are needed for future success in school and adult life" (Hoy & Miskel, 1982, p. 330).

In overview, the goals model focuses on the degree to which a goal is attained as a measure of effectiveness. Consequently, it is meaningful in organizations where goals are specific and clearly articulated, where they are stable over time, and where organizational performance can be objectively measured. Those organizations that possess these characteristics tend to adopt the goals model because it is rational.

> **In Brief**
>
> In the goals model of effectiveness, goal attainment is the criterion of effectiveness. The model is useful only to the extent that goals are specific and unambiguous and goal attainment can be easily measured.

When a professional sport team fires its coach, it is usually because the organization has not achieved its goal of winning a minimum number of games. Whatever else the coach might have accomplished is irrelevant. From the organization's point of view, the bottom line on effectiveness is the win–loss ratio. It is an output that is clear and easily measurable. Many organizations, however, either do not possess the luxury of clearly defined goals or have goals whose attainment cannot be objectively measured. When this is the case, other models of effectiveness must be employed.

SYSTEM RESOURCE MODEL

An alternate model of effectiveness, the **system resource model**, focuses on the inputs of the organization (see Exhibit 13.2). Yuchtman and Seashore (1967), who proposed this model, defined effectiveness as "the ability of the organization, in either absolute or relative terms, to exploit its environment in the acquisition of scarce and valued resources" (p. 898). Every organization must compete with other organizations for resources from the larger society. Thus, an effective organization is one that gains an advantageous bargaining position relative to other organizations that share the same environment. The significance of the organization's bargaining position in the context of its environment was highlighted in Chapter 8. It was suggested that the members of the institutional and managerial subsystems must be able to influence the elements in the distal and task environments respectively.

Consider the case of a university seeking large donations and government subsidies to finance the building of a new athletics arena. It has to compete with other universities and other nonprofit organizations in the region for donations and subsidies. According to the system resource model of effectiveness, the university will be considered effective if it secures the resources necessary for the construction of the arena. That, of course, is a function of the relative influence and bargaining power of the competing organizations. The case would be the same with professional sport franchises seeking financial support from municipal governments. They are competing with other elements in the environment for municipal dollars.

When a university assesses the relative superiority of its first-year students or the relative amount of research grants secured by its faculty, it has

Sidebar

The recently popular *resource based view* (RBV) of organizations focuses on the system resources model. The RBV holds that an organization can gain and sustain competitive advantage if it can garner critical resources and exploit those resources profitably (Barney, 1991, 1995). Resources are "all assets, capabilities, organizational processes, firm attributes, information, knowledge, etc. controlled by a firm that enable the firm to conceive of and implement strategies that improve its efficiency and effectiveness" (Barney, 1991, p. 101). According to Barney (1991, 1995), these resources can be *physical capital* (e.g., facilities, equipment, geographic location), *human capital* (e.g., the expertise and experience of managers, coaches, the talents of athletes), *organizational capital* (e.g., history, tradition, and culture of the university and its athletic department), or *financial capital* (e.g., reserves, debt, surplus revenue).

Resources are either *tangible* (e.g., facilities, raw materials, and other equipment), or *intangible* (e.g., organizational culture, reputation, and motivation of employees or players). As Carmeli (2004) noted, an organization can easily acquire tangible resources (or imitate them) and put them to various uses. In contrast, intangible resources take time to develop and cannot be easily imitated. Hence, "intangible, more than tangible, resources have potential for competitive advantage creation" (p. 112). For example, the sale of licensed merchandise is a source of income for many universities. Universities like the University of Notre Dame and the Ohio State University make more money through the sale of such merchandise than some other universities. This advantage is based not on the quality of the products (other universities produce equally good if not better quality merchandise) but on intangible resources such as university tradition and the loyalty of alumni and fans.

The criticalness of a given resource for competitive advantage is based on how *valuable, rare, imperfectly imitable,* and *hardly substitutable* it is (Barney, 1991). A resource is valuable only if it can contribute to organizational performance and goals. For instance, height of an individual as a resource may be very valuable in the context of basketball and volleyball, but it does not have any relevance to conducting research. Similarly, a large stadium is valuable only in the context of a football, baseball, or soccer competition; its value is suspect in the context of a hockey game.

The second attribute of resources that create competitive advantage is their rarity. If all organizations can have a resource (i.e., the resource is not rare), then a particular organization cannot gain a competitive advantage through that resource. For example, we can understand the significance of the 7-foot, 6-inch Yao Ming to the Houston Rockets basketball team. If there were hundreds of players as tall and talented as Yao, then his height would not be a rare resource—other teams could recruit such tall players and nullify the advantage Yao Ming provides for the Rockets. This explains why there is such intense and expensive effort to recruit or draft talented athletes.

Imperfect imitability refers to the inability of other organizations to imitate a given resource. It is not possible to imitate height in basketball, say, for example, by equipping players with stilts. Even if the rules would permit such a tactic, the players on the stilts could not be as fast or agile as Yao Ming.

The fourth attribute of a resource contributing to competitive advantage is low substitutability. That is, a basketball coach may exploit other resources (e.g., speed, skills, or strategies) to make up for lack of height and to nullify the advantages of height. Take the case of the NBA Championship series of 2004, which the Detroit Pistons won against the Los Angeles Lakers. The Pistons' coach, Larry Brown, employed strategies of "hustle and bustle" and of double-teaming or triple-teaming Shaq O'Neal and Kobe Bryant, the stars of the Lakers. In other words, the coach substituted the speed and agility of his players for Shaq's height and Kobe's shooting ability. According to Bacon (2004), "The Pistons transformed the game itself from a star-centered run-a-thon to a selfless, disciplined game of Brown ball" (p. 40).

The RBV framework has been the basis of studies in sport management. Smart and Wolfe (2000) noted that at that time the Penn State football program was very successful among Big 10 football programs (i.e., it had a sustainable competitive advantage over the other teams in the Big 10). They argued that physical resources (e.g., stadium, training facilities and equipment, dormitories, information management systems for recruiting and game analysis) and human resources (e.g., athletic ability of student–athletes, coaches' experience) were valuable but not rare among the Big 10 universities. They concluded that the Penn State football team's history, culture, and coaching staff's long tenure (i.e., organizational resources) were the sources of the sustained competitive advantage enjoyed by that program. Cunningham (2003) used the average of the coaches' salaries and the recruiting budget as indicators of human resources and found that this measure was related to the success of athletic programs as indicated by the Sears Directors' Cup scores. In another study, Cunningham and Sagas (2004) found that the coaching experience and racial diversity of coaching staff (strength of human resources) were related to football program success.

In a more comprehensive study, Won and Chelladurai (2005) investigated the influence of several types of resources contributing to competitive advantage in intercollegiate athletics with reference to two sets of outcomes—*athletic and academic performance*. They found that the intangible resources of an athletic department (e.g., athletic and academic reputation of the university) were the *contributing resources* that facilitated the generation of other more tangible resources (i.e., human and financial resources). The tangible resources were found to influence the attainment of athletic performance goals (i.e., winning record) and athlete development goals (i.e., graduation rates and gender equity).

adopted the perspective of the system resource model. Similarly, when coaches use the number and quality of athletes who tried out for the various teams or athletic administrators cite the season tickets sold as a measure of effectiveness, they are also using a system resource approach. By the same token, the athletic department itself may use the donations, endorsements, and sponsorships it receives as indicators of effectiveness.

System Resource versus Goals Model

It might appear at first glance that the goals model and the system resource model are significantly different—the former emphasizes the outputs of the organization, whereas the latter emphasizes the inputs. This is not the case, however. They are integrally linked if the organization is viewed as an open system. This idea of a link between the outputs of a system and its inputs is illustrated as the feedback loop from outputs to inputs (see Exhibits 3.2 and 13.2). That is, the feedback loop indicates the acceptability of organizational outputs and the availability of needed resources.

Any organization, as an open system, must be in a profitable exchange position with its environment. That is, it must be able to obtain essential inputs from the environment. However, this is possible on a continuing basis only when its outputs are acceptable to the environment. Thus, a measure of the degree to which the system is able to obtain its resources is, in fact, a measure of the acceptability and utility of its outputs. When large numbers of students wish to enroll in a particular university, it is presumed that the programs offered by that university are of high quality. Similarly, when clients select one tennis club over another, it is implied that the facilities and services in that club are superior.

In short, the quality of the services provided by organizations may be inferred from the quantity of demand for their services. These demands, in turn, translate into inputs for the organization. As another example, if a university athletic department is able to secure a large number of donations from the public, it is probably because the public appreciates what the department is doing and achieving. Thus, the system resource model quantifies one element (inputs) and uses it as a surrogate or substitute measure for another element (outputs), which is not as easily quantifiable (see Exhibit 13.3).

Obtaining System Resources as an Operative Goal

Viewed from a different perspective, an operative goal of an organization might be to obtain resources from the environment. Thus, measuring the extent of resource acquisition is the equivalent of measuring goal attainment. Yuchtman and Seashore (1967) made reference to this when they noted:

> The better the bargaining position of an organization, the more capable it is of attaining its varied and often transient goals [operative goals], and the more capable it is of allowing the attainment of personal goals of members. Processes of "goal formation" and "goal displacement" in organizations are thus seen not as defining ultimate criteria of effectiveness, but as strategies adopted by members for enhancing the bargaining position of their organization. (p. 898)

It is important to note the emphasis on "goal formation" and "goal displacement" in the above quote. Earlier we noted that the operative goals are set by the dominant coalition. The dominant coalition would, of course,

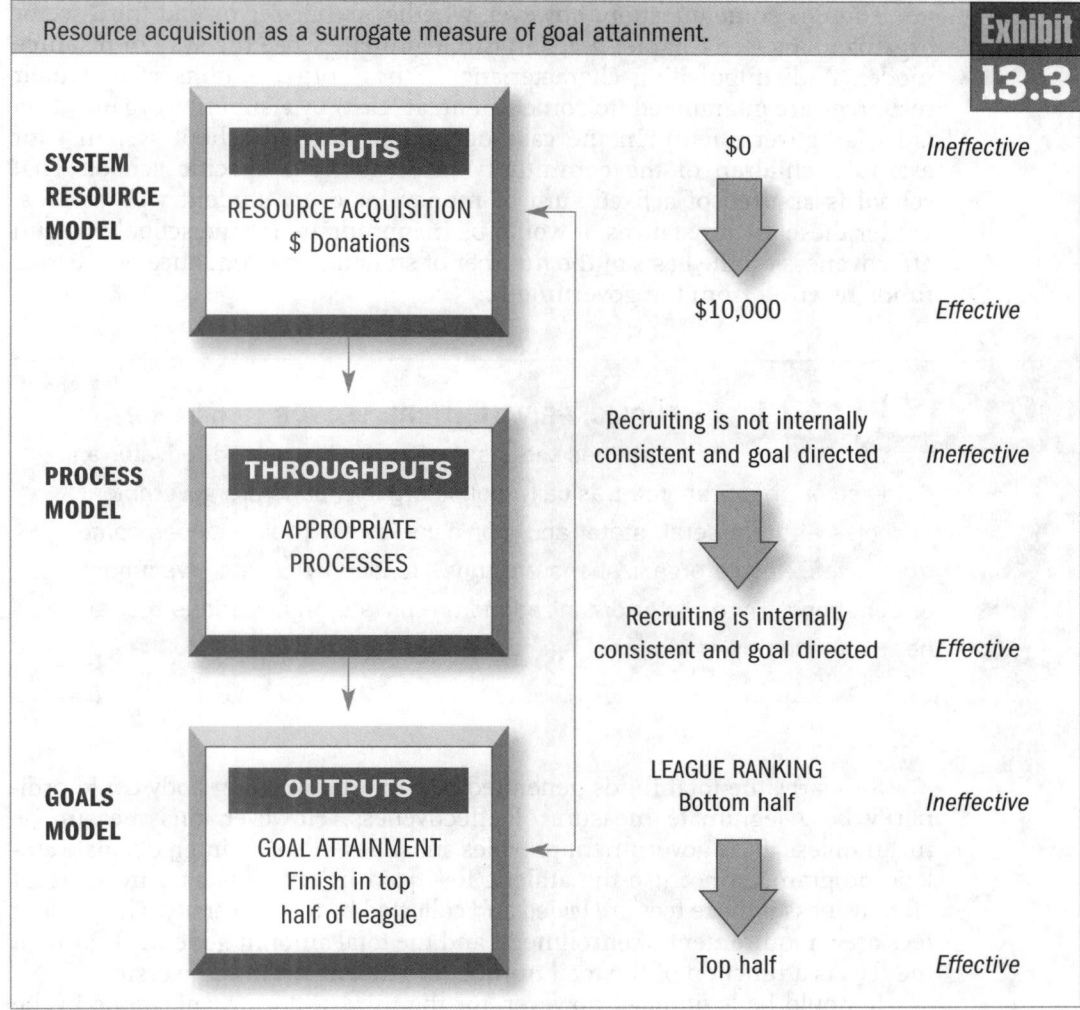

Exhibit 13.3 Resource acquisition as a surrogate measure of goal attainment.

include the resource providers, who would influence the formation or displacement of organizational goals.

Applicability of System Resource Model

When Yuchtman and Seashore outlined the system resource model of organizational effectiveness, they felt that it was valid and applicable to all organizations. It is true that the model provides a useful framework in many instances. For example, the system resource model is highly relevant for professional/human service organizations because their output cannot be objectively measured. Consequently, their effectiveness is best measured by the demand for their services. Similarly, the system resource model is also relevant for volunteer, nonprofit organizations. Their major source of funding is the contributions and donations of members of the larger community. Consequently, the degree to which these organizations are able to attract financial support is a measure of their effectiveness. The number of volunteers in the organization (input of human resources) is also an indicator of organizational effectiveness.

There is some question, however, whether public-sector and third-sector organizations (see Chapter 2 again) can legitimately use the system resource model. A distinguishing characteristic of these organizations is that their resources are guaranteed (to some extent, at least) by a superior organization (such as government). In the case of publicly funded school systems, for example, children of the community must attend a specific school. That school is assured of a fixed sum of money for every student who attends. Under these circumstances, it would be inappropriate for the school to claim effectiveness on the basis of the number of students in attendance or the total funds received from the government.

To Recap

PUBLIC, PRIVATE, THIRD SECTOR Chapter 2 described the distinctions among public, private, and third-sector organizations. Basically, public organizations are government agencies at the federal, state, and municipal levels. Their finances come from taxes. Private organizations are those funded by private investments or donations. Third-sector organizations are private organizations that are heavily funded by government agencies.

Similarly, the total funds generated by a sport governing body could ordinarily be a legitimate measure of effectiveness. However, this measure is meaningless if the government provides subsidies. Also, an intercollegiate athletic program cannot use the athletic fees paid by students as a measure of effectiveness if those fees are levied and collected by the university. The student fees are a requirement of enrollment, and the total amount generated through the fees is a function of the total number of students in the university.

It would be legitimate, however, for the third-sector organizations in the above examples to claim effectiveness on the basis of the acquisition of resources outside of government support. A sport governing body might generate a considerable amount of money through corporate sponsorships and private donations. It might also secure superior human resources in terms of athletes and volunteer coaches and officials. Some universities are famous for the resources they garner. These all would be legitimate indices of effectiveness.

In overview, the system resource model supposes that the degree to which an organization influences environmental elements and secures necessary resources is a measure of its effectiveness. This emphasis on the input phase is meaningful only to the extent that the organization's outputs cannot be easily measured and its resources are not assured through legislative authority.

In Brief

In the system resource model, the input of resources is the measure of organizational effectiveness because these inputs are indicative of the acceptability of the outputs. However, the model's applicability is limited when an organization's inputs are underwritten by a superior authority.

PROCESS MODEL

If an organization cannot use the goals model because it cannot objectively measure its outputs, and if it cannot use the system resource model because its resources are underwritten by a superior organization (such as a government), how can it evaluate effectiveness? A number of authors (e.g., Pfeffer, 1977; Steers, 1977) have suggested, as a partial solution, that the focus should be directed toward the internal processes of the organization rather than on its proposed end states. From a systems perspective, this involves an emphasis on the throughputs, which link the inputs to outputs (see Exhibits 3.2 and 13.3).

The underlying rationale for the **process model** of effectiveness is that the conversion of inputs into acceptable outputs is based on the throughput processes adopted by the organization. If those throughput processes are internally logical, consistent, and without friction, then it can be assumed that the organization is effective. Further, as Mott (1972) pointed out, organizational processes are expected to be adaptable to changes in the environment and flexible to accommodate fluctuating workloads. That is, the organization is doing what is rational in the context of its goals and its environment.

The process model can be illustrated by a school system, which has as its purpose the education of youth. As noted before, neither the goals model nor the system resource model can be validly used to assess the school system's effectiveness. The most crucial processes within the school system are the efforts that go into curriculum design, the logical progression within the total curriculum, and the teaching and evaluation methods employed. Similarly, an athletic program can be judged on the basis of such processes as recruiting, training, scheduling competitions, and so on. An evaluation of these processes would be one measure of the relative effectiveness of the respective systems. Another measure would be the general policies and procedures, the satisfaction expressed by both coaches and athletes, and the lack (or presence) of conflict within the athletic department.

As another example, consider a weight-loss clinic. Whether clients lose weight after a period of participation in the program can be objectively measured. However, such weight loss or the failure to lose weight can be attributed to many factors, including a client's biology, heredity, personal eating and exercise habits, and adherence to directions from instructors, even though the processes adopted by the fitness club in terms of exercise prescription, nutritional guidelines, and leadership can be judged to be appropriate and adequate.

The arguments for the process model of effectiveness are equally applicable to private, profit-oriented organizations. In fact, the identification and specification of appropriate processes are the foundation of the movement labeled total quality management (TQM). In this approach, the quality of a product is best judged by the extent to which the processes specified by experts are strictly followed (Crosby, 1985; Deming, 1986). Any deviations from the specifications will detract from the quality of the product. Assembly lines are based on the notion of appropriate processes strictly followed. We can also take the case of traffic and crowd control before, during, and after a professional football game. After careful analysis of the problem, experts come up with a set of processes to be followed by all involved. Strict adherence to these specifications is necessary to ensure the safety of spectators and the public. Of course, the success of the event management is judged on the basis of the smooth flow of traffic without any bottlenecks, as well as on the orderly behavior of the spectators. Such successes are attributed to the processes adopted by the sport franchise.

Pros and Cons of the Process Model

As was the case with the goals and system resource models, the process model of effectiveness has some advantages. However, the evaluation of internal processes also poses problems. Consider again a public school system. The process model presupposes that a body of experts can judge the appropriateness of specific processes. And, because experts' judgments are accepted as correct, there is a tendency to specify the "appropriate" processes and procedures in advance for all schools to follow. When this happens, every school or school system must be judged as effective if it followed the specified processes.

This trend is evident in third-sector organizations that depend heavily on the government for financial support. For example, many governments offer financial assistance to sport governing bodies for specific programs. These programs are assumed to lead to better management of the sport governing bodies, better recruitment and training of the national team, and so on. The sport governing bodies in turn must follow these guidelines and institute the suggested programs in order to receive government grants. Thus, all sport governing bodies tend to become identical in terms of their internal processes. In a similar manner, the traffic and crowd control processes adopted by various athletic departments and professional sport franchises tend to become similar across the country because these organizations "benchmark" and adopt the best practices of other organizations.

Weber's concept of a bureaucracy is another instance in which the problems associated with the use of internal processes are highlighted. Weber's bureaucratic prescriptions are normative in the sense that they suggest that all organizations must be bureaucratized in order to be efficient (see Chapter 7). However, the best judgment that can be made about an organization using the process model is whether the organization is more or less bureaucratized. To relate the degree of bureaucratization to effectiveness would be inappropriate.

The process model emphasizes the logic of the internal processes linking inputs to desired outcomes. However, the danger lies in treating a process as the one best way, thereby making it an end in itself.

Thus, the danger in the use of the process model of effectiveness is that organizations tend to deify the processes irrespective of their relationship to effectiveness. An emphasis on processes could be counterproductive from a systems perspective. The concept of equifinality (see Chapter 3) suggests that two organizations adopting two different sets of processes can both be equally effective. For example, the structures and processes of two different city recreation departments of equal size may vary considerably, yet they may serve their respective citizen groups quite effectively. Consequently, it would be inappropriate to judge one department as effective and the other as ineffective based on their internal structures and processes.

In overview, the process model of effectiveness emphasizes the significance of the throughput processes that link the inputs and outputs of an orga-

> **EQUIFINALITY AND MULTIFINALITY** As we noted in Chapter 3, *equifinality* refers to the idea that two systems starting from different positions can end up at the same final position. Any two systems (organizations) can differ in the number and nature of their subsystems and the environments they face. Therefore, the particular internal processes within each system may also differ. The concept of equifinality suggests that the systems can be equally effective, because in each system the subsystems and their processes might be consistent with each other and with the task environment. On the other hand, the concept *multifinality* suggests that any two organizations following the same processes may still vary in the degree to which they achieve their goals.

nization, and the need for the internal throughput processes to be congruent and goal-directed. If these processes are internally consistent and goal-directed, they are considered to contribute to goal attainment. As a consequence, they also can be used as indicators of organizational effectiveness. However, when specific processes are designated as most effective, there is a strong likelihood that uniform procedural prescriptions will be set out for all organizations.

MULTIDIMENSIONALITY OF ORGANIZATIONAL EFFECTIVENESS

Given the difficulty in exclusively applying either the goals, system resource, or process model, it may be necessary to assess the effectiveness of an organization from a **multidimensional** perspective. Evan (1976) suggested that "to appraise the effectiveness of an organization with the aid of systems theory . . . one must measure its performance with respect to all four systemic processes as well as their interrelationships" (p. 19). The four systemic processes that Evan referred to are the inputs, throughputs, outputs, and feedback of a system (see again Exhibits 3.2 and 13.2).

Evan also proposed a sample set of systemic indicators of effectiveness for various types of organizations. For example, he suggested that colleges and universities could use the number of students who graduate (output), the annual budget (input), and the cost of the information system (throughput) as effectiveness indicators. Also, it may be necessary for some organizations to measure effectiveness at different points in the input–throughput–output cycle since no (or only a few) output measures may be available or feasible.

In fact, many university athletic departments proclaim their effectiveness by pointing out several positive elements from the input, throughput, and output stages of their operations. Number of graduating athletes, win–loss ratio, championships won, and awards to athletes and coaches are among the effectiveness indicators for the output stage (goal attainment). The academic and athletic quality of incoming athletes, the recruitment of quality coaches, and the dollars generated through donations and gifts are some of the indicators of quality from the input stage. Finally, the construction and maintenance of quality facilities, the quality of the academic counseling, and the efficiency of the athletic trainers are some of the effectiveness indicators from the throughput stage.

To illustrate further how different dimensions of effectiveness can be superimposed on the input–throughput–output cycle (i.e., system resources model, process model, and goals model), let us consider Karteroliotis and Papadimitriou's (2004) five dimensions of the effectiveness of sport governing bodies in Greece. These dimensions are (1) caliber of the board and external liaisons, (2) interest in athletes, (3) internal procedures, (4) long-term planning, and (5) sport-science support. Readers will recall that in Parson's hierarchical differentiation of subsystems in Chapter 8, the major function of the institutional system was to interact effectively with elements in the distal environment. That point is highlighted by the first of the dimensions listed above. The caliber of the board can be seen as the input of human resources. The second dimension, interest in athletes, is the goal of the organization and thus can be mapped to the output stage in Exhibit 13.2. The other three dimensions are the processes in the throughput stage.

For another example, Kushner and Poole (1996) suggested that the performance of a nonprofit organization can be evaluated on four components—resource acquisition, efficiency, goal attainment, and client satisfaction. Resource acquisition relates to the input stage, reflecting the system resource model; efficiency to the throughput stage or the process model; and goal attainment and client satisfaction to the output stage or the goals model.

The need to measure organizational effectiveness at various stages in the input–throughput–output cycle may be greater in organizations with more than one domain of activities, in which each domain has its own distinctive goals. In those cases, the three models of effectiveness may be differentially relevant to the domains of organizational activity. For example, Chelladurai, Szyszlo, and Haggerty (1987) identified the relative importance attached by the administrators of national sport organizations (NSOs) in Canada to six dimensions of effectiveness. These dimensions were derived by superimposing the three phases of the input–throughput–output cycle on the two domains of NSO activities—mass sport (promotion of public participation in the sport) and elite sport (promotion of excellence in the sport and winning in international competitions). Thus, the six dimensions were input-human resources, input-monetary resources, throughput-mass, throughput-elite, output-mass, and output-elite. These administrators rated input-human resources, throughput-mass, throughput-elite, and output-elite as the more important effectiveness dimensions than input-monetary resources and output-mass. (See Exhibit 13.4.)

It is significant that the input of monetary resources was not considered as important as the other dimensions. At the time of this study, the Canadian government contributed an average of 75 percent of the budget of the national sport governing bodies. Hence, the administrators did not place much importance on that dimension. These administrators also did not place much emphasis on the output dimension of

> **In Brief**
>
> Given the difficulties associated with each model, organizations tend to use all three models to assess and portray their effectiveness. Different models may also be applied to evaluate different programs of an organization.

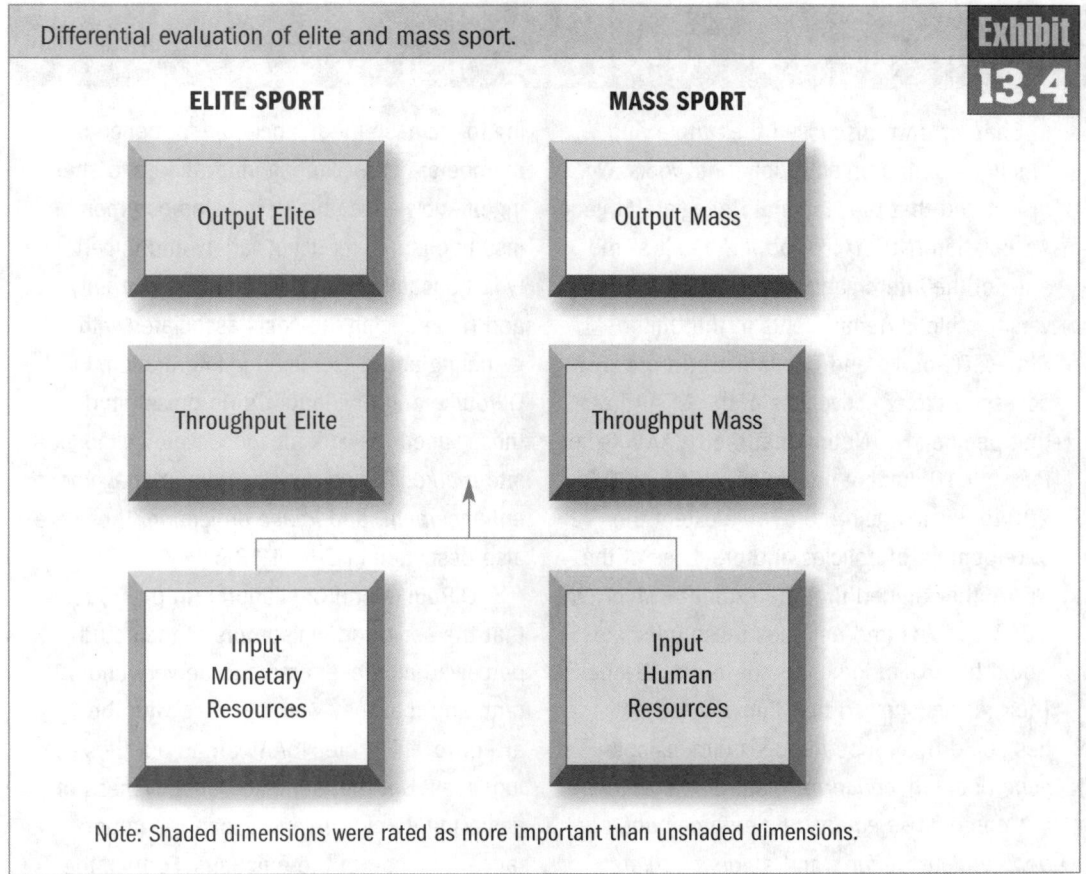

Exhibit 13.4 Differential evaluation of elite and mass sport.

Note: Shaded dimensions were rated as more important than unshaded dimensions.

mass sport. The goal of sport governing bodies is to promote their respective sports among the public. The attainment of this goal—that is, the extent of public participation in the sport—is hard to judge. The number of fee-paying members could be considered a measure of input of monetary or human resources.

In essence, the administrators of Canadian sport governing bodies endorsed a goals model approach for evaluating their elite sport programs. However, this approach was rejected for the evaluation of mass sport programs. This, of course, reflects the fact that an objective measure for the goal attainment of an elite program is readily available (for example, the performance record of the national team in international competitions). However, an objective measure is not available for mass sport programs. We also noted that third-sector organizations should not use the securing of monetary resources as a measure of effectiveness, because governments contribute most of the financial resources, and, therefore, finances lose their potency as an effectiveness indicator. Consistent with this perspective, these authors found that sport administrators did, in fact, emphasize the input of human resources to a greater extent than the input of monetary resources as effectiveness indicators of both the elite and mass sport programs. Finally, the administrators in this study rated the process model of effectiveness as important for the evaluation of both elite and mass programs. In essence, they took a multidimensional approach to evaluating sport governing bodies.

Sidebar

In Chapter 8 we discussed the nature and functions of interorganizational networks. We also noted that the National Collegiate Athletic Association (NCAA) is a powerful unit at the apex of the interorganizational network of university athletic departments in the United States. O'Rourke and Chelladurai (in press) assessed the effectiveness of the NCAA from that perspective. Noting that the NCAA has set for itself 16 guiding principles (NCAA, 2004a, 2004b), which guide to a large extent the development of policies and practices of the NCAA, they argued that the extent to which the NCAA upholds and enforces these principles would be a valid indication of its effectiveness. Their results showed that these varied activities could be grouped into six dimensions: *general equity concerns, institutional autonomy, competitive equity, rule enforcement, student–athlete welfare,* and *student–athlete status*. These are described in Exhibit 13.5.

In addition, they included the critical functions of a network organization noted in Chapter 8. These were (1) creating greater access to resources for member organizations; (2) helping to increase the financial performance of members; (3) facilitating innovation and sharing of knowledge and learning among member institutions; (4) reducing variety and uncertainty in transactions and economic uncertainty; and (5) reducing the costs associated with gathering and disseminating information. In O'Rourke and Chelladurai's (in press) study, these varied network functions were collapsed into *marketing and development, management enhancement,* and *image projection*. These are also described in Exhibit 13.5.

O'Rourke and Chelladurai (in press) found that the senior administrators of their study perceived all these factors to be very important, and that they were satisfied with the extent to which the NCAA carried out these functions. But the ratings on effectiveness of achieving them were lower than the importance attached to the functions. Further, the factors of image projection, student–athlete status, and marketing and development were the more dominant influences in administrators' perceptions of NCAA effectiveness.

THE MULTIPLE-CONSTITUENCY MODEL

Connolly, Conlon, and Deutsch (1980) criticized both the goals and system resource models of effectiveness for their assumption that "it is possible, and desirable, to arrive at a *single* set of evaluative criteria, and thus at a *single* statement of organizational effectiveness" (p. 212). Instead, they proposed:

> a view of organizational effectiveness in which several (potentially, many) different effectiveness statements can be made about the focal organization, reflecting the criterion sets of different individuals and groups we shall refer to as "constituencies." (p. 212)

The constituencies they refer to are the owners, managers, employees, clients, suppliers, and other stakeholders. The constituent groups may be

> **Exhibit 13.5** Dimensions of effectiveness of NCAA based on its principles and functions.
>
> | DIMENSION | DESCRIPTION |
> |---|---|
> | **Based on NCAA Principles** | |
> | General equity concerns | Promotion of gender equity, commitment to gender and ethnic diversity, and activities being free of biases |
> | Institutional autonomy | Encouraging member institutions to conform to their own constitutional bylaws, allowing members to control their own programs, and promoting the financial stability of member institutions |
> | Competitive equity equity | Creation of competitive equity by ensuring that athletes are bona fide students, stating clear recruiting rules, encouraging reporting of violations, and deterring athlete–agent contacts |
> | Rule enforcement | Consistent enforcement of its rules, hiring qualified administrative personnel, and specifying clear academic requirements and eligibility |
> | Student–athlete welfare | Ensuring harassment-free interactions of athletes with their coaches, their academic eligibility, the quality of their experiences, accountability of member institutions, and appropriate recruiting rules |
> | Student–athlete status | Emphasizing the athletes as an integral part of the student body, their dignity, and their rights |
> | **Based on Network Functions** | |
> | Marketing and development | Helping members develop and market new products and services, and securing funds through donations, sponsorships, and grants |
> | Management enhancement | Assisting member institutions to enhance their managerial skills and techniques, and improve their day-to-day operations |
> | Image projection | Protecting the integrity of and projecting a positive image for intercollegiate athletics and member institutions |

within the organization (senior administrators, employee groups), or they may belong to the environment (consumer groups, suppliers). In the case of a department of sport management, the students, the faculty, the staff, and the dean and other administrative heads would form the internal constituencies. External constituencies would include university administrators, the senate, alumni, and other faculties. Beyond the university, the external constituencies would be professional and semiprofessional sport franchises, city recreation departments, fitness clubs, and other organizations that have a stake in how the sport management department operates and in the type of graduates that come out of it. These constituencies will have varying perspectives on what the focal sport management program should achieve.

Sidebar

That each of multiple stakeholders (or constituents) would hold their differing judgment of the effectiveness of an organization as the truth was humorously illustrated by Herman and Renz (1999) in the story of the three baseball umpires:

> The first says he calls balls and strikes 'as they are," and the second says, "I call 'em as I see 'em." The third says, "They ain't nothing 'til I call 'em." (p. 110)

> There are pitches, but a pitch is neither a ball nor a strike until the umpire calls it. . . . Of course, unlike the baseball analogy, in NPOs there is no single umpire (all stakeholders are permitted to determine effectiveness, although some stakeholders may be considered more credible than others) and no regular procedure for determining effectiveness (all stakeholders are free to send messages, with varying degrees of justification, about effectiveness and to focus on different activities as more relevant for determining effectiveness). Effectiveness is stakeholder judgment, formed and changed in an ongoing process of sense making and negotiation. (p. 118)

Connolly, Conlon, and Deutsh (1980) pointed out that the multiple-constituency approach to effectiveness incorporates the notion that different goals will be held by different groups in an organization. Insofar as differences in the perception of goals exist, there will also be differences in the perception of organizational effectiveness. Connolly and his colleagues noted that it was "somewhat arbitrary to label one of these perspectives a priori as the 'correct' one" (p. 212) and suggested that effectiveness must be considered as a plural concept—it is *effectivenesses* that should be considered, not *effectiveness*.

To Recap

MULTIPLE STAKEHOLDERS/CONSTITUENCIES The **multiple constituencies** referred to by Connolly, Conlon, and Deutsch (1980) are the same as the stakeholders discussed in Chapter 3. Stakeholders were defined as "persons or groups that have or claim ownership, rights, or interests in a corporation and its activities, past, present, or future" (Clarkson, 1995, p. 106). In Chapter 5 on planning, we also noted that the stated goals of an organization tend to be global and vague. It was said this vagueness allowed for the accommodation of varied expectations of multiple stakeholders or constituencies. Thus it is not surprising that the problems associated with specifying organizational goals also arise in the case of evaluating organizational effectiveness.

Note that the Connolly, Conlon, and Deutsch (1980) approach hinges on the idea that different constituents hold different goals. It implies that different constituents will use different criteria or indices in evaluating the effectiveness of a given organization. For instance, the faculty and alumni of a university may hold different goals for their intercollegiate department. Therefore, they may be expected to apply different criteria in judging the effectiveness of the athletic department. Hypothetically, the alumni may hold the view that intercollegiate athletics should be concerned with only the major sports such as football and basketball. Accordingly, their effectiveness criteria would be focused on football and basketball operations. The faculty, in contrast, may emphasize the breadth of the athletic program and greater opportunities for more students to pursue excellence in sports. Thus, their effectiveness criteria are likely to be broad-based. This multiplicity of criteria is born out of the different goals held by different constituents (see Exhibit 13.6).

In Brief

As different constituents of an organization may hold different goals for the organization, their perspectives on organizational effectiveness will also differ.

Exhibit 13.6 Multiple-constituency model.

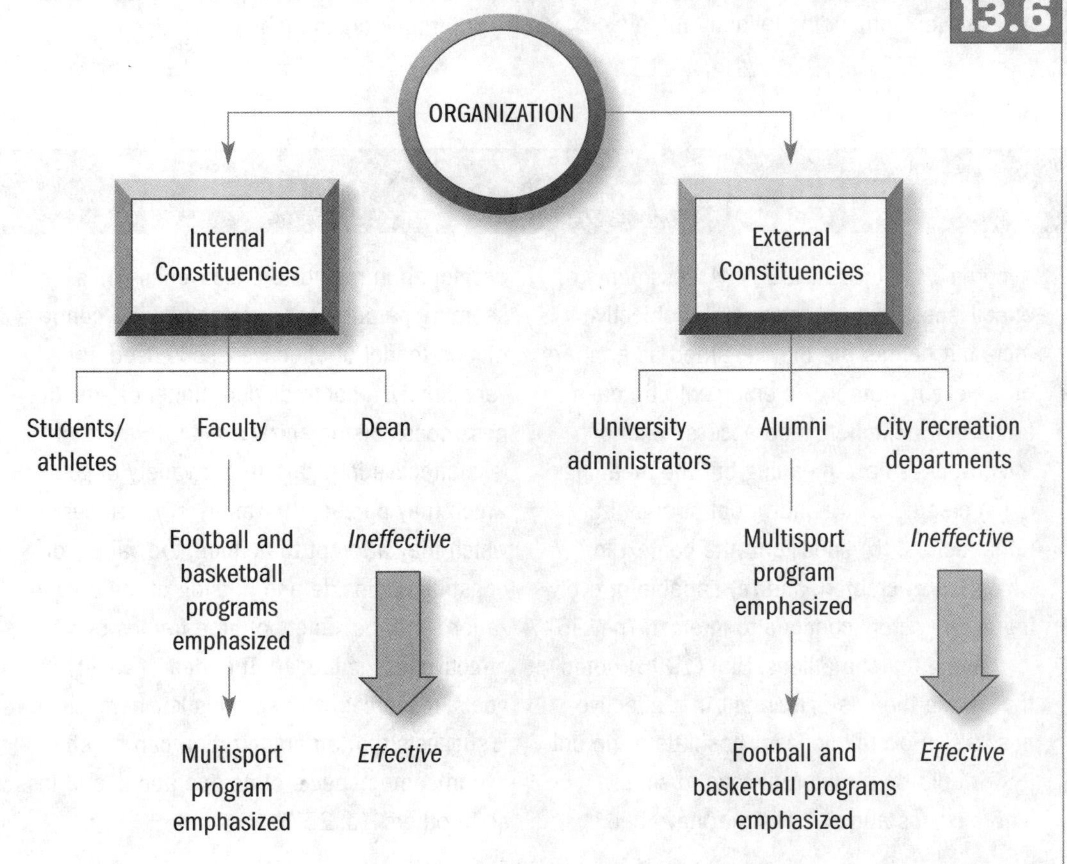

ORGANIZATION

- Internal Constituencies
  - Students/athletes
  - Faculty → Football and basketball programs emphasized → *Ineffective* / → Multisport program emphasized → *Effective*
  - Dean
- External Constituencies
  - University administrators
  - Alumni → Multisport program emphasized → *Ineffective* / → Football and basketball programs emphasized → *Effective*
  - City recreation departments

Sidebar

Based on the notion of multiple perspectives of organizational effectiveness held by the multiple stakeholders, Herman and Renz (1997) recommend the following for the managers of NPOs:

> We have suggested to these managers that the basic implication of our results is that they recognize that different constituencies are judging their organizations' effectiveness in different ways and that they (the managers) should find out what criteria are important to the different constituencies and provide favorable information on how their organizations are doing on those criteria. In effect, we are recommending tailoring the effectiveness message to each audience. Some managers tell us this is not something they have not thought of or already done. The more cynical have stated that all good managers are "spin doctors."

Herman and Renz also advocate

> Recognizing that how and on what bases different constituencies reach effectiveness judgments varies and that differentially emphasizing information of interest to differing constituencies is not tantamount to advocating lying. Managers can (and many do) present information that is as accurate as possible while still presenting it in ways that make a good case for their organization. (p. 202)

Sidebar

According to Forbes (1998), "Assessments of effectiveness are not regarded as objective facts but neither are they regarded as arbitrary or irrelevant. Rather, the emergent approach holds that definitions and assessments of effectiveness have meaning but the meaning is (a) created by the individual or organizational actors, (b) specific to the context in which it was created, and (c) capable of evolving as the actors continue to interact" (p. 195).

Along the same lines, Hall (1996) noted that "while there is agreement that effectiveness as an overall concept has little or no utility, it would be a major mistake to simply ignore issues and findings that have been developed in regard to effectiveness. This seeming paradox can be resolved if a contradiction model of effectiveness is used. Put very simply, a contradiction model of effectiveness considers organizations to be more or less effective in regard to the variety of goals which they pursue, the variety of resources which they attempt to acquire, the variety of constituents inside and outside of the organization, and the variety of time frames by which effectiveness is judged. The idea of variety in goals, resources, and so on is key here, since it suggests that an organization can be effective in some aspects of its operations and less so in others" (p. 257).

The problem of multiple goals and thus the multiple conceptions of organizational effectiveness is much more pronounced in nonprofit organizations than in commercial enterprises. Commercial enterprises have at least one objective and quantitative bottom-line criterion of effectiveness—making profits for the owners or shareholders. Herman and Renz (1999, p. 107) highlighted this when they advanced the following six theses about the effectiveness of nonprofit organizations (NPOs):

- Nonprofit organizational effectiveness is always a matter of comparison.
- Nonprofit organizational effectiveness is multidimensional and will never be reducible to a single measure.
- Boards of directors make a difference in the effectiveness of NPOs, but how they do this is not clear.
- More effective NPOs are more likely to use correct management practices.
- Nonprofit organizational effectiveness is a social construction.
- Program outcome indicators as measures of NPO effectiveness are limited and can be dangerous. (p. 107)

MULTIDIMENSIONALITY PERSPECTIVE VERSUS MULTIPLE-CONSTITUENCY MODEL

The multiplicity of effectiveness criteria stemming from different goals should not be confused with the criteria stemming from the issue of measuring effectiveness at the input, throughput, and output stages. For instance, the alumni group in the previous example may be unanimous in emphasizing football and basketball, but they may be split in emphasizing the winning percentage of the teams (goals model), the revenue generated by the department (system resources model), or the recruiting and training of athletes or marketing of the programs (process model). By the same token, members of a constituent group that supports a wider range of sports may be divided among themselves in emphasizing the input, throughput, or output dimensions of effectiveness. Thus, it is important to distinguish between the two sources of effectiveness criteria—multidimensionality of effectiveness versus **multiple perspectives** on effectiveness.

For an example from the commercial sector, the Nike Corporation is quite well known for its creativity and entrepreneurial efforts to offer quality footwear and apparel for public consumption. However, it has a constituent group that criticizes it for the production of its goods in sweatshops in developing countries. While other groups (athletes, general consumers, business analysts, shareholders, sport organizations) may consider Nike to be effective, this particular constituency evaluates it very negatively. Similarly, it is not uncommon for the owners and shareholders of a professional sport franchise to consider their franchise effective because it generates large revenues and profits, while the fans evaluate the franchise as a failure based on its poor win–loss record.

Although Connolly and his colleagues emphasized the flexibility of the multiple-constituency model in terms of its accommodating various perspectives among the constituencies over time, they did not clarify how an organization could use the differing evaluations (by the constituencies) to improve its performance. The fact that managers have to make choices from among these perspectives is not addressed in their model. We will address this issue later in this chapter.

COMPETING VALUES MODEL

The foregoing discussion shows that the issue of effectiveness becomes more complex when the various interest groups (the multiple constituencies) hold a number of incompatible goals for the organization. Because multiple constituencies could have different preferences for organizational performance, and therefore would select different criteria for assessing organizational effectiveness, the values underlying these differing sets of criteria are important (Quinn & Rohrbaugh, 1983; Zammuto, 1984). As Zammuto (1984) suggested:

> Organizational effectiveness fundamentally is a value-based concept in that the whole of the evaluation process requires the application of value judgments, from the selection of constituencies and the weighting of their judgments to the development of recommendations for future organizational performance. (p. 614)

Campbell (1976) was more emphatic when he pointed out that "there is no algorithm of science that will specify which variables should be labeled as criteria of organizational effectiveness. That begins as a value judgment and ends as a political decision" (p. 40). Values held by key decision makers and their judgments about effectiveness are related to operative goals that are, in the first place, subjective. This is reality, and we must realize that all the objective computations and calculations cannot mask this fact.

Connolly, Conlon, and Deutsch (1980) and Zammuto (1984) underscore the significance of values underlying multiple perspectives on organizational effectiveness. This suggests that the issues surrounding the concept of organizational effectiveness can be framed as a set of competing values. This was Quinn and Rohrbaugh's (1983) basis in proposing their **competing values** approach to organizational effectiveness. They selected 17 of 30 effectiveness criteria collated earlier by Campbell (1977). Then they asked a group of experts to judge the similarity between pairs of criteria. These similarity judgments were subjected to multidimensional scaling (a statistical procedure appropriate for such data). The results showed that the criteria could be grouped in the space defined by three dimensions: (1) internal versus external, (2) flexibility versus stability, and (3) means versus ends.

Internal versus External

The first dimension reflects the organizational focus, "from an internal, micro emphasis on the well-being and development of people in the organization to an external, macro emphasis on the well-being and development of the organization itself" (Quinn & Rohrbaugh, 1983, p. 369). Thus, this dimension has the people and the organization as its polar ends.

For example, a university athletic department may be more concerned with generating revenue. Therefore, its processes may reflect cost reduction in all its operations. This, in turn, may negatively affect the athletes, coaches, and other staff of the department. Another university athletic department, with a greater focus on the welfare of its athletes and coaches, may spend more money on positively enhancing the experiences of its people. In the process, the department's surpluses may be reduced. Much of the debate on intercollegiate athletics is focused on this pair of competing values. Different constituencies of the athletic department may employ either of the focuses in evaluating an athletic department. The divergent focuses on people versus the organization are also relevant to other sport organizations, including commercial organizations such as a professional sport franchise, a commercial fitness club, or a sport-marketing consulting firm.

Flexibility versus Stability

The second dimension derived by Quinn and Rohrbaugh (1983) reflects the competing views on organizational structure, "from an emphasis on stability to an emphasis on flexibility" (p. 369). The decision makers in a city recreation department may be more concerned with the stability and consistency of their operations. Therefore, they may structure their department to ensure greater control of their operations. Such a structure would emphasize centralized decision making. In contrast, decision makers in another city recreation department may be concerned with being open to client demands and satisfying their needs. They may also be interested in identifying and implementing new trends in recreation. Accordingly, they are likely to make the structure more flexible to permit decentralized decision making. It follows that different constituents (including the decision makers) may apply either of the competing orientations toward structure in evaluating the effectiveness of the departments.

Means versus Ends

The third dimension of Quinn and Rohrbaugh (1983) pertains to organizational means and ends, "from an emphasis on important processes (e.g., planning and goal-setting) to an emphasis on final outcomes (e.g., productivity)" (p. 369). The ends sought by a commercial fitness club may be profit or market share. The means employed by the club may be extensive planning to streamline its operations, offer new programs, and install new equipment. The dichotomy represented by this dimension reflects the distinction between the goals and process models of organizational effectiveness discussed earlier in the chapter.

In Brief

All the values guiding organizational analysis can be grouped under three dimensions: internal versus external focus, flexibility versus stability, and ends versus means.

In overview, these three dimensions of competing values highlight (a) attention orientation (internal/external focus), (b) structural preferences (flexibility/control or centralization/decentralization), and (c) the means–ends dichotomy. When these three dimensions are crossed with each other, they yield eight cells as shown in Exhibit 13.7. Note that each cell combines one extreme of each of the three value dimensions.

Quinn and Rohrbaugh (1983) went a step further to propose four models of effectiveness, each consisting of two of the eight cells shown in Exhibit 13.7.

Exhibit 13.7 Competing values model of organizational effectiveness.

PEOPLE				ORGANIZATION			
Flexibility		Stability		Flexibility		Stability	
Means (1)	Ends (2)	Means (3)	Ends (4)	Means (5)	Ends (6)	Means (7)	Ends (8)

	CELL	EMPHASIS
Human Relations Model	Cell 1 (PFM):	Group cohesion, morale, member commitment
	Cell 2 (PFE):	Human resource management processes
Internal Process Model	Cell 3 (PSM):	Information management, communication
	Cell 4 (PSE):	Stability, control, continuity, equilibrium
Open System Model	Cell 5 (OFM):	Flexibility, readiness, adaptability
	Cell 6 (OFE):	Resource acquisition, external support
Rational Goal Model	Cell 7 (OSM):	Planning, goal-setting
	Cell 8 (OSE):	Productivity, efficiency

The **human relations model** focuses on flexibility and internal focus with a view to enhance human resource development (ends) through such means as cohesion and morale (Cells 1 and 2). The **internal process model** reflects an emphasis on control and internal focus to bring about control and stability (ends) through the means of information management and communication (Cells 3 and 4). The **open system model** emphasizes flexibility and external focus in order to secure resources and external support (ends) through such means as being ready for and adaptable to environmental changes (Cells 5 and 6). Finally, the **rational goal model** features a heavy emphasis on control and external focus to ensure productivity and efficiency (ends) through such means as planning and goal-setting (Cells 7 and 8).

As Robbins (1990) noted, the competing values approach

> goes significantly beyond merely acknowledging diverse preferences. It assumes [demonstrates] that these diverse preferences can be consolidated and organized. The competing-values approach argues that there are common elements underlying any comprehensive list of OE [organizational effectiveness] criteria and that these elements can be combined in such a way as to create basic sets of competing values. Each one of these sets then defines a unique effectiveness model. (p. 69)

In addition, the competing values model identifies three dimensions that reflect the perennial dilemmas faced by managers. That is, the three dimensions of competing values have an impact on all managerial functions. For instance, in the planning function of selecting goals for the organization, what priority would be given to the welfare of the personnel relative to corporate welfare (that is, the polar ends of Quinn and Rohrbaugh's first dimension)? Similarly, their means–ends dimension affects the setting of goals and the choice of activities (or programs) to achieve those goals. Their second dimension relates to the organizing function, where the rigidity or flexibility of the organizational structure and coordinating mechanisms is determined. From this perspective, Quinn and Rohrbaugh's competing values model provides a global perspective on all of management—not just on the concept of organizational effectiveness.

A differing perspective on Quinn and Rohrbaugh's model is that "it is not so much a theory of organizational effectiveness but more an account of where managers put their major emphasis in conducting the affairs of an organization, which by implication tells us something about how they evaluate its effectiveness" (Rollinson, 2002, p. 474). That is, the model can be seen as a scheme contrasting approaches managers can take in carrying out the different functions of management, such as planning, organizing, and leading. For instance, one fitness club manager, in contrast to another, may focus on the means (e.g., offering different programs and ensuring the quality of services offered) of achieving a given set of goals (e.g., making a 20 percent return on investment) rather than on the goals themselves. This illustrates Quinn and Rohrbaugh's means–ends distinction (see Chapter 5 on planning, which discusses setting goals and generating alternative courses of action to achieve those goals).

Similarly, one manager of a professional sport franchise may set up a bureaucratic structure to ensure stability and consistency of operations, while another may adopt the systems approach in making the structure more flexible to adapt to environmental conditions (see Chapters 7 and 8, which explain classical forms of organizing and systems-based organizing). These differing approaches are what Quinn and Rohrbaugh label the flexibility–stability dimension.

Finally, one athletic director may be more interpersonally or people-oriented in leading the members of the organization, while another athletic director may be more task- or organization-oriented in the leadership function (see Chapters 10 and 11 for a discussion of the different approaches to leadership). This illustrates what Quinn and Rohrbaugh call the people versus organization focus or the internal versus external focus.

From the above perspective, one can see the competing values model as a depiction and classification of the structures and processes adopted by organizations and their managers. However, the thrust of the model is that the adoption of different configurations of structures and processes also leads to the selection of criteria for evaluating the effectiveness of the organization. In one sense, the structures and processes adopted by the organization reflect the goals the organization has set for itself, and thus an effectiveness evaluation could legitimately focus on how well those structures and processes are implemented.

PARADOXICAL NATURE OF ORGANIZATIONAL EFFECTIVENESS

hen the focal organization has to satisfy contradictory sets of criteria, it is forced to engage in activities that may mutually undermine each other's effects. This exemplifies what Cameron (1986) calls **organizational paradox.** According to him, "organizational effectiveness is inherently paradoxical. To be effective, an organization must possess attributes that are simultaneously contradictory, even mutually exclusive"

> In a sense, the paradoxical model [and the competing values model as well] can be viewed as a more complex form of its predecessors—it allows for the likelihood of organizations operating simultaneously in different environmental domains, with each domain conveying different expectations. Whereas contingency theory assumed a single domain, for the sake of matching organizational and environmental characteristics, the paradoxical extension allows for multiple domains requiring multiple, simultaneous, and inherently contradictory matches.
>
> **WHETTEN & CAMERON,** *1994, p. 141*

(p. 545). Although Cameron uses the notion of paradox mainly to refer to conflicting organizational processes, the concept is relevant to the contradictions inherent in the viewpoints of the multiple constituents. The organization faces paradox, and its activities are paradoxical when it attempts to satisfy those "contradictory, even mutually exclusive" viewpoints. In fact, Cameron (1986) found that:

> The organizations that achieved the highest levels of effectiveness were also those that satisfied the most separate constituency group expectations, even when different constituencies held contradictory expectations. Highly effective organizations were paradoxical in that they performed in contradictory ways to satisfy contradictory expectations. (p. 550)

Consider university athletics. The expectations of the alumni, the student body, and the athletes could be divergent and even conflict with each other. Many universities have succeeded in bringing about a balance between these opposing and "paradoxical" expectations. Other universities, on the other hand, have allowed one of the constituencies—the alumni—to assume a dominant position that has resulted in great repercussions for athletics as well as the universities concerned. This situation is akin to what Cameron calls *schismogenesis*, "a process of self-reinforcement where one action or attribute in the organization perpetuates itself until it becomes extreme and therefore dysfunctional" (p. 546). The problem with the emphasis on dominant coalitions in the assessment of organizational effectiveness is that it sets the process of *schismogenesis* in motion. Choosing the criteria of the most powerful groups makes them more and more dominant, until they are able virtually to dictate what the organization should do. Organizations and their administrators need to be concerned about such negative processes.

PRIMACY AMONG MULTIPLE PERSPECTIVES

he foregoing discussion shows that there are multiple perspectives on organizational effectiveness, and that these differing perspectives are rooted in the values held by different groups. While this is doubtless the case, these discussions do not provide any guidelines for the practicing manager. Given a multitude of claims and counterclaims, the manager has to give one or more of these perspectives greater force than the others. Zammuto (1984) suggested that the writings on multiple constituencies and their perspectives can be synthesized into four classes, each one giving a particular constituency primacy in the evaluation of organizational effectiveness. These classes are described below.

Relativistic Perspective

The **relativistic perspective** holds that the evaluations by all of the various constituencies are legitimate, and therefore the primacy of one view over the others cannot be established. As explained earlier, Connolly, Conlon, and Detsch (1980) strongly supported this perspective. In suggesting that the evaluator's task is only to collect effectiveness ratings from multiple constituencies for the use of the superiors, the relativistic approaches do not really address the distributive issue. That is, the suggestion that the various constituencies may emphasize different values, which lead to differential emphases on organizational goals, does not provide any guidelines for the top administrators or the researchers who have to select a specific perspective to guide their actions.

Power Perspective

The **power perspective** (see Miles, 1980; Pennings & Goodman, 1977; Pfeffer & Salancik, 1978) is categorical in asserting that the preferences of the most powerful constituents, or of the coalition of powerful constituents, need to be satisfied. The models that subscribe to the power perspective emphasize the identification of the critical goals held by different constituents. For instance, Miles (1980) would require the preferential ordering of the various goals held by different constituencies, based on the relative power of the constituencies. In the case of a university's intercollegiate athletic program, for example, the significant constituencies (or power centers, as Miles calls them) would include the athletes themselves, the coaches, the wider student body, the university administrators, the alumni, the media, the immediate community, and the local government. Information on the powerful or strategic constituencies is sought from the top administrators of the program and then corroborated by other sources.

> **In Brief**
>
> In addressing different perspectives of its constituents, an effective organization engages in contradictory activities, which contributes to the paradox of organizational effectiveness.

The relative power of a constituency depends on its ability to influence or control the activities of the focal organization. Power is often, but not always, a function of the resource contributions made by that constituency. For example, in many American universities, the alumni association has considerable influence in the affairs of the athletic programs because of its significant contribution of resources. In contrast, the athletic programs in many Canadian universities are financed through the activity fees paid by the students. The students, however, do not possess the degree of influence and power commensurate with their resource contribution. This is analogous to the citizens who pay the taxes not having a say in the distribution of the taxes. These and similar situations could be an artifact of the diffusion of power among a large number of benefactors, or of benefactors' disinterestedness.

According to Miles (1980), once the priorities of the powerful constituents are identified, effectiveness is evaluated on the basis of attainment of these prioritized goals. However, despite the model's sophistication in the assessment of relative power of the constituent groups and the establishment of priorities among the goals they hold, it still does not solve the problem that arises when two equally strategic interest groups hold conflicting values or goals for the organization.

Social Justice Perspective

The focus of the **social justice perspective** (Keeley, 1978) is on satisfying the needs of the less powerful or the less advantaged constituents. The social welfare programs of many countries, aimed at assisting disadvantaged citizens, rise out of this perspective. Many critics of intercollegiate athletic programs in America take this stance when they point to the inequity in the distribution of resources to various sports. For example, the social justice perspective would suggest that the use of the gymnasiums be equally distributed among basketball, volleyball, and badminton teams.

Evolutionary Perspective

Finally, the emphasis in Zammuto's (1984) **evolutionary perspective** is on "the continual process of becoming effective rather than on being effective" (p. 608). That is, organizational effectiveness is viewed in terms of how the organization attempts to satisfy the divergent needs over the long term as the constituents and their needs change over time. For example, an athletic department in a smaller institution may buy new equipment and uniforms for its teams in successive years. In any one year, only a few teams may get the new equipment, but in the long run every team gets its turn.

PRIME BENEFICIARY APPROACH

s we noted, the major concern of the multiple-constituency approaches is the question: which of the multiple perspectives should prevail? The various approaches discussed above tend to be mutually exclusive, and at times seem to ignore organizational purposes. Chelladurai (1987) proposed an alternate approach based on Blau and Scott's (1962) criterion of **prime beneficiary** (see Chapter 2 for a discussion of Blau and Scott's work).

With the relatively clear specifications developed by Blau and Scott, it is easier and more justifiable to uphold the perspective of the prime beneficiary in the evaluation of organizational effectiveness.

The players' unions in various sports are examples of mutual benefit associations, and the players are the prime beneficiaries. Accordingly, the players' views on the union's effectiveness should reign supreme as the measure of effectiveness. Similarly, evaluations of the organizational effectiveness of a private golf club should be based on members' views, because they are the prime beneficiaries.

In the case of a professional sports club (a business concern), the prime beneficiaries are the owners. The notion that their view should reign supreme is generally accepted in North American society. For instance, when the former Cleveland Browns football team was moved to another city, the city administrators, the fans, and the media expressed concerns. In the end, however, the primacy of the owners' views was upheld. By the same token, the owners also are the supreme judges of the effectiveness of their own respective organizations.

To Recap

PRIME BENEFICIARY Blau and Scott argued that although several groups may benefit from the organization, one group can be identified as the prime beneficiary—that is, whose benefit is the primary reason for the organization's existence. Accordingly, the organizational and managerial concerns are aimed at ensuring that the benefits to the prime beneficiary are not diverted or thwarted.

To extend the argument further, Blau and Scott's (1962) four-level classification of organizations facilitates the identification of prime beneficiary with respect to any one type of organization. That is, the rank and file members are the prime beneficiaries in mutual benefit associations, such as an exclusive golf club or a players' union. The owners are the prime beneficiaries in business concerns. The public in contact are the prime beneficiaries in service organizations, such as a school, a community hospital, or a city recreation department. And the public at large is the prime beneficiary in commonweal organizations, such as the police force or the prison system.

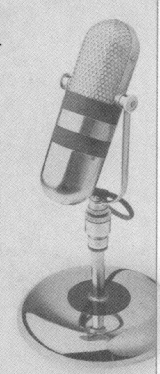

An example of a service organization (in Blau and Scott's terminology) would be a city or university recreation department. The department provides facilities and programs for the benefit of local residents or students. Thus, as the prime beneficiaries of the department, their judgments about the effectiveness of the department should be of paramount influence in managerial decisions. In a similar manner, many organizations offer sport and recreation programs to the disabled and disadvantaged. All of these organizations exist to serve the people who come into contact with them. There are no good examples of a commonweal organization in sport and recreation; however, many sport and recreation programs for youth may be considered to benefit the larger community if they are designed to "keep kids off the street."

The foregoing examples show that the prime beneficiary approach includes two of the various approaches suggested by Zammuto (1984). Because the owners of a professional sports franchise are the prime beneficiaries of the organization, they hold the power to make decisions. Therefore, the notion of prime beneficiary encompasses the power perspective suggested by Zammuto. In mutual benefit associations (such as labor unions or recreational clubs) where members are the prime beneficiaries, fairness among all members is paramount. Therefore, Zammuto's social justice perspective is applicable. In a similar manner, the social justice perspective on the primacy of constituents would hold in service organizations whose prime beneficiaries are the clients

In Brief

One way to decide on the primacy of different perspectives on organizational effectiveness is to focus on the prime beneficiary of that organization (i.e., the constituent for whose benefit the organization exists).

Sidebar

It is important to distinguish between the concept of primary stakeholder (discussed in Chapter 3) and prime beneficiary (discussed in Chapter 2).

Primary stakeholder refers to any group without whose cooperation and participation the organization cannot survive. Thus, the coaches and athletes of a professional sport franchise are primary stakeholders because without them the franchise cannot produce the contest and the entertainment thereof. Similarly, the coaches and athletes of a university athletic department are primary stakeholders. In both examples, the coaches and athletes are treated equally as primary stakeholders.

However, the *prime beneficiaries* of professional sport franchises are the owners, while the players and coaches are "costs" of running the business. That is, the coaches and athletes are paid their salaries with a view that their performances will result in profits for the owners. In the case of intercollegiate athletics, the athletes are the prime beneficiaries, while the coaches are "cost" items. The coaches are paid their salaries so that they will serve the athletes—the prime beneficiaries—by coaching, instructing, and training them to be better athletes.

Although sport managers must satisfy the needs and preferences of primary stakeholders in order to make an organization more effective, they should base their judgment of organizational effectiveness on how well the prime beneficiaries are served.

in contact. It must be noted that Zammuto's (1984) other two approaches do not really establish the primacy of any one constituent. The relativistic perspective simply says that all perspectives of the multiple constituents are legitimate, and, therefore, primacy of any one cannot be established. In a similar vein, the evolutionary approach implies that all perspectives are legitimate, and that the organization should attempt to satisfy as many constituents as possible in a sequential manner.

To recommend the perspective of the prime beneficiary is not to minimize the need for any organization to seek and secure required resources by catering to the wishes of other constituent groups. From Cameron's (1986) perspective of organizational effectiveness as a paradox, it is necessary for an organization to accommodate some of the expectations of other groups even though they may be inconsistent with the needs of the prime beneficiaries. The essential point is that an effective organization attempts to satisfy these contradictory expectations only with a view to increase the payoffs to its prime beneficiaries. In one sense, satisfying the other constituents may be viewed as a cost incurred by the organization in order to serve the prime beneficiaries better. For instance, if an athletic department raises the salaries of its coaches, it satisfies that constituency. But the additional cost is incurred only to make sure that the coaches serve the athletes, the prime beneficiaries. "To keep the prime beneficiary in perspective is to keep the ultimate purpose of the organization in perspective" (Chelladurai, 1987, p. 45).

A final comment on the need to distinguish between a multidimensional approach and the multiple-constituency approach to effectiveness: The multidimensional approach simply suggests that an organization should be evaluated on different dimensions—resource acquisition, productivity, smooth functioning of internal processes, and so on (Evan, 1976; Steers, 1975). The problems associated with it are *scientific* to the extent they are concerned with *what* is to be measured and *how* it should be measured. In the multiple-constituency model, however, various groups evaluate a focal organization on the same dimensions. For example, the national team preparations of a sport governing body might be evaluated differently by the athletes, the clubs, and the administrators. Similarly, a university athletic department is subject to differential evaluations by athletes, the student body, the faculty, the alumni, the media, and the general public. Thus, the multiple-constituency approach focuses on *whose perspective or preferences* should be the basis for evaluation rather than on *what* should be evaluated. The critical issue addressed here is *political* in nature to the extent that it focuses on appeasing various claimants and their perspectives.

AN OVERVIEW OF ORGANIZATIONAL EFFECTIVENESS

We noted at the beginning of the chapter that the various models of effectiveness can be synthesized into a gestalt view of effectiveness. As Yuchtman and Seashore (1967) pointed out, since the three processes of an open system—acquisition of resources, transformation of the inputs (throughputs), and disposal of the outputs—are integrally linked to each other, the effectiveness of the system can be measured at any point in the input–throughput–output cycle. This is highlighted by the fact that each model of effectiveness focuses on one of the elements in the cycle (see Exhibit 13.2). In addition, the chapter discussed the issue of multiple constituencies and their differential evaluations of organizational effectiveness. We also noted that the values individuals have underlie their perspectives on organizational effectiveness. The critical issue of the primacy of these different views was discussed from the perspective of prime beneficiaries of organizations.

To Recap

EFFECTIVENESS MODELS All models of effectiveness utilize either direct or substitute measures of goal attainment. Therefore, the goals model is appropriate for those cases where goals are clear and their attainment is measurable. In cases where specific goals are either not identifiable or not measurable, the practical solution is to adopt the system resource model, because there is a direct link between resource acquisition and output acceptance. The process model of effectiveness should be considered only if the former two models cannot be profitably used. Even then, managers must take care to avoid placing undue emphasis on predetermined processes.

A careful examination of the five models discussed in the chapter shows that all of them have goal attainment as the primary concern in the assessment of effectiveness. For example, the underlying assumption of the system resource model is that the ability of the organization to secure resources reflects the environment's acceptance of the organization's outputs. Thus, the degree to which the organization secures its resources reflects its goal attainment. Similarly, the process model of effectiveness links organizational processes to the outputs. Finally, the multiple-constituency and the competing values models also emphasize the operative goals held by different groups. The degree to which the organization achieves the goals of the various constituencies is a measure of its effectiveness.

In short, in choosing the criteria of effectiveness for their organizations, managers should focus on what Campbell (1976) calls *closeness to the final payoff*. That is, a criterion that is more closely related to the goal should be selected over those more remotely connected. For instance, if the academic achievement of the athletes is set as a significant goal, then the actual graduation rate is a more suitable effectiveness criterion than is the existence (or not) of a study table for the athletes. The former reflects goals attainment (it is actually the payoff), whereas the study table reflects only the process to attain that payoff.

SUMMARY

Various models of effectiveness—the goals, system resource, process, multiple-constituency, and competing values models—were shown to be related to the systems view of organizations. The goals model focuses on achieving organizational goals, the system resources model on securing required resources, and the internal process model on the smooth functioning of the organization's processes. The multiple-constituency model emphasizes the views held by different stakeholder groups, and the competing values model stresses the values held by decision makers. Four different perspectives were advanced with regard to the varying preferences of multiple constituencies. The relativistic perspective holds all views as legitimate and equal, the power perspective endorses the views of the constituency with greatest power, the social justice perspective considers the needs of the least powerful and the disadvantaged, and the evolutionary perspective suggests that organizational effectiveness requires satisfying different constituencies over time.

We noted that all models are more or less goal oriented, but the difficulty encountered in measuring goal attainment leads to a focus on different surrogate (substitute) measures. We also discussed the organizational conditions under which each model would be appropriate. Finally, we considered that the selection of effectiveness criteria must be based on the degree to which the criteria reflect the ultimate criterion—the attainment of goals to serve the prime beneficiaries.

Developing Your Perspectives

1. Select a sport organization. What criteria would you use to evaluate its effectiveness? Why?

2. Give examples of sport organizations where each of the four models of effectiveness—goals, system resource, process, and multiple-constituency models—would be appropriate.

3. List as many criteria of effectiveness as possible for a sport organization. Place them on Campbell's (1976) continuum of closeness to the final payoff.

4. According to your perceptions, what are the effectiveness criteria used in evaluating your faculty or department? Who decides on these criteria? Can you infer their operative goals from these criteria?

5. Select a variety of sport organizations and identify the prime beneficiaries of each organization. Explain the extent to which their views are upheld in the evaluation of organizational effectiveness, and the manner in which this occurs.

References

Bacon, J. U. (2004). New balance. *NWA World Traveler, 36* (12), 36–40.

Barney, J. (1991). Firm resources and sustained competitive advantage. *Journal of Management, 17* (1), 99–120.

Barney, J. (1995). Looking inside for competitive advantage. *Academy of Management Executive, 9* (4), 49–61.

Blau, P. M., & Scott, W. R. (1962). *Formal organizations.* San Francisco: Chandler.

Cameron, K. S. (1986). Effectiveness as a paradox: Consensus and conflict in conceptions of organizational effectiveness. *Management Science, 32* (5), 539–553.

Campbell, J. P. (1976). Contributions research can make in understanding organizational effectiveness. In L. S. Spray (Ed.), *Organizational effectiveness: Theory–research–utilization.* Kent, OH: Graduate School of Business Administration, Kent State University.

Campbell, J. P. (1977). On the nature of organizational effectiveness. In P. S. Goodman and J. M. Pennings (Eds.), *New perspectives on organizational effectiveness.* San Francisco: Jossey-Bass.

Carmeli, A. (2004). Assessing core intangible resources. *European Management Journal, 22* (1), 110–122.

Chelladurai, P. (1987). Multidimensionality and multiple perspectives of organizational effectiveness. *Journal of Sport Management, 1,* 37–47.

Chelladurai, P., & Danylchuk, K. E. (1984). Operative goals of intercollegiate athletics: Perceptions of athletic administrators. *Canadian Journal of Applied Sport Sciences, 9* (1), 33–41.

Chelladurai, P., Inglis, S. E., & Danylchuk, K. E. (1984). Priorities in intercollegiate athletics: Development of a scale. *Research Quarterly for Exercise and Sport, 55* (1), 74–79.

Chelladurai, P., Szyszlo, M., & Haggerty, T. R. (1987). Systems based dimensions of effectiveness: The case of the national sport organizations. *Canadian Journal of Sport Sciences, 12,* 111–119.

Connolly, T., Conlon, E. J., & Deutsch, S. J. (1980). Organizational effectiveness: A multiple-constituency approach. *Academy of Management Review, 5,* 211–217.

Crosby, P. B. (1985). *Quality without tears.* New York: Signet.

Cunningham, G. B. (2003). Human resources as sources of competitive advantage: A resource-based view of the athletic department. *Applied Research in Coaching and Athletics Annual, 203,* 37–58.

Cunningham, G. B., & Sagas, M. (2004). People make the differences; the influence of the coaching staff's human capital and diversity on team performance. *European Sport Management Quarterly, 4,* 3–21.

Deming, W. E. (1986). *Out of the crisis.* Cambridge, MA: MIT Press.

Etzioni, A. (1964). *Modern organizations.* Englewood Cliffs, NJ: Prentice Hall.

Evan, W. M. (1976). Organization theory and organizational effectiveness: An exploratory analysis. In L. S. Spray (Ed.), *Organizational effectiveness: Theory–research–utilization.* Kent, OH: Graduate School of Business Administration, Kent State University.

Forbes, D. P. (1998). Measuring the unmeasurable: Empirical studies of nonprofit organization effectiveness from 1977 to 1997. *Voluntary and Nonprofit Sector Quarterly, 27* (2), 183–202.

Hall, R. H. (1996). *Organizations: Structures, processes, and outcomes* (6th ed.). Englewood Cliffs, NJ: Prentice Hall.

Hasenfeld, Y. (1983). *Human service organizations.* Englewood Cliffs, NJ: Prentice Hall.

Herman, R. D., & Renz, D. O. (1997). Multiple constituencies and the social construction of nonprofit organization effectiveness. *Nonprofit and Voluntary Sector Quarterly, 26* (2), 185–206.

Herman, R. D., & Renz, D. O. (1999). Theses on nonprofit organizational effectiveness. *Nonprofit and Voluntary Sector Quarterly, 28,* (2), 107–126.

Hoy, W. K., & Miskel, C. G. (1982). *Educational administration: Theory, research, and practice* New York: Random House.

Inglis, S. E., & Chelladurai, P. (1983). Student perceptions of goals of intercollegiate athletics: The case of a Canadian university. *Proceedings of the FISU Conference–Universidade '83,* pp. 778–787. Edmonton, Alberta, Canada.

Karteroliotis, K., & Papadimitriou, D. (2004). Confirmatory factor analysis of the sport organizational effectiveness scale. *Psychological Reports, 95,* 366–370.

Keeley, M. (1978). Social justice approach to organizational evaluation. *Administrative Science Quarterly, 22,* 272–292.

Kushner, R. J., & Poole, P. P. (1996). Exploring structure–effectiveness relationships in nonprofit arts organizations. *Nonprofit Management and Leadership, 6* (2), 171–180.

Lawrence, P. R., & Lorsch, J. W. (1967). *Organization and environment: Managing differentiation and integration.* Cambridge, MA: Harvard Graduate School of Business Administration.

Miles, R. H. (1980). *Macro organizational behavior.* Santa Monica, CA: Goodyear.

Molnar, J. J., & Rogers, D. L. (1976). Organizational effectiveness: An empirical comparison of the goal and system resource approaches. *Sociological Quarterly, 17,* 401–413.

Mott, P. E. (1972). *The characteristics of effective organizations.* New York: Harper & Row.

NCAA, (2004a). The National Collegiate Athletic Association's purposes. www.ncaa.org/about/purposes.html. Retrieved on February 16, 2004.

NCAA (2004b). Principles for conduct of intercollegiate athletics. www.ncaa.org/library/membership/division_i_manual/2000-01/article_2.pdf. Retrieved on February 16, 2004.

O'Rourke, S.M., & Chelladurai, P. (in press). Effectiveness of the National Collegiate Athletic Association: Perceptions of Intercollegiate Athletic Administrators. *International Journal of Sport Management.*

Ostroff, C., & Schmitt, N. (1993). Configurations of organizational effectiveness and efficiency. *Academy of Management Journal, 36,* 1345–1361.

Pennings, J. M., & Goodman, P. S. (1977). Toward a workable framework. In P. S. Goodman & J. M. Pennings (Eds.), *New perspectives on organizational effectiveness.* San Francisco: Jossey-Bass.

Perrow, C. (1961). The analysis of goals in complex organizations. *American Sociological Review, 26,* 854–866.

Pfeffer, J. (1977). Usefulness of the concept. In P. S. Goodman & J. M. Pennings (Eds.), *New perspectives on organizational effectiveness.* San Francisco: Jossey-Bass.

Pfeffer, J., & Salancik, G. R. (1978). *The external control of organizations.* New York: Harper & Row.

Price, J. L. (1972). The study of organizational effectiveness. *Sociological Quarterly, 13,* 3–15.

Quinn, R. E., & Rohrbaugh, J. (1983). A spatial model of effectiveness criteria: Towards a competing values approach to organizational analysis. *Management Science, 29* (3), 363–377.

Robbins, S. P. (1990). *Organization theory: Structure, design, and applications* (3rd ed.). Englewood Cliffs, NJ: Prentice Hall.

Robbins, S. P., & Coulter, M. (1996). *Management*. Upper Saddle River, NJ: Prentice Hall.

Rollinson, D. (2002). *Organisational behaviour and analysis: An integrated approach*. (2nd ed.). Harlow: Financial Times Prentice Hall.

Smart, D. L., & Wolfe, R. A. (2000). Examining sustainable competitive advantage in intercollegiate athletics: A resource-based view. *Journal of Sport Management, 14,* 133–153.

Steers, R. M. (1975). Problems in the measurement of organizational effectiveness. *Administrative Science Quarterly, 20,* 546–558.

Steers, R. M. (1977). *Organizational effectiveness: A behavioral view*. Pacific Palisades, CA: Goodyear.

Steers, R. M., & Black, J. S. (1994). *Organizational behavior* (5th ed.). New York: HarperCollins College Publishers.

Trail, G., & Chelladurai, P. (2000). Perceptions of goals and processes of intercollegiate athletics: A case study. *Journal of Sport Management, 14,* 154–178.

Whetten, D. A., & Cameron, K. S. (1994). Organizational effectiveness: Old models and new constructs. In J. Greenberg (Ed.), *Organizational behavior: State of the science* (pp. 135–153). Hillsdale, NJ: Lawrence Erlbaum Associates.

Won, D., & Chelladurai, P. (2005). *Competitive advantage in intercollegiate athletics: Roles of intangible resources*. Paper presented at the 20th Annual Conference of the North American Society for Sport Management, Regina, Canada, June 1–4, 2005.

Yuchtman, E., & Seashore, S. E. (1967). A system resource approach to organizational effectiveness. *American Sociological Review, 32,* 891–903.

Zammuto, R. E. (1984). A comparison of multiple constituency models of organizational effectiveness. *Academy of Management Review, 9* (4), 606–616.

CHAPTER 14

Managing Diversity

MANAGE YOUR LEARNING

After completing this chapter you should be able to:

- Define and describe diversity in the workplace and marketplace.
- Distinguish among forms of diversity.
- Differentiate among the concepts of affirmative action, valuing diversity, and managing diversity.
- Discuss the strategies of accommodation and activation in managing diversity.
- Identify the relationships between tasks and time factors in managing diversity.

STRATEGIC CONCEPTS

accommodation
activation
actualization
affirmative action
benefits of diversity
competence
cultural diversity
deep-level diversity
deficit

difference
diversity
legal requirement
managing diversity
strategies for managing diversity
surface-level diversity
task factor
time factor
valuing diversity

ORGANIZATIONS AND DIVERSITY

In the previous chapters, the descriptions of organizations and their management emphasized the variability associated with management. For instance the cooperation among different people performing different roles is the essence of some definitions of an organization (see Chapter 2). Chapter 3 described organizations as open systems. We defined a system as a set of interrelated and interdependent parts that differ in their attributes but are arranged in an organized manner to produce a unified whole (Immegart & Pilecki, 1973; Robbins, 1997; Waring, 1996). We also noted that one system might differ from another in terms of the parts and attributes of parts that make the system. An effective system is one in which different parts of the system and their attributes combine to make up a meaningful whole, and in which the activities of different parts are coordinated to facilitate the effective functioning of the system itself.

The notion of diversity also underlies the definition of sport management as "coordination of limited human and material resources, relevant technologies, and situational contingencies for the efficient production and exchange of sport services" (Chelladurai, 1994, p. 15). We noted that coordination is achieved through the functions of planning, organizing, leading, and evaluating (discussed in Chapters 5 through 13). A perusal of these chapters highlights the concept of diversity (variability) of the elements that need to be coordinated. Thus, the concept of diversity underlies all managerial actions (Thomas, 1996). However, we will confine this chapter's emphasis on management of diversity to a consideration of diversity in human characteristics. Accordingly, the focus of this chapter is on the variability or diversity among people with whom an organization interacts, including its employees and customers.

The variability among people was emphasized in our discussion of planning. For instance, in setting goals and choosing appropriate means to achieve those goals, managers need to be attuned to external as well as internal environmental conditions. The external conditions include individuals and groups (called constituents or stakeholders), who differ in their values and goal preferences (see Chapter 5). The internal conditions include the employees of the organization, who differ in their abilities, work experiences, goal preferences, and so on. Similarly, the organizing function entails breaking down the total work into distinct jobs and assigning those jobs to qualified individuals, and establishing a mechanism to coordinate these jobs and individuals (see Chapters 7 and 8). Implied in this description is the idea that the jobs as well as the people who perform them differ in terms of skills, abilities, and attitudes. Individual differences result in the varying preferences for leadership considered in the multidimensional model described in Chapter 13.

If we push the idea of differences among us far enough, we can conclude that each of us is distinct and different from anyone else in the world. This is certainly true in the biological sense, because our fingerprints and DNA compositions are unique in the universe. Even from a social–psychological perspective, we are characterized by differences in terms of abilities, attitudes, personality, values, and thinking styles. The factors that set us apart at the individual level are called *individual difference variables*. These variables help distinguish one individual from another of the same group, such as white Americans, African Americans, Asian Americans, males, and females. The individual difference variables have been the subject matter of study in fields such as human resource management, personnel psychology, and organizational behavior. In fact, individual differences are the subject of four entire chapters in Chelladurai's *Human Resource Management in Sport and Recreation*.

Individual differences affect every managerial action and its effectiveness. Thus, a critical function of management is to take advantage of the differences among employees and coordinate them for attaining organizational effectiveness. Because diversity in the workforce (differences among employees and customers) presents unique opportunities as well as obstacles for organizational effectiveness, it is useful for us to understand the dynamics of diversity in the workplace and how to mobilize it for greater organizational effectiveness.

> **In Brief**
>
> The definition of management implies that the diversity in resources, personnel, activities, and associated technologies needs to be coordinated. Thus, diversity underlies management.

DIVERSITY DEFINED

The following is a sampling of definitions of **diversity**:

> Diversity is "any mixture of items characterized by differences and similarities." (Thomas, 1996, p. 5)

Diversity refers to "individual human differences. In the context of organizational life, diversity is about individual differences that can be drawn on and developed to promote the goals and practices of an organization. This definition refers to individual and group differences that contribute to distinct social entities." (Arredondo, 1996, pp. 15–16)

Diversity is "the result of a broad range of complex, social, political, economic, and other forces that have put in close proximity people who have vastly different orientations, frames of reference, backgrounds, and perspectives." (Sonnenschein, 1997, p. 2)

Diversity is "a mix of people in one social system who have distinctly different, socially relevant group affiliations." (Cox & Beale, 1997, p. 1)

Diversity "encompasses any characteristic used to differentiate one person from others. Our conception of diversity includes differences across gender, race, age, physical ability, sexual orientation, religion, skills, and tenure in the organization." (Joplin & Daus, 1997, p. 32)

Note the subtle difference between Thomas's (1996) and the other definitions. Thomas's definition refers to a mixture of items including all organizational variables, material and human. In this broader view, diversity "applies not only to a company's people concerns but to many other critical areas" (Thomas, 1996, p. 5). For instance, Thomas would include acquisitions and mergers, cross-functional coordination, and managing change as issues of diversity. "The more lines of business you have, the more functions, the more races represented in your workforce, and the greater the differences among them, the greater the diversity" (Thomas, 1996, p. 9). As noted, Thomas's broader view is included in discussions of management in general. Many issues associated with diversity in products, structure and processes, and environments were discussed in previous chapters.

On the other hand, Arredondo (1996), Cox and Beale (1997), and Sonnenschein (1997) restrict their conception of diversity to human differences. Most scholars and practitioners take this perspective, restricting their discussion of diversity to human differences. We should also note that differences among people can be at the group level or the individual level. These differing orientations appear in the definitions of diversity proposed by Cox and Beale (1997), who emphasize group affiliations, and Arredondo (1996), who focuses on individual differences. Cox and Beale (1997) note that group affiliations may relate to gender, nationality, age, levels or types of physiological abilities or disabilities, ethnic identity, religion, and so on. Note also that a socially relevant group affiliation implies that some meaning is attached to interactions among members of the group. These

Diversity as used in this book refers to a myriad of characteristics that set apart individuals or groups from other individuals or groups.

authors note that wearing the same size shoes does not have the same effect or meaning as belonging to the same political party. Diversity at the individual level can be related to the abilities, talents, values, and beliefs an individual brings to the organizational context. The focus of this chapter will be on both group-level and individual-level diversity.

DIMENSIONS OF DIVERSITY

According to Schuler and Jackson (1996), there are many dimensions of diversity, including gender, ethnicity, culture, age, functional areas of expertise, religion, lifestyle, and so on. Similarly, Kossek and Lobel (1996) consider "diversity to be not only derived from differences in ethnicity and gender, but also based on differences in function, nationality, language, ability, religion, lifestyle, or tenure" (p. 2).

Milliken and Martins (1996) categorize these grouping characteristics as observable or readily detectable attributes, and less visible or underlying attributes. Observable attributes include race or ethnic background, age, and gender. Less visible attributes include education, technical abilities, and tenure in the organization. One reason they distinguish between observable and nonobservable attributes is that "when differences between people are visible, they are particularly likely to evoke responses that are due directly to biases, prejudices, or stereotypes" (p. 404).

In line with the above distinction between observable and nonobservable group characteristics, Hopkins (1997, p. 3) categorizes group characteristics as:

- *ethnographic* descriptors such as nationality, religion, and language
- *demographic* descriptors such as age, gender, and place of residence
- *status* descriptors such as social, economic, and educational background
- *sexual orientation* descriptors such as heterosexual, homosexual, or bisexual
- a range of other descriptors relating to formal or informal membership affiliations, such as functional specializations and part-time or full-time employment status

From a different perspective, Jehn, Northcraft, and Neale (1999) speak of three categories of diversity—informational diversity, social category diversity, and value diversity. *Informational diversity* refers to "differences in knowledge bases and perspectives that members bring to the group," which may arise from "differences in education, experience, and expertise" (p. 743). *Social category diversity* is

Social philosophers are still debating the merits of encouraging members of a multicultural society to perpetuate their ethnic identities versus the merits of encouraging them to amalgamate into the "American melting pot." In recent years this national debate has been dominated by a single theme: ethnic, racial, and social diversity. However, as groups other than those identified by race or ethnicity (e.g., feminists, homosexuals, the aged, and disabled individuals) intensify their efforts to be recognized as legitimate entities in America's mosaic of humanity, social philosophers have begun to move beyond the rhetoric of ethnic, racial, and cultural diversity and toward the new rhetoric of "diversity."

HOPKINS, *1997, pp. 3–4*

Sidebar

I come from a family of nine children (five girls and four boys). Sibling rivalry often led us to arguments of who was better and who was better liked by our mother. When we took our arguments to Mother, she would ask us to put up our right hand with fingers spread out. After pointing out that the five fingers are not alike, she would ask us which one of the five fingers we would not miss should it be cut off.

Extending this analogy, we can suggest that management of diversity consists of (a) recognizing the differences as well as similarities among people (the fingers), (b) realizing that each person, like a finger, has unique qualities that can contribute to the total effort, and (c) capitalizing on these unique features and coordinating them for productivity and effectiveness. Each finger is different, but it takes the coordination of all five to manipulate objects effectively.

---

born out of membership in specific social categories such as race and gender. *Value diversity* "occurs when members of a workgroup differ in terms of what they think the group's real task, goal, target, or mission should be" (p. 745). The idea of differences in information and knowledge people possess suggests that people specializing in functional areas (e.g., marketing, accounting, coaching, fitness leadership) may also be diverse (Pelled, Eisenhart, & Xin, 1999). That is, the specialized training and education and experiences with specific task contingencies may lead to *functional diversity*—diverse orientations regarding what activities are important and how they should be carried out.

As you consider the factors that underlie diversity, note two caveats. First, each of us can be described as diverse under specific circumstances. For instance, a young student renting an apartment in a complex predominantly occupied by retirees would be diverse from the "mainstream" occupants in terms of age. Similarly, a middle-aged person visiting a bar full of college students would be the odd one (that is, the old one). Second, because individuals belong to more than one group, judgments about individuals cannot be made on the basis of their membership in only one group. For example, the distinction between males and females implies that the males will be alike on certain characteristics in comparison to females. However, any two males may differ in their nationality, religion, or language. Similarly, contrasting white Americans from nonwhite Americans does not say anything about the sexual orientation, educational background, or religion of a white American or a nonwhite American. The issue of diversity and managing diversity is complex.

Another point of emphasis in Thomas's (1996) definition of diversity as "any mixture of items characterized by differences *and* similarities" (emphasis added) is that diversity includes both differences and similarities among groups. In his words,

> One way of conceptualizing this is to think in terms of a macro/micro continuum. A micro perspective looks at the individual component and a macro perspective looks at the mixture. To get at the true nature of diversity (comprising differences *and* similarities) requires an ability to assume both perspectives simultaneously; the micro facilitates identification of differences, and the macro enhances the ability to see similarities. (p. 6)

In a similar vein, Lawson and Shen (1998), noting that it takes longer to change a heart than a mind, suggested that "the critical challenge for each person and each organization around the world is to learn that diversity is a bridge to finding deeper similarities and interests among all human beings" (p. 69).

DIFFERENCES VERSUS DEFICITS

ny discussion of diversity or management of diversity must begin with the basic idea that **differences** are not **deficits**. The natural tendency to view anything different about an individual or a group of individuals as inferior to us must be resisted. As Weiner (1997) noted,

> For something to be "different," there must be a reference point, something for it to be different from. Typically "we" (whoever "we" are) see other cultures as different from "us," often unaware that we are different from them. . . . That is, we typically divide the world into an in-group (our group) and all other groups are out-groups; out-groups are seen as different. This would not be a problem except that in-group thinking typically defines those who are different as inferior, wrong or bad. (p. 2)

In Brief

Diversity can be described in terms of several dimensions such as gender, race, age, language, religion, and so on. It is important to note that differences in these dimensions are not deficits.

The same issue was illustrated by Hagar, the cartoon character. Hagar tells his stooge, Eddie, "Remember, Vikings are the chosen people." Eddie asks, "Who chose us?" The pat answer from Hagar is "We did." Such self-determined notions of the superiority of "our group" leads to stereotypes such as "members of certain groups lack leadership ability, have a propensity for certain kinds of work such as caring work or technical work, have good or poor work ethics and so on" (Weiner, 1997, p. 3). In this text, the term "different" carries no connotation of deficit. It simply means "not the same." "'Not the same' describes two or more things as being unlike or different; it does not mean that one is better than the other" (Weiner, 1997, p. 2).

WHY THE CONCERN WITH DIVERSITY?

he underlying reason for society's concern with diversity is that our society and workplaces are growing more diverse. In terms of overall population distribution, the U.S. Bureau of the Census predicts the following changes:

	2000	2050 (projected)
White	71.6%	52.8%
Hispanic	12.5%	24.5%
Black	12.3%	13.6%
Asian	3.6%	8.2%

These overall changes will be reflected in workplaces, of course. In addition, the workforce will continue to include growing numbers of women, individuals who are disabled, individuals of various sexual orientations, and others who may differ from what we define as the "norm." Just as importantly, this diversity will be reflected in those who buy products and services.

Sidebar

The negative effects of diversity on employees of intercollegiate athletic departments have been demonstrated by Cunningham and his associates (Cunningham & Sagas, 2004a, 2004b, 2004c; Fink and Cunningham, in press). Cunningham and Sagas (2004a) reported that greater diversity in terms of tenure and ethnicity was associated with lower occupational commitment and higher intention to leave the occupation among 235 Division IA football coaching staffs. However, diversity in age was not related to either of the outcomes. In another study of Division IA assistant football coaches, Cunningham and Sagas (2004c) found that coaches belonging to minority races perceived less career-related opportunity, were less satisfied with their careers, and had greater occupational turnover intentions than their white counterparts. They also found that perceived career opportunity affected career satisfaction, which, in turn, influenced the intention to leave the occupation.

Fink and Cunningham (in press) investigated the effects of differences in gender and race between subordinates (i.e., assistant/associate athletic directors, senior women's administrators, and coaches) and their athletic directors on an index of work experience. Their results showed that persons in mixed-gender dyads and those in mixed-race dyads had poorer work experiences than did persons in demographically similar dyads.

Cunningham and Sagas (2004) studied the effects of being in a predominantly white or predominantly black staff on organizational commitment of Division I assistant basketball coaches. They found that black coaches in predominantly white or black staff expressed greater commitment than did black coaches in staffs with a relatively equal distribution of whites and racial minorities. In contrast, white coaches on predominantly black coaching staffs were less committed than whites in other settings. Cumulatively these studies suggest that diversity in demographic characteristics could detrimentally affect the attitudes of minority members in workgroups. Hence it is important that managers recognize this and take steps to reduce the negative impact of diversity and enhance its potential benefits.

It is crucial that today's managers and leaders understand what diversity is and learn how an organization may take advantage of the diversity of its workforce, its clients, and its customers.

In Chapter 1, after describing the various products of sport organizations, we noted that sport management is concerned with producing and marketing sport services. Implied in this statement is the need to tailor an organization's products to be consistent with the needs of its customers, and to adopt marketing strategies that suit the characteristics of the customers. Marketers have long known that a market (i.e., the collection of customers) is not a unitary concept. That is, a market can be subdivided into segments based on specific characteristics such as gender, age, education, and so on; hence the terms *market segmentation* and *niche marketing*. Thus, any organization concerned with marketing its products must understand the nature of diversity in its market, and must learn appropriate marketing strategies, including market segmentation.

Weiner (1997) notes that globalization of industries and trade also directs a greater focus on diversity. If the United States itself is characterized by diversity, the global economy is much more so. To the extent an organization deals at the international level, it has to be attuned to the diversity in the global market. Moreover, as the global economy moves labor across national boundaries, organizations need to ensure smooth interactions among these diverse workers (Schneider & Northcraft, 1999).

In January 1999, the Clinton administration relaxed U.S. trade sanctions against Cuba. One element of the policy was to allow the Baltimore Orioles professional baseball club to compete with the Cuban national baseball team in Cuba. This move, labeled *baseball diplomacy*, is expected to be the forerunner of continued sport exchanges between the United States and Cuba. In that eventuality, it becomes imperative that sport organizations understand and appreciate the diversity between the two nations in terms of language, culture, and political ideology. Currently, the National Basketball Association, the National Hockey League, and Major League Baseball franchises have many players from European, Asian, and South American countries. The performance of these players and their teams is contingent on effective management of their diversity. By the same token, the National Basketball Association and the National Football League must be concerned with managing diversity as they extend their operations beyond North America. That is, they have to understand, accept, and effectively manage the diversity among employees, athletes, and the spectators.

Management needs to be concerned with diversity because of the increasing diversity in the American population and workforce, and the increasing globalization of the economy, as well as of sport.

BENEFITS OF MANAGING DIVERSITY

As we noted, diversity implies that the market and the workforce are composed of people of different demographic and ethnographic backgrounds, different socioeconomic status groups, and different sexual orientations. It also implies that such diverse people bring to the organization different beliefs, values, and attitudes. What is more important in our context is that these diverse groups bring different talents and perspectives relevant to organizational processes. Effective management of diversity is based on capitalizing on the diverse talents and perspectives in order to solve organizational problems and enhance the effectiveness of organizational processes, thus reaping the **benefits of diversity**.

Cox and Beale (1997) argue that revenue enhancement is achieved through effective marketing strategies, problem solving, creativity, and innovation. *Effective marketing strategy* refers to selling to increasingly diverse consumers. This is facilitated by a well-utilized, diverse workforce in two main ways: A diverse workforce will provide public relations value for the organization, and a well-managed, diverse workforce will enhance the reputation of the organization with its potential customers (Weiner, 1997). In addition, the organization will gain from the marketing insights available from diverse employees.

Problem solving is enhanced by diverse backgrounds and experiences, and by the insights from differing perspectives. These differing perspectives facilitate critical analysis and scrutiny of a given problem. By the same token, a diverse workforce is rich with creativity and innovation. Weiner (1997) echoes this view and underscores the many benefits to be derived from the contributions of talents of a multicultural workforce.

COSTS OF MANAGING DIVERSITY

Workforce diversity may increase the costs of running an organization if that diversity is not managed properly. Costs may arise from increased absenteeism and turnover because of the dissatisfaction and disenchantment of employees. Also, the positive contributions of a diverse workforce may not be realized owing to the reduced efficiency of communication among diverse workgroups. Unresolved issues in intergroup dynamics may further increase the costs. In addition, harassment behaviors are likely to increase, which in turn may lead to legal ramifications such as discrimination suits.

Effective management of diversity also involves some costs. As Weiner (1997) notes, the first obvious costs relate to monetary and material resources of the organization. In attempting to accommodate the needs of working mothers, for example, the organization may have to spend extra resources setting up a day care center. Similarly, it costs money to build a wheelchair ramp for the workers who need such a facility.

Less evident in the above examples is the time taken in the effective management of a diverse workforce. We noted that a diverse workforce contributes greatly to problem solving and good decision making, but such problem solving and decision making take time. Group decision making is notorious for the time it takes. This difficulty is more pronounced when diverse individuals are involved. It takes time to understand each other's perspectives and to arrive at a solution acceptable to all or at least to the majority. Another cost alluded to by Weiner (1997) is the discomfort experienced by members of a diverse team and the resistance of members to understanding and appreciating different perspectives. Such discomfort may lead to the biggest potential cost of all: conflicts among members of a diverse workforce.

PERSPECTIVES ON MANAGING DIVERSITY

Diversity in the workforce is not a matter of debate. It is a fact. But managing diversity may be a focus of debate. What are the effective ways of managing diversity? How do we capitalize on the advantages of a diverse workforce and minimize the disadvantages of diversity? These questions are of great concern among theorists and practitioners. Thomas (1991) noted that affirmative action, valuing diversity, and managing diversity are the three approaches to diversity in the workplace. While these processes are important in themselves, people at times are not clear about the distinctions among them. An effective manager needs to be clear about these terms and their implications for management. The following section describes these approaches.

Affirmative action. Affirmative action is a government policy aimed at eliminating the discriminating effects of managerial policies and practices that preclude equal employment opportunities for all without reference to group membership.

> It aims, through a variety of methods, to remedy discrimination and increase the representation of designated disadvantaged groups, namely women and ethnic minorities. The policy goes beyond advocating simple sex or color blindness in employment decision making by specifying that group membership be explicitly taken into account in such decisions. Thus, the assumption built into this policy is that nondiscrimination alone is not sufficient to counteract the consequences of prejudice and inequality—that something more is needed. (Heilman, 1994, pp. 126–127)

Valuing diversity. Valuing diversity refers to (a) a genuine acceptance of diversity as a given, (b) recognizing the advantages of a diverse workforce, and (c) a clear understanding that benefits of diversity can be derived only through appropriate managerial practices. "Valuing diversity is a philosophy about how diversity affects organizational outcomes that holds the presence of diversity represents a distinct organizational resource that, properly leveraged, can bring a competitive advantage against organizations that either are culturally homogeneous or fail to utilize their diversity" (Cox & Beale, 1997, p. 13).

> **Sidebar**
>
> "Dealing with differences in Canada is unique because Canada is the only country to have a legal commitment to multiculturalism. The federal *Multiculturalism Act* recognizes the diversity of Canadians with respect to race, national and ethnic origin, and religion as a fundamental characteristic of Canadian society. The Act commits the government to a policy of multiculturalism designed to preserve and enhance the multicultural heritage of Canadians while working to achieve equality for all Canadians in the economic, social, cultural and political life of Canada. The Act only affects the federal government and puts no requirements on work organizations. Still, it does provide a foundation and expectation for how work organizations will behave" (Weiner, 1997, p. 1).

Managing diversity. Managing diversity implies that "the organizational interventions that fall within the realm of this label focus on ensuring that the variety of talents and perspectives that already exist within an organization are well utilized" (Schuler & Jackson, 1996, p. 4). According to Cox and Beale (1997), managing diversity is "creating a climate in which the potential advantages of diversity for organizational or group performance are maximized while the potential disadvantages are minimized" (p. 2). In Arredondo's (1996) view, managing diversity is a strategic organizational approach, and it "represents a shift away from activities and assumptions defined by affirmative action to management practices that are inclusive, reflecting the workforce diversity and its potential" (p. 17).

In summary, affirmative action is a function of government regulations that are imposed on organizations to redress past discriminations as well to ensure equal opportunities for all in the present, whereas valuing diversity and managing diversity are learned processes with no reference to any governmental regulations. Affirmative action relates largely to the hiring of employees

Sidebar

For decades, governments at all levels have been concerned with maximizing the benefits of diversity in the workforce. To this end, these governments have promulgated laws and regulations to curb discriminatory employment practices and promote equal employment opportunities for all members of society. Fernandez and Barr (1993) list the following as a sampling of federal government initiatives in this regard:

- *Equal Pay Act of 1963*

  Prohibits gender-based pay differentials for equal work.

- *Title VII, 1964 Civil Rights Act (as amended in 1972)*

  Prohibits job discrimination based on race, religion, gender, or national origin.

- *Executive Order 11246 (1965)*

  Requires contractors and subcontractors performing work on federal or federally assisted projects to prepare and implement affirmative action plans for minorities and women, persons with disabilities, and veterans.

- *Age Discrimination in Employment Act (1967)—ADEA*

  Prohibits age discrimination in areas such as hiring, promotion, termination, leaves of absence, and compensation. Protects individuals age 40 and over.

- *Rehabilitation Act of 1973*

  Prohibits contractors and subcontractors of federal projects from discriminating against applicants or employees who are physically or mentally disabled, if qualified to perform the job. Requires the contractor to take affirmative action in the employment and advancement of individuals with disabilities.

- *Vietnam Era Veterans Readjustment Assistance Act of 1972 and 1974*

  Requires government contractors and subcontractors to take affirmative action with respect to certain classes of veterans of the Vietnam Era and Special Disabled Veterans.

- *Immigration Reform and Control Act of 1986 (IRCA)*

  Prohibits employers from discriminating against persons authorized to work in the United States with respect to hire or termination from employment because of national origin or citizenship status.

- *The Americans with Disabilities Act of 1990, Title I*

  Prohibits employers from discriminating against qualified applicants and employees with disabilities with regard to any employment practices or terms, conditions, or privileges of employment.

- *Civil Rights Act of 1991*

  Grants to plaintiffs the right to a jury trial and makes available compensatory and punitive damages (capped at $300,000).

(entry into the organization), whereas valuing and managing diversity deal with how diverse people are treated once inside the organization and how their varied talents and perspectives are utilized. Henderson (1994) provides an even more elaborate description of affirmative action, valuing diversity, managing diversity, and the differences among them. Henderson notes that affirmative action is *legally* driven, valuing diversity is *ethically* driven, and managing diversity is *strategically* driven. This fundamental distinction among the three concepts provides for other differences that are outlined in Exhibit 14.1.

Exhibit 14.1 Distinctions among affirmative action, valuing differences, and managing diversity.

AFFIRMATIVE ACTION	VALUING DIFFERENCES	MANAGING DIVERSITY
Quantitative. The achievement of equality of opportunity is sought by changing organizational demographics. Progress is monitored by statistical reports and analyses.	*Qualitative.* The emphasis is on the appreciation of differences and the creation of an environment in which everyone feels valued and accepted. Progress is monitored by organizational surveys of attitudes and perceptions.	*Behavioral.* The emphasis is on building specific skills and creating policies that get the best from every employee. Efforts are monitored by progress toward achieving goals and objectives.
Legally driven. Written plans and statistical goals for specific groups are used.	*Ethically driven.* Moral and ethical imperatives are the impetus for cultural change.	*Strategically driven.* Behaviors and policies contribute to organizational goals, such as increased profits and productivity.
Remedial. Specific target groups benefit as prior wrongs are addressed. Previously excluded groups have an advantage.	*Idealistic.* Everyone benefits by feeling valued and accepted in an inclusive environment.	*Pragmatic.* The organization benefits: morale, profits, and productivity increase.
Assimilation model. Assumes that groups that are brought into the system will adapt to existing organizational norms.	*Diversity model.* Groups retain their own characteristics, shape the organization, and are shaped by it to create a common set of values.	*Synergy model.* Diverse groups create new ways of working together effectively in a pluralistic environment.
Opens doors. The focus is on hiring and promotion decisions.	*Opens attitudes, minds, and the culture.* The emphasis is on inclusion, not assimilation.	*Opens the system.* Managerial policies and practices are affected.
Resistance. Resistance arises from perceived limits to autonomy in decision making and fears of reverse discrimination.	*Resistance.* Resistance arises from the fear of change and discomfort with differences.	*Resistance.* Resistance arises from the denial of demographic realities, of the need for alternate approaches, and of the benefits of change.

From *Cultural diversity in the workplace: Issues and strategies,* by G. Henderson. Westport, CT: Quorum Books. ©1994 by G. Henderson. Reproduced with permission of Greenwood Publishing Group, Inc., Westport, CT.

Valuing diversity and effectively managing it begin with a clear understanding of what diversity means and what implications it has for the organization and the people in it. In Weiner's (1997) view, *inclusivity* (i.e., valuing diversity) "requires recognizing differences while perceiving them as part of the whole.... The mind-set shift involves realizing that all groups are different and that all differences are equally valid, assuming they are relevant, and have something to contribute" (pp. 6–7). That is, the mindset that is bound to the in-group versus out-group dichotomy should shift to valued differences among subgroups.

In a similar vein, Cox and Beale (1997) view *diversity competency* as "a process of learning that leads to an ability to effectively respond to the challenges and opportunities posed by the presence of social–cultural diversity in a defined social system" (p. 2). Learning to manage diversity consists of awareness, meaning the recognition and acknowledgment of diversity and its effects; understanding, leading to a deeper grasp of the need for effective management of diversity; and action steps to change behavior. These stages (shown in Exhibit 14.2) relate to all managerial activities, including hiring and promotion decisions, training programs, performance evaluation and feedback, group formation and functioning, and conflict resolution.

Robbins and Coulter (1996, p. 507) also note that coordination of heterogeneous groups requires understanding of differences and the need to be fair and equitable; empathy, meaning recognition of others' perspectives and preferences; tolerance for different perspectives, values, and behaviors; and communication in order to discuss issues in non-threatening ways.

> **In Brief**
>
> Affirmative action is a **legal requirement** imposed by government. Valuing diversity is a philosophy that accepts diversity and believes in the value or usefulness of all people. Managing diversity is a strategy for making the best use of the talents, abilities, and perspectives of diverse workers.

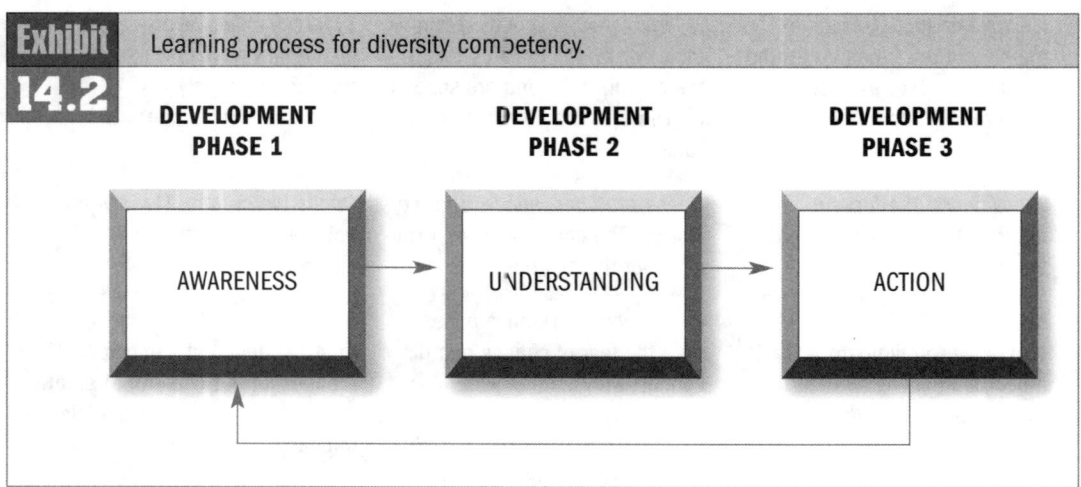

Exhibit 14.2 Learning process for diversity competency.

DEVELOPMENT PHASE 1: AWARENESS → DEVELOPMENT PHASE 2: UNDERSTANDING → DEVELOPMENT PHASE 3: ACTION

Source: Cox and Beale (1997, p. 5).

OPTIONS FOR HANDLING DIVERSITY

Thomas (1996) identifies the following eight options available to managers facing diversity issues. Note that diversity as defined by Thomas refers to a mixture of items characterized by differences and similarities. This view would include differences among organizational environments, structures, processes, and material as well as human resources. As noted, the focus in this book is on diversity in human terms, as seen in the workforce and the market.

Option 1: Include/exclude. In this option, either the number and variability of elements in the mixture are increased, or diversity is excluded by minimizing the variability in the elements of the mixture. Thomas (1996) notes that the option of exclusion is prohibited for the most part by existing laws prohibiting discrimination and requiring equal employment opportunities. Despite such laws, however, even today there are sport organizations that restrict their membership to certain categories of people.

Option 2: Deny. In this option, decision makers refuse to acknowledge differences among people; thus, there is less tolerance for gender or racial groupings. For instance, management may not encourage support groups for women or minorities. Again, as Thomas (1996) notes, this option is less prevalent as the workforce—both managers and employees—becomes more comfortable with ethnic and gender diversity.

Option 3: Assimilate. Managers operating under this option attempt to minimize diversity by insisting that the diverse elements conform to the dominant norms. Holding dominant norms and ways of operating as ideals, managers expect everyone to fit into a given mold. These managers also tend to emphasize organizational and task requirements as the basis for organizational behavior. While we cannot ignore organizational or task requirements, we must also recognize that such requirements include preferences and traditions. "The corporate mold, comprising true requirements and also these preferences, traditions, and conveniences, was developed sometime in the past, by whatever race was dominant then" (Thomas, 1996, p. 92). The problem here is the confounding of *true* requirements of the task or organization and preferences and traditions that are unrelated to the task.

Option 4: Suppress. In seeking to minimize diversity in the workplace, managers may attempt to suppress manifestation of any racial differences. These managers may acknowledge and accept gender or racial differences outside the organization but not in the workplace. For example, a manager of a fitness club may insist that all aerobic instructors conform to standard attire and music, suppressing preferences of minority employees for specific styles of dress and music.

Option 5: Isolate. One way of reducing the complexity of managing diversity is to isolate groups defined by gender or race. Thomas (1996) gives the example of how a predominantly white church handled diversity in the congregation. When confronted with an influx of Hispanics, the church hired a Hispanic minister and arranged special services for the Hispanic members.

Sidebar

Any discussion of diversity touches upon easily identifiable characteristics such as gender, color, and age as well as less discernible characteristics such as educational, economic, and social status. A more thorough analysis would show that the values, beliefs, and attitudes that individuals bring to the situation are also important sources of diversity in the workplace. Because people's beliefs, values, and attitudes stem partly from their cultures, the notion of **cultural diversity** has gained prominence in the discourse on diversity issues.

Culture is defined as a unique set of values, beliefs, attitudes, and expectations, as well as language, symbols, customs, and behaviors of individuals by virtue of some common characteristic(s) shared with others (e.g., DeSensi, 1994; Doherty & Chelladurai, 1999). When we speak of a "youth culture," a "gay culture," a "drug culture," an "African American culture," or a "Latino culture," we think of each culture as consisting of a unique set of values, beliefs, attitudes, language, symbols, and behaviors shared by members belonging to the defined group.

Although cultural diversity among groups of people defined by race, gender, age, and other such characteristics is readily apparent, there are some dangers to generalizing this conception to all people of a group. First we need to understand that considerable differences exist among members of a group in the extent to which they accept and adhere to the values, beliefs, and attitudes of the group in general (Allison, 1988; Fine, 1995). In other words, the differences among groups (*intergroup* differences) should not be allowed to hide the differences among members of any one group (*intragroup* or *interindividual* differences).

The significance of the distinction between intergroup and intragroup differences is shown in Exhibit 14.3. The mean of Group A on a given cultural value such as authority relations is shown to be lower than that of Group B (intergroup difference). At the same time, there are considerable differences between members within each of the groups (intragroup differences). While the scores for most members of Group A cluster around the mean for that group, the scores for A1 and A2 from Group A are far apart from each other. This is the same case with members B1 and B2 in Group B. Notice also that the scores for A1 and B1 (and those of A2 and B2) are almost the same, although they belong to two different groups.

A second confounding issue is that any one individual may belong to more than one distinguishing group. Consider these four individuals: an African American female, an African American male, a white female, and a white male. Each one of them belongs to different groups defined by race and gender. If we were to make any judgments about any one of them based on cultural indicators, we would be at a loss; any such judgment could be terribly wrong. In *All in the Family,* a popular television show of the 1970s, the white male Archie Bunker and the African American male George Jefferson were constantly arguing about the superiority of their respective races, making liberal use of racial epithets. However, they shared very similar and intense gender biases in dealing with their wives.

The point is that an individual may identify with more than one culture group based on a number of different personal characteristics (see Doherty & Chelladurai, 1999; Cox, 1993). For example, an individual may belong to several groupings simultaneously, such as males or females, Christians or Buddhists or Muslims, whites or nonwhites, and so on. The basic premise is that every group has its own culture, and therefore, a person may belong to several cultures at the same time (Doherty & Chelladurai, 1999). That is, an individual's personal culture is multifaceted. One view is that individuals will emphasize those facets of their personal culture that are associated with permanent characteristics such as gender, race, and age. Another view is that individuals may focus on different facets of their personal culture in different contexts (such as work and nonwork settings). The important thing for sport managers is to recognize the complexity and multifaceted nature of personal cultures that employees bring to the workplace. It would be inappropriate and counterproductive to pigeonhole an employee into any specific cultural box.

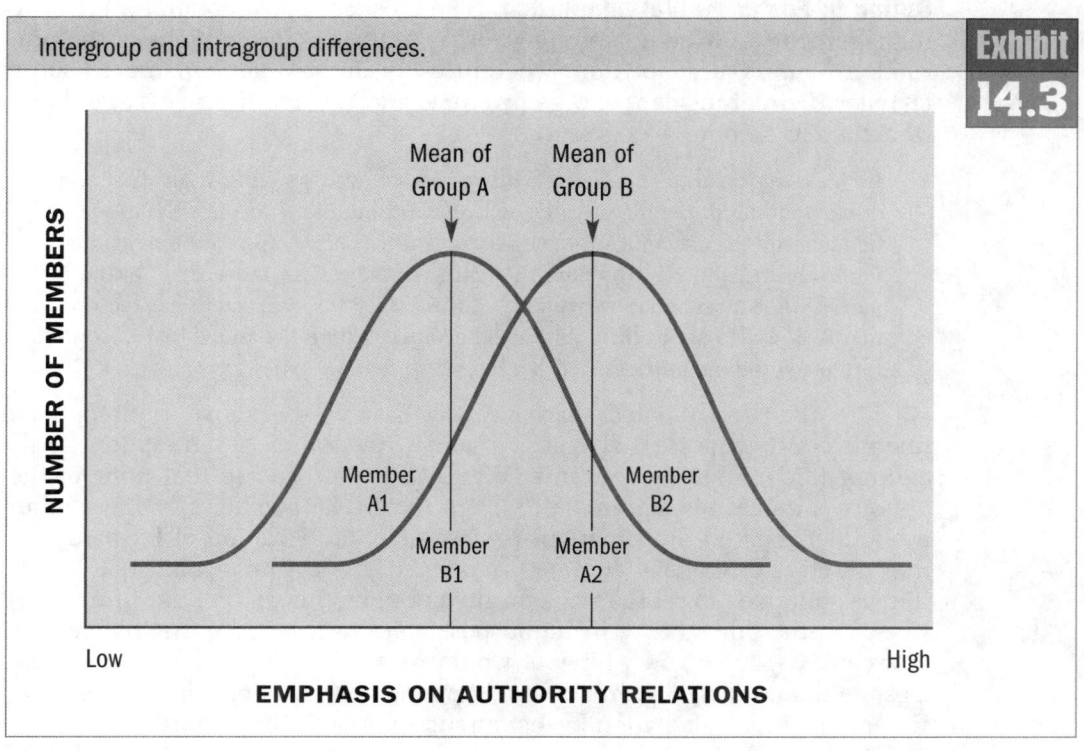

Exhibit 14.3 Intergroup and intragroup differences.

MANAGING DIVERSITY

One may argue that the move was based on good intentions because the Hispanic members are likely to be better served by a minister who speaks their language and understands their culture. Consider a fitness club that caters to young adults as well as senior citizens. Is it not reasonable for the management to schedule separate exercise sessions for the two groups? Similarly, it is not uncommon for a city recreation department to organize soccer competitions for different age groups and for males and females.

However, in the workplace such segregation may be less defensible. For instance, if individuals are relegated to specific departments or tasks based on gender or race, discrimination is being practiced.

Option 6: Tolerate. Managers operating under this option acknowledge gender and racial differences, perhaps because of affirmative action equal employment regulations. Ostensibly, the attitude represented by this option is that there is room for all. However, while all are included in the workforce, they are not treated equally. They do not become full partners in organizational processes. As Thomas (1996) noted, "to be tolerated is to be kept in limbo between full participation and exclusion" (p. 93).

Option 7: Build relationships. This option reflects management's efforts to manage diversity effectively. With acceptance and understanding of diversity, managers try to cultivate positive relationships and harmony among members of the diverse workforce with a view to enhancing productivity and effectiveness of the organization as a whole. Thomas (1996) notes that this is a significant and necessary—but not sufficient—step for effective management of diversity.

Option 8: Foster mutual adaptation. The most advanced option for effective management of diversity among Thomas's (1996) eight options is the promotion of mutual adaptation, wherein every diverse element makes some changes in order to adapt to organizational and task requirements and thereby achieve common objectives.

> By focusing on *true requirements* [italics added] and pushing individual and organizational preferences, conveniences, and traditions to the side, the parties identify the essentials for the relationship and free up room for negotiations around the *nonrequirements* [italics added]. This movement by both parties allows assimilation where it is necessary for organizational requirements and also some flexibility in other areas where the individual is comfortable with being different (Thomas, 1996, pp. 94-95)

Thomas (1996) noted that only this last of the above eight options unequivocally endorses diversity, whereas the other seven options only attempt to eliminate or minimize diversity. He also noted that none of the options is inherently legitimate or illegitimate. The goodness/badness of an option depends on the situation. For example, the isolation of Hispanics in the church referred to by Thomas can be seen as a legitimate and good option if it was intended to set the stage for further reorganization of the church services. On the other hand, if the purpose were to minimize the interactions between Hispanics and whites, it would be an illegitimate and bad option. Despite the possible legitimacy of all options, the focus of this chapter is on fostering mutual adaptation in the pursuit of organizational goals.

In the above quote, I have added the emphasis to two significant terms—*true requirements* and *nonrequirements*. The requirements that Thomas (1996) refers to are those required for the effective functioning of the organization and successful performance of the job at hand. You may recall the glory days of the Chicago Bulls professional basketball franchise with Michael Jordan, Scottie Pippen, and Dennis Rodman. Rodman was quite different from the other two players in values, beliefs, and behaviors. The management, the coaches, and the players accepted this divergence in attitudes and behaviors insofar as they did not violate the organizational and task requirements. Thus, Rodman was free to color his hair and pierce his body as he deemed fit. However, he was required to abide by the organizational requirement of wearing the team uniform, as well as the task requirement of following the rules of the game. It is also noteworthy that management, coaches, and players made the best use of Rodman's defensive and rebounding skills while accommodating his idiosyncratic preferences and behaviors, which were unrelated to task performance. This example highlights two distinct strategies in managing diversity—*accommodation* and *activation*. We will discuss these two strategies in detail in a later section of the chapter.

CONCEPTUAL FRAMEWORKS OF DIVERSITY IN SPORT

The study of diversity in sport organizations has been rather limited. Notable exceptions are the works of DeSensi (1994, 1995), Doherty and Chelladurai (1999), Fink and Pastore (1999), and Fink, Pastore, and Riemer (2001, 2003). Patterned after Chesler and Crowfoot (1992) and Cox (1991), DeSensi (1995) identified three forms of organizations in which diversity is differentially managed—monocultural, transitional, and multicultural organizations. *Monocultural organizations* tend to emphasize one culture and expect the employees of different cultural backgrounds to adapt to the dominant culture. At the other extreme are *multicultural organizations,* where all cultural backgrounds are valued and accommodated. In between are the *transitional organizations,* which are changing in order to accommodate the increasing diversity in the workforce and customer base. These three forms of organizations are said to vary along the five dimensions of mission, culture, power, informal relations, and major change strategies, as shown in Exhibit 14.4.

Doherty and Chelladurai (1999) maintain that individuals bring to the organization their own "personal culture," composed of a unique set of values and beliefs about the world around them. Individuals derive these values and beliefs from their association with different cultural groups, and they are not necessarily confined to one cultural group. This perspective differs from viewing employees as belonging to one specific cultural group and assuming one set of values and beliefs for all members in that group. In these authors' view, the benefits and problems associated with personal cultures are accentuated by how diversity is managed, which in turn is a function of the culture of the organization.

The organizational *culture of similarity* is characterized by the values and assumptions of parochialism, ethnocentrism, rigidity, task orientation, and intolerance of ambiguity. This type of organizational culture is manifested in closed group membership, one-way or closed communication, and unilateral decision making. In contrast, the organizational *culture of diversity* is characterized by flex-

Exhibit 14.4 Organizational stages of multiculturalism.

DIMENSION	MONOCULTURAL	TRANSITIONAL	MULTICULTURAL
Mission	Deliberately exclude or ignore diversity.	Announce desire/need for diversity.	Positively value diversity. Link diversity to "bottom line" and social justice values. Global perspective.
Culture	White, male, and Eurocentric norms prevail. Prejudice and discrimination evident. Encourage assimilation into dominant community. Emphasize individualism.	White and male norms are questioned but prevail. Prejudice and discrimination are lessened, but still exist. Seek accommodation to and comfort/tolerance for minorities. Reify particular group identities.	Prejudice and discrimination constantly confronted publicly and negatively sanctioned. Alternative norms are publicized and embraced. White, male, and Eurocentric symbols are changed. Synthesis of individual characteristics, group identities, and a transcendent community.
Power	White and male throughout. Others excluded or at bottom. Access limited to the "club." Strong hierarchy.	A few minority members who can adapt reach higher status. White and male sponsors of minorities and women. Narrow access.	Multicultural team of leaders. Relatively flat and multilevel decision making. Wide access. Value different decision-making styles.
Informal relations	Exclusionary with segregated social events. Communications within racial/gender groups. No external intergroup contact.	Distant but cordial relations. Open to assimilated minorities. Communication on deeply held issues mostly within social identity groups. Some external intergroup social contact.	Proactive inclusiveness. Homogeneous and heterogeneous groupings coexist. Much communication across race/gender lines. Sense of community (yet differentiated).
Major change strategies	Litigation and countersuit. External demand/protest and coercion. Some listening by elite.	"Awareness" and training programs evident. Administrative mandate. Affirmative action programs. Assessments and audits.	Continuous (re)education and growth of individuals and organization. Reward multicultural work. Multicultural norms and leadership. Coalition formation. Combat external social oppression.

Reprinted, by permission, from J. T. DeSensi, 1995. "Understanding multiculturalism and valuing diversity: A theoretical perspective," *Quest*, 47 (1): 37–38. Originally from *Visioning Change: Stages in the movement from monocultural to multicultural organizations*, by M. Chesler and J. Crowfoot, 1992, University of Michigan, Ann Arbor. Used with permission.

ibility, people orientation, a high degree of respect for differences, and tolerance for ambiguity. Such an organizational culture encourages two-way, open communication; multilevel decision making; and open group membership.

Fink and Pastore (1999) proposed a framework that outlines four different levels of managing diversity in the context of intercollegiate athletics. At the lowest end is the strategy of noncompliance to regulations relating to diversity, a characteristic of monocultural organizations. The next level of strategy is simply compliance to all existing regulations with a view to avoid litigation and other conflicts. The organization itself is still largely monocultural in its orientation. At the third level is the reactive strategy, where any problem arising out of diversity in the workplace is immediately addressed and solved. At the top is the proactive strategy, where diversity is defined more broadly than race and gender, and is valued to a great extent. Accordingly, this strategy would involve changing policies to attract and retain diverse people and to benefit from diversity.

Based on Fink and Pastore (1999), Fink and colleagues (2001) investigated the beliefs of top management people (athletic directors, senior women's administrators, assistant or associate athletic directors) and softball and baseball coaches at Division IA athletic departments about managing diversity. In general, top administrators believed in the benefits of diversity. Further, these beliefs were reflected in the extent of diversity management practices. That is, strong beliefs in the benefits of diversity were associated with proactive management practices. In contrast, the other respondents (baseball and softball coaches) perceived that their institutions were characterized by compliance strategies to a fair extent and by proactive strategies to a lesser extent. Based on these and other findings, Fink and colleagues (2001) came to a general conclusion that Division IA athletic departments operate in a culture that values similarity as defined by Doherty and Chelladurai (1999).

In a subsequent study, Fink, Pastore, and Riemer (2003) examined the dynamics of diversity management and individual and organizational outcomes at the level of NCAA Division III intercollegiate athletics. They found that perceptions of proactive diversity management were significantly associated with enhancement of all outcomes, which included organizational outcomes of

1. attraction of talented employees
2. retention of talented employees
3. attraction of a diverse customer (fan) base
4. avoidance of discrimination lawsuits
5. a diverse workforce

and individual outcomes of

1. a creative organization
2. an organization in which all employees are involved in decision making
3. an organization in which employees are satisfied
4. a productive organization.

Interestingly, they found that perceptions of enhanced diversity management contributed more to individual level outcomes than to organizational level outcomes. Further, the strategy of compliance was also related to these outcomes, while the reactive strategy was unrelated to any of the outcomes.

AN INTEGRATIVE FRAMEWORK

In the following sections, we will use a framework that integrates various approaches to managing diversity. We propose that managers can better manage diversity if they take a contingency perspective and consider the forms of diversity they must deal with, diversity management strategies, and the task and time factors that will impact diversity management. Exhibit 14.5 illustrates the integrative framework. Before discussing these elements of the framework and their interrelationships, we must emphasize a fundamental principle underlying all of management, including management of diversity: that of competence as the basis for involvement of members in specific jobs.

Competence as the Cornerstone

You will recall the notion of **competence** as one of the tenets of bureaucracy discussed in Chapter 7. Theorists have also emphasized the significance of competence in diversity management. For instance, Thomas (1996) noted that competency must be a primary consideration in managing diversity. Similarly, Lawson and Shen (1998) believe that a focus on job performance–related skills and abilities in hiring and promotion processes would prove beneficial to both the individuals and the organization. On the other hand, a preferential focus on job-irrelevant attributes would prove detrimental for the organization and the individuals themselves. In Lawson and Shen's view, competence, commitment, and compassion should be the cornerstones for harnessing diversity. From this perspective, these authors state the rule as:

> Seek competence first, keep an open mind, pursue a mix of members, and rely on job performance-related data. No one group of members has a monopoly on competence: rather, different persons have different competencies. You will not do your organization, yourself, or others any favor if you hire and promote individuals who lack competence unless they agree to participate in competence-enhancement education provided by the organization. (Lawson & Shen, 1998, p. 80)

Forms of Diversity

Earlier in the chapter, we discussed the different forms of diversity. We noted that some forms of diversity are observable (color, gender, age, height, and so on) and some are nonobservable (values, beliefs, education). Some authors have used the term **surface-level diversity** to refer to observable differences and the term **deep-level diversity** to refer to non-observable differences. For the purposes of the framework for managing diversity, it is useful to consider diversity in the forms of:

1. Appearance or visible features of individuals, such as gender, age, color, and race. These are some of the surface-level differences noted earlier.
2. Behavioral preferences (such as dress and food preferences). These also belong to the category of surface-level differences.
3. Value and attitudinal differences (individualism versus collectivism, attitudes toward athletics, and so on). These belong to the deep-level differences alluded to earlier. These differences can be identified only

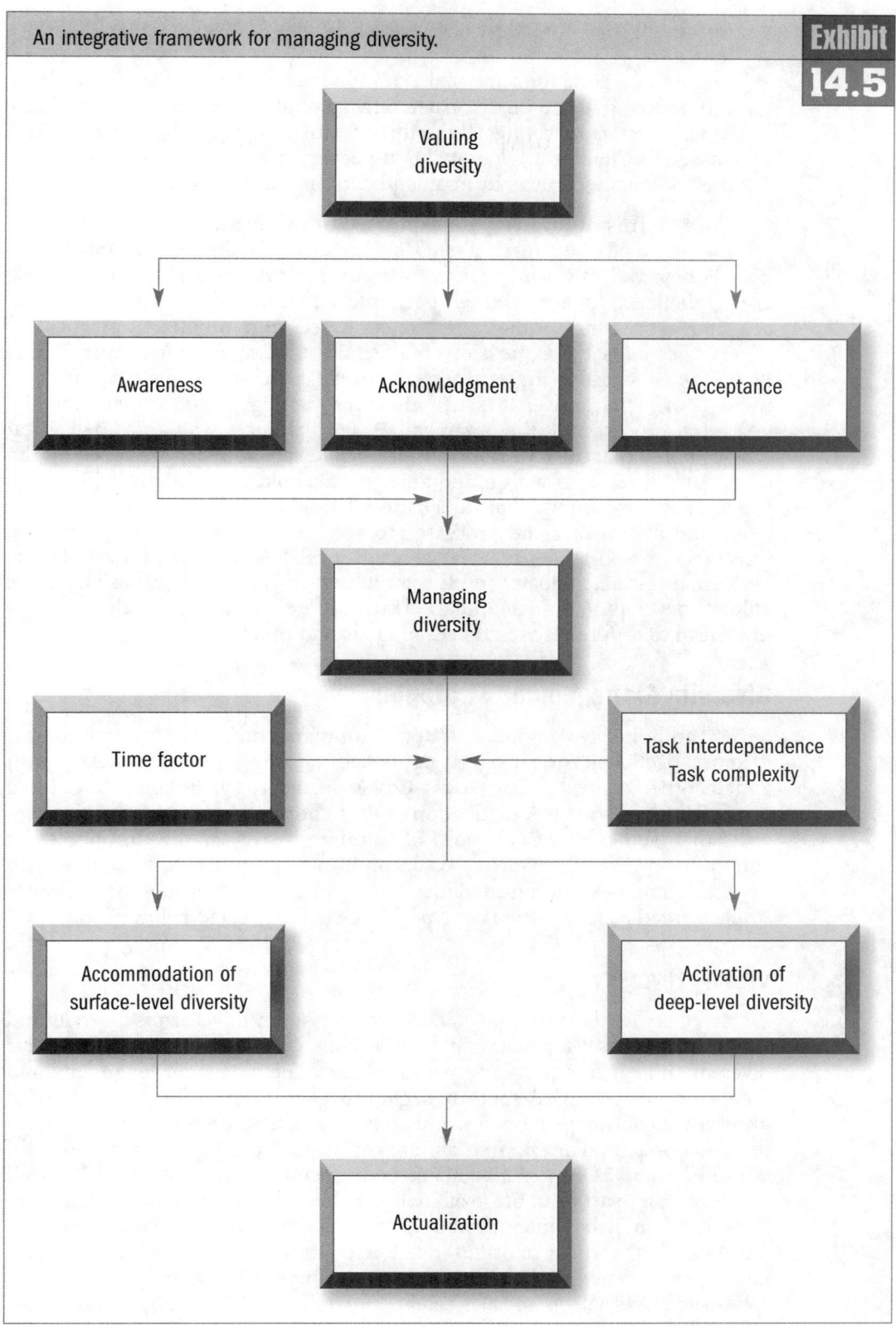
Exhibit 14.5 An integrative framework for managing diversity.

through observation of decisions people make or the positions they take on specific issues.
4. Cognitive orientations and skills of individuals. These are also deep-level differences that can be discerned only through observing the individuals in task performance. Recall the three forms of managerial skills we discussed in Chapter 4. We noted that people differ in the extent to which they possess technical, human, and conceptual skills.

These forms of diversity are expressed in two significant ways. We may call the first type of expression *symbolic,* because it is identified through symbols. For example, the unique dress worn by many Arabs, Indians, or Chinese are symbolic expressions of their background. Similarly, the foods people eat are often expressions of their preferences based on tradition and practice.

The second set of expressions of diversity is substantive in nature. I label it *substantive* because these expressions reflect the values, beliefs, and attitudes people hold on vital issues affecting the organization, including the goals and processes of the organization. For instance, Trail and Chelladurai (2000) noted that calls for reform in intercollegiate athletics are based on the divergent values both within and among stakeholders of intercollegiate athletics. They have shown that values are related to the choice of goals for athletics and approval of the processes to achieve those goals. In their study, those faculty and students who held power-related values endorsed athletic performance-related goals, and those high on universalism values chose the student development-related goals. Thus, differences between value orientations lead to differences in choices of goals and processes.

Diversity Management Strategies

Several authors have proposed **strategies for managing diversity** in the context of sports (DeSensi, 1995; Doherty & Chelladurai, 1999; Fink & Pastore, 1999) and in other contexts (Cox, 1993; Cox & Beale, 1997; Robbins & Coulter, 1996; Thomas, 1996). A distillation of these perspectives and strategies suggests that we begin with the idea of valuing diversity as the first necessary condition for managing diversity. Second, managing diversity includes two distinct strategies—accommodation and activation—that can be variously implemented based on the task type. These are explicated below.

Valuing Diversity

We noted earlier that valuing diversity is a philosophy that accepts diversity and views it as an asset for the organization. This basic requirement for effective diversity management is composed of awareness, acknowledgment, and acceptance of diversity. A sport manager must first be aware of the existence of diversity, acknowledge it openly, and accept the diversity with all its opportunities and obstacles. For example, a manager may see two men or two women of the same color. The most obvious diversity factor is color, and the color itself sets each pair apart from those of another color. However, the individuals within each pair may be quite different from each other on several other diversity factors such as country of origin, religion, political leanings, and language. As Lewis (2002) noted, "a healthier sense of belonging in contemporary organizations requires a deep, social acceptance of differences, aided by critical exam-

> **Sidebar**
>
> Here is an example of the principle of accommodation. In September 2004, there was a furor when Andrea Armstrong, a recent convert to Islam, requested to wear long pants, long sleeves, and a scarf *(hijab)* during basketball practices and competitions. To her, this was an expression of her religious beliefs and convictions. After some discussions and consultations, the University of South Florida was willing to accommodate her preferences and asked the NCAA to grant an exemption to its policy on uniforms. Armstrong felt that her clothing would not distract other players nor hamper her play. Despite the approval of the University of South Florida, Armstrong quit the team because she did not want to be at the center of a controversy. But the incident highlights the wisdom of the University of South Florida authorities in recognizing and reconciling individual preferences with the overall aim of the team, and accommodating those preferences.
>
> Incidentally, the five pages devoted to uniforms in the NCAA basketball rules book do not address religious preferences relating to uniforms. That does not mean that such preferences are not accepted. For instance, Tamir Goodman, a basketball guard at Towson University, wore a yarmulke on the court during practices and games *(USA Today,* 2004). Similarly, many athletes wear chains bearing a cross as expression of their Christian faith. Further, it is not uncommon to see basketball players (both men and women) wearing long-sleeve shirts underneath the team uniform or players wearing a hairnet. As these practices do not interfere with performance on the court, organizations have generally not taken issue with them. It is unfortunate that practices that express nonmainstream religious or cultural beliefs do spawn controversies.

ination of artificial distinctions" (p. 770). Thus, effective diversity management would require that management be aware of these differences, acknowledge them, and accept them as legitimate and beneficial to the organization.

As we noted earlier in the chapter, Thomas (1996) outlined several options an organization can undertake in dealing with diversity. He also noted that only one of those options—mutual adaptation—was focused on true understanding of diversity and on maximizing the benefits of diversity. Extending this line of reasoning, we find that there are two broad classes of strategies for managing diversity: accommodation and activation.

Accommodation

Accommodation simply refers to permitting and facilitating the symbolic expression of behavioral preferences of diverse individuals. For instance, if women of Indian origin wish to wear saris to work and if task performance would not be affected by wearing saris, then management should permit it. Similarly, if workers of Islamic faith prefer to pray during lunch break, management can accommodate those preferences by setting aside a room for such

purposes. If some workers would prefer vegetarian food, management could accommodate this preference by making such food available in the cafeteria. In essence, the strategy of accommodation is aimed at satisfying preferences for symbolic expressions of diversity. As this strategy reflects the reactions of management to preferences of diverse individuals, it is to some extent similar to the reactive strategy of Fink and Pastore (1999). This strategy would also be part of the organizational culture of diversity proposed by Doherty and Chelladurai (1999).

Activation

Activation is the process of deliberately bringing divergent perspectives to bear on a task or project. In other words, management consciously encourages members to express their preferences for specific goals or courses of action, or their perspectives on a problem and solutions thereof. In fact, management facilitates substantive expressions of diversity (the effects of less observable elements such as values, beliefs, and attitudes) with a view to capitalizing on the strengths of diversity.

Of course, managing these substantive expressions is relatively more difficult. At the same time, this task is more important because these substantive expressions represent unique and innovative ways of perceiving and thinking about organizational affairs. The varying substantive expressions lead to debates and discussions necessary for optimal decisions and creative problem solving. Thus, it is necessary to activate the richness of the resources offered by diversity toward actualizing the full potential of the members and the organization.

It was noted that producing and marketing of any sport service need to be geared to the increasing diversity in the marketplace. Suppose a fitness club is operating in an area where several immigrant groups reside. Suppose also that the club has hired a few employees from these immigrant groups. If the club wants to make its operations culturally sensitive, it would make sense to engage these immigrant employees in group discussions because they bring to the situation perspectives that are culturally derived. If management activates this special expertise and these unique insights, it is likely to make more informed and practically useful decisions. In the context of marketing spectator sports to African Americans, Armstrong (1998) alludes to the notion of activation. She suggests that African American experts in consumer behavior, media, and African American culture should be involved in designing and implementing these marketing strategies because they bring unique perspectives that are relevant to the African American segment of the market.

Task Factors

While the management strategies of accommodation and activation are somewhat straightforward, the issue of *what* to accommodate and *when* to activate is more complex. A useful way to address this issue is to look at the nature of the task in which culturally diverse people are involved. The following sections discuss two significant **task factors** that moderate the effects of diversity on performance. Doherty and Chelladurai (1999) include *task complexity* and *task interdependence* as moderators of the effects of diversity on organizational and group outcomes.

Sidebar

Based on a report by Lapchick (1991), DeSensi (1995) noted that racial discrimination was evidenced in the stacking of African American players in professional football. The term *stacking* was first introduced by Loy and McElvogue (1970) to refer to the finding that playing positions were staffed differentially by race. That is, black players were disproportionately represented in the so-called noncentral positions—cornerbacks, running backs, and wide receivers. In contrast, white players, more than black players, tended to occupy the so-called central positions—quarterback, center, linemen, and linebackers. Stacking was said to be the process of excluding African American players from central positions and stacking them in the noncentral positions. Note that central positions are those at the center of the configuration of all players at the time of the snap (geographic centrality). Lapchick's (1991) data showed that such stacking was evident as recently as 1990. According to this data, blacks constituted only 8 percent of quarterbacks, 13 percent of centers, and 24 percent of offensive guards, whereas 66 percent of linebackers, 96 percent of cornerbacks, 90 percent of running backs, 86 percent of wide receivers, 83 percent of safeties, and 72 percent of defensive ends were blacks.

Regardless of whether or not this practice is continuing, the argument that stacking is a manifestation of discrimination is suspect. The fundamental basis for this argument is that the so-called central positions are more important than the noncentral positions. Chelladurai and Carron (1977) argued that geographical centrality in football does not parallel the functional centrality of the game itself. In football, it is the running backs and wide receivers that are engaged in advancing the ball for a touchdown. Thus, these positions are central to the functions of the offensive unit. Although the quarterback is the most central position both geographically and functionally, all actions initiated by the quarterback have to be completed by one of the geographically noncentral but functionally central positions. The other positions jointly play only a supporting role. Thus, the assertion that there is discrimination against black players in football cannot be sustained by these data. In fact, it can be argued that it is whites who are precluded from the functionally central positions.

On the other hand, any data showing that African American players are paid less than white players in comparative playing positions, or that disproportionately fewer blacks are found in coaching and administrative positions, would indicate discrimination.

Simplicity and Complexity of Tasks

A task is said to be simple when the purposes and processes of executing the task are relatively straightforward. Examples of simple tasks are those of the locker room attendants and ticket takers at a sports venue. In these cases, the persons deal with a narrow set of activities that can be made routine and standard. As Jehn, Northcraft, and Neale (1999) noted, "when a task is simple and well understood group members can rely on standard operating procedures" (p. 746). Thus, the effects of diversity (both positive and negative) are mini-

mal in simple and routine tasks. Insofar as there is no room for substantive expressions while performing simple tasks, effective management of diversity is restricted to accommodating the symbolic expressions of individuals.

Task complexity refers to difficult and multifaceted tasks (such as policy development, project management, and so on), where the environment is not stable and information is lacking. Such complex tasks are not well understood and do not have prior procedures to handle them. More important, they require problem-solving skills (Jehn et al., 1999). In Doherty and Chelladurai's (1999) view, the beneficial effects of diversity are enhanced in complex tasks because members bring different perspectives and understandings to addressing the issues posed by the task and to proposing and revising solutions. Jehn and his colleagues (1999) refer to *informational diversity*, meaning "differences in knowledge bases and perspectives that members bring to the group" (p. 743). These authors maintain that education, experience, and expertise are the bases of informational diversity. We can extend that argument and suggest that the personal values and beliefs of members of a group also bring different perspectives to bear on the task at hand. That is, substantive expressions of diversity are critical in complex tasks. Harnessing these differing perspectives and their expressions toward accomplishment of group and organizational tasks is management's task. By the same token, proper management of the negative effects of diversity can prevent these from becoming a problem.

Task Interdependence

Doherty and Chelladurai (1999) state that insofar as people of diversity are engaged in relatively independent tasks involving little or no interaction with others, the effects of diversity (both positive and negative) will be neutralized except in the case of symbolic expressions. Accommodating these symbolic expressions need not be a major concern in independent tasks.

In contrast, the effects of diversity can be enhanced in interdependent tasks, where members need to rely on one another to complete their tasks. Interdependent tasks require smooth interaction among group members, who need to communicate, cooperate, and coordinate their efforts (Jehn et al., 1999). Management needs to promote the use of the strengths of such diversity and garner its potential benefits. That is, management needs to facilitate the substantive expressions (creativity, innovative solutions, and so on). If management does not value diversity but rather attempts to stifle it, the potential benefits of diversity are minimized, and the negative effects of diversity (miscommunication, mistrust, confusion, and stress) will increase.

Time Factor

In attempting to harness the benefits of diversity, managers must also consider the **time factor** and its impact on the effects of diversity. In general, members of a newly formed group tend to categorize others based on surface-level differences (such as gender, race, or age), and to make judgments about them based on stereotypes (see Harrison, Price, & Bell, 1998). Given some time, members develop a better understanding of the others' psychological features or deep-level differences and similarities. Any perceived similarity in values, beliefs, and attitudes between the focal person and the others would strengthen the bond between them. Then, even if members perceive differences in values and beliefs, judgments about the others and interactions with them will be based more on observed behavior than on stereotypes (Harrison et al., 1998).

As group members become familiar with each other, they may also become more disposed to hear out different perspectives and develop an understanding and appreciation for those perspectives (Pelled et al., 1999). By the same token, individuals may cultivate the ability to frame and state their views in juxtaposition with others' perspectives. Thus, members may develop a shared understanding of the task and its requirements, as well as of the processes involved in solving problems. The development of such understandings leads to the blurring of the in-group and out-group boundaries. In fact, over time, all members may come to think that they belong to the in-group (that is, the entire group) and to perceive members of the other groups as the out-group (Pelled et al., 1999). All this positive transformation takes time, however. Research has shown that homogeneous groups perform well in the short run, while diverse groups perform well in the long run (see Harrison et al., 1998; Pelled et al., 1999; Schneider & Northcraft, 1999). Note that the negative effects of diversity may take hold in the short run, causing the group to experience conflict and discomfort. Thus, the interactions early on among members of a diverse group may be contrived and artificial. Members may also be restrained from freely expressing their views for fear of rejection.

As Harrison and colleagues (1998) noted:

> Time merely allows more information to be conveyed. . . . That is, time provides the opportunity to acquire interpersonal information; the amount of information acquired is a function of the length of shared experience for group members, the breadth of group activities, the depth of task interdependence, and other factors. These exchanges allow group members to learn deeper-level information about their psychological similarity to or dissimilarity from their coworkers, where before they would have used surface-level demographic data as information proxies. (p. 104)

A CONTINGENCY PERSPECTIVE

We have looked at two distinct forms of expressions of diversity—symbolic and substantive. After discussing two strategies for managing diversity (accommodation and activation), we identified task and time factors as moderators of the effects of diversity on task performance. Given performance imperatives, sport managers need to take a contingency view in deciding on the extent to which the strategy of activation will be practical or beneficial. As we noted earlier, those task situations characterized by low interdependence and low complexity may not require activation of substantive differences. That is, when tasks are well defined and the processes of completing the tasks are clear cut, there is little need to exchange opinions and discuss options (Pelled et al., 1999). Thus, the utility of the strategy of activation may be minimal. In contrast, creative problem solving in a complex task may call for activation of the substantive expressions of divergent perspectives. Such a process would yield the benefits of divergent perceptions, orientations, and problem-solving skills.

Note that task factors have more effect on the extent and utility of the strategy of activation of substantive expressions of diversity. The strategy of accommodation is not affected to the same extent by task factors because accommodation deals with symbolic expressions of cultural diversity that do not normally affect task performance. For this reason, accommodating symbolic expressions of diversity can be more easily implemented. Thus, the strategy of accommodation can be thought of as a universal process. That is, the strategy of accommodation should be adopted as a general policy, whereas the strategy of activation should be linked to task factors. Exhibit 14.6 shows these differential approaches to the two strategies.

While the notion of universal application of the strategy of accommodation is generally true, there may be circumstances where even the principle of accommodation would be circumscribed by organizational or task factors. For instance, wearing of a sari by a soldier in a combat situation is not conducive to effective performance in that situation. Similarly, the redcoats in a sporting event may be required to wear red coats so as to be identifiable by supervisors, coworkers, and spectators. Under these circumstances, the organization may not be able to accommodate the behavioral preferences of its members.

The time available for making decisions or solving problems also influences the extent to which management may activate substantive expressions of diversity. As we noted, diverse groups take more time to understand their differing orientations and come to some common understanding of the problem at hand and possible solutions. Therefore, managers may assign decision making and problem solving to homogeneous groups. If a diverse group has to deal with them at all, a useful strategy for managers is to be more directive in structuring the problem and channeling discussions. That is, the substantive expressions of diversity are minimized with a view to saving time. If there is more time, managers are well advised to employ the strategy of activation in order to generate creative and more productive ways of tackling the problem.

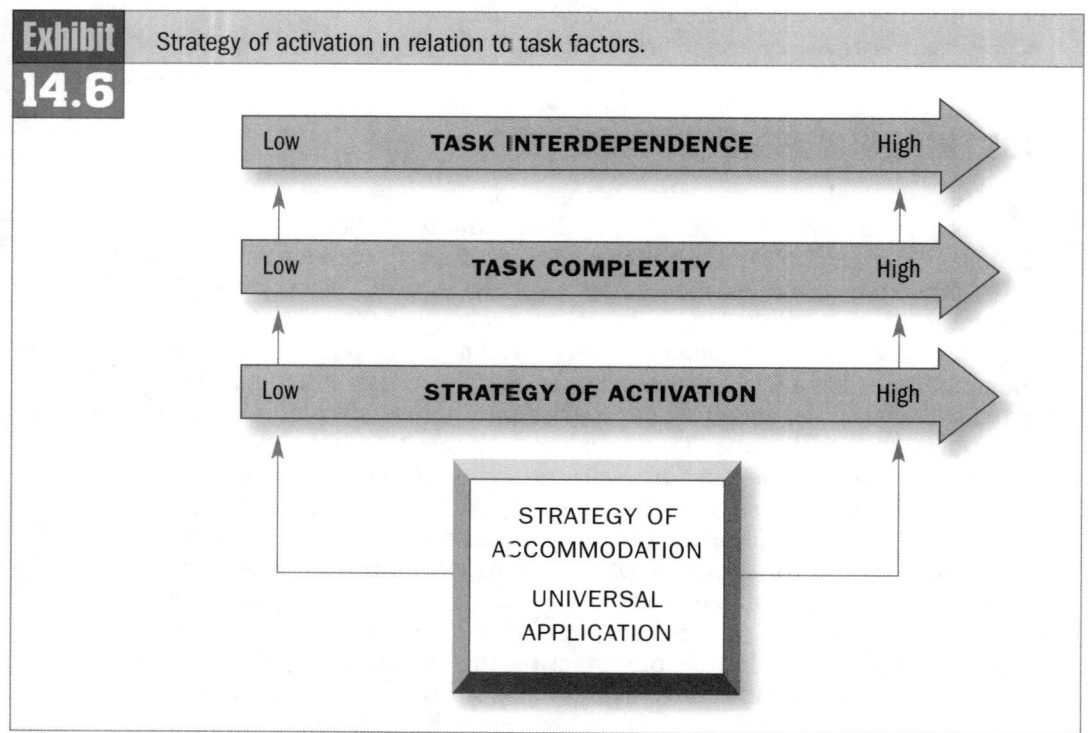

Exhibit 14.6 Strategy of activation in relation to task factors.

Sidebar

Chelladurai (2001) employed the metaphor of the solar system to illustrate and highlight the diversity management strategies of accommodation and activation. Two forces are operating in the solar system: the centripetal force created by gravity pulls the planets toward the sun, while the centrifugal force created by the velocity of the planets causes them to pull away from the sun. If the centripetal force exceeded the centrifugal force, the planets would be sucked into the inferno of the sun. If, on the other hand, the centrifugal force were greater than the centripetal force, the planets would break loose and hurtle away from the sun. The point is that the dynamic equilibrium among the planets and the sun is maintained by the equality of these two forces.

In our context, the planets correspond to the individuals and groups, and the to the organization with its purposes. The "centrifugal forces"—the different sets of values and beliefs of the groups—can impel the individuals and groups outward, away from the purposes of the organization. In contrast, "centripetal forces" from organizational structures and processes can integrate the groups into collective action and pull them toward organizational purposes. Valuing diversity means recognizing, accepting, and allowing the centrifugal forces to operate. Managing diversity requires the creation of the centripetal forces to draw the groups toward the organization and create the dynamic equilibrium and integration of diversity. It is the balance between the two forces that makes for effective diversity management.

Sidebar

Cunningham (2004) and Cunningham and Chelladurai (2004) have suggested that one method to reduce the possible negative effects of group diversity is through the formation of a common in-group identity, such that group members come to consider the aggregate (i.e., the total group) as representing a single, superordinate group. Indeed, within the context of cross-functional teams, Cunningham and Chelladurai (2004) found that the presence of a common in-group identity resulted in greater coworker satisfaction and a stronger preference to work with the team. Therefore, managers seeking to mitigate diversity's negative effects should seek to reinforce the common identity of all members of the group.

Readers will note that this strategy of creating common in-group identity is employed by coaches. As Cunningham (2004) noted, quite often they achieve this by identifying a common goal of athletic excellence, a common enemy (e.g., the rival basketball team), or a common fate (i.e., everybody loses if the team loses, or everybody gains when the team wins). Please note that politicians also whip up support by extolling the virtues of the in-group, and the need to unite to defeat the other group.

ACTUALIZATION

Borrowing from Maslow (1943), we use the term **actualization** to refer to the attainment of the full potential of the members, the groups within the organization, and the organization as a whole. Managing diversity is about improving organizational performance by optimally utilizing every member's abilities and by leveraging diversity as an organizational resource (Cox & Beale, 1997). Thus, the most important rationale for management of diversity is the optimization of individual potential and the quality of life for all. A critical caveat here is that the concern with diversity should not be mistaken for concern with minority issues. On the contrary, our earlier discussion shows that diversity in certain dimensions (such as values, beliefs, attitudes, education, age, and so on) can be found even within the majority group. Thus, the central purpose of managing diversity should be the promotion of the potential and quality of life of all members. In sum, the concept of actualization refers to management's relative success in optimizing individual potential, enhancing quality of life for all, and thus increasing organizational productivity.

SUMMARY

This chapter highlighted the need for sport managers to be aware of the significance of diversity in the workforce and marketplace. The dimensions of diversity include observable or surface-level diversity such as gender, race, and color, and less observable or nonobservable differences in behavioral preferences, values and attitudes, and cognitive orientations. In discussing these dimensions of diversity, we emphasized that differences are not deficits. Affirmative action can be compared to a genuine sense of valuing diversity and managing that diversity. Strategies for managing diversity include the negative options of denying the existence of diversity and suppressing or isolating diversity. Positive strategies include building relationships and fostering mutual adaptations among diverse members.

The final sections of the chapter present an integrative framework for managing diversity. The two cornerstones of managing diversity are a genuine valuing of diversity and a focus on competence. All dimensions of diversity are expressed in two significant ways—symbolic expressions, such as preferences for specific dress and food, and substantive expressions, such as expressions of one's values, attitudes, and preferences for certain courses of action.

The two major strategies for managing diversity are (a) accommodating symbolic expressions of diversity, such as specific attire, food, language, and so forth, and (b) activating substantive expressions of diversity in values, needs, and preferences as well as diversity in information and expertise. We noted that the employment of these two strategies is contingent on the nature of the task. In independent or simple tasks, the strategy of accommodation of symbolic expressions is necessary and sufficient. In the case of interdependent and complex tasks, in addition to accommodating symbolic expressions, management must also activate substantive expressions of diversity. This leads to better decisions acceptable to most participants.

DEVELOPING YOUR PERSPECTIVES

1. Consider your closest friends. In what ways are they similar to you? In what ways do they differ? What specific similarities and differences affect your relationships, and in what ways? How do you and your friends manage the diversity among you?

2. Identify a sport organization you are familiar with. Describe the diversity among members of that organization. Explain the effects of this diversity on the functioning of the organization. What conscious efforts is that organization making to capitalize on the strengths of its diversity?

3. Can you identify situations in sport management in which the strategy of accommodation of symbolic expressions can easily be followed without disrupting the work processes? Similarly, can you identify circumstances in sport management where accommodation would be detrimental to work performance?

4. The strategy of activation is fruitful only in some circumstances. Identify and describe some circumstances in sport management that require activation and some that prohibit it.

References

Allison, M. T. (1988). Breaking boundaries and barriers: Future directions in cross-cultural research. *Leisure Sciences, 10*, 247–259.

Armstrong, K. L. (1998). Ten strategies to employ when marketing sport to Black consumers. *Sport Marketing Quarterly, 7* (3), 11–18.

Arredondo, P. (1996). *Successful diversity management initiatives: A blueprint for planning and implementation.* Thousand Oaks, CA: Sage Publications.

Chelladurai, P. (1994). Sport management: Defining the field. *European Journal of Sport Management, 1*, 7–21.

Chelladurai, P. (2001). Athletic teams as models for managing diversity. Opening Keynote presentation at the 9th Congress of the European Association for Sport Management. Vittoria-Gasteiz, Spain. September 19–23, 2001.

Chelladurai, P., & Carron, A. V. (1977). A reanalysis of formal structure in sport. *Canadian Journal of Applied Sport Sciences, 2*, 9–14.

Chesler, M., & Crowfoot, J. (1992). *Visioning change: Stages in the movement from monocultural organizations.* Ann Arbor: University of Michigan.

Cox, T. (1991). The multicultural organization. *Academy of Management Executive, 5*, 34–46.

Cox, T. (1993). *Cultural diversity in organizations: Theory, research, and practice.* San Francisco: Berrett-Koehler.

Cox, T., Jr., & Beale, R. L. (1997). *Developing competency to manage diversity: Readings, cases, & activities.* San Francisco: Berrett-Koehler.

Cunningham, G. B. (2004). Strategies for transforming the possible negative effects of group diversity. *Quest, 56*, 421–438.

Cunningham, G. B., & Chelladurai, P. (2004). Affective reactions to cross-functional teams: The impact of size, relative performance, and common in-group identity. *Group Dynamics: Theory, Research, and Practice, 8* (2), 83–97.

Cunningham, G. B., & Sagas, M. (2004a). Group diversity, occupational commitment, and occupational turnover intentions among NCAA Division IA football coaching staffs. *Journal of Sport Management, 18*, 236–254.

Cunningham, G. B., & Sagas, M. (2004b). Racial differences in occupational turnover intent among NCAA Division IA assistant football coaches. *Sociology of Sport Journal, 21*, 84–92.

Cunningham, G. B., & Sagas, M. (2004c). The effect of group diversity on organizational commitment. *International Sports Journal, 8* (1), 124–131.

DeSensi, J. T. (1994). Multiculturalism as an issue in sport management. *Journal of Sport Management, 8,* 63–74.

DeSensi, J. T. (1995). Understanding multiculturalism and valuing diversity: A theoretical perspective. *Quest, 47,* 34–43.

Doherty, A. J., & Chelladurai, P. (1999). Managing cultural diversity in sport organizations: A theoretical perspective. *Journal of Sport Management, 13,* 280–297.

Fernandez, J. P., & Barr, M. (1993). *The diversity advantage: How American business can outperform Japanese and European companies in the global marketplace.* San Francisco: Jossey-Bass. First published by Lexington Books.

Fine, M. G. (1995). *Building successful multicultural organizations.* Westport, CT: Quorum Books.

Fink, J. S., & Cunningham, G. B. (in press). The effects of racial and gender dyad diversity on work experiences of university athletics personnel. *International Journal of Sport Management.*

Fink, J. S., Pastore, D. L., & Riemer, H. A. (2003). Managing employee diversity: Perceived practices and organizational outcomes in NCAA Division III athletic departments. *Sport Management Review, 6* (2), 147–168.

Fink, J. S., Pastore, D. L., & Riemer, H. A. (2001). Do differences make a difference? Managing diversity in Division IA intercollegiate athletics. *Journal of Sport Management, 15,* 10–50.

Fink, J. S., & Pastore, D. L. (1999). Diversity in sport? Utilizing the business literature to devise a comprehensive framework of diversity initiatives. *Quest, 51,* 310–327.

Fiske, A. P. (1992). The four elementary forms of sociality: Framework for a unified theory of social relations. *Psychological Review, 99,* 689–723.

Harrison, D. A., Price, K. H., & Bell, M. P. (1998). Beyond relational demography: Time and the effects of surface- and deep-level diversity on work group cohesion. *Academy of Management Journal, 41* (1), 96–107.

Heilman, M. E. (1994). Affirmative action: Some unintended consequences for working women. *Research in Organizational Behavior, 16,* 125–169.

Henderson, G. (1994). *Cultural diversity in the workplace: Issues and strategies.* Westport, CT: Quorum Books.

Hopkins, W. E. (1997). *Ethical dimensions of diversity.* Thousand Oaks, CA: Sage Publications.

Immegart, G. L., & Pilecki, F. J. (1973). *An introduction to systems for educational administrators.* Reading, MA: Addison-Wesley.

Jehn, K. A., Northcraft, G. B., & Neale, M. A. (1999). Why differences make a difference: A field study of diversity, conflict, and performance in workgroups. *Administrative Science Quarterly, 44,* 741–763.

Joplin, J. R. W., & Daus, C. S. (1997). Challenges of leading a diverse workforce. *Academy of Management Executive, 11* (3), 32–47.

Kossek, E. E., & Lobel, S. A. (1996). Transforming human resource systems to manage diversity: An introduction and orienting framework. In E. E. Kossek & S. A. Lobel (Eds.), *Managing diversity: Human resource strategies for transforming the workplace* (pp. 1–19). Cambridge, MA: Blackwell Business.

Lapchick, R. E. (1991, summer). Professional sports: The racial report card. *Center for the Study of Sport and Society Digest, 2* (1), 4–8.

Lawson, R. B., & Shen, Z. (1998). *Organizational psychology: Foundations and applications.* New York: Oxford University Press.

Lewis, M. (2002). Exploring paradox: Toward a more comprehensive guide. *Academy of Management Review, 25,* 760–776.

Loy, J. H., & McElvogue, J. F. (1970). Racial segregation in American sport. *International Review of Sport Sociology, 5,* 5–24.

Maslow, A. H. (1943). A theory of human motivation. *Psychological Review, 50,* 370–396.

Milliken, F. J., & Martins, L. L. (1996). Searching for common threads: Understanding the multiple effects of diversity in organizational groups. *Academy of Management Review, 21,* 402–433.

Pelled, L. H., Eisenhart, K. M., & Xin, K. R. (1999). Exploring the black box: An analysis of work group diversity, conflict, and performance. *Administrative Science Quarterly, 44,* 1–28.

Robbins, S. P. (1997). *Managing today!* Upper Saddle River, NJ: Prentice Hall.

Robbins, S. P., & Coulter, M. (1996). *Management* (5th ed.). Upper Saddle River, NJ: Prentice Hall.

Schneider, S. K., & Northcraft, G. B. (1999). The social dilemmas of workforce diversity in organizations: A social identity perspective. *Human Relations, 52,* 1445–1467.

Schuler, R. S., & Jackson, S. E. (1996). *Human resource management: Positioning for the 21st century* (6th ed.). Minneapolis, MN: West.

Sonnenschein, W. (1997). *The practical executive and workforce diversity.* Lincolnwood, IL: NTC Business Books.

Thomas, R. R. (1991). *Beyond race and gender: Unleashing the power of your total workforce by managing diversity.* New York: AMACOM.

Thomas, R. R. (1996). *Redefining diversity.* New York: AMACOM.

Trail, G., & Chelladurai, P. (2000). Perceptions of goals and processes of intercollegiate athletics: A case study. *Journal of Sport Management, 14,* 154–178.

USA Today. (2004). www.usatoday.com/sports/college/womensbasketball/cusa/2004-09-16-muslim-quits. Retrieved on September 27, 2004.

Waring, A. (1996). *Practical systems thinking.* London: International Thomson Business Press.

Weiner, N. (1997). *Making cultural diversity work.* Scarborough, ON, Canada: Carswell (Thompson Professional Publishing).

Adams, J.S., 242, 256, 257, 258, 259
Affholter, D.P., 333
Allison, M.T., 398
Amis, J., 39, 92, 94, 222
Andre, J., 148
Argote, L., 44
Arkers, H.R., 168
Armstrong. K.L., 408
Arnold, J.A., 307
Arnott, M., 178, 181
Arredondo, P., 386, 393
Ashley, F.B., 94
Avolio, B., 305

Bacon, J.U., 353
Bailey, W.S., 148
Ball, D.W., 61
Barney, J., 352
Barr, M., 394
Bass, B.M., 279, 305, 306, 307, 314
Basu, R., 304
Battista, R., 31
Baxter, P.R., 181
Beale, R.L., 391, 393, 396, 405, 413
Belasco, J.A., 83
Bell, M.P., 410, 411
Ben-Ner, A., 89
Bennis, W.B., 306, 307
Berry, L., 339
Bies, R.J., 260
Birkinshaw, J., 227
BKB Services, 231
Black, J.S., 123, 130, 133, 166, 167, 246, 273, 345, 347, 349
Blanchard, K.H., 313
Blau, P.M., 66, 69, 202, 204, 374, 375
Bowen, D.E., 24, 25, 339
Bowers, D.G., 277
Bowman, C., 57, 73, 86
Branch, D., 153
Branch, D., Jr., 275
Branscombe, N.R., 38
Briere, N.M., 31
Brockner, J., 168
Broughton, L., 7, 10, 14, 49
Brown, M., 6
Broyles, J.F., 36, 147
Burnham, D.H., 279, 284, 285, 286, 287, 315
Butler, T., 98, 106
By the numbers, 10

Byars, L.L., 46, 101, 113, 114, 123, 125, 151, 153, 154

Camerer, C.F. 168
Cameron, K.S , 371, 372, 376
Campbell, J.P., 251, 347, 368, 378
Camy, J., 96
Carlson, S., 108
Carroll, L., 140
Carroll, S.J., 121
Carron, A.V., 290, 409
Cashman, J., 103
Certo, S.C., 76, 78, 189
Chairncross, A., 151
Chelladurai, F., 11, 12, 20, 22, 24, 30, 35, 45, 48, 61, 62, 90, 94, 113, 143, 144, 146, 147, 168, 176, 178, 181 251, 278, 279, 282, 283, 290, 303, 309, 311, 313, 323, 339, 353, 360, 362, 374, 376, 385, 398, 399, 401, 403, 406, 407, 409, 410, 413
Chesler, M., 401
Cialdini, R.B. 38
Clarkson, M.B.E., 86, 88, 89
Cleave, S., 251
Columbus Dispatch, 37, 39
Conger, J.A., 305, 306
Conlon, E.J., 362
Connolly, T., 362, 364, 365, 368, 373
Coons, A.E., 275
Coulter, M., 347, 396, 406
Cox, T., 386, 401, 406
Cox, T., Jr., 391, 393, 396, 406, 413
Crompton, J.L., 39
Crosby, P.B., 357
Crow, R.B., 153
Crowfoot, J., 401
Crowson, R.A., 63
Cunningham. G.B., 94, 353, 390
Cusins, P., 85
Cyert, R.M., 148

Dansereau, F , 303
Danylchuk, K.E., 94, 113, 143, 146, 147, 309
Daus, C.S., 386
David, F., 135
David, F.R., 127, 133
De Knop, P., 10
Deming, W.E., 357

DeSensi, J.T., 20, 398, 401, 402, 406, 409
Dessler, G., 278, 288, 289, 314
Deutsch, S.J., 362
DiMaggio, P., 92
Doherty, A.J., 282, 283, 309, 398, 399, 401, 403, 406, 407, 410
Donaldson, T., 89
Downey, H.K., 278
Drazin, R., 81
Drucker, P.F., 62
Duchon, D., 304
Duda, J.L., 32
Dunham, R.B., 73, 76, 133, 135
Dunnette, M.D., 251

Eilon, S., 149
Eisenhart, K.M., 388
English, R.A., 29
ESPN, 87
Etzioni, A., 65, 345, 348
Evan, W.M., 359, 377
Evans, M.G., 288

Farley, M., 333
Fayol, H., 102
Ferguson, A., 11
Fernandez, J.P., 394
Fiedler, F.E., 279, 280, 281, 282, 283, 284, 294, 315
Fielding, L.W., 64, 65
Filley, A.C., 130, 174, 190
Fine, M.G., 398
Fink, J.S., 390, 401, 403, 406, 407
Fink, L.F., 137, 189, 191
Folger, R., 259
Forbes, D.P., 366
Ford, C.E., 38
Fortier, M.S., 31
Fottler, M.D., 66
Freeman, S., 86
Friesen, P., 310
Frisby, W.M., 204, 205, 336
Fulks, D.L., 10

Gannon, M.J., 140, 151, 153
Gerrard, B., 234
Gibson, H.J., 10
Gill, D.L., 31
Gillen, D.J., 118
Goes, J.B., 234

Goetsch, D.L., 339
Goodman, P.S., 373
Graen, G., 303
Green, S.G., 304
Greenberg, J., 259, 260
Gresov, C., 81
Griffin, M.A., 307
Gronröös, C., 23, 24, 28
Gross, J.B., 31
Guest, R.H., 108
Gui, B., 89
Gummesson, E., 25, 26, 27

Haga, B.A., 303
Haggerty, T.R., 139, 176, 178, 181, 360
Hakel, M.D., 251
Hall, R.H., 142, 189, 227, 231, 366
Halpin, A.W., 275
Hambrick, D.C., 22
Hammersley, C.H., 153
Hardy, S., 22
Harrison, D.A., 410, 411
Hasenfeld, Y., 29, 30, 31, 33, 141, 148, 349
Hatry, H.P., 331
Hay, R.D., 36, 147
Heene, A., 73
Heilman, M.E., 393
Heitman, H.M., 31
Hemphill, J.K., 275
Henderson, G., 395
Hendry, L.B., 176, 282
Herman, R.D., 345, 364, 366, 367
Hersey, P., 313
Herzberg, F., 240, 242, 247–250
Hesterly, W.S., 22
Hinings, C.R., 92, 222
Hoang, H., 168
Hoeber, L., 25
Hollander, E.P., 274
Hopkins, W.E., 64, 387
House, R.J., 278, 279, 288, 289, 294, 305, 314
Howard, D.R., 10, 14, 15, 39
Howell, J.M., 305
Hoy, W.K., 350, 351
Huddleston, S., 31
Hulin, C.L., 251
Human, S.E., 234
Hunsaker, P.L., 315
Hunt, J.G., 279, 293, 295, 302, 311, 312, 315

IEG, 328, 335
IHRSA, 10
Immegart, G.I., 73, 79, 80, 384
Inglis, S.E., 143, 146
Ivancevich, J.M., 274

Jackson, S.E., 387, 393
Jago, A.G., 178
James, D.N., 148

Jarrett, M.G., 57, 73, 86
Jehn, K.A., 387, 409, 410
Jermier, J.M., 292
Jewett, A.E., 31
Johns, G., 273
Joplin, J.R.W., 386
Julian, J.W., 274

Kahn, R.L., 73
Kanfer, R., 241, 243, 259
Kanter, R.S., 227
Kanungo, R.N., 305, 306
Karteroliotis, K., 360
Katz, D., 73, 106, 107, 210, 276
Keating, J.W., 204
Keeley, M., 374
Keidel, R.W., 62
Kent, A., 309
Kerr, S., 183, 292
Kestner, J.L., 333
Keuning, D., 57, 100, 123, 140
Khandwalla, P.N., 74
Kikulis, L.M., 222
Klemp, G.O., Jr., 108
Knight, P.A., 241, 274
Knoke, D., 50, 51, 68, 94, 95, 227
Koontz, H., 76, 101, 189
Kossek, E.E., 387
Kraatz, M., 234
Kraut, A.I., 112
Kuga, D.J., 251
Kushner, R.J., 360

Lambrecht, K.W., 153
Lapchick, R.E., 409
Larson, L.L., 284
Lassegard, M.A., 38
Lawler, E.E., 242, 261–265, 290, 292
Lawrence, P.R., 210, 211, 213, 226, 237, 349
Lawson, R.B., 388, 395, 404
Leventhal, G.S., 259
Li, M., 153
Liebeskind, J., 22
Likert, R., 104
Litttleton, T.D., 148
Lobel, S.A., 387
Lorsch, J.W., 210, 211, 213, 226, 237, 314, 349
Lovelock, C.H., 24, 26, 27
Loy, J.H., 409

Maccoby, N., 276
MacLean, J.C., 61
Mahony, D.F., 10, 14, 15
Major League Soccer, 136
March, J.G., 148
Margulies, N., 28, 63, 67, 69
Martins, L.L., 387
Maslow, A.H., 240, 242–246, 413
Mathes, S.A., 31
Mathews, A.W., 147

Matsuoka, H., 168
Matteson, M.T., 274
Mayo, E., 101
McCaskey, M.B., 154, 155
McClelland, D.C., 108, 279, 284–287, 315
McDonald, M.A., 38
McElvogue, J.F., 409
McGill, M.E., 65
McGuire, R., 143
McKelvy, B., 63
Meek, A., 6, 7, 10, 13, 14, 17, 49
Megginson, L.C., 133
Melnick, M.J., 37, 38
Mero, N.P., 274
Meyer, J., 92
Miles, R.E., 227
Miles, R.H., 373
Miller, D., 310
Miller, L.K., 64, 65
Milliken, F.J., 387
Mills, P.K., 28, 63, 67, 69, 225, 226, 265
Milne, G.R., 38
Milstein, M.M., 83
Mintzberg, H., 44, 108, 109, 111, 112, 189, 210
Miskel, C.G., 350, 351
Mitchell, T.R., 91, 278, 288
Moag, J.S., 260
Molitor, G.T.T., 15, 16
Molnar, J.J., 347
Mondello, M.J., 5
Moore, K., 310
Moorman, R.H., 259
Morden, A.R., 150
Morecroft, J., 73
Morse, N., 276, 315
Mott, P.E., 357
Mullin, B.J., 21, 22, 38
Myers, A.M., 324, 328
Myers, P.S., 227

NASPE/NASSM Joint Task Force on Sport, 5
National Council of Youth Sports, 11
Naylor, J., 75, 123, 170
NCAA, 87, 235, 236, 327, 335, 362
Neale, M.A., 387
Newcomer, K.E., 324, 331
Niehoff, B.P., 259
Nike, 135, 136
Noll, R.G., 135
Northcraft, G.B., 387, 391, 411
Nutt, P.C., 177

O'Rouke, S.M., 362
O'Bryant, C.P., 251
Ogasawara, E., 62
Ogilvie, B.C., 176, 282
Oldham, G.R., 251
Olsen, R.P., 23

Osborn, R.N., 154, 279, 293, 295, 302, 311, 312, 315
Ostroff, C., 345
Owen, J.M., 325, 331, 334

Papadimitriou, D., 360
Pappas, A.T., 65
Parasuraman, A., 339
Park, S.H., 233, 234
Parks, J.B., 20
Parsons, T., 210, 215, 218–221, 226, 237
Pastore, D.L., 401, 403, 406, 408
Paton, G.A., 4, 139
Pearce, J.A., II, 135
Pelled, L.H., 388, 411
Pelletier, L.G., 31
Pennings, J.M., 373
Perrow, C., 141, 142, 146, 156, 197, 201, 203, 349
Pettinger, R., 101, 125, 128
Pfeffer, J., 357, 373
Pierce, J.L., 76, 133, 135
Pillecki, F.J., 73, 79, 80, 384
Pinder, C.C., 241
Pitts, B.G., 14, 21, 22
Podsakoof, P.M., 305
Poole, P.P., 360
Porter, L.W., 2, 73, 123, 130, 133, 166, 167, 242, 261–265, 290, 292
Powell, W., 92
President's Council, 327
Preston, L.E., 89
Price, K.H., 348, 349, 410
Priesmeyer, H.R., 150
Prince, C., 44
Provan, K.G., 234
Putler, D.S., 90

Quarterman, J., 20, 108, 112
Quek, C.B., 178, 181
Quinn, R.E., 368, 369

Rabbino, H.T., 73
Rafferty, A.E., 307
Reeves, T.C., 81, 82
Reimer, E., 276, 403
Renz, D.O., 345, 364, 366, 367
Reynolds, R.G., 64
Richards, M.D., 140
Richman, J.M., 153
Riemer, H.A., 61, 339, 401
Ritzer, G., 200
Robbins, S.P., 2, 57, 73, 100, 101, 102, 105, 113, 115, 123, 125, 128, 138, 141, 154, 192, 210, 347, 349, 370, 396, 406
Roberts, G., 31
Rogers, D.L., 347
Rohrbaugh, J., 368, 369
Rollinson, D., 57, 104, 371
Rosen, R., 125, 128, 133, 148
Roth, W., 81, 82

Rowland, K., 284
Royse, D., 333
Rue, L.W., 101, 113, 114, 123, 125, 151

Saal, F.E., 241, 274
Sagas, M., 353, 390
Salancik, G.R., 373
Salas, E., 44
Sanchez, R., 73
Sasser, W.E., 23, 24, 28
Scheirer, M.A., 333
Schermerhorn, J.R., 171, 241
Schmitt, N., 345
Schneider, B., 24, 28, 339
Schneider, S.E., 391, 411
Schuler, R.S., 387, 393
Scott, R., 92
Scott, W.R., 65, 69, 92, 374, 375
Seashore, S.E., 277, 351, 354, 377
Shamir, B., 305
Shank, M.D., 38
Shapiro, D.L., 260
Shaskin, M., 307
Shaw, S., 251
Shen, Z., 388, 395, 404
Sheridan, J.E., 278
Shilbury, D., 38
Silk, M.L., 92, 94
Sills, D.L., 68
Simon, H.A., 57, 163, 169, 170–173
Slack, T., 20, 21, 50, 76, 92, 222
Slocum, J.W., 278
Smart, D.L., 353
SMG, 231
Smith, P.A., 251
Snow, C.C., 227
Snyder, C.R., 38
Soelberg, P., 173
Sofer, C., 58
Sonnenschein, W., 386
Sperber, M., 148
Sport Canada, 66
Standeven, J., 10
Staw, B.M., 168
Steers, R.M., 246, 345, 347, 349, 357, 377
Stern, R.N., 233
Stewart, R., 108, 302, 303, 315
Stier, W.F., 4
Stogdill, R.M, 278
Stotlar, D.K., 14, 21, 22
Street & Smith, 8, 9
Stuart-Kotze, R., 113
Sutton, W.A., 22
Szilagyi, A.D., 275
Szyszlo, M., 360

Taber, T.D., 304
Task Force on Sport Management Curriculum & Accreditation, 21
Taylor, J.C., 277
Taylor, W.F., 201

Telander, R., 148
Theobald, W., 335, 339, 340
Thibault, L., 77, 222
Thomas, R.R., 385, 386, 388, 392, 397, 400, 401, 404, 406, 407
Thompson, J.D., 44, 210, 215–217, 220, 226, 237
Thyer, B.A., 333
Tosi, H.L., 274
Trail, G., 90, 143, 144, 406
Treasury Board of Canada, 331
Turner, A.N., 162
Tuson, K.M., 31
Tutko, T.A., 176, 282
Tyler, T.R., 260
Tynon, J.F., 153

Vallerand, R.J., 31
Van Fleet, D.D., 274, 305, 310, 314
Van Gils, M.R., 231
Vecchio, R.P., 175
Vroom, V.H., 176, 178, 179, 181, 182, 242, 251, 253, 254, 255, 256, 315
Vuolle, P., 31

Waldroop, J., 106
Wallace, M.J., 275
Wann, D.L., 38
Waring, A., 73, 84, 210, 384
Warriner, C.K., 142
Weber, M., 197, 226, 237
Weber, R.A., 168
Webster's Ninth New Collegiate Dictionary, 86
Weese, W.J., 306
Wehrich, H., 76, 101, 189
Weiner, N., 389, 391, 392, 393, 396
Wholey, J.S., 331, 333, 334
Whyte, D.N.B., 153
Williamson, J., 30
Winer, B.J., 275
Winter, D., 284
Wolfe, R.A., 90, 353
Wooten, L.M., 65
Wyckoff, D., 23
Wynne, B.E., 315

Xin, K.R., 388

Yetton, R.N., 176, 178, 181
Yuchtman, E., 351, 354, 377
Yukl, G.A., 274, 278, 285, 305, 310, 314

Zakrajsek, D., 61
Zalesny, M.D., 44
Zammuto, R.E., 368, 372, 374, 375, 376
Zeigler, E.F., 3, 107
Zeithaml, V.A., 339
Zenger, T.R., 22
Zimalist, A., 135

Abilities and traits, effective performance and, 261
Abstract rules, in bureaucracy, 199, 199–201
Academic environment, 213
Academic performance, 353
Access:
 market, 39
 physical, 27
Accessibility, program, 338
Accommodation, 406–407, 412
Accuracy, 260
Achievement, need for, 285–286
Achievement-oriented behavior, 289
Activation, diversity and, 408, 412
Activity, program of, 58
Actual leader behavior, 315–316
Actualization, 414
Adaptation, mutual, 400–401
Adaptive behavior, 294
Adaptive-reactive theory, 293–296
Administration of physical education, 3
Administrative person model, 171–173
Advertising, 8, 138 (*see also* Marketing)
Affiliation, need for, 285
Affirmative action, 393, 394, 395
Age Discrimination in Employment Act, 394
Agnostic activities, 30
Alternatives:
 evaluating, 124, 130–132, 166
 generating, 124, 129–130, 154, 166
 selecting, 124, 132
American Sport Education Program, 329
American Youth Soccer Organization, 39, 42, 233
Americans with Disabilities Act, 394
Anticipatory skills, 108
Appraisal, of performance, 323–324

Arenas, new, 10 (*see also* Facility construction)
Armed forces, 13
Armstrong, Andrea, 407
Asian Association for Sport Management, 5
Assimilate, diversity and, 397
Assimilation model, 395
Association, creating, 40
Athlete Satisfaction Questionnaire (ASQ), 61, 339
Athletic departments:
 Canadian, 112–113
 managerial roles and, 112–113
 Thompson's model and, 217
Athletic environment, 213
Athletic performance, 353
Athletic teams, as organizations, 61–62
Athletics, distinguished from sport, 204–205
Attributes:
 of problem situations, 179–184
 organizational, 57–61
Authority, 225
 hierarchy of, 197–198, 199
 hierarchy of in organizations, 60
Authority relations, 399
Authority structure, 221
 in service organizations, 224–226
Autocratic decision making, 178
Availability bias, 175

Bachelor's program in sport management, 337
Basketball Canada, 218
BCS, 10, 87
Behaviors, 241, 243
 adaptive, 294
 instrumental, 288, 290, 291
 leadership, 288–289
 participative, 289, 291
 reactive, 294–296
Behavioral approach to leadership, 274, 275–278

Benchmarking, 130
Bias suppression, 259–260
Biases, in decision making, 175
BIRGing, 38
BKB Services, 231
Black-box model, 84
Boundaries, 74–75
 organization's, 59
Boundary-spanning units, 215, 216, 217
Bounded rationality, 171–172
Bowl Championship Series (BCS), 10, 87
Boys and Girls Clubs, 13
Brainstorming, 153, 154
Branada Sports Communication, 125
Budgeting:
 planning and, 138–140, 325
 rational-comprehensive, 139–140
Buffer agents, 216, 217
Bureaucracy, 197–205
 criticisms of, 199–202
 defined, 197
 purposes of, 203
 in sport organizations, 204–205
 tenets of, 197–199
Bureaucratization, 200, 358 (*see also* Bureaucracy)
Business concerns, 66

Calculability, 200
Canada:
 athletic departments of, 112–113
 basketball and, 218
 bureaucracy in sport organizations in, 205
 Coaching Association of, 329
 Kamloops Women's Action Project, 336
 multiculturalism and, 393
 PARTICIPATION program, 40, 327
 university athletic department in, 199–201

421

Interuniversity Sport (CIS), 231
Capital, 352
Career, sport management opportunities, 13–14, 144
Centralization, 222
Certainty of the environment, 211
Change, magnitude of, 151
Character, credible, 307
Characteristics:
  group, 387–389
  leader, 315–316 (see also Leadership)
  member, 314–315
  situational, 312–314
Charismatic leadership, 310–311
CHOICES, 327
Citizenship, as goal, 144
Civil Rights Act of 1991, 394
Client satisfaction, 126, 339–340
Clients, 45
  motives for participation, 31–33
Clinton, Bill, 391
Coercive isomorphism, 92–93
Collegiate sports, 3–4
Commitment:
  escalating, 168
  likelihood of, 180, 182
Commonweal organizations, 67
Communication:
  channels, 227
  interactional justice and, 260
Communist bloc countries, athletes and, 218
Community, 47
Competence:
  diversity and, 404
  technical, 199, 201
Competence/expertise, of worker/supervisor, 191
Competing values models, 369–370
Competing values, 368
  model of organizational effectiveness, 368–371
Competition component of operating environment, 78
Complexity, 222
Conduct, norms and codes of, 313 (see also Leadership)
Confirmation, of decisions, 174
Congruence, three states of leader behavior, 316–317
Consideration, 275
Consistency, 259
Constituencies, external and internal, 363

Constraints:
  goals and, 149
  identifying, 124, 127, 129
Consultants, 43–44
Consumer health/fitness services, 35
Consumer involvement, 31–33
Consumer-pleasure services, 34
Consumer services, 28–29, 265–266
Content of work, 248
Content theories of motivation, 242
Contest, sport, 36–37
Context:
  coordination and, 46–47
  of work, 248
Contingency effects, 281
Contingency model of leadership effectiveness, 279–284
  criticisms of, 284
Contingency perspective, 411–412
Contributing resources, 353
Control, 200
Cooperative unit, 57
Coordinated effort, 57
Coordination, sport management as, 44–47, 48
CORFing, 38
Correctibility, 260
Cost-benefit, 338–339
Cost-benefit analysis, 332–333
Cost-effectiveness, 333
Criteria, specifying performance, 124, 130–131
Critical incident method, 250
Cuba, trade and, 391
Cultural diversity, 398 (see also Diversity)
Culture, 47
  builder, 307
  of similarity, 401
  transmission of, 144, 145
Curative motives, 33
Curriculum, sport management, 21
Customer component of operating environment, 78

Decisional roles, of manager, 109, 100–111
Decision confirmation, 174
Decision makers, and evaluating decisions, 172
Decision making, 161–184, 273
  administrative person model of, 171–173

  as social process, 176–184
  autocratic, 178
  biases in, 175
  defined, 163
  diversity and, 392
  economic person model of, 170–171
  group, 178
  implicit favorite model, 173–176
  models of, 170–176
  participation in, 278, 287
  participative, 177–178
  rationality in, 169–176
  steps in, 164–166
  style of, 278
Decision significance, 179–180, 182
Decision styles, 176, 178–184
Decisions:
  examples of, 163
  programmed/nonprogrammed, 167
  significance of, 167–168
Deep-level diversity, 404
Deficiency needs, 246
Deficits, vs. differences, 389
Degree programs, sport management, 5, 337
Delphi technique, 152–153, 177
Demand, 151
Demand-side stakeholders, 89–90
Demands-constraints-choices theory, 302–303
Democracy:
  bureaucracy in, 202–203
  organizational vs. political, 183
  purposes of, 202, 203
Demographic descriptors, 387
Dempsey, Cedric W., 335–336
Deny, diversity and, 397
Departmentation, 192–196, 199
Design, of organizations, 210–224
Developmental goals, 143, 144
Differences, vs. deficits, 389
Differentiated units, in a professional sport franchise, 214
Differentiation, 211, 222
Direction, of behaviors, 241
Directional planning, 154–156
Discretionary influence, 296
Discrimination:
  identifying, 409
  incentives against, 394 (see also Diversity)
Dissatisfiers, 248
Disseminator, manager as, 109, 110

Distal environment, 75–78, 220, 221
Distributive justice, 259–260
Disturbance handler, 210
    manager as, 109, 110
Diversity, 144, 383–415
    accommodation and, 406–407, 412
    activation strategy, 408, 412
    actualization and, 414
    affirmative action, 393, 394, 395
    benefits of managing, 391–392
    competence and, 396, 404
    contingency perspective, 411–412
    costs of managing, 392
    cultural, 398
    deep level, 404
    defined, 386–387
    differences, vs. deficits, 389
    equilibrium in managing, 413
    forms of, 404, 406
    growing, 389–391
    in sport, 401–403
    informational, 387
    in-group identity and, 413
    integrative framework for managing, 404–411
    management of, 177
    management strategies, 406–411
    managing in college athletics, 403–404
    marketing and, 390–391
    nondiscrimination initiatives, 394
    options for handling, 397–401
    organizational stages of, 401–403
    perspectives of managing, 392–396
    social category, 387–388
    surface level, 404
    task factors, 408–410
    time factor, 410–411
    valuing, 393, 395, 406–407
    within diversity, 398–399
Division of labor, 59–60, 197, 199
Doctoral program in sport management, 337
Donor services, 33, 40
Dream Team, 36
Drug culture, 398

Economic:
    activities, satellite, 49–50
    component of environment, 76
    significance of sport industry, 6–12
Economic person model, of decision making, 170–171
Economics:
    big five growth areas, 15–17
    organizational, 22
Effectiveness:
    assessments of, 366
    defined, 345–346
    organizational, see Organizational effectiveness
Efficiency, 125, 200
    defined, 345–346
    management and, 347
    need-based theories and, 251
Effort, 261
Effort–performance relationship, 261–263
Effort–reward probability, 264
Ego orientation, 32
Elite sport programs, 361
ELQ, 307
Employee orientation, 276, 279
Employee–customer interface, 63, 67, 223, 224
Employees, 45
    appraisal of, 323–324
    competence of, 191
    defining organization, 32
    relationship with supervisor, 191–192
Empowering Leadership Questionnaire (ELQ), 307
Empowerment:
    leadership, 307–308
    skills, 108
Enacting vs. forecasting, 149
Endorsements, 8
Ends and means, 137
Energy, for actions/behaviors, 241
Entertainment, as goal, 144, 145, 156
Entrepreneur:
    manager as, 109, 110
    role, 210
Entropy, negative, 79–80
Environment:
    academic, 213
    distal, 220, 221
    external, 75–78
    general, 220, 221
    influences on organizations, 86–95
    internal, 78–79
    recreational/athletic, 213
    task, 75, 77–78, 220, 221

Environmental:
    factors, 290
    influences, 209
    stability, 215–216
Equal Pay Act of 1963, 394
Equifinality, 81–82, 358, 359
Equilibrium:
    in managing diversity, 413
    punctuated, 310
Equipment/apparel, 8, 11
Equity, 263, 264
ESPN, 87, 88, 89
Esteem needs, 244
Ethicality, 260
Ethnic Minority Enhancement Program, 327, 333
Ethnographic descriptors, 387
European Association of Sport Management (EASM), 5
Evaluating:
    alternatives, decision making and, 124, 130–132, 166
    management and, 105
Evaluation, 322–340 (see also Program evaluation)
    of organizations, 344–345 (see also Organizations)
    standards of, 334–340
Event management, 13
Evolutionary perspective, 374
Excellence, pursuit of, 32
Executive director, 221–222
Executive Order 11246, 394
Expectancy, 252–253
Expectancy theory, 252–256
External:
    constituencies, 363
    environment, 75–78
    events, 228–229
    feedback, 82, 84–85
    networks, 227, 229–231
Extrinsic rewards, 263, 264

Facility:
    construction, 8, 10, 15
    management, 13
    physical access to, 27
Feedback, 82, 84–85
FIBA, 233
FIFA, 233
Figurehead, manager as, 109, 110
Final payoff, closeness to, 378
Financial capital, 352
Financial security, as goal, 144, 145
Fitness clubs, 23, 26
Five C Model of leadership, 307

SUBJECT INDEX **423**

Flexibility versus stability, as dimension of competing values, 369
Flexiform model, 225, 226, 265
Focus group, 339–340
Footwear, 8, 11
Forces within an individual, 241
Forecasting, 149–153
Formalization, 222
Framing the problem, decision making and, 164–166
Functional departmentation, 193
Functional power, 226
Functions, of networks, 234–236
Funding:
　governmental, 65–66
　source of, 63, 65–66

Gambling, 9
Gandhi, Mahatma, 307, 311
Gender equity, studies of, 333, 335–336
General environment, 220, 221
General Motors, 50
Generating alternatives, decision making and, 124, 129–130, 154, 166
Generation, 130
Globalization, 391
Goal emphasis, 277
Goal-oriented departmentation, 193–194
Goals:
　attainment of, 378
　clarity of, 349–350
　complementary, 145
　conflicting, 145
　constraints and, 149
　continuum of for activity/leisure, 31
　developmental, 143, 144
　displacement of, 354
　formal statements, 142
　formation of, 354
　intangible, 350
　intercollegiate athletics and, 143–144
　management and, 101
　measurement of, 349, 350
　multiple, 349–350
　organizational, 140–149
　performance, 143, 144
　setting, 124, 125–126
　stated, 141–142, 156
Goals model, of organizational effectiveness, 348–351

Goods:
　defined, 23
　rental of, 26–27
Government, 47
　agencies as open systems, 77
　funding, 65–66
　involvement in sport, 93
Gratification, 244
Gross domestic sports product (GDSP), 6
Gross national product, 151
Group:
　characteristics, 387–389 (see also Diversity)
　decision making, 178, 392
　expertise, 180, 182
　support for objectives, 180, 182
Growth, 125
　needs, 246

Health/fitness, as goal, 33, 144
Heterogeneity, 24, 25, 28
Hierarchical authority structure, 197–198, 199
Hierarchical suborganizations, 218–220
Hierarchy:
　absence of strict, 227
　of needs, 243
High school sports, 3–4
Higher-order needs, 246
Horizontal differentiation, 222
Human:
　behavior, 241
　capital, 352
　relations model, 370
　resources 45
　services, 28, 29–30
　skills, management and, 107
Human-curative services, 35
Human-excellence services, 35
Human-skill services, 35
Human-sustenance services, 35
Hygienes, 248

Identity, of organizations, 58
Imitability, of resources, 353
Immigration Reform and Control Act of 1986, 394
Impacts, of a program, 330–331
Imperfect imitability, of resources, 353
Impersonality, 199, 201
Implicit favorite:
　bias, 175

model of decision making, 173–176
Importance of commitment, 180, 182
Incentives, 252
Individual motivation, 241, 290–292
Individual outcomes, diversity and, 390
Individual-level performances, 323–324
Inequity, 257
Inequity theory, 256–259
Influence, 274
　discretionary, 296
Information:
　directional planning and, 156
　gathering, 149–154
Informational:
　diversity, 387
　roles, of manager, 109, 110
In-group, 304
　diversity and, 413
Initiating structure, 275
Input/outcome balance, 256–257
Inputs, 82, 83, 256–257, 354, 356, 357, 359
Input-throughput-output cycle, 360, 377
Input-throughput-output model, 347–348
Inseparability, 25, 28
Institutional isomorphism, 92–93
Institutional subsystem, 220
Institutional theory, 92–94
Instrumental behavior, 288, 290, 291
Instrumentality, 253
　of organizations, 58
Insulation, 218, 224
Intangibility, 24, 28
Integration, 211–214
Intensity, of behaviors, 241
Interactional justice, 260
Interaction facilitation, 277
Intercollegiate athletics, and Olympic sports, 146
Interdependence, 410
Intergroup differences, 398, 399
Interindividual differences, 398
Internal:
　constituencies, 363
　environment, 78–79
　feedback, 82, 84–85
　networks, 227–229

processes, 229–230
process model, 370
versus external, competing values and, 368–369
International Olympic Committee (IOC), 40, 139, 233, 309, 326
Internet, 8
Interorganizational network, 47, 231–236
Interpersonal roles, of manager, 109, 110
Interventions, programs as, 331
Intragroup differences, 398, 399
Intrinsic rewards, 263, 264
Intuitive skills, 108
Involuntary stakeholders, 88–89
Involvement, consumer, 31–33
IOC, 40, 139, 233, 309, 326
Irrationality of rationality, 200
Isolate, diversity and, 397–398
Isomorphism, 92–94

Japanese Society of Sport Management (JSSM), 5
Job enrichment, 250, 266
Job types, 13
Jordan, Michael, 311
Journals, sport management, 5–6
Just do it, 328
Justice and fairness theories, 259–260

Kamloops Women's Action Project, 336
Kennedy, John F., 311
King, Jr., Martin Luther, 311
Knight, Philip, 311

Labor:
    division of, 199
    operating environment and, 78
Lawrence and Lorsch model of designing organizations, 210–215
Leader (see also Leadership):
    expertise of, 180, 182
    manager as, 109, 110
Leader–member exchange theory, 303–305
Leader–member relations, 280
Leadership, 271–296, 301–318
    actual leader behavior, 315–316
    behavior, 288–289
    behavioral approach to, 274, 275–278
    charismatic, 310–311

concepts of, 272–273
contemporary theories of, 302–318
contingency model of effectiveness, 279–284
defined, 273–275
demands-constraints-choices theory, 302–303
ELQ, 307
Five C model, 307
function, 289
leader-member exchange theory, 303–305
market, 126
motivation and, 240–268 (see also Motivation)
multidimensional model of, 279, 311–318
path-goal theory, 314
performance and satisfaction, 316–317
preferred leader behavior, 314–315
required leader behavior, 311–312
situational approach to, 275, 278–296
steady-state, 310
style, 279–280
substitutes for, 292–293
trait approach to, 274, 275
transactional theory, 303–305
transactional vs. transformational, 305
transformational, 305–310
visionary, 306
Least preferred coworker (LPC), 279
Legal component of environment, 76
Legitimacy, of stakeholders, 91
Leisure time, 16
Liaison, manager as, 109, 110
Licenses, seat, 138
Life sciences era, 16
Likelihood of commitment, 180, 182
Limbaugh, Rush, 87, 88, 89
Little League, 39, 42
LMX, 303–305
Lombardi, Vince, 311
Lopiano, Donna, 308
Loss-aversion bias, 175
Love needs, 244
Low substitutability, of resources, 353

Lower-order needs, 246
Luxury boxes, 138

Macro variables, 293, 312
Maintenance outputs, 84
Maintenance-interactive, 67
Management:
    correspondence of functions/skills/roles, 114
    defined, 100–102
    efficiency and, 347
    evaluating and, 105
    four functions of, 102–105
    human element of, 101–102
    human skills and, 107
    leading and, 104–105 (see also Leadership)
    levels of, 112
    Mintzberg's roles, 108–111, 112–113, 114
    of attention, 306
    of meaning, 306
    of self, 306
    of trust, 306
    organizing and, 103–104
    overview of process, 113–114
    planning and, 102–103 (see also Planning)
    roles in athletic contexts, 112–113
    roles of, 108–113, 210
    skills of, 106–108
    tasks, 112–113
    technical skills and, 106
    transforming skills, 108
    vs. marketing, 116
    women in, 184
Manager:
    decisional roles of, 109, 100–111
    informational roles of, 109, 110
    interpersonal roles of, 109, 110
Managerial:
    models, comparison of, 287–288
    motivation, model of, 284–287 (see also Motivation)
    roles, 108–113, 210
    subsystem, 219
Mandela, Nelson, 307, 311
Market:
    access, 39
    conditions, 47
    leadership, 126
    segmentation, diversity and, 390
    share, 125

SUBJECT INDEX **425**

Marketing, 138
  diversity and, 390
  effective strategy, 391
  of sport services, 41
  vs. management, 116
Mason, James G., 308
Mass sport programs, 361
Master's program in sport management, 337
Matrix, departmentation, 195–196
MBA programs, 93
McDonaldization, 200
McJobs, 200
Means and ends, 137
Means versus ends, competing values and, 369
Mechanization, progressive, 80–81
Media, broadcast rights, 8
Medical treatment, 9
Mega-materials era, 16
Member factors, 289
Membership, of organization, 58–59
Micro variables, 293
Mimetic isomorphism, 93–94
Ministry of sports, French, 93
Minorities, see Diversity
Mintzberg's managerial roles, 108–111, 112–113, 114
Mission statement, 135–137
MLS, mission statement, 135–136
Models:
  leadership, see Leadership
  of decision making, 170–176
  of organizational effectiveness, 347–371
Monitor:
  manager as, 109, 110
  role, 210
Monocultural organizations, 401
Motion studies, 101
Motivation, 273
  client, 31–33
  content theories of, 242
  defined, 241–242
  in sport organizations, 264–267
  individual, 290–292
  leading and, 240–268
  model of managerial, 284–287
  needs-based theories of, 242–251
  Porter and Lawler model of, 261–264, 290–292
  process theories of, 242

work, 241
Motivational effect of leadership, 289–290
Motivation-hygiene theory, 247–251
Motivators, 248
Motives:
  curative, 33
  sustenance, 33
Multicultural organizations, 401
Multiculturalism:
  Canada and, 393 (see also Diversity)
  organizational stages of, 401–403
Multidimensional model of leadership, 279, 311–318
  transformational leadership within, 317–318
Multidimensionality:
  and multiple-constituency model, 367–368, 377
  of organizational effectiveness, 359–361, 367–368
Multifinality, 81–82
Multiple constituencies, 364, 368
  model of organizational effectiveness, 362–368
Multiple perspectives, 367, 372–374
Mutual adaptation, 400
Mutual benefit associations, 66

NASPE, 5, 40, 46, 336–337
NASPE/NASSM Task Force on Sport Management Curriculum, 21
NASSM (North American Society for Sport Management), 4, 21, 46, 336–337
National Federation of State High School Associations, 233
National sport organizations (NSOs), 360
NBA, 125, 135, 167–168, 233, 328, 353
NCAA, 10–11, 15, 60, 64, 81, 93, 94, 127, 132, 209, 231, 233, 275, 287, 294, 314, 326–327, 362, 363
  BCS and, 87
  diversity management and, 403, 407
  drug education program, 338
  Ethnic Minority Enhancement Program, 327, 333

functions of, 235–236
gender equity and, 333, 335
goals and, 143
Women's Enhancement Program, 333
Needs, 241–242
Needs-based theories of motivation, 242–251
Needs hierarchy theory, 243–247
Negative entropy, 79–80
Negotiator, manager as, 109, 110
Network functions, 234–236
Network organizations, 226–236 (see also Networks)
Networks:
  external, 227, 229–231
  internal, 227–229
  interorganizational, 231–236
  inter-organizational, 47
New atomic age, 16
New space age, 16
NFL, 76, 88, 133, 233
Niche marketing, diversity and, 390
Nike, 50, 311, 328, 367
  mission statement, 135–136
Nominal group technique, 152
Nondiscrimination, 394
Nonprofit organization, 64
Nonprogrammed decisions, 167
Nonrequirements, 400, 401
Normative isomorphism, 93–94
NPOs, 364
  effectiveness of, 367
  managers of, 366

Objectives:
  group support for, 180, 182
  management and, 101
  meeting, 335–336
Official goals, 141–142
Ohio State University, The, 212, 275–276, 277, 278
  mission statement, 135–136
Ohio University, 4
Olympics, 36, 37, 40
  intercollegiate athletics and, 146
  International Committee (IOC), 40, 139, 233, 309, 326
  Special, 45, 316
Open doors, affirmative action and, 395
Open system model, 370
Open systems, 72–82, 210, 279 (see also Systems)
  defined, 74

perspectives, 208–224
processes in, 79–82
thinking, 226
vs. closed, 74
Operating environment, 75, 77–78
Operational planning, 137–138
Operational units, 225–226
Operative goals, 142–149
Opportunities:
    analyzing, 129
    decisions and, 164
    identifying, 124, 126–127
Organizational:
    capital, 352
    contexts, 13
    democracy, 183
    economics, 22
    field, 50
    paradox, 371
    set, 290
    society, 50
Organizational effectiveness, 344–378
    as managerial concern, 346–347
    models of, 347–371
    multidimensionality of, 359–361, 367–368
    multiple constituency model, 362–368
    paradoxical nature of, 371–372
    process model of, 357–359
Organizational-level performances, 323–324
Organizations:
    athletic teams as, 61–62
    attributes of, 57–61
    authority structure in, 224–226
    boundaries of, 59
    classical view of, 56–69
    classifying, 63–68
    commonweal, 67
    consumer service, 265–266
    defined, 57
    defined by employees, 32
    design theorists, 210–224
    diversity and, 383–415 (see also Diversity)
    division of labor, 59–60
    environmental influences on, 86–95
    external environment of, 75–78
    formal rules and procedures, 60–61
    goals of, 140–149
    growth of, 125

hierarchy of authority, 60
identity of, 58
institutional theory and, 92–94
instrumentality of, 58
isomorphism and, 92–94
management of, see Management
marketing function of, 116
membership of, 58–59
monocultural, 401
network, 226–236 (see also Networks)
nonprofit, 64
as open systems, 72–82 (see also Open systems)
performance of, 323–324
permanency of, 59
planning and, see Planning
population of, 50
prime beneficiary, 63, 66–67
private sector, 356
production function of, 116
professional service, 265–266
profit orientation of, 63–65
program of activity, 58
public sector, 356
resource based view (RBV) of, 352
resource dependence theory, 94–95
service, 66, 224–226
source of funding, 63, 65–66
stakeholders of, 86–92
subsystems and boundaries, 74–75
as systems of inputs-through-puts-outputs, 82–85
systems view of, 71–95
third-sector, 333, 356
Thompson's model of design, 215–218
transitional, 401
turf wars in, 194
volunteer, 266–267
volunteer participation in, 63, 67
Organizing, 103–104, 273
    defined, 188–190
    principles of, 190–197
Orientation:
    employee, 276, 279
    product, 276
    task, 279
    task vs. ego, 32
Outcomes, 252, 257
Out-group, 304

Outputs, 82, 83–84, 330–331, 354, 356, 357, 359
Outsourcing, 230–231, 232, 233
Ownership, transfer of, 26, 27, 28

Parson's model, 218–220, 360
Participant services, 33, 34–35
Participant sport, 10–12
Participation:
    client motives for, 31–33
    in decision making, 177–178, 287
PARTICIPACTION, 40, 327
Participative behavior, 289, 291
Participative decision making, 177–178
Path-goal theory of leadership, 288–293, 314
People-changing services, 30–31
People-processing services, 30
People-sustaining services, 30
Perception, 253
Performance, 243, 261, 264
    academic, 353
    appraisal, 323–324
    criteria, specifying, 124, 130–131
    goals, 143, 144
    of leader, 316–317 (see also Leadership)
Performance-reward relationship, 263
Perishability, 24–25, 28
Permanency, of organization, 59
Persistence, of behaviors, 241
Personal experience bias, 175
Personal-interactive, 67
Personnel, player, 138
Physical capital, 352
Physical education, administration of, 3
Physical fitness, program promoting, 327
Physiological needs, 243
Plan, standing, 139
Planning, 102–103, 121–157, 273
    benchmarking and, 130
    budgeting and, 138–140, 325
    defined, 123–124
    directional, 154–156
    document, 124, 132–133
    forecasting and, 149–153
    function, 188, 210
    generating/evaluating alternatives, 124, 129–132
    identifying opportunities, 124, 126–127

mission statement and, 135–137
operational, 137–138
organizational goals and, 140–149
programming and, 325
rational, 140–154
setting goals, 124, 125–126
specifying performance criteria, 124, 130–131
steps in the process, 124–133
strategic, 133–137
tactical, 137–138
Planning-programming-budgeting system (PPBS), 139–140
Player personnel, 138
Pleasure, pursuit of, 32
POLE, 103
Political component of environment, 76
Pop Warner Football, 39, 42
Population, organization, 50
Porter and Lawler model of motivation, 261–264, 290–292
POSDCORB, 103
Position power, 281
Power:
  centers, 373
  differential, 94
  need for, 286–287
  perspective, 373
  stakeholders and, 91
PPBS, 139–140
Predictability, 200
Preferred leader behavior, 314–315
President's Challenge of the Youth Physical Fitness Program, 327
Pressure for production, 192
Prestige, as goal, 144, 145
Primary stakeholder, 89, 142, 376
Prime beneficiary, 63, 66–67, 374, 375, 376
Private inurement, 64
Private-sector organizations, 65, 356
Problem, as occasion for making decisions, 164
Problem attributes, 179–184
  decision significance, 179–180, 182
Procedural justice, 259–260
Procedures, organizational, 60
Process model of organizational effectiveness, 357–359
Process theories of motivation, 242, 252–260

Process-oriented departmentation, 193
Production orientation, 276
Production:
  function of organization, 116
  pressure for, 192
  of sport services, 41
Productive capacity, 26
Productivity, 125
Product-oriented departmentation, 193–194
Products:
  as goods and services, 23–24
  sport industry, 22–28
Professional judgment, 336–337
Professional services, 8, 28, 29
  organizations, 224–225, 265–266
Professional sport franchise, functions of, 234–235
Profit orientation, 63–65
Program evaluation, 331–340, 345
  accessibility/safety, 338
  ASQ, 339
  client satisfaction, 339–340
  cost-benefit analysis, 332–333, 338–339
  defined, 322–324
  defining programs, 324–328
  meeting objectives, 335–336
  program profiles, 334
  socioeconomic evaluation, 337–338
  standards of, 334–340
Program logic, 334
Program profile, 334
Programmed decisions, 167
Programs:
  accessibility of, 338
  commercial, 328
  cost-benefit analysis, 332–333, 338–339
  defined, 324–328
  evaluation of, see Program evaluation
  nonprofit, 326–328
  for profit, 328
  public, 325–328
  safety of, 338
  in small organizations, 328
  as social interventions, 331
  from a systems perspective, 329–331
  vs. projects, 326
Progressive:
  mechanization, 80–81

segregation, 80
Projects, vs. programs, 326
Prolonged activities, 30
Proximal (task) environment, 75, 220, 221
Psychic benefits, 40
Public relations, goals and, 144, 145
Public sector, 65, 356
Publication, 9
Public-sector organizations, 356
Punctuated equilibrium, 310
Pursuit of excellence, 32
Pursuit of health/fitness, 33
Pursuit of pleasure, 32
Pursuit of skill, 32

Rarity, of resources, 352
Rate of return, 138
Rational goal model, 370
Rational planning, 140–154
  information gathering and, 149–154
  operational goals and, 140–149
Rational-comprehensive budgeting, 139–140
Rationality:
  bounded, 171–172
  in decision making, 169–176
  defined, 169
  of ends, 170
  irrationality of, 200
  subjective, 173
Reactive behavior, 294–296
Real goals, 142–149
Recreation programs, 327
Recreational environment, 213
Recreational sport, 10–12
Red Cross, 61, 126
Red tape, 199, 202
Reebok, 50
Rehabilitation Act of 1973, 394
Relationships, building, 400
Relativistic perspective, 373
Rental of goods/services, 26–27
Representative bias, 175
Representativeness, 260
Required leader behavior, 311–312
Research, on leadership, 275–278
Resource allocator, manager as, 109, 110
Resource based view (RBV), of organizations, 352
Resource dependence theory, 94–95

Resource imbalance, 95
Resources, 352–353
    defined, 352
    imperfect imitability of, 353
    low substitutability of, 353
Responsibility/authority, as principle of organizing, 196–197
Return, rate of, 138
Reward, 252, 261
    intrinsic/extrinsic, 263, 264
Reward-satisfaction relationship, 263
Rivalry, interdepartmental, 199
Role perception, effort-performance relationship, 262
Rules:
    abstract, 199
    and procedures, organizational, 60–61
    strict reliance on, 201

Safety and security needs, 243
Safety, of programs, 338
Salvation Army, 126
Samaranch, Juan Antonio, 309
Satellite economic activities, 49–50
Satisfaction, of leader, 316–317
Satisfice, 172, 173
Satisfiers, 248
Scalpers, 330
Schismogenesis, 372
Season tickets, 138
Secondary stakeholders, 89, 142
Segregation, progressive, 80
Selective perception bias, 175
Self-actualization, 244
Self-regulation, 79–80
Service:
    attributes, 24
    defined, 23
    organizations, 66
Services:
    consultant, 43–44
    consumer, 28–29, 265–266
    donor, 33, 40
    human, 28, 29–30
    participant, 33, 34–35
    production and marketing of, 41
    professional, 8, 28, 29
    rental of, 26–27
    satellite, 43
    separable, 26
    social ideas, 33, 34, 40
    spectator, 33, 34, 35–38
    sponsorship, 33, 34, 38–40

Sexual orientation descriptors, 387
Similarity, culture of, 401
Simultaneity, 24, 25
Situational approach to leadership, 275, 278–296
Situational characteristics, 312–314
Situational favorableness, 280–281
Skill, pursuit of, 32
Skills:
    human, 107
    leadership, *see* Leadership
    management, 106–108 (*see also* Management)
    technical, 106
    to transform, 108
Sport management:
    career opportunities, 13–14
    as coordination, 44–47, 48
    curriculum, 21
    defining the field of, 19–52, 40–48
    degree programs, 5, 337
    diversity and, *see* Diversity
    educational institutions and, 3–4
    emergence of, 3
    forecasting and, 153
    future of, 14–17
    history of, 2–4
    introduction to, 2–17
    journals, 5–6
    landmark thrusts, 4
    planning and, *see* Planning
    professional associations, 5
    professional status of, 4–6
Sport Management Association of Australia and New Zealand (SMAANZ), 5
SMG, 231
Social:
    awareness, 126
    category diversity, 387–388
    component of environment, 76
    ideas, 33, 34, 40
    justice perspective, 374
    process, decision making as, 176–184
Socioeconomic evaluation, 337–338
Span of control, 190–192
Spatial differentiation, 222
Special Olympics, 45, 316
Specialization, 190
Spectacle, 37
Spectator services, 33, 34, 35–38

Spectator sports, 11
Spokesperson, manager as, 109, 110
Sponsorship, 9, 10, 328
    measuring impact of, 335
    services, 33, 34, 38–40
Sport industry:
    economic significance of, 6–12
    products, 22–28, 41–42
    segments of, 7–12
    size of, 6–12
Sport managers:
    and adaptive-reactive theory, 296
    contingency model and, 281–284
    differentiation and integration and, 214–215
    expectancy theory and, 255–256
    inequity theory and, 257–259
    justice and fairness theories, 260
    need-based theories and, 251
    needs hierarchy theory and, 247
    Thompson's model and, 217
    two-factor theory and, 248–250
Sport Motivation Scale (SMS), 31
Sport organizations (*see also* Organizations)
    bureaucracy and, 204–205
    defined, 20
    motivation in, 264–267
Sport:
    products, 22–28, 41–42
    programs, elite, 361
    services, classifying, 33–41
    distinguished from athletics, 204–205
    diversity in, 401–403 (*see also* Diversity)
    tourism, 10
SportCoach, 329
SportDirector, 329
Sport-governing bodies, international, 13
SportParent, 329
Sports:
    collegiate, 3–4 (*see also* NCAA)
    high school, 3–4
    teams, 14
    youth, 11–12
Stability, 202
    environmental, 215–216
Stacking, 40
Stakeholders, 86–92, 142, 364
    classifications of, 88–92

demand-side/supply-side, 89–90
primary/secondary, 89
voluntary/involuntary, 88–89
Stakeholder theory, 86–92
Standards:
of evaluation, 334–340
set by experts, 336
Standing plan, 139
Status descriptors, 387
Steady-state leader, 310
Strategic planning, 133–137 (see also Planning)
Strengths, analyzing, 129
Student-athletes, 3–4, 45 (see also NCAA)
Subjective rationality, 173
Substitutability, of resources, 353
Subsystems, 74–75
Super Bowl, 15
Supervisor:
competence of, 191
relationship with employees, 191–192
Supplier component of operating environment, 78
Supply-side stakeholders, 89–90
Support, 277
Support units, 46
Supportive behavior, 288, 291
Suppress, diversity and, 397
Surface-level diversity, 404
Sustenance motives, 33
SWOT, 128–129
System boundaries, 74–75
System resource model of organizational effectiveness, 351–356
applicability of, 355–356
Systems:
of inputs-throughputs-outputs, 82–85
open, see Open systems thinking, 73
view, of organizations, 71–95
Systems perspective, 237
programs from, 329–331

Tactical planning, 137–138
Task:
environment, 75, 77–78, 220, 221
factors, diversity and, 408–410, 412
interdependence, 410, 412
orientation, 32, 279

structure, 280–281
Task-interactive, 67
Tasks:
managerial, 112–113
simplicity, complexity of, 409–410, 412
Taylorism, 200
Teams:
building, 62
competence of, 180, 182
large- vs. small-market, 14
as organizations, 61–62
Technical:
competence, 199, 201
core, 215–216, 217, 222–223
skills, 106
subsystem, 218–219
Technologies, 46
Technology component of environment, 76
Tenets of bureaucracy, 197–199
Tennis club, SWOT and, 128–129
Theories, leadership, see Leadership
Third place experience, 37–38
Third-sector organizations, 333, 356
Thompson model of designing organizations, 215–218
Threats, analyzing, 129
Throughput processes, 357
Throughputs, 82, 83
Ticketing operations, 13
Time factor, diversity and, 410–411
Time/motion studies, 101
Tolerance, diversity and, 400
Total-quality management (TQM), 357
Tourism, sport, 10
Trade, globalization of, 391
Trait approach to leadership, 274, 275
Transactional theory, 303–305
Transfer of ownership, 26, 27, 28
Transformational leadership, 305–310
Transitional organizations, 401
Travel, sports, 9
Trends, changes in, 151
TRIM movement, 40
True requirements, 400, 401
Turf wars, in organizations, 194
Two-factor theory, 247–251

United States Cycling Federation, 218, 233

Unit-level performances, 323–324
Units, organizational, 324
Unity of command, 196
University of Michigan, 276–278
Urgency, stakeholders and, 91–92
Utility, 252

Valence, 252
Value congruence skills, 108
Value, of resources, 352
Values, competing, 143–146, 368–371
Variability, 26
Variables of organizational system, 293
Variables, macro, 312
Vertical differentiation, 222
Vertical job loading, 250
Videos, 9
Vietnam Era Veterans Readjustment Assistance Act, 394
Visibility, as goal, 144
Visionary leadership, 306
Visioning skills, 108
Voluntary stakeholders, 88–89
Volunteer:
employees, 45
organizations, 266–267
participation in organizations, 63, 67, 266–267

Weaknesses, analyzing, 129
Winning, as goal, 144
WNBA, 135
Women managers, 184
Women's Enhancement Program, 333
Women's Sport Foundation, 308–309
Women's World Cup, 16
Work:
content of, 248
context of, 248
facilitation, 277
motivation, 241
processes, 227–228
types done, 191
World Cup, 15, 16, 36

YMCA, 13, 40, 64–65, 66, 89
Youth culture, 398
Youth sports, 11–12

Zeigler, Earl F., 308